Your fully reengineered Microso…

The all-new learning format of your Microsoft study guide delivers in-depth preparatio… objective review—along with great new study tools to help prepare you for the job. F…

- Relevant exam objectives highlighted at the start of each chapter

- "Why This Chapter Matters" and "Real World" sidebars on how you can apply learning concepts to the job

- Practices and design activities where you work through multi-step, real-world solutions

---

3-14   Chapter 3   User Accounts

Lesson 2: Creating Multiple User Objects

There occasionally situations that require you to create multiple user objects quickly, such as a new class of incoming students at a school, or a group of new hires at an organization. In these situations you need to know how to effectively facilitate or auto-mate user object creation so that you are not approaching the task on an account-by-account basis. In Lesson 1, you learned how to create and manage user objects with Active Directory Users and Computers. This lesson will extend those concepts, skills, and tools to include user object creation through template objects, imported objects, and command line scripting of objects.

> **After this lesson, you will be able to**
> - Create and utilize user object templates
> - Import user objects from comma-delimited files
> - Leverage new command-line tools to create and manage user objects
>
> **Estimated lesson time: 15 minutes**

Creating and Using User Templates

It is common for objects to share similar properties. For example, all sales representa-tives may belong to the same security groups, are allowed to log on to the network during the same hours, and have home folders and roaming profiles on the same server. In such cases, it is helpful when creating a user object for that object to be pre-populated with common properties. This can be accomplished by creating a generic user object—often called a *template*—and then copying that object to create new users.

To generate a user template, create a user and populate its properties. Put the user into appropriate groups.

 Security Alert   Be certain to disable the user, since it is just a template, to ensure that the account is not used for access to network resources.

To create a new user based on the template, select the template and choose Copy from the Action menu. You will be prompted for properties similar to those when you create a new user: first and last name, initials, logon names, password, and account options. When the object is created, you will find that properties are copied from the template based on the following property-page based description:

- **General**   No properties copied.
- **Address**   All properties except Street address are copied.

- "Off the Record" sidebars bridge the gap between how things *should* work and how they *do* work

- Planning Tips you can apply in the real world

- Chapter summaries help ensure you understood main points

- Exam highlights—key points and terms you should know

- Exam tips written by an industry insider

---

3   User…

Exam Objectives in this Chapter:

- Create and manage user accounts.
  - Create and modify user accounts by using the Active Directory Users and Computers MMC snap-in.
  - Create and modify user accounts by using automation.
  - Import user accounts.
- Manage local, roaming, and mandatory user profiles.
- Troubleshoot user accounts.
  - Diagnose and resolve account lockouts.
  - Diagnose and resolve issues related to user account properties.
- Troubleshoot user authentication issues.

Why This Chapter Matters

Before individuals in your enterprise can begin to access resources they require, you must enable authentication of those individuals. Of course, the primary com-ponent of that authentication is the user's identity, maintained as an account in Active Directory. In this chapter, you will review and enhance your knowledge related to the creation, maintenance, and troubleshooting of user accounts and authentication.

Each enterprise, and each day, brings with it a unique set of challenges related to user management. The properties you configure for a standard user account are likely to be different from those you apply to the account of a Help Desk team member, which are different still from those configured on the built-in Adminis-trator account. Skills that are effective to create or modify a single user account become clumsy and inefficient when you are working with masses of accounts, for example when managing the accounts for a number of new hires.

To effectively address a diverse sampling of account management scenarios, we will examine a variety of user management skills and tools including the Active Directory Users & Computers snap-in and powerful command-line utilities.

3-1

Lesson 3   Managing User Profiles   3-29

 Note   Be sure to configure share permissions allowing Everyone Full Control. The Windows Server 2003 default share permissions allow Read, which is not sufficient for a roaming pro-file share.

On the Profile tab of the user's Properties dialog box, type the Profile Path in the for-mat: **server**>\<**share**>**%username%**. The %*username*% variable will automat-ically be replaced with the user's logon name.

It's that simple. The next time the user logs on to their system, the system will identify the roaming profile location.

 Exam Tip   Roaming user profiles are nothing more than a shared folder and a path to the user's profile folder, within that share, entered into the user object's profile path property. Roaming profiles are not, in any way, a property of a computer object.

When the user logs *off* of their system, it will upload the profile to the profile server. The user can now log on to their system, or any other system in the domain, and the documents and settings that are part of the RUP will be applied.

 Note   Windows Server 2003 introduces a new policy: Only allow local user profiles. This pol-icy, linked to an OU containing computer accounts, will prevent roaming profiles from being used on those computers. Users will, instead, maintain local profiles.

When a user with an RUP logs on to a new system for the first time, the system does not copy its Default User profile. Instead, it downloads the RUP from the network loca-tion. When a user logs off, or when a user logs on to a system on which they've worked before, the system copies only files that have changed.

 Real World   **Roaming Profile Synchronization**

Unlike previous versions of Microsoft Windows, Windows 2000, Windows XP, and Windows Server 2003 do not upload and download the entire user profile at logoff and logon. Instead, the user profile is *synchronized*. Only files that have changed are transferred between the local system and the network RUP folder. This means that logon and logoff with RUPs are significantly faster than with ear-lier Windows systems. Organizations that have not implemented RUPs for fear of their impact on logon and network traffic should reevaluate their configuration in this light.

MCSE: Designing Security for a Microsoft Windows Server 2003 Network Exam 70-298

Objective	Pages
Creating the Conceptual Design for Network Infrastructure Security by Gathering and Analyzing Business and Technical Requirements (1.0)	
Analyze business requirements for designing security. Considerations include existing policies and procedures, sensitivity of data, cost, legal requirements, end-user impact, interoperability, maintainability, scalability, and risk.	
■ Analyze existing security policies and procedures.	1-6 to 1-11, 1-17 to 1-19
■ Analyze the organizational requirements for securing data.	1-19 to 1-22
■ Analyze security requirements of differing types of data.	1-19 to 1-22
■ Analyze risks to security within current IT administration structure and security practices.	1-12 to 1-15, 1-21 to 1-24
Design a framework for designing and implementing security. The framework should include prevention, detection, isolation and recovery.	
■ Predict threats to your network from internal and external sources.	1-34 to 1-35
■ Design a process for responding to incidents.	1-36 to 1-38
■ Design segmented networks.	1-38 to 1- 42
■ Design a process for recovering services.	1-42 to 1-44
Analyze technical constraints when designing security.	
■ Identify capabilities of existing infrastructure.	1-50 to 1-52
■ Identify technology limitations.	1-52
■ Analyze interoperability constraints.	1-52 to 1- 53; 1-15 to 1-17
Creating the Logical Design for a Security Network Infrastructure (2.0)	
Design a public key infrastructure (PKI) that uses Certificate Services.	
■ Design a certification authority (CA) hierarchy implementation. Types include geographical, organizational, and trusted.	2-11; 2-15 to 2-25
■ Design enrollment and distribution processes.	2-35 to 2-46
■ Establish renewal, revocation, and auditing processes.	2-50 to 2-63
■ Design security for CA servers.	2-3 to 2-13; 2-65 to 2-72
Design a logical authentication strategy.	
■ Design certificate distribution.	2-42 to 2-46
■ Design forest and domain trust models.	6-5 to 6-25
■ Design security that meets interoperability requirements.	6-26 to 6-36
■ Establish account and password requirements for security.	6-37 to 6-51
Design security for network management.	
■ Manage the risk of managing networks.	4-5 to 4-16
■ Design the administration of servers by using common administration tools. Tools include the MMC, Terminal Server, Remote desktop for Administration, Remote Assistance, and Telnet.	4-17 to 4-38
■ Design security for Emergency Management Services.	4-39 to 4-44
Design a security update infrastructure.	
■ Design a Software Update Services infrastructure.	5-3 to 5-26
■ Designing group policy to deploy software updates.	5-27 to 5-34
■ Design a strategy for identifying computers that are not at the current patch level.	5-35 to 5-47
Creating the Physical Design for Network Infrastructure Security (3.0)	
Design network infrastructure security.	
■ Specify the required protocols for a firewall configuration.	3-9 to 3-14 3-17 to 3-22
■ Design IP filtering.	3-34 to 3-38
■ Design an IPSec policy.	3-38 to 3-62
■ Secure a DNS implementation.	3-27 to 3-33
■ Design security for data transmission.	3-14 to 3-34
Design security for wireless networks.	
■ Design a public and private wireless LANs.	12-5 to 12-17
■ Design 802.1x authentication for wireless networks.	12-18 to 12-33

Objective	Pages
Design user authentication for Internet Information Services.	
▪ Design user authentication for a Web site by using certificates.	13-32 to 13-39
▪ Design user authentication for a Web site by using IIS authentication.	13-32 to 13-35; 13-40 to 13-44
▪ Design user authentication for a Web site by using RADIUS for IIS authentication.	13-32 to 13-34; 13-40
Design security for Internet Information Services.	
▪ Design security for Web sites with different technical requirements by enabling the minimum required services.	13-5 to 13-12
▪ Design a monitoring strategy for IIS.	13-21 to 13-26
▪ Design an IIS baseline based on business requirements.	13-5 to 13-19; 13-27 to 13-31
▪ Design a content management strategy for updating an IIS server.	13-19 to 13-20
Design security for communication between networks.	
▪ Select protocols for VPN access.	7-3 to 7-12
▪ Design virtual private network (VPN) connectivity.	7-13 to 7-26
▪ Design demand-dial routing between private networks.	7-27 to 7-43
Design secure communication with external organizations.	
▪ Design an extranet infrastructure.	7-44 to 7-50
▪ Design a strategy for cross-certification of Certificate Services.	2-17 to 2-30
Design security for servers with spcific roles. Roles include domain controllers, network infrastructure servers, file servers, Internet Information Services servers, Terminal Servers, and POP3 mail servers.	
▪ Define a baseline security template for all systems.	8-14 to 8-27
▪ Create a plan to modify baseline security templates according to role.	8-28 to 8-32; 8-3 to 8-13

Designing an Access Control Strategy for Data (4.0)

Design an access control strategy for directory services.	
▪ Create a delegation strategy.	9-27 to 9-35
▪ Analyze auditing requirements.	9-36 to 9-53
▪ Design the appropriate group strategy for accessing resources.	9-3 to 9-11; 9-14 to 9-19
▪ Design a permission structure for directory service objects.	9-4 to 9-11; 9-27 to 9-31
Design an access control strategy for files and folders.	
▪ Design a strategy for the encryption and decryption of files and folders.	9-61 to 9-71
▪ Design a permissions structure for files and folders.	9-4 to 9-14; 9-20 to 9-22
▪ Design security for a backup and recovery strategy.	9-54 to 9-60
▪ Analyze auditing requirements.	9-36 to 9-53
Design an access control strategy for the registry.	
▪ Design a permission structure for registry objects.	9-4 to 9-11; 9-22 to 9-47
▪ Analyze auditing requirements.	9-36 to 9-53

Creating the Physical Design for a Secure Client Infrastructure (5.0)

Design a client authentication strategy.	
▪ Analyze authentication requirements.	10-3 to 10-17
▪ Establish account and password security requirements.	10-15
Design a security strategy for client remote access.	
▪ Design remote access policies.	10-23 to 10-36
▪ Design access to internal resources.	10-18 to 10-23
▪ Design an authentication provider and accounting strategy for remote network access by using Internet Authentication Service (IAS).	10-36 to 10-44
Design a strategy for securing clients. Considerations include desktop and portable computers.	
▪ Design a strategy for hardening client operating systems.	11-3 to 11-32
▪ Design a strategy for restricting user access to operating system features.	11-33 to 11-39

Note   Exam objectives are subject to change at anytime without prior notice and at Microsoft's sole discretion. Please visit Microsoft's Training & Certification Web site (*www.microsoft.com/traincert*) for the most current listing of exam objectives.

Microsoft

MCSE Self-Paced Training Kit (Exam 70-298): Designing Security for a Microsoft® Windows Server™ 2003 Network

Roberta Bragg

PUBLISHED BY
Microsoft Press
A Division of Microsoft Corporation
One Microsoft Way
Redmond, Washington 98052-6399

Library of Congress Cataloging-in-Publication Data
Bragg, Roberta.
    MCSE Self-Paced Training Kit (Exam 70-298) : Designing Security for a Microsoft
    Windows Server 2003 Network / Roberta Bragg.
        p. cm.
    Includes index.
    ISBN 0-7356-1969-7
    1. Computer networks--Security measures.   2. Microsoft Windows Server.   I. Title.

TK5105.59.B72   2003
005.8--dc21   2003065183

Printed and bound in the United States of America.

1 2 3 4 5 6 7 8 9   QWT   8 7 6 5 4 3

Distributed in Canada by H.B. Fenn and Company Ltd.

A CIP catalogue record for this book is available from the British Library.

Microsoft Press books are available through booksellers and distributors worldwide. For further information about international editions, contact your local Microsoft Corporation office or contact Microsoft Press International directly at fax (425) 936-7329. Visit our Web site at www.microsoft.com/mspress. Send comments to *tkinput@microsoft.com*.

Active Directory, FrontPage, Georgia, Microsoft, Microsoft Press, MS-DOS, MSDN, MSN, NetMeeting, Outlook, SharePoint, Visual Studio, Windows, the Windows logo, Windows Media, Windows Mobile, Windows NT, and Windows Server are either registered trademarks or trademarks of Microsoft Corporation in the United States and/or other countries. Other product and company names mentioned herein may be the trademarks of their respective owners.

The example companies, organizations, products, domain names, e-mail addresses, logos, people, places, and events depicted herein are fictitious. No association with any real company, organization, product, domain name, e-mail address, logo, person, place, or event is intended or should be inferred.

Acquisitions Editor: Kathy Harding
Content Development Manager: Lori Kane
Technical Editor: Jim Cochran
Project Manager: Julie Pickering
Indexer: Seth Maislin

Body Part No. X10-09380

Roberta Bragg

Roberta Bragg, MCSE: Security, CISSP, Security +, and Security Curmudgeon or Security Therapist, depending on her mood, is a 25-year veteran of the computing industry. She has sold, programmed, administered, secured, taught, and written about computing systems. Roberta has taught programming languages at the university, trade school, training company, and junior college levels; client server technologies, object oriented design, and Microsoft networking technologies for training companies; and information security at seminars and conferences around the world. As a programmer for CopyWrite, she wrote programs for law firms, insurance companies, hotels, and public utilities. As the network administrator of a Midwestern consulting firm, she single-handedly trashed its phone system and UNIX Web server in a single night, and then put them back together in a more secure configuration. As chief cook and bottle washer of Have Computer Will Travel, Inc., she is currently an author and consultant specializing in information security. She has authored Microsoft Certified Professional Magazine's "Security Advisor" column for five years, writes a column for 101 Communication's *Security Watch* newsletter (for which she provides security tips and commentary for over 55,000 people on a weekly basis), and has written several books on information security. She is also the Security Expert for the SearchWindows2000 Web site, where she answers readers' questions. You can find Roberta sitting in a wading pool in the back yard of her Grain Valley, Missouri, home with her cat Perrin (who thinks he is a fish) or in line at airport security—she's the one with the combat boots removed, wiggling her toes in her orange toe socks, and refusing to be scanned unless her laptops are brought to her.

Contents at a Glance

Practices

Tables

Design Activities

Contents

3   **Designing the Network Infrastructure for Physical Security**   **3-1**

Section III # Creating a Security Design for Management and Maintenance of the Network

4 Designing Security for Network Management   4-3

5   Designing a Security Update Infrastructure   5-1

Section IV Creating a Security Design for Basic Network Functions

6   Designing a Logical Authentication Strategy   6-3

8   Designing Security by Server Role   8-1

10   Designing a Secure Client Infrastructure   10-1

Section V   Creating a Security Design for Wireless Networks and Web Servers

12   Designing Security for Wireless Networks   12-3

Acknowledgments

Thanks are such easy rewards to give for the tremendous job that the team did on this book. I wish I could do more. I wish I knew who all of you were. For those I've had direct contact with and to those I have not, wow!

I couldn't have asked for a better team nor better use of the team approach. This is the way that books should be created, and I hope to have the pleasure of working with all of you again. You all deserve raises and public recognition for the work that you have done. I cannot give you the former, so to the best of my ability, I'll provide the latter.

Kathy Harding: If you hadn't invited me I never would have had this marvelous opportunity. If you hadn't visited with me several times about the book, I know I couldn't have done my part. Then, like the best acquisition editors, once the team was assigned and the author primed, you stood back and let us all do our jobs.

Roger LeBlanc: Like most authors I have my little quirks and sometimes-odd ideas about how sentences and paragraphs should be constructed. Most copy editors just correct my writing and allow me to complain if the technical meaning gets changed. Instead, you gave me the reasons behind many of your changes. You also did this with great tact. I find myself writing better because of you.

Julie Pickering: When Lori and I fudged up the schedule because we wanted to do a better book, you found the slack, in a tight schedule, to give us the time. I appreciate it, and I know someone had to work harder because of it. Thank them for me, OK?

James Cochran: Working with a good tech editor is like walking a tightrope with a net; it's like making an arrest with proper backup; it's like trashing your server and finding that the backup is good. You were all of those things. I appreciate your playing Tonto to my Lone Ranger.

Ben Smith: Peer review is often provided for technical books—during the outline and proposal stage, and after the book has been published. You reviewed every word I wrote, before anyone at Microsoft Press saw them. Your insightful comments, additions, corrections, and pats on the back were one of the highlights of this book's process. I am honored that you took the time to review my work.

Lori Kane: When I met you, I was a poor innocent author whose theory of education was provided by students, both ecstatic and disgruntled, and by her struggles to help people learn. You truly rocked my world when you suggested we transform this book into one that used modern educational theory. Imagine that—actually use what is known about the learning process to help people learn a highly technical subject. A simple idea really, and such a process is long overdue in the certification guide genre. Ever the eager glutton for punishment, I agreed. The process resembled the transition I had to make when switching to object oriented programming. Both processes require a new way of thinking and a lot of false starts before you have a usable product, but I think this mental re-org was harder. I'm sure there were points at which you must have felt as if you had made a mistake in trying to teach this old woman new tricks. I know there were times I felt like I was a rat in a maze. Lori dear, you did almost kill me, but look what we have produced! This has got to be the best certification guide ever written, and I am proud to have been a part of it.

—Roberta Bragg, Security Curmudgeon or Security Therapist (depending on her mood), Grain Valley, MO, October 26, 2003

About This Book

Welcome to *MCSE Self-Paced Training Kit (Exam 70-298): Designing Security for a Microsoft Windows Server 2003 Network.*

Information systems and networks that are designed without security in mind are destined for failure. Information systems and networks that incorporate security in their design will remain robust and defensible long after their counterparts have been destroyed. Information systems where security is considered hand-in-hand with business and technical needs will be easier to defend, manage, and maintain and will stand a better chance of surviving attacks. To design such Microsoft Windows–based networks, you must be knowledgeable in the technical underpinnings of security technologies and the Windows implementation of them, but it is even more crucial that you understand how to consider business needs and existing technical constraints in your design. This book will teach you how to do so. It will also help you prepare to take the exam 70-298.

Each chapter addresses an important aspect of network security design and a range of exam objectives. The goal of both the objectives and the chapter orientation is to provide a complete guide to Windows-based network security design. The book does not concentrate on technical details, except as they relate to the design. You will not find extensive implementation information. There are many excellent resources that can provide that. Instead, this book concentrates on the design process.

 Note For more information about becoming a Microsoft Certified Professional, see the section "The Microsoft Certified Professional Program" later in this introduction.

Intended Audience

This book was developed for information technology (IT) professionals who plan to take the related Microsoft Certified Professional exam 70-298, *Designing Security for a Microsoft Windows Server 2003 Network,* as well as IT professionals who design, develop, and implement software solutions for Microsoft Windows–based environments using Microsoft tools and technologies.

 Note Exam skills are subject to change without prior notice and at the sole discretion of Microsoft.

Prerequisites

This training kit requires that students meet the following prerequisites:

- Have a solid understanding of the networking and security technologies in Windows Server 2003. Although information about new security technologies for Windows Server 2003 and security technologies that cause many experienced Windows administrators problems are detailed in this book, this book should not be your first introduction to security technologies.

- Have at least one year of experience implementing and administering a network operating system in environments that have the following characteristics:

  ❑ At least 250 users

  ❑ Three or more physical locations

  ❑ Three or more domain controllers

  ❑ Network services and resources such as messaging, database, file and print, proxy server, firewall, Internet, intranet, remote access, and client computer management

  ❑ Connectivity requirements such as connecting branch offices and individual users in remote locations to the corporate network and connecting corporate networks to the Internet

- Have at least one year of experience in the following areas:

  ❑ Designing a network infrastructure

  ❑ Implementing and administering a desktop operating system

About the CD-ROM

For your use, this book includes a Supplemental CD-ROM, which contains a variety of informational aids to complement the book content:

- The Microsoft Press Readiness Review Suite Powered by MeasureUp. This suite of practice tests and objective reviews contains questions of varying degrees of complexity and offers multiple testing modes. You can assess your understanding of the concepts presented in this book and use the results to develop a learning plan that meets your needs.

- An electronic version of this book (eBook). For information about using the eBook, see the section "The eBook" later in this introduction.

- An eBook of the *Microsoft Encyclopedia of Networking, Second Edition* and of the *Microsoft Encyclopedia of Security*, which provide complete and up-to-date reference materials for networking and security.

- Sample chapters from several Microsoft Press books. These chapters give you additional information about Windows Server 2003 and introduce you to other resources that are available from Microsoft Press.

- Supplemental information, including:

  ❑ The "Windows Server 2003 Security Guide," which provides templates and instructions for securing Windows Server 2003.

  ❑ The "Windows XP Security Guide," which provides instructions and templates that can be used to secure Windows XP.

  ❑ "Threats and Countermeasures: Security Settings in Windows Server 2003 and Windows XP," which details every security setting.

  ❑ The "Windows 2000 Security Operations Guide," which provides similar information and templates for Windows 2000.

A second CD-ROM contains a 180-day evaluation edition of Microsoft Windows Server 2003, Enterprise Edition.

Caution   The 180-day evaluation edition provided with this training kit is not the full retail product and is provided only for the purposes of training and evaluation. Microsoft Technical Support does not support this evaluation edition.

For additional support information regarding this book and the CD-ROM (including answers to commonly asked questions about installation and use), visit the Microsoft Press Technical Support Web site at *http://www.microsoft.com/mspress/support/*. You can also e-mail tkinput@microsoft.com or send a letter to Microsoft Press, Attention: Microsoft Press Technical Support, One Microsoft Way, Redmond, WA 98052-6399.

Features of This Book

Each chapter of this book identifies the exam objectives that are covered within the chapter, provides an overview of why the topics matter by identifying how the information applies in the real world, and lists any prerequisites that must be met to complete the lessons presented in the chapter.

The chapters are divided into lessons. Each lesson ends with a practice to test your knowledge of the material presented in the lesson. Most practices use real-world scenarios to help you see if you can apply what you learned to real-world situations.

After the lessons, you are given an opportunity to apply what you've learned in a chapter-ending design activity. In this activity, you must work through a more lengthy and detailed real-world scenario to see if you can apply what you learned from all the lessons to a real situation. Each chapter ends with a summary of important concepts and a short section listing key topics and terms that you need to know before taking the exam.

> ### Real World **Helpful Information**
> You will find sidebars like this one that contain related information you might find helpful. "Real World" sidebars contain specific information gained through the experience of the author and other IT professionals just like you.

Informational Notes

Several types of reader aids appear throughout the training kit.

Tip   contains methods of performing a task more quickly or in a not-so-obvious way.

Important   contains information that is essential to completing a task.

Note   contains supplemental information.

Caution   contains valuable information about possible loss of data; be sure to read this information carefully.

Warning   contains critical information about possible physical injury; be sure to read this information carefully.

See Also   contains references to other sources of information.

Planning   contains hints and useful information that should help you to plan the implementation.

On the CD   points you to supplementary information or files you need that are on the companion CD.

Exam Tip   flags information you should know before taking the certification exam.

Off the Record   contains practical advice about the real-world implications of information presented in the lesson.

Notational Conventions

The following conventions are used throughout this book:

- Characters or commands that you type appear in **bold** type. Bold is also used for lead-in text to bulleted lists.

- *Italic* in syntax statements indicates placeholders for variable information. *Italic* is also used for introducing new terms and for book titles.

- Names of files and folders appear in Title caps, except when you are to type them directly. Unless otherwise indicated, you can use all lowercase letters when you type a file name in a dialog box or at a command prompt.

- File name extensions appear in all lowercase.

- Acronyms appear in all uppercase.

- Monospace type represents code samples, examples of screen text, or entries that you might type at a command prompt or in initialization files.

- Square brackets [ ] are used in syntax statements to enclose optional items. For example, [*filename*] in command syntax indicates that you can choose to type a file name with the command. Type only the information within the brackets, not the brackets themselves.

Keyboard Conventions

- A plus sign (+) between two key names means that you must press those keys at the same time. For example, "Press ALT+TAB" means that you hold down ALT while you press TAB.

- A comma (,) between two or more key names means that you must press each of the keys consecutively, not together. For example, "Press ALT, F, X" means that you press and release each key in sequence. "Press ALT+W, L" means that you first press ALT and W at the same time, and then release them and press L.

Getting Started

The exercises for this training kit emphasize security design and not implementation; however, the book does contain a few hands-on exercises to help you learn about designing security for a Windows-based network. Use this section to prepare your self-paced training environment.

Caution The computers that you use for your work should not be connected to a production network. If your computers are part of a larger test network, you *must* verify with your test network administrator that the computer names, domain name, and other information used in setting up Windows Server 2003 and the completion of the exercises in this book do not conflict with network operations. If they do conflict, ask your network administrator to provide alternative values and use those values throughout all of the exercises in this book.

Hardware Requirements

Each computer must have the following minimum configuration. All hardware should be on the Microsoft Windows Server 2003, Enterprise Edition Hardware Compatibility List.

- **Computer and processor**   133 megahertz (MHz) minimum is required. Use the Intel Pentium/Celeron family, the AMD K6/Athlon/Duron family, or a compatible processor. (Windows Server 2003, Enterprise Edition supports up to eight CPUs on one server.) 733 MHz is recommended.

- **Memory**   128 megabytes (MB) of memory is the minimum required (maximum 32 gigabytes [GB] of RAM). 256 MB or more is recommended.

- **Hard disk**   1.55 to 2 GB of available hard-disk space is required. (More room will be required to install additional operating system features and to practice some of the techniques described.)

- **Drive**   A CD-ROM or DVD-ROM drive is required.

- **Display**   VGA or hardware that supports console redirection is required.

- **Peripherals**   A keyboard and Microsoft mouse, or a compatible pointing device, or hardware that supports console redirection is required.

- **Miscellaneous**   Internet access and networking requirements:

  - Some Internet functionality might require Internet access, a Microsoft Passport account, and payment of a separate fee to a service provider. Local and/or long-distance telephone toll charges might apply. A high-speed modem or broadband Internet connection is recommended.

❑   For networking, you must have a network adapter appropriate for the type of local-area, wide-area, wireless, or home network to which you want to connect and access to an appropriate network infrastructure. Access to third-party networks might require additional charges.

Software Requirements

The following software is required to complete the procedures in this training kit. (A 180-day evaluation edition of Windows Server 2003, Enterprise Edition, is included on the CD-ROM.)

■   Windows Server 2003, Enterprise Edition

Caution   The 180-day evaluation edition provided with this training kit is not the full retail product and is provided only for the purposes of training and evaluation. Microsoft Technical Support does not support these evaluation editions. For additional support information regarding this book and the CD-ROMs (including answers to commonly asked questions about installation and use), visit the Microsoft Press Technical Support Web site at *http://mspress.microsoft.com /mspress/support/*. You can also e-mail tkinput@microsoft.com or send a letter to Microsoft Press, Attn: Microsoft Press Technical Support, One Microsoft Way, Redmond, WA 98502-6399.

Setup Instructions

Set up your computer according to the manufacturer's instructions.

For the exercises that require networked computers, you will need two computers that can communicate with each other. The first computer must be configured as a primary domain controller (PDC) and should be assigned the computer account name DC1 and the domain name wingtiptoys.com. This computer will act as a domain controller and can be used to provide the following services: Internet Information Services (IIS), Internet Authentication Service (IAS), certificates, and Routing and Remote Access Services (RRAS).

The second computer will act at various times as a server in the wingtiptoys.com domain, a second domain controller in the wingtiptoys.com domain, or a domain controller in the tailspintoys.com forest for most of the procedures in this course.

Caution   The computers that you use for your work should not be connected to a production network. If your computers are part of a larger test network, you *must* verify with your test network administrator that the computer names, domain name, and other information used in setting up Windows Server 2003 and the completion of the exercises in this book do not conflict with network operations. If they do conflict, ask your network administrator to provide alternative values and use those values throughout all of the exercises in this book.

The Readiness Review Suite

The CD-ROM includes a practice test made up of 300 sample exam questions. Use these tools to reinforce your learning and to identify any areas in which you need to gain more experience before taking the exam.

▶   **To install the practice test**

1. Insert the Supplemental CD-ROM into your CD-ROM drive.

Note   If AutoRun is disabled on your computer, refer to the Readme.txt file on the CD-ROM.

2. Click Readiness Review Suite on the user interface menu.

The eBook

The CD-ROM includes an electronic version of the training kit. The eBook is in portable document format (PDF) and can be viewed using Adobe Acrobat Reader.

▶   **To use the eBook**

1. Insert the Supplemental CD-ROM into your CD-ROM drive.

Note   If AutoRun is disabled on your machine, refer to the Readme.txt file on the CD-ROM.

2. Click Training Kit eBook on the user interface menu. You can also review any of the other eBooks that are provided for your use.

The Microsoft Certified Professional Program

The Microsoft Certified Professional (MCP) program provides the best method to prove your command of current Microsoft products and technologies. The exams and corresponding certifications are developed to validate your mastery of critical competencies as you design and develop, or implement and support, solutions with Microsoft products and technologies. Computer professionals who become Microsoft certified are recognized as experts and are sought after industry-wide. Certification brings a variety of benefits to the individual and to employers and organizations.

> **See Also**   For a full list of MCP benefits, go to *http://www.microsoft.com/traincert/start /itpro.asp.*

Certifications

The Microsoft Certified Professional program offers multiple certifications, based on specific areas of technical expertise:

- *Microsoft Certified Professional (MCP).* Demonstrated in-depth knowledge of at least one Microsoft Windows operating system or architecturally significant platform. An MCP is qualified to implement a Microsoft product or technology as part of a business solution for an organization.

- *Microsoft Certified Desktop Support Technician (MCDST).* Individuals who support end users and troubleshoot desktop environments running on the Windows operating system.

- *Microsoft Certified Solution Developer (MCSD).* Professional developers qualified to analyze, design, and develop enterprise business solutions with Microsoft development tools and technologies, including the Microsoft .NET Framework.

- *Microsoft Certified Application Developer (MCAD).* Professional developers qualified to develop, test, deploy, and maintain powerful applications using Microsoft tools and technologies, including Microsoft Visual Studio .NET and Web services.

- *Microsoft Certified Systems Engineer (MCSE).* Qualified to effectively analyze the business requirements, and design and implement the infrastructure for business solutions based on the Microsoft Windows and Microsoft Server 2003 operating systems. For systems engineers who specialize in designing, planning, and implementing security on the Microsoft platform and who focus on creating a secure computing environment, the new MCSE: Security on Microsoft Windows 2003 certification has been created.

- *Microsoft Certified Systems Administrator (MCSA).* Individuals with the skills to manage and troubleshoot existing network and system environments based on the Microsoft Windows and Microsoft Server 2003 operating systems.

- *Microsoft Certified Database Administrator (MCDBA).* Individuals who design, implement, and administer Microsoft SQL Server databases.

- *Microsoft Certified Trainer (MCT).* Instructionally and technically qualified to deliver Microsoft Official Curriculum through a Microsoft Certified Technical Education Center (CTEC).

Requirements for Becoming a Microsoft Certified Professional

The certification requirements differ for each certification and are specific to the products and job functions addressed by the certification.

To become a Microsoft Certified Professional, you must pass rigorous certification exams that provide a valid and reliable measure of technical proficiency and expertise. These exams are designed to test your expertise and ability to perform a role or task with a product and are developed with the input of professionals in the industry. Questions in the exams reflect how Microsoft products are used in actual organizations, giving them "real-world" relevance.

- Microsoft Certified Professionals (MCPs) are required to pass one current Microsoft certification exam. Candidates can pass additional Microsoft certification exams to further qualify their skills with other Microsoft products, development tools, or desktop applications.

- Microsoft Certified Desktop Support Technicians (MCDSTs) are required to pass two core client operating system exams. Elective exams are not required.

- Microsoft Certified Solution Developers (MCSDs) are required to pass three core exams and one elective exam on the Visual Studio 6.0 track. MCSD: Microsoft .NET track candidates are required to pass four core exams and one elective.

- Microsoft Certified Application Developers (MCADs) are required to pass two core exams and one elective exam in an area of specialization.

- Microsoft Certified Systems Engineers (MCSEs) are required to pass five core exams and two elective exams. MCSE: Security candidates on the Microsoft Windows 2003 certification track are required to pass five core exams and three security specialization exams.

- Microsoft Certified Systems Administrators (MCSAs) are required to pass three core exams and one elective exam that provide a valid and reliable measure of technical proficiency and expertise.

- Microsoft Certified Database Administrators (MCDBAs) are required to pass three core exams and one elective exam that provide a valid and reliable measure of technical proficiency and expertise.

Technical Support

Every effort has been made to ensure the accuracy of this book and the contents of the companion disc. If you have comments, questions, or ideas regarding this book or the companion disc, please send them to Microsoft Press using either of the following methods:

E-mail: tkinput@microsoft.com

Postal Mail: Microsoft Press
Attn: *MCSE Self-Paced Training Kit (Exam 70-298)* Editor
One Microsoft Way
Redmond, WA 98052-6399

For additional support information regarding this book and the CD-ROM (including answers to commonly asked questions about installation and use), visit the Microsoft Press Technical Support Web site at *http://www.microsoft.com/mspress/support/*. To connect directly to the Microsoft Press Knowledge Base and enter a query, visit *http://www.microsoft.com/mspress/support/search.asp*. For support information regarding Microsoft software, please connect to *http://support.microsoft.com/*.

Evaluation Edition Software Support

The 180-day evaluation edition provided with this training kit is not the full retail product and is provided only for the purposes of training and evaluation. Microsoft and Microsoft Technical Support do not support this evaluation edition.

Caution The evaluation edition of Windows Server 2003, Enterprise Edition, included with this book should not be used on a primary work computer. The evaluation edition is unsupported. For online support information relating to the full version of Windows Server 2003, Enterprise Edition, that *might* also apply to the evaluation edition, you can connect to *http://support.microsoft.com/*.

Information about any issues relating to the use of this evaluation edition with this training kit is posted to the Support section of the Microsoft Press Web site (*http://www.microsoft.com/mspress/support/*). For information about ordering the full version of any Microsoft software, please call Microsoft Sales at (800) 426-9400 or visit *http://www.microsoft.com*.

Section I
Documenting the Impact of Business and Technical Constraints on the Security Design Process

Considering the impact of business and technical constraints on the security design process might be your least favorite part of your role as a security designer. As a technical person, you might have little patience for those who cannot speak your language or who do not intimately understand how technologies work. You might be frustrated because you know exactly what to do to secure your organization's networks and operating systems but have not been given the money, time, staff, or training to do it right. You might also have met with resistance when proposing essential changes to security practices.

This section can help you overcome the objections of business management, provides insight into the business needs that constrain every information system design and the minds that can approve or deny any security proposal, and can help you identify and explain technical constraints and security requirements to management. Management is not going to suddenly become technically astute or security smart. You, however, who already possess the technical knowledge, can learn how to express

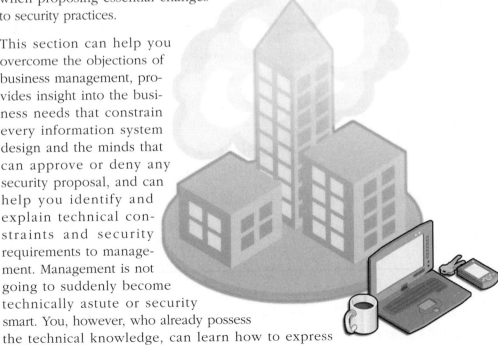

security needs in business language. To do so, you must start with Chapter 1, "Creating a Conceptual Design for Network Infrastructure Security," which includes a discussion of business and technical constraints in the broader framework that is security design. It provides:

- Instruction on analyzing business requirements
- A discussion about the impact of laws on security design
- A discussion about the cost of security
- Instruction about how to categorize data to properly protect it
- Definitions of technical terms that business people can understand
- Considerations of the impact of legacy technologies on security
- Information about risk analysis and threat modeling
- Considerations of the impact of interoperability issues on security design
- A framework against which all other security design topics are built

1 Creating a Conceptual Design for Network Infrastructure Security

Exam Objectives in this Chapter:

- Creating the conceptual design for network infrastructure security by gathering and analyzing business and technical requirements.
    - Analyze business requirements for designing security.
        - Analyze existing security policies and procedures.
        - Analyze the organizational requirements for securing data.
        - Analyze risks to security within current IT administration structure and security practices.
    - Design a framework for designing and implementing security. The framework should include prevention, detection, isolation, and recovery.
        - Predict threats to your network from internal and external sources.
        - Design a process for responding to incidents.
        - Design a process for recovering services.
    - Analyze technical constraints when designing security.
        - Identify capabilities of existing infrastructure.
        - Identify technology limitations.
        - Analyze interoperability constraints.

Why This Chapter Matters

Unless your business has a properly designed security framework, it is doomed to failure. The primary purpose of information security is to make sure that a business remains in business. And whether you are tasked with designing a security framework for an entire organization or with designing the best possible security solution for a soon-to-be-implemented business process, you must start with an understanding of your organization's business model, technical infrastructure, and existing security policies. To understand these things, you must gather the pertinent business and technical information, evaluate how well existing security policies meet business needs, design a security solution by using the principles of security design, and then evaluate technical, legal, social, and management constraints, which often require you to make adjustments to the ideal solution.

This chapter lays a crucial foundation for the rest of the chapters in this book. This chapter provides the big picture and teaches you how to design a framework against which you will perform all security design.

Lessons in this Chapter:

Before You Begin

This chapter presents the skills and concepts related to creating a security design framework. This training kit assumes that you have a minimum of 1 year of experience implementing and administering desktop operating systems and network operating systems in environments that have the following characteristics:

- At least 250 supported users
- Three or more physical locations
- Typical network services such as messaging, database, file and print, proxy server or firewall, Internet and intranet, remote access, and client computer management
- Three or more domain controllers
- Connectivity needs that include connecting branch offices and individual users in remote locations to the corporate network and connecting corporate networks to the Internet

In addition, you should have experience designing a network infrastructure.

Many design exercises are paper based; however, to understand the technical capabilities that a design can incorporate, you should have some hands-on experience with products. Where specific hands-on instruction is given, you must have at least two computers configured as specified in the "Getting Started" section at the beginning of this book.

Lesson 1: Analyzing Business Requirements for Information Security

When business managers state business requirements for an IT department, their requirements often do not consider security. Instead, managers ask for things such as quick turnaround, return on investment, and reduction in expenses—requirements that often lead to reduced security. As a security designer, you are responsible for aligning these business requirements with the IT department's goals to design and deploy secure systems.

Planning   Whenever possible, security design should start at the beginning of each IT project. If you add the security design at the end of an existing project, you might not be able to provide the best solution and might not be able to provide sound security at all.

After this lesson, you will be able to

- Explain the process of analyzing business requirements.
- Describe common business drivers for security design.
- Explain the guidelines for:
  - Mitigating the cost of security.
  - Managing legal requirements.
  - Determining how security design affects end users.
  - Using the security design to mitigate risk.
  - Reducing the impact of interoperability on security.
- Describe threats to security introduced by maintainability issues.
- Analyze existing security policy and procedures.
- Categorize and secure data based on organization's needs.
- Use data flow to determine where data is at risk.
- Analyze risks to security in the existing IT administration structure.

Estimated lesson time: 90 minutes

The Process: Analyzing Business Requirements

To analyze business requirements:

1. *Review business requirements stated by management.* Business requirements might be stated in terms of the budget for the project, the connectivity and types of data that must be available for use by partners, etc. Make sure you understand the stated purpose.

2. *Make note of additional business requirements discovered during the review.* Asking questions about the stated requirements, for example, might turn up additional requirements. Questions about the type of data to be shared, for example, might reveal the limitations of who can read the information, who is allowed to change it, and so on.

3. *Analyze the business requirements.* You do this so that you can make sure that the security design stays true to its goal of supporting the business. To help you analyze the business requirements, perform the following tasks:

   a. Develop a list of common business drivers—the objectives that propel the business forward and continue to make it profitable. (Examples of common business drivers are shown in the following section.) You can use this list to help you analyze all projects.

   b. Research how the business drivers will affect the security design and vice versa.

   c. Analyze existing security policies and procedures.

4. *Document what you learn.* If you document what you learn, your security design can start with an orderly discussion of the business drivers and business requirements and how you have considered them. This information will make it easier for business decision-makers to accept and support your design recommendations.

The rest of this lesson provides information that you can use to help you analyze business requirements.

Common Business Drivers for Security Design

For an organization to stay in business and maximize profits, its management must consider certain business drivers for each business activity the organization undertakes. Common business drivers that the security design must address include the following:

- **The initial and ongoing cost of security**   The real and perceived cost of security will always be a driving factor in the implementation of security.

- **Legal requirements for security**   Legal requirements affect implementation of security and other IT operational aspects, and the impact of these legal requirements is increasing. Deciding how much security is necessary and convincing management to accept the recommendation is not an easy chore. However, current and proposed laws support the design and development of sound security practices. Consequently, legal requirements often can be an ally to security designers rather than a burden.

- **The impact security decisions will have on end users**   For purposes of considering the effect of security on end users, *end user* is defined as an individual who uses a system to obtain, manage, or distribute information but is not limited to employees who work directly for the company. Customers who access their banking or other information via the Internet, partners who cross gateways to access shared information, and public use of company Web sites are all examples of end users relying on information systems. Security designers must consider the impact that security policies will have on end users. For example, changing the password policy to require the use of symbols, letters, and numbers in password, when users were not required to do so before, can greatly upset a large number of users. If users are not warned that such a change is coming and told what they need to do to, the uproar and complaints can affect productivity and even force a roll-back to a less secure password policy.

■ **How security will mitigate risk**   *Risk* is often defined as the probability of suffering a loss. Risk management involves identifying risk and deciding what to do about it. Even if a risk cannot be eliminated, it can be addressed. Mitigation of risk is one the goals of information security.

In addition to these common business drivers, the IT department has business drivers of its own to consider:

■ **Maintaining interoperability**   The best security design might not be implemented because it failed to take into account the nature of all operating systems and applications that are part of the organization's network.

■ **Achieving security maintainability goals**   Any operations design must achieve certain maintainability goals, and this is even more important with security designs. Security devices and procedures that are not maintained will eventually become ineffective.

■ **Addressing scalability needs**   Many security designs can be implemented in a test network or small business with great success, but are impractical or fail when rolled out across more extensive systems. While you can't always forecast system growth, you can evaluate a security design in light of the environment it will be deployed in and simply assume moderate growth over time.

The guidelines that follow will help you analyze these business and IT-specific drivers.

Why the Cost of Information Security Inhibits Its Use

The real and perceived cost of security has always been a key factor in the poor implementation of security. Security-specific products, such as firewalls and intrusion detection systems (IDS), appear to cost a lot of money and do not produce results that non-technical people can easily understand.

The average cost of security-specific products can range from a few dollars to tens of thousands of dollars per product. They can require training for staff and are complicated to explain to the layman. What's more, the data that security products produce is often difficult to explain to end users and management. What, for example, does it mean to the average employee that there is evidence of hundreds of blocked packets in the firewall logs or that a large number of alarms are generated by the IDS?

Other examples of identifiable costs attributed to security include the downtime experienced because users forget passwords and the reduced or perceived reduction in performance when auditing is turned on or when data is encrypted. But the largest inhibiting factor, by far, has been the perception that security is overhead—something that brings no direct improvement to the bottom line and something that is expendable when the company is economically stressed.

Guidelines for Mitigating the Cost of Security

Follow these guidelines to minimize the cost of security:

- **Always insist on a clear and complete statement of the cost that security adds to any project.**   Whether the cost is prepared by vendors, internal IT staff, management, or the security designer, it must be complete.

- **Look at security solutions that reduce cost.**   Are there security technologies suitable for this project that can reduce overall cost and thus improve profitability? An example of such technologies is the use of Secure Sockets Layer (SSL) encryption accelerator cards in e-commerce projects. People rarely doubt the need for secure servers to protect the transmission of sensitive customer or partner financial information during an e-commerce transaction. However, SSL encryption does reduce the number of transactions that can be processed per minute. Slowing the processing of monetary transactions is not a good thing, but removing SSL encryption is not an acceptable solution. SSL-encryption accelerator cards are the answer. Although these cards add cost to a security project, they pay for themselves because they allow the number of possible SSL-encrypted transactions to increase and provide the required care of customer information as it traverses the Internet.

- **Look for security technologies that, if not employed, absolutely will result in the failure of the project or will result in large, unnecessary expenses.**   No one today can imagine running an e-mail gateway without antivirus protection. However, it was not long ago that the purchase of such products was seen only as an expense that *might* be useful. Many organizations learned the hard way that not providing and frequently updating antivirus protection on both the gateway and the end-user machine leads to business interruptions and larger expenses than the cost of providing protection in the first place.

- **Look for other tangential business drivers that, if not analyzed, can lead to increased expense.**   For example, confidentiality and integrity—or perhaps the lack of confidentiality and integrity—are becoming increasingly larger legal issues. Ignorance of relevant laws and regulations is not an excuse not to follow them. Potentially large fines and lawsuits can be the result of failure to follow current laws. Another example is that although designing and deploying security can be expensive and require significant expertise, the lack of security can cost even more. The hard costs of the security design—such as costs for equipment, training, and so on—should always be a part of the project cost-benefit analysis. In some cases, it can be shown that adding security reduces the cost of doing business.

The Cost of Virus and Worm Attacks

According to Computer Economics (as quoted in Investors Business Daily, August 28, 2003, http://biz.yahoo.com/ibd/030828/feature_1.html) and various new articles on the Internet, the worldwide cost of various malicious code attacks is estimated as follows:

- $11.2 billion in 2002
- $13.2 billion in 2001
- $17.1 billion in 2000

Although other organizations dispute these exact figures—citing difficulties in estimating the spread of infection as well as the costs of cleanup—these attacks clearly have a tremendous negative economic impact.

Guidelines for Managing Legal Requirements

Follow these guidelines to manage legal requirements:

- Have the organization's legal team review each security design.
- Improve the security design team's awareness of current legal requirements.
- Require the security design team to prepare legal compliance as part of its design.
- Have a frank discussion with IT-knowledgeable attorneys early in each product or process development cycle.

Legal Requirements that Influence Security Design

To make time spent with legal advisors efficient and productive, the security framework should include a living document that includes concise, IT-friendly statements about each law that might affect IT projects. Here is an example of current laws that might be examined for their relevance to projects. The review of such a list might point out, for example, the need for better technical controls on access to patient or employee data, or the need for discussion on improving integrity controls on financial data. Any discussion of whether the law might affect how the project should be designed should ultimately involve the organization's legal advisors. This short list of laws to be explored is not intended to be a comprehensive list:

- **Health Insurance Portability and Accountability Act (HIPAA) of 1996.** A summary of this act can be found at *http://www.hhs.gov/ocr/privacysummary.pdf*. HIPAA is a U.S. national standard for the protection of health information. The act describes privacy and security standards for electronic exchange of patient health information. This applies to the IT department at doctor's offices, hospitals, and insurance carriers, but might apply to others as well (for example, to businesses that have benefit plans, because their healthcare plans might come under the restrictions of the law). Government-provided decision tools are available at *http://www.cms.hhs.gov/hipaa /hipaa2/support/tools/decisionsupport/default.asp*.

- **Graham Leach Bliley.** Financial institutions (that is, any company that provides financial products or services) have their own set of legislation that controls how they must manage the privacy of customer financial information. It restricts use and disclosure of non-public personal information.

- **Sarbanes-Oxley Act of 2002 (Public Company Accounting Reform and Investor Protection Act).** This act targets publicly traded or registered companies. Private firms are also complying. Many restrictions are related to the operation of public accounting firms, and the act also includes strict requirements for records retention to prevent document destruction. For example, if a firm is engaged by a company to do an audit, that firm cannot also provide development of financial services or accounting software for the company. The CEO and CFO must sign a statement that accompanies the company's annual report stating that all information in the report is correct. This might sound tangential to information security until you consider the question, "How can they attest to accuracy if they are not prepared to defend the security of their financial computer programs and attest to the integrity of the data?" The act also requires that internal controls be reported. Internal controls = security infrastructure.

■ **Homeland Security Act of 2002 (Provision Computer Security Enhancement Act).** This act provides increased surveillance powers for law enforcement agencies, including surveillance conducted on the Internet. The act includes provisions to make it easier for federal agencies to obtain customer information from Internet service providers (ISPs).

■ **USA Patriot Act.** This act was established to deter and punish acts of terrorism. The act includes a directive for the U.S. Secret Service to develop a national network or electronic crime task force; amends the federal criminal code to allow wire, oral, and electronic communications when the case includes terrorism offenses, chemical weapons, and computer fraud and abuse; amends federal criminal code to include surveillance and interception of computer trespassing; and amends federal criminal code to include wiretaps to intercept teleconferences. In one famous case quoted to support passage of the act, a hacker stole teleconference services from a company and used them to plan and execute hacking attacks. Law enforcement agencies could not get authority to tap into the teleconferencing session. The act now gives investigators the ability to request that authority. The act also extends definitions to include cable companies, who, during the passage of earlier bills, were not providing Internet access services but who now are.

■ **California law SB 1836.** This law is an amendment to the California Information Practices Act that says if you do business with residents of California, have their unencrypted information in your databases, and are then hacked, you must notify each of those California residents that their personal information might have been compromised. This law is a California law that affects every state in the U.S.

Considerations for Determining How Security Design Affects End Users

To help you determine how a change in security can affect end users, ask yourself these questions:

■ **How will a stronger password policy actually work at the end-user level?** Will requiring a longer password mean more passwords are written on paper where unauthorized users might discover them? Will it mean loss of productivity or additional help desk labor because of an increased need to reset passwords?

■ **What will adding an account lockout policy do to users?** Account lockout policies lock accounts after a number of incorrect password attempts. The number of false attempts allowed is adjustable. Will the number of allowed attempts accommodate remote users, or will fumble-fingered sales personnel be unable to enter their orders because their account gets locked out? How long will the policy keep accounts locked out? Local users might be able to wait the 10 minutes or until the help desk can reset their account. Can the traveling executive seeking critical information on a dial-up line afford to waste that much time attempting to contact the help desk?

- **What will be the side-effects of moving to smart cards?**   What will happen when users forget their smart cards at home and attempt to use an office mate's card? If restrictions on card removal (sessions are logged off when smart cards are removed) are set, two users cannot use the same smart card and maintain consecutive sessions. This solves a long-standing dilemma as well—that is, how to restrict each user to one session at a time on the network. These are positive side-effects that affect users. However, smart cards can also have a negative effect. In the Microsoft Windows 2000 environment, smart card certificate renewal is not automatic. This situation can have a major impact on end users because they must figure out how to renew certificates. Although this is not a difficult chore, it can be for some users. When thousands of users must do so, many of them will have problems. This will put a large strain on the help desk and might affect the productivity of the users, as after certificates expire users cannot work until they renew the certificate. In Windows Server 2003, you *can* implement automatic renewal. If you do not consider the impact of security on end users, you might miss this critical step.

Guidelines for Using the Security Design to Mitigate Risk

Follow these guidelines to incorporate risk mitigation strategies into your security design:

- Look at IT operations with an eye to risk. This approach can help in the development of more secure systems.

- Develop a risk model for IT operations as a part of any security framework.

- Don't limit risk modeling to the evaluation of potential security risks, but incorporate the development of a long-term risk management strategy into the company's IT operations.

- Find out who manages risk for the organization. You will find them to be a ready source of information on risks to your organization.

- Incorporate other people's knowledge about risks into security designs.

- Require continuous risk assessment and response. Your security design should continually search for new risks and periodically evaluate known risks. Consider that viruses and worms, historically perceived as risks related to e-mail, are now spread by attacks against vulnerable services such as Web and database services exposed to the Internet. Modern malicious code is a blended threat and targets various segments of the computing environment, and as such, requires constant vigilance.

- Integrate risk management into all roles, including IT roles and those of every process owner. Process owners can take responsibility for identifying risks and managing them. If end users circumvent security, for example, by sharing passwords, they put systems at risk. Human Resources can be involved by ensuring that employees are aware of security risk factors, and if dictated by policy, by enforcing sanctions against people who do not comply.

> **See Also**   For more information about risk management for IT, see "MOF Risk Model for Operations" on the TechNet page of the Microsoft Web site at *http://www.microsoft.com/technet /itsolutions/tandp/opex/mofrl/MOFRisk.asp*. This white paper, which parallels a similar white paper about software development, explores the Microsoft Operations Framework risk model. This model seeks to embed risk management practices into every IT team role and process.

The Process of Risk Evaluation

To evaluate which risks to address first, risk managers use the strategy of determining the cost of risk and then ranking risk by using a combination of cost and probability. Two methodologies are used: informal and formal.

In the informal methodology, two steps are taken:

1. People familiar with the process of risk evaluation perform an evaluation to determine whether there is a risk and what might be done about it. For example, it does not require a lot of calculation to determine that risk of infection via some new worm or virus is high if a network is connected to the Internet and you are not using any antivirus programs. Mitigating the possibility, and certainly the severity, of such attacks is easily accomplished and it is usually not a problem to justify the cost. The exact calculation of risk, in dollars and cents, can require expertise, access to actuary tables, and perhaps specific proprietary software, and it is not considered necessary in an informal risk evaluation.

2. Risks are ranked to determine which ones should be addressed first. Ranking risk involves determining which risks are larger so that the worst risks can be addressed first and receive the most attention. Informal risk ranking is accomplished by assigning each risk two numbers: one number for how critical the threat is and the other for how likely the threat is to happen. These numbers are arrived at partially by instinct and partially as a result of past experiences of you and your peers. Multiplying the two numbers gives us one way to assess and compare risk. For example, the threat of a hurricane wiping out a data center is a critical risk and on a scale of 1 to 10—with 10 being the most severe—the potential damage might rank as a 10. However, the possibility of this happening ranges from slight to near impossible in many locations. The number for likely occurrence might be assigned a 1. Hence, the risk number for the hurricane threat is a 10. Because a maximum threat index in this scale is 100, the hurricane will be placed well down on the list of threats that need to be mitigated.

This process might seem simple, but a more formal risk evaluation follows a similar plan. More time is spent on each operation, and the process gets more specific. The following steps are taken in a formal evaluation:

1. A formal financial impact statement is prepared for each risk. This includes calculating the potential for monetary loss if the risk becomes a reality.

2. A business impact analysis (BIA) is prepared:

   a. For each risk, it is determined what will happen if risk becomes reality.

   b. For each risk, it is determined exactly how much time in days or hours can pass before the business goes out of business.

   c. Each risk is ranked according to this time factor. It is more important to first address risks that have the most devastating impact on the business—that is, which cause a faster demise of the business.

3. A risk mitigation plan is prepared. The risk of intrusion via the Internet, for example, might be reduced by the deployment of firewalls and intrusion detection systems, or the risk might be transferred to another company by outsourcing the management and procurement of these security defenses. Risk might also be avoided by not taking an action. Plans to develop a Web site that allows customers to manage their own data might be stopped if the project is deemed too risky.

Identifying the Sources of Risk: It's Not as Simple as It Seems

Many risk management experts caution that we should look for all sources of risk. They identify the sources of risk as people, processes, and technology. Other experts include things beyond our control, such as your ISP's lax password policy that could be a risk to the security of your organization's data. Identifying the sources of risk, however, is not always simple.

In 1998, a small Midwestern consulting firm's telephone system was rendered inoperable in the middle of a business day when the system administrator changed the account used to run the service for the software-based Private Branch Exchange (PBX) system. The change was made, in accordance with the PBX system documentation, to facilitate the delivery of voice mail directly to the employees' mailboxes. However, when the PBX system was brought back on line, the phones were all dead. Fortunately, the administrator was able to determine that the problem could be rectified by granting the new account appropriate permissions on the database. Nowhere in the PBX system documentation was that step listed or even alluded to.

It is easy to see, after a loss occurs, how it happened. Yet if you had been evaluating the risks associated with the PBX, which source of risk would you have identified?

- Was the source of the risk people related? The systems administrator has to make changes to systems configuration from time to time—did she make a mistake or proceed without all the information? Did the administrator make a change to the configuration without thinking of the possible consequences? If she had reviewed the process with others, she might have questioned why permissions were not being reassigned.

- Was the source of the risk technical? The system might have failed because its configuration was in error. Wouldn't a better design have warned the administrator that a change in accounts might cause a problem? New error messages in Microsoft Windows Server 2003 and Windows XP Professional seek to warn users and administrators of nonreversible operations, such as password resets, that might damage the ability to access critical data such as encrypted files.

- Was the source of the risk process related? Should the operational procedures have been required to be tested or at least reviewed before they were implemented? Or, perhaps such a major change should have been made during less critical business hours.

Guidelines for Reducing the Impact of Interoperability on Security

Use the following guidelines to reduce the impact of interoperability on security. These guidelines refer to the process of encrypting data but also highlight the need to consider interoperability.

Note   To make this example simple, this discussion is restricted to communications across the data network.

- **Determine what current processes will be part of the design.**   This is a good first step.

- **Develop a list of the hardware and software that will be used in the design.**   This list can be compiled by addressing the following issues:

  - ❏ What computers will be used? Are products such as routers, firewalls, and other network devices currently separating computers that must share information?

  - ❏ What operating system and version will be used? Is specific application software used? For example, is Microsoft Word used for documents? Is Microsoft Excel used for spreadsheets? Will documents be copied across the network? Collected from an intranet site? And will they be attached to e-mail messages or be in the body of e-mail messages?

❑ Will the hardware and software used affect which security protocols can be used? Consider, for example, that IPSec is implemented at a lower layer than SSL. IPSec can be used to encrypt all data without any need to redesign the application. SSL, however, must be designed into the application.

■ **Evaluate the capabilities of current processes, hardware, and software.** The list of possible solutions that can be used in any particular security design depend on the capabilities of existing hardware and software and the capabilities of planned purchases of hardware and software. Use the following questions to evaluate current system capabilities and available products:

❑ What security software and mechanisms currently exist? In today's networks, the use of IPSec should be considered, as should virtual private networks (VPNs) for remote communications, SSL for access to intranet servers, and e-mail encryption. The use of SSH (secure shell) is also a possibility for encrypting communications that might be used to manage databases and file servers where information resides. Many of these products and processes are built into Windows Server 2003

❑ Are proprietary encryption products already a part of the network infrastructure?

❑ Can all clients that will be used participate when specific communication protocols are selected? This will narrow the field of possibilities or determine the need for hardware and software upgrades.

❑ Evaluate other communication protocols and software if no solution exists for your current configuration and if funding exists for additional purchases.

■ **Review existing standards for communication protocols.** How old is the standard? Do vendors adhere to it? Which vendors? Is there a wide range of implementation decisions to be made? Is the standard volatile or stable?

■ **For each protocol, determine where interoperability issues exist.** One way to make this determination is to contact other individuals and organizations that are already using the protocol you are considering. Ask your current vendors to provide you with contact information for customers who are using their products with the products that you already have or plan to purchase. Ask the contacts that they provide if both products work well together.

■ **Determine the best communications protocol for each need.** For each of your needs, rank the possibilities by determining cost to implement, availability, relative security offered, and interoperability issues. This process will show you how a protocol that seems best in one scenario is not well-suited to another scenario. For example, Internet Protocol Security/Layer Two Tunneling Protocol (IPSec/L2TP) is a better choice for VPNs than Point-to-Point Tunneling Protocol (PPTP) if security is the only parameter measured. However, other factors—such as the ability to transit Network Address Translation (NAT) or the cost to upgrade all client computers—might prevent it from being selected.

See Also   For information about the interoperability of Microsoft products, use the keyword "interoperability" to search the Microsoft Web site at *http://www.microsoft.com*. For specific support for the interoperability between Windows systems and Unix, Macintosh, and Novell systems, see the TechNet page of the Microsoft Web site at *http://www.microsoft.com/technet/treeview/default.asp?url=/technet/prodtechnol/windowsserver2003/proddocs/datacenter /works_with_existing_systems.asp*. For information about other companies' IPSec products, see the ICSA labs Web site at *http://www.icsalabs.com/html/communities/ipsec/certification /criteria/IPsecCertCriteria10B.shtml*. The systems listed on this Web site indicate compliance with the ICSA standard, one requirement of which is interoperability with other systems.

Off the Record   How can interoperability affect security design? When you use nonstandard or unproven sources without adequate testing, you might find that you have an unusable system. You have only to look at the variety of implementations of IPSec to understand how this can be a problem. IPSec is a standard, but various implementations have strayed from that standard and interoperability between two devices using IPSec is often a challenge.

Often, interoperability of heterogeneous systems results in using the least common denominator for security. For example, with IPSec, you might have to use shared secrets, rather than digital certificates, for mutual authentication. During the design phase, it is important to understand the consequences of maintaining interoperability of heterogeneous systems (including legacy systems), because you will need to alter the overall design to prevent building weaknesses into the infrastructure.

Threats to Security Introduced by Security Maintainability Issues

Any operations design must satisfy maintainability goals, and this is even more important with security design. If security cannot be maintained, it might be eliminated. The following threats to security can result when security designers forget to consider maintainability:

■ If a security design has a high reliance on people following a written policy that cannot be enforced via technical controls, it is unlikely that adherence to the policy will continue over time.

■ If a technical control is difficult to maintain, its enforcement might weaken over time. If there is no way, for example, to prevent the introduction of modems into the network and strict restrictions on Internet access are enforced via the local area network (LAN) connection, users might use modems as alternative paths to access the Internet. In doing so, they breach security by avoiding filters, access controls, and logging.

- When controls must be renewed and it is difficult to do so, business productivity will be disrupted. Can certificates be automatically reissued before they expire, or must new certificates be manually obtained? Who will manage the intrusion detection systems when the person who received training and cared for the intrusion detection systems for three years leaves the company?

Important   Support for security maintainability is important. In Windows Server 2003, functions such as Group Policy can be used to reapply security settings on a periodic basis. Computer and user certificates can be automatically deployed. Security templates can be reapplied to stand-alone systems and used to audit security compliance.

Considerations for Analyzing Existing Security Policies and Procedures

The ability to analyze existing security policies is necessary to the development of security design. Ask the following questions to analyze security policies:

- Does the security policy meet business needs? Does an existing policy on Web sites, for example, cover the use of SSL to protect customer data? How about the security of that data once it is in the organization's database? Are there policies that cover all aspects of the business's operations? Are there, for example, policies to cover access to the Internet by employees or policies that cover the use of privately owned Personal Digital Assistants (PDAs) for storage of company, customer, or patient data?

- Do the written policies follow the definition of a policy, or are they precise in defining exact implementation details or technology choices? There was concern, for example, that HIPAA regulations would specify the use of digital signatures on the transport of any patient or healthcare data and would specify what technologies and equipment should be used for enforcement. The bill did not do either. While HIPAA is a U.S. federal law and not a security policy, analyzing the law's effects on healthcare organizations offers some of the same challenges as evaluating the effects of security policy on an organization, and a wealth of commentary can be found on the law to assist you in determining whether your analysis is in tune with experts in the field of law and information security.

- How can the policy be enforced using technology? Policy should be written without undue consideration to what is technically possible. However, an analysis of the policy should result in a precise statement on what can and cannot be enforced with the technology currently in place, what additional technology might be purchased to fulfill the technical enforcement of the policy, the cost of purchasing additional technology for enforcement, and alternatives to the policy that can be recommended.

■ Is one security policy more important than another security policy? Is a policy that restricts user access to the Internet more or less important than a policy that requires customer data to be encrypted? Remember to evaluate whether the need for encryption is high because of risk of attack or whether encryption is being used for some other reason. For example, some have suggested that encrypting customer data may protect a company from having to follow the demands of a California law that requires a report be given to California customers if an attack is successful against your organization. You might determine that encryption is overkill given the nature of the information you are protecting and the layers of company infrastructure that would have to be penetrated to successfully attack it. You might, therefore, recommend a policy change or prioritize implementation differently when you understand the policy's driver.

What Are Security Policies and Procedures?

To analyze existing security policies and procedures, you must first be able to distinguish between the two. *Security policies* are concise statements of required behavior. *Security procedures* detail how the policies are carried out. Because security policies do not dictate the implementation of security procedures, the best technology can be selected for the job, more than one technology can be used, and better technology can be used as it is developed without having to rewrite the policy.

Policy is usually the product of a management committee and should be approved by the highest level of management. However, although IT management often participates in the development of security policy, the analysis and implementation of security policies are often performed by non-management, technical personnel.

How to Categorize and Secure Data Based on an Organization's Needs

The security designer can further assist data protection efforts by developing methods for categorizing data. This section explains why data must be secured and then describes how to categorize and secure data based on an organization's needs.

Why Secure Data?

Data, or to be more precise, information, is the lifeblood of most organizations. Without billing information, a company cannot collect its debts. Without customer information, a company might lack the ability to secure future sales. Without correct product information, customers might not purchase products from the company. If this information becomes unavailable or is lost, the business might not survive.

To Categorize Data

Three characteristics of data—*purpose*, *integrity*, and *sensitivity*—will help you define a categorization scheme that can be used in all security designs. Categorizing data will help you determine the extent to which it should be protected. Think of these as the dimensions that define the data. Just as height, width, and depth define objects such as blocks and boxes, purpose, integrity, and sensitivity define data.

> **Note**   In the real world, data owners should be responsible for classifying data, but being familiar with the process will allow you to question or to assist the data owners.

Use the following guidelines to categorize and secure data:

1. *Determine how the data is used (its purpose) and what will happen if the data is unavailable.* Here, it's important to identify what the data is used for. Some information gathered during the organization's risk analysis process or in the development of the BIA will be of great assistance to you here. Data can then often be categorized by its purpose—its importance to the survival of the business.

2. *Determine the impact of errors in the data.* What will happen if the integrity of the data cannot be ensured? If my name is spelled incorrectly in your customer database, I might get annoyed. If my bill is incorrect, I can guarantee you I'll be upset. But these issues are correctable and might be due to small clerical errors. If, however, every customer's bill is only half of what it should be, there is a serious system error somewhere that will affect the company's profitability and, likely, its ability to remain in business. Clearly, some data must be protected more securely than other data.

> **Off the Record**   An example of why determining the impact of errors is important is evident in the early use of computer-controlled radiation machines. These machines controlled the amount of radiation directed to a cancerous tumor by calculations based on an operator setting and an internal table. Unfortunately, because of system-design errors coupled with operator error, there have been cases of accidental megadoses of radiation burning a hole through a patient's shoulder instead of merely destroying cancerous cells.

3. *Determine the sensitivity of the data.* What will happen if the data becomes available to unauthorized individuals? In government operations, data is often classified as secret, top secret, and for these eyes only, and the protection of the data is arranged accordingly. In a business, care should also be taken to classify the sensitivity of data and arrange for its protection. If there is not time to formally classify

data, you should at least make yourself aware of the nature of sensitive data. Financial factors that might affect the stock market price of a company are, for example, more sensitive than information about employee vacation times (and even that depends on whose vacation time people might gain knowledge of).

How to Use Data Flow to Determine Where Data Is at Risk

After data is categorized, to protect data, you must first determine where and when the data is exposed. If you do this, you will be able to develop a security design that meets each data type for every location or path it takes. A good way to determine where and when data needs protection is to study the data flow. Data flow describes where data enters the system and where it is validated, processed, stored, and eventually destroyed. Despite being the keepers of systems, IT professionals do not always have a clear picture of how this happens. A good resource for examining data flow is in the documentation of in-house software development projects, infrastructure designs and maps, and process charts that describe how processes work within the organization.

Figure 1-1 shows a process flow chart for an e-commerce site. Notice the designation of data entry at specific pages of the site; the storage and manipulation of data at a database in the organization's internal network; the storage of customer information; and order-tracking and manual-processing information and activities such as the availability of phone orders, customer help desk, and shipping operations. What areas would you note on the chart as areas of concern for making the system more secure? The shaded areas in Figure 1-2 mark the junctures where security should be applied to keep data safe.

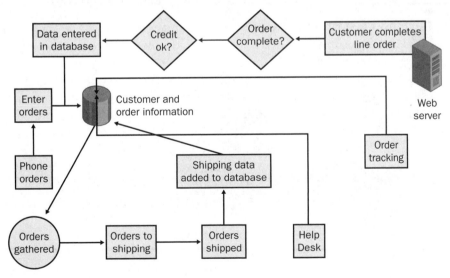

Figure 1-1   Reading a process chart

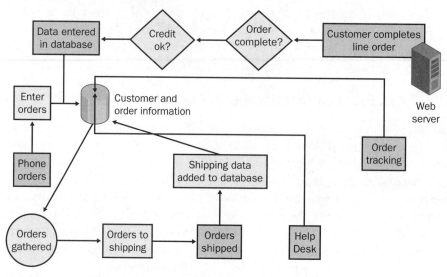

Figure 1-2   Identifying areas for data security

Guidelines for Analyzing Risks in the Existing IT Administration Structure

IT personnel often have greater knowledge of and access to systems and data than any other employees, most company managers, and certainly any outsiders. Yet they are often treated as if they never make mistakes and should always be above suspicion. When designing security, you must accumulate and evaluate information about the administrative structure of IT. Use the following guidelines to do so:

- **Develop a list of who the players are and what authority they hold.**   An organization chart will show you the management structure. Knowing who reports to whom is important. Figure 1-3 shows an organization chart for Wingtip-toys.com, a large toy manufacturer. From this chart, we can see that the company has provided good separation of duties within its structure. Information security personnel report to the CSO, not to the IT department. When information security personnel report to the very organization that they need to monitor, it becomes too easy to underestimate security needs or have trouble providing reports on security status within IT impartially. An organization chart typically shows only the overall management hierarchy. It might be more difficult to determine the identities of nonmanagement personnel within a department, but this information is also important.

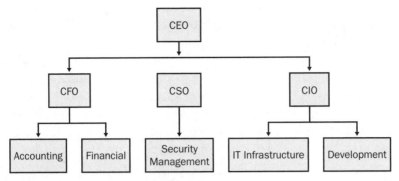

Figure 1-3   Reviewing the organization chart

- **Create a chart of network and Active Directory directory service responsibilities.**   This chart should include other system permissions and privileges. This level of detail will provide a clearer picture of who within IT can do what within which systems. A brief security analysis might not be able to uncover documentation that outlines these responsibilities, but nevertheless the need for such documentation still exists. A clear understanding of how permissions are granted to objects—including files, folders, registry keys, and Active Directory objects—and to whom permission is granted is a necessary part of the security designer's function when analyzing business requirements. In a security design, this knowledge is important, as it helps to design a system of administrative responsibility that mitigates the abuse of administrative privilege.

- **Create a logical diagram that details the existence of all divisions and offices and identifies the administrative needs for each.**   The diagram should also detail the existence of administrative personnel.

- **Determine where security boundaries lie.**   In the Windows 2000 and Windows Server 2003 world, the security boundary is the forest. Tight coupling of Active Directory structures means that a rogue administrator could compromise the domain boundary in a single forest environment. Legal, political, customer, Internet, and internal boundary needs require the use of multiple forests within an organization. A forest trust can be created between Windows Server 2003 forests. The trust can be restricted to mitigate the risk of providing access across forest boundaries. Knowledge of how security boundaries work—where they exist (the forest) and where they do not exist (the domain)—is part of the knowledge necessary to analyze the risk in an IT administrative structure.

Example: Using Network Diagrams to Evaluate the Impact of Administrative Authority

Figure 1-4 shows a section of the logical network diagram for Tailspintoys.com. Notice the existence of two offices: the Corporate Headquarters office and the Warehouse office. In the diagram, communications between the two offices are distinguished by the existence of VPN servers at both sites. An analysis of administrative responsibility should show that the individuals with administrative privileges on each VPN server have equivalent levels of permission. Their cooperation is necessary to ensure access between the sites, and their understanding of the security requirements and compliance with security policy means a weakness at either end could result in the compromise of their systems.

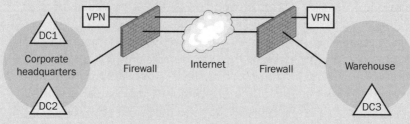

Figure 1-4   Evaluating the impact of administrative authority via network diagrams

Practice: Analyzing Business Requirements for Information Security

In this practice, you will analyze business requirements and evaluate a security policy for a fictitious company, place documents in data categories, identify noncompliant security policies, and decide how to secure public access to a company Web site. If you are unable to answer a question, review the lesson materials and try the question again. You can find answers to the questions in the "Questions and Answers" section at the end of this chapter.

Exercise 1: Analyzing Business Requirements

Read the scenario and then answer the questions that follow.

Scenario   Tailspin Toys and Wingtip Toys have formed a partnership to provide consumer information on toy safety. The project plan states that the companies will engage in joint research on toy safety and will produce joint investigatory and information reports. The information will be distributed several ways, including on a joint Web site, in brochures, and in leaflets that will be included in product packaging. The distribution of these materials is a service to the public and will also help the companies maintain a positive image. Each company will provide access to some of its research data and will provide communications venues for the researchers.

You are a new security designer for Tailspin Toys. Your boss has just asked you to review the project plan. Your boss would like you to list the business requirements that will drive the security design for this project.

Review Questions   Answer the following questions.

1. What text or parts of the project plan will help you in your task of creating a list of business requirements?

_____

_____

_____

_____

_____

_____

_____

_____

_____

_____

_____

2. What are the new IT functions that will be built because of this partnership?

_____

_____

_____

_____

_____

_____

3. Promoting a positive image is a stated business driver. What are the unstated drivers that set the parameters for the security design?

_____

_____

_____

_____

Exercise 2: Evaluating the Current Security Policy

Read the scenario and then answer the questions that follow.

Scenario   Your boss pulled the following key parts out of the Tailspin Toys security policy and sent them to you to evaluate:

- "Some form of authentication other than passwords must be used for all internal systems."

- "Direct access by non-employees to data on the company intranet is not allowed."

- "Communications from outside the corporate network must be encrypted and authenticated."

- "Employee access to the Internet shall be restricted and audited."

- "Wireless networks are not allowed without the approval of IT."

Review Questions   Answer the following question.

1. What are the implications of these statements in the Tailspin Toys security policy for the proposed IT projects that you listed in Exercise 1?

_____

_____

_____

_____

_____

_____

_____

_____

_____

_____

_____

_____

Exercise 3: Placing Documents in Data Categories

Match the data categories listed below to the list of documents in the following table. In the real world, data owners should be responsible for classifying data, but being familiar with the process will allow you to question or to assist the data owners. The data categories are:

- Public (OK for anyone to read)
- Internal (employee access only)
- Confidential (limited access)

Table 1-1   Matching Documents to Data Categories

Document	Data category
Company Internet Web site home page articles	
Statements being prepared for the annual report	
An announcement of the company picnic	
Company intranet Web site home page	
Employee names, addresses, phone numbers	
The published annual report	
Product development research	
Employee benefits plan information	

Exercise 4: Identifying Noncompliant Security Policies

Answer the following question.

1. Your company has the following security policy: "All access to external resources such as the Internet shall be through company gateways and shall be restricted and audited." Which of the following items do not comply with this security policy? Choose all that apply.

   a. An unapproved wireless network is established by the Accounting department.

   b. An employee uses a modem to access a personal e-mail account.

   c. An employee opens Internet Explorer on his company-provided desktop computer. The computer has been configured to use the company-provided gateway.

   d. An employee uses a company-provided laptop from home to access the company intranet.

Exercise 5: Deciding How to Secure Public Access to a Company Web Site

Answer the following question.

1. Wingtip Toys manufactures and sells toys. The company Web site provides product information, company information, and links to online retailers who sell the company's toys. Public access to the site should be secured by using the following items:

   a. A firewall, SSL, operating system and Web site hardening, and an intrusion detection system.

   b. A firewall, operating system and Web site hardening, and an intrusion detection system.

   c. A firewall, a VPN, operating system and Web site hardening, and an intrusion detection system.

   d. A firewall, a VPN, SSL, operating system and Web site hardening, and an intrusion detection system.

Lesson 2: Creating the Security Design Framework

A security design framework is a structure on which all future security designs can be built. As a security designer, you should create a base security design framework on which your security designs can be built or you (or your design team) might end up with incomplete assessments, lack of follow-through, and an incomplete picture of the changing security landscape.

After this lesson, you will be able to

- Describe the components of a security design framework.
- Describe the process for creating a security design framework.
- Identify the principles of information security design.
- Explain the purpose of threat modeling.
- Perform threat modeling.
- Design a process for responding to incidents.
- Design the use of segmented networks.
- Design a process for recovering services.

Estimated lesson time: 80 minutes

Components of a Security Design Framework

A security design framework is a collection of items or components that should be considered when creating any information security design. Parts of a security design framework typically include the following concepts, which will be defined more fully in later sections:

- Prevention, detection, isolation, and recovery.

- The principles of information security design. These are concepts that should be reviewed when examining any IT process. If they can be applied, a more secure process will result.

- Threat modeling. If you understand how a network or one of its components might be attacked, you can develop a better defense.

- Incident response. When an attack occurs, what should be done?

- Segmented network design. Isolating parts of the network can contribute to security. Each design should question the need for segmentation and propose how to isolate sensitive data and the computers that store or manage it.

- Recovery processes. An attack, or even an accident, can mean the destruction of data, computers, or network infrastructure. Planning for the recovery of data, computers, and network infrastructure can prevent the loss from becoming a disaster.

- Life-cycle review. Every security design has a life cycle. Security design, policy and procedure development, implementation of the security design, and management of the design and policies form the basis of a sound security framework. However, this is not a linear process. Each new product, process, and threat means re-analysis and possible revision. Security is not a job that is ever done.

Example: Using the Concepts of Prevention, Detection, Isolation, and Recovery

These considerations should be worked into the security framework and should also be a part of each security design. The framework serves as the list of items that should be considered in every design. This does not mean that every security design will have its own processes for all four but that all four issues should be addressed in the security design.

If, for example, you are charged with ensuring that a new Human Resources system is deployed and maintained in a secure manner, policies and procedures might already be in place that cover the hardening of the operation system (a common approach to preventing successful attacks), detection of attack (via auditing and intrusion detection systems), and response to an incident, including isolation of the affected computers (by the appointed incident response team). Current backup and recovery plans might be sufficient to ensure that systems can be efficiently replaced and brought on line. Your security design might only need to address the uniqueness of the Human Resources software, the sensitivity of the data it contains, and provide an evaluation of its place in a business continuity recovery plan.

The Process: Creating a Security Design Framework

There are many ways to create a security design framework. Here is one process for creating a security design framework:

1. Use the components of a security design framework from the preceding topic as a starting point. This list includes the basic elements of the framework.

2. Question experienced designers to obtain additional items or more examples of how to apply these items.

3. Review security designs, and add the common elements you find in the designs to your framework.

4. After each successful design, look for and record any new items you feel should be reviewed when creating new designs.

The rest of this lesson teaches the key concepts and skills to complete this process.

> ### The Impact of the Framework on the Design
>
> All sound security designs seek to prevent security failure, but designers of well-formulated security plans also realize that good security allows for the detection of attempted or successful intrusions and provides a method for coping with such events. Sound security designs include instructions on how to isolate compromised systems and how to recover should the worst nightmare become a reality.
>
> Many, but not all, experienced designers know that detection and incident response are necessary parts of a design. Less experienced designers might not consider these things. Having and using a framework that states the importance of these things allows all designers to approach each design as if they were wise beyond their own experience and knowledge.

What Are the Principles of Information Security Design?

You can use several well-known security design principles to help you design security for information systems. These principals have their roots in the design of security for business system processes. Although you might not be able to apply every principle to every security design situation, you will find that using these principles will allow you to quickly see where security can be added. These principles should be part of your framework. Use these security design principles to help you design security for information systems:

> **Tip**   Throughout this book, these principles will be used to explain specific security designs.

- **Separation of duties.**   Whenever possible, separate the functions of critical operations and assign different parts of the operation to different roles within the organization. For example, programmers should not have network administration privileges; those with backup rights shouldn't have restore rights; and auditors shouldn't be able to modify systems.

- **Least privilege.**   Give people only the privileges and access to data that they absolutely need. For example, users shouldn't be administrators on their desktops. Delegate administrative authority at the organizational unit (OU) level where possible, not domain-wide.

- **Reducing the attack surface.**   The fewer avenues of attack that are available, the less there is to protect and the less chance there is of the network being compromised. For example, disable unneeded services, don't install unnecessary services or applications, and protect sensitive data with encryption.

- **Defense in depth.**   Do not rely on one defense. Use many. If one fails, the other might prevent the intrusion or at least give you time to deal with it. For example:

  - Require authentication, use permissions on shares, use permissions on folders, and use permissions on files.

  - Use a firewall, use gateway filters for e-mail, harden servers and client computers, train administrators, train users, and create an incident response team.

- **Diversity of mechanism.**   If every computer is the same and if every defense mechanism is the same, then they will fail the same way. Use a variety of mechanisms. This is also addressed by providing redundancy and multiple paths. For example, design a classic perimeter network (also known as a DMZ, or demilitarized zone, and a screened subnet) or border network with two firewalls. One firewall should be between the Internet and the border network and the other should be between the border network and the internal network. Do not use the same firewall at each border. If an intruder successfully penetrates the external firewall, you do not want her to be able to use the same attack on the internal firewall.

- **Use of fail-safe defaults.**   Systems should always be configured to choose the most secure default action. For example:

  - Ports on firewalls should always be closed by default. You must open those for which you want to provide access.

  - No access, such as access to a file, should be possible unless it is explicitly given.

- **Economy of mechanism.**   Complexity is the enemy of security. The more complex security is, the more likely it is to fail. When a security strategy is hard to understand, people don't use it or configure it incorrectly. For example, if a smart card must be in the smart card reader to keep a session going, make the smart card the employee ID badge. Because an ID badge must be worn at all times, the user's smart card will always be available to the user. Only one card is therefore necessary for both approved entrance to the building and free access to building facilities and the logon for the computer. In addition, when a user leaves his desk, he must remove the smart card to retrieve the necessary badge for building access. If the computer is configured to log the user off when the card is removed, another security activity is automatically used and the user doesn't have to remember to do it.

- **Use of open designs.**   Security through obscurity generally doesn't work if it is the only security strategy. Security designs should use well-understood algorithms. Well-known algorithms have been examined by many security experts, and it is more likely that the flaws have been discovered and corrected. This does not mean that you should expose the security mechanisms in place for your organization, network, applications, and so on. It means that you should choose well-known algorithms and products that have been inspected by others and use generally accepted practices and principles. An example of this is to use IPSec for communication security or Kerberos for authentication, as opposed to using proprietary protocols.

Note   It is often difficult to decide which principle to apply, and sometimes it may seem as if one principle contradicts the other. For example, diversity of mechanism and economy of mechanism appear to say that lots of different things are a good idea and also that complexity is a bad idea. This is why security principles are not rules. Each case must be weighed. For example, the previous information about using two firewalls (diversity of mechanism) makes it harder for an attacker to penetrate the inner network. However, it also can make it harder for administrators to secure the network. If no one knows how to configure the different firewalls, then the complexity of the approach can get in the way of good security. The firewall may not be correctly configured and the attacker may be able to more easily get by its defenses. The answer? In this case, providing expertise on both firewalls supports the diversity principle; however, if that cannot be done, then using the same firewall in both places (economy of mechanism) is the best answer.

- **Complete mediation.**   Complete mediation means that:

  ❑ All access avenues should be checked. Program input should be checked by the program; administrators should protect shares with proper permissons; users should not be allowed to install un-approved software; and auditors should be reviewing whether all of these things, and any other access controls, are being implemented properly. Each entry point requries checking by those responsible for them, as well as by those responsible for reviewing what others are doing.

  ❑ You should review firewall controls, DNS security, network authentication, modem and other out-of-band communications access, PDA devices, wireless devices, remote computer connections, file and folder permissions, physical security, and so on.

- **Psychological acceptability.**   Recognize that the human element is the most important security asset. Make security unobtrusive, hide its complexity, use acceptable processes, and obtain user buy-in. For example, if you choose to use biometrics, which might include fingerprinting and retinal scans, consider user acceptance. Your users might find the processes to be an invasion of personal privacy. Voice recognition and hand geometry might be more readily accepted by users.

- **Trust but audit.**   Users and administrators must have the privileges they need to do their job, but no one is completely and permanently above suspicion. Remember that people change, temptation can be great, and anger can make some people overstep their usual reluctance to break the rules. Provision for auditing should be part of any security design. Reviewing audit logs can provide valuable information. The following examples show how audit data can be used:

  ❑ Match computer restarts with approved maintenance requests. Investigate the discrepancies. Who rebooted? Why? Many attacks require the reboot of systems. This is an activity that is particularly wise to track.

❑ Monitor the use of administrative functions such as group and user management. Understanding what normal activity is and ensuring that only approved changes are made can go a long way to detecting abuses of privilege.

■ **Keeping up to date.** Systems change, and new bugs and insecure practices are discovered all the time. Systems must be patched, and administrators need to be knowledgeable about the latest defense mechanisms. For example, applying security patches is sound preventative advice—many of the major Internet-based attacks of the past years did not impact companies where patching processes were in place.

What Is Threat Modeling?

Using the principles of security design can result in the development of a sound security design that will mitigate the risk from attacks that have not been developed yet. However, the wise security designer will not rely on good design alone to thwart future attacks. A wise security designer will continually refine these principles by evaluating the threats to the security of the systems she is assigned to protect.

Threat modeling is the act of brainstorming about new threat conditions by using known lists of possible attacks. When you perform threat modeling, you ask the questions: "What type of attacks do I need to defend against?" and "What conditions might lead to a hacker successfully compromising my network?" Just evaluating and protecting against well-known threats assumes that every network is the same and that every attacker will attempt the same types of access and has the same skill set. Threat modeling seeks to use the security administrator's intimate knowledge of specific networks and applications and both logical and chaotic thinking to come up with potential scenarios. What, for example, could a knowledgeable insider who developed your accounting systems do with that knowledge—both as an employee and after leaving the company? How about contractors to whom security management is outsourced? What practices need to be implemented to make code more secure? Not just secure from the potential implant of a back door by a malicious programmer but secure from immature coding practices that introduce vulnerabilities an attacker might exploit.

The goal of threat modeling is the same as the goal for using known preventative security disciplines: to reduce overall risk. Microsoft has adopted threat modeling as part of its product development process and has found it extremely useful. Threat modeling done during software design introduces security early in the development process and results in a more robust and secure product. In fact, testers report that 50 percent of the bugs found in code can be found by doing threat modeling—simply by looking at the system design and imagining how it could be corrupted. For threat modeling to be an effective security tool, it must be incorporated early in the network and system design process and in the development of security policies and procedures.

See Also   Michael Howard and David LeBlanc's book, *Writing Secure Code* (Microsoft Press, 2002), includes additional information about threat modeling with respect to the development process. Although the book deals with writing secure code, it embodies principles and practices that can easily be applied to designing secure networks.

How to Perform Threat Modeling

Fortunately, threat modeling is a simple process. It takes time to do it right, but this time is well spent if it uncovers vulnerabilities in proposed or existing systems and allows you to protect systems from those threats. The threat modeling process consists of the following steps:

1. *Assemble a team.* The team should be composed of people who know the current network and its systems well; people who know the proposed new hardware, software, or infrastructure; people who use the systems; and informed outsiders. Team membership should not be restricted to IT professionals. Computers, applications, and networks are used by many people within your organization, and these people often know the shortcuts or quick ways of doing things and the workarounds that they, as users, tend to use. Knowledge of common user practices can suggest new areas for threat investigation.

2. *Understand the process.* Use existing and new flow charts and diagrams to thoroughly document the process. You want to know how data flows through the system, where all components are located, who administers them, and who has access to them. Because current processes are often incompletely documented, this is a good opportunity to discover more information about the systems, and the process might lead to discovering other areas where security design is necessary.

3. *Determine threats.* Use brainstorming techniques to list all possible threats, no matter how bizarre they might sound. At this point, every possible threat mentioned should be recorded.

4. *Rank threats by risk.* This is the point at which you determine the threats that are most likely to damage systems or allow successful intrusion. Like a business impact analysis, the ranking of threats allows you to calmly deal with the most likely scenarios first.

5. *Determine a response for each threat.* Should you respond? How much effort should be spent? What mitigation techniques—such as data encryption, smart cards, VPN, hardening techniques, and so on—are already in place to deal with this threat? Are they adequate?

6. *Use technology and security processes to mitigate the threat.* After threats worthy of response have been ranked and mitigation techniques have been designed, choose and implement the techniques that can do the job.

How to Design an Incident Response Process

No matter how careful you are in implementing preventative processes and techniques, no matter how extensive your threat modeling is, and no matter how well you respond to an attack and prevent its success, there will always be the possibility that an attack on your system will succeed. Furthermore, an attack does not have to succeed to be of interest. Is an increase in port scanning the prelude to a directed attack? Are a number of Web defacements indicative of a possible elevation in politically motivated attacks on government targets? Your security design needs to be able to respond to both successful attacks and activities on your system that may indicate an attack is in progress.

See Also   The Computer Emergency Response Team (CERT) of the Carnegie Melon Software Engineering Institute was formed in 1988 in response to the first Internet worm (the Morris worm). For information about current vulnerabilities, educational materials, and classes about incident handling, see the CERT Web site at *http://www.cert.org.*

Because you cannot protect yourself from compromise if you don't know that you are under attack and because you must make a decision about how to respond to attacks before they occur, an incident response process should be part of every security design framework. The time to formulate an incident response process is before you have an incident. To design an incident response process, use the following steps:

1. *Form a Core Computer Security Incident Response Team (CCSIRT).* Team membership depends on your organization's risk management strategy. In general, the team is composed of members of your security team and positions include (but are not limited to) the following:

   ❑ Team Leader—Responsible for activity of CCSIRT and coordinating review of actions.

   ❑ Incident Lead—Responsible for coordinating response to incident. This person represents CCSIRT to outsiders. The person serving in this role might change depending on the nature of the incident.

   ❑ Associate Members—Handle and respond to particular incidents. They might be members of other departments and specialize in areas affected by incidents. They are indirectly involved with incident handling. Associate members are people such as contacts from the IT department, the Legal department, the Communications department, and management.

2. *Develop a response procedure.* Although every incident can be different, a standardized procedure helps the team coordinate its efforts. The procedure is not always followed in a linear fashion. Indeed, many parts—such as communication, documentation, and assessment—happen throughout the incident.

3. *Raise awareness of security.* This involves communicating with members of the IT department and with employees and managers throughout the organization

4. *Train the IT department and the entire organization how to respond to an incident.* IT is usually the first department to identify an incident. CCSIRT should be the respondent, but the IT department should know how to report incidents internally. End users of systems should report suspicious activity to IT.

See Also   For more information about incident handling, see Chapter 10, "Responding to Incidents," in the Patterns and Practices guide *Securing Windows 2000 Server,* on the Tech-Net page of the Microsoft Web site at *https://www.microsoft.com/technet/treeview /default.asp?url=/technet/security/prodtech/Windows/SecWin2k/10respnd.asp.*

Components of a Typical Response Procedure

Typical response procedural steps will include:

- Initial assessment—The Incident Lead and the IT contact begin the process of determining the nature of the incident. The incident might even turn out to be a false alarm.

- Communications—The Incident Lead alerts the entire CCSIRT to the incident and they identify who else needs to be contacted. At this stage, you should keep the number of people contacted to a minimum. False reports of security breaches can do as much damage as real security breaches.

- Initial response—A decision is made by the CCSIRT team as to what action to take—for example, removing the affected computer from the network, shutting down the affected computer, or doing nothing. Associate members are apprised of the actions. The goal is to contain the damage and minimize the risk.

- Collect initial evidence—The Incident Lead begins the process of collecting evidence with the help of the IT department. The Incident Lead should limit her collection to items that can be collected without damaging or contaminating the evidence. Examples of such evidence might be the number of computers that appear to be affected, statements from employees, or any data that was recorded or copied prior to the event being labeled as an attack. The goal is to understand the type and severity of the attack, the point of origin, and the intent of the attack, and to identify systems that have been compromised. Legal representatives can be contacted at this time if the incident warrants it. For example, an Internet worm attack might be an ordinary occurrence and not rate the involvement of legal counsel. However, if it appears that the worm was directed specifically at your organization, or appears to be copying customer credit card numbers, then the involvement of legal counsel is warranted.

- Protect evidence—To be able to take legal action against perpetrators, the CCIRT team must protect evidence that will support their conviction. Systems need to be backed up, and a skilled computer forensics persons should be utilized to collect and examine some types of evidence. A skilled forensic person will know how to properly protect evidence while collecting and examining it. For example, he might make a copy of a hard drive and examine the hard drive copy, not the original drive. Examining a drive can change data, and that would make the evidence inadmissible in court.

- Implement a temporary fix—The IT department does what is necessary to ensure continuation of operations. The CCSIRT might need to advise them on how this will affect the investigation. Management approval and advice might need to be solicited.

- Notify external agencies—The corporate communications officer releases private and public information as directed by management after consultation with IT, CCSIRT, and Legal. The corporate communications officer might also have to notify local and national law enforcement agencies, external security agencies, and virus experts.

- Recover systems (implement permanent fix)—The IT department completes the system's return to a normal level of functionality.

- Determine financial impact on business—Management assesses information. Costs include the loss of business, legal costs, labor costs, lost employee productivity, replacement of hardware and software, and loss of reputation or customer trust.

- Review response and update policies—As the security designer and administrator, you need to learn from the incident what needs to be done better and modify the incident response plan accordingly.

Considerations for Designing Segmented Networks

This topic presents design considerations for segmented networks and provides guidelines for using internal segments to improve network security design.

Design Considerations

For both border segments and internal segments, the important considerations for design are:

- Should a segmentation or joining occur?
- Where should the connection or segmentation be?
- What type of device will manage the connection?

- What types of communications are allowed to travel from one network to the other?

- Who is allowed to access the segment?

- How is access authenticated and authorized?

- Should communications between networks be encrypted?

- Should intrusion detection systems be deployed? If so, to what degree and where?

The answers to these questions will vary—often depending on the degree to which each network trusts the other. When designing segmented networks for security, the rationale is usually one segment is trusted and the other is not trusted, although it could just be that one segment is less trusted than the other.

> **Note**   The design of different types of segmented networks is explored further in this book. Secure wireless network design is detailed in Chapter 12, "Designing Security for Wireless Networks." Access to networks via traditional gateways—including firewalls, perimeter networks, and VPNs—is discussed in Chapter 7, "Designing Secure Communications Between Networks."

Segmented Network Terminology

Before you start working with segmented networks, you must be able to define what they are and define certain terms and phrases used in this area of computing.

What Is a Segmented Network?

Segmented networks are networks separated by devices that might obstruct the free flow of communications between computers on opposite sides. Devices such as routers, switches, firewalls, NAT servers, VPN servers, and proxy servers are often used to segment networks. Networks are often segmented to obscure the existence of and composition of the network, to protect elements of one network from another, or for both reasons. In other words, segments are created to define areas of trust.

It is those nodes, and how they are segmented from Internet, that commonly is the subject of a discussion on designing segmented networks. In these designs, a border between the internal, or trusted, network and the external, or untrusted, network is created either by inserting a gateway such as a firewall or by creating border segments more commonly known as a perimeter network or DMZ. However, it is also a good practice to segment the internal, trusted network into different areas of trust.

What Is a Border Gateway?

A border gateway is a gateway that separates an organization's internal, private network from a network that does not belong to them, such as the Internet. Because this is a connection to the outside world, a high degree of security must be designed into it. The designer has no ability to affect the operations of the external network and so must design a gateway that provides the most protection for the internal network. In most organizations, this means a firewall will be used and configured to allow only specific types of traffic into and out of the internal network. External access might be simple Web site access and e-mail or communications with business partners. Often different gateways are designed for specific types of traffic. For example, a proxy/firewall gateway might provide access to the Internet while not allowing access from the Internet to the internal network. This configuration might be coupled with a separate firewall that protects access to a Web server or e-mail server but which does not allow end users to traverse the gateway.

Typically, policy mandates use of the gateway for access to the Internet; however, many opportunities for accessing points outside of the internal network exist, and control of these opportunities needs to be planned. Additional opportunities are internal modems, wireless cards, and wireless access points. In addition, authorized direct connections to other networks—including VPN gateways—might exist or be necessary. Figure 1-5 shows multiple points of egress and ingress into the wingtiptoys.com network.

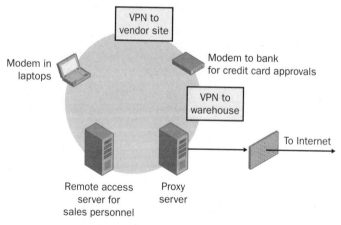

Figure 1-5   Mapping ingress and egress points

What Is a Perimeter Network?

A *perimeter network*, also known as a DMZ because of its resemblance to a demilitarized zone agreed upon between hostile nations, defines a network that is neither part of the organization's internal network nor part of the external network, but is under the control of the organization.

Wingtiptoys.com uses the classic perimeter network, which is flanked by two firewalls, as shown in Figure 1-6. Another possible design is the three-pronged network. A firewall with three network interfaces is part of the Tailspintoys.com network (shown in Figure 1-7) and is used to provide a connection to the external network, the internal network, and the perimeter network. In either case, systems that need to communicate with the external network are placed on the perimeter network. This configuration provides another layer of protection for the internal network, as an attacker must first penetrate the perimeter network. In the pure, classic design, no access to the internal network is allowed from the perimeter network or external network. The inner firewall allows only access from the internal network to the perimeter network, and the outer firewall allows limited access in both directions.

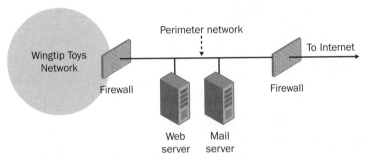

Figure 1-6   Examining the classic perimeter network

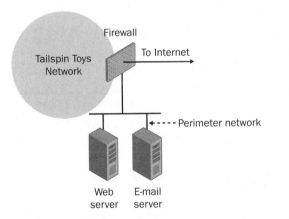

Figure 1-7   Segmenting three networks with a single firewall

Guidelines for Using Internal Segments To Improve Network Security Design

Traditionally, few internal networks are segmented for security reasons. The internal network has often, in the past, been described as the "trusted" network, and thus communications were not restricted within its boundaries. Today there is a growing realization that even internal networks are "hostile" networks, and one way to offer protection to sensitive data and operations is to use traditional security gateways to internally segment the network. In this way, access to sensitive data and operations can be restricted to those trusted with it, and exposure of information is curtailed. Figure 1-8 shows a proposed internal network segmentation for Tailspintoys.com.

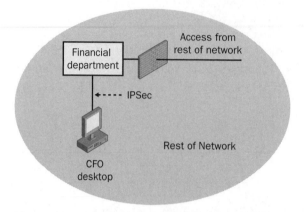

Figure 1-8 Inspecting a proposed internal network design

Examples of portions of the network that might be segmented are the financial, research, and product development departments. However, the rationale is to separate areas of trust, and each organization needs to make those decisions. Indeed, many questions will need to be asked, including those of concern for all segmented networks and any additional ones necessitated by the uniqueness of the area of trust.

> **Note** Segmenting networks can bring interesting problems, such as difficulties in communications between services across networks. For more information about issues specific to Active Directory, see Chapter 3, "Designing the Network Infrastructure for Physical Security," and the article "Active Directory in Networks Segmented by Firewalls" on the Downloads page of the Microsoft Web site at *http://www.microsoft.com/downloads/details.aspx? FamilyID=c2ef3846-43f0-4caf-9767-a9166368434e&DisplayLang=en*.

Guidelines for Designing a Recovery Process

In the rush to design secure systems that respond to the business needs of the organization, the ability to recover systems in the event of failure might be overlooked. It should not be. Recovery processes, including emergency management of remote servers, are often seen as a network administration process and are not included as part of a security designer's purview. However, one aspect of security is ensuring the availability of data and systems, and dealing with the risk of systems failure—whether due to hardware or software malfunction or attack—is something that should be a part of every security design. Use the following guidelines to help you design for recovery:

- **Understand the capabilities of the systems for recovery.**   All systems should be considered, and a comprehensive strategy should be developed for each. However, each platform presents specific benefits and challenges. Windows Server 2003 offers many features to assist in recovery, including volume shadow copy, backup and restore processes, Automated Systems Recovery (ASR), and Emergency Management Services.

- **Divide systems by computer role on the network.**   What a computer is used for dictates what type of backup and restore plan needs to be developed for it. Databases, for example, might contain extremely sensitive data, large amounts of data, require special backup software, and take a long time to back up and restore. Desktop computers, on the other hand, might not store any data locally and might simply require a fresh imaging or replacement should they fail.

- **Have written procedures for each computer role.**   Don't trust any one person's knowledge of how computers must be backed up or how they can be restored. This person might not be available when needed. Written plans are critical.

- **Practice recovery steps.**   Provide test systems, and require IT personnel who recover systems to practice the recovery steps. Keep records of which IT personnel have completed practicing the recovery steps. Provide a drill. Simulate the loss of a domain controller, for example, and require IT personnel to recover the system. Provide feedback about how well they responded to the drill. If systems are lost and then recovered or not recovered, provide postmortem discussions on the process.

- **Determine when to use volume shadow copy.**   This service empowers the end user with the ability to recover previous editions of files or to restore files that have been accidentally deleted.

- **Design a backup strategy.**   Windows Server 2003 has backup and restore processes built into it, and other companies' products are available as well. Determining which product to use will depend on the availability of the services necessary to your design. Backup strategies include decisions to be made about frequency, comprehensiveness, storage of backup media, offsite storage, personnel, logging, number of copies, security for backup media, and audits of backup processes.

- **Rank systems to determine how critical they are.**   In a formal business continuity plan, a business impact analysis (BIA) is constructed to determine which systems are the most critical to an organization's survival. The BIA is an interdepartmental project. Without this information, an IT design for recovery might consist of the identification of critical IT resources such as domain controllers, messaging servers, firewalls, and the like. The reason for this qualification is to create more comprehensive recovery plans for these systems and to determine the order of recovery efforts should multiple systems be affected at the same time.

Exam Tip   Recovery of systems at remote locations can be accomplished via the use of Emergency Management Services (EMS) and specialized hardware. Providing such access to systems could result in malicious activity if the systems are not properly secured. EMS, auxiliary hardware connections, or both could be used to connect to and disrupt the normal services provided by the server. Any design that provides such access should include security.

- **Determine special systems strategies that are the result of the server role or location.**   Domain controllers, e-mail servers, firewalls, Internet Information Services (IIS), Domain Name System (DNS) servers, and other network server roles require backup and recovery techniques in addition to the backup and recovery required by the base operating system. Servers located at remote locations might require processes as provided by the Emergency Management Services available with Windows Server 2003.

- **Complete the recovery process plan.**   All the information gathered is formulated into a comprehensive plan. The plan includes procedures and schedules for each type of product and systems—both backup and recovery. It also defines the order of recovery during times of multiple failure, assignment of responsibilities, and a plan for continuous testing and auditing of recovery plans.

- **Test each piece of the plan.**   Testing each piece of the recovery process ensures adequate backups are being prepared and that the procedures are valid. Testing might also show that alternative procedures or additional processes need to be added.

- **Audit backup processes.**   Designing an adequate plan is a good start, but even better are plans that are actually implemented, maintained, and reviewed. There should be processes in place—including logging—to monitor backup.

Practice: Creating the Security Design Framework

In this practice, you will predict threats to a company, design a segmented network, and design a recovery process for a fictitious company. You will then match security plan elements to parts of a security framework and identify devices that segment internal networks into zones. If you are unable to answer a question, review the lesson materials and try the question again. You can find answers to the questions in the "Questions and Answers" section at the end of this chapter.

Exercise 1: Predicting Threats to a Company

Read the scenario and then answer the question that follows.

Scenario   You are a new security designer for Tailspin Toys. Your boss has asked you to begin the process of threat modeling for a proposed shared research project between Tailspin Toys and Wingtip Toys. The project will allow researchers from both companies to access to Tailspin Toys documents. Your job is to predict the threats to the company when allowing this type of non-employee access to internal documents.

Review Question   Answer the following question.

1. What types of threats should you think about?

_____

_____

_____

_____

_____

_____

_____

_____

_____

_____

_____

_____

_____

_____

Exercise 2: Designing a Segmented Network to Provide Extra Security

Read the scenario and then answer the questions that follow.

Scenario   The Wingtip Toys Financial department has requested further protection for its databases and files. Upon investigation, you found that 90 percent of the employees with authorization to this information are located in one physical area of the company. The other 10 percent are located in branch offices or in upper management offices in another building. Your boss has asked you to begin the design of a segmented network that will provide added security. In her e-mail, she reminded you not to forget to provide access to the segmented network for the employees who do not work in the main area and access for all employees to the company intranet and gateway to the Internet.

Review Questions   Answer the following questions.

1. What steps will you take to begin designing the segmented network to provide added security?

_____

_____

_____

_____

_____

_____

_____

_____

_____

_____

_____

_____

_____

_____

_____

_____

_____

_____

_____

2. Sketch a proposed design, incorporating your decisions from the previous steps.

Exercise 3: Designing a Recovery Process

Read the scenario and then answer the question that follows.

Scenario   Tailspin Toys does not have formal disaster recovery and business continuity plans. Your boss has asked you to begin the process of creating these plans. As a first step, you must translate your knowledge about proper backup and recovery processes into tasks for the IT department to perform. You'll need to list those tasks and provide a sentence or two that describes what each task should accomplish. Assume for brevity's sake that all systems are using Microsoft Windows.

Review Question   Answer the following question.

1. What tasks must the IT department perform to back up and recover data securely?
   Describe each task in one to two sentences.

_____

_____

_____

_____

_____

_____

_____

_____

_____

_____

_____

_____

_____

_____

_____

_____

_____

_____

_____

_____

_____

_____

_____

Exercise 4: Matching Security Plan Elements to the Parts of the Security Framework

Match the security plan elements that follow to the prevention, detection, isolation, and recovery parts of the security framework in the following table. Some elements might fall in more than one category.

Security Plan Elements   The security plan elements include:

- Using Group Policy to enforce the security configuration

- A backup procedure

- Sending incident handling team (CCSIRT) members to a class about forensics

- Installing an Intrusion Detection System (IDS)

- Removing a network cable from the back of a computer system

- Unplugging the firewall's interface to the Internet

- Training end users how to create strong passwords

- Deploying smart cards and readers, and requiring their use for all external access to the corporate network

Table 1-2   Categorizing Security Design Features

Prevention	Detection	Isolation	Recovery

Exercise 5: Identifying Devices that Segment Internal Networks into Zones of Trust

Answer the following question.

1. Which of the following devices can be used to segment internal networks into zones of trust—zones that are secured against intrusion from each other? Choose all that apply.

   a. A firewall

   b. A switch

   c. A packet-filtering router

   d. A hub

Lesson 3: Analyzing Technical Constraints that Affect Security Design

The security designer must analyze the situation and understand the limitations imposed by factors such as legacy infrastructure, currently installed software, and the interoperability requirements. If she does not, she will not produce a workable design and may even promote one that reduces, instead of increases, security on the network.

After this lesson, you will be able to

- Identify capabilities of legacy infrastructure and integrate them into the design.
- Identify technology limitations.
- Analyze interoperability constraints.

Estimated lesson time: 30 minutes

Guidelines for Integrating Legacy Infrastructure in Security Designs

Very few security designers get to pick and choose hardware, operating system software, security devices, and processes from scratch. Instead, they must make sure that security designs consider legacy computers, operating systems, network devices, or other infrastructure components. These considerations are often a large part of security design work. This section describes what a legacy system is and then provides guidelines for integrating legacy infrastructure in security designs.

What Is a Legacy System?

A *legacy system* is any infrastructure component such as hardware, operating system software, network device, or application that is technically out of date. Often legacy systems cannot be replaced either because they still provide a service, they provide a service that cannot be provided by another system, funds do not exist to bring them up to date, or there is no compelling reason to bring them up to date. Legacy systems can be old technologies that preceded recent versions of the software or operating system—for example, older versions of Windows or a version of an application that is no longer supported. Many capabilities and constraints introduced by non-Windows systems are discussed in the "Guidelines for Analyzing Interoperability Constraints" section later in this lesson.

Integration Guidelines

To successfully integrate legacy systems into your security design, you must recognize their capabilities and then work within those constraints. Use these guidelines to integrate legacy systems into security designs:

- **Do not compromise the security of these systems.**   The security of these systems must not be compromised when you add new systems. For example, when Linux or Windows operating systems are run on mainframe systems, care should be taken to make sure that security on the mainframe is not reduced. Adding new software adds new vulnerabilities, which must be mitigated. Another example is that adding new applications might require opening new ports on a firewall, ports that might be used to attack legacy systems.

- **Recognize that the accommodation of legacy system capabilities could mean full compliance with security policy and directives might not be accomplished.**   For example, if a system is not capable of using 10-character passwords, you cannot fulfill that criteria of a security policy or design.

- **Increase the security of legacy systems by incorporating, wherever possible, any changes that can make them more secure.**   Upgrades or the installation of new utilities might provide this extra security.

> **Note**   When can legacy systems be eliminated because of security concerns? It is not up to the designer to determine the end of the life cycle for legacy systems, but the designer can report the inability to fulfill mandated security policy because of the limitations of these systems and recommend a solution. Management must then make the decision about when and where legacy systems should be eliminated. The designer can also recommend legacy system placement or use so as to mitigate the risk of its use.

Each legacy system difference must be examined to determine where these systems will either cause a change in the configuration in Windows Server 2003 (and possibly reduce the level of security), require an alternative security solution, require an upgrade to services, or require removal of the legacy system before security policy can be met. The security designer's goal, is, as always, to provide the best, most secure solution while being mindful of the constraints and the need to support business requirements.

How a Legacy System Can Be Integrated into a Security Design

An example of a legacy system issue is LAN Manager (LM) authentication. Windows 98 systems cannot natively use Windows NT LAN Manager (NTLM) for authentication; instead they use its predecessor, LM. Windows Server 2003 systems eliminate, by default, the use of LM. The security design decision might then be to reconfigure Windows Server 2003 to allow the use of LM or install the Active Directory directory service client on Windows 98 systems and configure them to use NTLM.

> If the design decision is based only on immediate financial cost, the choice will be to allow the use of LM, which will greatly reduce the security of the forest. It will take money, in the form of administrative time, to implement the client and configure the systems. However, this will result in better security. The necessary configuration can be automated, which will reduce its cost. The benefits of maintaining security are sometimes difficult to quantify, but in this case, there are many ways the security team can make the point. One way would be by using cracking tools on a test system that uses LM and on one that does not. Doing this would show how quickly the LM database passwords can be cracked in comparison to those on the system where LM is not used. Care should be taken to make sure this test, which takes very little time to set up, is done on a test system and that no real passwords are exposed.

Considerations for Identifying Technology Limitations

Every system has its technology limitations—factors that restrict what can and cannot be done. When these limitations affect a security operation, the security design must account for them. To identify technology limitations, you must consider:

- **Existing hardware limitations.** If an operating system upgrade is required, can the existing hardware meet minimum requirements of the proposed operating system? Will security services put additional demands on the hardware? Can the hardware be upgraded or replaced?

- **Existing operation system limitations.** If the operating system cannot be upgraded, what part of the security policy or security design cannot be met?

- **Existing software constraints.** Does existing application software impose requirements, such as administrative access, to run or require that specific hardware be installed?

- **Existing legal requirements such as FIPS.** The Federal Information Processing Standard (FIPS) is mandated for some U.S. government operations. This standard specifies cryptographic algorithms and other security-related processing functions. Meeting these standards might require special software, certain cryptographic algorithms, and security devices such as Fortezza cards.

Guidelines for Analyzing Interoperability Constraints

Few organizations are lucky enough to have systems that come from only one company. Most networks now include operating systems, hardware platforms, and additional devices and services from a variety of vendors. These complex networks can be the result of natural growth, consolidation, or mergers. Follow these guidelines to analyze interoperability constraints:

See Also   Windows Server 2003 incorporates standard technology implementations in many areas. Areas of concern for security designs are detailed in the following chapters: Kerberos (Chapter 6), IPSec (Chapter 3), VPNs (Chapter 7), PKI (Chapter 2) and client access (Chapter 9 and Chapter 11).

■ Perform an inventory on the types of existing and proposed systems that might affect the design. Attaining knowledge that spans the entire organization is important. Even if not all systems will affect the proposed design, knowledge of all systems allows you to ask the right questions. In addition, few organizations restrict digital communications to their employees only. Most have some digital interface with customers, vendors, and partners. Before starting a design, determine what types of systems exist. Here is a list of things to check or to check for:

   ❑ Windows, Linux, Unix, other midrange systems, and IBM-style mainframes

   ❑ Existing network infrastructure, network devices, and appliances

   ❑ Various specialized network roles, such as databases, Web servers, and e-mail servers

   ❑ Specialized access scenarios, such as telecommuters, mobile personnel (such as sales staff), branch offices, foreign offices, and warehouses

■ If the system will interface with customer or partner systems, understand the types of systems that customers and partners will have. The security design must include recommendations on how to securely interoperate with devices outside of your network.

■ For each proposed design, evaluate computers, software, and network infrastructure that will need to interoperate with computers targeted for new software or processes by following these steps:

   ❑ Evaluate which systems are a part of the new design.

   ❑ Identify how the implementation of the proposed technology differs on each system.

   ❑ Review product documentation that details how interoperability is supported. Find, if possible, evidence of actual systems or certifications that support this interoperability.

   ❑ Perform internal testing between the new and existing computers, software, and network infrastructure to work out additional constraints.

   ❑ Develop designs that incorporate lessons learned from each project that you do.

Practice: Analyzing Technical Constraints that Affect Security Design

In this practice, you will analyze legacy infrastructure constraints and identify operating system clients to upgrade for a fictitious company. If you are unable to answer a question, review the lesson materials and try the question again. You can find answers to the questions in the "Questions and Answers" section at the end of this chapter.

Exercise 1: Analyzing Legacy Infrastructure Constraints

Read the scenario and then answer the question that follows.

Scenario   Wingtip Toys has decided to segment its Financial department from the rest of its network. Your boss has sent you the following information and has asked you to analyze the technology constraints on the design:

- For authorized employees whose office location is separated from the main Financial department, IPSec has been chosen as the necessary requirement for protecting communication. The desktop systems used by these employees are Windows NT 4.0 Workstation, Windows 98, and Windows XP Professional.

- No part of the budget is available for upgrading any desktop systems at this time.

Review Question   Answer the following question.

1. What are the technology constraints on this proposal? How might the design be affected by these constraints?

_____

_____

_____

_____

_____

_____

_____

_____

_____

_____

_____

_____

_____

_____

Exercise 2: Identifying Operating System Clients to Upgrade

Read the scenario and then answer the question that follows.

Scenario   You're a security designer for Wingtip Toys, and you receive a proposal to change the security policy for Wingtip Toys, which includes the requirement that the LM authentication protocol be phased out.

Review Question   Answer the following question.

  1. Which Windows operating system clients absolutely must be upgraded to another operating system before LM can be eliminated from the network?

Design Activity: Developing a List of Security Issues

In this activity, you must use what you've learned in all three lessons and apply it to a real-world situation. Read the scenario, and then complete the exercise that follows. You can find answers for the exercise in the "Questions and Answers" section at the end of this chapter.

Scenario

Wingtip Toys and Tailspin Toys are proceeding with their plans to jointly research and publish information about toy safety. They want to develop the resources and begin the project. Then, they plan to provide their toy safety reports to other concerned parties, including citizen and parent groups, the media, other toy manufacturers, and providers of the products and services that the toy manufacturers use. The following requirements must be met:

- **Requirement 1**   Researchers from both companies must have access to shared data.

- **Requirement 2**   Both companies will provide resource servers to store gathered information.

- **Requirement 3**   Public access to information will be provided by a new Web server that will be co-located at each organization's site.

You are asked to develop a list of security issues that should be addressed as part of this project.

Exercise 1: Develop a List of Security Issues

In this exercise, you will develop a list of security issues. To do this, answer the questions that follow.

1. What are the business requirements of the project that may pose a security risk? Why do these things pose a security risk?

2. Are there any legal issues concerning the security of the information?

3. Are there any interoperability issues that concern the security of the information?

4. Are there administration-related risk issues?

5. Are there network location issues?

Chapter Summary

- The security design must consider the constraints imposed by legacy systems.

- Building a security design framework is a good way to ensure that all possible areas are addressed in a security design. Concepts to include in your security framework include:

    - ❑ Threat modeling. This is a good tool to know how to use because it can help you develop a well-rounded approach to security design.

    - ❑ Prevention, detection, isolation, and recovery. These are all pieces in the security design process. None of them, on their own, can provide a comprehensive approach to security design.

    - ❑ Analysis of existing security policies and procedures. This is a good first step for any design and might also result in you discovering weaknesses in the existing security policies and procedures.

    - ❑ Security procedures should be performed in accordance with security policies. Both should support business needs.

    - ❑ The type of data that must be protected dictates what type of security will be used to protect the data.

    - ❑ IT administration practices should be considered when performing risk analysis, threat modeling, and security design.

- The security design must consider the constraints imposed by interoperability requirements.

- The security design must consider the constraints imposed by technical limitations.

Exam Highlights

Before taking the exam, review these key points and terms. You need to know this information.

Key Points

- Administrative authority should be considered as a possible security risk.

- Business operations and needs must be considered in the security design.

- Existing security policies and procedures should be reviewed.

- Threat modeling is a way to discover gaps in security.

- Prevention, detection, isolation, and recovery are components of a well-rounded security design.

Key Terms

Legacy system Any infrastructure component such as hardware, operating system software, network device, or application that is technically out-of-date. For example, Windows 2000–based computers might be defined as legacy systems in a predominately Windows XP Professional and Windows Server 2003 network, and an IBM mainframe that hosts hundreds of Linux servers running Apache Web sites would not be defined as a legacy system (at least not until the next version of Linux is placed on the market).

Segmented networks Networks that are separated into zones of trust. Access between the networks is restricted. Gateways such as VPN servers, firewalls, proxy servers, and other devices can provide and restrict access between networks. For example, they can provide or restrict access between the Internet and a business internal network.

Technical constraint Any technical reason why a security design cannot be implemented as designed. The reason for the technical constraint can be insufficient interoperability between disparate systems, legacy system issues, or simply the existence of applications and hardware components that pose conflicts or that cannot support the proposed design.

Threat modeling The process of brainstorming all possible risks to a system so that countermeasures can be developed.

Questions and Answers

Pg 1-24 **Lesson 1   Exercise 1: Analyzing Business Requirements**

1. What text or parts of the project plan will help you in your task of creating a list of business requirements?

You should begin by reading the project goals or mission statement in the project plan for statements that appear to give the companies some benefit. In this example, "help the companies maintain a positive image" is the main statement of benefit. The other benefit you will find in the project plan, providing consumer information on toy safety, is a consumer benefit, not a business benefit, and is therefore not relevant to your assignment.

Also, look for statements or phrases that suggest a change to standard security practices might be necessary. In this example, the phrases "joint research," "access to some of its research data," and "provide communication venues" indicate that changes to standard security practices will be necessary. All of these findings can be added to the list of business requirements.

2. What are the new IT functions that will be built because of this partnership?

A database or file server for storing research must be created and made available to both companies.

It is possible that news groups, chat rooms, and Web sites for team interaction will need to be created.

A joint Web site and perhaps links on the new Web site to the companies' existing Web sites may be necessary. New data on the companies' Web sites will need to be created.

3. Promoting a positive image is a stated business driver. What are the unstated drivers that set the parameters for the security design?

Unstated drivers include: 1) the need to limit partner access to the joint research and keep other company data secured from partner access, 2) the need to set up secured communication for partners and keep the rest of the world out, and 3) the need to prevent the blurring of lines between the two companies.

Pg 1-26 **Lesson 1   Exercise 2: Evaluating the Current Security Policy**

1. What are the implications of these statements in the Tailspin Toys security policy for the proposed IT projects that you listed in Exercise 1?

The policy might require issuance of certificates or the preparation of some other form of authentication so that partners can access resources. However, the policy states "internal" resources. If the research data is totally segmented from other internal data, you might decide that it does not come under this restriction.

Because non-employees are not allowed to access the company intranet, the research site will have to be separated from internal resources.

Cryptographic support for communications must be designed into your solution. This requirement might mean using SSL or VPNs, but it definitely must be part of the overall project design.

However Internet access is restricted within Tailspin Toys, the restriction will have to be adjusted to allow internal researchers to access the other partners' research materials.

If the internal researchers want to set up a wireless network, it must be reviewed by the IT department.

Pg 1-27 **Lesson 1 Exercise 3: Placing Documents in Data Categories**

Match the data categories listed below to the list of documents in the following table. In the real world, data owners should be responsible for classifying data, but being familiar with the process will allow you to question or to assist the data owners. The data categories are:

The following table shows the correct answers.

Table **Matching Documents to Data Categories—Answer Key**

Document	Data category
Company Internet Web site home page articles	public
Statements being prepared for the annual report	confidential
An announcement of the company picnic	internal
Company intranet Web site home page	internal
Employee names, addresses, phone numbers	confidential
The published annual report	public
Product development research	confidential
Employee benefits plan information	internal

Pg 1-27 **Lesson 1 Exercise 4: Identifying Noncompliant Security Policies**

1. Your company has the following security policy: "All access to external resources such as the Internet shall be through company gateways and shall be restricted and audited." Which of the following items do not comply with this security policy? Choose all that apply.

    a. An unapproved wireless network is established by the Accounting department.

    b. An employee uses a modem to access a personal e-mail account.

    c. An employee opens Internet Explorer on his company-provided desktop computer. The computer has been configured to use the company-provided gateway.

    d. An employee uses a company-provided laptop from home to access the company intranet.

    Items a and b are not compliant with the policy. A wireless network does not usually, by default, provide access to external resources. However, depending on its location and strength and depending on how employees use wireless cards in their computers, access to external resources might be provided or might be accidentally obtained. A modem uses a telephone line and goes around any company-provided gateway. Option c is not correct because the company has configured the computer to use approved resources. Option d is not correct because the employee is not accessing resources external to the company.

Pg 1-28   **Lesson 1   Exercise 5: Deciding How to Secure Public Access to a Company Web Site**

1. Wingtip Toys manufactures and sells toys. The company Web site provides product information, company information, and links to online retailers who sell the company's toys. Public access to the site should be secured by using the following items:

    a. A firewall, SSL, operating system and Web site hardening, and an intrusion detection system.

    b. A firewall, operating system and Web site hardening, and an intrusion detection system.

    c. A firewall, a VPN, operating system and Web site hardening, and an intrusion detection system.

    d. A firewall, a VPN, SSL, operating system and Web site hardening, and an intrusion detection system.

b is the correct answer. Options a, c, and d are incorrect because SSL and a VPN connection are not needed. The Web site does not sell toys, nor are there any other business needs described that indicate SSL or VPN connections for the public are necessary.

Pg 1-45   **Lesson 2   Exercise 1: Predicting Threats to a Company**

1. What types of threats should you think about?

Answers will vary. Some examples of threats you should be thinking about include:

1) Think about threats related to the data. Data that is not complimentary about the company might be exposed to the public. Also, internal documents might provide the other company with information that allows them to be more competitive with yours.

2) Think about threats to the systems that are shared. The other company's employees might introduce worms and viruses. They might maliciously attack the system. They might accidentally delete information. Opening the system to external access might provide access for people other than those who have been approved. The administrators of the shared system might unknowingly provide outsiders, or unauthorized insiders, with privileges that would enable them to destroy or manipulate data. Outsiders might be able to elevate their privileges and thus do damage or access data on the shared system that they are not authorized for.

3) Think about threats to other company systems. If there is a trust between the shared system and the company forest, outsiders might accidentally be given access to resources outside the intended shared system. Viruses, worms, and other malicious code might infect other company resources. If outsiders are given (or able to assume) elevated privileges within the shared systems, they might be able to leverage this to obtain elevated privileges in the company forest.

Pg 1-45   **Lesson 2   Exercise 2: Designing a Segmented Network to Provide Extra Security**

    1. What steps will you take to begin designing the segmented network to provide added security?

        Answers will vary. Here is one solution:

        a. Develop a solution for the 90 percent of people working in one physical area. Because they are physically located in one area, it's possible to segment the network by providing a gateway between their area and all others. A firewall can provide that gateway and be configured to allow the Financial department users access to trusted sites. For example, a firewall could be configured to allow the Financial department users access to the company intranet servers and possibly to servers on the Internet that have been approved for access by Financial department users.

        b. Decide how you will allow authorized users outside the internal segment to access resources. You have two choices: IPSec or VPNs. IPSec does not require user authentication; however, it might be judged adequate because it protects the communication, and other controls (access control lists, for example) should already define access to resources within the segment. A VPN does require user authentication and can provide secure access for authorized employees who are not on site.

        c. Consider other communications that must pass through the gateway. Where will user mailboxes be located, and how will they send and receive e-mail? How will Active Directory be accessed? Users must authenticate to a domain controller and Group Policy must be downloaded. If the size of the segment is large enough or important enough, should a domain controller be placed within the segment? If so, how will replication be secured?

        d. Consider administration issues. Will IT administrators be able to access financial systems remotely, or will they need to locally log on to systems? If remote access is allowed, should terminal services be considered? Or should a VPN connection be considered?

    2. Sketch a proposed design incorporating your decisions from the previous steps.

        Your answer should look something like Figure 1-8 in the lesson, but it may be a little different.

Pg 1-47   **Lesson 2   Exercise 3: Designing a Recovery Process**

    1. What tasks must the IT department perform to back up and recover data securely? Describe each task in one to two sentences.

        1) Divide computers into categories according to network roles such as domain controller, server, and desktop computers.

        2) Within each category, determine whether separate recovery processes are needed for the operating system and various services, such as e-mail server, DNS, and so on.

        3) For each category, write procedures for recovery. List the tools available, the steps to be taken when determining which tool to use, and what to do before using the tools. Also provide detailed, step-by-step procedures about how to use the tools.

        4) Provide test systems, and require IT personnel who recover systems to practice the recovery steps. Keep records of which IT personnel have completed practicing the recovery steps.

5) Provide a drill. Simulate the loss of a domain controller, for example, and require IT personnel to recover the system. Provide feedback about how well they responded to the drill.

6) If systems are lost and then recovered or not recovered, provide postmortem discussions on the process.

7) Assume recovery will not be possible. For each category defined in step 1, develop a backup policy. Provide information about each system, including what should be backed up, when the backup should occur, how and where (for example, onsite or offsite) backups should be stored, and who (using their job title) should perform backups.

8) Provide detailed procedures that explain how to perform the required backups. Include logging and storage requirements.

9) Document how to meet the requirement that those tasked with backup receive training and supervision until they can complete backups according to policy.

10) Document how to meet the requirement to periodically test backup media by restoring to test systems.

11) Document how the audit of backup and recovery processes will be conducted.

Pg 1-48 **Lesson 2   Exercise 4: Matching Security Plan Elements to the Parts of the Security Framework**

The following table shows the correct answers:

Table   Categorizing Security Design Features—Answer Key

Prevention	Detection	Isolation	Recovery
Using Group Policy to enforce security configuration	Installing an IDS	Removing a network cable from the back of a computer system	A backup procedure
A backup procedure	Sending incident handling team (CCSIRT) members to a class on forensics	Unplugging the firewall's interface to the Internet	
Sending incident handling team members to a class on forensics			
Training end users how to create strong passwords			
Deploying smart cards and readers, and requiring their use for all external access to the corporate network			

Pg 1-49   **Lesson 2   Exercise 5: Identifying Devices that Segment Internal Networks into Zones of Trust**

Answer the following question.

1. Which of the following devices can be used to segment internal networks into zones of trust—zones that are secured against intrusion from each other? Choose all that apply.

   a. A firewall

   b. A switch

   c. A packet-filtering router

   d. A hub

   Options a and c are correct. Option b is incorrect because although a switch can be used to segment networks, there are well-known attacks that easily penetrate this configuration. Option d is also incorrect because a hub connects multiple computers and simply rebroadcasts all data to all computers.

Pg 1-54   **Lesson 3   Exercise 1: Analyzing Legacy Infrastructure Constraints**

Answer the following question.

1. What are the technology constraints on this proposal? How might the design be affected by these constraints?

   1) A specific technology, IPSec, is required. Some operating systems used in the network don't have the ability to use IPSec. Only Windows XP professional has built-in IPSec capability. However, a download that will enable users of Windows NT 4.0 and Windows 98 to use an L2TP/IPSec VPN is available on the Product Support Services page of the Microsoft Web site at *http://www.microsoft.com/downloads/details.aspx?displaylang=en&familyid=6A1086DC-3BD0-4D65-9B82-20CBE650F974.*

   2) But, you must delve further. Do the existing clients meet the requirements of the downloadable client mentioned in step 1? Windows NT 4.0 must be service pack 6, and Windows 98 must have Internet Explorer 5.01 or later and the Dial-up Networking client version 1.4 upgrade. Each system will need to be checked and upgraded as required.

   3) Other technical adjustments will need to be handled. L2TP/IPSec VPNs require machine certificates. You must figure out how clients will obtain the certificates. You must also decide how to audit the use of IPSec. You also need to determine whether there are compatibility issues with other products (such as network cards or software programs) the clients might be using.

Pg 1-55   **Lesson 3   Exercise 2: Identifying Operating System Clients to Upgrade**

Answer the following question.

1. Which Windows operating system clients absolutely must be upgraded to another operating system before LM can be eliminated from the network?

   Answer: Windows for Workgroups

Design Activity: Developing a List of Security Issues

Pg 1-56   **Exercise 1: Develop a List of Security Issues**

In this exercise, you will develop a list of security issues. To do this, answer the questions that follow.

1. What are the business requirements of the project that may pose a security risk? Why do these things pose a security risk?

    1) Results of research will be shared with another company and eventually with the public. Depending on the category of data that will be shared, there may be a risk that something is shared that should not be.

    2) Data will be placed on public Web servers that belong to each company. Neither company will have any control over the other's Web server. Will both meet the security standards of their partner?

    3) Each company will set up servers and provide access to researchers from the other company as well as their own company. Will the security on each server be adequate? How will access be authorized? Authenticated?

2. Are there any legal issues concerning the security of the information?

    Laws address privacy concerns about any data that might identify individuals. Since this is research data, questions should be asked about this issue.

3. Are there any interoperability issues that concern the security of the information?

    There may be. As the issues of authentication and authorization are addressed, interoperability concerns will need to be addressed.

4. Are there administration-related risk issues?

    1) Computer administrators are always a risk. This project involves the sharing of data between different companies—both on Web servers and other servers. Care will need to be taken in assigning administrators.

    2) The location of the servers will need to be considered. Will they belong to a domain in the forest? To a separate domain? To a separate forest?

5. Are there network location issues?

    Where are the shared servers located? On a perimeter network? Inside the firewall? Outside the firewall? How will network access be protected?

Section II
Creating a Security Design for the Network Infrastructure

When a civil engineer designs a highway intersection, she knows the materials she has to work with and the physical forces that she must support. She knows this from study, education, and experience. She knows how to design structures from concrete and steel to support the weight of many vehicles traveling at high rates of speed. There are standard lane sizes, cants to the curve, a correct numbers of beams, and a proper thickness of surface. There are safety features too: rounded side rails that taper to the ground at the ends of bridges and ramps, paved shoulders, and gentle curves.

When you design security as the foundation for your network, you have fewer precise rules to work with and less concrete laws to reinforce your decisions. Opinions vary widely about what tools you should choose and what path you should follow. Nevertheless, reliable guidelines exist and a solid security infrastructure can be designed. The chapters in this section will tell you how.

Business and technical constraints must form the framework for security design, but no security design can ignore the technical foundation upon which it must rest. This foundation-the network infrastructure-is composed of logical and physical components. This section addresses both of these components. Chapter 2, "Designing the Logical Infrastructure," provides one solution for implementing the logical elements of network infrastructure design: authentication, authorization, confidentially, and integrity. Chapter 3, "Designing the Network Infrastructure for Physical Security," explores infrastructure designs that consider border controls, Domain Name System (DNS), and the security of internal communications.

2 Designing the Logical Infrastructure

Exam Objectives in this Chapter:

- Create the logical design for a security network infrastructure.
- Design a public key infrastructure (PKI) that uses Certificate Services.
- Design a Certification Authority (CA) hierarchy implementation. Types include geographical, organizational, and trusted.
- Design enrollment and distribution processes.
- Establish renewal, revocation, and auditing processes.
- Design security for CA servers.

Why This Chapter Matters

If you don't base your security design on solid logic, it will fail. Before you think about protocols and proxies, you must think about authentication, confidentiality, and integrity. Before you think about hardware and software, you must think about availability, security, and privacy—and what these things mean to your organization. If you cannot describe the purpose of a secure network infrastructure, what it is made up of, and how it will support business without hindering it, you doom your design (not to mention your career as a designer) from the start.

Lessons in this Chapter:

Before You Begin

This chapter presents the skills and concepts related to designing the logical security infrastructure. This training kit assumes that you have a minimum of 1 year of experience implementing and administering desktop operating systems and network operating systems in environments that have the following characteristics:

- At least 250 supported users

- Three or more physical locations

- Typical network services such as messaging, database, file and print, proxy server or firewall, Internet and intranet, remote access, and client computer management

- Three or more domain controllers

- Connectivity needs, including connecting branch offices and individual users in remote locations to the corporate network and connecting corporate networks to the Internet

In addition, you should have experience designing a network infrastructure.

Many design exercises are paper-based; however, to understand the technical capabilities that a design can incorporate, you should have some hands-on experience with products. Where specific hands-on instruction is given, you must have at least two computers configured as specified in the "Getting Started" section at the beginning of this book. This chapter presents additional topics and practices to teach you how to complete the major steps to put the design into production.

Lesson 1: Building a Logical Security Infrastructure by Using Certificate Services

Every network has a security infrastructure. Every network has rules about who can use what resource and what they can use it for. The difference between most networks and a network in which the logic of security has been designed is that the network with designed security has a strong foundation on which to build its controls. Each piece of the security puzzle can be snapped into place with minimum disruption to the network. To build this strong foundation, you must first understand certain key concepts. This lesson teaches those concepts.

After this lesson, you will be able to

- Describe the pillars of information security.
- Apply the pillars of information security to your designs.
- Build a logical security infrastructure by using certificate services.
- Identify the components of a public key infrastructure.

Estimated lesson time: 60 minutes

The Pillars of Information Security

To create a logical design, the vague notion of "secure" must be replaced with concrete maxims. These, in turn, must be explained and interpreted so that you can use them as you create your designs. The pillars of information security include authentication, authorization, confidentiality, integrity, and nonrepudiation. These pillars are described in Table 2-1. Your ability to express each one of these concepts is a part of the foundation on which network security rests.

Tip   When you develop a logical design, think of the things that are available to fulfill these needs. Remember, however, that technologies change, as do the ways they are expressed.

Table 2-1   The Pillars of Information Security

Pillar	Definition
Authentication	The way that security principals (users, computers, processes) can prove their identity before connecting to the network or to some resource contained by the network. In a traditional network, authentication is supported by technologies that rely on passwords. Today, additional authentication tools—such as certificates, smart cards, biometrics, tokens, and even unique devices—are supported.

Table 2-1   The Pillars of Information Security

Pillar	Definition
Authorization	The process that dictates what a security principal can do after it is authenticated. System privileges and object-based access control lists (ACLs) are the primary methods of authorization used in the Microsoft Windows 2003 family of operating systems.
Confidentiality	The process that keeps private information private. Data, communications, and even code can have requirements for protection. While authorization can protect digital information, there are many ways to subvert authorization, including taking ownership of an object, placing a copy of the data on another computer, capturing information as it flows across a network, and so forth. Providing layers of security is a maxim of good security. Confidentiality allows you to do this. Confidentiality is most often obtained on a network by using encryption. Classic symmetric key encryption uses a single key and an algorithm to make plain text, which is easily understood, into ciphertext, which is not. One of encryption's weaknesses is the problem of keeping the encryption key safe. Today, a public key/private key algorithm is often incorporated for that purpose, and certificates are used to map the keys to a security principal.
Integrity	The ability to guarantee that information is not arbitrarily changed. Changes can be made to data, but only when authorized. Many networks and systems maintain integrity by providing authentication and authorization controls. When data is sent over a network, additional controls are needed. Network communications has long supported the use of algorithms that check integrity by comparing the result of a calculation that includes the data sent with the result of that same calculation that includes the data received. If there is a difference in results of the two calculations, then the data has changed. These calculations detect accidental changes made because of poor communications and require a repeated transmission. It cannot protect the integrity of data from malicious interference. Modern communication protocols such as IPSec use encryption to protect the data that is sent from being tampered with.
Nonrepudiation	A method of providing undeniable proof that a security principal is the source of some data, action, or communication. Nonrepudiation can cement the assertion that I did use my credit card to make an online purchase or that the boss did send the e-mail giving me the day off. In both of these cases and in many other digital situations, the use of public key/private key technologies can provide implementation of nonrepudiation.

> **Note**   An access token, which contains the user's authorization material, is attached to each process the security principal runs and does not traverse the network. Instead it is created at each computer the security principal visits. However, the information that is used to build the access token does traverse the network. For example, it is incorporated in the authorization field of a Kerberos ticket.

Guidelines for Applying the Pillars of Information Security to Your Designs

Each one of the pillars of information security should become a part of your information security design. How you use them will depend on what your design is for and the technology that is available to implement the design. To apply the pillars of information security to your designs, follow these guidelines:

- Give the process of authentication prime importance. The process of authentication is what protects your network and its data. Spend time improving the authentication process. Selecting the best available means and training people in its use will provide more rewards than the same amount of attention paid to any other pillar. Think about it this way. If the lock on your front door keeps people out of your house, the strength of any locks or security measures inside your house are of no consequence.

- Don't ignore the other pillars of information security. Eventually, every lock can be broken. You do need the protection provided by the other pillars.

- When applying authorization to the logical design, consider the following questions: How are the security principals' authorization credentials presented, and how are they available to the security monitor for evaluation? In Windows Server 2003, as in other versions of Windows, the security reference monitor checks security principal privileges and group membership against object ACLs and the process the security principal has requested. In the Microsoft Windows world, the authorization material is returned with the authentication approval and traverses the network with each authentication process.

- When designing confidentiality for a system, remember that different types of data require different types of protection. To simply encrypt all data is not a solution.

- A network infrastructure design needs to protect the integrity of data whether the data is in a file system, database, operating system core, or being transported between devices.

- Nonrepudiation is becoming a more important part of information security. Look for the ability to apply this pillar in the areas of communications, systems administration, and software modification.

- Although you might not see the need or be able to apply all the pillars to all design projects, you should always examine the need for each pillar and apply all of them to the entire information system security design. All of them are necessary.

Guidelines for Building a Logical Security Infrastructure Using Certificate Services

To implement every one of the pillars of information security in your design, you can use certificate services. *Certificate services* are services through which public key/private key algorithms are implemented. Although not every such algorithm requires the use of digital certificates, all of them can do so. Digital certificates are one component in a public key infrastructure (PKI).

To implement certificate services in Windows Server 2003, you design a public key infrastructure. Follow these guidelines for using certificate services:

- To create a strong, logical security infrastructure design, incorporate the use of PKI technologies:
  - ❏ Where possible
  - ❏ Where it is the best design decision for the enterprise
  - ❏ Where it is dictated by operating system, application, or other operational requirement.
- Use certificates for computer authentication by implementing IPSec.
- Use certificates for user authentication by implementing smart cards.
- Use certificates for authorization by using the Encrypting File System (EFS).
- Use certificates to provide confidentiality for data stored in files by using EFS.
- Use certificates for data communications to provide computer authentication.
- Use certificates for integrity by using digital signatures.
- Use certificates for nonrepudiation by using digital signatures.
- Use certificates to protect Active Directory replication by implementing SMTP transport.
- Use certificates to protect the Active Directory by implementing secured LDAP queries.
- Do not use self-signed certificates (certificates that are not signed by a Certification Authority). A CA provides increased control and recoverability. EFS, by default, uses self-signed certificates that can be configured to use those issued by a CA.

The Components of a Public Key Infrastructure

A *public key infrastructure* is the sum of the components implemented to provide certificate services on a network. Certificate services include the issuing, use, and maintenance of certificates. You must be able to identify and define the components of a public key infrastructure to successfully and securely implement certificate services on your network. The components of a PKI include:

- Digital Certificates

- Certification Authority (CA)

- Certification Hierarchy

- Certificate Revocation List

- Certificate Policy Statement

The following sections describe these components in detail.

What Is a Digital Certificate?

A digital certificate is a collection of related data that binds an identity to a cryptographic key pair. Certificates can be used for authentication, authorization, nonrepudiation, and other security controls. Figure 2-1 shows the Details tab from an EFS certificate.

Figure 2-1   EFS Details tab

Certificates contain information such as:

- A name that indicates to whom or to what the certificate belongs. If the certificate is issued from a CA that is integrated with Active Directory directory services, the name might be the name of a server or a user with Active Directory credentials.

- A copy of the public key from a cryptographic key pair.

- The name of the CA that issued the certificate.

- The purpose or purposes for which a certificate can be used.

- The signature of the CA that issued the certificate.

Depending on the type of PKI that is implemented, specific types of certification might be issued that have specific uses on the network. Types of certificates include the following:

- EFS, which is used by the Encrypting File System

- Certification Authority, which is used to sign certificates and Certificate Revocation Lists (CRLs) produced by the CA

- IPSec, which is used for IPSec authentication

- User, which can be used for EFS, authentication, and other purposes

- Domain Controller, which is used to identify a domain controller

- Server, which is used to authenticate a server

What Is a Certification Authority?

A Certification Authority (CA) can be an entity or an organization that manages and controls the production of public or private certificates. *CA* is also the name used to describe the computer device and the software that produces or controls the issuance or revocation of certificates and the infrastructure for their use in the network. Windows Server 2003 provides such a service as an optional component or server role. In this book, unless otherwise noted, the use of the term Certification Authority or the initials CA will mean the computer and software that produces or controls the issuance or revocation of certificates and the infrastructure for their use in the network.

A single CA can provide all the certificate services required, or multiple CAs can be arranged in a CA hierarchy. Windows CAs are either root CAs or subordinate CAs. A *root CA* creates its own certificate; a *subordinate CA* receives its CA certificate from another CA. The following four types of CAs can be installed:

- A root stand-alone CA, which is not integrated with Active Directory. It can be installed on a Windows Server 2003 server or a Windows 2000 server that is or is not a member of an Active Directory domain.

- A root enterprise CA, which is integrated with Active Directory and can only be installed on a Windows Server 2003 or Windows 2000 server that is a member server in an Active Directory domain.

- A subordinate stand-alone CA, which is not integrated with Active Directory and receives its CA certificate from a root CA. The subordinate stand-alone CA can be installed on a Windows Server 2003 or Windows 2000 server that is or is not an Active Directory domain member server.

- A subordinate enterprise CA, which is integrated with Active Directory.

What Is a Certification Hierarchy?

A certification hierarchy, or *CA hierarchy*, is an organized collection of CAs. The first CA in a CA hierarchy is the root, and there can be only one root. All other CAs joined in the hierarchy are subordinate to the root and must receive a CA certificate from another CA. A CA hierarchy can contain both stand-alone and enterprise CAs. For more information about CA hierarchies, see Lesson 2.

What Is a Certificate Revocation List?

A *certificate revocation list (CRL)* is a list of certificates that have been revoked along with the reason they were revoked. Certificates are issued with a predetermined validity period (the length of time for which they can be used). However, a certificate can be revoked if it should no longer be accepted and has not yet reached its expiration date. Reasons for revocation might be suspicion or knowledge of certificate compromise, an employee leaves the company, and so on. A CRL can therefore be used as one step in the process used to determine whether a certificate is valid.

What Is a Certificate Policy Statement?

A *certificate policy statement (CPS)* is a formal document that specifies how the PKI will be operated and managed. It is, as the American Bar Association states, "A statement of the practices which a certification authority employs in issuing certificates." The CPS might include information such as:

- Physical and procedural security for the CA
- Security for the network on which the CA exists
- Network identification of the CA (including DNS address, CA name, and server name)
- Certificate policies implemented by the CA, and each type of certificate issued by that CA
- Policies and procedures for issuing, renewing, and recovering certificates
- Certificate lifetime of each certificate
- Policies for revocation
- Policies for CRLs, including CRL distribution point and publication period
- Policy for CA renewal

Request for Comments (RFC) 2527, "Internet X.509 Public Key Infrastructure Certificate Policy and Certification Practices Framework," is an informational RFC that provides a framework for certificate policy writing. This RFC is a good source of information on items that might be covered in a certificate policy definition or certificate practice statement, and it provides sample statements that might be used in developing a CPS.

In addition to including statements about the overall management of the PKI, the CPS should outline, for each certificate, a certificate practice policy statement that states information such as:

- How users are authenticated to the CA
- The intended purpose of the certificate
- Requirements for certificate enrollment and renewal
- Maximum length for public key and private key pairs
- Legal issues that might arise if the CA is compromised
- Legal issues that might occur if the certificate is not used as intended
- Private key management, such as archiving details, export processes, or requirements that smart cards or other hardware devices be used
- Obligations of users of the certificates, such as what to do if keys are lost, damaged, or compromised

Although the CPS is a formal written document, in Windows Server 2003, the CAPolicy.inf file can be used to document certificate policy statements. This file must be copied to the system directory of the CA before the CA is installed or renewed.

See Also For more information about the CAPolicy.inf file, see the "Distributed Services Guide" of the Windows Server 2003 Resource Kit and the Resource Kit page of the Microsoft Web site at *http://www.microsoft.com/reskit*.

Practice: Using Certificates for Authentication and Authorization

In this practice, you will explore uses for certificates in authentication and authorization. If you are unable to answer a question, review the lesson materials and try the question again. You can find answers to the questions in the "Questions and Answers" section at the end of this chapter.

Exercise 1: Investigating Authentication and Authorization Certificate Usage

Read the following articles in the Windows Server 2003 Help documentation:

- Authentication Methods: Internet Protocol security
- Authentication and Smart Card Support
- Encrypting and Decrypting Data

After you've finished reading the articles, answer the following questions:

1. When designing an IPSec policy, when would you use one authentication strategy above another?

_____

_____

_____

_____

_____

_____

_____

_____

_____

_____

_____

_____

_____

_____

2. You must create an authentication design in which smart card usage is required. What authentication choices are available, and which would you pick for your design?

_____

_____

3. In your design of the authorization and confidentiality systems, what part can EFS play?

_____

_____

_____

_____

_____

_____

Exercise 2: Matching Windows Server 2003 Technologies to the Pillars of Information Security

1. Match specific Windows Server 2003 technologies with the pillars of information security listed in Table 2-2. Technologies include:

   ❑ IPSec Encapsulating Security Protocol (ESP)

   ❑ Certificates in IPSec authentication

   ❑ Secure Sockets Layer (SSL)

   ❑ Rights

   ❑ Digital signatures

   ❑ Transport Layer Security (TLS)

   ❑ Certificates for authentication

   ❑ EFS

   ❑ ACLs

   ❑ VPNs

   ❑ Authentication Header (AH)

   ❑ ESP protocols in IPSec

Table 2-2   Technologies Associated with the Pillars of Information Security

Pillar	Supporting Technologies
Authentication	
Authorization	
Nonrepudiation	
Confidentiality	
Integrity	

Lesson 2: Designing a CA Hierarchy

A single CA can be installed and used to provide all the certificate services a network requires. However, this single CA must be a root CA and must remain online so that its services can be used. This is not an ideal security situation. The root CA is the seat of all trust in your public key infrastructure. It is possible, for it to become the seat of all trust for the entire organization. If an attacker can compromise the root CA, he then can access any thing and do anything in the organization. You can improve security, scalability, and flexibility by implementing a CA hierarchy. This lesson teaches you how.

After this lesson, you will be able to

- Describe how a CA hierarchy works.
- Protect the root CA hierarchy infrastructure.
- Install an offline root CA.
- Describe the different types of CA hierarchies.
- Design different types of CA hierarchies.
- Explain the certificate chaining process.
- Explain the purpose of qualified subordination.
- Secure CAs.

Estimated lesson time: 60 minutes

How a CA Hierarchy Works

A CA hierarchy works as follows:

1. A CA hierarchy is created by installing a root CA and one or more subordinate CAs in an organization. Two or more levels of CAs can be implemented.

> **Tip**   A root CA can be installed on a Windows Server 2003 or Windows 2000 computer that is either a stand-alone computer, or a domain member.

2. The root CA is the only CA on the first level. The root CA issues CA certificates for one or more subordinate CAs, which then make up the second level.

3. Subordinate CAs, in turn, can issue CA certificates for CAs that will make up a third level.

More than three levels are possible; however, it is generally agreed that three levels provides the most flexibility, efficiency, and scalability in a CA hierarchy.

Example: A Typical CA Hierarchy

Although there is no single right way to create a CA hierarchy, the most secure designs limit the types of certificates that each CA in the hierarchy can issue. A typical design of this type is shown in Figure 2-2. It follows this best practice configuration:

- A root CA is only allowed to issue other CA certificates.

- The root CA is protected.

- The middle layer or *intermediate CAs* can only issue CA certificates.

- The bottom layer CAs issue end-use certificates and thus are called *issuing CAs*.

- Issuing CAs are each limited in the types of end-use certificates they issue.

- Issuing CAs do not issue CA certificates.

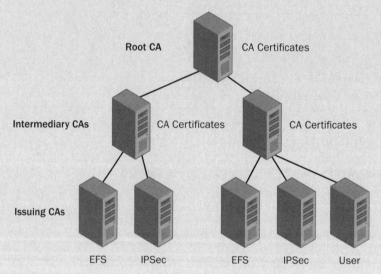

Figure 2-2 Examining a simple, best practice CA hierarchy

This example shows how the layers of CA hierarchies should be implemented and specifies two important practices: protecting the root CA and limiting the types of certificates that any CA can issue. It does not, however, provide the information that will help you accomplish that, nor does it inform you of typical CA hierarchy implementation types and when they should be used. Review the guidelines in this lesson to get the full picture.

Guidelines for Protecting the CA Hierarchy Infrastructure

The CA hierarchy computers require security above and beyond that of other servers in the network. The root CA requires special protection. The root CA is the seat of all trust in a PKI. This CA issues all other certificates used in the enterprise. If the root CA is compromised, all other certificate usage is suspect. The only method of recovery is to rip and replace—that is, to revoke all certificates produced by the CAs in the hierarchy, remove all CAs in the hierarchy, and start all over again. The root CA therefore requires a higher degree of protection than any device or service on the network. To protect the CA infrastructure, follow these guidelines:

- **Protect the root CA.**   To do this:
    - ❑ Establish at least a two-tier hierarchy composed of a root CA and one or more issuing CAs. Figure 2-3 shows a simple two-layer CA hierarchy that can be used to provide protection for the root CA, and hence for the rest of the trust network. The connection between the two CAs illustrates their hierarchical connection; it does not represent a network connection.

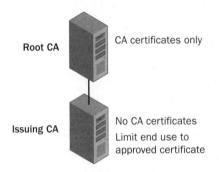

Figure 2-3   A two-layer hierarchy

    - ❑ Install the root CA as a Windows Server 2003 stand-alone root CA. This type of CA does not need to be on a network.
    - ❑ Take the root CA offline. When the root CA is not connected to the network, it cannot be attacked across the network. You will need to take care in configuring the root CA so that it can function offline and so that the services—such as a certificate revocation list—and access to a copy of its certificate are available online.
    - ❑ Physically protect the root CA. Consider placing the root CA in a vault or in another extreme protection area. Use a hardware device for storage of the CA keys.
    - ❑ Limit access to the root CA. Access to the root CA is necessary only for limited maintenance activities and can be restricted to a few trusted employees.
    - ❑ Restrict the root CA so that it can issue only CA certificates. The ability to issue any other kind of certificate should be removed.

- **Protect all the CAs.**   To do this:

  ❑ If intermediate CAs are used, place them on the network in a secure location and provide those servers with much more security than normal servers.

  ❑ If intermediate CAs are used, restrict them to issuing CA certificates.

  ❑ Place issuing CAs on the network, and provide them with a physically secure location and additional security beyond what you'd provide for other, more mundane network servers.

  ❑ Restrict the issuing CAs so that they are able to issue only end-use certificates.

  ❑ Restrict access to and administrative authority for all CAs.

Guidelines for Installing an Offline Root CA

Protecting the root CA is very important. Best practices recommend installing the root CA on a stand-alone computer, never placing it on the network, and protecting it in a vault. To install a root CA to be used for a hierarchy in this manner, use the following guidelines:

- Ensure that the computer that will be used for the root CA is not placed on the network. Remember that:

  ❑ In a production environment, this computer does not have to be installed on the network at all.

  ❑ By isolating the computer during installation and not connecting it to the network, you reduce the possibility that the computer can be compromised.

- Ensure that the stand-alone CA is not a domain member. This is illustrated by the following points:

  ❑ Once a computer takes on the role of CA, you cannot change its name or domain membership.

  ❑ Because this computer will be kept separate from the network anyway, it should not be a domain member and its name should be decided and established before certificate services are installed.

  ❑ The CA name does not have to be the same as the computer name.

- When installing certificate services, view its components: Certificate Services CA and Certificate Services Web Enrollment Support. Remember that:

  ❑ If IIS is installed on the computer, you can use either the web interface or the Certificates snap-in to request new CA certificates. The web interface is not necessary.

  ❑ The computer will not be on the network, so adding IIS does not present the risk that it might while on the network.

■ When prompted, always select a stand-alone root CA. To do this, follow these guidelines:

❑ Although you can create either an enterprise-root or a stand-alone root CA, an enterprise-root CA would have to be integrated with Active Directory. Removing such a computer permanently from the network would mean excess processing and errors as the member server keeps trying to find its domain controller.

❑ Use Custom settings, as shown in Figure 2-4, to select special cryptographic service providers (CSPs).

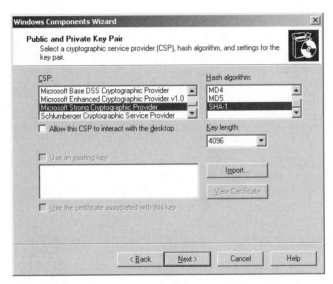

Figure 2-4   Selecting key strength and algorithms

❑ If special CSPs are not required, select the Microsoft Strong Cryptographic provider.

❑ Special CSPs are provided by vendors so that their devices will work with certificate services. By default, three third-party CSPs (Schlumberger cryptographic service provider, Infinean SICRYPT Base Smart Card CSP, Gemplus GemSAFE card CSP v1.0) are available, but vendor CSPs can be added as needed.

❑ Select a 4096-bit key. The default is 2049, but a longer key length is recommended.

❑ If you need to recover or rebuild a CA, you can install the CA and import an existing key pair.

❑ Carefully consider the validity period, location of the certificate database, log, and shared folder because they cannot be changed after set up.

■ After the installation, configure the CA to support network locations for A.I.A. and CRL.

Types of CA Hierarchies

Before you can design a CA hierarchy, you must understand the types of hierarchies that you can use. There are three types of CA hierarchies: geographical, organizational, and trusted. Which type of hierarchy you choose depends on what you need to accomplish for your organization. The needs of your organization might also require you to accommodate combinations of these hierarchies. The following sections describe the types of CA hierarchies.

Geographical Hierarchies

Geographical hierarchies accommodate a geographically dispersed organization. In the example shown in Figure 2-5, the root CA is located at corporate headquarters in New York. The intermediary CAs are located in each major geographical area, and each geographical area has one or more issuing CAs. Multiple layers support the design, so a European CA issues CA certificates for issuing CAs placed in Belgium, London, and Paris, while a South American CA provides CA certificates for São Paulo and Santiago.

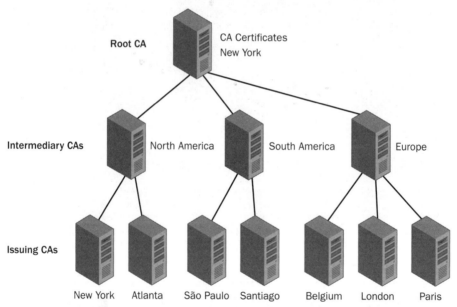

Figure 2-5   Providing a geographically dispersed network with CA services—a multi-tiered hierarchy

This type of structure can also be used if the organization's operations are geographically volatile. A part of the structure can be removed without having to tear out the entire system. Reasons for removing a part of the hierarchy include compromised security or divestiture of assets. If the European operations are sold, for example, the certificates published in that area can be revoked and the CAs decommissioned. The rest of the hierarchy remains intact.

Organizational Hierarchies

Organizational hierarchies accommodate an organization's need for autonomous areas. Figure 2-6 shows this type of hierarchy.

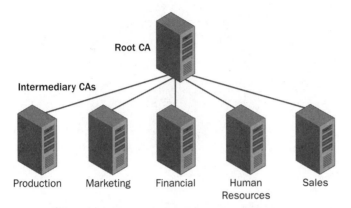

Figure 2-6   An organizational hierarchy with autonomous areas

Another type of organizational hierarchy is based on assigning certificate functions to a CA. Figure 2-7 shows another organizational CA, a divisional design that includes CAs that only issue certificates for specific functions. The two types of organizational CAs are often combined as shown in Figure 2-8.

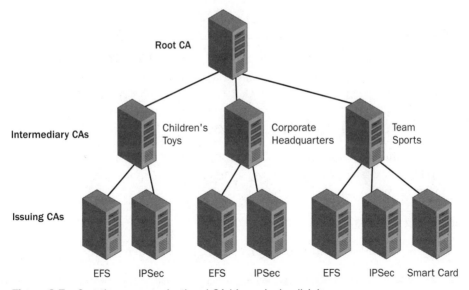

Figure 2-7   Creating an organizational CA hierarchy by divisions

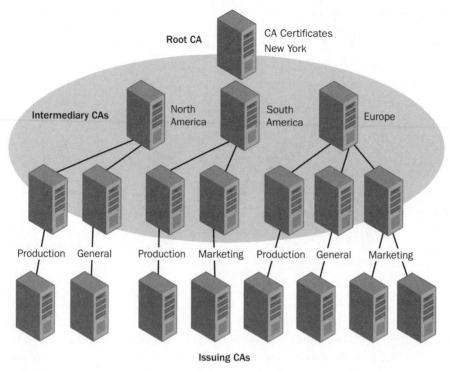

Figure 2-8 Combining the geographically dispersed and functionally diverse organizational CA hierarchies

Trusted Hierarchies

Trusted hierarchies extend trusts to other CA hierarchies. Trusted hierarchies are discussed further in the sections "Designing a Trusted Hierarchy" and "What Is Qualified Subordination?" later in this lesson.

Guidelines for Designing CA Hierarchies

The guidelines for designing CA hierarchies differ depending on which type of CA hierarchy you design. The following sections present guidelines for designing the different types of CA hierarchies.

Designing a Geographical Hierarchy

Follow these guidelines if your enterprise is dispersed across a large geographic area:

- Provide CAs at strategic locations. Doing this will make the regular function of certificate services operations more efficient, and it allows you to avoid having to access certificate revocation lists (CRLs) and obtain certificates across the WAN.

Note   CRLs can be published to local network file servers and intranet servers, and are, of course, replicated as part of Active Directory. Finding a local copy of a CRL is not the problem. Ensuring that locally available revocation information is up-to-date might be. While we like to think of the transfer of digital information as being instantaneous, with many operations and circumstances it is not. Active Directory replication, for example, has a latency factor. In a larger Active Directory environment, this latency factor can be significant. Distance can also result in delays or the inability to access information as networks outside of local control have interruptions and downtime. The use of a local, or geographically specific, CA can improve the chances that CRLs are available in a more timely fashion.

■ Use a multiple-tier hierarchy to easily support the widely dispersed enterprise. Refer back to Figure 2-5 for an example of just such a geographical hierarchy.

Designing an Organizational Hierarchy

Follow these guidelines if your organization needs autonomous areas:

■ Limit issuing CAs to specific types of certificate issuance. The design might include a CA used for issuing smart card certificates, another for EFS certificates, and a third for machine certificates used for authentication.

■ Place CAs under departmental or divisional control. In this design, the root CA issues CA certificates for each part of the organization, and each of these CAs can be used either to issue CA certificates for issuing CAs under their control or to directly issue end-use certificates.

■ Use two types of distributed hierarchies together when you need to both organize distribution by division (organization) and types of certificates that are issued.

Designing a Trusted Hierarchy

Follow these guidelines when you must design relationships between CA hierarchies:

■ Question the need for seeking such a relationship. If both hierarchies are within the same organization, there might be a solid reason for designing such a relationship. There are many possible reasons for this. Perhaps the reason is simple politics, a recent acquisition or merger, or even one party's lack of knowledge of the existence of the other. The reason for two different hierarchies could also be to protect a more sensitive area of the company, or simply to separate the use of certificates in a public-facing network or in a network that serves as an extranet of partners. Arbitrarily cross-certifying hierarchies (providing a trust relationship between them) is not a wise or secure thing to do. Ask these questions:

❑ If hierarchies lie in different companies, is a total trust relationship required?

❑ Can the need to use certificates to provide access to jointly owned resources or shared resources be provided by mapping certificates to Active Directory accounts? If the need is merely to provide trust in one direction this might be a better answer.

If two organizations require a way to trust certificates from one another, cross-certification might be the answer. However, cross-certification requires strict management and a need to set limits on the trust relationship. One organization might need to trust the other to fulfill some partnership agreement; however, that does not mean either party wants to put its infrastructure at risk.

■ Understand that cross-certification between hierarchies will increase network-related (IPSec, SSL, and so on) traffic by lengthening the certificate chaining process. *Certificate chaining* is the process by which certificates are traced back to their roots as part of the validation process. The deeper the CA hierarchy is, the longer the certificate chain is. Cross-certification creates longer chains. Attention must be paid to ensure the design results in the shortest certificate chain possible and that the chain length and the time it takes to create the chain does not exceed an application time-out limit.

Multiple constraints are possible, from complete trust between two hierarchies to limited trust assigned to a single CA within a single hierarchy. Care should be taken to limit trust to what is needed.

The more complicated and restrictive the constraints are, the more difficult it is to get the process correct and ensure it is maintained. The lengths to which you should go in determining and restricting trust will depend on the risk tolerance of the operations concerned. Spend time during the design process to determine the constraints that are necessary.

■ Obtain mutual agreement on the nature of the trust that is desired and ensure equal care is practiced on each side of the trust. No security solution can provide complete protection from malicious action or neglect by another party to the trust. Therefore, each side needs to understand the other, and care should be taken to determine the trustworthiness of the other organization before trust is extended.

■ Create an issuance policy for each hierarchy, and identify the extent of trust extended between them. Issuance policies can be added to version 2 certificate templates, but best practices require creating an issuance policy file, policy.inf, for the qualified subordinate CA. (Version 2 certificate templates are new in Windows Server 2003 Enterprise Edition. They are customizable.) This prevents you from creating multiple template policies.

The Certificate Chaining Process

You must understand how trust is validated by cross-certification before you can design the cross certification. However, before considering the unique design issues that accompany the decision to join two hierarchies, consider the way in which trust is validated in a single hierarchy. To validate a certificate, many steps are taken. One of them is certificate chaining and the accompanying validation of each certificate in the chain. A certificate chain defines the path from the root CA through the layers of the intermediary and issuing CAs to the specific certificate being validated. The process of determining the path back to the root CA is called *certificate chaining*. The following sections describe how the certificate chaining process works and when cross certification can be used.

How Certificate Chaining Works

The certificate chaining process includes these steps:

1. Each CA uses its private key to digitally sign every certificate that it issues. Hence the public key of the CA can be used to prove that a certificate was issued by it.

    a. If there is only one CA, the root CA, then all certificates will chain or lead directly to it.

    b. If a hierarchy consists of two levels, a root CA and an issuing CA, then all end-use certificates will chain back to the root CA, but each chain will have an additional link, the issuing CA. The public key of the issuing CA, obtained from its certificate, can be used to validate the signature on the certificate, and the root CA public key can be used to validate the signature on the issuing CA's certificate.

    c. If a hierarchy is deeper than two levels, each layer in the hierarchy will represent a link in the certificate chain but all valid chains will eventually lead back to the root. All certificates can be validated by using the public key of the CA that issued them.

    Each link in the chain is determined by locating the CA that issued the current certificate. This CA is called the parent CA or issuing CA. The operating system can locate the parent CA because the parent CA's name is on the certificate. Figure 2-9 shows the Issuer information for the certificate.

2. Eventually, each certificate in the chain is validated because its chain leads to a trusted root CA. For a root CA to be trusted, its certificate must be in the certificate store of the computer that is attempting to validate a certificate issued by its hierarchy, or the trust must be granted by some user action.

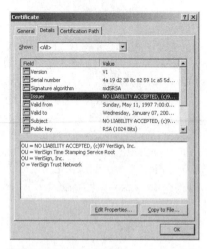

Figure 2-9   Viewing issuer information

See Also   For more information about the certificate chaining process in Windows, see the "Troubleshooting Certificate Status and Revocation" white paper on the TechNet page of the Microsoft Web site at *http://www.microsoft.com/technet/security/prodtech/pubkey /tshtcrl.asp*.

3. When a certificate is presented that cannot be chained back to one of the trusted root CAs, the chain is considered broken, and strictly speaking, the certificate won't be trusted. However, an application could be written that does not check the chain, accepts a chain that does not extend back to a trusted root, or allows the user to accept a certificate regardless of the state of the chain. To understand what will happen in each case requires understanding these elements for the application. Indeed, there are other factors that will also come into play such as CRL checking.

Certificate Chaining on the Internet

The certificate chaining process is managed across the Internet by including the root CA certificate in the certificate store of the browser, and hence, on Windows systems, in the certificate store of the computer. When the browser is first installed, the certificate store includes the root CA certificates of public CAs. When the browser connects to any site that has a certificate that can be chained back to a certificate in its certificate store and then authenticated, a secure channel can be negotiated. If an untrusted certificate (that is, the root CA certificate is not in the store) is presented, it is rejected. However, if the root CA is not present in the Trusted Root or Untrusted Root containers, the user will be prompted to select whether to trust the certificate. The user, in many cases, can accept the certificate without proof of trust, but that is another story.

How to Solve the Certificate Acceptance Problem

What prevents the acceptance of a certificate from another certificate hierarchy, and what needs to be done to guarantee its acceptance? Although major public CA certificates are present in the certificate store of the Windows computer, CA certificates from private CAs are not. Therefore, when a certificate from another hierarchy is not accepted, it is because it comes from a source that is not yet trusted.

To ensure that a certificate from another certificate hierarchy can be accepted, you must make sure that the certificate is trusted and, depending on the application, that a certificate chain is available. To do this, you can do one of the following:

- Place a copy of the other hierarchy's CA certificates in the certificate stores of all computers that might be asked to verify them.

- Create a cross-certification between two hierarchies. In this case, when a trusted hierarchy's certificate is presented, it chains to a trusted CA.

What Is Qualified Subordination?

Windows Server 2003 certificate hierarchies can be cross-certified. The process involves the setting of constraints and is therefore called *qualified subordination*. A qualified subordination can use multiple constraints and even limit which types of certificates from a partner will be trusted. The process is outlined in RFC 2459 and 3280. The following sections describe the types of constraints and provide examples of qualified subordination.

Types of Constraints

Each instance of qualified subordination can be limited by the following four types of constraints:

- A *Basic* constraint, which limits the path length for a certificate chain by specifying the maximum number of CAs that can exist below the CA where the constraint is assigned. Best practices include limiting the certificate chain for subordinate CAs but not for root CAs. (Changing the constraint on a root CA would require redeployment of the hierarchy, while changing the constraint on a subordinate CA means only redeployment of CAs below it in the hierarchy.)

- A *Name* constraint, which designates namespaces that are permitted in the certificates presented. The CA enforces all constraints defined in its certificate. This allows specification of which namespaces from the other hierarchy will be trusted. Specific namespaces can also be excluded. For example, a common best practice would be to prevent the partner hierarchy from issuing certificates that use your namespace. Doing that ensures all certificates issued by the partner hierarchy chain to their namespace. If a partner hierarchy were able to chain to your namespace, the certificate might gain privileges you do not want to extend.

- An *Application* constraint, which requires that a certificate must contain the application constraint or it will not be recognized. This allows an application to define which certificates will be accepted for the purpose of authentication, encryption, signing device drivers, and so forth.

- A *Policy* constraint, which specifies levels of trust in issuance policies. These limit trust to only certificates that contain a mappable object identification (OID) value to the other organization. An example of this might be a constraint that limits the certificate holder to some spending limit in a business-to-business e-commerce relationship.

Examples of Qualified Subordination

Hierarchies created in this manner extend the trust boundaries of the organization's PKI. Typical scenarios for qualified subordination include the following:

- Allowing trust between all CAs in the two hierarchies

- Limiting the trust to specific CAs in each hierarchy

- Limiting a specific CA within a hierarchy in the types of certificate it can issue and which security principals it can issue them to

Figure 2-10 shows cross-certification between two hierarchies. In the design, CA hierarchies in the Tailspin Toys and Wingtip Toys networks allow certificates produced by CAs in either hierarchy to be trusted by entities in either forest. This trust relationship was created when each root CA issued a cross-certification certificate that was then installed at the other's root CA. This is a fairly simple configuration and reasonably easy to troubleshoot.

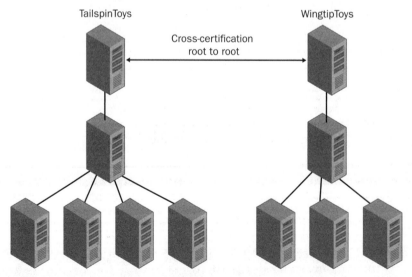

Figure 2-10 Providing cross-certification with full trust between two hierarchies at the root CA

If an organization does not want to extend comprehensive trust like this, a cross-certification certificate can be issued by a subordinate CA to the trust partner's root CA (see Figure 2-11). This is also a good practice if revocation of the cross-certification certificate is possible. Because root CAs generally issue CRLs more infrequently than subordinate CAs, information about a revocation will be available to clients more quickly. Both methods extend full trust between the hierarchies except where any constraints might be set.

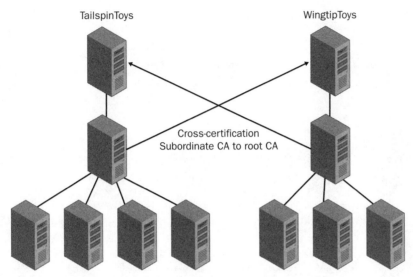

TailspinToys

WingtipToys

Cross-certification
Subordinate CA to root CA

Figure 2-11   Cross certification between the subordinate CA of one hierarchy and the root CA of another

> **Note**   In addition to creating total trust between both hierarchies, a cross-certification can extend the trust to a new CA. The trust is extended to any new CA that is added if its certificate is signed by a CA that is part of the cross-certification. If cross-certification certificates are issued by root CAs, any new CA will be trusted. If cross-certification certificates are issued by subordinate CAs, any new CA whose certificate chain leads to the subordinate CA will be trusted.

To complete a trust, a policy.inf file is configured on the CA that issues a cross-certification certificate. In the example of cross-certification shown in Figure 2-10, this means each root CA; in Figure 2-11, this means the subordinate CAs. The cross-certification certificate defines any name, issuance, and application constraints between the hierarchies.

Trust, in all these cross-certification examples, is established because the certificate presented can be chained to a root CA that exists in the local hierarchy. That is, a certificate can be issued by Tailspin Toys, but if cross-certification exists and it is used within the Wingtip Toys organization, it will chain ultimately to the Wingtip Toys root CA. However, if a subordinate CA is used and it is not the only direct child of the root CA, the partner hierarchy will not be able to validate certificates issued by CAs that do not chain to the cross-certification CA.

Figure 2-12 shows an example of limited trust between two hierarchies. This design pictures a limited trust, and the circles show the portion of the hierarchy trusted by the partner hierarchy.

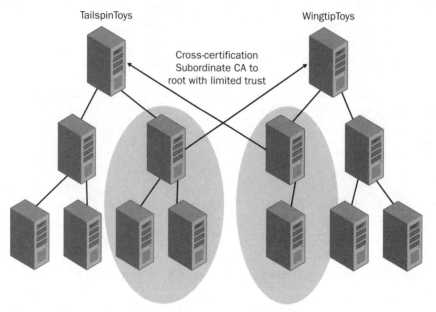

Figure 2-12   Providing cross-certification with limited trust between two hierarchies

Another type of qualified subordination limits a single CA's certificate issuance. This type of qualified subordination is quite interesting. It doesn't represent cross-certification at all, but more effectively limits the ability of a specific CA within a single hierarchy. So, for example, an issuing CA named GrainValley, which is located in the CA hierarchy for Tailspin Toys, is limited by a name constraint to producing only certificates that have a Domain Name System (DNS) name of GrainValley.midwest.tailspin-toys.com.

Guidelines for Securing CAs

Follow these guidelines for securing CAs:

- Implement constraints by using rules on both CAs in a trust relationship. These constraints provide an additional control over CAs. For example, normal CA configuration provides the ability to limit a CA so that it can issue only end-use certificates. However, an administrator with appropriate privileges can change this. If trust is placed in the CA only, new types of trusted certificates might be introduced where they shouldn't be. If, for example, a basic constraint that limits the CA to creating end-use certificates is placed on the CA's certificate, an administrator cannot accidentally or maliciously simply provide the CA with the ability to issue CA certificates.

■   Restrict the right to renew a CA certificate, and separate it from the right to add new certificate types to an issuing CA. This will help foil attacks in which a rogue administrator renewed the CA certificate to then change its issuing ability. For more information, see Lesson 5, "Designing Security for the Certification Authority," later in the chapter.

See Also   Requests for Comments (RFCs) are part of the Internet standardization process and can be read by visiting *http://www.ietf.org*. Knowledge of exact RFC wording is not part of this examination, but reading RFCs can provide in-depth understanding of protocols and processes used in security as well as in all aspects of IT.

Important   If trust between multiple organizations is required, a simpler design can be developed using a *Bridge CA*. A Bridge CA is simply a CA that becomes the link between multiple hierarchies. If the Bridge CA is part of the certificate chain, the certificate will be validated. Bridge CAs also make it easier to add a new hierarchy to an existing Bridge CA relationship. Using Bridge CAs can rapidly create a web of trust between hierarchies because certificates need to be exchanged only between the Bridge CA and the designated trusted hierarchy CAs. Once the Bridge CA is published in the newly trusted hierarchy organizations, the web is complete.

See Also   To learn more about cross-certification, read the "Planning and Implementing Cross-Certification and Qualified Subordination Using Windows Server 2003" article located at *http://www.microsoft.com/technet/treeview/default.asp?url=/technet/prodtechnol /windowsserver2003/plan/ws03qswp.asp*.

Practice: Designing a CA Hierarchy

In this practice, you will design a certificate hierarchy for the fictitious company Tailspin Toys, design cross-certification between Tailspin Toys and Wingtip Toys, and then install an offline root CA. If you are unable to answer a question, review the lesson materials and try the question again. You can find answers to the questions in the "Questions and Answers" section at the end of this chapter.

Exercise 1: Designing a Certificate Hierarchy for Tailspin Toys

Read the following scenario and then answer the questions that follow.

Scenario   You are a new security designer for Tailspin Toys, a large toy company that has 26 locations in the United States and international offices and warehouses in Belgium. The company divisions are geographically based (four regions) and have a large degree of local autonomy. Your boss wants you to create a design for a flexible and secure certificate hierarchy for the company. He gives you the following information:

- Immediate plans are to establish IPSec-based VPN connections between all locations and establish smart-card usage for IT employees.

- Future plans are to have all design and financial employees use EFS to secure data and smart cards for authentication.

Review Questions   Answer the following questions.

1. Tailspin Toys has a securable vault used for storing backup tapes. Could this vault be used to secure the root CA? Why or why not? How will you protect the root CA?

_____

_____

_____

_____

_____

_____

2. What type of CA hierarchy do you recommend? Why?

_____

_____

_____

_____

_____

_____

_____

_____

_____

3. Sketch a likely design.

Exercise 2: Designing a Cross-Certification Hierarchy between Tailspin Toys and Wingtip Toys

Read the following scenario and then answer the questions that follow.

Scenario   Your company, Tailspin Toys, and another toy company, Wingtip Toys, are involved in a joint project, and both companies require the ability to securely exchange communications. The companies also need to be able to validate one another's digital signatures on documents and e-mail messages. The partnership between the companies is formed for the operation of a specific project, providing complete trust is not a goal of this project. Both parties are reluctant to trust the other, and each wants maximum control over the relationship. The CA hierarchy consists of three levels. Your boss asks you to design a cross-certification hierarchy.

Review Questions   Answer the following questions.

1. What must you determine as you develop the design?

_____

_____

2. Develop a cross-certification design.

_____

_____

_____

_____

Lesson 3: Designing the Certificate Enrollment Process

Creating CA hierarchies is only the first step in the design of certificate services for an enterprise. You must also design the process of certificate enrollment and certificate distribution. *Certificate enrollment* is the process used to obtain a certificate. You can design enrollment to happen via user request or to be automatic. There are two parts to the enrollment process that you must consider during design: first, who and how a request can be made, and second, whether the request will be approved. *Certificate distribution* is the process of getting the certificate to the device from which it will be used. Windows Server 2003 can distribute many certificates across the network to the computers on which they will be used. You can also export a certificate to a file, transport it where it needs to go, and manually install it on the device.

After this lesson, you will be able to

- Explain the certificate enrollment process.
- Explain the considerations for designing certificate enrollment.
- Design the certificate enrollment and distribution policy.
- Configure enrollment and certificate distribution for the offline root CA.

Estimated lesson time: 90 minutes

How the Certificate Enrollment Process Works

Before you begin your design, you must understand how the certificate enrollment process works. The enrollment process consists of two main steps: request and approval or denial. The process varies depending on the type of certificate, the type of CA and its configuration, and whether it is automatic or manual. Typical certificate enrollment processes include:

- The CA enrollment process
- The manual end-user enrollment process
- The automatic end-user enrollment process

The following sections describe these processes in detail.

The CA Enrollment Process

The root CA certificate enrollment process is simple. During installation, a key pair is generated and the certificate is created and then signed by the root CA. When subordinate CAs are created, the process is different. The CA from which the certificate will be requested is called the *parent CA*. The server requesting the certificate is called the *child CA*.

> **Important**   Remember that the root CA and any CAs that have been so configured can issue CA certificates.

If the root CA is online, the following steps will occur during the installation of the subordinate CA:

1. The administrator installing the subordinate CA (the child CA) selects the type of CA to be installed as either stand-alone subordinate CA or enterprise subordinate CA.

2. The installation process prompts the administrator, who then selects or enters the parent CA (the CA from which to request the subordinate CA certificate).

   If the parent CA is a member of the same Active Directory infrastructure as the server that will become the child CA, the administrator might be able to browse to the CA.

3. A key pair for the CA certificate is generated by the child-to-be CA.

   a. If the parent CA can be accessed online, the child-to-be CA is authenticated.

   b. If the parent CA has been configured to automatically issue CA certificates, the child-to-be CA has been authenticated, and the process is being carried out by an authorized administrator, the request is approved. A CA certificate, which includes the child CA's public key, is signed by the parent CA.

4. The certificate is sent to the child CA.

5. The child CA installs the certificate in its certificate store.

6. The installation process is completed, and the certificate services are started.

If, however, the intended parent CA is not accessible online, a different process must be followed. This process is used when creating the second level in a CA hierarchy in which the root CA has been taken offline:

1. The administrator installing the subordinate CA selects the type of CA as either a stand-alone subordinate CA or enterprise subordinate CA.

2. The administrator requests that a certificate request form be created.

3. The installation process will prompt the administrator, who then enters the name of the parent CA.

4. A certificate request is created and can be saved to a floppy disk.

5. The installation process will continue, but the certificate service will not start and no certificates can be issued by the CA until its certificate is installed.

6. The administrator takes the certificate request to the offline CA and uses it to request a CA certificate.

If the administrator has the permission to obtain a CA certificate, a certificate is created that includes the child CA's public key. The certificate can be saved to the floppy disk. This is the approval step.

7. The administrator returns to the subordinate CA, installs the CA certificate, and starts the service.

The Manual End-User Enrollment Process

Automatic enrollment is available for some types of certificates. But if automatic enrollment is not possible or is not part of the design, each certificate request must be initialized by a user or by an enrollment agent. An *enrollment agent* is a user who requests certificates for another user or for a computer or device. Administrators can request certificates for computers; however, special enrollment certificates must be obtained before a user can request other types of certificates for another user. Requests can be made via the browser or via the Certificates snap-in. To do this, follow these steps:

1. The user, or an enrollment agent, initiates a request by using the certificates console or by visiting the enrollment pages of the CA's enrollment site.

2. The user, or the enrollment agent, must complete a form:

   ❑ If an enterprise CA is selected, the types of certificates needed can be selected from a list or form.

   ❑ If a stand-alone CA is used, more information must be completed to provide the CA with the data needed to create the certificate.

3. The certificate is either issued or set to pending:

   ❑ If an enterprise CA is used and it is configured to automatically approve or deny certificate requests, the certificate will be approved and issued if the following things occur: the requestor is authenticated, the CA is able to issue the requested certificate type, and the requestor has permission to obtain this type of certificate.

   ❑ If a stand-alone CA is used and it is configured to automatically approve or deny certificate requests, a properly configured and submitted request will be approved.

   ❑ If a CA is not configured to require administrator approval, the certificate will be marked as pending.

   ❑ If a certificate is configured to require administrative approval (even if the CA that issues it is configured to automatically approve requests), then it will be set to pending.

4. If a certificate is marked as pending, an administrator must manually approve or reject the request before the certificate is issued.

5. If an automatic approval or rejection cannot be given, the requesting user or enrollment agent must check back later to either obtain the certificate or find out whether the request has been rejected.

The Automatic End-User Enrollment Process

When automatic enrollment is available, certificates are automatically issued for intended users or computers. It is not necessary to make a manual request. The exact process—when the certificate must be requested and what has to happen before it can be installed—will depend on the type of certificate.

Automatic enrollment for computer certificates and Encrypting File System (EFS) certificates was introduced in Windows 2000. In Windows 2000, if automatic computer certificate enrollment is configured, a certificate is issued to and installed by a computer when it joins the domain. If a CA is configured to issue EFS certificates, a certificate is issued to and installed by a user's computer when the user first requests to encrypt a file. If no CA is present to issue an EFS certificate, and EFS is not disabled, a self-signed certificate is issued for the user.

Windows Server 2003 expands the use of automatic enrollment to users. However, for certificates to be automatically enrolled, custom certificate templates must be created and configured for automatic enrollment. The process of automatic enrollment will vary. For example, to complete the enrollment process, the certificate must be distributed to the users. In the case of certificates for smart cards, for certificates to be installed, the user must have a smart card reader/writer and must insert a new smart card into the reader at the proper time. Thus, the process cannot be completed until the user is prompted to insert a smart card (signifying that the process is ready) and then inserts the smart card. Remember, however, that the process of enrollment is automatic here. Enrollment is the request and the approval or denial. Distribution delivers the certificate, and installation installs it. It is the later part of the process that must be completed, in this case, by a manual operation.

Considerations for Designing Certificate Enrollment

You have to consider many things as you design certificate enrollment. First among these considerations are the constraints on the process. The following sections describe the constraints that limit the certificate enrollment process and then provide additional considerations for designing certificate enrollment.

Constraints that Limit the Certificate Enrollment Process

Constraints are of two types: those that are built-in to the product and are unchangeable and those that can be configured. Consider the following constraints when designing the certificate enrollment process:

- Built-in constraints are controls that already exist.

  - If a user can authenticate to an enterprise CA, he or she can make a certificate enrollment request for a user certificate such as an EFS certificate, user certificate, and so on.

  - To request a computer or service certificate, a user must have administrative privileges.

  - To request a CA certificate, a user must have administrative privileges on the CA.

- Configurable constraints are under your control. They might have a default configuration, but they are meant to be configured to suit the policy and risk posture of the organization. These are the configurable constraints:

  - Certificate types can be restricted to users and groups of users by adding or removing the Enroll permission on the certificate template for the specific certificate type. For example, EFS Recovery Agent certificates can be restricted to a specific group of users by giving the group the Enroll permission on the EFS Recovery Agent certificate and not including any other group. A best practice is to pay careful attention to who can request each certificate type and who is given permission, via use of groups, to obtain certificates.

  - A CA can be restricted in the types of certificates it issues. In general, the root CA and intermediary CAs should issue only CA certificates. Further, issuing CAs should not issue CA certificates and should be configured to issue only the certificate types that are approved. This guideline, however, might not work in some circumstances. In smaller environments, for example, a single CA might serve all purposes or a two-tier hierarchy made up of two CAs might be present.

  - The policy of the issuing CA can be set to require manual approval of each certificate request. In a large enterprise where thousands of certificates must be issued, this is not a workable solution. However, even in a large enterprise, some CAs, such as the root CA, can be set to require manual approval.

  - Automatic enrollment of computer certificates can be configured in Active Directory Group Policy.

  - In a cross-forest trust, a Windows Server 2003 CA will not by default *chase*, or attempt to find, user information necessary to approve a certificate request from a trusted forest. This constraint improves performance and also security because you might not want to issue certificates directly to users in the trusted forest. *Cross-forest referral*, or referral chasing, can be enabled via a **certutil** command on the CA. The **certutil –setreg policy\EditFlags +EDITF_ENABLELDAPREFERRALS** command must be issued at the command prompt on the CA, and then the service must be stopped and started.

❏ An enrollment agent role can be configured by assigning a Windows group permission to obtain an enrollment agent certificate. A user in possession of this type of certificate can obtain a certificate on behalf of other users. For example, if automatic enrollment for smart card certificates is not wanted or configured, a smart card enrollment agent can produce smart cards for employees. This takes the process out of the hands of the end user, who might have problems understanding the enrollment process, and provides another degree of control over who is issued a smart card, as well as who is issued replacement smart cards. However, this approach provides the enrollment agent with a very powerful right. An enrollment agent might not be necessary if auto-enrollment can be established for certificate needs in which an agent might have been required.

❏ An enrollment agent can be restricted. Enrollment agents by default have sweeping powers and are able to issue certificates for anyone in the organization. Certificates can be restricted by permissions set on the certificate templates; however, for stricter control, the ability of the enrollment agent to issue certificates can be constrained by identifying both who can perform the enrollment and who an enrollment agent can enroll. To implement these additional restrictions, version 2 certificates are required.

Additional Considerations for Designing Certificate Enrollment

In addition to the constraints that limit the certificate enrollment process, you must consider the following issues in the design:

■ **Is there a cross-forest trust? If so, should referral chasing be enabled?**   Not enabling referral chasing can assist in restricting enrollment. You must decide whether users and computers in a trusted forest should be able to obtain certificates issued by the trusting forest, or whether a separate CA hierarchy should exist in the trusted forest and a separate trust relationship be established via qualified subordination.

■ **Are Netscape browsers used by clients authorized to request certificates?**   If Netscape browsers are used, you must change a Windows Server CA to permit Netscape browsers to be used for enrollment. You must decide whether the incorporation of this change should be part of the design, based on the official policy of the organization about which browsers are allowed to be used. In addition, because the version of the Netscape browser must be 6.2.2 or later, the decision to configure the CA might result in a need to upgrade client browsers. Alternatives to making the CA configuration change are using the Certificates snap-in on these computers, or where possible, providing auto-enrollment.

- **Should extensions be blocked or allowed in certificate requests?**   Extensions can be used to restrict certificate issuance. If they are used, they will be ignored by Windows Server 2003 unless configuration changes are made. Extensions provide a valuable way of tightening controls on certificate issuance. The decision to use them might depend on interoperability issues.

- **Are e-mail addresses required in certificates?**   If so, e-mail addresses can automatically be added to certificates produced by enterprise CAs based on information in Active Directory. However, stand-alone CAs must be configured to add e-mail addresses to certificates. This issue might be one more factor that pushes a design to an Active Directory–integrated model, or it might simply be another consideration in the design of the stand-alone CA.

- **What should be the validity period of issued certificates?**   The validity period is the period of time from the certificate becoming valid until it expires. An enterprise CA certificate validity period can be configured via settings on certificate templates. However, the certificate validity periods of stand-alone CAs must be adjusted via changes to the registry.

- **Which types of end-use certificates can be issued by the CA and to whom?**   The type of end-use certificate to be issued by a CA often plays a roll in the design of the CA hierarchy, but these questions are part of the certificate request process.

- **Should certificate issuance be automatically or manually approved?**   An enterprise CA, by default, is configured to automatically issue a requested certificate if all constraints are met. The assumption is that if the user can be authenticated by Active Directory and is authorized to request the certificate, the certificate should be issued. Manual approval can be required, however. Manual approval in a large enterprise or in a scenario where many certificates must be issued will result in additional administrative work. The administrator must manually visit the CA and accept or reject the certificate on a regular basis or the requests will expire. An option might be to establish a separate CA for the types of certificates that require tighter control. This CA can require manual approval for all certificate requests, but it provides tighter control. Another possibility, when greater control over certificate issuance is required, is to use version 2 certificates.

- **Which types of certificates should be used?**   Two types of certificates are available. Version 1 certificates are available for use with Windows 2000 and Windows Server 2003 CAs. They cannot be modified or secured, but they do provide end-use specificity. Each version 1 certificate can be used only for its designated purpose or purposes. A smart card certificate can be used only with a smart card, an IPSec certificate can be used only for authenticating a computer attempting to negotiate an IPSec policy, and so forth. Version 2 certificates are available only with an enterprise CA installed on a Windows Server 2003 Enterprise Edition computer. Version 2 certificates allow customization of enrollment policies, key archiving, template usage, authentication, and so on. Version 2 certificates must be used if key archival is needed.

■ **If Web-based enrollment is allowed, should the Web server used for enrollment reside on the CA? If not, where should it be placed?**   The computer used for Web enrollment is also called the *Registration Authority (RA)* or *CA Web enrollment proxy* or sometimes *Web enrollment station*. Should other services also be offered from the RA? If IIS is present on the CA computer when the CA is installed, Web-enrollment pages are installed by default. However, it is possible to install Web-enrollment services on an IIS server that is not on the CA computer. Doing so will allow you to restrict access to the CA computer, as all users will no longer need to directly interface with the CA. Communications between the CA and the RA can be protected. The RA, if separate from the CA, must be trusted for delegation in Active Directory, which might present additional security issues. In either case, ASP must be enabled on the RA computer and IIS should be installed before the Web-enrollment pages are installed to ensure the creation of the necessary virtual roots. The roots can be created after the fact.

Guidelines for Designing the Certificate Enrollment and Distribution Policy

A policy should be designed that specifies how certificate enrollment and distribution will occur. Although some parts of the process are not configurable, others are. Enrollment and distribution can be automated for some certificates, such as computer certificates. Enrollment can be manual or automatic depending on the operating system and on the CA, Group Policy, and certificate template design. You can even require that one or more administrators must approve a specific type of certificate request. Follow these guidelines to design a certificate enrollment and distribution policy:

■ When a large number of certificates must be distributed, configure an automatic enrollment process. Automatic distribution will occur for most certificates that are automatically enrolled. For example, do this when a new project is implemented in which every employee must obtain a certificate to continue to do their job.

■ Configure automatic enrollment of computer certificates if a Windows 2000 CA is used.

■ Configure the use of CA-generated EFS certificates.

■ Configure auto-enrollment for certificates that are used by large numbers of people. If a Windows Server 2003 CA is responsible for certificate issuance, a member of the Enterprise Admin group can specify the types of certificates that can be auto-enrolled by creating version 2 certificate templates and assigning the auto-enroll permission to the user groups that he wants to auto-enroll.

- Provide users with Windows XP clients. Windows XP clients will examine the templates in Active Directory, and if the client has the Enroll permission on the template and the template is configured for automatic enrollment, Windows XP will automatically enroll those certificates. (If the permission to Enroll has not been granted on the certificate template, the certificates will not be enrolled.)

- Restrict automatic enrollment when greater control is wanted. For example, IPSec policies can be configured to prevent rogue computers from accessing resources on the network. However, if certificates are used for authentication, the rogue computer can be joined to the domain; and if automatic enrollment of machine certificates is established, the rogue computer will automatically receive a certificate and not be prevented from accessing resources via the IPSec policy.

- Use an RA for Web-based enrollment. Separating the enrollment process from the issuing CA allows you to provide better protection for the CA computer. End users do not need access to the CA, and communications between the CA and the RA can be secured via IPSec.

Guidelines for Configuring Enrollment and Certificate Distribution for the Offline Root CA

The root CA must also be configured to support enrollment and certificate distribution. It is especially important that an offline root CA be configured to support the distribution of its root CA certificate and CRL to the network. Follow these guidelines to support the design of a CA hierarchy with an offline root:

- **Configure distribution before any certificates are issued.**   A summary of this process is as follows:

  ❑ The location of the root CA certificate and CRL are published on certificates issued by the CA. This information might be needed by applications to validate the issued certificate.

  ❑ If the location of the root CA and CRL are changed after a certificate is issued, there is no way for the application to know this and locate these important items.

- **Configure distribution of the root CA certificate.**   Following are key facts to keep in mind about this process:

  ❑ Distribution is configured by changing information of the Authority Information Access (AIA) property of the root CA as shown in Figure 2-13.

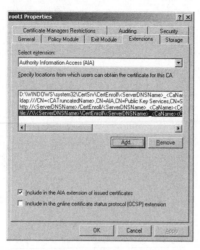

Figure 2-13   Modifying the AIA publication location

❑   AIA specifies the location from which clients can download a copy of the CA certificate. The AIA default location is on the CA computer. Because this CA will be offline, you must change the publication location of the AIA to the network so that it is accessible by clients.

❑   The location must be changed before certificates are issued because the AIA location is published on the certificate.

❑   Use the example syntax, and enter a URL that maps to a location on a Web server on the network. Figure 2-14 shows the process.

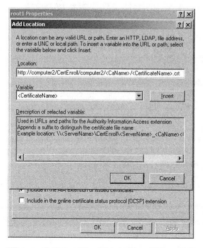

Figure 2-14   Modifying the AIA publication location URL

❑   Make sure the new URL is selected, and click the Include In The AIA Extension Of Issued Certificates check box. Don't forget this step! The location of the AIA must be available, and for it to be used, the information must be published on the certificate.

❑ Remove the old URL, which points to the local computer. The root CA will not be accessible on the network.

❑ Add an AIA LDAP location, and make sure it's included in the published certificates. The default LDAP location on a stand-alone server that is not a member server will not have this item checked, as it makes no sense for that server. However, because the typical hierarchy design will include enterprise subordinate CAs, the root CA certificate should be available in Active Directory.

❑ Don't forget to obtain a copy of the root CA certificate and publish it in the Active Directory on the Web server.

❑ Remove the file location, because the root CA will not be on the network where this could be accessed.

- **Configure the distribution of the root CA CRL.**   To do this, use the following procedures:

    ❑ This is the extension named the CRL Distribution Point (CDP).

    ❑ Remove the old Web location.

    ❑ Remove the file location from the locations published in the certificate, but do not remove the location. The root CA will not be accessible to computers, so publishing the file location in the CDP extension of certificates is useless. The Publish CRLs To This Location check box should remain checked. The published CRL must be retrieved from this location in order to publish it elsewhere.

    ❑ Add an LDAP location and a Web location, and make sure they are published to the certificate by checking the Include In The CDP Extension Of Issued Certificates check box (as shown in Figure 2-15).

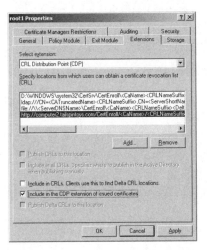

Figure 2-15   Adding an HTTP location for the CDP

❑ An Active Directory location will ensure that the CRL is available to all sites and that it will be replicated to all domain controllers.

❑ A very large CRL, however, might have an impact on replication, and alternatives might need to be considered. If the organization has a well-developed intranet Web server system where all company locations are serviced, publishing a copy of the CRL to the company intranet is a solid idea. However, consideration must be given to usage issues related to intranet downtime or simple unavailability to some locations.

❑ Remember that because the CA is offline, each location must be manually updated.

■ **Requests for CA certificates should always be manually approved.**   Stand-alone CAs cannot use Active Directory to authenticate the user and determine whether she is allowed to be issued the certificate. When certificate requests are marked "pending" (which is the default), the CA administrator will have to approve them.

■ **Set the CRL Publication Interval to several months.**   The CRL will be published to the file system of the root1 CA. You will need to copy them and manually ensure they are published to Active Directory and the Web server designated in the root CA interface. The first CRL, which is an empty CRL, is published to the file system when the CA is installed.

Practice: Designing the Certificate Enrollment Policy

In this practice, you will design an enrollment policy, design the use of an RA, and map certificates to enrollment types. If you are unable to complete an exercise, review the lesson materials and try the question again. You can find answers to the questions in the "Questions and Answers" section at the end of this chapter.

Exercise 1: Designing an Enrollment Policy

Read the following scenario and then answer the questions that follow.

Scenario   You are a new security designer for Tailspin Toys. Your boss needs you to come up with design recommendations for an enrollment policy for the company. He told you that Tailspin Toys will need the ability to provide certificates for EFS, for encrypting data in transit, and to secure administrative accounts using smart cards.

Review Questions   Answer the following questions.

1. What items should be considered?

_____

_____

2. Why should these things be considered?

3. What are your design recommendations for the enrollment policy?

Exercise 2: Designing the Use of an RA

Read the following scenario and then answer the questions that follow.

Scenario   You've given your boss at Tailspin Toys your recommendations for designing the enrollment policy, and he asked if an RA should be part of the design. You have the following information to work with:

■ The Web-enrollment pages are installed by default during the installation of the CA. However, you can, instead, install them on a separate computer. Doing so creates a separate registration authority (RA) to support enrollment.

■ Enrollment can be via the Certificates snap-in or via Web-enrollment pages on IIS. Either option allows you to reduce access requirements for the CA because all users can obtain certificates by visiting the RA.

Review Questions   Answer the following questions.

1. Should you recommend an RA? Why or why not?

_____

2. What things should you consider before making this recommendation?

_____

_____

_____

_____

_____

_____

_____

_____

_____

_____

_____

_____

_____

_____

Exercise 3: Mapping Certificates to Auto-Enrollment Types

Indicate which certificates you would recommend be auto-enrolled by entering one of the following auto-enrollment choices into Table 2-3 next to the certificate type. One auto-enrollment type gets used three times. Auto-enrollment types include:

■ Auto-enrollment

■ Auto-enrollment user input

■ Do not provide auto-enrollment

Table 2-3   Certificates that Map to Auto-Enrollment Types

Certificate	Which Auto-Enrollment Type Would You Recommend?
IPSec	
EFS	
CA	
User	
Certificates to test auto-enrollment	

Lesson 4: Designing the Renewal, Revocation, and Auditing Processes

Certificates have a life cycle. They are created and have a *validity period*, which is a time during which they can be used and after which they expire. Many certificates can be renewed, and the process can be automated. Even if a certificate cannot or should not be used, but it has not expired, it can be revoked. Finally, certificate use and CA activity can be audited—if auditing has been configured. This lesson teaches how to design the renewal, revocation, and auditing processes.

After this lesson, you will be able to

- Explain what renewal, revocation, and auditing are.
- Explain the considerations for designing the renewal policy.
- Explain how the revocation process works.
- Explain how a delta CRL works.
- Explain the considerations for designing the revocation process.
- Design a revocation policy.
- Explain the considerations for designing the auditing process.

Estimated lesson time: 50 minutes

What Are Renewal, Revocation, and Auditing?

The following sections describe what each of these components is.

Renewal

Renewal is the process by which certificates are approved for continued use. The renewal process can be automatic or manual. It can be triggered because a certificate is about to expire or because of a policy change. The expiration date is assigned when the certificate is issued. The validity period is the time between when the certificate can be used and the time it expires. The certificate validity period varies with the type of certificate, with the validity period established during the installation of the CA, and with the validity period configured on the version 2 certificate template. Your design of the certificate renewal process includes the design of the validity period.

Revocation

Revocation is the process by which a valid certificate that has not expired is made invalid. All certificates have an expiration date that marks the end of their validity period. However, it will sometimes be necessary to revoke certificates or make certificates invalid before that time. During the phase in which you design PKI, the various reasons for revocation should be discussed and a policy should be written that spells out when a certificate will be revoked and for what reasons. Revoked certificates are added to a certificate revocation list (CRL). The CRL can then be examined to determine whether a certificate is valid. Before you can design the CRL management process, learn more about how it works, including learning about a new Windows Server 2003 PKI component known as delta CRLs.

Auditing

Auditing is a chronological recording of events that makes it possible to reconstruct and reexamine an event. An audit can also be a formal study of systems for the purpose of determining that the system is securely operated and that it complies with security policies. This type of audit can also be used to detect new processes that might require changes in policy and procedure to make systems more secure. Auditing can also be used on a day-to-day basis to detect attacks and to discover instances of compromised security.

To provide records that can be used for these purposes, audit records of the CA activities must be collected. Turning auditing on is a simple process, while determining what to audit is not. Designing auditing for PKI is important. As with determining policies and procedures that dictate the CA operation, the audit of CA activities should also be carefully determined.

Considerations for Designing the Renewal Process

As you design the renewal process, consider the issues outlined in the following sections.

Renewal Considerations

Ask yourself these questions:

- Should all certificates that expire be renewed? Might it be better to have some certificates require the creation of a totally new certificate? As an example, consider the certificates issued for qualified subordination. These certificates might provide an outside organization access to your system, and you might want to ensure this trust is limited in time and is thoroughly examined before it is continued.

- Should certificates be automatically renewed? Automatically renewing certificates still requires some kind of authentication, so if an account no longer exists or is disabled, no certificate will be issued. However, can you guarantee that all invalid accounts are actually disabled or deleted?

Validity Period Considerations

The validity period considerations are:

- A validity period is always established to limit the amount of time that a certificate is exposed to possibly being compromised. A certificate is compromised not when an unauthorized individual obtains the certificate, but when the associated private key is compromised. The usefulness of the private key is controlled by the expiration of the certificate. In some cases—for example, EFS—the private key can be used after the expiration of the certificate to decrypt files. Because new files, however, are being protected by the new public key, the usefulness of the old private key extends only to files encrypted using the old public key. Best practices include a recommendation to decrypt files and then encrypt them after a new EFS certificate is issued.

- There are maximum certificate validity periods. When version 2 certificates are used, Subordinate CA, IPSec, Enrollment Agent, and Domain Controller certificate validity periods can be as long as five years. Of course, the validity period cannot exceed that of the root CA. All other version 2 certificates can have a validity period of up to one year, but again, it can't have a validity period longer than that of the root CA.

- Establishing the expiration date of a CA certificate is one of the configuration steps necessary during its installation. To determine an appropriate validity period for the CA certificate, consider the necessary validity period for the types of certificates it will issue.

- No CA can issue a certificate that will remain valid beyond the CA's validity period. This restriction ensures there will be no orphaned certificates. If a CA certificate is not renewed and expires, all certificates it has issued have already expired. This means, however, that as the expiration date for the CA certificate approaches, the validity period of the certificates issued might be less than the desired length of time.

- The validity period of the CA should be established and its renewal scheduled so that certificates are issued as close to the certificate validity period desired as possible. Consideration must also be given to the CA certificates that a CA can issue.

- Any design for certificate renewal should start with an estimate of the best times for end-use certificate renewal and work backwards. Because the subordinate CA's validity period will depend on the root CA's validity period, you need to set the root CA validity period long enough. For example, if the decision is made to issue smart-card certificates and EFS certificates that are good for a period of one year and IPSec machine certificates that are good for a period of six months, giving the root CA a validity period of five years is more than adequate. If the issuing CA certificate is renewed after one year, all new and renewal smart-card, EFS, and IPSec certificates will most likely receive their full validity period. If, however, the

CA certificate is not renewed and one and a half years has passed, when a new smart-card certificate is issued it will be good for less than six months.

■ How long of a validity time is the right amount of time? The length of an adequate, yet limited, validity period will depend on the nature of the service the certificate is used for.

❑ Certificates issued for authentication, for example, should not be issued for a validity period of several years if most employees leave the company after one year.

❑ A cross-certification certificate might be issued for a period of a few months. The certificate can be renewed, but if it is not, the short validity period provides a definitive way to end the trust relationship.

Certificate Revocation Considerations

The certificate revocation considerations are:

■ Certificates can be revoked, but not all applications check revocation lists. In addition, many things can delay the distribution and downloading of new CRLs.

■ Remember to design validity periods based on finding the sweet spot between minimizing exposure and opportunities for compromise and allowing for the administrative tasks that might be necessary during renewal. Where auto-enrollment reduces the administrative task of renewal, time frames can be shorter, but keep in mind that auto-enrollment means fewer certificates will expire on their own if the issuing CA is still available on the network.

■ An additional decision must be made at CA renewal time. When a CA is renewed, a new key pair can be generated or the old pair can be reused. Remember the reason for CA certificate renewal: the minimizing of opportunity for key compromise. Creating a new key pair is a good way to continue limiting opportunities, but the decision should be based on the strength of the key and the status of computer technology. A large key size is typically harder to crack and therefore more desirable. Larger keys, however, take a longer time to generate and encrypt information. The root CA certification, however, will be used only to sign new subordinate CA certificates, so this point is moot.

Off the Record   How large should the key for the root CA be? Should it always be regenerated when the certificate is renewed? One estimate concludes that a 4096-bit key might take about 15 years to crack with today's computing equipment. If the root CA is given a 4096-bit key and a five-year validity period, when the administrator renews the certificate after four years, she can reassess the key based on thoughts of cryptography experts at that time. She can then make a decision about whether to renew by using the current key pair or by generating a new key pair.

- *Intermediate CAs*, those CAs that do not issue end-use certificates, must also renew their certificates, and you can choose whether or not to renew their keys. On one hand, they are not the root and have no power to issue end-use certificates. However, if they are compromised, every issuing CA they have issued a CA certificate for must be replaced. They are also more exposed than the stand-alone root CA. In addition, if cross-certification with another CA hierarchy is performed at the intermediary CA level, their being compromised might result in more risk and greater negative implications than with a CA that has not issued a cross-site certificate.

- When a new key pair is generated for a CA, a new CRL distribution point is created. This is done to ensure the CRL is signed by the current CA private key. This can also be used to advantage in environments where many certificates are issued and revoked. CRLs can become large in these cases, and although the old CRL will continue to be issued until every certificate that was issued using the old keys has expired, it will eventually be of no use.

- Certificate renewal is necessary to implement policy change:

  - If, for example, you want a cross-certificate, a new policy file can be created only for an existing CA when the certificate is renewed.

  - Other changes, such as adding the ability to archive private keys, will result in the certificates previously issued being superceded and new certificates being issued.

  - When a policy changes, and thus CA renewal is necessary, plan the renewal for off-peak hours when the request for certificates will likely not be as high.

  - Policy changes cannot always be anticipated, but the process required to handle them can be a part of the design of the renewal process. Consider how the change will affect certificate requests and whether current certificates should be used until they expire or whether the new certificates should supercede them.

How the Revocation Process Works

After you design the renewal process, you must design the revocation process. There are two parts to this process: when and how certificates should be revoked and how applications learn that certificates have been revoked. Because a certificate is usually revoked to prevent it from being used, the process of how applications learn that a certificate is no good (has been revoked) is critical. But before you can design the revocation process, you must understand how the process works. The revocation process looks like this:

1. The decision is made to revoke a certificate.

2. The CA administrator revokes the certificate by right-clicking the certificate in the CA console, choosing Revoke, and selecting a reason for revocation.

3. The revoked certificate is placed in the Revoked container of the CA database, and its information is added to the CRL.

4. The CA administrator can manually publish the CRL, or it will automatically be published at the specified CRL publication period.

5. When a certificate is presented for use and the application to which it is presented requires certificate revocation checking, the computer will check for a cached copy of the appropriate CRL, the one issued by the CA that has signed the certificate.

   ❑ If a cached copy of the appropriate CRL is present and has not been expired, the list is checked. If the certificate is not on the list, this part of the revocation check is passed.

> **Exam Tip**   If a cached CRL is available and it has not expired, a new CRL will not be downloaded. If the certificate has recently been revoked, even though the administrator manually published a new CRL, this information will not be available to the computer until the current, cached CRL expires. Therefore, it is possible that a revoked certificate will be validated.

   ❑ If a cached copy of the appropriate CRL is not present, the computer checks the certificate for the location of a downloadable CRL, downloads the CRL, and checks it.

6. The process is repeated for other certificates in the certificate chain.

7. Depending on how the application is written and configured, whether or not the certificate or any of its chained certificates are on any retrieved list, and whether a list can be retrieved, the certificate might or might not be validated.

> **Exam Tip**   CRL checking is not always carried out. Even when it is, a perfect result is not always required for the certificate to be validated.

How a Delta CRL Works

Another important thing to understand before you design the revocation process is how a delta CRL works. This section describes what a delta CRL is and how it works.

What Is a Delta CRL?

In a large and volatile network, CRLs can become quite large. If the publication period is short, in an attempt to more securely manage the knowledge of revocation, clients will be downloading the large CRLs quite frequently. Remember that each CRL includes all revoked certificates that have not expired, not just the newly revoked ones. If security is less important than performance, and the publication period is long, the information on revoked certificates can become seriously outdated. If the information is outdated, then a revoked certificate, possibly one that has been compromised, can be used. The issue of performance vs. security can be partially solved by the use of delta CRLs. A *delta CRL* is a CRL that is published within the normal publication period of the CRL. Delta CRLs contain only newly revoked certificates. Delta CRLs are a new function that is available only in Windows Server 2003 CAs.

How Do Delta CRLs Work?

When delta CRLs are used, the client keeps the main CRL in its cache and downloads new delta CRLs. The lists are combined when the certificate verifier seeks to validate presented certificates. Figure 2-16 shows this process. When a new main CRL is issued, all the revoked certificates published in delta CRLs will be in the new main CRL. The old delta CRLs are no longer needed and are deleted.

The client application must understand delta CRLs to use them. (All applications that use Crypto-API in Windows XP and Windows Server 2003 can use delta CRLS.) However, if a client cannot use delta CRLs, the client can still use the main CRL in the normal way. The client just will not be able to see newly revoked certificates until the old CRL expires and a new CRL is downloaded. Figure 2-16 shows how the use of delta CRLs by the CA is interpreted in a delta CRL–aware application vs. one that is not. As you can see, at time t1 both clients download a current main CRL. At time t2, a new delta CRL is published that includes, among others, the revoked "Jeff" user certificate. At this time, client A, which is delta CRL–aware, downloads the delta CRL. Client B, which is not delta CRL–aware does nothing. At time t3, a new main CRL is published, which includes the information on the revoked "Jeff" certificate. At time t4 the old main CRL validity period ends. Both client A and B download the new main CRL. During the time between time t2 and t4, client B has no knowledge of the revoked "Jeff" certificate. If the certificate were presented, it might be validated. However, client A, which downloaded the delta CRL, would not validate the certificate.

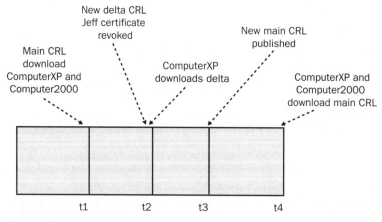

Figure 2-16   Examining delta CRLs

Considerations for Designing the Revocation Process

As you design the revocation process, think about the following things:

■ Consider the use of delta CRLs—they can improve security and performance.

❑ Consider that some applications will not benefit from the use of delta CRLs because some legacy applications do not know how to use them. If no applications can use the delta CRLs, setting them up might be pointless and might even do harm because the use of delta CRLs might result in longer times between the publication of regular CRLs.

❑ If the use of delta CRLs will not change the publication period of CRLS, and if new operating systems and applications are planned in the near future, it does no harm to include the use of delta CRLs in your design.

■ Consider revocation limitations.

❑ Understand that all applications do not use revocation checking. For some processes, such as checking SSL certificates on the Internet, it may be quite impractical, and for others, it is just not built into the application.

❑ Other applications might have revocation checking built in, but they might respond differently if a valid CRL cannot be located. Some of these applications might fail to validate the certificate if the CRL is not valid or cannot be located; other applications issue warning messages that empower users to accept certificates anyway; and still others might silently accept certificates.

❑ Knowing what applications are used on the network and how they respond is important in the design of PKI. If certificate revocation checking cannot be used, some other methodology must be relied on—for example, user account expiration. If the user's account has expired, it won't matter if his certificate is still valid—he still will not be able to access resources on the network.

❑ If applications cannot use CRLs, perhaps other applications can be selected.

■ When certificates are revoked, knowledge of their revocation is not immediately available to applications that might use them. There are a number of reasons for this:

❑ The CRL is published periodically. Each publication will include all the certificates revoked at that time, but certificates revoked after the publication will wait until the next publication.

❑ A CRL publication period, by default, is one week, but it can be adjusted by the CA administrator. Publishing more frequently means revocation lists are more up to date and thus a higher degree of security can be maintained. However, the more frequent the publication, the more burden there is on the network.

❏ It takes time for the CRL to reach all areas of the network. When one of the CRL distribution points is Active Directory, time is needed for replication. In recognition of this latency, a CRL also has a validity period that is longer than the publication period. By default, the validity period is a 10 percent extension of the publication period. (Registry entries allow adjustment of this time period to allow for slow Active Directory replication.) The validity period is the time the CRL is considered to be authoritative by certificate verifiers.

Guidelines for Designing a Revocation Policy

As a designer, you are not a security policy writer; however, you are often working with products and new processes for which there is no policy and for which few other people have the knowledge necessary to write one. You might also need to make design decisions that are really the purview of a policy. If no policy exists, as part of your design, use the following guidelines to design a policy for management approval:

■ Ensure that the policy specifies which of the reasons for revocation will be used and when. Having defined reasons will help prevent misunderstandings. If certificates are revoked and new certificates are required when specific job changes are made, users won't think having their certificates revoked means they have done something wrong.

■ Decide whether certificates should ever have their revocation removed. Policy might dictate that to avoid confusion this strategy should not be used, and operations might also play a role. For example, in a large infrastructure, lag time will always exist between when a certificate is revoked and when that information is actually available to the applications that depend on it. You will also see a delay between the time you revoke a certificate and the time it is actually removed, and this might make using this process inconvenient. On the other hand, if all revocations are final, the CA Manager or administrator might be reluctant to revoke a particular certificate, and that is not desirable either. Providing guidelines for the policy on when to revoke a certificate is an important part of the revocation process design.

■ Decide who will make the revocation decision and who will implement it. This policy can list things such as "all user certificates will be revoked when the employee leaves the company," "if an employee forgets her smart card, a new smart card will be issued and the certificate assigned to the old smart card will be revoked," and so on. As the smart-card statement hints, in addition to blanket statements, each use of certificates should be examined to determine when revocation is appropriate.

■ Determine when the CA administrator should manually publish a CRL. Reasons for doing so include: a large number of new revocations have occurred, or revocation happened because of suspected or actual key compromise. However, if a verifier of a certificate has a valid CRL in its local cache, it does not attempt to retrieve another CRL from the CA. This means that even though a new CRL is published, it won't be retrieved until the current CRL validity period expires.

- Design the location of CRL publication points.

  ❑ By default, an enterprise CRL is published in the Active Directory and to the Web-enrollment pages.

  ❑ Additional or different publication points need to be established before certificates are issued, as the CRL publication point must be part of the certificate. (Certificate verifiers use the publication point on the certificate to access a CRL if necessary.)

  ❑ Consider the size of the implementation and the geographic dispersion to determine whether additional points are necessary. CRLs can be published to file locations, URLs, and LDAP directories.

  ❑ Special consideration should be taken for offline root CAs. Their CRL publication points must be established on the network, and automatic publication must be turned off because the offline CA cannot publish to the network. A manual process must be established for periodic publication of the CRL. A long publication period should be established so that the manual publication and manual placement of the CRL on the network will be an infrequent chore. This approach is perfectly acceptable because it would be rare to revoke the root CA certificate.

- Consider normal CRL processing by the certificate verifiers. Because they do not access a new CRL until the currently cached CRL expires, if it becomes necessary to revoke a certificate and a long publication period is established, the time needed for news of the CA revocation to reach certificate verifiers will be longer. The effect of this delay can be tempered by ensuring that the procedure for revoking a CA certificate includes the revocation of its entire certificate list first and a delay in revoking the CA certificate until all certificate verifiers have downloaded the new CRL.

Revocation Checking on the Internet

Checking the revocation status of certificates on the Internet is considered to be problematic. The following items partially explain the problem:

- Older versions of Internet Explorer do not turn on revocation checking by default.

- Some versions of Netscape browsers cannot automatically check for revocation status.

- Given the size of the Internet and the erratic availability of some sites and some connections, it might not be possible to locate a CRL when necessary.

- Not all certificates can be issued with the location of their CDP in the certificate. Microsoft applications as well as others look for the CDP information in the certificate in order to find the CRL. If no CDP is present, the CRL cannot be located.

Considerations for Designing the Auditing Process

After you design the revocation process, you can design the auditing process. As you design the auditing process, think about the following things:

- Consider the configuration of auditing.

  ❏ Auditing of CA activity requires configuration in the Certification Authority console, but it is dependent on the establishment of object access auditing in the Windows Settings, Security Settings, Local Policies, Audit policy of the appropriate Group Policy Object (GPO).

  ❏ If object access auditing is not turned on, specific CA activity will not be recorded in the Security event log. If the CA exists on a member server, the Audit policy should be set using Group Policy. The GPO should be linked to the domain or organizational unit (OU) that the CA computer is a member of. (The design of Group Policy is discussed in Chapter 5 and Chapter 8.)

- Consider the events that can be audited. These are configured from the CA audit properties page as shown in Figure 2-17.

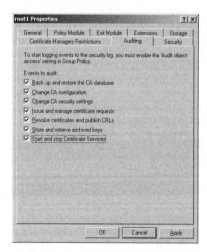

Figure 2-17   Selecting CA audit events to monitor

❑ *Back Up And Restore Of The CA Database.* Auditing these events provides a solid record of backup. Checking for successful backup is always a sound activity. In addition, an unexpected restore of the CA database located by the audit might be an indication of tampering and should be investigated.

❑ *Change CA Configuration.* Auditing these events allows for the tracking of successful and unsuccessful changes to configuration against planned and approved changes and provides a record of proper maintenance. Possible tampering can also be confirmed. Configuration events audited include adding and removing templates, configuration of the CRL publication schedule, configuration of the CDPs and AIAs, changes to policy modules, and key archival and recovery.

❑ *Change CA Security Settings.* These events include the configuration of CA roles for role-based administration, setting of restrictions on Certificate Managers, and the configuration of auditing. It's important to note that these configuration events are not recorded by turning on the Changes In Configuration settings—you must turn on Changes In CA Security Settings Auditing.

❑ *Issue And Manage Certificate Requests.* Auditing these events will record successful and failed attempts at issuance of certificates and their management. A record can be produced for each certificate requested, issued, or imported.

❑ *Revoke Certificates And Publish CRL.* Auditing these events will record successful and failed attempts to revoke certificates and publish CRLs.

❑ *Store And Retrieve Archived Keys.* If key archival is configured, auditing these events will record successful or failed attempts at storage and retrieval. Access to archived keys should be performed only according to strict policy to ensure that only authorized administrators retrieve the keys and that they are returned to the correct owner. There are technical controls to ensure this; however, checking the audit of the process against documented approved need will enable discovery of unauthorized attempts and compromised keys.

❑ *Start And Stop Certificate Services.* Stopping and starting certificate services is necessary to accomplish some configuration and policy changes, as well as CA key renewal. The actual events should always be audited against approved maintenance.

■ Consider which events to audit.

❑ To decide which events to audit, determine how much knowledge is needed. The amassing of large volumes of records that might never be examined is counterproductive. The policy, and therefore the design, of the audit should keep these things in mind. One way to make a determination is to examine the impact of auditing each event and make decisions based on impact vs. value.

❑ You should also work with your organization's legal department to determine whether auditing certain types of events are required by law or regulation and what the retention period is for keeping records of those events.

❑ The first attempt at decision making can be based on which audited events produce few records and yet provide valuable and critical security information. Items such as the stopping and starting of Certificate Services, storage and retrieval of archived keys, backup and restore, and configuration changes should not overwhelm event logs with activity, and all provide information that is critical to understanding the security status of the CA and being able to reconstruct major CA security policy operations.

❑ Gathering the events just listed costs little but produces a large benefit. However, recording each certificate request, issuance, and revocation and each CRL publication might have little value in many environments and the current information can be found in the Certification Authority console. Collecting such information in the security log would seem to be useful only for reconstruction of events and for keeping permanent records of activity. Collecting the information in the security log will vastly increase the amount of records and thus the amount of space needed to maintain logs and log archives. It might also overwhelm those whose responsibility it is to review the logs. Important events can be hidden in a sea of ordinary activity.

■ Consider using correct auditing techniques or ways to review the information.

❑ Using correct techniques can counter the negative effects of massive logs. When events are filtered according to their importance, critical events are easily discernible.

❑ In addition, while reviewing large amounts of ordinary activity is often fruitless, examining the trends shown in the collected information can be valuable. If knowledge of what is ordinary exists, the abnormal can trigger further investigation. What, for example, is the meaning of a sudden large increase in revocation? Or in certificate request denial? These trends are not observable via simple viewing of the CA console.

■ Write a security log review process. Collection of records is an exercise in futility if records are not reviewed.

■ Before CA-specific auditing events will be recorded, object auditing must be turned on in the Audit Policy portion of Group Policy. Consider where this should be done. The offline root CA will require object auditing to be turned on to capture local information. The other CAs should be placed in a designated OU so that the entire security baseline for CAs can be easily applied. A GPO can be linked to this OU, and the GPO's audit policy can be set to audit object access for success and failure.

See Also   Careful consideration of the meaning of events will enable the development of the best audit design for each CA implementation. For more information about designing audits in general, see Chapter 9.

Practice: Designing a CRL Location and Publication Periods

In this practice, you will design a CRL location and publication periods. To do so, read the following scenario and then answer the questions that follow. If you are unable to complete this practice, review the lesson materials and try the question again. You can find answers to the questions in the "Questions and Answers" section at the end of this chapter.

Scenario   You are the security administrator for Contoso. You have been asked to design the publication period and location of CRL for the Contoso PKI. You have the following information to work with:

- The publication period and location of each CA's CRL must be considered separately.

- Locations must be decided before the CA issues certificates because the certificate verifier will use the location listed on the certificate to download a new CRL.

Review Questions   Answer the following questions.

1. What decisions do you need to make as you design the CRL location and publication periods?

   _____

   _____

   _____

   _____

2. What should you consider as you make each of these decisions?

   _____

   _____

   _____

   _____

   _____

   _____

Lesson 5: Designing Security for the Certification Authority

A certification authority can be used to provide security for many parts of the logical security infrastructure of an organization. To secure the CA infrastructure, you must design security for CA computers and for securing the CA administration practices. Many regular security practices devised for standard servers can be used to secure the CA computer. In addition, you should enable role separation for CA administration and design specific computer security strategies for the CA computer.

After this lesson, you will be able to

- Describe the available CA-specific administration roles and operating system roles.
- Use CA administration roles.
- Explain how an operating system administrator can enable CA role separation.
- Design additional security for CA servers.

Estimated lesson time: 45 minutes

Available CA-Specific Administration Roles and Operating System Roles

When privileged use of a resource, such as administration, is necessary, the best security designs will separate the activity into two or more task-based roles and assign these roles to different groups of people. This fulfills the principle of separation of duties. Administering Certificate Services is a sensitive and privileged process. Those with ultimate authority over the CA have an enormous amount of trust placed in them by the organization. To mitigate the risk that any individual can misuse this power, design the use of CA administration roles. Built-in roles exist for administration and for ordinary use of certificate services. CA roles consist of CA-specific roles and operating system roles. Role separation, a technical control that prevents a single user account from performing all CA administration roles, can also be enforced. The following sections describe CA-specific administration roles and operating system roles that can use Certificate Services.

See Also   Role Separation, and the ability to enable its enforcement in Windows Server 2003, is a feature that is in compliance with the Certificate Issuing and Management Components Family of Protection Profiles (CIMC), which can be examined at *http://csrc.nist.gov/pki /documents/CIMC_PP_20011031.pdf*. Protection profiles are descriptions of approved lists of security standards that are used in the Common Criteria certification process. Common Criteria is an internationally recognized security standard for certifying the suitability of computer systems for specific uses. Notice of compliance with a specific protection profile does not imply or prove certification with any Common Criteria standard to any standard level. It does, however, show attention to commonly agreed upon security standards. If you are going to design security for computer systems, you should be aware of and knowledgeable in current existing security standards.

CA-Specific Administration Roles

CA-specific roles are administration roles. The CA-specific roles are:

- CA Administrator—Configures and maintains the CA by performing the following tasks:
    - Configures policy and the exit module
    - Stops and starts certificate services
    - Configures extensions and roles
    - Defines key recovery agents
    - Configures Certificate Manager's restrictions
    - Deletes a single row in the CA database when necessary
    - Enables, publishes, or configures CRL schedule when necessary
    - Assigns other CA roles when necessary
    - Renews the CA certificate
    - Uses the "Manage CA" permission
- Certificate Manager—Manages certificates by performing the following tasks:
    - Approves and denies certificate enrollment and revocation requests
    - Reactivates certificates placed on hold
    - Recovers archived key
    - Uses the "Issue and Manage Certificates" permission

When a CA is installed on a domain member computer, three administrative groups have authority to administer the CA: members of the local Administrators group on the server that hosts the CA, members of the Domain Admins group, and members of the Enterprise Admins group. If the CA is not a domain member, only members of the local Administrators group have authority to administer the CA. However, before certificates are issued, an operating system administrator should assign CA management roles, enforce role separation, and remove the operating system administrator's ability to manage CAs.

Exam Tip   Even if the operating system administrator's ability to manage the CA has been removed, she can regain control of the CA. There is no way to remove this implicit privilege from operating systems administrators. If the operating system administrator uses this privilege, and auditing has been configured, a record of this event will be posted to the security log.

Operating System Roles That Can Use Certificate Services

In addition to using the CA-specific roles, you can use several operating system roles to strengthen the role-based security model for certificate services. The roles either exist as default groups or can be created as custom groups that have been granted specific user rights and permissions. Operating system roles are:

- **Backup Operator**   Has the backup files and directories right and the restore files and directories right. Backup operators can also stop the Certificate Service (but they cannot start it again).

- **Auditor**   Has the manage auditing and security log permission. Users with this permission can configure, view, and maintain the audit logs. The role of auditor should be held by someone outside of normal IT operations as well as by IT employees.

- **Enrollees**   Have the authority to request certificates from the CA. By default, the Enroll permission is granted to Authenticated Users. This can be changed by granting the Enroll permission to some other built-in or custom group or groups and removing the permission from Authenticated Users. Note that Enrollees are authorized to request certificates. Certificate requests can be refused. If certificates are manually accepted, each request can be reviewed and either granted or denied. If certificates are automatically issued, permissions on certificate templates should be used to restrict issuance to authorized security principals.

- **Administrator**   Has full control by default. If separation of roles is enabled, the Administrator retains the right to renew CA keys and certificates, and perform bulk deletion of rows in the CA database.

By default, all CA roles are assigned to Administrators of the CA computer. Enterprise CAs are always domain member computers and thus can be managed by members of the local Administrators group of the CA computer, the Enterprise Administrators group, and the Domain Administrators group. Stand-alone CAs are managed by Domain Administrators and local Administrators when joined to a domain, and by local Administrators when their systems are stand-alone. CA-specific roles are assigned to groups or users (local or domain, depending on computer domain membership) by using the Certification Authority console. Operating system roles are assigned in the usual manner, by using Active Directory Users and Computers in a domain, and Computer Management on a stand-alone system.

The operating system administrator is not the same as the CA Administrator. However, while the computer administrator role might be necessary to perform some duties necessary for the CA, the assignment of the CA Administrator role does not provide a user with computer Administrator privileges. The CA Administrator role applies only to specific CA-related tasks.

Off the Record   Key archival provides an example of how the role separation between CA Administrator and Certificate Manager provides separation of duties. When key archival is used, the copy of the private key is encrypted and the key "blob" (the encrypted key) is stored in the CA database. Only the Certificate Manager can retrieve this blob, but only the valid Key Recovery Agent can decrypt the key data. This is an example of separation of duties. The Key Recovery Agent role is not a CA administrative role, but it is important to proper CA functioning. The Key Recovery Agent cannot, on his own, retrieve user keys and decrypt them. The Certificate Manager can retrieve the key blob but cannot decrypt it. Thus either, on his own, cannot obtain and use private keys that belong to others. One would have to be in cahoots with the other, a situation that is not likely to happen.

Guidelines for Using CA Administration Roles

You assign the CA Administrator and Certificate Manager roles by giving the Security permission to the Windows group you have created for this purpose. Follow these guidelines for using CA administrative roles:

- Assign these permissions to a group rather than to a user.
- Remove CA-specific roles from the Administrators group.

Important   The Administrators group retains the right to renew the CA certificate.

- Assign trusted users to fulfill the roles. When designing the use of CA administrative roles, remember their purpose: separation of roles and increased security of operations. The difficulty in implementing roles to fulfill these purposes is the inconvenience and the need in smaller organizations to identify sufficiently trusted individuals to perform the roles. It does no good to require role separation and then give the trusted role to someone who has not earned that trust.

- Enable role separation:

  - If you cannot enforce role separation, wherever possible, dictate that privileges be separated.

  - If role separation between the CA Manager and Certificate Manager cannot be established because of an organization's small size, separate operating system administration from CA administration.

  - Because those who have full administrator privileges on the CA computer can regain administrative control of the CA, give only highly trusted individuals this ability. Do not allow all current members of the Administrators group to have this ability.

How an Operating System Administrator Can Enable CA Role Separation

The operating system administrator can enable CA role separation by removing operating system administrators from CA administration roles and separating CA Administrator and Certificate Manager roles so that no single account can hold both titles. To do this, the administrator must perform the following steps:

1. Create two custom groups—CA Admin and Certificate Managers—one for each role.

2. Assign the Manage CA permission on the CA node in the Certification Authority console to the CA Admin group.

3. Assign the Issue And Manage Certificates permission on the CA node in the Certification Authority console to the Certificate Manager group.

4. Assign appropriate users to each group.

5. Use the following command to apply role separation:

   certutil -setreg ca\RoleSeparationEnabled 1

6. Stop and then start Certificate Services.

> **Caution**   Make sure to create the roles prior to applying role separation. Otherwise, no one will have the ability to manage the CA. The administrator would then have to remove role separation and start over.

Role Assignment vs. Role Separation

There are several processes embodied in CA role management:

- Assigning the roles of CA Administrator and CA Manager
- Removing the operating systems administrators CA administration rights
- Enforcing role separation

Assigning different groups to each role and removing CA administration privileges from the computer administrator results in better security. This fulfills the "separation of duties" dictum. However, there is nothing in place, with simple role assignment, to prevent one individual from being assigned both roles. If an individual is assigned both roles, you have lost as much as you have gained. The only role separation is that of separating the computer administrator from the CA managers.

> However, if a second step—role separation—is taken, security is greatly
> improved. If CA role separation is in place, a user must only be assigned a single
> CA role. If multiple role assignments are made, the user will not be able to per-
> form any operation on the CA. Care needs to be taken to ensure that a user is not
> assigned to both the CA Administrator and CA Manager role when role separation
> is enforced. If an individual has both roles, she will be unable to do any of the
> duties of either. To enable correct assignment of her role, role separation will
> have to be removed, group membership will have to be adjusted, and then role
> separation will need to be re-enabled.

Guidelines for Designing Additional Security for CA Servers

In addition to securing administrative roles and implementing auditing, CA servers
themselves should be secured. You do this through a combination of configuration,
physical protection, and, sometimes, network segmentation. This section describes
things to think about and things to do as you design additional security for CA servers.

Considerations

As you design additional security for CA servers, ask yourself these questions:

- Should the CA be protected by a firewall?

- Should the RA be placed on a different computer?

- Should communications between the RA and the CA be secured? What about communications between the client and the RA?

- Should SSL be used? IPSec?

- What about CA recovery? Are any special updating instructions or practices necessary?

Guidelines

Follow these guidelines for securing CA servers:

- Place database and transaction log files on separate hard drives. The CA database
  uses transaction logs to record events before posting them to the database. Keeping log files separate from database files might enable more complete and easier
  recovery should hard-disk failure occur. Using separate hard drives is also important because it improves performance.

- Keep the root CA offline, and secure its signing key by use of hardware. Keep the
  CA in a vault to minimize the possibility of it being compromised.

- Use the Certification Authority console to change permissions. The use of other
  tools is not supported and might produce unpredictable results.

- Back up the CA database, the CA certificate, and the CA keys on a regular basis. The backup period should be based on the number of certificates issued—the more certificates issued, the more frequently the database should be backed up. Use a full system backup to provide the fastest system recovery and to provide the most reliable data redundancy.

- Use SSL between the client and RA when using Web enrollment to provide confidentiality and integrity for the certificate request and response.

- Ensure that the default file access control permissions are retained. Doing this ensures the proper operation and protection of the database.

- Physically protect all online CAs and RAs. To physically protect them, locate them in a secure facility where access is limited. The objective is to prevent unauthorized access to the CA server.

Practice: Designing CA Administrative Roles

In this practice, you will design administrative management for a CA. To do this, read the following scenario and then answer the questions that follow. If you are unable to answer a question, review the lesson materials and try the question again. You can find answers to the questions in the "Questions and Answers" section at the end of this chapter.

Scenario

You are the security engineer for Tailspin Toys. As part of the design process for the Tailspin Toys CA hierarchy, you must design CA administrative roles. The following requirements must be met:

- The administration of the CA should be separate from computer administration.

- The administrative duties of the CA should, if possible, be split to enforce separation of duties.

Review Questions

Answer the following questions.

1. What decisions must you make as you design administration of the CAs?

   _____

   _____

   _____

   _____

   _____

_____

_____

_____

_____

_____

_____

_____

_____

_____

_____

_____

_____

_____

_____

_____

_____

_____

_____

2. Design administrative management for Tailspin Toys. What recommendations will you make?

_____

_____

_____

_____

_____

_____

_____

Design Activity: Designing the Logical Infrastructure

In this activity, you must use what you learned in all five lessons and apply it to a real-world situation. Read the scenario and then complete the exercises that follow. This is a paper-based activity. You are not required to implement the design, but it must be implementable. If you are unable to complete an exercise, review the lessons and try the question again. You can find answers to the questions in the "Questions and Answers" section at the end of this chapter.

Scenario

You are a new security designer at Wingtip Toys. It's your first week, and your boss wants you to design a PKI for Wingtip Toys. The implementation is limited and has a small budget. As she hands you the requirements, she mentions that all requirements must be met. The requirements are as follows:

Requirement 1   Certificates are required for IPSec policy authentication. IPSec policies will be used to protect communications between VPN gateways and between a limited number of traveling user client systems and VPN servers. IPSec policies might be developed for use between computer systems on the LAN.

Requirement 2   Design for efficiency and low cost of implementation.

Requirement 3   Provide for future growth.

Requirement 4   Provide a complete infrastructure design, including hierarchy (if necessary), enrollment, revocation, and CA security components.

Your boss will be presenting your design to upper management next week, and she tells you that she wants you to be at the meeting. She warns you to be prepared to explain all your decisions because she might defer to you when management has questions about design decisions.

Exercise 1: Design the CA Hierarchy

Given the requirements, design a CA hierarchy for Wingtip Toys. Answer the following questions:

1. What is your recommendation?

_____

_____

2. What are your reasons for making this recommendation?

_____

_____

_____

_____

_____

_____

_____

_____

_____

_____

_____

_____

Exercise 2: Design Enrollment and Revocation

Given the requirements, design enrollment and revocation for Wingtip Toys. Answer the following questions.

1. What are your recommendations?

_____

_____

_____

_____

_____

_____

_____

_____

_____

_____

2. What are your reasons for making these recommendations?

_____

_____

_____

_____

_____
_____
_____
_____
_____
_____
_____
_____
_____
_____

Exercise 3: Design Security for the CA

Given the requirements, design security administration for Wingtip Toys. Answer the following questions.

1. What are your recommendations?

_____
_____
_____

2. What are your reasons for making these recommendations?

_____
_____
_____
_____
_____
_____
_____
_____
_____
_____
_____
_____

Chapter Summary

- Certificate hierarchies can provide security for the root CA and separation of duties, solve geographical and political design issues, and provide load balancing and efficient operation.

- Best practices include using an offline root CA protected in a vault and using a hardware device for key storage.

- It is a good practice to separate CA certificate issuing and end user certificate-issuing CAs.

- Many of the advanced features of Windows Server 2003 PKI are available only with level 2 certificates. Level 2 certificates can only be produced if the CA is installed on a Windows Server 2003 Enterprise edition server.

Exam Highlights

Before taking the exam, review these key points and terms. You need to know this information.

Key Points

- Level 2 certificates are only available when the CA is installed on a Windows Server 2003 Enterprise edition computer.

- Level 2 certificates can be customized to provide key archival, specify that certificate issuance must be approved, and many other options.

- CA hierarchies are used to provide protection for the root CA and to scale the infrastructure geographically and functionally.

- Auto-enrollment and automatic certificate issuance are excellent ways of distributing most certificates when Active Direcory is used for authentication.

- CA certificate issuance, any certificates issued from a stand-alone CA, and any highly sensitive certificates should not be automatically issued when requested. Instead, they should require administrative approval.

- Enforced role separation will prevent a computer administrator from managing the CA with the exception that he can renew the CA certificate.

Key Terms

Authority Information Access (AIA)   A location—such as a URL, file system path, or LDAP—where a copy of the CA certificate can be obtained.

Certificate enrollment   The process by which a certificate is obtained. It consists of two parts, a certificate request and the denial or issuance of the requested certificate.

Certificate Practice Statement (CPS)   A statement of the practices that indicates how a certificate is used, how keys are managed, requirements for enrollment, requirements for revocations, and so on.

Certificate Revocation List (CRL)   A list of certificates that have been revoked.

Certification Authority   The computer system that issues and manages certificates.

CRL Distribution Point (CDP)   A location—such as a URL, file system path, or LDAP—where the CRL can be found.

Delta CRL   A partial CRL that can be published in between the times when the main CRL is published. While the main CRL includes all the revoked certificates that have not expired, the delta CRL includes only certificates revoked after the last main CRL was published.

Role separation   The assignment of two or more critical parts of a process to at least two individuals. This can prevent the abuse of privilege, as two or more people have to cooperate to perform some critical operation.

Questions and Answers

Pg 2-12 **Lesson 1   Exercise 1: Investigating Authentication and Authorization Certificate Usage**

1. When designing an IPSec policy, when would you use one authentication strategy above another?

   Use preshared key authentication when testing IPSec policies, but do not use it in a good production solution because the key is visible in the interface and log files, and it might be known to a large number of people. Because Kerberos can be used only by computers that are members of a Windows Server 2003 or Windows 2000 domain, it cannot be used to test policies used on computers that are not Windows Server 2003 or Windows 2000 domain members. In addition, special attention needs to be paid to configuration to ensure that the client initiates the communication; otherwise, authorization will not be performed. (The authorization considered here is authorization for one computer to access another across the network—access controls on computer resources will still be functional.) Use certificate authentication if devices and IPSec implementations are interoperable. Do not use certificates if the appropriate root CA certificate is not in the device certificate store. If it is not present, the certificate cannot be validated. To summarize: Use preshared keys only for tests. Use Kerberos only on domain members. Use certificates only where compatible IPSec is found and where the root CA certificate can be provided.

2. You must create an authentication design in which smart-card usage is required. What authentication choices are available, and which would you pick for your design?

   Smart-card usage requires the use of certificates; therefore, use of certificates must be part of the CA design.

3. In your design of the authorization and confidentiality systems, what part can EFS play?

   EFS can be used to encrypt files that are stored in the Windows Server 2000 and later versions of the NTFS file system. When files are copied by the user who encrypted them to a drive formatted with FAT or across the network to a file server, the files are unencrypted. EFS can therefore be used to assist authorization controls on file-based data because it limits access to the possessor of the private key. EFS needs to be supplemented with some other protocol when transported across the network, and users need training to ensure they don't accidentally decrypt a file. ACLs should also be set to increase security.

Pg 2-14   **Lesson 1   Exercise 2: Matching Windows Server 2003 Technologies to the Pillars of Information Security**

The following table provides the answers:

Table   Technologies Associated with the Pillars of Information Security—Answer Key

Pillar	Supporting Technologies
Authentication	Certificates in IPSec authentication, Secure Sockets Layer (SSL), and Transport Layer Security (TLS) use of certificates for authentication
Authorization	EFS, ACLs, and rights
Nonrepudiation	Digital signatures
Confidentiality	EFS, VPNs, and IPSec Encapsulating Security Protocol (ESP)
Integrity	Use of Authentication Header (AH) and ESP protocols in IPSec

Pg 2-32   **Lesson 2   Exercise 1: Designing a Certificate Hierarchy for Tailspin Toys**

1. Tailspin Toys has a securable vault used for storing backup tapes. Could this vault be used to secure the root CA? Why or why not? How will you protect the root CA?

Although placing the offline CA in a vault would provide adequate protection, access to the vault could not be restricted to CA administrators. A separate locked room or vault is recommended. A design compromise might be to provide a locked area within the vault for the root CA. Access to the CA could thus be further restricted as access to the vault would not provide direct physical access to the root CA.

2. What type of CA hierarchy do you recommend? Why?

Four regional U.S.-based offices and one European office, all with local autonomy, appear to dictate the location of regional intermediary CAs. However, the first implementation of certificate services does not call for the extensive use of certificates. Providing an immediate implementation of a broad intermediary layer would seem to be overkill. Instead, a single intermediary CA should be deployed. As certificate usage grows, additional geographically located intermediate CAs can be installed. Although several functional areas are mentioned, the small size of the initial deployment offering dictates no immediate division of functional use. A single issuing CA should be installed.

3. Sketch a likely design.

Answers may vary. The following graphic shows a recommended design.

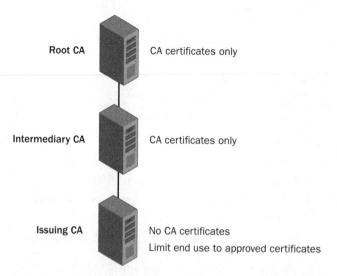

Root CA — CA certificates only

Intermediary CA — CA certificates only

Issuing CA — No CA certificates
Limit end use to approved certificates

Pg 2-33 **Lesson 2 Exercise 2: Designing a Cross-Certification Hierarchy between Tailspin Toys and Wingtip Toys**

1. What must you determine as you develop the design?

You must determine where the cross-certification certificate should be issued and determine the constraints for qualified subordination.

2. Develop a cross-certification design.

Answers may vary:

1) Determine where the cross-certification certificate should be issued. Because complete trust is not wanted and because of the lack of trust between the companies, issue the cross-certification certificate from the intermediary CAs.

2) Determine constraints for qualified subordination. Because the depth of each hierarchy is shallow, to prevent future additions of CAs from enlarging the trust areas, a basic constraint is used to limit the certificate trust path length to 1. Each company also assigns a designated namespace and excludes its own company's namespace to prevent the other company from issuing certificates using its partner's namespace.

Pg 2-46 **Lesson 3 Exercise 1: Designing an Enrollment Policy**

1. What items should be considered?

What types of certificates are approved for use in the CA hierarchy? Can the process of enrollment and distribution be automated? Are there any certificates—such as enrollment or key recovery agent certificates—that should not be automatically approved and distributed? Is the process of CA enrollment protected? Is arbitrary CA installation prevented?

2. Why should these things be considered?

Decisions to be made regarding requests to the offline root CA include who will create the CA certificate request, what media will be used, how the media will be taken to the root CA, and how the media with the CA certificate will be transported back to the subordinate CA.

3. What are your design recommendations for the enrollment policy?

The policy should include:

1) Separate CA certificate enrollment from end-use certificate enrollment. The best practices for CA certificate enrollment are to insist on manual approval for requests made at the root CA. By doing that, the CA administrator will have to approve the request.

2) Requests for CA certificates for issuing CAs are made to the subordinate CAs that are online. There is no need to create offline requests. However, a policy should be created that identifies how a new issuing CA is approved, who can install a new issuing CA, and the parameters necessary.

3) By default, the Authenticated Users group has Enroll permissions on end-use certificates. Therefore, enrollment policy should define who can be issued each type of certificate. Not making this assignment would allow unauthorized users to obtain certificates. After a decision is made about who should obtain what type of certificate, the administrator should be instructed to set the permission on templates. Custom groups might need to be created. If so, a domain administrator or enterprise administrator should create the groups. Decisions that these individuals need to make include what the group scope should be or which users from which domain should be able to be members in the group.

4) Adding new templates to each CA and removing unnecessary templates from each CA.

5) A policy regarding how requests are made for certificates that must be manually requested. Should an enrollment agent be used? An enrollment agent simplifies the process for the end user. Instead of having to learn a procedure—for example, how to request a smart-card certificate—and possibly having to learn how to use a device, the user has to make certificate requests through an enrollment agent. Using an enrollment agent can result in tighter control over certificate enrollment because the enrollment agent has to approve the request and the user identity must be authenticated by Active Directory. Creating enrollment agents, however, creates opportunities for misuse of power. An enrollment agent might create certificates for nonexistent employees, or the agent might create certificates for employees but then keep the certificates for her own use or sell or give them to others.

Pg 2-48   **Lesson 3   Exercise 2: Designing the Use of an RA**

1. Should you recommend an RA? Why or why not?

Yes. Using an RA is a more secure choice.

2. What things should you consider before making this recommendation?

You should consider:

1) Whether Web enrollment will be allowed. In the case of the root CA, Web enrollment is useless because no user will be able to or should visit the Web pages to request a certificate. Obtaining computer certificates does not have to be done via a Web browser either. Computer

certificate enrollment can be automated. However, using Web enrollment is a simpler process for end-use certificate requests and must be used for certain types of certificate requests. Since end-user certificates will be required, Web enrollment should be allowed.

2) Where the IIS server that serves these pages will reside. IIS can be installed on the CA computer to provide enrollment pages, or it can be installed elsewhere. If it is installed on the CA computer, all users who need to request certificates must be able to access the CA computer from the network. If the RA is established separately, access to the CA over the network can be restricted and protecting the CA computer becomes easier. Communications between the RA and the CA can be protected via an IPSec policy.

Pg 2-49   **Lesson 3   Exercise 3: Mapping Certificates to Auto-Enrollment Types**

The following table provides the answer:

Table   Certificates that Map to Auto-Enrollment Types—Answer Key

Certificate	Which Auto-Enrollment Type Would You Recommend?
IPSec	Auto-enrollment
EFS	Auto-enrollment
CA	Do not provide auto-enrollment
User	Auto-enrollment
Certificates to test auto-enrollment	Auto-enrollment user input

Pg 2-63   **Lesson 4   Practice: Designing a CRL Location and Publication Periods**

1. What decisions do you need to make as you design the CRL location and publication periods?

   You must decide where the root CA CRL should be located, the root CA CRL publication period, intermediary root CA publication locations, whether to have an intermediate root CA publication period, the location of end-user CA CRLs, and how long the CRL should be.

2. What should you consider as you make each of these decisions?

   You should consider the following:

   a. *The root CA CRL location.* If this CA will be kept offline, the CDP location must be changed to be somewhere accessible. Possible locations are Active Directory, the file system, and URLs.

   b. *The root CA CRL publication period.* Because the root CA will issue only CA certificates, there should be infrequent if any changes to the CRL. However, a valid CRL must be present on the network. Because publication will be a manual process, a long publication period is recommended. Should a CA certificate need to be revoked, all the certificates of the CA to be revoked should first be revoked, and then the CA's CRL should be published.

   c. *Intermediary CA publication locations.* Because they are online, default locations will work; however, consider whether there is a need for additional locations. Are there clients that are not part of Active Directory that might need to obtain the CRL? Are locations diverse and dispersed? Perhaps some intranet and file system locations will need to be added for redundancy.

   d. *An intermediate CA publication period.* These CAs issue CA certificates for end-use CAs. Because there might be more possibilities for the revocation of an end-use CA than for an intermediary CA, the publication period should be shorter. The size of the CRL will always be small, and therefore, frequent publication should not cause a replication performance issue.

   e. *The location of end-use CA CRLs.* Each end-use CA might have different requirements. Indeed, each might serve a different population. In addition to having the default publication in Active Directory, potential publication to areas that are closer to the user population might make sense.

   f. *The potential length of the CRL.* A large CRL will mean potential replication issues, and the more frequently it is published, the more problems are likely to occur. However, a long publication period is not wise either. Because many certificates might be revoked, there's a good chance that knowledge of a revoked certificate might not reach a certificate verifier and a revoked certificate might get validated.

Pg 2-71   Lesson 5   Practice: Designing CA Administrative Roles

   1. What decisions must you make as you design administration of the CAs?

1) Consider all CA roles. No management or end user role should be lightly assigned. Each role, whether CA specific or related to the operating system but used for CA management, should be identified and decisions should be made on what type of user should fulfill the role.

2) Decide on group structure and usage. Each role should be fulfilled by assigning individual user accounts to groups. Where possible, it might be acceptable to use built-in operating systems groups, but each role should be separately considered. The ability to perform a role is based on the permissions granted to the group on the CA and certificate objects. If built-in groups will be used, consider any preexisting permissions that these groups have. For example, the Backup Operators group seems perfect to fulfill the backup role for a CA. However, the Backup Operators group also includes the permission to restore as well as back up files. Separation of duties requires the separation of these roles. This separation can be accomplished by creating two groups and providing them with the appropriate privileges. However, this approach might not be appropriate in all designs.

3) Decide how individuals will be selected for group membership. The individuals that will fill the CA Administrator and CA Manager roles will be given a very trusted status. Employees and potential employees should be examined, and choices should be made carefully. A security design can include parameters such as recommended background checks and so on.

4) Determine whether role separation should be enforced. Role separation will enforce separation of duties; however, in a small environment where only one individual must do both roles, role separation would prevent that person from doing either. Convenience, availability of personnel, and risk tolerance are all factors in your decision.

2. Design administrative management for Tailspin Toys. What recommendations will you make?

1) Three CA administration positions will be used: Computer administrator, CA administrator, and Certificate manager.

2) The role of backup operator should be split into backup operator and restore operator.

3) Groups should be created for all roles and implemented by granting permissions to the groups.

4) Individuals should be carefully selected for each role based on their experience and integrity.

5) Role separation should be enforced.

Design Activity: Designing the Logical Infrastructure

Pg 2-73 **Exercise 1: Design the CA Hierarchy**

1. What is your recommendation?

Recommendation: Wingtip Toys should implement a two-tier hierarchy with an offline root.

2. What are your reasons for making this recommendation?

Answers may vary. Here are some reasons:

1) Because of the small size and scope of the project, it is tempting to establish a single enterprise root CA. This would be the most efficient and least costly design to implement. However, it does not provide for future growth. If a more extensive CA hierarchy is required in the future, the root CA cannot be taken offline. Wingtip Toys might end up with multiple hierarchies or the CA might have to be decommissioned and replaced.

2) An enterprise CA cannot be protected as well as an offline stand-alone root. The computer used to implement the root can be a less expensive system because its usage will be limited.

3) An offline root will add to the complexity of the process and to management overhead. However, it will meet the need for future growth, be more secure, and, after it is established, will require little administrative overhead.

Pg 2-74 **Exercise 2: Design Enrollment and Revocation**

1. What are your recommendations?

1) The root CA should issue only CA certificates. Any request should always be set to pending.

2) The enterprise subordinate CA should issue only IPSec certificates. All other certificate templates should be removed.

3) The CDP and AIA for the offline root should be changed to network-available sites.

4) The CRL publication periods for the offline CA should be set to 6 months and only manual publication should be permitted.

5) The publication period for the enterprise CA should be shorter, perhaps the default of one week.

6) Auto-enrollment for IPSec certificates should be configured.

2. What are your reasons for making these recommendations?

Answers may vary. Here are some reasons:

1) Other certificate templates can be restored if future requirements dictate it. Leaving them out for now prevents some possible forms of abuse.

2) Moving the CDP and the AIA of the offline root to the network allows them to be found as required.

3) Manual publication of the CRL is necessary because the offline CA can't publish to network sites.

4) The Enterprise CA CRL publication period should be small so that revocation numbers should be small, and thus interference with Active Directory replication nonexistent. Having a short publication period improves security, as information on revoked certificates will be available sooner to certificate verifiers.

5) Although not every computer needs an IPSec certificate at the current time, there does not seem to be a security risk at this time with providing each machine with a certificate. If IPSec policies are developed, there will be one less step in their deployment.

Pg 2-75 **Exercise 3: Design Security for the CA**

1. What are your recommendations?

Recommendations:

1) Enforce role separation.

2) Provide full auditing.

2. What are your reasons for making these recommendations?

Reasons include:

1) To require enforced role separation in a tiny startup company might provide little benefit. However, in a company the size of Wingtip Toys, having role separation—that is, CA administration vs. computer administration—is manageable and provides benefits.

2) Auditing should not be compromised. Full auditing of all CA procedures, including certificate enrollment, is necessary. Automated processes for collecting audit logs and filtering significant events and trends should be purchased or developed. Auditors, trained individuals outside of the IT department, as well as IT management, should be involved from the start in the review of security logs, tracking of events, and investigation of anomalies or potential attacks or abuses of privilege.

3 Designing the Network Infrastructure for Physical Security

Exam Objectives in this Chapter:

- Create the physical design for a secure network infrastructure.
    - Design for network infrastructure security.
    - Specify the required protocols for the firewall configuration.
    - Design Internet protocol filtering.
    - Design an IPSec policy.
    - Secure a DNS implementation.
    - Design security for data transmission.

Why This Chapter Matters

If an attacker can launch a denial of service (DoS) attack against your Domain Name System (DNS) server or poison its database, she doesn't need to go any further to disrupt your network. If the attacker can step across your network boundaries and access your most sensitive data with impunity, she has the ability to put you out of business. If all communications on your internal network can be captured and read, your network is a prime target for a sudden destructive attack—for example, by some disgruntled employee who was just laid off. This chapter teaches you how to design the network infrastructure for physical security—completing what you must know to create a security design for the network infrastructure.

Lessons in this Chapter:

Before You Begin

This chapter presents the skills and concepts related to creating a network infrastructure for physical security. This training kit assumes you have a minimum of 1 year of experience implementing and administering desktop operating systems and network operating systems in environments that have the following characteristics:

- At least 250 supported users

- Three or more physical locations

- Typical network services such as messaging, database, file and print, proxy server or firewall, Internet and intranet, remote access and client computer management

- Three or more domain controllers

- Connectivity needs that include connecting branch offices and individual users in remote locations to the corporate network and connecting corporate networks to the Internet

In addition, you should have experience designing a network infrastructure.

Many design exercises are paper-based; however, to understand the technical capabilities that a design can incorporate, you should have some hands-on experience with products. Where specific hands-on instruction is given, you must have at least two computers configured as specified in the "Getting Started" section at the beginning of this book.

Lesson 1: Designing Network Border Control

The first barrier to those who would penetrate the security of your network are the areas at which your network touches another network. The borders need to be clearly defined and protected. If you can control access to your network, you have won the first battle in the fight to protect your network's resources. To control network borders, you must understand the resources that you need to protect, the places where borders should exist, and how to select and effectively configure and manage the devices that provide border control.

After this lesson, you will be able to

- Describe the process of designing network border control.
- List common categories of data.
- Determine resource needs.
- Classify data.
- Explain what logical infrastructure support is.
- Design network segments for security.
- Design effective border controls.
- Explain the considerations for choosing border controls.
- Select and use effective border controls.
- Explain the considerations for designing Active Directory replication over firewalls.
- Secure Active Directory traffic.

Estimated lesson time: 60 minutes

The Process of Designing Network Border Control

There are four steps to designing network border control:

1. *Assessing resources.* Thoroughly review all resources on the network. Doing this will make it clear what needs to be protected and ensure that network segmentation is not limited to natural borders, such as the border between the private network and the public network. Instead, it will reveal the need to segment the internal network as well. To assess resources, perform the following steps:

   a. Perform an initial classification of data. Quickly separate mundane data from crucial data and public data from private data.

   b. Determine what resources need to be accessed, who needs to access them, and when the resources need to be accessed. By reviewing and documenting these needs, you can make sound decisions about which resources should be further protected.

    c. Classify data.

    d. Identify where the resources are located.

    e. Identify associated infrastructure necessary to provide secure access to these resources.

2. *Designing network segments for security.* The information you have gathered on your resources reveals which ones require more protection. It will also suggest where areas of the network can be separated. In many cases, critical resources are already protected by their location in separate buildings, floors, and areas. Connections with outside resources, such as digital connections with partners and connections to the Internet, also provide clear borders.

3. *Selecting effective border controls.* For each border between segments, you must select a method of controlling the flow of data across it. To do so, you must know what types of border controls are available and what they are best at doing.

4. *Designing Active Directory traffic, including directory service replication over firewalls.* Some borders will be protected by firewalls. If creating a border—such as that between perimeter networks and your internal network—will mean that you have separated some domain member computers from Active Directory domain controllers, or separated domain controllers from each other, you must design a method for allowing replication over firewalls. To do so:

    a. Understand the protocols that must be able to cross the firewall.

    b. Understand the risks of opening the firewall to allow these protocols to cross.

    c. Review alternative methods for enabling this communication.

    d. Select the best method for getting the job done.

The following topics provide guidance for performing these steps.

Common Categories of Data

The first step in assessing resources and designing network segmentation is to quickly divide your data into categories. This is just an initial step—you will refine and expand on this as you continue your work. You can use the common categories listed here or others that are determined by your organization:

- Resources that all employees might need access to, such as most printers and file servers, the intranet Web sites, and so on

- Information that most employees receive only limited access to, such as financial information, payroll information, human resources information, research, and so on

- Information that your organization gladly shares with the public, such as public company data, product information, and perhaps access to online product sales

- Data that is meant for partner access

Guidelines for Determining Resource Needs

The next step in assessing resources and designing network segmentation is determining resource needs. Review and document which resources need to be accessed by whom so that you can make an informed decision about which resources should be further protected. Guidelines for determining resource needs are as follows:

- **Use the same principles for determining overall resource needs as you do for determining who should have access to a single server.**   That is, employees should not be able to access anything that is not necessary to their jobs; partners should not be able to access anything not specifically designated as available to them; and the public should be limited to information the organization wants them to have.

- **Express logical barriers via the acquisition and management of physical controls.**   The decisions about what hardware, software, or other protection is needed, as well as when and where it is needed, depend on the resource that needs protection and where it must be placed. For example, the root Certification Authority computer for the organization should be protected by many physical borders—that is, placing it in a vault, taking it offline, restricting access to it to a limited number of employees, and placing its keys in a secure physical device. On the other hand, ordinary printers should be conveniently located in rooms on every floor.

Guidelines for Classifying Data

After you have determined resource needs, you are ready to begin classifying data. Follow these guidelines for classifying data:

- Investigate and document exactly what the terms *public data* and *private data* mean for your organization. When you clearly understand these terms, the need for separating the internal network into areas of trust might become more obvious, and the need for stronger protection on the natural borders between company and public and between company and partner might become more distinct. For example, Tailspin Toys might want current product information to be available to the public to encourage them to buy its products, but the company does not want to expose information on any unique manufacturing processes, customer lists, material sources, financial information, employee data, and so forth. A bank or a hospital will have information that must be made public by law, as well as strict regulations on how it must control access to other information.

- Identify and catalog data by its level of sensitivity. This guideline supports the development of boundary controls that match data classification levels. For example, data classified as public data can be placed on a public Web site. On the Web site, you will provide controls to protect the data from unauthorized modification (maintain its integrity), to protect the Web server itself from damage (by means of denial of service attacks, defacement, physical harm, deletion of site information and controls, and so on), and to protect internal sites from being compromised.

■ Document the current location of the resources.

■ Document who requires access to the resources and when they require that access. Some people will require access to all resources all the time. Some will require access to some resources all the time. Others will require no access to any of the resources at any time. You must know these things to grant access only where and when it is needed.

■ Document what logical infrastructure is necessary to support them. Documenting such dependencies allows appropriate consideration to be made—and there's often more than one choice. It's far better to be aware of the issues and make an informed decision than to simply put up a border device and find out later that domain clients cannot connect to a domain controller or other resource.

Levels of Data Sensitivity

Classifying data by level of sensitivity is one of the most effective ways to classify data. Military and government operations often use one particular list of data-sensitivity categories (shown below), while many public-sector organizations often opt to use a different list of categories (shown below).

Military and Government Levels of Data Sensitivity

This list is in order of sensitivity, with the least sensitive data category at the top of the list.

1. Unclassified

2. *N*-data. *N*-data is data that is classified by a specific topic. Just as mathematicians use 'n' to designate any number—for example, by using 2 * *n* to mean multiply 2 times whatever number you have—this classification represents innumerable classifications, each one named by the project or topic it covers. Data can reside at any level and can also represent security categories that are above the top-secret level. A person might be classified for the top secret level but not for some specific *n*-data resource.

3. Confidential

4. Secret

5. Top secret

Business and Nonmilitary Levels of Data Sensitivity

Most businesses adopt the following categories, which are somewhat different than the government and military categories:

1. Public—anyone can know

2. Partner—external-partner-project joint information (might be several partner projects further identified by the partner members)

3. Employee Only—organization information for internal use only

4. Confidential—private financial data or private employee data, such as Social Security number, home address, medical history, and so on

5. Legal—information that must be shared only with organization's legal department

6. Secret—top executive knowledge only

What Is Logical Infrastructure Support?

Logical infrastructure support is the access to data resources or services that is necessary to obtain or use classified data. A resource that needs to be protected by using a boundary control must not be separated from its logical infrastructure support. For example, if there is a need for authenticating employees who will be accessing internal resources from remote sites, a normal setup might include the use of a Microsoft Windows Server 2003 Routing and Resource Access Server (RRAS). This server might be placed on a perimeter network behind a firewall so that it is available to users across the Internet and to protect the private network from the outside world. However, if users must authenticate, the RRAS will need access to a domain controller and a way to connect across the firewall.

Real World   What Happens When Infrastructure Support Is Missing?

In a recent engagement, I visited with a company that provides access from the Internet for its employees. The company uses an Internet connection to access company resources, including an e-mail server, file servers, and a product database. An Active Directory domain manages authentication. When the company decided there was a need to control Internet access to its intranet, it added a firewall. However, doing that resulted in users outside the firewall not being able to authenticate. What was the company's immediate solution? Take out the firewall. Eventually, the company added the firewall back and added a virtual private network (VPN). Now all employees use the VPN to tunnel through the firewall and access corporate resources. The same solution could have been arrived at initially with a little bit of study, and the lost productivity and potential risk from harm would have been avoided.

Items that need to be accessed from outside an organization's boundaries and common dependencies are listed in Table 3-1. Some of these resources might also have a dependency on the location of a certificate revocation list (CRL). Figure 3-1 shows this interdependency of services.

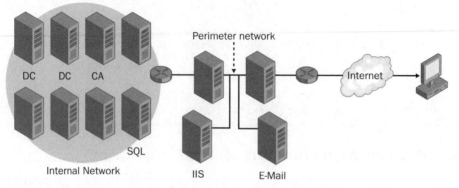

Figure 3-1   Discovering service interdependencies

Table 3-1   Common Resources That Need Remote Access

Resource	Dependencies
E-mail, Microsoft Exchange	Active Directory, therefore domain controller and Global Catalog (GC) server.
Public Web server	Possibly SQL database, application servers, domain controller
Intranet server	Possible SQL database, application server, domain controller
SQL database	Domain controller
Remote access server	Domain controller, Internet Authentication Service
VPN server	Domain controller, Internet Authentication Service

Some of these resources, depending on their use, might be made more secure by the segmentation of the internal network and the boundaries established by adding devices or other protective measures, such as requiring IPSec for communication. Each resource, its dependencies, and its current location should be identified along with any protection or boundary devices that isolate it. For example, list current perimeter networks (DMZs), internal segments, remote locations, and so on.

Guidelines for Designing Network Segments for Security

After you have classified data and identified who needs access to the data, you can begin the process of determining where the network should be segmented. Providing greater network segmentation makes it easier to provide good network security by designating areas between which border controls can be placed. It also makes it easier to provide stronger physical security controls. In some cases, where network segmentation cannot occur, stronger physical security controls can be implemented. Follow these guidelines to design network segments for security:

- Ignore existing segments. You will find that the network is already segmented for various reasons, but you should at first ignore these divisions and determine the best segmentation design for security.

- Design natural boundaries, such as those between the Internet and your network and those between partner networks and your network.

- Consider segments to form an area around sensitive data (such as financial data, research data, and so on). This can prevent unrestricted movement of data in and out of the area.

- Consider placing on a separate network the computers used by administrators to administer the network.

- Consider separating servers and workstations. This technique can be effective in preventing worms and other malicious code that might infect user systems from infecting servers. You accomplish this by using border controls to restrict traffic.

- Separate developers (computer programmers, software developers, software architects, and other members of the software development teams) from the general population, creating a separate development network.

- Create a separate test network that is not connected to the production network.

- Review current network segmentation, and align it with recommendations.

Considerations for Choosing Border Controls

After you design network segments, you must review the border controls that are in place and then choose effective border controls for new network segment junctures. Many border controls are available for managing data flow between segments of your network. The following sections describe what you should know as you begin to choose border controls.

What Are Border Controls?

Border controls are controls that sit at the junction between trusted and less trusted segments of a network. They can be firewalls, remote access servers, intrusion detection systems (IDSs), packet filtering routers, VPN servers, or a combination of these things that are located on a border between the internal private network and an external network such as the Internet. They can be the same controls used to protect gateways between geographically dispersed segments of a single organization's network or to link partner networks into an extranet. They can also be the same devices used to segment internal networks into areas of trust.

Note Most IT professionals are familiar with IDSs—security screening devices that alert the administrator to potential attacks on the network. Recently, a new type of device known as an intrusion protection system (IPS), which is built to react to and stop an attack without administrative intervention, has emerged on the market. These products detect attacks and can be programmed to respond to them. For example, the device might immediately block all traffic from the identified interloper. In addition, specific types of packets, such as those that are improperly formed (empty, inconsistent, too short, too long, arriving on the wrong ports, and so on) are dropped. Examples of these systems are Jasomi Networks' PeerPoint Intrusion Prevention System (*http://www.jasomi.com/peerpointintrusion.html*), Psynapse Technologies' Checkmate Intrusion Protection System (*http://www.psynapsetech.com/.*)

Some capabilities of these new products have been featured in firewalls and IDSs in the past. For example, some IPSs will proactively block data from an IP address or IP address range that appears to be being used in an attack. The difference with these products is the extent to which the product can and does go and the fact that the product is a separate device. The IPS idea is catching on—even the IDS manufacturers are now also touting new IPS features on their IDSs. Read about Cisco's efforts in this area at *http://www.cisco.com/en/US /products/sw/secursw/ps2113/* and Internet Security System's efforts at *http://www.iss.net /products_services/enterprise_protection/*.

Firewall Considerations

Many types of firewalls are available. Most, such as Microsoft Internet Acceleration and Security server, start with the premise that all traffic should be blocked by default and require that the administrator configure access rules. Many provide additional services such as intrusion detection/protection and VPNs. Several issues reduce the effectiveness of firewalls as border controls:

- To provide access to resources, ports must be opened, and the more ports that are opened, the less protection the firewall can offer.

- Common ports, such as port 80, are used for other types of traffic for many things other than anonymous access to Web sites—the original use of the port. Because many organizations open this port to allow access to a Web site, much additional traffic, some which might not be harmless, is allowed through.

- Far too many organizations still believe that because they use a firewall, they are protected from everything—even though they might not have even properly configured the firewall. These organizations believe the firewall is security.

To mitigate these issues, use the following best practices:

- Carefully control which ports are opened. Ports should not be arbitrarily opened to serve some whim. A formal approval process must be followed that will ensure there is a legitimate business reason for opening the port and the security ramifications have been properly evaluated.

- Where protocols, such as remote procedure calls (RPCs), would require opening a wide range of ports, alternative solutions should be sought. Can the traffic be tunneled inside Secure Sockets Layer (SSL) or a more traditional VPN? In general, protocols that require extensive use of secondary ports are ill-suited to traverse a firewall.

- Consider using an application-layer firewall that inspects traffic at the application layer to determine whether it is really what it appears to be. Thus, traffic of a malicious nature that uses port 80 might be detected and blocked, while valid traffic will be allowed.

- Open ports for connection with a specific server or servers. Don't give unconditional access across a network. By following this rule, the risk engendered by the introduction of harmful traffic is reduced because only one or a few servers will be affected.

- Use a firewall capable of stateful inspection. Stateful inspection keeps track of the state (new request, response to previous traffic) of a connection and dynamically opens ports when necessary, rather than leaving them open.

Packet-Filtering Router Considerations

Considerations for using packet-filtering routers include the following:

- Most routers are capable of performing packet filtering and were often used as the first firewalls.

- They are often used to specifically restrict traffic-only segments for performance reasons.

- They are effective border controls, but they do not offer the many additional features that are present in modern firewalls and shouldn't be used instead of a firewall at a border between the private network and the Internet.

- A good use for these routers is to segment sensitive areas on the internal network. As with firewalls, care needs to be taken to prevent excessive opening of ports.

- They are often susceptible to Internet Protocol (IP) spoofing; they should not be relied on as the sole means of protection between networks.

Proxy Server Considerations

In the traditional sense, a proxy server simply proxies, or passes on, traffic from one party to another and serves as a way to expedite traffic across a gateway, not to inhibit it. Considerations for using proxy servers include the following:

- Modern proxy servers serve as border controls. They might require authentication, and they might restrict access to resources—for example, restricting a specific Microsoft Windows user group from accessing a range of Internet addresses, or preventing the download of specific file types.

- Many Internet filtering products act as add-ins on proxy servers or firewalls.

- Many proxy servers, such as Microsoft ISA Server, do not allow any connection to simply pass though. Rather, the proxy server creates a connection to the requested resource, such as a Web server, and relays it to the client. The client itself never actually connects to the Internet.

- The primary issue with proxy servers is that they are not firewalls and should not replace firewalls.

- Many proxies include the use of Network Address Translation (NAT). While NAT does hide the internal addresses, it is not a security control.

IDS and IPS Considerations

Intrusion detection systems (IDSs) alert administrators of suspected attack traffic or attempts to enter the network. Intrusion protection systems (IPSs) can be configured to respond to an attack. They can, for example, block traffic from the source of the attack. Considerations for using IDS and IPS include the following:

- Both systems can be effective additions to the securing of border control, and they can be used to detect internal attacks.

- IDS and IPS systems can be dedicated agents, computer systems, devices; however, the process of intrusion detection also incorporates inspection of process logs and security logs. Information about monitoring by using Windows logs is included in Chapter 9.

VPN Considerations

VPNs are often thought of as tunnels through the firewall. In that respect, they might be seen as tools that circumvent border controls. However, properly designed VPNs protect access to resources because they require authentication and encrypt traffic, thus protecting data that travels between two trusted networks or between a trusted client and a trusted network. Another way of looking at it is to see VPNs as processes that extend the network beyond traditional borders. For more information about VPNs, see Chapter 7.

Considerations for IP Protocol Packet Filtering with IPSec

IPSec is often used to protect communications between devices or as the encryption protocol of choice in VPNs. The IPSec Request for Comments (RFCs) also describe the use of IPSec to block or allow specific protocols from entering or leaving a specific device's Transmission Control Protocol/Internet Protocol (TCP/IP) stack. Often referred to as *IP protocol filtering with IPSec*, this process is available in Windows when using IPSec policies. Within the policies, filters can be constructed to allow or block specific ports that have a source or destination of a specific IP address or range of addresses.

Just as a firewall or a packet-filtering router can be used to determine which ports can be used by traffic entering or leaving the network, an IPSec policy can be used to specify which ports can be used to send or receive traffic for a specific device. These types of policies can protect a specific computer in the following ways:

- A Web server can be limited to receiving traffic on ports 80 (HTTP) and 443 (SSL), or a computer could be limited to receiving telnet traffic from only one specific computer.

- SQL server ports could be blocked on systems that do not need to allow network connections but run software which does so by default.

- Two types of policies can be written. Either the policy can block everything and then allow only specific ports, or the policy can allow everything and block only specific ports.

- When allow all/block some policies are used, only the specific ports that are blocked will be affected. A new filter must be written for each port that needs to be blocked.

- If a block all/allow some policy is written, care must be taken to understand exactly which ports must be open to enable the specific functioning of the device.

- It is rarely productive to attempt to apply IPSec block and allow policies to an entire network of computers, but policies can be applied via Group Policy or through scripts to apply the policies to many computers easily.

ICF Considerations

Internet Connection Firewall (ICF) is a stateful filter firewall based on service definitions and is available on Windows XP Professional and Windows Server 2003. ICF provides logging and is capable of providing inbound access to services running on the computer, such as a Web server. It is an excellent security resource on a desktop system. It is not, however, an enterprise solution, primarily because it does not provide any egress filtering capabilities.

TCP/IP Filtering Considerations

TCP/IP filtering can be configured on the network interface. It is stateless packet filtering and protocol filtering. It is rarely recommended because there are many other solutions that are superior.

Considerations for IPSec in Transport Mode

IPSec policies can also be created to protect traffic between Windows computers on a network. Windows 2000, Windows Server 2003, and Windows XP Professional have IPSec built in. A client for Layer Two Tunneling Protocol/Internet Protocol security (L2TP/IPSec) is provided as a download for Windows 98 and Windows NT 4.0. IPSec communications provide machine authentication, privacy, integrity, and protection from replay-based attacks. For more information, see "Lesson 3: Designing Security for Internal Data Transmissions," later in this chapter.

Considerations for Remote Access and RADIUS Servers

Remote access to internal networks can be provided via dial-up and network resources by using Windows Routing and Remote Access Services (RRAS) and Windows Internet and Authentication Service (IAS). Dial-up access provides for user authentication and data encryption. Remote access policies can restrict who can access the network, when they can access it, and by what means. Internet Authentication Services can centralize authentication and accounting (auditing) information for many RRAS servers.

Considerations for Network Access Quarantine Control

Network Access Quarantine Control is a new feature of Windows Server 2003. It can be used to delay remote connections while a script is run to determine whether the computer meets criteria designated in an administrative script. If the criteria are met, the connection proceeds in a normal manner. If the criteria are not met, the user can be redirected to a location where instructions are given on how to meet the criteria and information is given as to where the proper tools can be downloaded and installed. Alternatively, the user can be given instructions on how to comply and the connection can be terminated upon providing the instructions. Items that might be tested include the following:

- The correct service pack
- Correct and updated antivirus software and signatures
- Routing disabled
- Firewall software installed
- Password-protected screen saver

See Also   For more information about Network Access Quarantine Control, see Chapter 7.

Guidelines for Selecting and Using Effective Border Controls

Just understanding what current controls can do suggests where they are appropriate. However, there's more to the process of selecting and using effective border controls than just being able to define them. Follow these guidelines to select and use border controls:

- Determine which controls are already in place and whether they are effective and properly managed. The security architect will not often have the opportunity of starting from scratch and must learn to deal with inherited structures.

Often, however, there is nothing wrong with inherited structures except that they are ill-managed or improperly configured.

■ Document the current border controls. Many organizations have acquired various security devices with little thought to the necessary management and training required for them to work properly. It's as if they thought firewalls were like seat belts—if networks had them, people would eventually use them, and using them was just as easy as buckling up. In documenting current border controls, determine the following information about each control:

□ Manufacturer, make, model, and serial number—Knowing this information will assist in understanding the control's configuration and capabilities and in locating support.

□ Training received—Find out who received training on the product and when.

□ Product documentation—Find out the location of product documentation and information about its availability.

□ Use and location—Determine what the control is used for and where it is used (for example, external firewall of DMZ, or IDS in DMZ).

□ Configuration—Each device configuration will be different, but thorough documentation is necessary to compare what is to what should be.

■ When selecting border controls and designing their use, strike a balance between the needs of employees, customers, and partners to access and manipulate the organization's data and the organization's need to protect its data.

■ If secure access, which provides acceptable protection, cannot be designed and implemented, consider disallowing external access.

■ Consider the location of the VPN/remote access server. Choices include locating the VPN server outside the firewall (after which accepted communications are then given access through the firewall), locating the VPN server in the DMZ and tunneling VPN traffic through the external firewall, and locating the VPN server directly on the internal network with its own connection to the Internet. While its location in the DMZ can provide the VPN server with protection, some see location on the internal network as a better choice. With this approach, the VPN server is protected by configuring packet filters or IP protocol filters using IPSec directly on the VPN server and allowing only VPN traffic to connect. Both scenarios can be secured, but it's important to note that traffic that does not pass through a firewall or other border device after leaving the VPN server is not filtered or inspected. Trojan horses, viruses, and other malware, as well as attacks, can transit into the network. The VPN server is only meant to authenticate the user, and possibly authenticate the computer and protect the data in transit, not to inspect the data once it has arrived.

■ When IPSec is used as the protocol of choice for the VPN server and it is configured to require a certificate, consider the issues related to location of the certification revocation list (CRL):

❑ If Point-to-Point Tunneling Protocol (PPTP) is used in the VPN and a NAT server sits between the VPN server and the client, the NAT server must have a NAT editor that can translate PPTP tunneled data.

❑ If IPSec is used for the VPN and a NAT server sits between the VPN server and the client, do the VPN client and VPN server both support IPSec NAT traversal? Is the NAT server compatible? Early versions of IPSec in Windows could not be used across NAT, but more current versions are designed to do so.

❑ The VPN needs an authentication and accounting provider. A Windows VPN can use Windows or RADIUS. If Active Directory accounts are used, is access to the Active Directory available?

❑ Is name resolution available in the DMZ?

❑ Should a classic DMZ using two firewalls be used or a single firewall with three network interfaces?

❑ What type of VPN should you use? Should you use a remote access VPN (one in which VPN clients connect to VPN servers), a site-to-site VPN, or both?

❑ Where should supporting services be located? For example, if access to Active Directory is necessary, should a domain controller be placed in the DMZ or in a separate forest? Or should access to Active Directory be configured across the firewall?

❑ Who should receive access and how much access should they receive? If partners are provided access, should a separate forest be deployed or is a separate domain all that is required? What controls should be in place? Who should manage the forest? Should partners have administrative access?

❑ For each border control, what controls should be used? Should different controls be in place for public access vs. employee or partner access?

❑ What type of authentication should be allowed? Are passwords sufficient? Smart cards? Biometrics?

❑ When employees connect to remote services, what control should the organization have over their client machines if company-issued machines are not required? What control should the company have if company-issued machines are required? How can this control be implemented? Are there privacy issues? Should split-tunnel VPNs (that is, VPNs in which the user can be tunneling to the corporate intranet and yet access the Internet directly) be allowed?

The Way It Was

Early firewalls formed outward-facing solid barriers. They existed to prevent any traffic from entering the network. Access from the internal network to other networks was permitted. In fact, few controls if any prevented anyone from accessing other networks. However, if the communications arriving at the external side of the firewall was not an answer to some request from inside, it was not allowed. Designing this type of border control is easy, but it is not useful for most firewall installations today. Today firewalls allow some access from the Internet to corporate resources: either to resources on a DMZ, such as a web server, or to internal resources, such as Web server access to an internal database. Selecting and designing appropriate controls requires matching them to the needs of the organization and then providing the most secure configuration.

Considerations for Designing Active Directory Replication over Firewalls

This section discusses the considerations for designing Active Directory replication over firewalls and the protocols and ports used by Active Directory.

Considerations

If you work for an organization that operates from multiple locations, Active Directory replication might at least have to take place across firewalls. In some cases, this can be avoided—for example, when remote locations are small and authentication over the WAN is acceptable, or when users can work locally without WAN connections for long periods of time. In these cases, no domain controller is placed at the remote site and no replication has to occur. However, users do need access to Active Directory services, and providing this access across a firewall is also important. In other circumstances, however, domain controllers must be placed at geographically distant locations or otherwise exist where traffic boundaries are determined by firewalls. In these cases, you must plan for replication.

Before a solution is implemented, its design should take into account the security implications and the best, most secure solution selected. As for any situation where traffic should be permitted across physical boundaries, the design should first review the necessary protocols, determine whether changes can be made that will improve security, list the approaches that can be used, and then select the best solutions from among the approaches listed. Considerations include performance, new threats that can result from the actions taken, and the financial impact of the solution.

Protocols and Ports Used by Active Directory

Active Directory replication must occur between domain controllers within the domain and between the domain and global catalog servers. Two protocols can be used: remote procedure calls (RPC) and Simple Mail Transfer Protocol (SMTP). The use of protocols for replication can be divided into four types of data that must be replicated and the protocols that are available for each. Table 3-2 provides this information.

Table 3-2   Replication Data and Protocols

Type of Data Replication	RPC	SMTP
Schema	Yes	Yes
Configuration	Yes	Yes
Global catalog	Yes	Yes
Domain naming context	Yes	No

Exam Tip   You cannot secure Active Directory replication by insisting that all Active Directory replication take place by using SMTP. Domain naming context replication requires the use of RPC.

As this table shows, you cannot fully replicate all types of Active Directory data using SMTP alone. Any approach to securing replication data across a firewall should have a plan for both RPC and SMTP data.

For replication to occur, additional ports must be opened. Table 3-3 lists all services and their respective ports.

Table 3-3   Ports Used by Active Directory

Service	Port and Protocol
DNS	53 TCP and User Datagram Protocol (UDP)
Global Catalog Lightweight Directory Access Protocol (LDAP)	3268 TCP
Global Catalog LDAP over SSL	3269 TCP
Kerberos	88 TCP and UDP
LDAP	389 TCP
LDAP over SSL	636 TCP
Network basic input/output system (NetBIOS) name service	137 TCP and UDP
NetBIOS datagram service	138 UDP
NetBIOS session service	139 TCP

Table 3-3   Ports Used by Active Directory

Service	Port and Protocol
RPC dynamic assignment	1024-65535 TCP
RPC endpoint mapper	135 TCP and UDP
Server Message Block (SMB) over IP (Microsoft Directory Services)	445 TCP and UDP
Windows Internet Naming Service (WINS)	1512 TCP and UDP
WINS replication	42 TCP and UDP

There are two problems here. Opening of NetBIOS and SMB ports is generally a good way to help attackers break into your network. Also, opening of all high ports (the ports between 1024 and 65535) to allow RPC dynamic assignment is an unacceptable solution because the risk of also allowing unwanted traffic to enter is high. The following guidelines will present ways to solve these problems.

Guidelines for Securing Active Directory Traffic

The final task that you will perform as you design network border controls is to secure Active Directory traffic. Are there ways to reduce the total number of ports necessary to allow replication? There are. Follow these guidelines to design the secure transport of Active Directory traffic:

- If WINS, WINS replication, or both are necessary for a specific network, drop the requirement to open the ports that WINS requires.

- If a HOSTS file (for DNS) and an LMHOSTS file (for WINS) name resolution can be adopted, do not open the ports for DNS or WINS on the firewall.

Note   HOST and LMHOSTS files are located in the %windir%\system32\drivers\etc folder on each server. Sample files provide instruction for how to use them.

- Choose the appropriate technique for securing your Active Directory traffic: use full dynamic RPC, limit RPC ports, or tunnel replication traffic. See the sidebar at the end of this list for more information.

Tip   When creating an IPSec policy to be used for Active Directory replication, the use of authentication is a critical choice. While either Kerberos or machine certificates can be used, if you must perform the initial replication of data when a server is promoted to domain controller, you cannot use Kerberos. When the new domain controller is being created, it does not yet have the ability to use Kerberos for authentication, and the IPSec connection will fail. Kerberos can be used for authentication if all domain controllers have already been promoted.

- Consider requiring domain controllers to be built at headquarters and then shipped to alternative locations. This means that the initial replication will already have occurred, and Kerberos can be used for authentication in the IPSec policy created for replication.

- Consider promoting domain controllers at remote locations by using the special dcpromo /adv switch. This technique will prompt you, and you can select "restore from backup". In this case, you must supply a backup of Active Directory from headquarters to be used in the initial promotion. The Active Directory data in the backup will be used to update the Active Directory database. There is no need for the initial replication of domain data to occur over the WAN.

Note   To use certificates for authentication, each domain controller that will participate must obtain a certificate. You can build a Windows 2000 Certification Authority for this purpose. Information on doing so is available in Chapter 2. Information on using the certificate for authentication in an IPSec policy is in Lesson 3.

Techniques for Securing Active Directory Traffic

There are three techniques for securing Active Directory traffic:

- Use full dynamic RPC.
    - A firewall's role traditionally is to present a barrier. Each port that must be opened for traffic reduces the firewall's effectiveness as a barrier.
    - Full dynamic RPC requires random incoming high-port connections. This means there is no way to know which ports must be open on the firewall to enable the connection.
    - Allowing dynamic RPC across a firewall means that all high ports must be opened. This approach is often referred to as "making Swiss cheese out of the firewall" because it provides an attacker with a large number of holes to use.

- Limit RPC ports.
    - To understand how it's possible to limit the use of RPC ports, consider how RPC works. The RPC service has a universally unique identifier (UUID) in the registry. The UUIDs are well-known—that is, they are unique for each service and are the same across multiple platforms. For the services to be used, this UUID must be associated with a port.
    - Port association is done when the RPC service starts. A free high port is obtained and registered with the UUID. The same port will be used for the service until it is stopped. However, the same port or a different port can be used the next time. This is why all ports must be open—it is impossible to predict which port will be used.

❑ For a client to connect and use the service, it must discover the port. This is done by connecting to and querying the server portmapper service (in Windows systems on port 135) for the port in use for the specific UUID. The portmapper service returns this information to the client, and the client then attempts to connect to the specific RPC service.

❑ You can, for some services, assign the port that the service will use. Doing this allows the firewall configuration to be restricted to a small number of required open ports, which is a much more acceptable solution.

❑ To assign a port in Windows Server 2003, you must make a registry entry to assign the port that will be used. Refer to Table 3-3, "Ports Used by Active Directory," to see the possible port assignments. When you assign a port for the RPC dynamic assignment entry, this becomes the RPC static port for Active Directory replication. You can change your table of required ports to include your port in the dynamic assignment cell of the table. Exercise 2 of this lesson details the specifics of creating the registry entry.

■ Tunnel replication traffic.

❑ An alternative solution, tunneling replication traffic, will reduce the number of ports that are required to be open to permit the tunneling protocols, DNS, and Kerberos. Table 3-4 lists these ports. Note that both PPTP and IP Security (IPSec) ports are not required if only one tunneling protocol is used.

Table 3-4 Services and Ports Needed for the Tunneling Method

Service	Tunnel	Port/Protocol
DNS	N/A	53 TCP and UDP
PPTP	PPTP	1723 TCP
Generic Routing Encapsulation (GRE)	PPTP	IP protocol 47
Kerberos	N/A	88 TCP and UDP
Internet Key Exchange (IKE)	IPSec	500 UDP
IPSec Encapsulated Security Payload (ESP)	IPSec	IP protocol 50
IPSec Authenticated Header (AH)	IPSec	IP protocol 51

❑ Tunneling can be accomplished either via a gateway-to-gateway VPN using PPTP or IPSec over L2TP, or by using an IPSec transport mode policy that manages communications between domain controllers. In some cases, a VPN gateway might already be established between company locations. In such a case, the protocol access might already be configured for the firewall and Active Directory replication would simply need to use the secure path that is already established.

> ❑ If no gateway is present, the choice is either to create one or to configure IPSec policies. Gateway-to-gateway tunnels are discussed in Chapter 7.
>
> ■ The choice of an IPSec policy has the following advantages:
>
> ❑ Few ports need to be opened on the firewall.
>
> ❑ The data is tunneled not just across the border but from an Active Directory domain controller to an Active Directory domain controller.
>
> ❑ IPSec requires mutual authentication between the servers.
>
> ❑ IPSec configuration can be made more secure by the choice of key size, length of time a key is used, and the choice of authentication, integrity, and encryption algorithms.

Practice: Designing Network Border Controls

In this practice, you will design the Internet data center network for a fictitious company and restrict the ports used for Active Directory replication. Complete the following exercises. If you are unable to answer a question, review the lesson materials and try the question again. You can find answers to the questions in the "Questions and Answers" section at the end of this chapter.

Exercise 1: Designing an Internet Data Center Network

Read the scenario and then answer the questions that follow.

> **Tip**   Remember, the best design is not always the one that appears to provide the most security. Other factors such as risk, performance, and cost can affect the decision.

Scenario   Coho Winery is a large distributor of premium wines and is considering adding a consumer access online retail store. Wine will be sold from its www.cohowinery.com Web site by the bottle, by the case, or via wine clubs that send automatic monthly shipments. The network architects have asked you to help them make sound security decisions as they design the physical infrastructure for the site. They e-mailed you these questions:

- Should Coho Winery consider full redundancy or just do as much as possible?

- Should Coho Winery use routers programmed with traffic policies or should it simply select fast routers?

- Should Coho Winery simply have a large, fast implementation of Web sites and firewalls providing hardware redundancy and spreading data over multiple servers as the site grows, or should it invest in a load-balancing solution (even if this means, at first, having smaller, less powerful servers)?

- Should Coho Winery use hardware duplication for fault tolerance?

- Should Coho Winery use the more traditional DMZ design (which provides two firewalls: one between the Internet and the DMZ, and one between the DMZ and the internal network), or should it use a three-pronged approach (in which the firewall has three network interfaces: one for the DMZ, one for the Internet, and one for the internal network)?

- How should security management of the DMZ be performed?

- Should Coho Winery use a separate management network and use scripts to lock down and manage servers? Or should it simply provide scripts to lock down servers, set them up to automatically refresh, and then use the local user account database for authentication and access control? Or should the company use Active Directory and Group Policy to manage security, including authentication and authorization?

- How should access to Active Directory be provided? Which of the following strategies should be employed?

  - ❑ Authentication takes place across the firewall into the internal network. The corporate Active Directory will be used for authentication.

  - ❑ Authentication takes place across the firewall and into the internal network. The Active Directory of a separate forest will be used for authentication.

  - ❑ The DMZ has its own domain, and a domain controller is placed in the DMZ.

  - ❑ The DMZ has its own forest, and all domain controllers in the forest are inside the DMZ.

Review Questions   Answer the following questions.

1. Should Coho Winery opt for full redundancy or just do as much as possible?

_____

_____

_____

_____

_____

_____

_____

_____

_____

2. Should Coho Winery use routers programmed with traffic policies that determine what sort of traffic can enter and leave the network, or should they simply select fast routers?

_____

_____

_____

_____

3. Should Coho Winery simply have a large, fast implementation of Web sites and firewalls providing hardware redundancy and spreading data over multiple servers as the site grows, or should they invest in a load-balancing solution?

_____

_____

_____

_____

_____

_____

_____

_____

_____

_____

_____

_____

_____

4. Should Coho Winery use the more traditional DMZ design or use a three-pronged approach?

_____

_____

_____

_____

_____

_____

_____

_____

5. How should security management of the DMZ be performed?

_____

_____

_____

_____

_____

_____

_____

6. Assuming the use—now or in the future—of Active Directory for authentication, how should access to Active Directory be provided?

_____

_____

_____

_____

_____

_____

_____

_____

_____

_____

Exercise 2: Restricting the Port Used for Active Directory Replication

Complete the following steps to restrict the port used for Active Directory replication:

1. Log on to DC1.

2. To open the registry editor, click Start, click Run, and then type **regedit** in the Open box.

3. Navigate to the following path:
   HKEY_LOCAL_MACHINE\SYSTEM\CurrentControlSet\Services\NTDS\Parameters

4. On the Edit menu, select New, and then select DWORD value.

5. Enter the name **TCP/IP Port**.

   Note that the space is required.

6. Double-click the new value, and click Base, Decimal.

7. Set the value data to the port number 50000 (as shown in Figure 3-2).

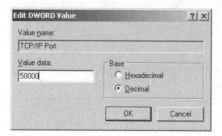

Figure 3-2   Setting the Active Directory replication port

The port number should be a number between 49152 and 65535.

> **Note**   These ports are set aside by the Internet Assigned Numbers Authority (IANA) for use by private and dynamic assignments. The use here of 50000 denotes nothing special; it's just an easy number to type and remember.

8. Click OK to close the dialog box.

9. On the File menu, click Exit to close registry editor.

10. Repeat this operation on DC2.

> **Off the Record**   In the real world, many domain controllers might exist. The change taught above can be automated by writing a script and applying it to all domain controllers that require it. Creating a script and applying it to all domain controllers eliminates the possibility of configuration error. The change could also be incorporated if a separate image has been created for the automated production of new domain controllers. If changes are made to production systems, be sure to verify that replication is occurring.

Lesson 2: Securing DNS

Securing DNS is a crucial part of ensuring the operation and security of an Active Directory network. If DNS is compromised, an attacker can prevent normal operations, route computers to spoof resources and services, and gain information that identifies additional crucial or sensitive hosts that can be attacked.

After this lesson, you will be able to

- Describe how DNS is used in an Active Directory network.
- Describe common attacks on DNS.
- Describe methods for securing DNS deployments.
- Secure DNS zone replication.

Estimated lesson time: 60 minutes

How DNS Is Used in an Active Directory Network

DNS has three uses in an Active Directory network:

- It is used by all clients to locate services such as a domain controller. DNS must be functional for users and computers to authenticate and access other services on the network.

- It is used for name resolution, to translate computer names into IP addresses for computers on the network.

- It is used to locate resources, such as Web servers and mail servers on the network.

Common Attacks on DNS

The first step in securing DNS is to understand the types of attacks that are typically used against it. Attacks on DNS include:

- **Footprinting**. An attacker obtains DNS zone data and thus has domain names, computer names, and IP addresses. This information can be used to further compromise systems.

- **Redirection**. By changing the IP addresses of legitimate servers, an attacker can redirect clients to spoofed servers, which are servers under the attacker's control.

- **Denial of service (DoS)**. An attacker might attempt to prevent legitimate clients from obtaining name resolution by flooding the DNS server with a large number of recursive queries. Eventually the DNS server can become overwhelmed and the DNS service will not be available.

- **Data modification/IP spoofing**. An attacker might attempt to use a valid IP address obtained from DNS zone information in IP packets created by the attacker. Because these packets now appear to come from a legitimate source on the network, the attacker might be able to use them to gain information or compromise other resources.

- **DNS cache poisoning**. Additional name resolution information might be returned with a query and placed in the DNS server cache of names and addresses that it is not authoritative for. Clients might be able to resolve names by using the DNS cache. An attacker might attempt to poison the cache by returning incorrect addressing information. Clients are then redirected either to a computer under the control of the attacker, or they are simply sent to an incorrect address.

Methods for Securing DNS Deployment

Placement of DNS servers and data on the network is important. The more easily available the data is, the more likely it is to be attacked and the more likely network disruption or other successful attacks will occur. One of the easiest ways to foil attacks is to split DNS functions between external and internal DNS services. This can be done in two ways: either internal DNS services can use a delegated subdomain or records for services that must be accessible externally can be hosted externally (perhaps by your ISP) and everything else is hosted on an internal DNS server or servers.

The Split DNS Method

In the split DNS method, the namespace is divided and a subdomain is used for internal addressing. The internal DNS namespace is a subdomain of the external DNS namespace. For example, if the fictitious company Humongous Insurance uses this structure, then humongousinsurance.com is the external domain and local.humongousinsurance.com is used as the internal DNS subdomain.

An Alternative Method

In an alternative method, the records for those services that must be accessible externally are hosted by an external DNS server or servers. An internal DNS server(s) hosts the names and IP addresses of internal, private network clients. The internal server(s) should include the resource records for essential services such as locating domain controllers. Configure the internal server(s) to forward requests from internal clients for external servers to the external DNS server. The external DNS server(s) can be a DNS server(s) hosted by the organization in the DMZ or perimeter network, or can be hosted by the organization's ISP. An external DNS server should not have any records for internal servers or clients. Tailspin Toys uses this system in our sample scenarios.

> **Note**   If clients cannot resolve names on the Internet or are not allowed to, eliminate DNS communication with the Internet. Use only a private DNS namespace, and host it entirely within your network. (If the organization's Web servers and other services are available from the Internet, they should be physically separated from the internal network and their DNS records should be hosted in a separate DNS server, perhaps the ISP's server.)

Guidelines for Securing DNS Zone Replication

You must make available multiple copies of DNS data or zone information. These copies provide backup, redundancy, and load balancing. The information needs to be the same on each server, and the traditional method of synchronization is to provide one zone replication between primary and secondary DNS servers. That is, all changes to zone data are made on the primary DNS server and replicated to one or more secondary servers. An alternative method is provided by Windows Server 2003 and Windows 2000 DNS services when they are installed as Active Directory Integrated. In this case, zone information is shared using Active Directory replication.

The early DNS servers on the network that became the Internet were configured to allow zone replication to any DNS server. This configuration is not the one to use on your DNS servers today. Many years ago, there were few DNS servers, and letting everyone know how to reach you on the Internet was most important. No one envisioned that they would need to protect this knowledge.

> **Note**   Dnscmd.exe is a utility that can be used at the command line or incorporated into a script. If many DNS servers must be secured, writing a script that includes these commands is useful. Dnscmd commands are identified in the practice.

For today's networks, however, there is no reason to leave this opportunity for information theft open. If you expose your internal DNS data via zone replication, an intruder might use a zone transfer to find out information about the servers on your network, such as the names and IP addresses of domain controllers, mail servers, internal web servers and databases, and more. This information might be used to mount an attack against critical or sensitive servers on your network.

Securing DNS zone replication must be done. If Windows Server 2003 DNS servers are used, use one of the following configurations:

- **Use Active Directory replication.**   The best benefits are obtained by using Active Directory replication. This traffic is automatically encrypted; therefore, zone replication traffic also is. Domain controllers authenticate to each other, ensuring that the zone replication traffic goes to authorized servers. To use Active Directory replication, select Active Directory Integrated zones when configuring DNS. When this is done, zone transfer is disallowed, as shown in Figure 3-3.

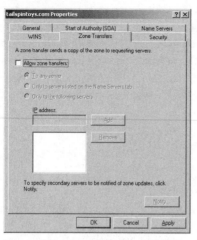

Figure 3-3 Confirming that DNS has disallowed zone transfer

■ **Restrict zone transfer.** If Active Directory integrated DNS is not used, restrict zone transfer to authorized servers. To restrict Microsoft DNS zone transfer to specific secondary DNS servers, use the Zone Transfer tab.

> **Note** An additional security configuration, secure cache against pollution (shown in Figure 3-4), is set by default. It can be found on the Advanced page of the DNS server properties. This setting prevents some referral DNS information from being added to the cache. Normally, when a query for name resolution is made, additional names and IP addresses might also be returned. If these addresses are not correct, the cache is said to be polluted or *poisoned*. The addresses might not be correct because of an attempt by an attacker to redirect communications to servers under her control. When this setting is used, the DNS server will not place referral names in its cache unless they are in the same domain as the query. That is, if a query for myserver.tailspintoys.com returned addressing information for yourserver.wingtiptoys.com, the information would not be cached.

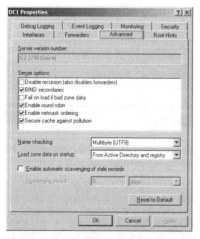

Figure 3-4 Confirming that the cache is secured against pollution

- **Encrypt replication traffic.**   Replication traffic can be encrypted by either setting up a gateway-to-gateway VPN tunnel between the server locations and routing DNS zone transfer traffic over the tunnel, or by creating an IPSec transport mode policy that is triggered by communications between the primary and secondary servers. Using an IPSec tunnel has the advantage of authenticating the traffic. Each server must authenticate to the other before any transfer of data occurs. The tunnel also does not have the additional overhead of creating the VPN gateway.

- **Use secure dynamic registration.**   An attack on a DNS server might attempt to change the IP address for a registered server, service, or client. If successful, connections would then be redirected to a spoofed server or client and additional harm might be done. By using secure dynamic registration, the modification of an IP address is restricted and the address cannot be arbitrarily changed.

- **Secure DNS clients.**   All computers that are joined to a domain are DNS clients and should be secured. Best practices indicate that static IP addresses should be specified in the DNS configuration for the DNS client. The addresses for preferred and alternate DNS servers should be entered. If they are not, clients can be configured to obtain DNS server information by using Dynamic Host Configuration Protocol (DHCP); however, this means that the security of DNS services for these clients is dependent on the security of the DHCP server. If the DHCP server were to be compromised, incorrect information on DNS services could be provided to clients and thus either cause DoS or direct the clients to spoofed servers. In addition, you should limit clients that can access the DNS server by configuring the DNS server to listen only on specific IP addresses. Then only clients configured to use the DNS server will do so.

Practice: Securing DNS

In this practice, you will configure secure dynamic registration, secure zone replication, and then use dnscmd to secure DNS. Complete the following exercises. If you are unable to answer a question, review the lesson materials and try the question again. You can find answers to the questions in the "Questions and Answers" section at the end of this chapter.

Exercise 1: Configuring Secure Dynamic Registration

Complete the following steps to configure secure dynamic registration:

1. Log on to the Tailspintoys.com domain as an administrator.

2. Open the Start, Administrative Tools, DNS console.

3. Right-click the zone that you want to configure, and then select Properties.

4. On the General tab, in the Dynamic Updates area, select Secure Only from the list, as shown in Figure 3-5.

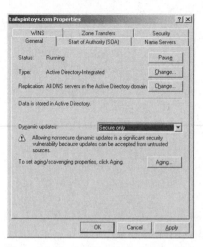

Figure 3-5   Configuring secure dynamic registration

5. Click OK.

Exercise 2: Securing Zone Replication

Complete the following steps to secure zone replication:

1. Log on to the Tailspintoys.com domain as an administrator.

2. Open the Start, Administrative Tools, DNS console.

3. Right-click the zone, choose Properties, and then click the Zone Transfer tab.

4. On the Zone Transfer tab, select the Allow Zone Transfers check box and click Only To Servers On The Name Servers Tab, as shown in Figure 3-6.

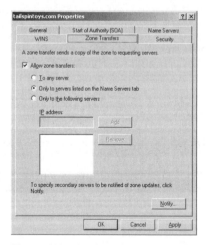

Figure 3-6   Configuring secure dynamic registration

5. Click OK.

Exercise 3: Using dnscmd to Secure DNS

Answer the following question.

1. How can dnscmd be used to secure DNS?

_____

_____

_____

_____

_____

_____

_____

_____

_____

_____

Lesson 3: Designing Security for Internal Data Transmissions

Every bit of data that crosses your network is important; but not all data needs to be hidden from view. Some data, however, is sensitive, and the risk of its exposure requires additional protection. For example, financial data, passwords, and patient healthcare information fall into this category. Although passwords are not transmitted in the clear during domain authentication, some applications might be found that do so. In these cases and others, additional security is necessary.

After this lesson, you will be able to

- Select methods to secure data transmission.
- Explain how Internet protocol filters are created.
- Design Internet protocol filters.
- Create a negotiating IPSec policy.
- Explain the purpose of IPSec startup protection.
- Design IPSec startup protection.
- Design an IPSec negotiation policy.
- Explain the considerations for selecting and configuring negotiation policies.
- Explain the guidelines for overall IPSec policy design.

Estimated lesson time: 60 minutes

Guidelines for Selecting Methods to Secure Data Transmission

VPNs, SSL, and IPSec can be used to secure internal data transmissions. Follow these guidelines to determine which method is appropriate for your organization:

- When access is required between two segments of the internal network that represent different trust levels, consider using VPNs to secure connections across internal firewalls. Doing so will require setting up a VPN server and managing client connections. However, both the user and computer can be authenticated, a distinct advantage over IPSec. For information about using VPNs, see Chapter 7.

- When communications between specific computers can be defined, consider using an IPSec policy. For more information about IPSec policies, see the section "Guidelines for the Overall IPSec Policy Design."

- When transmissions to and from specific ports should be absolutely blocked, use IPSec blocking policies. IPSec blocking policies are a way to create Internet Protocol filters.

- When transmissions to and from specific computers must be secured, use IPSec negotiation policies.

- Consider SSL to secure communications between users and intranet servers when sensitive information must be secured. SSL can be configured to require server authentication or both server and client authentication.

Note   IPSec is a protocol that can provide authentication, integrity, encryption, and protection from replay attacks. It is part of the native IP stack on Windows Server 2003, Windows 2000, and Windows XP Professional.

Tip   It's probably not feasible or cost efficient to entirely secure all data transmissions on the LAN. Performance, legacy systems, the need to troubleshoot network activity, and the time it would take to create, maintain, and troubleshoot the numerous techniques are prohibiting factors. In most cases, it's also just not necessary. A great deal of data crossing the LAN is of minimal importance, and more important data is already encrypted. In addition, good security practices provide reduction in risk for data on the LAN—for example, limiting access to cable plants and network access points and restricting by policy the use of protocol analyzers (and using tools to look for unauthorized use of them). In addition, segmenting the LAN into areas of trust, reduces potential access to transmissions. As with evaluating most security, the current risk and the consequences of not doing anything further should be weighed to help determine the need for further protection.

How IPSec Works

IPSec is implemented via the creation and assignment of IP Security policies. These policies can be created at the local level or established as part of a Group Policy object (GPO). When they are part of a GPO, they are applied to all computers whose account is within the site, domain, or organizational unit (OU) to which the GPO is linked. Policies are complex, and designing the correct policy for a specific situation requires knowledge of how policies work and the specifics of the parameters that can be configured. This is how IPSec works:

1. When assigned, IPSec policies are used only when triggered by the filters included within them. Filters are designations of computers, ports, protocols, and so forth. For example, an IPSec policy might include a rule with a filter on the destination TCP port 23. If the policy is assigned on the computer belonging to a user named Jeff, when Jeff attempts to make a Telnet connection to server 192.168.7.56, the policy is activated.

> **2.** What happens next depends on the filter action selected in the policy. Filter actions available are *block*, *permit*, or *negotiate*.
>
> ❑ If the filter action selected is block, all packets bound for TCP port 23 will be dropped.
>
> ❑ If the filter action is permit, packets bound for port 23 will be allowed.
>
> ❑ If the filter action is negotiate, Jeff's computer will attempt to negotiate a connection by using the specifics included in the policy. If the computer 192.168.7.56 has an IPSec policy assigned and it has a compatible rule, negotiate will probably be successful and Jeff will be able to connect to the computer. However, if no policy is assigned on the remote computer or the policy is not compatible, no connection will occur.

Elements of an IPSec Policy

Each IPSec policy has the following elements:

- **One or more *rules***. A rule is a collection of filters. Each rule can contain multiple filters but only a single filter action. If multiple actions are involved—such as "block all telnet, but negotiate a Telnet connection from computer at 192.168.7.33"—two rules are required.

- **A *filter list***. Each rule can have multiple filters. Filters specify information about the source and destination computers. Filters also provide information about the protocol, including source and destination ports, source and destination IP addresses, and source and destination mask.

- **Filter action**. Each rule must have one and only one filter action. The filter action is taken if the policy is triggered because of something in the filter list. If a filter list contains filters that include the destination port on the local computer for telnet ftp and nntp and a filter action of block, any traffic received that is destined for these ports is dropped.

- **General configuration**. Each policy can be configured to use specific protocols for integrity and authentication. Likewise, they must indicate things such as authentication type, frequency of key change, and *Diffie-Hellman group* (strength of key used to secure the Quick Mode negotiation).

How Internet Protocol Filters Are Created

There are several tools that can be used to create an Internet Protocol filter, but the basic process is the same:

Note   Tools that can be used to create Internet Protocol Filters and IPSec Negotiation policy are

- The netsh command line tool
- The IP Security Policy Management MMC snap-in
- The IP Security Policies on Active Directory container in a GPO
- The IP Security Policies on the Local Computer container in a Local Group Policy

1. Create the IPSec policy on a test computer:

   a. Create a blocking rule or a permit rule.

   b. Create a filter that indicates the source address of the packet that will trigger the rule, the destination address of the computer or computers that will block or permit traffic, and the protocol type and port.

   c. Create a filter action (either block or permit).

   d. Add as many filters as are required.

Important   Only one filter action is possible per rule. Therefore, if you require blocking and permitting Internet Protocol Filter, you must create two rules in the policy—one for blocking and one for permitting.

2. Assign the policy on the test computer.

3. Test the policy.

4. If the policy works, deploy the policy in the production network as required.

Guidelines for Designing Internet Protocol Filters

Internet protocol filters are implemented by writing IPSec policies that contain rules with either block or permit as the filter action. These policies do not require a compatible policy on other computers because no negotiation will occur. The policy will just block or permit the specified protocols. The filters can be written to block or allow transmissions either leaving the computer or attempting to connect to it. Follow these guidelines when designing Internet protocol filters:

- Consider using such a policy to block connections to port 80 on all servers except Web servers.

- Incorporate the policy in a GPO linked to the OU that includes server computer accounts.

- Consider using a policy to block all traffic, and then allow only certain types. The decision on whether to block all and then allow, or just specifically block individual protocols, will depend on the number of protocols that need to be blocked and the sensitivity of the data on the computer. A good example of such a policy is one that blocks all telnet communication.

■ When designing protocol filters for firewalls, the usual recommendation is to block all traffic and then open only the necessary ports. A similar approach can be used with IPSec. A policy might have one rule that specifies to block all communications and another rule that specifically allows only protocols that this specific computer requires. Care should be taken to ensure that all necessary protocols are made available.

■ Consider using similar policies to block or permit traffic from specific computers or ranges of IP addresses.

■ Consider how many protocols must be blocked. If more protocols must be blocked than permitted, rather than writing numerous filters—one for each protocol to block—a single rule is written that blocks all traffic, and then another rule will include a filter list with one filter for each protocol that is allowed.

■ When Internet protocol filters are created using IPSec policies, do not set any of the parameters that are used for negotiation because no negotiation occurs. For each rule, the block or allow filter action must be set. For each filter, the following information must be configured:

❑ protocol

❑ source port

❑ source IP address

❑ source mask

❑ source DNS name

❑ destination port

❑ destination DNS name

❑ destination IP address

❑ destination mask

How to Create a Negotiating IPSec Policy

Any of the IPSec policy tools can also be used to create an IPSec negotiation policy. To do so, follow these steps:

1. Create the IPSec policy on a test computer:

    a. Create a rule.

    b. Indicate whether a tunnel endpoint is required.

> **Important**   If a tunnel mode policy will be created, two rules are necessary—one to specify each side of the tunnel. If a transport mode policy will be created, no tunnel endpoint is necessary.

   c. Select the network connections that will enforce the rule. Choices are Remote, LAN, or all.

   d. Create a filter that indicates the source address of the packet that will trigger the rule, the destination address of the computer or computers that will block or permit traffic, and the protocol type and port.

   e. Create a negotiate filter action.

   f. Select an authentication method. Methods are Kerberos, certificate, or shared key.

   g. If encryption should be used, select the acceptable encryption types.

   h. Select integrity types.

   i. Select key change periods.

2. Assign the policy on the test computer.

3. Test the policy.

4. If the policy works, deploy the policy in the production network as required.

What Is IPSec Startup Protection?

To understand IPSec startup mode, think in terms of the three phases of startup. The first stage is when the computer is booted, before the IPSec driver is loaded. (There's no IPSec protection at this stage.) The second stage is after the driver is loaded but before the IPSec service starts. (This stage includes IPSec driver startup modes.) The third stage is after the IPSec service has started. (Domain or local policies, if assigned, will be in effect.) IPSec driver startup modes, new to Windows Server 2003, consist of the following:

■ Permit all inbound and outbound traffic. This is the default. However, once a persistent, local, or domain IPSec policy is started, the permit mode is no longer in effect.

■ Block all inbound and all outbound traffic (except traffic that matches filters configured using the `netsh dynamic set config bootexemptions` command and DHCP). Traffic is blocked until a persistent policy is applied.

■ Stateful allows DHCP and all outbound traffic initiated by the computer during startup, as well as inbound traffic that is sent in response to outbound traffic. The `netsh dynamic set config bootexemptions` command can also be used to add other filters. This mode is set if a persistent, local, or domain policy is present, and it is not in effect once they are loaded.

How to Design IPSec Startup Protection

When designing the use of IPSec, you need to consider IPSec startup modes. As it becomes increasingly impossible to capture meaningful traffic on the network, attackers will focus on the endpoints of communications, much as they focus on VPN endpoints today. Close holes in IPSec protection before this happens. You can set the startup mode by using the `netsh ipsec dynamic set config bootmode value={state-ful |block  | permit}` command by editing the registry or by implementing a persistent policy. The computer must be restarted after changing the startup mode.

The netsh command can be used to create, assign, monitor, and troubleshoot IPSec policies. In addition, there are tasks that can be done only by using netsh, including making an IPSec policy, instituting computer startup security, performing computer startup traffic exemptions, running diagnostics, performing default traffic exemptions, performing strong CRL checking, performing IKE (Oakley) logging, and creating persistent policies.

Just as you use the wizards and create local and domain policies by configuring IKE parameters and adding rules that are composed of filter lists, filter actions, and other configuration parameters, you use netsh to do the same.

You can create IPSec policies using netsh at the command lines or within scripts. The following steps will create an IPSec policy that blocks access to shares. It is a blocking policy only (meaning that no negotiation is required) and is meant only to prevent access to shares until the domain policy, which allows and protects administrative access from specific computers, can be loaded. Because it is for blocking only, it needs to be created only on the file servers and not on clients. You can implement this policy one command at a time. Alternatively, you could build a batch file and run it to implement the policy.

> **Important**   After you enter each command in the step-by-step exercise, press the ENTER key. If you receive an error message, correct your syntax. If you need to start over, you can delete the policy with the command `Delete Policy Name=`.

1. Open a command prompt on Computer2.

2. Enter the Netsh Ipsec Static context.

   Netsh

   Netsh>ipsec static

3. Create a policy on Computer2 by entering the following command:

   ```
   Add policy name="shares" description="block access to shares "
   activatedefaultrule=no mmsecmethods="3DES-MD5-3"
   ```

4. This policy needs a single rule. It will block all NetBIOS communications. To add the rule, you must first add the filter list, its filters, and a filter action. If you create a filter for a filter list that doesn't exist, the filter list is created. To create a filter list with a filter that triggers on NetBIOS ports, enter the following commands:

```
Add filter filterlist="shares" srcaddr=ANY dstaddr=Me description="block port"
protocol=TCP mirrored=yes srcmask=32 dstmask=32 srcport=0 dstport=135
Add filter filterlist="shares" srcaddr=ANY dstaddr=Me description="block port"
protocol=TCP mirrored=yes srcmask=32 dstmask=32 srcport=0 dstport=136
Add filter filterlist="shares" srcaddr=ANY dstaddr=Me description="block port"
protocol=TCP mirrored=yes srcmask=32 dstmask=32 srcport=0 dstport=137
Add filter filterlist="shares" srcaddr=ANY dstaddr=Me description="block port"
protocol=TCP mirrored=yes srcmask=32 dstmask=32 srcport=0 dstport=138
Add filter filterlist="shares" srcaddr=ANY dstaddr=Me description="block port"
protocol=TCP mirrored=yes srcmask=32 dstmask=32 srcport=0 dstport=139
Add filter filterlist="shares" srcaddr=ANY dstaddr=Me description="block port"
protocol=TCP mirrored=yes srcmask=32 dstmask=32 srcport=0 dstport=445
Add filter filterlist="shares" srcaddr=ANY dstaddr=Me description="block port"
protocol=UDP mirrored=yes srcmask=32 dstmask=32 srcport=0 dstport=135
Add filter filterlist="shares" srcaddr=ANY dstaddr=Me description="block port"
protocol=UDP mirrored=yes srcmask=32 dstmask=32 srcport=0 dstport=136
Add filter filterlist="shares" srcaddr=ANY dstaddr=Me description="block port"
protocol=UDP mirrored=yes srcmask=32 dstmask=32 srcport=0 dstport=137
Add filter filterlist="shares" srcaddr=ANY dstaddr=Me description="block port"
protocol=UDP mirrored=yes srcmask=32 dstmask=32 srcport=0 dstport=138
Add filter filterlist="shares" srcaddr=ANY dstaddr=Me description="block port"
protocol=UDP mirrored=yes srcmask=32 dstmask=32 srcport=0 dstport=139
Add filter filterlist="shares" srcaddr=ANY dstaddr=Me description="block port"
protocol=UDP mirrored=yes srcmask=32 dstmask=32 srcport=0 dstport=445
```

5. Type the following command to add a filter action to block access:

```
Add filteraction name="block NetBIOS" inpass=yes action=block"
```

6. Add a filter action to block all telnet:

```
Add filteraction name="block all telnet" inpass=yes action=block
```

7. Add a rule that will manage the filter list:

```
Add rule name="block shares" policy="noshares" filterlist="shares"
filteraction="block NetBIOS"
description="this rule blocks access to NetBIOS shares2"
```

8. Assign the policy:

```
set policy name="block shares" assign=yes
```

To make a policy persistent, you add it to the persistent storage. To do so, use the set store location command. The assigned policy will be stored in the registry.

Enter the following command:

set store location=persistent

Guidelines for Designing an IPSec Negotiation Policy

IPSec negotiation policies include rules, filter lists, filters, and filter actions just like the Internet protocol filters just described. In addition, they include many settings that determine how the transmission will be negotiated and how it will occur.

Use negotiation policies in the following situations:

- **Computer authentication is required before a connection is allowed.**   Because IPSec negotiation policies require authentication, connections from computers that cannot authenticate or do not have the policy assigned can be blocked. In this type of policy, data is not encrypted. A policy might be constructed, for example, to ensure only domain member computers can connect to shares on file servers. By default, if a user knows the location of a share and the credentials of an authorized user of the share, a connection will be made. However, if an IPSec policy must be used and the authentication process cannot be accomplished by the computer used, the connection will fail.

- **Sensitive data must be transmitted.**   IPSec policies can be required to negotiate encryption type and thus ensure all data is protected. If the data is captured by a protocol analyzer, the data cannot be read. In addition, data can be tunneled, offering transmission across networks.

- **You want to ensure connection from specific computers only.**   Authentication can limit connections. Each authentication type has its own plusses and minuses. Explicit filters can limit the connections to specific computers using their IP addresses.

To design the use of configuration details, remember that each configuration must match that of the policy present on the other computer or the connection will fail. Also consider that:

- If one computer has Kerberos authentication configured and the other has only shared secret configured, the negotiation will fail.

- If one computer is set to use only Data Encryption Standard (DES) and the other is configured to only use triple DES (3DES), then negotiation will fail. If DES and 3DES are encryption protocols that can be selected in the policy, 3DES is more secure.

- If one computer policy changes keys at a different time than the other, a connection might occur, but it will eventually fail because one computer has changed keys and the other has not.

- If a filter list includes a filter for TCP port 23 and the other filter list does not, negotiation will fail.

Considerations for Selecting and Configuring Negotiation Policies

Many items make up the configuration part of a negotiation policy. To write a policy that fits its use, you must make decisions about which ones to use. The following sections list the things you should consider as you select and configure negotiation policies.

Computer Authentication Considerations

Authentication considerations include the following:

- The authentication process can be either Kerberos, shared key, or certificates.
  - ❑ If Kerberos is used, only computers with accounts in the forest or with accounts in trusted domains can be used. Kerberos is the default choice and works well in domain environments.
  - ❑ If, however, computers have accounts from domains that are trusted by the same domain, forest, or trust relations, they will not be able to authenticate using Kerberos. This authentication process can also be a problem where Active Directory is not available—for example, in cases where a traveling user attempts to make an IPSec connection across the Internet back to the office. (This type of connection might be best made with a VPN or some other remote access solution.)

- The use of shared keys for authentication is not advised in a production environment.
  - ❑ Shared keys are useful while testing or troubleshooting IPSec.
  - ❑ The problem with using shared keys is that they are clearly visible in the policy interface, and they can be obtained by using troubleshooting tools. If users are administrators working from their own desktops and the shared key is used for authentication on policies on the desktop, users can easily find the key. A secret is no secret if it's widely known.
  - ❑ In troubleshooting, or in a test prior to deployment, using shared secrets can eliminate the possibility of problems with Kerberos or certificate authentication. This allows the rest of the policy to be thoroughly tested. Then, when problems in other areas are resolved or when there are no problems, authentication can be changed to Kerberos or certificates. If problems then occur, they are most likely authentication issues. The scope of the problem can therefore be narrowed, and it will be easier to troubleshoot.

- If certificates are used, three issues can cause a problem.
  - ❑ First, of course, certificates must be obtained. If a Windows public key infrastructure (PKI) is implemented, certificates can be issued by an Active Directory–integrated Certification Authority. Third-party certificates can also be used.
  - ❑ Second, the root certificate authority (CA) certificate for the CA hierarchy that issued the IPSec certificate must be available in the certificate store of the

computer that will use the IPSec policy. This means that, if the same CA hierarchy did not issue the certificates used by both computers, a root CA certificate from both the CA hierarchy that issued the current local machine certificate and one from the root CA of the hierarchy that issued the remote computer must be in the local computer's certificate store.

❑ Certificate Revocation Lists must be available.

❑ CRL checking is automatically done during IKE certificate authentication. However, computers can be configured so that a successful CRL check is not necessary for the certificate to be accepted. (This is not a best practice but is available in case certificates from third-party CAs, which do not add the CRL location to the certificate, must be used.)

❑ Modify this default when data is sensitive or there is a need for absolute certainty that the computers used have valid certificates.

❑ CRL checking can cause delays and might result in failures for authorized and unrevoked certificates.

❑ Without CRL checking, a compromised and revoked machine certificate might be used to authenticate a connection. The requirement for security will have to be weighed against the factors involved in ensuring correct and efficient CRL checking.

Protocol Considerations

Several protocols were originally excluded from the Windows implementation of IPSec. These excluded protocols are as follows:

■ In Windows 2000, Kerberos, IKE, RSVP, multicast traffic, and broadcast traffic was excluded, although a registry entry could specify differently. An IPSec policy configured to "block all" protocols, therefore, would not block these. These protocols were excluded to allow Kerberos and IKE to function and to allow Quality of Service (QoS) to be signaled (RSVP) even when traffic is secured by IPSec.

■ In Windows Server 2003, these default exemptions are not present, with the exception of IKE. If IKE traffic were not excluded, every IPSec policy would need a rule that permitted IKE to function.

Off the Record If IPSec policies implemented under Windows 2000 will be migrated to Windows Server 2003, the Windows 2000 computers should be configured with the *NoDefaultExempt = 1* registry key. (The key location is at HKLM\SYSTEM\CurrentControlSet\Services \IPSEC.) This key is supported in Windows Server 2003 for backward compatibility and will be preserved in an upgrade. The key can be modified by editing the registry or by using netsh at the command prompt as follows:

netsh ipsec dynamic set config ipsecexempt value=0.

Values for the key are:

0 = Multicast, broadcast, RSVP, Kerberos, and IKE traffic are exempt (the Windows 2000 default configuration).

u1 = Kerberos and RSVP are not exempt.

2 = Multicast and broadcast are not exempt, but RSVP, Kerberos, and IKE are.

3 = Only IKE is exempt (Windows Server 2003 default).

IPSec Sub Protocol Considerations

Two IPSec protocols are used: Authentication Header (AH) and Encapsulating Security Protocol (ESP). Both provide *data origin authentication* (which verifies whether each packet came from the server that negotiated the connection), *data integrity* (which checks to see whether the data changed), and *anti-replay protection* (which ensures authentication and other successful negotiation packets cannot be re-used by another computer to form a successful connection). Choose IPSec protocol based on authentication and encryption needs. The two protocols are similar in the protection they offer except:

- The IPSec subprotocol, AH, provides superior packet authentication. This is because AH provides protection for the data packet and the IP header. The AH header contains a field, Authentication Data, that includes an integrity check value (ICV) or authentication code. This value is checked to validate message authentication and integrity. The ICV is calculated over the IP header, the AH header, and the data payload. ESP, in contrast, does not sign the whole packet, only the payload—so only the integrity of the data can be validated.

- AH lacks the ability to encrypt data.

- Specify ESP when encryption is necessary.

Managing Certificates for IPSec Policies

Figure 3-7 shows just such a scenario. In the figure, two computers—one from tailspintoys.com and one from wingtiptoys.com—are attempting to negotiate an IPSec connection. Computer1.tailspintoys.com has an IPSec certificate from an enterprise CA in tailspintoys, and computera.wingtiptoys.com has an IPSec certificate from the enterprise CA in its domain. For each computer to authenticate to the other, each must have a root CA certificate from the other's root CA as well as their own. Arrows from the respective CAs point to each computer, showing that this is so.

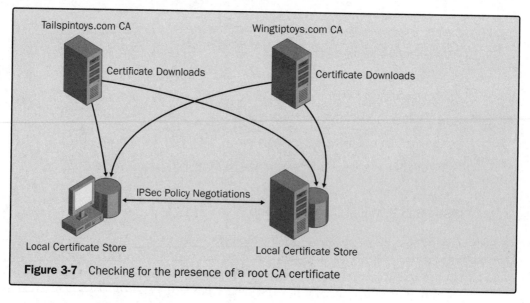

Figure 3-7   Checking for the presence of a root CA certificate

Tunnel-Mode Considerations

Tunnel-mode considerations include the following:

- IPSec traffic does not require that it be tunneled. When traffic travels from one computer to another, tunneling might or might not be necessary.

- By default, when IPSec is used for encryption in a Windows VPN, L2TP is used for the tunnel. IPSec tunnel mode is not used.

- When a negotiation policy is implemented, you can choose to use tunnel mode. This might be useful if the communication must take place over an intermediary network, such as the Internet when connecting a remote office to the main office.

Connection-Type Considerations

Connection-type considerations include the following:

- IPSec policies can specify that, if triggered, all such traffic will be negotiated or that only remote or only LAN connections will be negotiated.

- Use the remote choice if remote connections introduce a higher level of risk.

- Negotiation policies must exist on both computers that need to communicate using IPSec.

- Negotiation policies must match for successful connection and communication to occur.

Encryption Considerations

Encryption considerations include the following:

■ Encryption can be either DES or 3DES.

■ 3DES, or triple DES, offers better protection. However, if communications with systems that are not capable of using 3DES is required, DES must be used. Many policies will make both encryption protocols available to ensure communication with mixed client bases.

■ The encryption protocol might also be mandated by an organization's security policy.

■ The IPSec subprotocol, ESP, provides encryption while the AH protocol does not. ESP is specified by default, but you should ensure that it is being used by checking the policy and by testing.

■ SPecSNetwork cards designed to perform IPSec encryption are available and can offset the load that IPSec can put on the CPU of heavily used servers.

■ When encryption is required, the ESP IPSec subprotocol must be used.

Integrity Considerations

Integrity considerations include the following:

■ Integrity is accomplished using one of two protocols: MD5 or SHA1. Both are considered sound integrity algorithms, and the decision to use one or the other might depend on the ability of the computers that must communicate to use IPSec.

■ Using SHA1 will increase the processor overhead slightly, but it is required for organizations subject to Federal Information Processing Standards (FIPS) regulations.

Diffie-Hellman Group Considerations

The considerations for the Diffie-Hellman group include the following:

■ The Diffie-Hellman group indicates the size of the key used to secure the Quick Mode negotiation when the master key is being calculated. The larger the group number, the larger the key. Groups include the following:

❑ Low (1)

❑ Medium (2)

❑ High (3)

■ The larger the size of the key, the better the security. However, the larger the size of the key, the longer it will take to calculate the key. These keys are not the keys used to encrypt the data, however, and while data encryption keys are likely to change during data transmission, the key used by IKE is not.

- Restrict the policy to Diffie-Hellman group 3 only if all computers that must successfully negotiate the policy are Windows Server 2003 computers. If other computers or devices will need to communicate using the policy, use group 1 or 2.

Key Change Frequency and Re-Authentication Considerations

The considerations in these areas are as follows:

- Both master key and encryption keys can be scheduled to change during data transmissions, and re-authentication can be required.

- In general, the more frequently the session is authenticated and the more frequently master and encryption keys are changed, the more secure the data will be. For example, if an attacker were able to deduce one of the encryption keys, he would be able to decrypt only the packets encrypted with this key. If the key is changed frequently, little data will be available. However, each of these options reduces performance and puts additional burdens on the CPU. Choices should be made based on sensitivity of data, and additional performance requirements should be met by additional hardware support.

- Choices include the following:

  ❑ Perfect forward security. The key must be regenerated before each use.

  ❑ Authenticate and generate a new key every so many minutes. On a periodic basis, re-authenticate and generate a new master key.

  ❑ Authenticate and generate a new key every session. Each time a new session is requested, authentication must occur and a new master key is generated.

  ❑ Generate a new key every so many Kbytes. A number of Kbytes is entered, and then each time this number of Kbytes has been transmitted, a new encryption key will be generated.

  ❑ Generate a new key every so many seconds. A number of seconds is indicated, and at the end of this period a new encryption key will be generated.

How IPSec Negotiation Policies Work

If you understand how the negotiation process works, you will be able to design policies that work and take advantage of the negotiation process in your design. Processing can be divided into two phases: Phase I, known as *IKE Negotiation Mode* or *IKE Main Mode* (and sometimes just Main Mode), and Phase II, known as *Quick Mode*. The computer names One and Two are used for expediency.

The Steps in Phase I

1. Computer One sends a packet to computer Two.

2. The IPSec driver on computer One checks its outbound IP filter lists, detects that the packets match a filter, and determines the filter action is negotiate.

3. The IPSec driver notifies IKE to begin negotiations.

4. Computer One checks its policy for IKE Main Mode settings (authentication, Diffie-Hellman group, encryption, and integrity) to create a proposed negotiation specification to send to computer Two.

5. Computer One sends the IKE message to computer Two using UDP source port 500 and destination port 500.

6. Computer Two receives the IKE Main Mode message requesting secure negotiation. It uses the source IP address and the destination address of the packet to look up its own Policy IKE settings. It can accept the settings computer One sent only if they match its active policy settings.

7. If the security settings are compatible, negotiation of the IKE security association begins. A *security association (SA)* is a secured communication path between two computers.

8. Both computers participate in the negotiation, exchange identities, and authenticate to each other. A master key is generated, and the IKE SA is established.

The Steps in Phase II

1. Computer One does an IKE Negotiation Mode policy lookup to obtain full policy information. (IKE negotiation does not concern itself with which ports or other Quick Mode settings there are.)

2. Computer One proposes its options, including encryption and integrity algorithms (if used) and filter to computer Two.

3. Computer Two does its own IKE Negotiation Mode policy lookup. If it finds a match with the options proposed by computer One, it completes the Quick Mode negotiation to create a pair of IPSec SAs. There is one inbound SA and one outbound SA for each port required. Each SA is identified by a unique number, known as a Security Parameters Index (SPI).

4. Computer One's IPSec driver uses the outbound SA, signs, and if specified, encrypts the packets.

5. The IPSec driver passes the packets to the network adapter driver.

6. The network adapter driver puts the packets on the network

7. The network adapter on computer Two receives the packets from the network.

> 8. The packet SPI is used to find the corresponding SA. This step is necessary because multiple SAs might exist and only the corresponding SA has the associated cryptographic key necessary to decrypt and process the packets.
>
> 9. Computer Two's IPSec driver uses the inbound SA to retrieve the keys and processes the packets.
>
> 10. The IPSec driver converts the packets back to normal IP packet format and passes them to the TCP/IP driver that passes them to the receiving application.
>
> 11. Quick Mode IPSec SAs continue processing packets. SAs are refreshed until they are no longer needed, and then they are deleted. IKE Negotiation Mode SAs are not deleted when idle. By default, they have a lifetime of 8 hours. Their lifetime can be configured to a minimum of 5 minutes and a maximum of 48 hours. New traffic will trigger a new Quick Mode negotiation.

Guidelines for the Overall IPSec Policy Design

Follow these guidelines when designing IPSec policies:

- **Use network cards that support encryption on servers.**   If a server must manage many connections and encrypt all data, the performance of that server might deteriorate. There are several network cards that can offload IPSec encryption to a built-in processor on the network card. Windows IPSec is designed to use these cards if they are present.

- **Do not encrypt traffic between domain controllers and their clients.**   To authenticate, the client must connect to the server. To do so requires the establishment of an IPSec connection. However, IPSec cannot be negotiated because it requires authentication.

- **Ensure that the protocols that are required are configured.**   Several protocols were originally excluded from the Windows implementation of IPSec. Most of these are no longer excluded. For every protocol that must be used in a communication, you must configure a filter.

- **Design a single policy for each computer.**   Only one policy at a time can be assigned to a computer. A policy can have multiple filters and multiple rules. By using multiple rules and filters, a policy can be designed for most circumstances. Select multiple choices for encryption, integrity algorithm, Diffie-Hellman group, and authentication process in a policy when this is necessary for communication with many different Windows clients. Part of the negotiation process is selecting a combination that both *IPSec peers* (two computers that consummate a successful negotiation) can use. Different Windows computers might not be capable of all possible selections, so you must provide those they can work with. Narrow the choices for encryption, integrity algorithm, Diffie-Hellman group, and authentication process when you want more secure policies. If many choices are possible, there is always the possibility that a weaker algorithm will be used between peers even if the peers support the more secure choices. To ensure the strongest choices are used, remove all other choices.

- **Back up IPSec policies by creating a persistent policy.**   There is no default way to require that a local policy take over if a domain policy cannot be downloaded or assigned. To counter the lack of backup, create a *persistent policy* by using netsh and establish a persistent policy that at least provides minimum protection.

- **Audit IKE activity for testing purposes or to log its use.**   Track success and failure of IKE negotiations by auditing logon events for success and failure in the audit policy of the computers that are using IKE.

- **Consider the impact of auditing IKE.**   Where IPSec is used extensively, a large number of records will be collected. If they are not reviewed or used, they might simply clutter and fill the security log.

- **Consider requirements for ping.**   Do you want ping to be allowed? Ping is used in various troubleshooting scenarios and to determine whether a system is reachable on the network. If ping is blocked by the policy, these uses are lost.

- **Consider routers and firewalls.**   IPSec traffic is formed in the normal manner and will happily be routed by routers. However, if a firewall or router is blocking all traffic and only allowing specific protocols through, the firewall or router must be configured to allow IPSec.

- **Consider interruptions to communications when policies are configured or modified.**   Do not schedule changes or implementation at peak network usage times, and test before being implemented.

- **Test authentication methods before rolling out an IPSec design.**   Authentication can be tricky. The time to find this out is during the testing phase. IPSec policies can be assigned at the OU level. This means you can design IPSec policies for a specific group of computers.

- **Ensure that CRLs are available on the network, and test the ability of IPSec peers to access them by testing the policy on the network after testing it in a test lab.**   If CRLs are not available on the network, policies using certificate for authentication might fail.

- **Don't use the provided default IPSec policies.**   These policies are good example policies. However, most production policies combine factors from these policies and introduce others to meet the custom secure communication needs of the network. Default policies are overwritten during an upgrade and when policies are imported.

- **Accept unsecured communications on Internet facing connections.** On Internet facing connections, it is not a good idea to have an IPSec policy that will not accept any unsecured communications, nor one that will respond by always requiring IPSec. If you set up the IPSec policy to accept no unsecure communications, a successful DoS attack can occur. To ensure that a policy does not cause this problem, make sure the Accept Unsecured Communications, But Always Respond Using IPSec and Allow Unsecured Communications With Non-IPSec Aware Computer check boxes are cleared.

- **Don't assume interoperability with all computers and devices on networks.** When designing IPSec policies, understand clients, servers, and other devices on the network and their IPSec capabilities. Some might not be able to use IPSec, or their IPSec implementation might not be compatible with Windows.

- **Learn how to use netsh.** Netsh is a good tool for troubleshooting IPSec. It can also be used to create, assign, and monitor IPSec Policies. Two modes exist: static and dynamic. Use dynamic mode netsh IPSec commands to configure filters on the fly.

- **Do not attempt to use IPSec to protect all communications on a network.** The process is just too complex and fraught with opportunities for error. The use of IPSec for some communications would seem to be the equivalent to providing bank vaults for pocket change—it's rather unwieldy and more costly than complete loss of the resource would be.

- **Configure IPSec protection for startup.** The use of startup mode will ensure that a problem with the network or with Group Policy will not leave the computer vulnerable.

Practice: Designing an IPSec Policy

In this practice, you will select policies, design an IPSec policy for a fictitious company, and create an IPSec policy by using wizards. Complete the following exercises. If you are unable to answer a question, review the lesson materials and try the question again. You can find answers to the questions in the "Questions and Answers" section at the end of this chapter.

Exercise 1: Selecting Policies

Table 3-5 provides a list of scenarios that might be solved by creating an IPSec policy. In the second and third columns of the table, enter the filter description and filter action or actions that you would implement. Your filter action choices are block, allow, and negotiate. If the filter action is negotiated, indicate whether negotiation or authentication is the most important.

Table 3-5   IPSec Policy Types

Scenario	Filter Description	Filter Action
Prevent normal Web traffic from server1.		
Only Ted can telnet to server2.		
Protect all traffic between server3 and authorized clients.		
Block all traffic to server4 unless it is to and from domain controllers and authorized clients. Protect traffic to and from all authorized clients.		
Assure that all connections to domain one computers are from other computers joined in the domain.		

Exercise 2: Designing an IPSec Policy for Wingtip Toys

Read the scenario and then answer the question that follows.

Scenario   You are a security designer at Wingtip Toys. The company wants to protect sensitive files that must be made available by using shares. You have gathered the following information and made the following decisions:

- Users who are authorized to read or read and modify documents of specific types are given appropriate permissions on the share, folder, and files by using discretionary access control lists (DACLs).

- The servers are segmented behind an internal firewall. However, Wingtip Toys realizes that this security can be breached by current users whose computers are on that network segment, and potentially by other employees, contractors, and intruders who might gain entry to the area and the ability to connect to the network. To provide an extra layer of protection, you decide to use IPSec. This can provide data encryption to protect the data in case it is captured during transmission, and it can restrict communications to specific computers. This is not ideal because it will prevent authorized users from accessing data if they are not using one of the authorized computers—but this inconvenience is small.

■ Your users understand the need for confidentiality, and most of them are required to work from the regular systems at all times. This restriction has advantages, as assigned computers can be more closely audited and secured. You have decided to design a policy to block access from computers that are not under the control of authorized users.

■ The 192.168.5.0/24 subnet has been reserved for IT administrators, and no other computers are assigned addresses within that range.

Review Questions Answer the following question.

1. What steps should you take to design the policy?

_____

_____

_____

_____

_____

_____

_____

_____

_____

_____

_____

_____

_____

_____

_____

_____

_____

_____

_____

_____

_____

_____

_____

Exercise 3: Creating an IPSec Policy Using the Wizards

In this exercise, you will implement the policy designed in Exercise 2. To do this, you create an MMC console, create the blocking rule, create a negotiation rule, and select authentication. Complete the following procedures.

> **Important**   Although a security designer might not be the individual who will implement IPSec policies on the network, IPSec policies can be quite complex. To design them, you must know what it is possible to do and what it is not possible to do. Reading rules, considerations, and guidelines is a good way to begin, but to understand how a complex policy that incorporates multiple rules—including permitting, blocking, and negotiating rules—cannot be done by simply imagining how it might work in your head or by using logical diagrams. The designer must have experience in making a complex policy work. If you have met the prerequisites for this exam, you should have been exposed to the concept of a simple IPSec policy and you should have stepped through the construction of one. You might not, however, have designed and implemented a complex policy. Much can be learned by doing so. This exercise provides the step-by-step instructions for creating such a policy. If you want to implement it and test it, you will need two computers configured as described in the "Getting Started" section of this book and placed on the same test network.
>
> In this exercise, the policy is created on one computer. When complete, it can be exported to a file and imported onto others. Remember that each file server and each authorized client will need a copy of the policy. Modification will have to be made to the policy to ensure that individualized information, such as certificates, is properly handled.

▶   **Create an MMC console**

Complete the following steps to create an MMC console:

1. Click Start, and then click MMC.

2. On the File menu, click Add/Remove Snap-in, and then click Add.

3. From Add Standalone Snap-ins, select IP Security Policy Management and then click Add.

4. In the Select Computer Or Domain dialog box, accept the default local computer selection and then click Finish. (See Figure 3-8.) Then click Close, and click OK.

5. From the File menu, click Save-As, enter the file name **IP Policy Management**, and click Save.

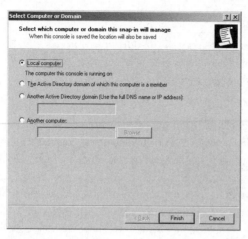

Figure 3-8 Selecting the IP security policy on the local computer

▶ **Create the blocking rule**

Complete the following steps to create a blocking rule:

1. In the IP Policy Management console just created, right-click the IP Security Policies on the Local Computer container and select Create An IP Security Policy from the context menu.

2. On the wizard welcome page, click Next.

3. Name the policy **Block File Share Access**, enter a description, and click Next.

4. Deselect the Default Response Rule check box, click Next, and then click Finish.

Note The default response rule allows insecure communication. In most cases, you will not want this, so it is good practice to remove the rule.

5. In the Blocking Web Server Access Properties dialog box, near the bottom of the Rules tab, clear the Use Add Wizard check box (shown in Figure 3-9), and click Add.

Tip When writing a blocking rule, further use of the wizard is counterproductive because it steps you through the creation of more complex policies and introduces confusion and extra work. By deselecting the wizard check box, the policy property pages are displayed after clicking Add.

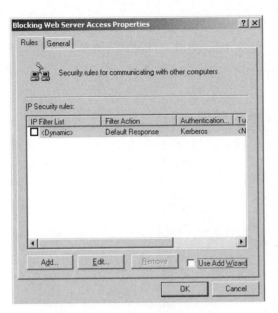

Figure 3-9   Deselecting the Add wizard

6. In the IP Filter List dialog box (shown in Figure 3-10):

   a. Click Add to create the filter list.

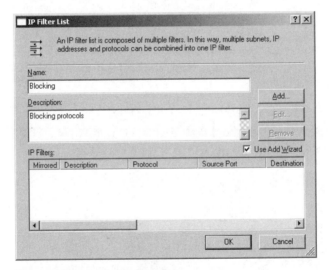

Figure 3-10   Adding a filter list

   b. In the Name text box, type **Blocking** to name the filter list, and in the Description box, type **Blocking protocols**

   c. Clear the Use Add Wizard box, and then click Add to add a filter.

7. In the IP Filter Properties dialog box:

    a. From the Source Address list, select Any IP Address.

    b. From the Destination Address list, select My IP Address (as shown in Figure 3-11).

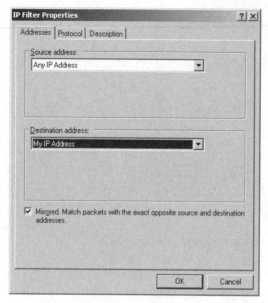

Figure 3-11   Creating the filter

8. Click Protocol.

9. On the Protocol tab:

    a. From the Select A Protocol Type list, select TCP.

    b. In the Set The IP Protocol Port area (shown in Figure 3-12), click To This Port, and in the text box, type **135** and then click OK.

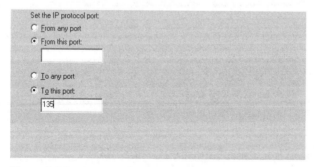

Figure 3-12   Defining filter ports

10. Repeat steps 8 and 9 for ports 136, 137, 138, 139, and 445. Then change the protocol type to UDP and create new filters for the same ports. When complete, click OK to close the IP Filter List dialog box.

11. Select the Blocking entry in the IP Filter lists box, and then click the Filter Action tab.

12. Deselect the Use Add Wizard option, and click Add to add a filter action.

13. In the New Filter Action Properties dialog box, on the Security Methods tab, click Block, as shown in Figure 3-13.

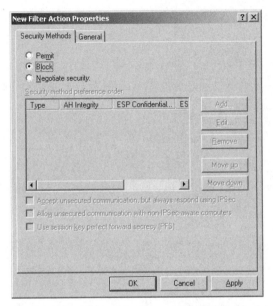

Figure 3-13   Creating the Block filter action

14. Click the General tab. In the Name text box, type **Block** to name the filter, and then click OK.

15. In the Filter Action dialog box, click Block Filter Action and then click Close. In the New Rule Properties dialog box, click Close.

Note   The preceding steps create a rule that will, if its policy is assigned, block all traffic to the file-sharing ports. Next, create a rule to provide negotiated connections between the file server and authorized clients. A blocking rule needs to be created only on the file server. A separate policy, one with just one rule, can be created for the clients. For now, create the second rule in this policy. This rule will have a filter action of negotiate.

▶   **Create a negotiation rule**

1. In the Policy dialog box, click General and then click Settings to locate and adjust the Key Exchange Settings. (See Figure 3-14.)

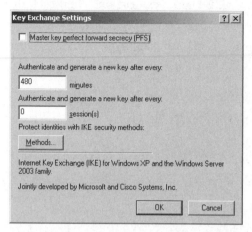

Figure 3-14   Locating the Key Exchange settings

2. In the Key Exchange Settings dialog box, click Methods.

The Key Exchange Settings page is the location for changing master key generation particulars.

3. In the Key Exchange Security Methods dialog box, select the fourth (last) default security method (shown in Figure 3-15) and click Remove. Select both the third and second method in turn and remove them as well. One method remains, as shown in Figure 3-16.

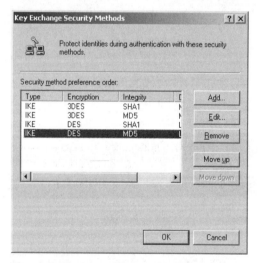

Figure 3-15   Inspecting security methods

Figure 3-16   Reducing the number of security methods

> **Note**   Removing three of the security methods reduces the opportunities for connection. Only a client that can negotiate 3DES and SHA1 using Diffie-Hellman group 2 can negotiate a connection. The Diffie-Hellman group could also be changed to high, but this would limit connections to Windows Server 2003 computers only.

4. Click OK twice to return to the General page, and then select the Rules page.

5. Make sure the Use Add Wizard check box is selected, and click Add to add a rule.

6. At the welcome page, click Next.

7. On the Tunnel Endpoint page, click Next.

    This policy will not use a tunnel.

8. Leave the All Network Connections option selected on the Network Type page, and click Next.

    This policy will remain effective no matter where the connection is coming from.

9. On the IP Filter List page, click Add to add a filter list.

10. Enter Negotiate as the name of the filter list, and enter a description.

11. Select the Use Add Wizard option, and click Add to add a filter.

12. On the Filter Wizard welcome page, click Next.

13. Enter a description for the filter, and click Next.

14. On the IP Traffic Source page, from the Source Address list, select A Specific IP Subnet and select a range of IP addresses. Enter the address **192.168.5.0** and the subnet mask of **255.255.255.0** (as shown in Figure 3-17), and then click Next.

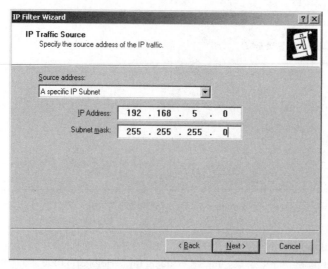

Figure 3-17   Entering an IP subnet as the source

15. For the IP Traffic Destination, select A Specific IP Address and enter the IP address for the file server. Then click Next.

16. Select the IP protocol type (in this case, TCP), and then click Next.

17. Select the To This Port option, enter **135**, and then click Next. Click Finish.

18. Click OK to return to the IP Filter List page in the wizard.

19. Repeats steps 11 through 18 for each TCP port. Repeat using UDP as the protocol type.

20. Select the New filter list, Negotiate, and then click Next.

▶ **Select authentication**

Complete the following steps to select authentication:

1. Click the default Require Security Filter action, and click Next.

2. Select Kerberos for the authentication method, click Next, and then click Finish.

3. Click OK to complete the rule, and then click OK.

   Authentication times out.

Design Activity: Designing the Network Infrastructure for Physical Security

In this activity, you must use what you learned in all three lessons and apply it to a real-world situation. Read the scenario, and then complete the exercises that follow. You can find answers for the exercises in the "Questions and Answers" section at the end of this chapter.

Scenario

The file-sharing IPSec policy for Wingtip Toys (that you developed in the previous practice) worked so well that administrators decided to do something similar to prevent ordinary connections to SMB ports on servers that are not file servers or domain controllers. The administrators use common administrative tools to manage, secure, and audit these computers, and they must leave ports open so that these computers can be managed.

They have come to understand that leaving the ports open is not a secure practice. While the use of these administrative tools is restricted to the Administrators group, leaving the ports open exposes access to the computers. Their thoughts are that an attacker might leverage this situation and compromise the server. They don't want to give up the use of their tools, so they implemented an IPSec policy that will allow only administrators working from their workstations to access the servers by this method. The IPSec Policy is implemented using Group Policy.

However, a consultant advised them on many ways in which Group Policy might not be downloaded or might otherwise become blocked, and the administrators realize this might be a problem. They want a solution that will always use the file-sharing policy, even if something happens to Group Policy. Only one policy can be assigned on a computer.

Requirement 1   An IPSec policy must be active on the server at all times, even if Group Policy fails.

Requirement 2   No connections on SMB ports are allowed unless they come from a very specific set of computers.

Requirement 3   Kerberos or certificates can be used for authentication.

Exercise 1: Determine How to Use Group Policy and Provide a Failsafe Method for Protecting Crucial Servers

Answer the following question.

1. How can this company use the Group Policy and still provide a failsafe method for protecting crucial servers?

Exercise 2: Determine the IPSec Startup Mode of Crucial Servers

Answer the following question.

1. If you want to enter and assign the policy, what should the IPSec startup mode of the critical servers be?

_____

Exercise 3: Determine if the Remote Desktop Protocol Can Be Used

Answer the following question.

1. Can the Remote Desktop protocol be used if the Group Policy IPSec policy does not get downloaded? If not, what could you do to make it possible?

_____

_____

_____

Exercise 4: Make a Policy Persistent

Answer the following question.

1. After the policy is configured using netsh, what must you do to make it a persistent policy?

_____

_____

_____

_____

Exercise 5: Explain Benefits of Persistent Policies

Answer the following question.

1. What are the benefits of persistent policies?

_____

_____

_____

_____

_____

Chapter Summary

- Designing border controls consists of evaluating remote access needs, understanding available border controls, examining the use of current controls, and creating a design that maximizes security according to the risk.

- Border controls consist of firewalls, IDS, IPS, VPNs, network access quarantine control, and IPSec policies.

- Securing DNS protects the physical network by preventing the capture of information about the network, or its modification.

- IP Packet protocol filtering can be implemented by using IPSec.

- IPSec can be configured to protect communications between two computers on a network. It can provide confidentiality, anti-replay protection, data origination authentication, and mutual machine authentication.

- IPSec should be used to protect sensitive communications.

- It is difficult, and not recommended, to attempt to use IPSec to protect every network communication.

Exam Highlights

Before taking the exam, review these key points and terms. You need to know this information.

Key Points

- Availability is a key concept in designing a network for physical security. Two factors that are important in ensuring availability are securing the border controls and services that operate on the border and using redundant hardware, software, and data.

- When numerous choices exist for specific border control implementation, the correct configuration of border controls is more important than which border controls are selected.

- Securing DNS can be accomplished by securing zone replication, using secure dynamic update, and keeping private internal data on internal DNS servers and by placing only Internet-accessible services on an Internet-accessible DNS server.

- IPSec packet protocol filtering using blocking policies is the best choice for implementing packet filtering directly on a server.

- To protect communications between two computers on a LAN, use IPSec.

Key Terms

IP protocol filtering   The use of IPSec to block or permit communication using specific protocols.

Network access quarantine control   The ability to quarantine clients attempting to remotely access a network until the configuration of the computer matches an organization's policy, as defined in a script.

Persistent IPSec policy   An IPSec policy that always remains in effect.

Questions and Answers

Pg 3-22   **Lesson 1   Exercise 1: Designing an Internet Data Center Network**

1. Should Coho Winery opt for full redundancy or just do as much as possible?

Answers may vary:

Coho Winery should consider full redundancy. Full redundancy provides at least one alternative way of operating for each network function. Full redundancy includes the use of two or more Internet service providers (ISPs) to ensure Internet access in the case of ISP business failure or network service interruption. In the most extreme cases, full redundancy means ensuring that the ISPs used are not obtaining their Internet access from the same provider.

It is unknown how successful Coho Winery's online store will be, and full redundancy might be too expensive to initially consider. Each component in the network design should be considered, and redundancy should be introduced when its cost can be justified.

2. Should Coho Winery use routers programmed with traffic policies that determine what sort of traffic can enter and leave the network, or should they simply select fast routers?

Consider using a router at the perimeter. These routers connect the Internet data center to the Internet. Traffic policy should be implemented on the routers to help secure access to the network. Fast routers can do this too. The important thing is taking the time to understand what can and cannot be done and doing it correctly.

3. Should Coho Winery simply have a large, fast implementation of Web sites and firewalls providing hardware redundancy and spreading data over multiple servers as the site grows, or should they invest in a load-balancing solution?

Consider load balancing. Load balancing can add resiliency and scalability for many network elements. Common implementations are for firewalls and Web servers. Load balancing requires the implementation of two or more duplicate systems and additional configuration and support. For example, Web site computers must be kept synchronized or a shared data resource should be used to ensure that each computer presents the same data.

Load balancing can spread the load over two or more devices of the same type, such as firewalls, Web servers, and so forth. In addition, should one of the devices be inoperable, all traffic is simply routed to the remaining devices. Load balancing can thus provide redundancy without the extra cost of providing "stand-by" or secondary systems. As the site grows, larger and faster systems can be added to the load-balancing solution. Plan on load balancing IIS, firewalls, and other systems as possible.

Also, plan hardware duplication for fault tolerance. Some hardware duplication can be done at a very low cost compared to the huge benefits it has. Full hardware duplication might prove to be too expensive, but some hardware duplication can be done. In the simplest design, two multilayer switches are used for hardware fault tolerance. Each server is equipped with two network adapters, and each one connects to one of the two switches.

4. Should Coho Winery use the more traditional DMZ design or use a three-pronged approach?

Answers will vary. The recommended answer is to use the traditional DMZ approach for an e-commerce site because it adds an extra layer of security. Although arguments can be made for both designs, the major issue with the one-firewall, three-pronged approach is that when this firewall is compromised, an attacker has direct access to both the DMZ and the internal network. In the traditional DMZ approach, an attacker who is able to penetrate the defenses of the external firewall still has the internal firewall to contend with. The downside of using two firewalls is the increased complexity and cost.

5. How should security management of the DMZ be performed?

All servers in the DMZ need to be locked down. Access to the management interface of servers needs to be authenticated and authorized.

If a single Web server were to be the only server in the DMZ, management of security could adequately be accomplished using the local account database and security templates and scripts. However, managing security on multiple servers can quickly become difficult. Using Active Directory imposes additional expense, but the benefits of consistent, periodic application of security is well worth it, as is the ability to use one account database and thus apply uniform access security.

6. Assuming the use—now or in the future—of Active Directory for authentication, how should access to Active Directory be provided?

The DMZ should have its own forest, and all domain controllers in the forest should be inside the DMZ. Active Directory placement is a difficult issue. If authentication must take place across the firewall, additional ports must be opened. If a domain controller is placed in the DMZ, there is more chance of the system being compromised, and replication across the firewall must occur. If the same forest is used by the DMZ as is used by all of the corporation, an attacker who manages to compromise an account used in the DMZ will then have access to the internal corporate network. If a new forest is designed for the DMZ, additional expense is incurred. In addition, decisions must be made on whether trust relationships between the corporate forest and the DMZ forest should be created, or whether the necessary users must be given separate accounts in each forest. There is more, however, to be gained—resources both in the DMZ and in the internal network are easier to secure if a separate forest is used for the DMZ.

Pg 3-33 **Lesson 2 Exercise 3: Using dnscmd to Secure DNS**

1. How can dnscmd be used to secure DNS?

Answer:

Dnscmd.exe is a utility that can be used at the command line or incorporated into a script. If many DNS servers must be secured, writing a script that includes these commands is useful. To use dnscmd to secure DNS, use the following commands to apply security with dnscmd.exe:

To limit zone transfer, use dnscmd to limit transfers to names servers for the zone as follows:

dnscmd /zoneresetsecondaries /SecureNS

To change to secure dynamic update, use the following command:

dnscmd /config /enablednssec 0

Pg 3-52 ## Lesson 3   Exercise 1: Selecting Policies

The following table shows the correct answers.

Table   IPSec Policy Types—Answer Key

Scenario	Filter Description	Filter Action
Prevent normal Web traffic from server1.	port 80 traffic with a destination address of server1	Block
Only Ted can telnet to server2.	1. All telnet traffic destined for server2 2. telnet traffic from Ted's computer to server2	1.block 2. allow
Protect all traffic between server3 and authorized clients.	All traffic destined for server3 and with a source of the IP address range for authorized clients.	Negotiate, use encryption
Block all traffic to server4 unless it is to and from domain controllers and authorized clients. Protect traffic to and from all authorized clients.	1. all traffic 2. traffic to and from domain controllers 3. traffic to and from authorized clients	1. block 2. allow 3. negotiate, use encryption
Assure that all connections to domain one computers are from other computers joined in the domain.	All traffic	Negotiate, require authentication only, use certificates

Pg 3-53 ## Lesson 3   Exercise 2: Designing an IPSec Policy for Wingtip Toys

Answer the following question.

1. What steps should you take to design the policy?

Answer:

a. Identify the ports used. Microsoft file sharing uses the Server Message Block (SMB) protocol. Historically, SMB uses the NetBIOS ports, User Datagram Protocol (UDP) ports from 137 through 139, and Transmission Control Protocol (TCP) ports from 137 through 139. Windows Server 2003, Windows 2000, and Windows XP can use direct-hosted SMB traffic. Direct-hosted SMB does not use the NetBIOS ports. Instead direct-hosted SMB requires port 445 (TCP and UDP).

b. Identify computers that are assigned to authorized users.

c. Determine authentication. Use certificates for identification because, by policy, computers are not automatically provided IPSec certificates. Certificates can be restricted. This will make it harder for an unauthorized computer to connect using the file-sharing ports.

d. Determine encryption, integrity algorithms, and the Diffie-Hellman group. All computers are capable of using 3DES, so 3DES is chosen. The default integrity algorithm, SHA1, is selected. The medium Diffie-Hellman group is chosen because the client systems cannot use Diffie-Hellman group 3.

e. Select key change timing and period. Accept the default changes because there is no indication in the information given that there is any reason to do otherwise.

f. Determine whether more than one rule is necessary. Remember, each rule can have only one filter action. This policy will require that all computers are blocked except those authorized, and it will require that those authorized must negotiate the connection. Because two filter actions (block and negotiate) are required, two rules will be necessary.

g. Review policy settings, and create a test policy.

Design Activity: Designing the Network Infrastructure for Physical Security

Pg 3-63   **Exercise 1: Determine How to Use Group Policy and Provide a Failsafe Method for Protecting Crucial Servers**

Answer the following question.

1. How can this company use the Group Policy and still provide a failsafe method for protecting crucial servers?

Use the netsh commands and create a persistent policy.

Pg 3-64   **Exercise 2: Determine the IPSec Startup Mode of Crucial Servers**

Answer the following question.

1. If you want to enter and assign the policy, what should the IPSec startup mode of the critical servers be?

The startup mode of the critical servers should be set to block.

Pg 3-64   **Exercise 3: Determine if the Remote Desktop Protocol Can Be Used**

Answer the following question.

1. Can the Remote Desktop protocol be used if the Group Policy IPSec policy does not get downloaded? If not, what could you do to make it possible?

The remote desktop protocol could be used only if another line is added to the startup script. The following line should be added:

netsh ipsec dynamic set config bootexemptions tcp:0:3389:inbound

Pg 3-64   **Exercise 4: Make a Policy Persistent**

Answer the following question.

1. After the policy is configured using netsh, what must you do to make it a persistent policy?

To make a policy persistent, you add it to the persistent storage. To do so, use the set store location command. The assigned policy will be stored in the registry.

Enter the following command:

set store location=persistent

Pg 3-64   **Exercise 5: Explain Benefits of Persistent Policies**

Answer the following question.

1. What are the benefits of persistent policies?

A persistent policy will be in place should the assigned policy have a problem. If, for example, the domain Group Policy fails to download or there is some other problem with the process, the default IPSec policy will always be in place.

If a persistent policy is active and a domain or local policy is assigned, the resultant IPSec configuration will be a combination of the two.

This protection will be loaded during startup before the local or domain policy.

Section III
Creating a Security Design for Management and Maintenance of the Network

Foundations and frameworks are great starters on the road to security, but how will you manage and maintain the secure systems that you design? If you cannot provide a design for secure administration, any gains in security as the result of new technologies or the hardening of old ones will be lost the first time an administrator changes a setting for his convenience, grants access to unauthorized individuals, or becomes frustrated with controls that he doesn't understand. Intruders will find it easy to circumvent technical controls if administrators have weak passwords or if their administrative workstations are readily available. Business needs will begin to be unconstrained by security requirements, and lack of attention to changes in technologies will leave the network subject to compromises that could have been easily avoided. This section contains these chapters:

- Chapter 4, "Designing Security for Network Management," which describes the issues and provides solutions that can become the cornerstone of successful network management security designs. It considers the risk that administrators pose, discusses the design of secure administrative practices, and introduces secure management of a technology new to Microsoft Windows Server 2003: Emergency Management Services.

- Chapter 5, "Designing a Security Update Infrastructure," which concentrates on designing the use of Software Update Services (SUS) to provide security patch management processing for a Windows-based network. It also addresses other necessary elements such as testing.

4 Designing Security for Network Management

Exam Objectives in this Chapter:

- Manage risk to managing networks.
- Design administration of servers by using common administration tools.
- Design security for emergency management services.

Why This Chapter Matters

The best security in the world can be negated by a single accidental or malicious action performed by an administrator. It only makes sense to take steps to make this less likely to happen. History teaches that simply providing rules, assuming loyalty, and relying on chance is not enough. Instead, you must examine the administrator, administration tools, and administration practices with a critical eye toward security. You must trust your administrators—there is no way around this—but there is no reason not to qualify that trust, secure operations, and monitor the practices of the people who touch the network the most.

Lessons in this Chapter:

Before You Begin

This chapter presents the skills and concepts related to designing security for network management. This training kit assumes you have a minimum of 1 year of experience implementing and administering desktop operating systems and network operating systems in environments that have the following characteristics:

- At least 250 supported users
- Three or more physical locations
- Typical network services such as messaging, database, file and print, proxy server or firewall, Internet and intranet, remote access, and client computer management
- Three or more domain controllers

- Connectivity needs that include connecting branch offices and individual users in remote locations to the corporate network and connecting corporate networks to the Internet

In addition, you should have experience designing a network infrastructure.

Many design exercises are paper-based; however, to understand the technical capabilities a design can incorporate, you should have some hands-on experience with products. Where specific hands-on instruction is given, you must have at least two computers configured as specified in the "Getting Started" section at the beginning of this book.

Lesson 1: Managing Administrative Risks

One of the best known security paradigms is the principle of least privilege. This principle can be applied in many ways, such as:

- Limiting how many administrators there are, and allowing most administrators to have only limited administrative capabilities

- Requiring that administrators log on with administrative credentials only when the elevated privileges are needed

- Limiting the number of operating system services that are used

- Disabling installed services on servers that will not use them

By just applying this principle to every proposed operation, you will significantly reduce the attack surface of the enterprise and make security less challenging. But designers must also understand how to manage administrative risks, and that is the focus of this lesson.

After this lesson, you will be able to

- Describe the process for managing administrative risks.
- Recognize common vulnerabilities in network management.
- Explain the difference between isolation and autonomy.
- Describe what a security boundary is.
- Explain what a security policy boundary is.
- Discover administrative security boundaries.
- Use Secure installation practices.
- Describe the security considerations associated with automated deployments.
- Determine which services to disable.

Estimated lesson time: 60 minutes

The Process of Managing Administrative Risk

The process for managing administrative risk is as follows:

1. *Recognize the vulnerabilities introduced by network administration.*

2. *Establish security boundaries.* Understanding the security boundaries provided by the operating system is essential in determining the scope of authority that administrators have. In addition to understanding where these boundaries are, you must also understand when to apply them. To do so, you need to know the key concepts of isolation and autonomy as they relate to service administration and data administration.

3. *Reduce the administration attack surface.* Reducing the attack surface is a sound security design principle that can be applied to any part of your security design. If you can reduce the number of things that can be attacked or the avenues that can be used to attack them, the network will be more secure. Reducing the attack surface can take many forms, but one of the easiest things to do is to eliminate things that are not needed. To reduce the ability of attackers to use administrative accounts and channels to attack networks, reduce the number of things in total that administrators must manage and reduce or partition the scope of their management by delegating authority. While these actions are also examples of least privilege, they illustrate a reduction in the attack surface quite nicely. If the administrator's account were to be compromised, the attacker would have less ability to do damage because the surface or range of things that can be attacked has been reduced.

4. *Evaluate and carefully judge your administrators.* The people who are trusted with the administration of your network must be trustworthy. Although you can limit authority, every bit of authority can be used to destroy important parts of your systems and data. In addition, at some point, someone must have absolute authority to keep systems running, correct errors introduced by others, troubleshoot problems, and so on. Checking the backgrounds of potential administrators and repeating the process periodically is crucial to the survival of your information systems.

5. *Monitor and audit administrative work.* Administrators are people: they make mistakes, they have needs and desires, they face temptations, and they are as likely to want to harm systems as any other employee. The difference is that administrators have the power and authority to harm systems easily. Often because an administrator has unlimited privileges, an attacker with administrative credentials or a malicious administrator can prevent operations from being audited or can delete the audit record of his activity by deleting the security log.

The following topics provide the information and guidelines you need to complete most of these tasks.

Note   Evaluating the trustworthiness of administrators is beyond the scope of this book, but it must be done. It is a topic for the legal and human resources departments of your organization to pursue. You can, however, protect your network from untrustworthy administrators by ensuring sound security principles are practiced, by designing an Active Directory infrastructure that meets your autonomy and isolation needs, and by auditing the actions of administrators. Auditing is discussed in Chapter 9.

Common Vulnerabilities in Network Management

> **Security Alert**   Remember that an administrative account is powerful—so powerful that its owner can use it to destroy a system as easily as she can use it to manage a system.

Common vulnerabilities introduced by administrators include:

- Accidentally making the organization's data available to those who should not have access.

- Using a weak password that allows the administrator account to be easily compromised.

- Inadvertently introducing a Trojan horse or virus into the system through ordinary tasks, such as checking e-mail and surfing the Web, performed while logged on as an administrator.

- Reducing security in favor of productivity or performance. When seeking a solution for poor network performance, for example, an administrator might turn off auditing or unassign IPSec policies.

- Sharing the administrator accounts so that there is no accountability for administrative actions.

- Giving the wrong administrative rights to the wrong people.

- Allowing administrator credentials to be captured when performing administrative tasks over the LAN, the WAN, or the Internet.

- Allowing the administrative session to be captured when remote administration is performed. If this happens, the attacker gains information that will assist him in compromising systems or deducing something about the network or the organization.

- Inadvertently deleting or modifying company or system data.

What Are Isolation and Autonomy?

Autonomy is a situation in which external control is possible even while local control is the way things are done. *Isolation* means that there is a clear, precise boundary and that there is no inherent connection or way for administrators from one network to administer another. This section provides guidelines for applying isolation and autonomy to administrative roles and provides several examples.

Guidelines for Applying Isolation and Autonomy to Administrative Roles

Defining administrative roles within organizations is difficult. One of the first decisions to make is how far authority will extend. In some organizations, centralized control is the norm. Although delegation of administrative authority might be applied, central administrative roles assign, supervise, and monitor all administrative functions. In other organizations, a more decentralized approach is used. The organization might be logically divided and different parts given autonomy over the management of their users and computers. Each part administers its own IT infrastructure.

In a decentralized organization, you must determine whether absolute isolation is required or whether simple autonomy is OK. That is, can each separate group, given its own sphere of management, accept that control over its function can be usurped by headquarters? Can the group work within such a framework, or do they need to exist in isolation? Must there be no connection that could possibly allow intrusion upon their administrative authority? In some organizations, this isolation is imperative. There might also be legal reasons that require it.

Examples: Where Autonomy and Isolation Can Be Used

Some examples of where isolation might be required include military organizations, Web or application hosting scenarios, businesses for which a public directory must be separated from a private directory, and organizations—such as financial organizations—that operate in international venues. For example, the Active Directory directory services for a company that provides investment banking and stock market analysis might need to be isolated to ensure that no information flows between the users or administrators of each group.

Autonomy might be used by corporations that are centrally managed and by smaller organizations in which there is one administrative management function. For example, while domain administrators in these scenarios might maintain the security configuration of all computers in the domain by using Group Policy, they might grant organization unit (OU) administrators the ability to further secure computers in the OU that they manage. The OU administrators would have autonomy but not isolation.

What Are Security Boundaries?

Security boundaries are borders beyond which security authority does not extend. Strictly speaking, no security principal, right, or privilege that is valid on one side of the border is valid on the other. Security boundaries provide isolation of administrative authority.

Examples: Security Boundaries

One example of a security boundary is the boundary between two Microsoft Windows Server 2003 computers that are not joined in a domain. The local Administrator account on one of these computers has no rights on the other. For one person to administer both servers, she would need an account in each of the local account databases and have the proper administrative privileges assigned. If both servers are file servers and a single user must be given access to files on both servers, the user must be given access to two separate accounts: one on each server

Another example of a security boundary is the boundary between two Windows Server 2003 or Windows 2000 forests. As in the single-server example, an administrator from one forest has no administrative authority in the other forest. Users from one forest have no access to resources in the other.

Non-Examples: These Things Are Not Security Boundaries

Although domains within a forest have their own separate account databases, two things prevent these domains from being security boundaries and from providing isolation:

- There are enterprise accounts in the forest that have rights and privileges in all domains in the forest. Examples of these groups are the Enterprise Admins group and the Schema Admins group.

- Because of the tight coupling between domains in the forest (that is, all domains in the forest trust all other domains in the forest), it might be possible, although it would be difficult, for a domain administrator to obtain elevated privileges in another domain.

Likewise, if administrative authority over organizational units (OUs) within a domain is assigned to a distinct group within an organization, this does not provide isolation. Enterprise Admins and Domain Admins can administer these OUs as well. Domains in a forest and OUs within domains can provide autonomy. That is, administration of each domain, OU, or both can be assigned to a distinct group of users. By agreement, those with the ability to administer these subunits, Enterprise Admins and Domain Admins, don't administer them.

However, if isolation is required, you must either keep servers apart from Windows Server 2003 or Windows 2000 domain membership or deploy multiple forests. Both techniques can be used within an organization as needed.

What Is a Security Policy Boundary?

Understanding the limits of administrative privilege is a necessary part of designing secure administration. When the operative scope of administrative power is understood, either the necessary monitoring controls can be used or a decision can be made to design a different infrastructure. However, much can be done by using a security policy, even though its boundary is not absolute. A *security policy boundary* defines an area (such as a domain or an OU) where a security policy will be enforced.

In many organizations, where autonomy is the requirement, a single forest with multiple domains might be adequate. The domain, however, must be seen as a security policy boundary, not as a security boundary. As described previously, domains in a forest cannot be totally isolated from intrusion by an administrator of other domains. This means that, by *policy*, domain segregation and autonomy can be structured, but there are technical means to subvert that authority. Unlike the forest, the domain boundaries in a Windows Server 2003 forest can be easily crossed.

Examples: Security Policy Boundaries

Domains have distinct security policy boundaries. The domain has a distinct Group Policy infrastructure—that is, Group Policy objects (GPOs) linked to domains and to OUs within domains have no influence over users and computers in other domains. There are even distinct parts of the GPO that are operative over the entire domain. The three policies that make up Account policies —the Password policy, the Kerberos policy, and the Account Lockout policy—are domain-wide policies, and each domain can maintain its own Account policy. Similarly, user rights within the domain are set at the domain level and do not affect the users in other domains.

Exam Tip   In most organizations, the one security requirement that will provoke the creation of multiple domains is the need for more than one password policy. If resources in some area of the organization require different password lengths—for example, to enforce a higher degree of security—separate domains will be necessary (unless you build custom application filters that require certain accounts to use passwords of longer length).

Off the Record   Security policy boundaries can also be created by another type of security policy—the written security policy of an organization. This type of policy specifies the security that the organization wants, but it might not be technically possible to implement it. One of my customers, for example, specifies that the Finance group's computers and users can be administered only by approved Finance group employees. The company created an OU named Finance and a Windows group named FinMan. It placed appropriate users in this group and granted full control of the Finance OU to the FinMan group. However, the company had to live with just obtaining an agreement from domain administrators to leave it alone, as there is no absolute, technical way to prevent a domain administrator from administering the OU.

How to Establish Administrative Security Boundaries

After you understand where security boundaries are and the difference between a concrete security boundary—such as the single server or the forest—and the policy boundary—such as that provided by using domains and OUs—designing the administrative model for security boundaries is straightforward.

To establish administrative security boundaries:

1. *Determine where there is need for isolation*. For each isolation need, create a forest, or if the need is small, create a single server.

2. *Determine where there is a need for autonomy:*

   ❑ Where autonomy is sufficient, or centralized control is required, create a single forest.

   ❑ In a centralized structure, when one account policy is sufficient, create one domain wherever possible. If more than one password policy is required, create multiple domains.

   ❑ In a decentralized structure, use OUs where possible instead of separate domains. Use separate domains where a high amount of decentralization is necessary.

3. *Review the security design to make sure it meshes with the performance design*. For example, requiring separate domains might not be necessary for security reasons, but network architects might have determined that, because of replication and the physical design of the network, having multiple domains is the best way to go. You will have to consider what implications this strategy has for security by reviewing any additional autonomy this approach gives administrators. An example of increased autonomy is the ability to create a distinct password policy.

Important   In an organization where control is decentralized, separating administrative control by using OUs instead of domains is most preferable because it reduces the administrative and financial overhead that establishing multiple domains would require. Where there is a large amount of decentralization, separate domains might be acceptable to provide groups the autonomy they want. But even in a decentralized organization, other factors—such as internal politics or the need to meet military, financial, or legal requirements—might require that you create separate domains or separate forests.

Guidelines for Reducing the Attack Surface

Reducing the attack surface can be accomplished in many ways, Here are a few:

- Using secure installation practices
- Using automated deployments
- Disabling unnecessary services

Guidelines for Securing Installation Practices

Secure installation practices will ensure that a server starts its productive life in an uncompromised state and that it presents the smallest attack surface possible.

> **Tip** Many security guidelines can be reinforced by creating and using an appropriate Group Policy infrastructure. However, servers should begin life already secure, and Group Policy should be used to keep them that way.

Follow these guidelines for securing installation practices:

- **Provide a secure place and infrastructure for server installation.** Servers should be installed in a physically secure area where access can be controlled. Only the people who are responsible for installing the servers should be able to physically access the server during installation. If installation is provided via network practice, such as by using Remote Installation Services (RIS) or Automated Deployment Services (ADS), a separate network should be provided—one that has no connection with the production network and absolutely no connection with the Internet. The server should not be physically moved until you have completed the initial installation and additional hardening.

- **Install only processes that are necessary for the server to function in its role.** The default installation of Windows Server 2003 does reduce the number of items installed (for example, IIS is not installed by default). However, each organization should inspect the default installation and review the necessity for each item that is installed by default. Is it necessary, for example, to install Notepad, WordPad, accessibility applications, Windows Media Player, and the calculator?

- **Do not install unnecessary services, or at least disable them.** Windows Server 2003 does not install many services that are unnecessary for server function, and it disables many more. You can modify the default security templates used at installation to modify the list of what is not installed and to modify what is installed but enabled or disabled. Guidelines specific to determining necessary services are provided in the section "Guidelines for Determining Which Services to Disable" later in this lesson. Guidelines for determining and implementing a security policy that implements this practice according to server role are discussed in Chapter 8, "Designing Security by Server Role."

- **Apply current service packs and critical security updates at the time of installation.** No new operating system installation is complete until service packs and security updates have been installed. The application of service packs and updates can be automated, just as installation can be. Even if a network solution for updating services is available in the production network, it is not a sound security practice to allow a new server on the production network before it has been updated. Always assume that attack code is available for announced vulnerabilities and might have penetrated the production network at any time. If no vulnerable servers are present on the network, however, the presence of the code will not mean it has successfully compromised a server.

- **Apply a security lockdown configuration.**   Everything required to lock down the system—such as security options, IPSec policies, user rights, file and registry permissions, and so on—should be configured before any server joins the production network. A discussion about determining what items should be locked down by server role is presented in Chapter 8.

- **Apply any required Internet access controls on your firewall to support the needs of the server you are installing.**   If the server manages content that is accessible via the Internet or via partner networks, any access to the server should be configured on the firewall for the server, not simply configured by designating access to the internal network via the required ports. Adding this new server might require a new firewall policy or an extension of the old policy to include this server.

Security Considerations Associated with Automated Deployments

Automated deployment is an excellent way to ensure standardization of installation and to provide quick and secure deployments, because the process of lockdown and provisioning with service packs and necessary updates is automated. However, there are factors that must be considered:

- **Initial states of bare metal deployment using DHCP and PXE are not authenticated.**   *Bare metal deployment* using Dynamic Host Configuration Protocol (DHCP) and Pre-boot Execution Environment (PXE) is the process whereby an operating system is installed on a new computer—a computer that has not previously had an operating system installed on it. To ensure that only authorized individuals and computers are installed and deployed, use a deployment network interface on a dedicated management network.

- **Communication between Automated Deployment Services (ADS) and the ADS controller can use a public key infrastructure (PKI) and Secure Sockets Layer (SSL) authentication to create private out-of-band management communication channels.**   This will ensure only authorized communication takes place during the deployment.

- **The ADS controller service uses the security context of a system service, which has the equivalent access to a local administrator.**   On managed devices, the ADS agent is installed by using the local machine Administrator account, which can be changed to any user with authority to run application and scripts for ADS jobs. If scripts must be run from network shares, the account must have access to network. The use of a privileged account is necessary to perform the functions of the install.

- **If an automated installation practice is incorrectly devised, its insecure practices will be perpetuated across all servers.**   The process of automated installation isn't what makes a server secure from the start, the actual configuration devised for the automated installation does that. If the configuration is insecure, all computers will have the same insecurity. If, for example, permission settings on files, folders, and registry keys are weakened in the default security template that is applied, servers will be less secure. Or, for example, if the setting that disallows LAN Manager (LM) authentication by default is changed to allow it, the weaker, LM password hashes might be present in the account database, making passwords easier to crack.

- **Automated installation scripts must be constantly reviewed.**   New vulnerabilities are discovered all the time, and scripts should seek to protect new computers against these vulnerabilities. New patches must be added to the list, and new security configuration will then be necessary.

Guidelines for Determining Which Services to Disable

With Windows Server 2003, many services are not installed or are disabled by default. Instead of installing a service by default under the assumption that users might someday want to use it, Windows Server 2003 is designed to assume that if users want to use a service, they will recognize that they need to install or enable it. This approach will cause people concerned with security to weep with relief, but it might cause others frustration as they attempt to determine what must be enabled to get something to work.

Follow these guidelines for determining which services can be disabled:

- **Know which services are used to do what.**   To determine what a service does and what happens if you disable it, see Chapter 7, "System Services," of the Threats and Countermeasures Guide (*http://www.microsoft.com/technet/treeview /default.asp?url=/technet/security/topics/hardsys/tcg/tcgch07.asp*).

- **Group services into three categories.**   The three categories are as follows:

  - ❑ Services that are needed for minimal server operations. Start with the default list that is enabled when a server is installed, and then whittle the list down.

  - ❑ Services that are needed for a server to perform a specific role. You will have many lists here.

  - ❑ Services that might or might not be needed, depending on which administrative tools are used. For example, the Remote Procedure Call service is required, as is the Remote Registry Service, if Microsoft Security Baseline Analyzer will be used to remotely scan servers for vulnerabilities.

- **List access requirements for services.**   ACLs on services should be adjusted to prevent start-up settings (automatic, manual, disabled) from being changed by anyone except for a small group of administrators.

- **Put changes in security templates, apply them during installation, and periodically use Group Policy.**   A security template is used during the installation process. The default for a new server is defltsv.inf. If the automated install is used, or if the network install installs from the installation files, this defltsv.inf file can be adjusted to meet a more stringent security policy and can be used during the installation.

If an automated update process starts with an image of an installed server or otherwise uses a preconfigured server as its base, security templates should be developed that implement the organization's security policy and can be applied to the server used as the image base.

Practice: Documenting the Process of Creating a Secure Installation

In this practice, you will document the things that a secure automated installation would need to do. To do this, answer the questions that follow. If you are unable to answer a question, review the lesson materials and try the question again. You can find answers to the questions in the "Questions and Answers" section at the end of this chapter.

Tip   The process does not require that you detail the steps to automatically install Windows Server 2003. Instead, list the steps that need to be automated. Begin by thinking of the things that are necessary to securely install a locked-down Windows 2003 server, and then group this information into broad steps that an automated installation would have to perform.

1. What are the steps in the process of creating a secure installation?

2. Where possible, list a security benefit of taking the steps you have listed.

_____

_____

_____

_____

_____

_____

_____

_____

_____

_____

_____

_____

_____

_____

_____

_____

_____

3. What is the benefit of producing a secure and secured automated installation?

_____

_____

_____

Lesson 2: Designing Secure Administration Practices

Designing secure administration practices is not that complex. It consists of applying sound security practices to the administrative process. Some of these principles are the same principles you would use to secure any kind of access (for example, applying the principle of least privilege and giving an administrator only the access she needs to do her job). Other principles are incorporated because of the type of access an administrator has. For example, securing all administrative communications between the administrator workstation and the server is important and should be the rule. However, applying that rule across the entire network—securing communications between all client and server access—is not necessary and might create more problems than it solves.

After this lesson, you will be able to

- Explain the process for securing administration practices.
- Reduce privileged group membership.
- Protect administrative systems.
- Protect PDAs used for administration.
- Secure administrative channels.
- Design division of management duties.
- Design secure administration practices.

Estimated lesson time: 60 minutes

The Process of Securing Administration Practices

The process of securing administration practices is as follows:

1. Reduce privileged group membership.

2. Protect administrative systems.

3. Protect PDAs used for administration.

4. Secure administrative channels.

5. Design division of management duties.

6. Design secure administration practices, including:

   ❑ Work practices for administrators

   ❑ Practices for securing the use of administrative tools

   ❑ Practices for remote administration

The following topics present the guidelines and procedures for completing these tasks.

How to Reduce Privileged Group Membership

Privileged groups are groups that have more access and authority than ordinary users. They might have these privileges by default or because they are assigned them via group policy, delegation of authority, or direct manipulation of resource ACLs.

> **Note**   The designation "administrative" group is not used on purpose. It is the assignment of privilege that designates a privileged group, not the artificial nomenclature of *admin* or *administrator*. It is possible in Windows Server 2003 to create a user group and assign it enough privileges and access so that, for all practical purposes, there is no right, privilege, or point of access the group does not have. Managing these groups is just as important as managing groups that are easily recognized as being privileged, such as Administrators, Enterprise Admins, and Schema Admins. The first thing that can be done to manage them is to reduce their membership.

To reduce privileged group membership:

1. Make a list of privileged groups. Don't forget to search among all group definitions to find such groups.

2. Rank groups by the amount and range of privilege and access they have. If you know who has the most power, you can concentrate on these groups first to obtain the most benefit the quickest.

3. Identify membership, and determine which members really need to be in the group. You must determine the following:

   ❏ Who has ownership of the group—that is, who tells IT who should be in the group?

   ❏ What is the group's procedure for determining membership? Is its security sound? For example: Do they carefully consider whether the proposed member really requires access to the resources the group can use? Do they determine whether an individual has the right to the privilege the group can exercise? Or do they just put someone in a group because that person has asked to be there?

   You might have to work with the owners of the group to help them understand when they should and should not be granting memberships.

4. Be especially careful when examining IT groups with administrative privileges. Do all members really need to be there? Do memberships represent the breaking of other security principles, such as separation of duties or the principle of least privilege?

5. Examine local Administrator groups. A common practice in many organizations is to assign all user accounts to be members of the local Administrators group on their desktop system. This practice has security implications both for that computer and for the domain. A local Administrator account can be used, for example, to find the

domain credentials of a domain service account, and then the credentials could be used to penetrate and compromise other domain computers. The reasons for this type of local Administrator group membership practice are many, and most reasons have no basis in fact or can be eliminated by using other techniques. You will have to investigate these reasons, but you can reduce, if not eliminate, this practice and make your network more secure.

6. Determine who can manage groups and accounts with administrative access. Providing administrative privileges should be carefully considered so that those given power to reset passwords or otherwise manage accounts can manage only specific types of accounts. Help Desk operators, for example, should not be able to manage the accounts of Domain administrators.

How to Protect Administrative Systems

Administrative systems are computer systems that are used by administrators to administer other computers. Typically, administrative systems are domain member Windows XP or Windows 2000 computers, but they can also be Personal Digital Assistants (PDAs), Windows Server 2003 computers, or other devices on the network. The steps to secure Windows administrative systems go beyond the hardening efforts that should be applied to all computers on the network.

To protect Windows administrative systems:

1. *Develop a security template that is specific for the computer role.* Include items that are developed for highly secure desktop computer roles.

2. *Provide physical security.* Administrative systems should exist in limited access areas. Only approved administrators should be able to access these areas. Systems should be locked to prevent their removal from the area. Remove floppy and CD-Rom drives to prevent possible disk-based attacks. If other physical security is good, you might decide that this step is unnecessary. As for all guidelines, you must evaluate the potential threats and your organization's risk tolerance.

3. *Provide smart card logon for these systems.* Smart card logon is a good security practice for the entire network. However, providing smart card logon is a large undertaking that requires additional expense. Providing smart cards for IT administrators and hardware for their administrative stations requires less work to implement and provides a lot of security for the investment.

   An additional benefit is that you can, to some extent, also prevent administrators from using systems other than their workstations for administration. This is possible because you can require that their accounts use a smart card, and not all computers will have the necessary hardware to provide smart card access. Be aware that this is not an insurmountable impediment—adding a single smart card reader that can plug into a universal serial bus (USB) port or serial port can be done relatively cheaply.

4. *Use IP security protocol filters to restrict the ingress and egress of packet types.* Using protocol filters provides protection for attacks that might use known ports. It can also prevent a compromised system from attacking other uncompromised systems on the network.

Guidelines for Protecting PDAs Used for Administration

PDAs can be used to administer Windows Server 2003 via a connection to terminal services. Unfortunately, there is no way to administer a PDA that is comparable to the steps that can be taken for administering via Windows desktop systems. PDAs cannot join the domain, for example, and therefore cannot be controlled via Group Policy. There are, however, things that can and should be done to secure this form of administration. Follow these guidelines for protecting PDAs used for administration:

- **At a minimum, use the power-on password provided by the PDA.** This password facility is not turned on by default, and studies show that few people turn it on. Although password protecting the PDA provides only weak security, it is far better than having no password protection at all. If sensitive information, such as a listing of accounts and passwords, is stored on the PDA, the power-on password might delay the attacker long enough to change passwords that could be exposed if the device is stolen.

- **Consider other products that extend authentication, including RSA tokens, biometrics, and other devices.** Some of these, if authentication fails, will destroy all data on the PDA and return it to factory condition.

> **Note** Some models of the Hewlett Packard Pocket PC provide a built-in fingerprint scanner that can be used for authentication. Once enabled, if an attempt at authentication fails, the PDA is returned to factory condition. That is, all software is refreshed on the system, but any personalization and data is destroyed.

- **Use an encryption product.** Many types of encryption products are available; some extend their charter by requiring validated logon within a short period of time. When the time period expires, the entire database on the PDA is destroyed.

- **Label the PDA.** Subscribe to one of the services that will provide a phone number to be used if the PDA is found. This, of course, works only if the finder is honest. However, hundreds of lost PDAs are turned into the Lost and Found departments of taxicab companies and airports but are never claimed. These companies do search items for phone numbers and make the necessary calls. If, however, there is no identifying information, no one can be called.

- **Physically protect the PDA**. Prevent PDA loss and theft by keeping it in a safe place when you're not using it. Locked drawers make good temporary locations. Use safes when staying in hotels. When carrying a PDA, keep it within a larger item that makes it harder to lose or to have stolen. For example, put the PDA in a locking briefcase, a purse or satchel that zips shut (as opposed to ones that hang open), or belt-attached hard cases that must be unsnapped or unzipped to remove the PDA.

- **Provide a VPN client, and use it for all connections used for administration.** PDA clients often expose passwords in clear text, or data can be easily captured.

- **Store as little confidential information on the PDA as possible.** Do not use the PDA as a storage place for account and password information.

- **Protect against rogue synchronizations.** Ensure that synchronizing of data between the PDA and desktop is linked to a specific desktop and that validation is provided.

- **Use antivirus protection.** To date, there are few PDA-specific viruses. That situation could change rapidly. In addition, a virus or Trojan horse could be planted on the PDA and transferred to the network when the PDA is synchronized to the administrator's station. Ensure that antivirus agents on the PDA and on the administrative station are up to date and in operation.

How to Secure Administrative Channels

Administrative channels are the communication connections that exist between administrative workstations and servers. If administrative sessions are captured, valuable information might be discovered. It is imperative that you secure administrative channels. To secure administrative channels:

1. *Use a VPN for remote administrative access that requires a connection from outside the network.* For example, use a VPN if administration of servers at a branch location is accomplished via WAN or Internet connection.

2. *Use a VPN for wireless administration.* Few wireless networks have adequate protection. Chapter 12, "Designing Security for Wireless Networks," establishes some guidelines for securing them. Even so, take no chances with administrative task information—secure the wireless connection via a VPN.

3. *Protect LAN administrative channels by using IPSec policies.* Ensure that administrative connections authenticate, preferably using certificates. Both Kerberos and certificate authentication ensure the identification of servers by more than IP address, and IPSec policies should require data encryption.

4. *On the server side, restrict connection to and use of specific services to appropriate administrative groups.* For example, if the only reason for running the remote registry service is to allow administrators to manage the server across the LAN, protect write access to registry keys. Give this access only to specific administrative groups. In this way, you can provide defense in depth—first by limiting registry changes to authorized administrators, and then backing it up with step 3, the use of IPSec policies.

You might be able to further restrict this type of connection if the ports used are made available only for administrative use. For example, the network configuration allowing file sharing might be needed only to allow remote administration. If this is so, use an IPSec policy similar to the one defined in Section III, "Creating a Security Design for Management and Maintenance of the Network," to protect the use of NetBIOS ports, and restrict port access to those machines dedicated to administrators.

Guidelines for Designing a Division of Management Duties

The objective of dividing management duties is to split administration functions that are dependent on each other and to reduce the administrative authority of administrators. *Dependent administrative functions* are functions of administration that can be split into two parts. For the job to be completed, both operations are necessary. Reducing administrative authority reduces the impact any single administrator can have and, by extension, lessens the impact on the network if an administrator's account is compromised. The following sections describe the guidelines for designing a division of management duties.

Split Dependent Functions to Improve Security

By splitting dependent functions, the risk of compromise and fraud is reduced. For example, if programmers have administrative authority in a separate network and only user privileges on the production network, the opportunity for the introduction of programmer-created malicious code on the production network is lessened. This statement is true because all code must be installed by production network administrators, who are different employees than programmers. While an administrator might not be inspecting code for malware (malicious software), he might be able to make the connection between the introduction of malware and the recent installation of new code. He knows who provided the code, and thus the investigation can begin. Accountability for actions is provided and should be a deterrent. If programmers have full administrative authority on all systems, an unethical programmer might introduce malicious code and not be discovered and held accountable.

Divide Administrative Duties

Splitting some administrative functions typically reduces the administrative authority of an individual, but other actions can do this as well. For example, when computer and user accounts are collected under OUs, the administration of the OU can be delegated to a user group of responsible people. This group will have control only over the OU and will have no powers in the domain or elsewhere in the forest, thus lessening the damage they might be able to do. In addition, their control over the OU can be restricted; they do not have to be given full control.

What Is the Difference Between a Data Administrator and a Service Administrator?

One of the primary modes of limiting administrative authority in a Windows forest is by splitting administrative duties between data administrators and service administrators. Data administrators are those who manage user accounts, computer accounts, printers, databases, and so forth. They will be assigned the administration of an OU, for example. Service administrators manage the infrastructure of the Active Directory network. They will be members of Domain Admins and Enterprise Admins.

Service administrators, because of their membership in domain and enterprise administrative groups, will have the authority to manipulate the data managed by data administrators. In this sense, they can also be data administrators. However, they should not exercise this authority except where necessary to correct improper data administration functions or to manage other service administrators and service administrator workstations. Data administrators can be prevented from administering network infrastructure services—that is, from performing the role of service administrators. Both types of administrative work should be monitored, and any attempts at misuse of authority should be investigated.

Protect Service Administrator Accounts

Although data administrators manage user and computer accounts, they should not be given authority over service administrator accounts or computers. Service administrators will have to be responsible for managing their own data. To protect service administrator accounts:

1. Create a top-level OU to be used for management of service administrator accounts and their computer accounts.

2. Place the computer accounts of service administrators in the OU.

3. Place the user accounts of service administrators in this OU.

4. Establish an account or group that will be responsible for the management of this OU, and provide them that control over the OU. Remove the ability of other administrative groups to exercise this type of control over the OU. Of course, service administrators might have the ability to take control of the OU and grant themselves this privilege. However, if you audit and look for these attempts, you can correct the situation.

5. Create a security baseline for computers in this OU, and apply it by using Group Policy. Include in this baseline and GPO the IPSec policy discussed previously for protection of administrative channels.

6. Create a security baseline for users in this OU, and apply it by using Group Policy.

Implement the Principle of Delegation of Authority

Default administrative groups can be used to implement service administrator practice, but they are not extensive enough to provide groups and appropriate responsibilities for data administrators. Instead, you should follow the practice of creating custom groups and providing them with the rights, privileges, and permissions that are necessary to do their job.

This practice, known as delegation of administrative duties, is not new. In the past, however, it often meant too much privilege was given and that written policy, not technical control, was the barrier to misuse of authority. In most cases, this worked fine. Trusted employees were given a job to do and didn't realize the power they really had, or understanding it, did not abuse it because they had a sense of what was proper or they feared being caught. The role of help desk operator illustrates this perfectly. Help desk operators are almost always required to be able to reset passwords and unlock accounts. In the past, they might have been given full administrative access so that they could perform these tasks. Now, instead of giving them full administrative privileges, you can delegate the rights to perform password and account resets by using the Delegation of Control Wizard. This tool can be used in many cases to provide the appropriate access required to complete an administrative role definition.

Guidelines for Designing Secure Administration Practices

This topic explains why it is important to design secure administration practices, explains the design process, and presents guidelines and recommendations for designing secure administrative practices, including securing the way administrators perform work practices, use of administrative tools, and practice remote administration. Many of the guidelines are best practices that should be added to any list. Others may need to be adapted according to your organization's security policy.

Why Design Secure Administration Practices?

Where sound, secure management practices are required by policy, enforced where possible by technical controls, and monitored for compliance, there is less chance of security breaches being the result of accidental or malicious malpractice. First, because the rules are written down, everyone can see what is proper and permitted. There is less room for accidental overstepping of administrative authority. Second, because there is less room for accidental overstepping of authority, improper action can be observed and reported where previously it might have been considered normal. Finally, by having rules, there is something to judge or monitor against.

The Design Process: Designing Secure Administration Practices for Administrators

To design secure administration practices for administrators:

1. *Identify administrative practices and group into common types.* Examples of task types include:

   ❑ Logon

   ❑ Remote access to servers and workstations

   ❑ Use of administrative workstation

   ❑ Use of administrative tools

2. *Determine ways in which you can make the practice more secure.* The guidelines in the following section suggest and explain ways to do so.

3. *Determine whether the proposed new way of working meets the security needs of the organization.* Every organization's approach to security and need for security are different. You would not expect security to be managed the same at a bank as it is in a small retail store. Administrative practices in a bank might require implementation of a majority of practices outlined below, while for a small retail store, strong passwords, Group Policy, and resource ACLs might be enough.

4. *Establish a list of secure work practices.* This is a list of practices that remain after applying the organization's security needs and security policy.

Guidelines for Designing Secure Work Practices for Administrators

The following recommendations and guidelines can serve as a starting place for designing secure work practices for administrators:

- **Use administrative accounts only for administration.**   Each user with elevated privileges should have an account that is to be used for those administrative practices and not for ordinary user activity such as reading e-mail.

  Administrators should log on using their nonadministrative account and use the runas command as needed.

- **End privileged sessions as soon as the administrative function is accomplished.**   Leaving a session operational longer than is necessary increases the risk that it might accidentally be used by someone else who might introduce malware or modify something. It also increases risk because, should the administrative session be left unattended, an unauthorized individual could perform administrative functions.

- **Administer critical, high-security servers directly from the console.**   The risk of performing these tasks remotely might be too high for some sensitive servers.

- **Always use administrative workstations for administration.** These stations are locked down and protected, so there is less risk of introducing malware or of exposing sensitive systems or information about sensitive systems than when using unprotected workstations. Furthermore, accounts with administrative privileges should be used only to log on to computers that have known trust states.

- **Never reduce security for convenience.** Security might mean extra work is involved in the administrative process, but security is established for a reason and should not be reduced without serious consideration. The competing pressures of demands for increased performance, efficiency, ease of access, and many others can tempt the administrator to change security practices. For example, persistently storing passwords for Web applications might be convenient, but it also introduces a new threat to the network.

- **When possible, take systems offline to troubleshoot them.** If you cannot take the system offline, take steps to reduce the risks associated with changes that might be made or tools that might be used to troubleshoot these systems. Never log on to a computer that you believe might have been compromised while it is attached to the network. You cannot trust a computer that has been compromised.

- **Do not add troubleshooting tools to servers.** Where possible, use external tools. Where tools must be loaded directly on the server, remove tools after problems are resolved.

- **Use administrative tools that can be secured, and use their security features.** If tools cannot be secured, use additional security practices to secure their operations. For example, use IPSec to secure telnet sessions.

Real World   Student Steals Administrator Password

A few months ago, I was doing some work for a public school system. The LAN administrator was concerned because it appeared as if a student had obtained his password and used it to attempt to change a grade. The administrator couldn't figure out how the student did this because he never wrote his password down or used it when students were present.

When questioned, the administrator told me that he had to frequently work on the student lab computers because students are constantly attempting and sometimes succeeding to add software, change settings, and so forth. To make some changes, he had to log on using his administrative account. At this point, his face brightened and then twisted with a strange smile. "Keystroke logger," he remarked. Later that week, the administrator told me that when he asked the student why he used a keystroke logger and recorded the administrator password, the student confessed and produced the device used. The administrator now monitors the lab computers for evidence of tampering and manages them remotely.

Guidelines for Securing the Use of Administrative Tools

Many administrative tools are snap-ins for the Microsoft Management Console (MMC). Other administrative tools are special administrative programs designed for a specific program or service. Still others are command-line tools that are either installed by default, provided as part of the support tools collection on the Windows Server 2003 installation disk, or provided as part of the Windows Server 2003 Resource Kit. Part of securing administrative practices is to secure the use of administrative tools. This consists of making sound choices in the tools that are used, in using their security features appropriately, and in adding security where necessary. The following sections describe the guidelines for securing the use of administrative tools.

Secure Administrative Tools   In addition to specifying practices for securing individual tools, you should take the following precautions:

- **Install tools only when necessary.**   If a tool is not necessary and not installed by default, don't install it. Think of auxiliary tools as you would the wide array of services that might be used on a specific computer.

- **Restrict access by setting Access Control Entries (ACEs).**   Where tools must exist, limit their use by controlling access. Reduce access to a particular tool to only those who need to use it.

- **Disable or restrict features of tools.**   Understand the risk of using specific tool parts, and reduce the risk by disabling unnecessary parts if possible.

- **Control access by disallowing remote access.**   Performing administration from the console reduces the risks involved with those activities because no information can be gained, nor credentials captured, over the network. In addition, remote access provides a way for an attacker to attempt to compromise the system or some part of it, and doing so is easy if the attacker has the proper credentials. If an attacker must go to a datacenter, however, he will have a harder time using these credentials without being discovered.

- **Provide a secure communication channel.**   Requiring SSL or IPSec to protect communications between the administrator's workstation and the server will prevent many types of attacks.

- **Specify that all administration either take place at the console, via a hardened and trusted computer on the LAN, or via a VPN.**   Making a distinction between internal computers and external computers or between specially prepared systems and those that are not can reduce the risks associated with administration.

- **Use administrative accounts only for administration.**   Use runas to temporarily authenticate using the privileged account to run administrative tools.

- **Don't change default security settings on system directories and registry keys without thorough knowledge.**   For example, the HKLM system registry subtree is protected because, by default, only members of the Administrators group in the Builtin folder and local system account have Full Control of this subtree. This is appropriate. Providing privileged access to other groups reduces the security. If this subtree is compromised, some resource might fail to start or some other problem might occur.

- **Use software restriction policies.**   Software restriction policies can prevent the use of tools and other files, or they can specify explicitly who can use them.

Secure the Use of Specific Tools   In addition to commonsense security restrictions, the requirements for securing many administrative tools are well documented. Examples of securing primary administration tools, as well as some other administration tools, are documented in this section. However, all administrative tools should be examined to find ways to secure their use.

In addition to developing security around specific tools, consider designating the *type* of tool that can be used or developing guidelines around how a tool is used, such as determining use based on where a tool is used from. For example, the use of Microsoft Management Console tools across a firewall would require opening up multiple ports on the firewall and therefore reducing overall network security. An argument can even be made for not using these tools on the LAN and to administer sensitive servers, because doing so requires that more services be enabled on a server and the server can be better secured if these services are not running. Possible alternatives to MMC use might be using terminal services when working remotely, or to require the use of VPNs when administering servers remotely. Using VPNs would obviate the need to open up extensive ports on the firewall.

Secure Administrative Tools That Use MMCs   Many Windows Server 2003 administration tools use the Microsoft Management Console. The most effective way of securing these tools is by limiting access to them. Then, to assist administrators, instead of using default Administrative tools for all administration, develop custom MMCs for use by specific administrative roles. For example, a custom MMC could be devised for administrators of computers in a specific OU. The MMC console could contain the snap-ins that they might use—for example, Computer Management. In this case, the Allow The Selected Computer To Be Changed When Launching From The Command Line check box (shown in Figure 4-1) should be checked to allow the administrator to select the computer to be managed. Permission to use the console can be granted to the user, and permission can be denied on the use of other consoles that are not necessary for this administrator to do her job.

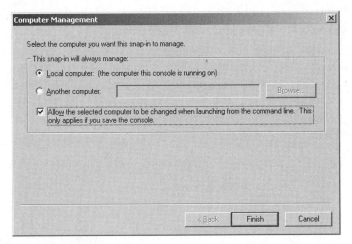

Figure 4-1   Making an MMC flexible

To secure administrative tools that use MMCs:

1. Add only snap-ins the administrator requires to do her job.

2. Reduce administration opportunities provided by this console by deselecting the Add All Extensions check box on the Extensions page of the Add/Remote snap-in page. (See Figure 4-2.)

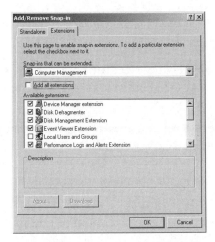

Figure 4-2   Restricting administration choices

3. Change the mode of the MMC console (File, Options, Console, Console mode drop-down box) to User mode; either User Mode – Limited Access, Multiple Windows, or User Mode – Limited Access Single Window. This prevents the user from changing the tools available in the console.

4. Authorize administrative groups to use only specific MMC consoles.

Using Group Policy to Restrict the Use of MMCs

To restrict the use of MMC tools, use Group Policy. Specifically, the User Configuration\Administrative Templates\Windows Components\Microsoft Management Console section of the GPO can be used to designate the Templates that can be used. (See Figure 4-3.)

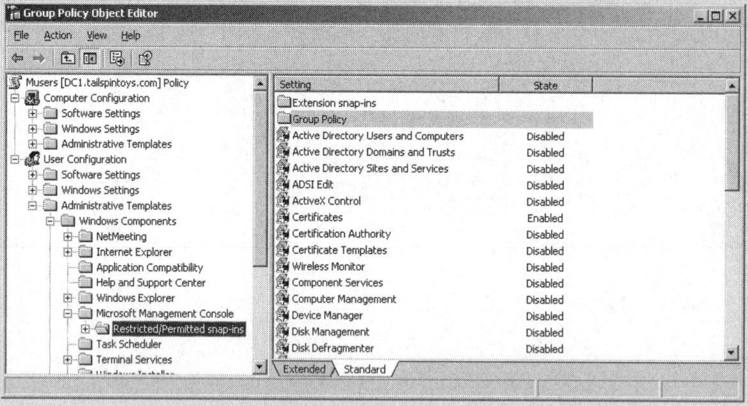

Figure 4-3   Using Group Policy to restrict the use of MMCs

Secure Group Policy Administration   Group Policy is an integral part of security administration. The ability to implement or block Group Policy is a security privilege that should not be given lightly to anyone. To secure Group Policy administration:

- **Restrict membership in the Group Policy Creator Owners group to a limited subset of service administrators.**   Membership in this group enables full administration of Group Policy in the Domain.

- **When decentralization empowers data administrators in the management of OUs, limit administrator's authority over Group Policy.**   When using the Delegation of Control Wizard, instead of providing data administrators with Full Control over their OU, limit them to specific administrative practices. With respect to Group Policy, guidelines for common task choices are as follows:

   ❑ Manage Group Policy Links—Do not give data administrators the ability to remove or add GPO links to their OU.

   ❑ Generate Resultant Set of Policy (Planning)—Do provide this ability if administrators are to be involved in planning new GPOs or if Logging mode cannot be used on all computers that administrators might manage.

   ❑ Generate Resultant Set of Policy (Logging)—Do provide this ability if administrators should troubleshoot GPO applications.

■ **Make custom delegation tasks explicit.**   In addition to the common tasks, custom delegation tasks—including Group Policy administration privileges—can be devised. When custom tasks are devised, they should not be broad; instead, they should be explicit in which objects administrators will manage and, within those objects, the specific things administrators can do. Do not delegate control to objects in the Delegation of Control Wizard by giving the right to control the This Folder, Existing Objects In This Folder, And Creation Of New Objects In This Folder option.

Secure the Administrative Use of Terminal Services   Client access to terminal services in Windows Server 2003 is via the Remote Desktop Connection (RDC). RDC can also be used to connect to a Windows XP Professional computer running the Remote Desktop. The connection provides full access to the file system, ports, printers, audio, and smart card sign on to Windows 2003 from Windows Server 2003, XP Professional, and Windows CE .NET. Additionally, the Remote Desktop Web Connection and Active X control/com object can be used.

What Is Remote Desktop for Administration?

Remote Desktop for Administration is a tool that can be used to administer Windows Server 2003. The Remote Desktop Tool that is provided in Windows XP and for Windows Server 2003 can be used to access a Windows Server 2003 computer and administer it. Terminal services on Windows Server 2003 does not have to be installed to use Remote Desktop for Administration. It is built on the Windows 2000 model of terminal services for administration. Although it works in a similar way, Remote Desktop for Administration can also connect to the "real" console of server. In other words, this type of terminal services session provides the exact same experience as a local console access using the server's keyboard and mouse. Items that were not available via the Windows 2000 terminal services for administration because it ran a virtual session are available when Windows Server 2003 Remote Desktop for Administration is used. To access this console, you run the remote desktop connection with the /console switch. Instead of using the GUI menu, enter **mstsc.exe /console** at the command line or create a remote desktop Web connection page and set the *ConnectToServerConsole* priority.

Remote Desktop for Administration is enabled by default, as can be observed in Figure 4-4. In some cases, where remote administration of a server is not needed, deselect the Allow User To Connect Remotely To This Computer check box.

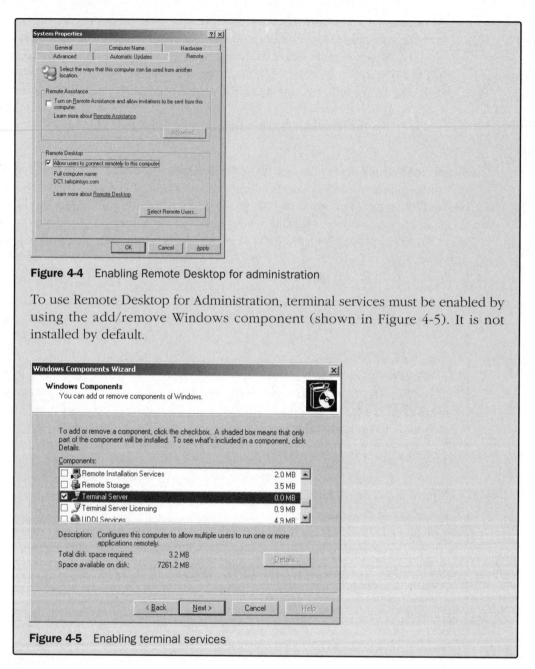

Figure 4-4   Enabling Remote Desktop for administration

To use Remote Desktop for Administration, terminal services must be enabled by using the add/remove Windows component (shown in Figure 4-5). It is not installed by default.

Figure 4-5   Enabling terminal services

To secure terminal services connections of administrators:

■ **Ensure use of the default 128-bit, RC-4 encryption to secure communications between clients and the server.**   Do this by only using clients capable of 128-bit encryption—such as Windows XP Professional and Windows 2000 Professional—and by configuring terminal services to only accept 128-bit connections.

- **If mutual authentication is required, connect to the Terminal Server only after creating a VPN tunnel to the network.** The protocol used for terminal services connections, the Remote Desktop Protocol (RDP), does not have a mechanism for authenticating the server that the client is connecting to. Consequently, an attacker could spoof the Terminal Server to intercept logon credentials.

- **Where required, use FIPS (Federal Information Processing Standard)—compliant encryption.** This choice will use the FIPS encryption algorithms, and it will provide compliance for organizations that require systems to be compliant with FIPS 140-1 (1994) and FIPS 140-2 (2001).

- **Where FIPS is specified, specify that only clients capable of 128-bit encryption can connect.** Figure 4-6 shows how to do this.

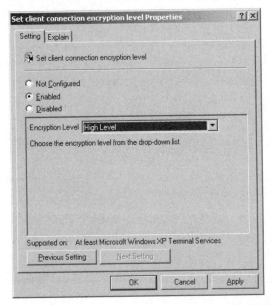

Figure 4-6   Restricting client connections to 128-bit encryption

- **Manage Remote Desktop for Administration and terminal services via Group Policy** Doing so will ensure standardization across all servers.

- **Create a group specifically for the use of Remote Desktop for Administration.** You can split administration of servers by using different groups.

- **Add the appropriate administrative accounts (accounts that are allowed to use terminal services for administration) to the group.** Using this process will allow you to more easily add or remove administrators who should have or no longer need to use the tool.

- **Add the group you have created to the Remote Desktop Users group.** In most cases, if a user is not a member of this group, he will be unable to use terminal services on this computer. The next two guidelines describe how to manage the exceptions.

- **Group Policy Editor can be used to assign user rights to individual users that will allow them to use terminal services without being a member of the Remote Desktop Users group.** An organization should decide which way it will control remote administration and use that method. This decision should be documented, but an audit of who can use Remote Desktop for Administration should require investigation of both methods described above instead of just tracking membership in the Remote Desktop Users group.

- **Remove the Domain Admins group from the local Administrators group, and replace it with the authorized administrators group for the specific server.** Members of the local Administrators group can access the computer remotely whether or not they are members of the Remote Desktop Users group. To ensure that only authorized administrators can access the computer remotely, reduce the membership of the local Administrators group.

What Is Remote Assistance?

Remote Assistance is a utility that allows users to send an invitation or request help with the system they are logged on to. The invitation, if accepted by the recipient, allows access to the system that sent the invitation. Although this might seem similar to Remote Desktop for Administration, remote assistance differs in several respects:

- Remote Assistance requires an invitation. Remote Desktop for Administration can be controlled, but it does not require a local user to send an invitation.

- Both the person sending the invitation and the invitee can see what is being controlled on the local machine. It can be used as a teaching mechanism. Remote Desktop for Administration does not do this.

- The user has a say in decisions made and is prompted to approve the take-over of her systems.

- A password is required to use the invitation. Remote Desktop for Administration requires that the user be an Administrator; Remote Desktop requires the knowledge of a distinct password, which should be passed to the administrator through an alternative medium (for example, over the telephone).

Remote Assistance can be controlled via the system applet properties or by using Group Policy. However, like the Remote Desktop for Administration utility, once Group Policy is in effect, changes cannot be made using system properties. A very sound security practice is to determine whether these models for administration should be used and by whom, and then document the process.

Secure Management of Network Load Balancing   Network load balancing and clusters exist to ensure availability, manage a large load, and provide redundancy. Typically, critical systems—such as firewalls, Web servers, and databases—are connected in this manner. Disturbance of these clustered systems via denial-of-service (DoS) attacks or system compromises can pose a major threat to network stability and security. It is important that they be secured and that sound and secure administrative practices are used.

To secure management of network load balancing:

- **Secure network load balancing (NLB) by leaving remote access to wlbs.exe disabled on all cluster hosts.**   Using wlbs.exe, the NLB control program, remotely is not recommended because of the risks it engenders. Unless wlbs.exe is protected by a firewall that blocks UDP ports 1717 and 2504, the possibility of fraudulent remote control messages reaching the hosts is present. Even on a protected network, local console use of wlbs.exe is preferred.

- **Instead of using wlbs.exe, use the Network Load Balancing Manager (NLM) administration tool.**   You should use this tool because it uses a secure method of communication to access NLB hosts.

- **Use a VPN connection if it is necessary to administer servers remotely.**   Connecting to servers across an untrusted network for administrative purposes presents additional risk. You can mitigate that risk by using a VPN.

- **Do not use the cluster service account to administer the cluster or allow this account to be a member of domain administrators.**   The service account should be a domain account (and it must be the same account on all cluster members), and when assigned, it will automatically be added to the local Administrators group on each cluster member and be given the additional privileges required (for example, the ability to act as part of the operating system, back up files and directories, increase quotas, increase scheduling priority, load and unload device drivers, lock pages in memory, log on as a service, and restore files and directories).

- **Specify a domain group that is allowed to manage the cluster, and put administrators in that group.**   When domain accounts are used for NLB management, Kerberos will be used for authentication. This is a more secure protocol.

- **Restrict access to the quorum disk to the cluster service account and members of the local Administrator group.**   Access to the quorom disk by others is not necessary.

- **At %windir@\syustem32\logfiles\cluster\ClCfgSrv.log, restrict access to the cluster log to cluster administrators and the cluster service account.**   This log has information about the cluster and should not be publicly available. Knowledge of the cluster might provide an attacker the means to successfully attack it.

Secure Administration of SharePoint Team Services   Sharepoint Team Services can be used for the collaborative efforts of groups within the organization. Exposing the content of one group's communications to others, allowing public access to communications, or unauthorized participation can expose critical privileged information. If Web sites are left unprotected, unauthorized individuals might delete them. To secure administration of these services:

- **Secure remote administration of Sharepoint Team Services by using SSL to protect names and passwords.**   Use the *https://sample.microsoft.com:1439 /fpadmdll.dll* to access the URL to connect.

- **Control access to fpadmdll.dll or fpadmcgi.exe.**   This code is used for administration. Use a nonstandard HTTP port for connection to fpadmdll.lll or fpadmcgi.exe. In Windows, by default, a nonstandard port is created for you, but this can be changed. If the extensions are used on UNIX, you must create the administration port. On Windows, don't use IIS to change the port, as this can break the shortcut to the HTML admin pages from the Start menu. Instead, use the setadminport operation:

```
owsadm.exe -o -setadminport -p <port>
```

Secure Administration of SQL Server   Microsoft SQL Server databases can include any type of data. When a SQL Server database is used as part of an e-commerce site, credit card numbers, private customer information, billing information, and thousands of pieces of important and critical information live within the database. Compromise of this system can mean more than just a few hours of downtime while the system is recovered, it can mean substantial loss of money, loss of customer trust, and even legal action. To secure administration of SQL Server:

- **Divide administrative responsibility into administration of the database and administration of the operating system.**   Database administrators should not be responsible for basic operating system maintenance, and network administrators have no business managing a database.

- **Assign a specific custom group as the SQL Server administrators, and remove the SQL logon for the default builtin\administrators group.**   Server administrators might know little about administering SQL Server, and the data stored there might be sensitive. Restricting administrative access to sensitive data is always a good idea.

- **Restrict cmdExec to sysadmin role.**   cmdExec is used by the SQL Server agent to execute Windows command-line applications and scripts. These are often scheduled tasks created by the system administrator.

- **Allow only members of the system administrator role to schedule jobs.**   Prior to the release of Service Pack 3 (SP3) for SQL Server, scheduling by a nonprivileged user was allowed. A nonprivileged user could run privileged commands in scheduled jobs.

■ **Do not install sample databases or unused stored procedures.** Default installations of SQL Server 7.0 and SQL Server 2000 include items such as the sample databases and stored procedures (including command-shell procedures) that could be used to compromise the server. This is another example of minimizing the attack surface.

■ **Always use Windows Authentication.** Because there are many common attacks against SQL Servers because of Mixed Mode authentication and other security weakness associated with SQL authentication, you should always use Windows Authentication for instances of SQL Server.

> **See Also**   For more information about SQL Server security, see the SQLSecurity.com Web site at *http://www.sqlsecurity.com/DesktopDefault.aspx.*

Secure the Administration of IIS   Securing administrative access to Internet Information Services (IIS) should be part of the overall Web site design. To secure administration of IIS:

■ Use IPSec policies to secure administrative connections.

■ Separate the administration of site content from the administration of site configuration. Knowledge necessary for creating and approving site content is different than that needed to ensure the correct configuration and security of the site.

■ Disable anonymous access on the default web IIS Admin Directory.

■ Enable basic authentication over SSL, or enable Windows Authentication.

■ Change the default port used for access to the administrative Web site and use IPSec to restrict access to only administrative computers, or disable the IIS admin site.

Guidelines for Securing Remote Administrative Practices

Remote administrative practices are any administration practices that do not take place at the console. However, some security practices change when the remote administration takes place over the WAN or Internet as opposed to over a local LAN. The risk of interception is higher during these "more" remote adventures, and additional security is required. Therefore, these guidelines are, in general, more applicable to administrative access over untrusted networks. Trust is relative.

Many of the guidelines for securing remote access can be applied to administrators working on the LAN. Follow these guidelines for securing remote administration practices:

■ **Manage IIS or other Web-based administration consoles remotely using SSL.**   SSL can provide authentication of the IIS server so that you know you have the correct server, not a spoofed one. Another benefit is that the communications are secured. No one can use a sniffer to discover credentials.

- **Use a VPN, terminal services, or terminal services over a VPN if access to administrative tools that require MMC is necessary.**   MMC access is not available over the firewall without opening Domain Name System (DNS) and remote procedure call (RPC) ports.

- **Restrict remote access to specific administrative accounts.**   Although some administrators might be restricted to administering from the console, others might be restricted to remote administration. Still others might require both types of access.

Practice: Inspecting Administration Tools and Securing Their Use

In this practice, you will create a list that can be used to inspect any administration tool. To do so, answer the following question. If you are unable to answer the question, review the lesson materials and try the question again. You can find the answer to the question in the "Questions and Answers" section at the end of this chapter.

1. Create a list that can be used to inspect any administration tool. What guidelines do you suggest for securing an administration tool's use?

_____

_____

_____

_____

_____

_____

_____

_____

_____

_____

_____

_____

_____

_____

_____

_____

_____

_____

_____

_____

Lesson 3: Securing Emergency Management Services

In addition to securing basic administration practices, unusual practices should also be considered so that they can be secured. Emergency management services is one of these practices.

After this lesson, you will be able to

- Explain the purpose of Emergency Management Services (EMS) and when to use them.
- Explain what out-of-band management is.
- Explain what an out-of-band infrastructure is.
- Describe the components of EMS.
- Explain the guidelines for securing EMS.

Estimated lesson time: 60 minutes

What Are Emergency Management Services?

Emergency Management Services (EMS) is a new feature in Windows Server 2003 that provides assistance in remote administration. Windows Server 2003 can start and operate without most video card support and, depending on the hardware, without legacy keyboard controllers. If properly equipped, the out-of-band management port (typically the serial port) can support Remote Installation Services (RIS).

Examples: EMS Tasks

An administrator can use EMS to administer a server—even a server without a mouse, keyboard, or display—as if there were a local console connection. She can restart the system and perform system-recovery tasks. Additional examples of recovery tasks that can be performed by using EMS include the following:

- View Stop errors
- Start or reset the server
- Switch between Windows Server 2003 command-prompt channel and Special Administration Console (SAC)
- Change basic input/output system (BIOS) settings
- View power-on self test (POST) information
- Install Windows by using Remote Installation Services (RIS)
- Use Windows Management Instrumentation (WMI), Terminal Services Remote Desktop for Administration, Microsoft Management Console (MMC), Telnet, Windows Script Hosts, and other tools
- Manage the operating system when it is not available via the network

When to Use EMS

EMS is not necessary when a server is functioning normally, but it is invaluable when a server is not functioning normally or when it cannot be reached over the normal network connection. To use EMS without using the normal network connection, EMS must be set up and configured with the appropriate out-of-band hardware (modem, service processor, or terminal concentrator) and be supported by the computer firmware. EMS can be a boot selection configured in boot.ini by using the /ems switch.

> **Note**   Firmware is low-level software, and input/output instructions are stored in read-only memory (ROM). ROM stays intact even when electrical power is removed. This means that firmware redirection, if supported, can be used with a service processor and EMS to manage the server remotely from the POST process to the operating system components initialization.

What Is Out-of-Band Management?

In-band management is the administration, either directly via the console or remotely via the network, of a server that is running normally. *Out-of-band management* is management by using a serial port or special device. Typically, the serial port is used as an out-of-band management port and devices designed for this type of support are attached. A secure connection can then be established, either through a phone line or a serial port connection through a null modem to a device (terminal concentrator or service processor) that allows out-of-band management via the network. Out-of-band management can be used to perform normal administration duties as well as EMS. One goal of using out-of-band access and EMS is to return the server to a functioning state, where in-band connection is then possible.

> **Off the Record**   Out-of-band remote administration is often used to provide an additional layer of security. Because most attacks on the server are attempted via the network connection, either from the LAN or through a connection to the Internet, some security experts advise preventing remote administration via the LAN and providing out-of-band capability. A secure, private telephone line can be implemented and used as the administration venue, or a separate administration network can be configured using serial ports and terminal concentrators or service processors. Out-of-band remote administration is not inherently more secure than remote administration over the normal network. Each process has its own risks, and many out-of-band administration services do not provide security at all. You must carefully weigh the risks of both methods and choose the one you can best secure and that fits the relative risk and relative sensitivity of the server to be administered.

What Is an Out-of-Band Infrastructure?

EMS is secured primarily by securing the out-of-band infrastructure. An *out-of-band infrastructure* is the support system that enables remote troubleshooting and repair of systems that do not complete the operating system boot. There are specific products that can connect via a serial port or other port and provide management options. These include terminal concentrators and service processors.

What Is a Terminal Concentrator?

Terminal concentrators are hardware devices that are used to provide serial access to several servers from a single networked device. This device can then be used to monitor a large number of servers from one location. Terminal concentrators typically include many serial ports that can be connected to servers over null modem cables, and they in turn can be accessed over the network by using telnet.

What Is a Service Processor?

When a server stops responding entirely, a remote-management medium that can function without the operating system is necessary. A service processor and a Peripheral Component Interconnect (PCI) adapter can provide this functionality. A service processor operates independently of the processors in the computer and can offer simple telnet style consoles or Web-based components. Service processors provide connections via out-of-band ports, which can be serial ports, usb ports, Ethernet ports, or modem connections. Service processors can be used to provide out-of-band administration for both normal administration and administration that requires EMS. Another name for a service processor is application-specific integrated circuits (ASICs).

> **Note**   An uninterruptible power supply (UPS) is not a service processor or a remote management system, but it can provide simple remote management capabilities such as shutting down the server or restarting it. It can also be used as a gateway to a management system—that is, a serial cable links the computer to the UPS, and another serial port on the UPS is used to connect to the management systems.

EMS Components

EMS components include:

- Normal Windows Server 2003 features to which console redirection functionality is added. (Output is redirected to an out-of-band management port and the video card if it exists, and keyboard input is still accepted if a keyboard is present.) Console redirection is available for Setup loader, text-mode setup, Recovery Console, RIS, loader, and Stop Error messages. A special version of the RIS startrom.com file is also available.

- Two unique remote-management command-line consoles. The EMS consoles are Special Administration Console (SAC) and !Special Administration Console (!SAC). They provide command-line support and can be accessed through an out-of-band remote management port using terminal software that supports VT-UTF8, VT100+, or VT100. SAC and !SAC are command-line consoles that are different than the Windows Server 2003 command-line environment. A comparison of SAC and !SAC is provided in Table 4-1.

Table 4-1   SAC and !SAC

Tool	When can it be used?	How can its commands be used?
SAC	Early part of boot process. Available as long as the kernel is running	Manage server during normal operation Use in Safe Mode Use during GUI setup Start or restart the server View active processes End processes Set or view IP address Generate stop errors to create a memory file dump Start and access command prompts
!SAC	Invoked by EMS when SAC fails to load or ceases to function	Redirect stop error message text Restart the computer if SAC becomes unavailable

Considerations for Securing EMS

A security standard for terminal concentrators does not exist. Often security consists of a password in the clear logon to telnet. In addition to any provided security features, other things to consider include:

- **Placing the networked device on a separate management network.**   The benefits of doing this include the following:

   ❑ It provides remote access or VPN connection to secure the communications.

   ❑ If access to the networked device is limited, there is less danger of it being misused.

   ❑ Protecting communications with a VPN is always a good idea.

- **Using a router to filter traffic that is permitted to go to the terminal concentrator.**   Do not allow traffic that does not originate from a management console to reach the terminal concentrator.

- **Requiring and using a service processor that provides management software that can be secured.**   Service processors often require the use of specific software for access to the computer. Investigate the security features provided by this software before purchase. Insist on secure procedures.

- **Requiring physical security between the servers and the terminal concentrators.** Restrict access to terminal concentrators and servers. Keep terminal concentrators locked away from all users except those who are authorized to manage them.

- **Using telnet over IPSec to secure communications.** Telnet or SSH can be used to connect to a terminal concentrator. HyperTerminal can be used to connect directly over a modem or null modem cable. Take steps to secure tools such as Telnet or HyperTerminal. Steps can include such things as requiring the use of logons and passwords.

- **Using terminal concentrators with security features.** Insist at least on the use of passwords, and if possible, smart cards or other security tokens.

- **Limiting physical access to the server and to out-of-band hardware.** Protecting access to the serial port will also protect the system from the use of unauthorized out-of-band hardware. Protect access to server racks, computer labs, server farms, and data centers.

- **Understanding the advantages and disadvantages of service processors designed to use normal network interfaces instead of serial ports.** These systems often have well-defined security implementations, but they also expose access to the typical TCP/IP and other protocol attack mechanisms. Make sure you are aware of the risks and know how to properly implement security on these devices.

- **Investigating the use of a separate network for management traffic, including EMS.** This network would include servers and only those secured workstations that are used to manage them. No connection to the Internet from this network should be allowed.

- **Using the dial-back configuration to ensure connection from an authorized computer when using a modem for EMS.** When a modem must dial-back to an administrator's workstation or company Remote Access Server, the remote administration connection by an individual who has discovered the phone number is prevented.

Practice: Securing EMS

In this practice, you will answer several questions to practice securing EMS. If you are unable to answer a question, review the lesson materials and try the question again. You can find answers to the questions in the "Questions and Answers" section at the end of this chapter.

1. You must specify security for the establishment of the remote use of EMS. A terminal concentrator and a serial connection will be used. Which statements should be added to your list? Choose all that apply.

      a. Secure special administrative software specified by the providers of the terminal concentrators.

      b. Use a version of telnet that provides secure authentication processing.

      c. Physically secure the connection between the device and the serial port.

      d. Physically secure the server case so that the special component cannot be tampered with.

2. You must specify security for the establishment of the remote use of EMS. A service processor will be used. Which statements should be added to your list? Choose all that apply.

      a. Secure special administrative software specified by the providers of the terminal concentrators.

      b. Use a version of telnet that provides secure authentication processing.

      c. Physically secure the connection between the device and the serial port.

      d. Physically secure the server case so that the special component cannot be tampered with.

Design Activity: Designing Security for Network Management

In this activity, you must use what you've learned in all three lessons and apply it to a real-world situation. Read the scenario, and then complete the exercises that follow. You can find answers for the exercises in the "Questions and Answers" section at the end of this chapter.

Scenario

You have been hired as a contract employee by Humongous Insurance. Your job is to help the company create a policy to govern administration practices and to ensure secure administration of its networks. You have gathered the following information to help you complete your job.

Current Environment

Humongous is fairly decentralized, and each internal group requires a considerable amount of autonomy. However, the company has adopted a single information security policy and requires all departments and divisions to adhere to it. A single Windows Server 2003 domain exists. All user accounts are in the Users container, and all computer accounts are in the Computers container.

Business Driver

Humongous does not believe in providing extensive training for IT professionals. It also believes that ordinary employees can learn to perform administrative duties and perform them adequately. The company does not pay well.

Problems

Last year, a former employee was able to penetrate the network and obtain confidential files. This type of intrusion needs to be prevented in the future.

Exercise 1: Establish Administrative Management of Users and Computers

Answer the following question.

1. What kind of organization of users and computers should be established? Why?

_____

_____

_____

Exercise 2: Establish Administrative Authority Level

Answer the following questions.

1. Some users in each division will need administrative authority. What is the best way to provide this? Why is this the best way?

_____

_____

_____

_____

_____

Exercise 3: Supervise Administrators

Answer the following question.

1. A methodology for ensuring that administrators don't overstep their authority is required. What would you suggest?

_____

_____

_____

_____

_____

_____

_____

_____

_____

_____

Chapter Summary

- Manage administrative risks by:
  - Developing secure work practices
  - Limiting administrative powers
  - Locking down administrative tools
- EMS provides a way to remotely recover a server that cannot be recovered by other means.
- The forest is a security boundary. The domain is not.

Exam Highlights

Before taking the exam, review these key points and terms. You need to know this information.

Key Points

- You should apply as many technical controls as you can. The use of separate forests, domains, and OUs can provide a variety of help.

- Use separation of duties to provide security. If two actions are required and each action must be completed by a different person, each person will be more responsible.

- If you reduce the attack surface by not installing unnecessary services and software, you will prevent attacks.

- All administrative activities should be monitored. Doing this can provide help when things go wrong and also give an early warning when administrative privilege is being overstepped.

- Emergency Management Services must be secured by securing the out-of-band infrastructure.

Key Terms

Autonomy   A situation in which external control is possible even while local control is the way things are done.

Isolation   A state in which there is a clear, precise boundary and in which there is no inherent connection or way for administrators from one network to administer another.

Security boundary   A boundary that isolates computer systems from each other.

Security policy boundary   A boundary that is logical. There can be a way to cross this boundary.

Questions and Answers

Pg 4-15   **Lesson 1   Practice: Documenting the Process of Creating a Secure Installation**

1. What are the steps in the process of creating a secure installation?

   Answer:

   1) Isolate the server. It should not be on the production network.

   2) Provide a way to prevent installation of optional items during the installation.

   3) Provide a way to add services that are required by this server that are options during instal-lation, such as promoting the computer to a domain controller.

   4) Provide a way to add services that are required for this server that are not part of a normal installation.

   5) Provide a way to apply security configuration settings determined by policy. Because default .inf files are used during a normal installation , these files could be modified and provided.

   6) Provide a way to apply additional security settings that cannot be configured in the default .inf files.

   7) Provide a way to add software such as service packs and security patches.

   8) Provide a way to add software such as Microsoft SQL Server or a third-party product.

2. Where possible, list a security benefit of taking the steps you have listed.

   Answer:

   For the step "Isolate the server," it should not be on the production network. The security ben-efit is that a separate network is free of contamination from servers and clients that might have already been compromised. It is free of attacks from outside the network because it is not con-nected to another one, and it should be free from attacks inside the network because the com-puters are installed on it from secure sources.

   For the step "Provide a way to prevent installation of optional items during the installation," the less unnecessary software there is running on the server, the less attack surface there is available.

   For the step "Provide a way to apply security configuration settings determined by policy," because default .inf files are used during a normal installation, these files could be modified and provided. Bringing up a server in a secure mode prevents the possibility that it can be com-promised before security settings are configured.

   For the step "Provide a way to apply additional security settings that cannot be configured in the default .inf files," bringing up a server in a secure mode prevents the possibility that it can be compromised before security settings are configured.

   For the step "Provide a way to add any additional software such as service packs, security patches," bringing up a server in a secure mode prevents the possibility that it can be compro-mised before security settings are configured. The security benefit is that if the installation itself is secure, each server installed from its image has the potential for similar security from the start.

3. What is the benefit of producing a secure and secured automated installation?

The security benefit is that the process is automated and thus repeatable in exactly the same manner, with the same results. An image cannot be modified (but it can be replaced).

Pg 4-38   **Lesson 2   Practice: Inspecting Administration Tools and Securing Their Use**

1. Create a list that can be used to inspect any administration tool. What guidelines do you suggest for securing an administration tool's use?

Answer:

■ **Determine whether another tool can be used to provide the same administrative choices.** You do this by considering the following:

❑ Determine whether this tool can be used in a more secure fashion than the other tool.

❑ Determine whether there is some reason the other tool should be used.

❑ Determine whether one tool might be better used remotely or locally.

❑ Look for built-in security in the tool.

❑ If the tool is used remotely, determine whether it can encrypt communications.

❑ Determine whether the tool can be restricted to use by administrators.

❑ Determine whether the tool requires installation.

❑ Determine whether the tool requires the addition of a new service.

■ **Search the Microsoft.com Web site and do a general Internet search to find out whether any security issues with the tool have been reported or whether secure use of the tool is documented.** If security issues exist, determine whether you can accept or mitigate the issues.

■ **Determine whether there is a need to access the tool through a firewall.** What ports might you need to open, and what risk does that entail? Can SSL or IPSec, or a traditional VPN be used to provide access to the tool?

Pg 4-43   **Lesson 3   Practice: Securing EMS**

1. You must specify security for the establishment of the remote use of EMS. A terminal concentrator and a serial connection will be used. Which statements should be added to your list? Choose all that apply.

a. Secure special administrative software specified by the providers of the terminal concentrators.

b. Use a version of telnet that provides secure authentication processing.

c. Physically secure the connection between the device and the serial port.

d. Physically secure the server case so that the special component cannot be tampered with.

Options b and c are the correct answers. Telnet is used to administer servers when terminal concentrators are used. Option a is incorrect—terminal concentrators are most likely used with telnet. Option d is incorrect. You might want to secure the case, but the terminal concentrator is a separate device.

2. You must specify security for the establishment of the remote use of EMS. A service processor will be used. Which statements should be added to your list? Choose all that apply.

   a. Secure special administrative software specified by the providers of the terminal concentrators.

   b. Use a version of telnet that provides secure authentication processing.

   c. Physically secure the connection between the device and the serial port.

   d. Physically secure the server case so that the special component cannot be tampered with.

   Options a and d are the correct answers. A service processor is most likely to provide or specify the use of unique tools. A service processor is a board that is installed within the computer. Option b is incorrect because special software is usually required. Option c is incorrect because the service processor can be a board inserted in the computer.

Design Activity: Designing Security for Network Management

Pg 4-45   **Exercise 1: Establish Administrative Management of Users and Computers**

1. What kind of organization of users and computers should be established? Why?

   Separate OUs, one for each division or department, should be established. This will allow the appointment of separate administrative groups for each OU and provide a good level of autonomy.

Pg 4-45   **Exercise 2: Establish Administrative Authority Level**

1. Some users in each division will need administrative authority. What is the best way to provide this? Why is this the best way?

   Create custom groups for each division and department that requires autonomy. Assign these groups only the privileges they need over their respective OUs. Do not make OU administrators members of any default administrative group—doing so would give them privileges that they don't need and give them those privileges in a larger part of the domain or forest.

Pg 4-46   **Exercise 3: Supervise Administrators**

1. A methodology for ensuring that administrators don't overstep their authority is required. What would you suggest?

   Audit administrators' activities on the network, and assign administrators membership in specific groups that are granted only the necessary privileges that they need to do their jobs. Check the background and employee performance of the administrators in the organization. Providing administrators with only the access and privileges that they need is a good way to limit the abuse they can perform.

5 Designing a Security Update Infrastructure

Exam Objectives in this Chapter:

- Design a security update infrastructure:
  - Design a Software Update Services infrastructure.
  - Design group policy to deploy software updates.
  - Design a strategy for identifying computers that are not at the current patch level.

Why This Chapter Matters

Ninety-five percent of all successful computer attacks where the cause can be determined are the result of vulnerabilities for which there already was a patch or other configuration mitigation (paraphrased from a statement made by CERT, the Computer Emergency Response Team, at Carnegie Melon University to Security Watch, a weekly newsletter produced by 101 Communications). Every day, someone new learns about a vulnerability in a system, a default setting that needs improvement, or another potential way to break into your systems. Every day, someone uses that information. You must be that person. To stop these attacks, you must incorporate new security information into your network in the form of security updates.

Lessons in this Chapter:

Before You Begin

This chapter presents the skills and concepts related to creating a security design framework. This training kit assumes that you have a minimum of 1 year of experience implementing and administering desktop operating systems and network operating system in environments that have the following characteristics:

- At least 250 supported users
- Three or more physical locations

- Typical network services such as messaging, database, file and print, proxy server or firewall, Internet and intranet, remote access, and client computer management

- Three or more domain controllers

- Connectivity needs that include connecting branch offices and individual users in remote locations to the corporate network, and connecting corporate networks to the Internet

In addition, you should have experience designing a network infrastructure.

Many design exercises are paper based; however, to understand the technical capabilities that a design can incorporate, you should have some hands-on experience with products. Where specific hands-on instruction is given, you must have at least two computers configured as specified in the "Getting Started" section at the beginning of this book.

Lesson 1: Introduction to Designing a Security Update Infrastructure

Updating security is not just patching, but patching does address the most immediate security needs. A well-designed, automated security-patch-updating infrastructure is a necessary component of your network. Microsoft Software Update Services (SUS) addresses many of the security updating needs for a Microsoft Windows–based network. But to create a well-designed security update infrastructure that includes SUS, you must first understand all methods available for updating security and how to choose the best combination of methods, know the general guidelines for designing a security update infrastructure, and know what SUS is and how it works. Only then can you design a security update infrastructure using SUS that will fit your network's needs.

After this lesson, you will be able to

- Explain the process for designing a security update infrastructure.
- List the changes that require security updates.
- Describe the methods for updating systems.
- Choose the best combination of update methods.
- Find the latest security vulnerability information.
- Explain the guidelines for designing a security update infrastructure.
- Explain the purpose of SUS and describe its components.
- Secure the SUS server.
- Design a software update infrastructure by using SUS.

Estimated lesson time: 60 minutes

The Process: Designing a Security Update Infrastructure

Implementing a security update infrastructure is a crucial part of any network security design. To make this happen, you must be able to not only identify what must be updated and how to do so, but you must also realize that there can be many processes involved and that you might need to use more than one process. This lesson provides the overall context and explicit instructions for using Microsoft Software Update Services as a primary component of a security update infrastructure.

To design a security update infrastructure, follow this process:

1. Determine the changes that require security updating, and document how to find this information.

2. Determine the methods for updating systems.

3. Select the best combination of update methods.

4. Use SUS to provide the security patching part of the security update infrastructure.

The rest of this lesson teaches the information and guidelines that you must know to complete the steps in this process.

Changes That Require Security Updates

Security updates are any updates that must occur that are in direct response to either new knowledge of a practice that will improve security or the release of a security patch that is provided as a response to a newly discovered vulnerability. *Security update processes* are the ways in which the changes can be made. Security patches, software that might be necessary to mitigate an impending attack, are only one part of the process. Security-related changes are as follows:

- Configuration changes to local and Active Directory Group Policy
- Configuration changes related to software not managed by Group Policy
- Routine software updates such as service packs (SPs)
- Engineering fixes provided by Microsoft in response to a specific customer need
- Security patches that mitigate a new vulnerability

Methods for Updating Systems

After you know what needs to be updated, you must learn how to do so. There are many ways to update systems. Most solutions cannot do the entire job. For example, Microsoft Software Update Services (SUS) Server is an excellent, automated approach to security patch deployment, but it cannot be used to change security configuration. And the Security Configuration and Analysis tool, which can be used to change security configuration, cannot be used to install software updates. Table 5-1 lists the methods for updating systems and answers questions about the types of updates that can be used to update systems.

Table 5-1   Security Update Methods

Security Update Method	Which Windows operating system can be updated?	Can security configuration be changed?	Can software be patched?	For how many systems should this method be used?
Windows Update	Windows 98 and later; some other software	No	Yes	When individuals must update their own systems
Manual Configuration	All	Yes	Yes	Small number
Automatic Update	Windows 2000 SP2 and later	No	Yes	50 or less
Custom Scripts	All	Yes	Yes	Dependent on delivery mechanism

Table 5-1   Security Update Methods

Security Update Method	Which Windows operating system can be updated?	Can security configuration be changed?	Can software be patched?	For how many systems should this method be used?
Security Configuration and Analysis	Windows 2000 and later	Yes	No	Single systems unless scripted
Group Policy	Windows 2000 and later; some software	Yes	Yes	Any number of Active Directory domain members
SUS	Windows 2000 and later	No	Yes	25 to several hundred
SMS with SUS Feature Pack	Windows 98 and later, can be customized for all software	Yes	Yes	Any size
Third-party products	Most products and software	Yes	Yes	Dependent on product

Guidelines for Choosing the Best Combination of Update Methods

Table 5-1 shows that few methods can be used alone to do all the security updating necessary. You will have to use one or more methods to change security configuration and a different method for updating computers with security patches. Follow these guidelines to determine the best combination of methods for updating security patches.

- **Make choices based on number of systems to update.** Guidelines for accomplishing this include the following:

  - In general, Windows Update, which can be used by visiting the Windows Update site, is useful only when a small number of systems—perhaps 50 or fewer—must be updated.

  - A manual updating procedure is even less scalable. A manual updating process consists of downloading patches and installing them one by one on each computer. It is too labor intensive to be used to update more than a few systems.

  - SUS can be used to update a few to many hundreds of systems. Using a SUS hierarchy will enable updating of many more.

  - SMS can be used to update any number of systems and is generally used only on large networks because of the complexity of installing and maintaining an SMS infrastructure.

  - Other companies' products, which are suitable for small and large operations, are available and vary widely in cost and complexity.

- ❑ Security configuration changes are best managed using Group Policy. However, organizations with only a few computers might not use a domain infrastructure and cannot use Group Policy.

- ❑ Security Configuration and Analysis can be used to update one computer at a time. If only a few computers exist, this might be OK.

- ❑ secedit can be used in a script and therefore applied to many systems, but it requires more work than Group Policy.

- **Make choices based on the ability of the system to update automatically coupled with the ability to review updates before installing.**   To help you do this, follow these guidelines:

  - ❑ Use Windows Update to automate multiple changes at a time. However, each system must be visited and pointed at the Windows Update site. A given update might be rejected or accepted, but because the update is meant for a single system, there is no way to review the update other than by reading about it.

  - ❑ Automatic Updates can be configured to download and install software updates immediately. Similar to using Windows Updates, the user can accept or reject individual updates, but the only review possible is by reading about the update.

  - ❑ SUS, SMS, and other products can be configured to update many computers automatically. Administrators can download, test, and review updates before approving updates for distribution.

  - ❑ Custom scripts assume any necessary testing is done before they are developed. Once developed and tested, the scripts can be automated for distribution.

  - ❑ After testing, Group Policy can be used to distribute patch deployment.

  - ❑ All security configuration changes and security patches should be tested before deployment.

- **Weigh choices as a whole.**   Keep the following things in mind when doing this:

  - ❑ More than one process will be needed. Choose a combination of processes that meet the size and needs of your organization.

  - ❑ For all but the smallest organizations, a combination of SUS and Group Policy is a good choice. All aspects can be covered, from scalability to diversity.

How to Find the Latest Security Vulnerability Information

To know which security patches or changes to make, you must know where to find out what is available and understand why the change is recommended. You must use multiple sources of update information to provide a sound security update infrastructure. Changes or security updates might be the result of a security alert (requiring the need to apply patches or service packs, make configuration changes, or update antivirus software), but they can also be initiated because of general security hardening efforts (applying security design principles such as reducing the attack surface by disabling unused services, updating antivirus programs, or installing service packs). To find security alert information:

- Sign up to receive Microsoft Security bulletins.
- Visit security alert lists.
- Visit security Web sites.
- Sign up to receive antivirus alerts from product vendors.

To find general security hardening information:

- Visit the Security and TechNet Security pages of the Microsoft Web site and other locations of security documentation.
- Perform vulnerability scanning with Microsoft Security Baseline Analyzer or other vulnerability scanning products.
- Visit security Web sites.

Sources of Security Vulnerability Information

Following is a list of sources of security alert information:

- Microsoft Security bulletins: *www.microsoft.com/technet/security/default.asp*
- Security alert lists, such as ntbugtraq (*www.ntbugtraq.com*) and SecurityFocus (*www.securityfocus.com*)
- Security Web sites, such as *www.SANS.org* and *www.securityfocus.com*
- Antivirus alerts from product vendors

Sources of general security hardening information are as follows:

- The Security (*http://www.microsoft.com/security/*) and TechNet Security (*http://www.microsoft.com/technet/security/*) pages of the Microsoft Web site
- Security links from product pages on the Microsoft Web site
- Results from running Microsoft Security Baseline Analyzer or other vulnerability scanning products

---

Guidelines for Designing a Security Update Infrastructure

After you know the changes that require security updates, the methods available, and how to find the latest security vulnerability information, you can begin to think about designing a security update infrastructure.

> **Important**   This topic provides the general guidelines for designing a security update infra-
> structure. Use this information in combination with knowledge of security tools and sys-
> tems—many of which are detailed in other chapters in this book—to design a security update
> infrastructure. You must design a security update infrastructure that encompasses the entire
> security infrastructure of your network. One part of a security update infrastructure is how the
> operating system code can be updated by applying security patches. This section is followed
> by specific information on how to design a security patching infrastructure using SUS.

Follow these guidelines for designing a security update infrastructure:

- **Assess the systems infrastructure.**   To do this:

  - ❏ Document which operating systems, applications, and versions are part of the
    network.

  - ❏ Determine how many systems exist, and rank them according to their critical
    nature. Ensure that systems, such as those that must have high availability or
    that manage critical or sensitive data, are documented and ranked at the top
    of the scale.

  - ❏ Document any systems that are no longer supported and any that are not
    managed.

  - ❏ Assess current network infrastructure and security infrastructure. Determine
    whether internal computers are protected from external threats and how that
    is accomplished. Include information on firewalls, intrusion protection sys-
    tems (IPS), and intrusion detection systems (IDS).

  - ❏ Document alternative network access paths such as wireless networks, trav-
    eling laptops, and modems. Are these paths secured?

  - ❏ Assess the security level of mobile computers such as laptop computers.
    These systems can be the source or infection and reinfection, introduction
    and re-introduction of vulnerabilities, and actual infection or compromise.

- **Assess the current vulnerability status.**   To do this:

  - ❏ Document the current updating strategy. If the status is "None," record that as
    well.

  - ❏ Determine the update status of current systems.

- **Assess current software installation processes.**   To do this:

  - ❏ Document any automated software installation processes.

  - ❏ Determine whether they can be used for installing updates.

- **Assess operations.**   To do this:
    - ❏ Document the change management process.
    - ❏ Determine the skill level of people who have the ability to modify systems. Are these individuals capable of making sound updating decisions? Are they capable of managing change?

- **Obtain management sponsorship and employee support.**   Without upper-management support, a security update system is doomed. Many updates can be smoothly integrated without any adverse affects, but you might have to make other choices that will result in changes to the way business is done, cost money, or disrupt user activity while changes are made. Employees need to understand the change management process, including security updates. The systems of employees who travel are especially vulnerable, and a way for updating these systems must be found.

- **Decide whether or not to update the system.**   Many sources of change knowledge are available. But which changes should be made? To determine this:
    - ❏ Devote time to assessing the nature of the threat. Is this something that systems might already be protected from? Are the systems that are affected part of the network? Does this require an update to settings? Use of a new feature? Or a patch for a vulnerability?
    - ❏ Quarantine security patches in a test environment until they can be tested for production.
    - ❏ Determine whether a countermeasure, other than applying a security patch, is available. Countermeasures might be more quickly applied and cause less disruption.
    - ❏ Design in a security update triage. Some updates might be more critical than others. If an updating triage is a part of your normal process, different time-frames can be scheduled. This might allow you the time necessary to update all systems with critical patches in a timely fashion.

Tip   Microsoft Security Levels of Vulnerability is published as part of the security bulletin. Other industry alerting organizations also attach some priority or severity rating with their alerts. Microsoft severity levels, with the most severe issues being "critical," are as follows: Critical, Important, Moderate, and Low. Integrate security severity ratings into your priority system by making "critical" updates number one and so forth. Take the time to evaluate items that might raise or lower priorities—for example, the high value of the assets on your systems, resources that have been targeted in the past, countermeasures in place, and so forth. It is not necessary to attempt to equate the alert severity ratings of different organizations with each other; it is more important to recognize whether every organization is giving the vulnerability a top level severity warning. If this is the case, these specific vulnerabilities should top your priority list.

- **Create solutions for all possible computer configurations.**   To do this:
  - ❑ Use a Remote Installation Service (RIS) or other automated installation solution to ensure production servers are placed on the production network with all currently approved service packs and updates.
  - ❑ Require updates for systems connecting via remote access and virtual private network (VPN) solutions. A Windows Server 2003 feature such as Microsoft Network Access Quarantine Control can be used to restrict access for systems that do not meet specific security requirements, such as having up-to-date patches.
  - ❑ Require updates for traveling systems. When systems return to the internal network, are they subject to a security review?

- **Create a solution that provides updating for all products.**   To do this:
  - ❑ Update all software. Because all software has vulnerabilities, all software must be updated to improve security and prevent successful attacks.
  - ❑ Ensure that the updating solution designates a process that attends to the updating of all systems and software.
  - ❑ Use SUS, Windows Update, and Automatic Updates to provide assessment for and the ability to patch the Windows operating system and operating system components such as Internet Explorer and Windows Media.
  - ❑ Use Office Update, a service similar to Windows Update, to update Microsoft Office 2000 and later.

- **Separate the process of vulnerability assessment into parts.**   To do this:
  - ❑ Assess all systems for vulnerability prior to update to determine which systems to patch (for what) and update.
  - ❑ Assess systems after updating to determine whether they got updated so that you can troubleshoot the problem.
  - ❑ Audit systems on a periodic basis to determine whether systems are being updated and to what extent.
  - ❑ Audit for specific problems when a threat appears imminent—for example, once a worm or other attack is confirmed as using a specific vulnerability.
  - ❑ Use tools such as Security Configuration and Analysis and Microsoft Security Baseline Analyzer to audit systems.
  - ❑ Use specific vulnerability testing tools released by Microsoft and other trusted third parties to test for common vulnerabilities.

- **Design regular update change initiation processes.**   To do this:
  - ❑ Provide a scheduled time for obtaining security update information and for reviewing proposed changes.
  - ❑ Obtain and review updates on at least a weekly basis.

❑ Ensure that the review process consists of searching for possible changes, reviewing changes for relevancy and severity, downloading software-based changes, and testing and/or analyzing changes against test systems.

❑ Schedule follow up to ensure approved changes were put into the update process and audit to determine whether the update was made.

What Is Software Update Services?

Microsoft Software Update Services (SUS) is a tool you can use to automate patch distribution and installation while retaining the right to decide which patches to apply. SUS is a service that can be installed on Windows Server 2003 or Windows 2000 Server and provides automated patch distribution to Windows 2000, Windows Server 2003, and Windows XP Professional computers that are running the Automatic Updates client.

SUS provides your organization a local version of the Windows Update site: a version that is under your control. This is very important. Instead of configuring your computers to automatically download and apply security patches across the Internet, you can configure your computers to automatically download only the security patches that you have approved from a local SUS server. This means you can save bandwidth. For example, if you manage the installation of security hotfixes on 250 computers configured with Automatic Updates, each computer would download each update. Consequently, for two 1-MB hotfixes that are released, clients on your network will download 500 MB of security updates. With SUS, the SUS server would download each hotfix once and distribute them to the clients, saving 498 MB of bandwidth. This feature is the primary advantage of SUS and a primary reason to use SUS for security updates. SUS provides additional benefits but is not a comprehensive answer to all security updates. This section explains what you can and cannot do with SUS, explains requirements for deploying SUS, and describes what the SUS client and SUS hierarchy are.

What You Can Do with SUS

Using SUS, you can

■ Download all security patches associated with security bulletins provided by Microsoft for Windows XP, Windows 2000, and Windows Server 2003 to the SUS server.

■ Synchronize the SUS patch database with Microsoft's patch database on a regular basis, either manually or automatically.

■ Decide which updates to distribute. Only security patches that you approve will be distributed to clients.

■ Point Windows XP, Windows 2000, and Windows Server 2003 computers to the SUS server for automatic download and installation of security patches.

■ Receive SUS update notifications. If you subscribe to the SUS notification list, each time a new or updated patch is added to the Microsoft database you will receive an e-mail notification.

What You Can't Do with SUS

You cannot use SUS to

- Apply configuration updates.

- Apply updates for Microsoft Office or other Microsoft products not listed previously.

- Apply updates to third-party products.

- Add new drivers or update existing drivers.

> **Important**   The next version of SUS is scheduled to provide Microsoft Office updates.

- Install service packs.

- Add updates to Windows from sources other than Microsoft.

- Apply a different set of updates to different computers. All computers that are directed to a specific SUS server will receive the updates approved for their operating system.

Clearing Up Update Terminology

Many words are used to describe updates, and you will find that many people use different words to describe the same thing or use the same word differently. The current Microsoft definitions for these terms, as paraphrased from the document "Microsoft Guides to Security Patch Management," are listed below. This book will use the words *security patch*, or *patch*, to describe patches related to security bulletins and provided by SUS. Updated term definitions are as follows:

- *Security patch*—A released fix that addresses a vulnerability in a specific product.

- *Microsoft Security Response Center (MSRC) severity rating*—A rating of the vulnerability.

- *Critical update*—A released fix that addresses a critical nonsecurity-related update.

- *Update*—A released fix that addresses a noncritical, nonsecurity-related bug.

- *Hotfix*—A package of one to many files that provides a fix for a product problem. A hotfix addresses a specific customer problem and is available only through a support relationship with Microsoft. Other terms that have been used are quick fix engineering (QFE) update, patch, and update previous.

- *Update rollup*—A collection of security patches, critical updates, updates, and hotfixes released together. They might be concerned with only one product component, such as Microsoft Internet Explorer.

- *Service pack*—A cumulative set of hotfixes, security patches, critical updates, and updates to the release of a product. It might include resolved problems not made available elsewhere, and it might include customer-requested design changes and features.

- *Integrated service pack*—A release or product with the service pack already applied.

- *Feature pack*—A new feature or features released for a current product. The feature pack only adds functionality and is usually part of the next release of the product.

Requirements for Deploying SUS

To deploy SUS, you must provide the following features and capabilities:

- A minimum of a Pentium 700 MHz CPU or equivalent
- 512 MB RAM
- A network adapter
- An NTFS partition of at least 100 MB free space for SUS installation and a minimum of 6 GB storage for updates if they are to be hosted locally
- Microsoft Windows 2000 Server SP2 or later or Windows Server 2003 member servers; or a Windows 2000 or Windows Server 2003 domain controller; or Small Business Server
- Microsoft Internet Information Services
- Microsoft Internet Explorer 5.5 or later

Note   SUS can be downloaded from the downloads page of the Microsoft Web site at *http://www.microsoft.com/downloads/details.aspx?FamilyId=A7AA96E4-6E41-4F54-972C-AE66A4E4BF6C&displaylang=en*.

What Is the SUS Client?

The Automatic Updates software is the SUS client. A separate client was provided for Windows 2000 Service Pack 2 computers. Automatic Updates is a feature of Windows 2000 Service Pack 3, Windows XP, and Windows Server 2003. To benefit from SUS server, all clients must be configured to use a specific SUS server. In addition, decisions must be made about automatic restarts, rescheduled updates, and so on.

See Also   For more information about the SUS client, see the "Policies in Group Policy That Can Be Used to Configure SUS Client Computers" section later in this chapter.

Exam Tip Windows Server 2003 uses an enhanced security configuration for Internet Explorer in which all Internet sites are placed in the Restricted sites zone. To access the local SUS administration Web site on a Windows Server 2003 server, you might need to place the http://*ipaddress* or http://*computername* of the SUS server in the Local intranet zone of Internet Explorer. If you want to remotely administer the SUS server from a Windows Server 2003 computer, enter the http://SUSServer_*computername* in the local intranet zone.

What Is a SUS Hierarchy?

A SUS hierarchy is an orderly collection of SUS systems. At the root of the hierarchy is the parent SUS server. The parent is the only SUS server that downloads patches from Microsoft. Many child SUS servers can be configured to download patches from the parent SUS server. Child SUS servers synchronize their patch databases with the parent patch database on a daily basis. A patch that is approved on the parent server is automatically approved on the client. Figure 5-1 shows a SUS hierarchy and its proper placement on the network. The figure shows the SUS parent server connection to Microsoft Windows Update across the organization's firewall, the SUS child servers, and production clients.

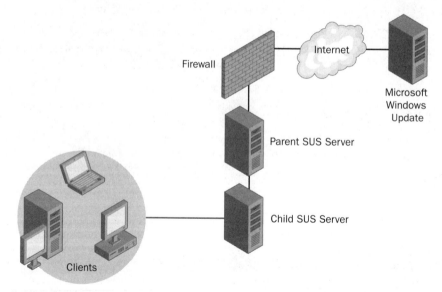

Figure 5-1 A SUS hierarchy

A SUS hierarchy might also be used to provide a test database of patches. Figures 5-2 and 5-3 show two options for testing patches. Figure 5-2 shows the test SUS server connected directly to Microsoft and making patches available to representative clients on its own test network. A separate SUS hierarchy makes patches available on the production network. After patches are tested in the test network, they are approved on the production parent for distribution to production clients. This design has the advantage of keeping the test network totally isolated from the production network.

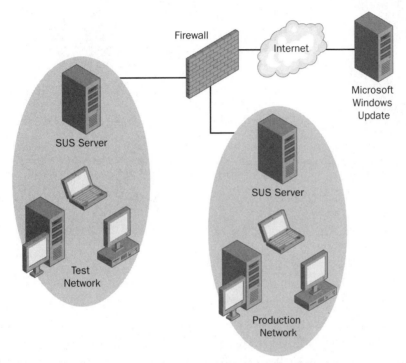

Figure 5-2   Using a separate SUS hierarchy for testing

In Figure 5-3, the test network's SUS server is a child SUS server. The production network also has a child SUS server in the hierarchy. The test network's child SUS server is set to automatically synchronize with the parent SUS server, but the production network's SUS server requires manual synchronization. Patches are tentatively approved on the parent SUS server. When the test network server is synchronized with the parent SUS server, the approved patches are ready for distribution to the test network. If a patch is not approved, its patch approval status is removed from the parent SUS server. If a patch is approved, the production network child SUS server is manually synchronized with the parent SUS server.

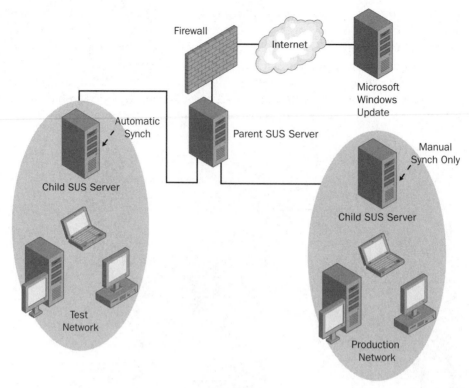

Figure 5-3   Using a SUS hierarchy for testing purposes

Guidelines for Securing the SUS Server

The SUS server itself must be protected. Although it is not likely that an attacker could cause the SUS server to issue non-Microsoft patches (and thus could not use it to launch a worm or virus attack), he could remove approval of security patches and thus prevent computers from being patched, block the SUS server's access to the Internet or to its parent SUS server, or otherwise prevent it from synchronizing. In addition to the normal security hardening and defensive processes that you adopt for all servers, follow these guidelines when securing the SUS server:

- Limit membership in the local Administrators group to reduce the number of accounts that can administer SUS. Only members of the local Administrators group on the SUS server can administer SUS by using the browser location http://*<servername>*/SUSAdmin.

- Limit the number of administrators by:
  - ❏ Removing the Domain Admins group from the local Administrators group
  - ❏ Creating a custom domain group for SUS administrators
  - ❏ Adding the accounts of selective members of Domain Admins to this group
  - ❏ Giving the new group membership in the local Administrators group

■ Consider using Secure Sockets Layer (SSL) to ensure server authentication. You must have a valid digital certificate and use it to configure SSL on the SUS server. The following directories must be configured to "Require 128-Bit Encryption":

- ❑ \autoupdate\administration
- ❑ \autoupdate\dictionaries
- ❑ \Shared
- ❑ \Content\EULA
- ❑ \Content\RTF

Guidelines for Designing a Secure Update Infrastructure Using SUS

It is simple to implement a single SUS server in a small, single-location network. Patches are automatically downloaded. You test them and mark some as approved. Clients obtain and install the patches. What could be easier? However, many networks are distributed and cannot use such a simple design. What can be done to patch remote systems and laptops that are primarily used away from the network or only connect through slow links? When is a hierarchy needed, and when might you use multiple parent SUS servers? How do you manage to update systems that must never be connected to the Internet or to networks that are? Follow these guidelines to design a secure update infrastructure by using SUS:

■ When designing the SUS network infrastructure:

- ❑ Consider the source of patches. A SUS server can download patches from Microsoft, approved patches from another SUS server, or approved patches from a content management server that is not running Internet Information Services (IIS). The content management server is an IIS server used to hold copies of approved patches. An IIS server in your perimeter network can then synchronize with the content management server.

- ❑ Use parent and child SUS servers to ensure that the same patches are available from each SUS server. In a parent/child hierarchy, the parent is the only SUS server that downloads patches from Microsoft.

- ❑ Place SUS servers in every data center and major business location.

- ❑ Consider where on the network to place these servers. A good location for child SUS servers is close to the clients that they will serve. Parent SUS servers need ease of access to the Internet. Child SUS servers and SUS clients do not need access to the Internet.

- ❑ Provide for serving SUS servers at locations where Internet accessibility is not provided. These sites can download from a content management server.

- ❑ Design the use of SUS servers for computers on perimeter networks. A content management server can be used on the perimeter network.

❑ Consider the use of network load balancing (NLB) for SUS servers. NLB can be used to automatically distribute the load over multiple SUS servers. Should one SUS server fail, the others will manage the load. If your infrastructure requires multiple SUS servers to serve a large number of clients, or it requires guaranteed 7 x 24 uptime, using NLB is the best solution. NLB requires the use of multiple servers and therefore is a more expensive solution. If NLB is used, configure child SUS servers with NLB. A separate, parent SUS server is used to download and stage updates. Figure 5-4 shows the arrangement.

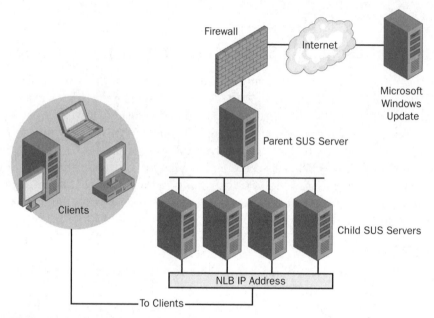

Figure 5-4   Using NLB for redundancy

Exam Tip   The SUS-to-SUS server synchronization is prevented from synchronizing through a firewall. This will prevent rogue SUS servers being set up on the Internet.

■ When designing SUS installation:

❑ Document constraints, including hardware and software.

❑ Provide a secure installation of the server before installing SUS, including current service packs and software updates.

❑ Install SUS server and any operating system updates to the SUS system in a quarantined space.

❑ Install the first SUS server in a test environment. Use test client and server computers to determine how SUS will be used. Working in a test environment allows administrators to learn how to effectively use and monitor the system before the health of their network depends on it.

❑ Consider running SUS as the only application on the server. While IIS can be used to host multiple applications, not all applications will be compatible with SUS. Applications that are compatible are FrontPage Server Extensions, SharePoint Team Services, and ASP.NET applications. However, remember that if the server is compromised because of problems with these applications, your patching infrastructure will also be compromised.

❑ Provide antivirus protection for the server, but ensure that SUS installation plans include turning off the antivirus protection.

❑ Acknowledge use of IIS Lockdown on Windows 2000 Servers. IIS Lockdown and URLscan are tools that add security to IIS. If they are not installed on IIS when you install SUS SP1, they will be installed during the process.

❑ If installing SUS on a domain controller, promote the domain controller before installing SUS or you will not be able to uninstall SUS.

❑ Consider the IIS location for the SUS server Web site. Generally, no other Web site function should be a part of the Web server that hosts SUS. If the SUS IIS server hosts a public Web site and it is compromised, the update structure of your entire network is also compromised.

❑ If you do not want SUS to install under the default Web site, either disable or remove the default Web site. SUS will always install to the default Web site if it is running. If no other Web site is running at port 80, SUS will create and install under a new Web site running at port 80.

■ When designing patch testing procedures:

❑ Patch testing procedures include testing the SUS server, testing the patch deployment process, and testing individual patches before they are approved for distribution.

❑ Consider how you will determine which patches to install. A good practice is to schedule a regular time to review patches. It is also wise, however, to spend time evaluating the threat of each vulnerability the patch represents mitigation for. If your patch reviews are scheduled too far apart, you might delay the implementation of a critical patch longer than is necessary.

❑ Plan to rate each patch against two things. First, determine whether you need the patch. Second, determine the severity of the vulnerability. Do you need to patch right away? Third, how critical are the systems that need to be patched.

❑ Consider how you will determine whether a patch is safe to install. Is it safe if you install it on one machine without problems? Or will you divide its testing into phases—first testing it on a plain install of the operating system (no additional special services or software applications) and then on a server that might have received engineering quick fixes? Will you also test deployment via SUS? Can patches be removed? Will patches overwrite custom configuration? What did the patch change?

See Also   The document "Patch Management Using Microsoft Software Update Services – Test Case Detail" (*www.microsoft.com/technet/itsolutions/msm/swdist/pmsus/pmsustc.asp*) outlines some test operations that can be carried out for SUS, including testing the SUS installation, the use of Microsoft Security Baseline Analyzer, and many of the SUS operations.

■ Determine the number of SUS servers necessary:

❑ A SUS server configured to the minimum hardware specifications can update approximately 15,000 clients.

❑ Add SUS servers to manage more clients or to cover multiple sites.

■ When designing a SUS hierarchy:

❑ Use multiple parent SUS servers if different levels of patch acceptance are desired by clients with the same operating system. For example, if you want to approve most updates for all systems but some updates should not be installed on all systems, you cannot do this with a single SUS parent. You could, however, have two SUS servers, each of which downloads its updates directly from Microsoft. In this case, most clients could point to the primary SUS server, and a few clients will point to a separate SUS server on which fewer patches are approved.

❑ Where all clients of each type of operating system can receive the same patches and there are many clients, design a parent/child SUS hierarchy.

■ When designing SUS operations:

❑ Best practices indicate that SUS should download patches on a regular, preferably daily frequency. The synchronization schedule is set from the Software Update Services administration site by visiting the Synchronize Server, Schedule Synchronization page. Figure 5-5 shows the page. Note that you can choose not to synchronize on a schedule. In this case, you must manually synchronize the SUS server.

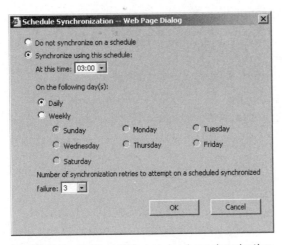

Figure 5-5   Setting SUS download synchronization

❑ Schedule child SUS servers to download patches from a parent SUS server as soon as possible by scheduling their download interval to occur after the parent SUS server downloads from Microsoft.

❑ In most cases, set SUS to download patches but not to automatically approve them. You should test patches before distribution.

❑ Design the testing process for updates. Test machines should be used that closely match the configuration of servers and clients on your network. Once a patch is approved for distribution, it must be marked approved in the Approve Updates page as shown in Figure 5-6. Approved patches are automatically made available for clients.

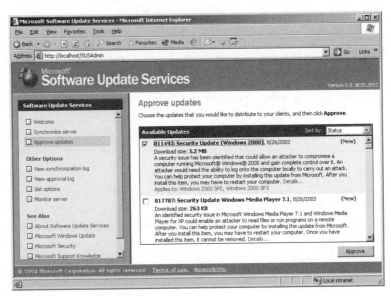

Figure 5-6   Approving patches

- When designing the client infrastructure:

  ❑ Some updates require a computer reboot before they are effective. No special precautions are necessary for logged-on users, as SUS will not automatically restart the computer when a user is logged on.

  ❑ Consider updating for one remote computer where the user is not Administrator on the computer. An administrator is notified of a pending update and can force an update. A nonadministrator is notified only when some action, such as allowing the system to reboot, is required. If these computers are not online when the scheduled update should take place, the system will not be updated.

  ❑ Consider situations where making a user an administrator and then limiting her rights on the system might serve the greater good.

- When designing backup and system recovery:

  ❑ Design a backup strategy. Backup should include the SUS Web site, the content directory, and the IIS metabase.

  ❑ Design a restore strategy. If there is total system failure and Windows must be restored, there is no solution except to reinstall SUS and download patches, but there might be recovery from less disastrous situations.

Exam Tip   If a SUS server fails and is beyond repair (a new installation of Windows is required), there is no supported method of restoration from backup for such a failure. Instead, reinstall SUS, download updates, and mark those previously approved as approved. Reconfigure SUS to precrash configuration.

- When designing for Redundancy Load Balancing for SUS:

  ❑ Consider the use of load balancing to serve large numbers of clients or to provide redundancy in the case of failure.

  ❑ Design for failure in parent/child relationships by providing an unlinked Group Policy object (GPO) that points the child SUS clients to the parent and another GPO that points the clients GPOs to the server. These GPOs can be linked to the proper domain or organizational unit or units should one of the SUS servers fail.

Security Alert   Do not select the Automatically Approve New Versions Of Previously Approved Updates option. If this setting is checked and a new version of a patch is released, it will be marked as approved and will be available for installation. There will be no option to test the patch before it is deployed and installed on clients.

■ When designing SUS administrative practices:

❑ Design the SUS baseline configuration.

❑ Consider the name resolution service available on the network. If NetBIOS name resolution is available, the NetBIOS name is all that is necessary. If DNS must be used, a DNS name must be entered.

❑ Consider which servers will synchronize content download updates from Microsoft and which from another SUS server. The synchronization partner for a SUS server is chosen in the Set Options page of the SUS server administration site. Figure 5-7 shows this page.

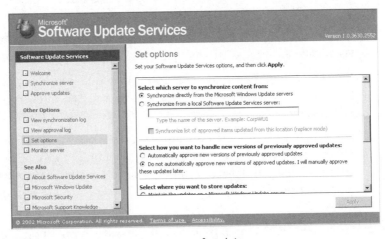

Figure 5-7   Configuring the source of updates

❑ Use the Set Options page, as shown in Figure 5-8, to enter proxy settings for SUS servers that must use a proxy server to reach the Internet. Consider languages that are required. All language-specific updates are available and will be downloaded and synchronized by default. To improve performance, select only the languages you will need. Take the time, however, to identify which languages are needed so that the appropriate language fix is available. Consider where content will be stored. In most cases, content will be stored on the SUS server, but you might decide that clients should be instructed to download updates directly from Microsoft. This might be the preferred solution for remote clients. In this case, a separate SUS server can be configured. When clients connect to the network, they will be notified that they need to obtain that patch directly from Microsoft.

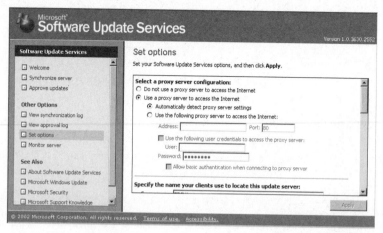

Figure 5-8 Pointing the isolated SUS server to the content management server

❑ Consider the administrative platform. If Windows Server 2003 is used, additional configuration for the browser—to add SUS sites to the local intranet zone—is necessary.

❑ Identify who will perform administrative practices such as auditing the reports in a production environment, monitoring for notifications, download reference files and review them, check security Web sites, monitor and record changes, and generate reports. Design and use a tracking log for this purpose.

❑ Review server actions and health. (Review synchronization and approval logs.)

Updating Isolated Network Segments Using Microsoft Content Management Server

SUS was designed to automate the process of updating Windows computers behind firewalls. Before it can do so, the SUS server must have access to the Internet to update its database of security patches. How, then, can you keep computers that do not have Internet access or WAN access to the rest of your network up to date? You configure a content management server to act as a repository of software updates. The content management server acts as a SUS distribution point. You then configure a SUS server on the isolated network segment to synchronize its content with the SUS distribution point.

The content management server must run IIS 5.0 or later but does not need to run SUS. You create the content management server by copying the content of a running SUS server's \Content folder to an IIS virtual directory created for this purpose. Copy the following items from a source server running SUS to a folder named \Content on the content management server.

- *<from the root of the SUS Web site>*\Aucatalog.cab

- *<from the root of the SUS Web site>*\Aurtf.cab

- *<from the root of the SUS Web site>*\approveditems.txt

- files and folders from the SUS folder \content\cabs (The SUS folder is the folder where update content is stored. This location is selected on the NTFS drive with the most room or, during a custom installation, it can be selected by the installer.)

Next create an IIS virtual directory root named *content*. (The location will be http://*<servername>*/content).

Finally, install a SUS server on the isolated network segment. Computers on this segment should be pointed to this SUS server to automatically download and install approved updates. To make the SUS server synchronize its database of updates with the content management server, you use the Set Options selection on the SUS administration Web site and add the content management server's name to the text box in the Select Which Server To Synchronize Content From area, as shown in Figure 5-7.

You must then configure computers on the isolated segment to obtain their updates from the SUS server. Be sure to manually update the content management server when new updates are approved.

Practice: Documenting Business and Technical Constraints for the SUS Infrastructure Design

In this practice, you will document constraints for an SUS infrastructure design for a fictitious company. Read the scenario and then answer the questions that follow. If you are unable to answer a question, review the lesson materials and try the question again. You can find answers to the questions in the "Questions and Answers" section at the end of the chapter.

Scenario

You are a new security engineer for Tailspin Toys. The company needs a solution to its security patching problems. Your boss asks you to use what you know and do some research on the Web to document the business and technical constraints for the SUS infrastructure design. He plans to use this information to compare SUS to other proposed solutions to the problem and to support his proposal of the adoption of SUS.

Review Questions

Answer the following questions.

1. What are the business constraints for the SUS infrastructure design?

   _____

   _____

   _____

   _____

   _____

   _____

   _____

2. What are the technical constraints for the SUS infrastructure design?

   _____

   _____

   _____

   _____

   _____

   _____

   _____

Lesson 2: Designing Client Configuration for the Security Update Infrastructure

Configuring the Automatic Update (SUS) clients is the second part of the security update infrastructure design. Although the local Group Policy or the client's registry can be modified to manage updates, the best and most flexible solution is Group Policy configuration.

After this lesson, you will be able to

■ Describe the methods available for configuring SUS clients.

■ Describe the policies in Group Policy that can be used to configure SUS client computers.

■ Describe user-specific settings that can be used to solve SUS issues for users.

■ Describe the registry values that can be used to configure SUS clients.

■ Design Group Policy management of SUS client operations.

Estimated lesson time: 45 minutes

Methods for Configuring SUS Clients

There are four options for configuring SUS clients. You can:

■ Use the Automatic Updates tab or Automatic Updates utility in Control Panel on each client.

■ Use the Local Group Policy.

■ Use a GPO.

■ Directly configure the registry on each client.

Using Active Directory–based Group Policy is the preferred method. In addition to reducing the administrative load, by using Group Policy you can ensure that the configuration is applied uniformly across all clients in a given Active Directory container.

Policies in Group Policy That Can Be Used to Configure SUS Client Computers

The administrative template wuau.adm must be present in the Administrative Templates container of the GPO that will be used to configure SUS clients. If the template is not present, it can be added by using the Add/Remove Templates selection from the shortcut menu. To access SUS client settings, click Computer Configuration, click Administrative Templates, click Windows Components, and then click Windows Update. The four policies that can be configured:

■ The Configure Automatic Updates policy, once enabled, can be configured to schedule a day and time for updating and dictate how updates should be managed. As shown in Figure 5-9, clients will automatically download and install new updates. Choices for update installation are:

  ❑ Updates should be automatically downloaded and the user notified.

  ❑ Users should be notified to download and update their systems.

  ❑ Updates should be automatically downloaded and installed.

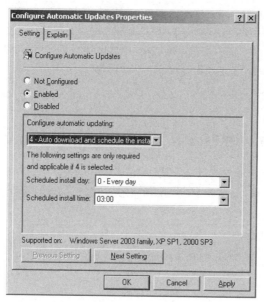

Figure 5-9   Configuring the Automatic Update schedule

Note   The user interface of the Setting tab is misleading because the three choices that you can make are numbered 2, 3, and 4.

■ The Specify Intranet Microsoft Update Service Location policy is used to specify the SUS server and the server where clients will upload statistics (information on their update status including download and installation status). The statistics server does not have to be a SUS server but must be an IIS server with logging enabled. If you use multiple SUS servers, you can use a single IIS server to collect update statistics. In Figure 5-10, this server is the same server.

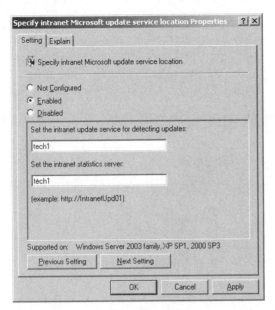

Figure 5-10   Specifying the SUS server

- The Reschedule Automatic Updates Scheduled Installations policy determines the number of minutes (shown in Figure 5-11) after the SUS service starts before updates are installed. This setting is used so that a computer that is offline when updates are made available will be updated when it is put back online.

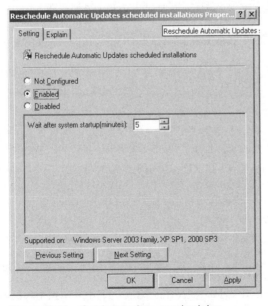

Figure 5-11   Setting update reschedules

■ The No Auto-restart For Scheduled Automatic Updates Installation policy, if enabled, prevents automatic restart if users are logged on and a patch that requires a computer restart is installed. (See Figure 5-12.) If the setting is not enabled, the user who is a local administrator will be prompted and can block the restart, while the nonadministrator will be notified that an automatic restart will occur.

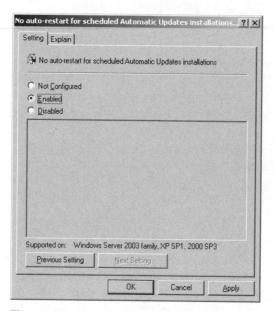

Figure 5-12   Requiring MBSA to use SUS server as the source of approved patches

User-Specific Settings That Can Be Used to Solve SUS Issues for Users

Most SUS client settings affect every user of the computer and are implemented in the Computer Configuration section of Group Policy. However, you can make these additional changes to user-specific settings:

■ In Windows XP only, the Remove Access To Use All Windows Update Features setting can be configured to prevent any user, even a user with membership in the local administrator group, from installing updates. Automatic updating will still work, but the user will not be able to visit the Windows Update site or download and install updates. Because this is a user-specific Group Policy, you can restrict its application to some users by filtering the application of the GPO that enables this setting by user groups. To access this setting, click User Configuration, click Administrative Templates, click Windows Components, and then click Windows Update.

■ Use the Remove Links And Access To Windows Update setting to prevent users from getting updates from Windows Update directly that you have not approved via SUS server. To access this setting, click User Configuration, click Administrative Templates, and then click Start Menu and Taskbar.

Registry Values That Can Be Used to Configure SUS Clients

When clients are not domain members or when you do not want clients to obtain their update policy through the domain, you can use Local Group Policy or configure registry entries. You can make registry entries directly, write a script, or configure registry entries by using a Windows NT 4.0–style systems policy.

To use the registry to configure SUS clients, use two sets of registry values. Add and configure the following Reg_SZ type entries under the registry key HKLM\software\Policies\Microsoft\Windows\WindowsUpdate:

- WUServer—The HTTP name of the SUS server

- WUStatusServer—The HTTP name of the SUS statistics server

Table 5-2 lists and explains the REG_DWORD values that can be configured at HKLM\Software\Policies\Microsoft\Windows\WindowsUpdate\AU.

Table 5-2   Update Client Registry Entries

Value Name	Value Range	Value Meaning
NoAutoUpdate	0 through 1	0 = Enabled (default); 1 = Disabled
AUOptions	2 through 4	2 = Notify of download and install 3 = Automatically download and notify 4 = Automatically download and schedule installation
ScheduledInstallDay	0 through 7	0 = every day Days of the week: 1 (Sunday) through Saturday (7)
Scheduled InstallTime	0 through 23	Time of day in a 24-hour format
UseWUServer	0 through 1	0 = Use Windows Update 1 = Use a SUS server
RescheduleWaitTime	1 through 60	Number of minutes after service startup before the rescheduled updates will be installed
NoAutoRebootWithLoggedOnUsers	0 through 1	Set to 1 to prevent automatic reboot if users are logged on

Guidelines for Designing Group Policy Management of SUS Client Operations

No one combination of Group Policy settings will work for all organizations or for all clients in the same organization. In addition, Group Policy provides a unique opportunity to plan for fault tolerance and redundancy. Follow these guidelines to develop a Group Policy design for SUS clients operations:

■ Design GPOs for updating clients using SUS:

   ❑ Consider developing a site GPO whose main function is to identify the local SUS server using the Specify Intranet Microsoft Update Service Location policy. When a site GPO is used, clients that move between sites will download the GPO and point to the SUS server nearest them.

   ❑ Create organizational unit–based GPOs to manage all other settings and to point clients to additional SUS servers if a hierarchy exists at the site. Because OU GPOs will take precedence over site GPOs, local clients will use the proper SUS.

   ❑ Consider what will happen to traveling laptops when both site and OU policies are in effect. The laptop receives the site policy, but it is overridden by the cached OU policy. To make sure the laptop uses the local site policy, set the site policy to NO OVERRIDE. You can filter the site policy by user groups so that local users continue to use their OU-assigned SUS server location.

   ❑ Use GPOs linked to OUs to set the time for clients to install downloaded patches. Set different times in different OU policies. In this way, patch installation can be staggered. (Clients poll the SUS server every 22 hours, minus up to 20 percent for randomization—this cannot be adjusted. Clients download and install new patches according to the schedule you set. Randomization of this activity is also advised.) Set a default time in the site GPO. OU-based GPOs will take precedence.

   ❑ Manage traveling laptops that are rarely in the office by linking a GPO to an organizational unit to which the laptop account belongs. Because the laptops might be used across a VPN and might not have an IP address in any site, they will not be affected by the site policy. The GPO policy, however, can provide them with the location of a SUS server to download updates from. When they are returned to the office, if site GPOs are used, they will receive updates from a local SUS server.

   ❑ Consider using client settings in a GPO to determine client update actions. If servers require different settings, different GPOs on different OUs can be used.

   ❑ Create GPOs for OUs that contain servers, to "not" automatically install downloaded patches. Instead, set them to download patches and notify. This means an administrator will need to manually approve patch installation on a server-by-server basis.

   ❑ Consider how systems that are turned off during their scheduled update time will get updated. By default, these systems will be updated at their next regularly scheduled update time. However, this can be changed by creating and setting the registry value RescheduleWaitTime or the Group Policy setting Reschedule Automatic Updates Scheduled Installation.

- Design GPOs for special issues:

  ❑ Consider that a typical patching schedule operates on a daily basis. Do you need to apply critical patches sooner? Create a temporary GPO for rapid patch installation. The temporary GPO can change the Configure Automatic Updates policy to an earlier time and also can automatically download and install the patch. The GPO can be linked to the domain or organizational unit when critical patches need to be distributed fast, and then unlinked to allow the normal GPO patch application to be used. Once the computers affected by the GPO refresh their policies, the new, approved, critical patch will download and be installed.

  ❑ Prepare for failure. Sooner or later a SUS server will fail. If more than one SUS server exists, use a temporary site GPO to point clients to an alternative SUS server. The temporary GPO must have a higher priority than the GPO that normally points clients to the local SUS server. When the local SUS server is operational again, remove the temporary GPO and clients will begin using the local SUS server after the next policy refresh. This policy can be used, for example, to point clients of a child SUS server to the parent SUS server should the child SUS server fail.

Practice: Designing GPOs

In this practice, you will design GPOs for a fictitious organization and explain why you made the decisions that you made. Read the scenario and then answer the question that follows. If you are unable to answer the question, review the lesson materials and try the question again. You can find an answer to the question in the "Questions and Answers" section at the end of the chapter.

Scenario

You are a security designer at Coho Winery. The winery has three locations: Boston, New York, and Paris. Boston and New York each have a single SUS server. Paris has three SUS servers: a parent SUS server, a child SUS server used in the testing environment, and a child SUS server used in the production network. Many users in New York and Boston work from home or are traveling a significant amount of the time. Users in Paris all work from a central location. Only a few users travel. You have been tasked with designing Group Policy objects for each location. You need to specify only the settings that are dictated by the information provided.

Review Questions

Answer the following questions.

1. What Group Policy objects will you design? Why?

_____

_____

_____

_____

_____

_____

_____

_____

_____

_____

Lesson 3: Monitoring and Improving the Security Patch Update Process

You design a security update process to ensure that systems are patched. But all the work spent designing and implementing the process is worthless if the patches applied cause problems for the systems they are applied to, are not actually being applied on all systems, or are not applied before an attack attempts to take advantage of the vulnerability the patch is meant to mitigate. The final important step in creating your security update infrastructure design is to specify how to resolve the testing, monitoring, and efficiency problems.

After this lesson, you will be able to

- Explain the goals of security patching programs.
- Audit the security patching process.
- Explain what MBSA can help you do.
- Use MBSA to scan computers for missing patches.
- Describe the requirements for MBSA scanning.
- Audit patching status using MBSA.
- Explain the considerations for using MBSA to audit patch applications.
- Determine patch status by using SUS and client logs.
- Test security patches.
- Monitor and improve the patch management process.

Estimated lesson time: 30 minutes

The Goals of Security Patching Programs

The goal of a security patching program is not just to patch systems. The goals of security patching programs are to:

- Determine which security patches should be applied
- Determine whether the patch installation process is working
- Not break computer systems by applying security patches
- Apply security patches before the weakness that they correct is attacked

The first two goals can be met by auditing the security patch status of computer systems. The third goal can be met by testing patches on test computers before deploying them to production computers. Finally, it will not always be possible to apply security patches to all systems before they are attacked. However, it is possible to make the security patching process more efficient. The following sections teach the information and guidelines that you will need to meet these goals.

How to Audit the Security Patching Process

Use the following steps to design the patch auditing process:

1. Use MBSA to determine which security patches need to be installed on which computers.

2. After your security patching procedures have completed, determine which security patches have been installed.

3. Use this information to refine the security patching process.

To determine which patches are needed, use Microsoft Baseline Security Analyzer (MBSA). This utility scans an entire network of computers and produces reports that list missing patches. To determine whether the patch installation process is working, do the following:

1. Use MBSA to scan against a list of approved patches to determine which ones have not been installed.

2. Enumerate patches installed on a specific computer by using a WMI script or other method. Information on a sample script is included in the sidebar "A Patch Management Equation."

3. Use other tools, data, and methods to determine why patches are not being installed and to validate the entire update process:

   ❑ Use SUS and client logs to troubleshoot patch installation and patch downloads.

   ❑ Use MBSA notes and Knowledge Base articles to investigate specific patch issues.

   ❑ Use the Resource Kit tool Gpresult, the Resultant Set of Policy tool, and the Group Policy Management Console tool to determine whether problems with Group Policy are interfering with the update process.

   ❑ Use normal network troubleshooting efforts to determine whether network issues are part of the problem.

A Patch Management Equation

How can you really tell whether all approved patches have been installed? MBSA reports patches that need to be installed but does not provide a list of patches that have been installed. You could assume that by simply subtracting this list of "need to be applied patches" from the list of approved patches, you will create a list of patches that have been applied. In most cases, this assumption is correct. However, you should spot check this equation to verify that your assumption is correct.

To verify that your list of patches that have been applied is complete, enumerate installed patches by using the Windows Management Instrumentation Service. A sample script is available from the TechNet Script Center at *http://www.microsoft.com/technet/scriptcenter/default.asp*. A script-writing primer can be downloaded from *http://msdn.microsoft.com/library/default.asp?url= /library/en-us/dnclinic/html/scripting06112002.asp* and is also included in the Windows Server 2003 Resource Kit.

Enumerate patches, and compare the list of patches applied to the list of approved patches for the computer. If patches are missing, you should determine why. If patches are missing, the list should match the list generated by MBSA. If it does not, you should try to figure out why.

A simple equation that expresses the result you should have for any single computer is: approved patches = MBSA list of not installed patches + enumerated list of patches determined by using the script. You might need to adjust this equation to account for the application of a cumulative patch. Because you can install cumulative patches instead of multiple patches, cumulative patches can confuse the issue of determining which patches have been applied.

What MBSA Can Help You Do

Using MBSA to identify systems that need patching is not a difficult process. But you must understand what it can do before you can determine the best way to gather the information and then interpret the results. This section describes the reporting functions of MBSA and the operating systems and software that MBSA can scan.

The Reporting Functions of MBSA

MBSA has two reporting functions. It can:

- Scan systems and report common security configuration vulnerabilities
- Determine whether patches are missing

MBSA can report information on a single computer, on a range of IP addresses, or on an entire domain. MBSA standard reports are HTML-based reports that identify security issues on a single system. However, you can also invoke MBSA from a script and report missing patches to a text-based file suitable for importing into a spread sheet or database. By default, the list of approved patches is the entire list of issued patches. A database of released patches is downloaded from Microsoft and used in the scan.

Operating Systems and Software MBSA Can Scan

MBSA can scan these systems and software for common security vulnerabilities:

- Windows NT 4.0

- Windows 2000

- Windows XP

- Windows Server 2003

- Internet Information Services 4.0, 5.0, and 6.0

- SQL Server 7.0 and SQL Server 2000

- Internet Explorer 5.01 and later

- Office 2000 and Office XP

Guidelines for Using MBSA to Scan Computers for Missing Patches

Follow these guidelines for using MBSA to scan computers for missing patches.

- If SUS is used to distribute patches, point the MBSA tool to the SUS server. The list of approved patches on the SUS server will be used in the scan.

- When you use MBSA at the command line or in a script, identify the SUS server by using the SUS parameter of the mbsacli.exe command. In the following command line, the SUS server to be used is johnstoe:

```
Mbsacli /d tailspintoys /SUS http://johnstoe
```

- When you use the MBSA GUI tool, indicate in the MBSA interface whether or not to use SUS, and identify the SUS server to use by entering its server name as shown in Figure 5-13.

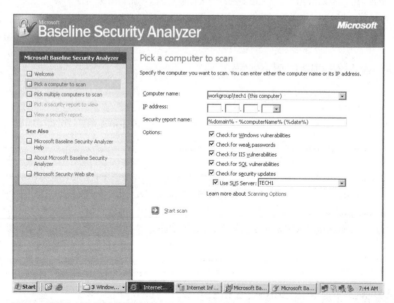

Figure 5-13 Telling MBSA to use the SUS server as a source of approved patches

Requirements for MBSA Scanning

MBSA can scan the local computer and other computers on the network. Requirements vary depending on the nature of the scan. Table 5-3 lists and compares the requirements. In the table, the Local Scan Only column indicates that a scan of the local computer only will be performed. The To Remotely Scan column lists the requirements for a computer that will scan other computers on the network. The Remotely Scanned column provides the requirements for computers that will be remotely scanned.

Table 5-3   MBSA Requirements

Item	Local Scan Only	To Remotely Scan	Remotely Scanned
Services	workstation, server	workstation, client for Microsoft Networks	server, remote registry, File and Print Sharing
Operating System	Windows 2000, Windows XP (if using simple file sharing), Windows Server 2003	Windows 2000, Windows XP, Windows Server 2003	Windows NT 4.0 SP4 and later, Windows 2000, Windows XP, Windows Server 2003
Browser	Internet Explorer 5.01 or later	Internet Explorer 5.01 or later	Internet Explorer 5.01 or later
XML Parser	Yes	Yes	No

How to Audit Patching Status Using MBSA

You can use MBSA as a graphical user interface (GUI)–based program that produces HTML reports to be viewed in the browser. In this case, each report represents the status of a single computer and is stored on the scanning computer. To obtain a more useful report, use the command-line version of MBSA, import the text file into a spreadsheet or database, and then produce reports. These reports will indicate which systems need to be patched and which patches are missing. An additional use of the reports is finding weaknesses in the design or implementation of your patching process. If, for example, no patches are being applied, the computer might not be properly pointing to a SUS server or some network issue might be preventing the computer from accessing the SUS server.

> **Using MBSA at the Command Line**
>
> The real power of MBSA is its ability to post the results of scanning to a text file. This information can be imported into a spreadsheet or database, and reports can be developed that provide an audit of the patching program. For each computer, the file will contain a listing of its missing patches. This information can be used to ensure that all computers are downloading and installing patches or determine that there are problems that must be investigated. For a full list of appropriate syntax,

refer to the article "Microsoft Baseline Security Analyzer (MBSA) Version 1.1 Is Available" at *http://support.microsoft.com/default.aspx?scid=kb;en-us;320454*. The following example command lines show how the mbsacli.exe command works:

- To scan computers based on their NetBIOS name:

  ```
  Mbsacli.exe /hf -h computer1, computer2, computer3, computer4
  ```

- To scan computers using their IP address:

  ```
  Mscacli /hf -I xxx.xxx.xxx.xxx, xxx.xxx.xxx.xxx
  ```

- To specify the name of a file (mycomputerip.txt) that contains IP addresses of computers to scan:

  ```
  Mbsacli /hf -fip mycomputerip.txt
  ```

- To specify a file (notthese.txt) that contains a list of Knowledge Base articles that represent security patches you do not want to scan for:

  ```
  Mbsacli /hf notthese.txt
  ```

- To specify a domain to scan:

  ```
  Mbsacli /hf -d tailspintoys
  ```

- To specify the name of a file (myscan.txt) to put output in:

  ```
  Mbsacli /hf -o tab -f myscan.txt
  ```

- To specify a password to be used for the scan. (Note that NTLM is used; the password is not sent in clear text over the network.)

  ```
  Mbsacli /hf -I xxx.xxx.xxx.xxx -u administrator -p password
  ```

- To specify the SUS server to use to identify approved patches:

  ```
  Mbsacli /hf -sus "http://susserver"
  ```

- To specify a scan of tailspintoys.com and place the results in the myscan.txt file:

  ```
  Mbsacli /hf -d tailspintoys.com -o tab f myscan.txt
  ```

Considerations for Using MBSA to Audit Patch Applications

As you design your security patch auditing process, think about these things:

- Consider the implications of remote scanning:
  - Remote scanning using MBSA requires that the remote registry service, server service, and File and Print sharing be running on the computers you will scan.

Two of these—the remote registry service and File and Print sharing—are often disabled to reduce the attack surface of the computer.

❑ Do the benefits of remote scanning counter the risk introduced by running these services? In many cases, the benefits surpass the risk. However, for critical servers—Internet-facing servers and other servers for which you want increased security—you might need to forego remote scanning.

❑ Instead of using remote scanning, you can use a terminal services connection and scan the computer locally. Local scanning requires the workstation and server service to be running.

■ Consider the need for the mssecure.xml file and, if necessary, ensure access to it:

❑ The mssecure.xml file is updated by Microsoft as new patches are released. If you intend to scan against the full list of patches, the MBSA software will need access to this file. MBSA can access this file on the Internet when a scan is made. (This means the most recent file will always be used.)

❑ You can also download the mssecure.xml file, place it on the local computer, and then instruct MBSA to use the local file.

❑ Alternatively, you can point MBSA to the local SUS server. (Shown earlier in Figure 5-13.) In this case, MBSA will audit the patch status of scanned machines against your approved list of updates on the SUS server. No access to the Internet will be required.

■ Consider how running MBSA on a domain controller differs from running MBSA on a member server:

❑ It is not recommended that you run MBSA on a domain controller. However, in smaller environments—especially those using Small Business Server (SBS)—you can do so.

❑ Updating SBS to Small Business Server Service Pack 1 will prevent errors that can be encountered by using MBSA on the SBS computer. Specifically, it addresses error messages related to restricting anonymous configuration.

❑ MBSA reports the use of services such as Remote Access Connection Manager, SMTP, and the World Wide Web Publishing Service as perhaps unnecessary. Yet they are part of many SBS installations. Administrators will need to be counseled not to disable these services if they are being used.

❑ MBSA might report that the IIS Lockdown tool has not been used. Because SBS also runs Exchange Server, administrators must be counseled on the proper use of IIS Lockdown on Exchange Server computers.

Guidelines for Determining Patch Status Using SUS and Client Logs

Follow these guidelines for determining patch status by using SUS and client logs:

- Use the client event logs. The client writes events to the system log to record operations being performed. These events can be collected and analyzed.

> **Tip** The error message "Error IUENGINE Querying software update catalog from http://servername/autoupdatedrivers/getmanifest.asp" error in a Windows XP update.log of a computer using SUS for updates is superfluous. SUS cannot update drivers. This error message can be safely ignored.

- Design SUS server log review:
  - ❏ The SUS server checks all the patches it downloads for a digital signature. If a signature cannot be validated, an error message—"The subject is not trusted for the specified action"—is written to the synchronization log. These errors might mean there is a problem with the official patch or an attempt to subvert the patching process.

> **Note** All downloaded patches are saved with a .tmp file extension until their digital signature is checked. If they pass the check, they are then stored with their original extension. This prevents an unsafe patch from accidentally being applied.

  - ❏ A properly configured virus-scanning product will delete any patch that is infected with a virus. Use a product that logs these actions, and review logs on a daily basis.
- Audit SUS clients:
  - ❏ Establish event log reviews that look for failures in downloading on SUS clients. Error messages are documented in the SUS deployment white paper, which can be downloaded from *www.microsoft.com/windows2000 /windowsupdate/sus/susdeployment.asp.*
  - ❏ Review the update.log file in the root of the system folder of the AU client. This file records the activities of the AU client.
  - ❏ Examine the SUS server IIS logs to find failed AU clients.
  - ❏ Examine the AU client status in the registry. The AUState value of 2 means the client will look for newly approved updates. A value of 5 means the client is pending installation of updates and cannot run a new detection. (The client resets itself after updates have been made. The AUState value is located in the registry key HKLM\SOFTWARE\Microsoft\Windows\CurrentVersion \WindowsUpdate\Auto Update.)

❑ Check that clients are in the correct location in Active Directory to receive the GPO that determines their update schedule and source. Use tools such as the Windows 2000 Resource Kit tool, Gpresult; Windows XP and Windows Server 2003 Resultnat Set of Policy (RSOP); or Group Policy Management Console (GPMC) to determine this information.

■ Audit the SUS implementation:

❑ Review the synchronization log to see that synchronization is taking place on a regular schedule: review failure notifications to verify that all update packages are being downloaded, and check the *<location of SUS Web site>* \AutoUpdate\Administration\History-Sync.xml file.

❑ Review the approval log. Are approved updates really those approved? Were they made by the assigned administrator? You can find the list of approved updates at *<location of SUS Web site>*\AutoUpdate\Administration\History-Approve.xml.

SUS Client Log Entries

Table 5-4 displays important events and their meaning.

Table 5-4   SUS Client Log Entries

Event ID	Event	Meaning
16	Unable to connect	The Automatic Update (AU) client cannot connect to the SUS server.
17	Install ready – no recurring schedule	An administrator must log on to install the updates. Updates are listed in the event.
18	Install ready – recurring schedule	Downloaded events are listed with the scheduled time when they will be installed.
19	Install success	Updates that have been installed are listed.
20	Install failure	Updates that failed to install are listed.
21	Restart required – no recurring schedule	The computer must be restarted. New updates will not be searched for or installed until the computer is restarted.
22	Restart required – recurring schedule	The computer will be restarted within five minutes.

Guidelines for Testing Security Patches

Testing security patches is much like many other testing processes. The following sections explain why security patches should be tested and present guidelines for testing security patches.

Why Security Patches Should Be Tested

Security patches are tested by Microsoft before they are released. However, this does not mean that a security patch will not cause problems when installed on a production system. There are many variables that make a security patch cause problems, including:

- A computer has an installed device that is incompatible
- A computer is using a device driver that is incompatible
- A computer has an installed hotfix that the security patch was not tested with
- A computer is using some combination of products that causes a problem

In addition, there could be a flaw in the security patch itself. To reduce the chance that a security patch will cause a problem for production systems, all security patches should be tested before they are used to update the computers on your network.

Testing Guidelines

Testing security patches is much like many other testing processes. Follow these guidelines to test security patches.

- Test security patches on test computers and not on production computers.
- Test security patches on computers that are installed on test networks.
- Test security patches on representative computer systems. Representative computer systems are computers that are running the same software and configured the same way that production systems are.
- Subscribe to lists and visit newsgroups frequented by your peers. These lists and newsgroups are the places that others report their security patch problems.
- Report security patch problems to Microsoft. Microsoft has and will fix and re-release security patches and/or help organizations to determine the cause of the patching problem.

Guidelines for Monitoring and Improving the Patch Management Process

When a patch management process does not exist or is poorly executed, every security bulletin can trigger anxiety, panic, and possibly even paralysis. Because of lack of proper management, more time is needed to respond and an attack is more likely to succeed. This reduces the amount of time that is available to respond. When patch management is under control, each new security bulletin can be calmly considered according to the normal security update process. The patch is more likely to be fully distributed before an attack occurs. However, even sound patch management processes do not always allow enough time to respond to a new threat. Is there a way to increase the speed or efficiency of responses to security bulletins?

Note   A regular process of security updating will ensure that systems are configured to meet threats that take advantage of system vulnerabilities. Often, by attending to sound security practices, you can even have proper mitigation in place and will either be unaffected by an attack based on the vulnerability or less affected than organizations that do not follow these practices. This does not mean that patching is not necessary, just that both efforts—patching and security practices—complement each other.

Real World   Blaster Worm and Change Management

In July 2003, a vulnerability was discovered with the Windows remote procedure call (RPC) service. The vulnerability was considered so severe that extraordinary measures were taken to notify Windows users. In addition to sending security bulletins to security bulletin subscribers, Microsoft took the unusual step of sending announcements and warnings to customers. Many security organizations, publications, and the mainstream press provided information and repeated the warnings. "Patch while there's time," everyone said. However, when a worm that exploited the vulnerability surfaced (the so-called Blaster, or LoveSan, worm), a large number of computers were infected nonetheless.

Microsoft Certified Professional Magazine did a quick survey in which they asked network administrators whether they were affected by the worm. More than 40 percent indicated they knew about the worm but were still affected. They just did not have the time necessary to patch all systems. (The patch was available three weeks before the worm was released.) A small percentage indicated they had not heard about the worm.

An independent survey at *www.howstuffworks.com* indicated that 27 percent of respondents had problems with the Blaster worm.

Symantec indicated that more than 330,000 computers were infected.

To make any operation more efficient, determine the steps in the process and then determine those you can change and ignore those you cannot. You cannot, for example, affect the time it takes to produce and make available a patch, and you cannot affect the time at which an attack based on the vulnerability becomes available. You can, however, influence the time it takes to approve a patch for distribution on your network (approval time), and you can influence the time it takes to distribute and apply the patch (patch time). Follow these guidelines to improve the efficiency component of your security update design:

■ Track the vulnerability/attack timeline. Record 1) the time that the bulletin and update is available, 2) that your test is done and application of the patch is approved, and 3) that patches are confirmed as deployed:

   ❏ *Approval time* is the time between the bulletin and patch release.

   ❏ *Patch time* is the time between the approval and confirmed patch deployment.

■ Look for ways to improve approval time. Before a patch is approved, you check for its relevance to your systems, determine how critical it is, and test it to determine how safe it is. Is information available that allows for a quick determination of relevance? Is a test system in place to test network or server issues with the update? Are there tools for acceptance testing, and is testing staffed? Can the priority of the update be easily determined? Who approves the change? If a change management team must meet to approve changes, do they meet frequently enough? Are there problems in patch downloads?

■ Look for ways to improve patch time. Are the necessary tools or skills available? Is there a system for rolling out the patch to your entire organization? How do you determine whether a release was successful? Do you have a way of dealing with errors? Must some servers be manually patched? Are remote users managed? What about traveling users?

Practice: Considering the Implications of Using MBSA

In this practice, you will consider the implications of using MBSA to scan computers. Read the scenario and then answer the question that follows. If you are unable to answer a question, review the lesson materials and try the question again. You can find answers to the questions in the "Questions and Answers" section at the end of the chapter.

Scenario

You are a security designer at Tailspin Toys, and you have been asked by a network administrator friend to help resolve a problem. The network administrators and the security administrators are arguing about the use of MBSA to scan their Windows network for patching status. Network administrators want to use MBSA on all systems across all networks so that they can accomplish the following tasks:

■ Compile the information in a central database

■ Use that information to audit the patching process—specifically, to find out which systems might be missing patches so that the systems can be corrected, and to figure out where the patching process itself can be improved

The security administrators claim that to use MBSA on the network will open up too many security vulnerabilities that they have fought to get closed. They are also worried about network administrator passwords being exposed on the network during scans, information leakage, and disruption of network activity.

Review Question

Answer the following question.

1. What would you tell the disputing parties? Support your conclusions.

_____

_____

_____

_____

_____

_____

_____

_____

_____

_____

_____

_____

_____

_____

_____

_____

_____

_____

_____

_____

Design Activity: Designing a Security Update Infrastructure

In this activity, you must use what you've learned in all three lessons and apply it to a real-world situation. Read the scenario, and then complete the exercises that follow. You can find answers for the exercises in the "Questions and Answers" section at the end of this chapter.

Scenario

You have been hired as a contractor to design a security update infrastructure for Tailspin Toys. You have collected the following information to help you complete the design.

Background

Tailspin Toys has a single location. Five hundred employees work from this location, but another 3,000 employees, contractors, and temporary workers work from home or on the road.

Existing Environment

There are 100 servers located in the data center. A research network serves the research department's 50 users and is isolated from the rest of the organization's network and the Internet. A single Windows Server 2003 domain serves the entire corporate infrastructure except the research department. Research department computers are domains in their own forest. Research department employees must leave their area and use a kiosk computer in another area if they need Internet or e-mail access. Telecommuters and traveling users use company-supplied computers.

Interviews

Following is a list of company personnel interviewed and their statements:

- **CIO**   "We have a major security problem. We have not been able to keep up with the patching required on our systems. We must have a system that will work as automatically as possible. No additional staff can be hired, and there is little money for new hardware and software."

- **Network administrator**   "Three of my buddies were laid off last week. I don't know how they expect me to put a new system into production. I've been telling them for months that they need to automate the patching process."

- **Employee**   "I'm tired of being blamed for every computer problem. I didn't click on it."

■ **Salesperson**   "Last week I came into the office for the first time in six months. They took my laptop away from me and kept it for two days. 'Updates,' they said. I can't be without my laptop like that."

Requirements

1. Must provide a way to automatically patch systems but allow IT to approve or not approve a patch.

2. Must provide an automated method of assessing which systems are actually getting patched and which systems are in need of patching.

3. Must accommodate traveling users and users who work from home. Many rarely, if ever, visit the office.

4. Must provide redundancy in case of failure.

Exercise 1: Choose a SUS Solution

Answer the following question:

1. Which SUS server installation will provide the best solution for Tailspin Toys? Choose the best answer.

    a. A single SUS server

    b. A parent and a single child SUS server

    c. A parent and single child SUS server, with the parent on the corporate network and the child in the research network

    d. A parent SUS server and a single child SUS server on the corporate network and an independent SUS server on the research network

Exercise 2: Design GPO Locations

Answer the following question:

1. What is the best GPO location design to ensure that computers used by telecommuters and traveling users who rarely visit headquarters receive updates? Choose the best answer.

    a. A site GPO that points to the research SUS server

    b. An OU GPO that points to the research SUS server

    c. An OU GPO that points to a child SUS server on the corporate network

    d. A site GPO that points to the child SUS server on the corporate network

Exercise 3: Solve the Isolated Network Patching Problem

Answer the following question:

1. You propose a separate SUS server for the research network. What is the best way to obtain software updates for the SUS server? Choose the best answer.

   a. Have the SUS server connect to Microsoft directly to download and synchronize patches.

   b. Have the SUS server download patches from the SUS server on the corporate network.

   c. When a security bulletin is issued, download patches from Microsoft to the kiosk machines and burn them to a CD-ROM. Then copy them to the research department SUS server.

   d. Create a content management server in the research department. Manually copy the content files from the corporate SUS server and then point the research department SUS server to the content management server.

Chapter Summary

■ A security update process is necessary. The process includes updating security configurations and patching the operating systems and other products that you use.

■ There are multiple ways to update security patches; however, SUS provides a way to automatically download and update multiple clients while maintaining control over which security patches are applied.

■ To implement the basic security patching process is easy. To make it work well requires monitoring to determine which patches actually get applied and to reduce the time between when the need for a security patch is made known and when the patch is distributed and applied.

Exam Highlights

Before taking the exam, review these key points and terms. You need to know this information.

Key Points

- SUS can be used to automatically download and distribute security patches for Windows XP, Windows 2000, and Windows Server 2003.

- You cannot add updates, service packs, or drivers to SUS server for deployment to client systems.

- Audit patch installation by using MBSA.

Key Terms

Critical update   Is a released fix that addresses a critical nonsecurity-related update.

Hotfix   Is a fix for a product problem that addresses specific customer problems and is available only through a support relationship with Microsoft. Previously called quick fix engineering (QFE) update.

Security patch   Is a release fix that addresses a vulnerability in a specific product.

Questions and Answers

Pg 5-25   **Lesson 1   Practice: Documenting Business and Technical Constraints for the SUS Infrastructure Design**

1. What are the business constraints for the SUS infrastructure design?

   The business constraints are:

   ❏ Resistance to any more control by IT of departmental computers.

   ❏ Money for deploying the infrastructure, including money for servers, test environment, and administrative time.

   ❏ Failure to recognize the importance of patching or the time used to do so with the current infrastructure.

   ❏ Fear of interference with user productivity. Managers have experienced down time in the past because of necessary patching and rebooting.

2. What are the technical constraints for the SUS infrastructure design?

   The technical constraints include the following:

   ❏ SUS cannot update all software.

   ❏ SUS does not provide self-auditing or reporting features.

   ❏ At least one SUS server requires Internet connectivity.

   Best practices advise against doing anything else on the SUS server that requires additional hardware and server licenses. The SUS software is free, but a licensed Windows 2000 or Windows Server 2003 server must be used to run it.

   You will not have the ability to limit some patches to some computers by using a single SUS server.

Pg 5-33   **Lesson 2   Practice: Designing GPOs**

1. What Group Policy objects will you design? Why?

   Design a site GPO, which points to the local SUS server and contains all other settings, for each location. The Boston and New York GPOs should be configured with NO OVERRIDE so that OU policies cached on visiting user computers will not direct the clients to attempt to use a SUS server across the WAN.

   For New York and Boston, design an OU GPO that points to their local SUS server for all users. If you do this and users visit a site other than their own, they will receive that site's policy, which will take precedence over their own OU policy; however, if they use a VPN to connect and receive no site policy, they will still have a SUS server to contact for updates.

   For Paris, design OU GPOs that will point to the production child SUS server for production systems, and OU GPOs that will point to the test child SUS server for test systems. The Paris GPO should not be set to NO OVERRIDE so that the OU GPOs will take precedence.

Pg 5-46 **Lesson 3   Practice: Considering the Implications of Using MBSA**

1. What would you tell the disputing parties? Support your conclusions.

The security administrators are correct that services might be enabled that were disabled in the past to close security vulnerabilities. MBSA does require that scanned systems have File and Print services and Remote Registry services run-ning. Both of these services have been the source of successful attacks on Win-dows computers in the past. They are often on a list of services that security mavens advise administrators to disable. However, the benefits of determining which systems are not being patched might outweigh the risk for many systems. For other critical systems and sensitive systems, these services can be disabled and a manual connection via terminal services can be used to run a local copy of MBSA. The results could then be made a part of the database.

Design Activity: Designing a Security Update Infrastructure

Pg 5-49 **Exercise 1: Choose a SUS Solution**

1. Which SUS server installation will provide the best solution for Tailspin Toys? Choose the best answer.

   a. A single SUS server

   b. A parent and a single child SUS server

   c. A parent and single child SUS server, with the parent on the corporate net-work and the child in the research network

   d. A parent SUS server and a single child SUS server on the corporate network and an independent SUS server on the research network

   Option d is the correct answer. Providing a parent and child SUS server on the corporate net-work allows for some redundancy. Client usage can be split between the two. If one fails, a cli-ent of the failed SUS server can be temporarily directed to the other one. The research network needs its own SUS server. There is no network connection to the corporate network. Answers a and b are incorrect because the clients on the research network cannot connect to any SUS server. Answer c is incorrect because the child SUS server cannot connect to its parent to download new patches.

Pg 5-49 **Exercise 2: Design GPO Locations**

1. What is the best GPO location design to ensure that computers used by telecom-muters and traveling users who rarely visit headquarters receive updates? Choose the best answer.

   a. A site GPO that points to the research SUS server

   b. An OU GPO that points to the research SUS server

   c. An OU GPO that points to a child SUS server on the corporate network

   d. A site GPO that points to the child SUS server on the corporate network

Answer c is correct. When VPN access is used, the user's computer might not receive an IP address that is in the site. Therefore, the site GPO will not be processed. An OU GPO can be retrieved, and the computer will have a SUS server to download updates from. Options a and b are incorrect. The research network is not accessible from the outside or from the corporate network. Option d is incorrect because the remote users might not get a site GPO.

Pg 5-50   ## Exercise 3: Solving the Isolated Network Patching Problem

1. You propose a separate SUS server for the research network. What is the best way to obtain software updates for the SUS server? Choose the best answer.

   a. Have the SUS server connect to Microsoft directly to download and synchronize patches.

   b. Have the SUS server download patches from the SUS server on the corporate network.

   c. When a security bulletin is issued, download patches from Microsoft to the kiosk machines and burn them to a CD-ROM. Then copy them to the research department SUS server.

   d. Create a content management server in the research department. Manually copy the content files from the corporate SUS server and then point the research department SUS server to the content management server.

   Option d is correct. Option a is incorrect. The research network is not allowed to connect to the outside world. Option b is incorrect. The research network is not allowed to connect to the corporate network. Option c is incorrect. You cannot directly copy patches to the SUS server. The SUS server must download them directly from Microsoft or from another SUS server. Patches copied to the SUS server will fail to be applied.

Section IV
Creating a Security Design for Basic Network Functions

After the logical and physical security architecture is in place and after the methods for secure administration and maintenance have been designed, it is time to design security for every network function. Chapters 6 through 11 will help you use the security foundations that you've created to design security. The chapters discuss:

- **Authentication**   The use of certificates for all authentication might not be possible or desirable. What then? You might also have computers that are not Microsoft Windows computers. What then? In addition, new trust models and trust limitations extend and limit authentication. What then? Authentication designs must consider more than simple domain logon. Chapter 6 will teach you how to do this.

- **Communication between networks**   Communication between networks is imperative but must be secured. Creating virtual private networks (VPNs) is one way to do that. They can even provide a method for quarantining client access until a security policy is met. Chapter 7 will teach you how to do this.

- **Server roles** Each server requires a different security design. With planning, server security can be customized to meet the needs of the role it plays on the network and yet be implemented quickly and automatically. Chapter 8 will teach you how to do this.

- **Data access control** Control at the server object level must also be provided. In Active Directory, object permissions do more than provide simple access; they can provide privileged access to servers, users, and services throughout the forest. Chapter 9 explores delegation of control, auditing, and file encryption designs.

- **Client computers** Clients are often ignored when security is considered. Not here. Chapters 10 and 11 define client security issues and present strategies for managing authentication, securing remote access, and hardening workstations.

6 Designing a Logical Authentication Strategy

Exam Objectives in this Chapter:

- Design forest and domain trust models.
- Design security that meets interoperability requirements.
- Establish account and password requirements for security.

Why This Chapter Matters

Poorly designed authentication strategies are a major source of successful, undetected attacks on the network. If an attacker can gain authenticated access to your network, he can operate with impunity and his activities will go unnoticed. Better authentication protocols, limited trust relationships, and strong password policies work to prevent attacks that result from compromised accounts. But to make your network even more secure, you must design and enforce a strong authentication strategy. This chapter teaches the best practices and guidelines that you'll need to create a strong authentication strategy.

Lessons in this Chapter:

Before You Begin

This chapter presents the skills and concepts related to creating a security design framework. This training kit assumes that you have a minimum of 1 year of experience implementing and administering desktop operating systems and network operating system in environments that have the following characteristics:

- At least 250 supported users
- Three or more physical locations
- Typical network services such as messaging, database, file and print, proxy server or firewall, Internet and intranet, remote access, and client computer management

- Three or more domain controllers
- Connectivity needs that include connecting branch offices and individual users in remote locations to the corporate network, and connecting corporate networks to the Internet

In addition, you should have experience designing a network infrastructure.

Many design exercises are paper based; however, to understand the technical capabilities that a design can incorporate, you should have some hands-on experience with products. Where specific hands-on instruction is given, you must have at least two computers configured as specified in the "Getting Started" section at the beginning of this book.

Lesson 1: Designing Forest and Domain Trust Models

It is often necessary to provide access to resources across domain and forest boundaries. To accomplish this, the first thing you must do is create trust relationships. Trust relationships allow accounts to authenticate across domain and forest boundaries and therefore provide the foundation on which authorized access to resources can be built. Trust models define the types of trust relationships appropriate for the organization.

After this lesson, you will be able to

- Describe the process for designing forest and domain trust models.
- Determine cross-boundary access requirements.
- Explain the purpose of different types of trusts.
- Explain the purpose of functional levels.
- Describe the guidelines for restricting trust relationships.
- Describe issues that can prevent networks from supporting trusts.
- Describe possible access requirements and the associated recommended trust types.
- Design appropriate trust models.

Estimated lesson time: 60 minutes

The Process: Designing Forest and Domain Trust Models

A *trust model* is the number and arrangement of trusts within as well as between forests, as well as the way in which these trusts are restricted. To design forest and domain trust models, follow this process:

1. Document the current forest and domain architecture. Before considering the creation of new trusts, determine the forest and domains that exist within your organization.

2. Determine where access is needed. If partner projects require access, determine the forest or domain structure within the partner's network that might become the partner in a trust.

3. Match access requirements to appropriate trust types. You must be prepared to select trust direction, meet trust requirements, and know how the trusts can be restricted.

4. Restrict trust relationships.

5. Design appropriate trust models.

Important   Make sure you understand why domains and forests are created—there might be a very good reason for maintaining isolation. Even in situations where the reason for separate forests appears ill-conceived, there might be a good reason not to establish trust relationships or to restrict those that are created. Regardless of the reason for multiple forests and domains, you should not simply provide full access across domain and forest boundaries.

The rest of this lesson provides information and guidelines that you need to complete key steps in this process. This lesson does not teach you how to document the current forest and domain architecture, because it is assumed that you have the prerequisite knowledge to do that task.

Reasons for Using Trusts

Chapter 4 discussed the design of forests and domains based on the need to provide isolation and/or autonomy. However, there are other reasons you might find yourself with multiple forests, legacy Microsoft Windows NT 4.0 domains, or partner networks you must provide access to:

- Separate forests might have been created by departments or divisions because there was no centralized decision-making over forest creation.

- Multiple forests might be the result of a merger or acquisition.

- Windows NT 4.0 domains might be required to provide for legacy applications that cannot yet be migrated to Windows Server 2003, or they might not be ready for migration or dissolution.

- Partner projects might require access to data within your domains or forests.

- Applications might reside on UNIX systems.

Guidelines for Determining Cross-Boundary Access Requirements

After you have documented existing forests and domains in your organization, you should determine where access is needed. Follow these guidelines to determine access requirements:

Important   A forest represents a security boundary and a trust pierces the security boundary, providing the ability for users of one forest to access resources in another. No trust should be made, nor access granted, to users across the security boundary. When authorized access is granted, only the access required should be given. If, for example, there is a requirement to provide users in one forest the ability to read documents in another, the users should only be granted read access, not full control.

■ **Determine whether access across boundaries is required.** There are three steps you can use to accomplish this:

❑ List stated access requirements. Requirements might be for access to applications or data that resides in another domain or forest or on another type of system.

❑ Question the need for access to determine whether it is really necessary. Just because a need is stated does not mean that it is necessary. By default, you should deny all access unless sufficient justification can be made and appropriate safety precautions are taken.

❑ Determine whether the information required is accessible without crossing the boundary. If information is already present or can be located without creating a new trust, there might be no need to create one.

Many times a request for access across security boundaries is not based on true need. Broad access might be seen as a symbol of power, or it might simply be requested to resolve curiosity. It might be simply something that "has always been that way." Document the reasons for access requests.

■ **Determine what type of access is required.** You can determine the type of access required by considering the following:

❑ Is access required in both directions? Do users on both sides of the boundary need to access resources on the other side?

❑ Determine whether access is required across the entire forest, a single domain, or a single server.

❑ Narrow the stated access requirements to machine and application.

■ **Determine whether current trusts are providing the required access.** To determine this, answer the following questions:

❑ Are trusts within the forest adequate to provide efficient access to resources where needed?

❑ Are previously created trusts efficient and meet access needs?

■ **Obtain granular information of access required.** Although implementing disk-level and file-level authorization is not part of the design process, knowing this information will allow you to restrict access to exactly what is required. You can fulfill this step by making the following determinations:

❑ Determine the files and applications that might be required. Knowledge of the required access can help determine the need for trust type.

❑ Determine the type of access required: read, write, or delete. Determine whether special rights are required.

■ **Determine who must approve the access.** You make this determination by doing the following:

❑ Identify data owners—that is, people in the organization who have responsibility for the data and its content—and determine who must approve data access. Generally, data owners must approve access to data but this is not always the case.

❑ Identify domain and forest owners. Domain and forest owners are those responsible for domain and forest administration. Domain and forest owners typically need to approve the creation of a trust.

Trust and Trust Direction Terminology

A number of terms are relevant to developing trust models. Following is a list of common terms and their definition:

■ Trust relationship—A conjoining of domains that allows authentication and access across domain boundaries, forest boundaries, or both.

■ One-way trust—A trust relationship that extends in one direction. All Windows trusts can be created in a single direction. However a bidirectional trust can be created by creating two trust relationships, one in each direction.

■ Trusted—In a one-way trust, the trusted domain is the domain whose accounts can be given access to resources in the trusting domain.

■ Trusting—In a one-way trust, the trusting domain is the domain whose resources can be accessed by accounts in the trusted domain.

■ Transitive trust relationship—Where multiple trust relationships exist, trust extends between all trusted and trusting domains. Windows 2000 and Windows Server 2003 domains within a forest are in a transitive trust relationship. All domains trust all other domains.

■ Nontransitive trust relationship—Where multiple trust relationships exist, trust does not extend from trust to trust. That is, if domains A and B trust each other and domains B and C trust each other, domains A and C do not trust each other. Windows NT 4.0–style trusts are nontransitive.

■ Local domain—In a Windows Server 2003 trust, the local domain is the domain from which the trust wizard is being run.

■ Specified domain—In a Windows Server 2003 trust, the specified domain is the domain that is the other domain in the trust relationship.

■ Incoming trust—In a Windows Server 2003 trust, the accounts in the local domain can be given access to resources in the specified domain.

■ Outgoing trust—In a Windows Server 2003 trust, the accounts in the specified domain can be given access to resources in the local domain.

■ Incoming forest trust builders—A default user group in Windows Server 2003 whose members can create incoming trusts. Incoming trusts are those in which users in the external forest can be granted access and privileges in the internal or local forest.

What Are Trust Types?

Trusts are relationships between domains that provide the ability to share resources across security boundaries. Within a bidirectional trust—a trust relationship that extends in both directions—users attain single sign-on (SSO), which is the ability to use one account to access resources across multiple domains.

Trust types define the possible relationships that can be formed

- between domains that exist in different forests
- between domains that are in the same forest
- between forests
- between Windows domains and Kerberos realms

The following section describes the trust types in detail.

Trust Types

There are six trust types:

- *No trust*—Windows NT 4.0 domains are created as solitary entities. By default, the Windows NT 4.0 domain has no trust relationships with other domains. Figure 6-1 shows an example of this. There are no trust lines extended between the Windows NT 4.0 domains or between the Windows NT 4.0 domain and the Windows Server 2003 forest.

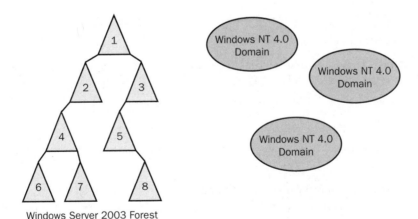

Figure 6-1   No trusts

- *Trusts between domains in a forest*—Windows Server 2003 and Windows 2000 domains within a forest have two-way, transitive trusts between every domain in the forest.

■ *Shortcut trust*—Even though every domain in the forest trusts every other domain in the forest, authentication requests must walk a *trust path* from child domain to parent domain. The trust path is explained in the sidebar "Walking the Trust Path." It might be more efficient to create a special trust, a shortcut trust between two domains within the same forest. This trust does not provide any new access benefits. It does, however, reduce the trust path length and make operations more efficient. Shortcut trusts are useful to optimize performance if a large number of domain trusts must be crossed for resource authentication or if a parent domain in the trust patch exists in a remote location over a slow WAN link. A shortcut trust is a one-way trust. Two one-way trusts can be created if trust is required in both directions. Figure 6-2 shows an example of a shortcut trust.

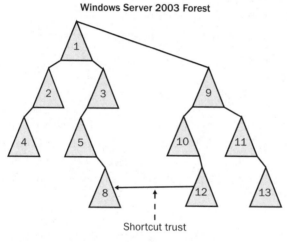

Figure 6-2   The shortcut trust

■ *External trust*—A trust is created between a domain in a forest and either a Windows NT 4.0 domain or a domain in another forest. Figure 6-3 shows several external trusts. Characteristics of external trusts include:

❑ The trust is a one-way, nontransitive Windows NT 4.0–style trust.

❑ If you want trust to extend in both directions, you must create two one-way external trusts.

❑ The trust is nontransitive—that is, the trust does not extend to other domains. If you want trusts between multiple domains, you must establish a trust between each domain. Figure 6-4 shows how a complete trust between all domains in two different forests would be created. It shows two one-way trusts extended between each domain.

❑ NTLM will be used to authenticate the trust.

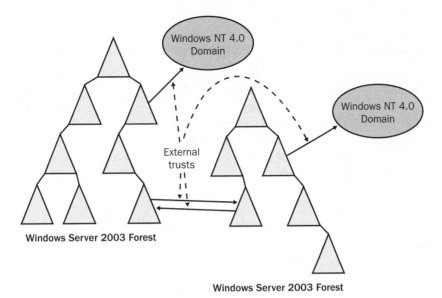

Figure 6-3   External trusts

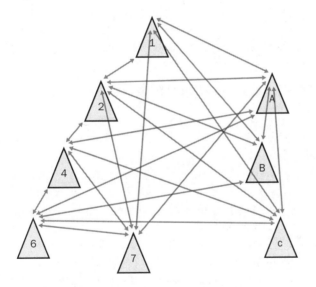

Windows 2003 Server Forest

Figure 6-4   Establishing complete trust

■ *External trust with a non-Windows Kerberos realm*—A realm is similar to a Windows domain. It is a logical collection of computers. If a realm trust is required, it can be created. A realm trust can be one-way or two-way, transitive or nontransitive, depending on the realm and the needs of the trust users.

> **See Also**   Instructions for creating a realm trust are at *http://www.microsoft.com/technet* */prodtechnol/windowsserver2003/proddocs/entserver/domadmin_createrealmtrust.asp*.

■ *Forest trust*—A forest trust can be created between two Windows Server 2003 forests. These trusts can be one-way or two-way trusts and are transitive. In a forest trust, every domain trusts every other domain in the other forests. Figure 6-5 shows an example of a forest trust. A forest trust can be created only between two Windows Server 2003 forests. Both forests must be at the Windows Server 2003 forest functional level.

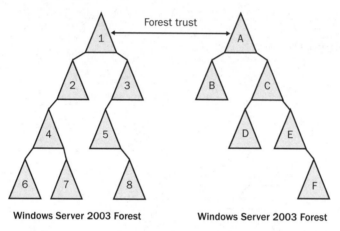

Figure 6-5   The forest trust

Walking the Trust Path

Within a Windows Server 2003 or Windows 2000 forest, every domain trusts every other domain. If Sally, a user from the west.mo.tailspintoys.com domain, wants to access a file in the newyork.west.worldwideimporters.com domain (assuming the worldwideimporters.com tree is part of the tailspintoys.com forest) and has been authorized to do so, she can access a file without the need to do anything special. However, for Sally to obtain access, her computer system must request a session ticket for the server in the east.newyork.worldwideimporters.com domain by making multiple requests. Although all domains trust each other, each domain has only cross-domain credentials to access its child domains or its parent domain.

Session ticket requests are said to "walk a trust path" until they can make the request of a domain controller in the same domain as the resource computer. In Sally's case, the trust path included the following computers, as shown in Figure 6-6.

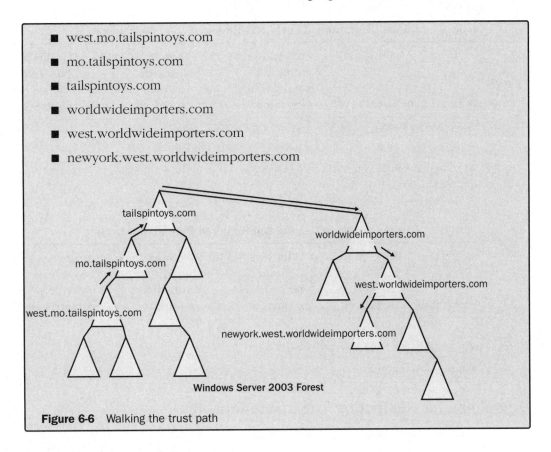

- west.mo.tailspintoys.com
- mo.tailspintoys.com
- tailspintoys.com
- worldwideimporters.com
- west.worldwideimporters.com
- newyork.west.worldwideimporters.com

Figure 6-6   Walking the trust path

What Are Functional Levels?

Before a forest trust can be created between two Windows Server 2003 forests, they both must have a Windows Server 2003 forest functional level. Functional levels are formal designations that cannot be set if their restrictions on domain controller operating systems are not met. Both domain and forest functional levels are available. In each case, a functional level can be configured when domains controller requirements are met. Forest trust creation is not the only benefit. Table 6-1 lists the domain, and Table 6-2 lists the forest functional levels and the type of operating system domain controllers required for each.

Important   On the domain controller, the operating system level is important in setting the functional level. Windows NT 4.0 and Windows 2000 servers and Windows NT 4.0 Workstation, Windows XP Professional, and Windows 2000 Professional computers can be joined in the domains and not affect the ability to raise functional level.

Table 6-1   Domain Functional Levels and Required Domain Controllers

Domain Functional Level	Windows NT 4.0 domain controllers required?	Windows 2000 domain controllers required?	Windows Server 2003 domain controllers required?
Windows 2000 Mixed	Yes	Yes	Yes
Windows 2000 Native	No	Yes	Yes
Windows Server 2003 Interim	Yes	No	Yes
Windows Server 2003	No	No	Yes

Table 6-2   Forest Functional Levels and Required Domain Controllers

Forest Functional Level	Windows NT 4.0 domain controllers required?	Windows 2000 domain controllers required?	Windows Server 2003 domain controllers required?
Windows 2000	Yes	Yes	Yes
Windows Server 2003 Interim	Yes	No	Yes
Windows Server 2003	No	No	Yes

Guidelines for Restricting Trust Relationships

After you create a trust, you must restrict trust relationships. This section describes how trust relationships are automatically restricted, defines Security Identifier (SID) filtering and selective authentication—important trust relationship concepts—and then provides guidelines for restricting trust relationships.

Ways That Trust Relationships Are Automatically Restricted

Trust relationships are automatically restricted in three ways:

- Direction—Trusts are one-way or made bidirectional by creating two, one-way trusts.

- Between specified domains or specified forests—The trust relationship created between two domains is not transitive. The trust relationship created between two forests is not transitive.

- Access to applications, files, folders, and other resources must be explicitly granted—The trust relationship does not change normal Windows Server 2003 authorization processes.

However, the trust relationship can be abused and unintended and perhaps unauthorized access can be gained across a trust. For each type of abuse, a trust restriction exists. The wise designer will use the following restrictions where appropriate.

What Is SID Filtering?

SID filtering is a process that does not allow the use of SIDs from outside the forest to be used to access resources within the forest. When a user attempts to access resources across forest boundaries SIDs are dropped from the user's access credentials if they do not come from the forest in which the user's account resides.

This process might be necessary to prevent forged SIDs, which might grant the user unauthorized access to resources. For example, a domain administrator from a child domain can add the Administrator SID from the parent domain of his SID History to gain domain administrator rights in the parent domain. If the parent domain is the root domain, the malicious domain administrator will have Enterprise Administrator rights. While there is no specific Windows interface to directly and arbitrarily add SIDs to the user's credentials, a malicious user might find a way to programmatically do so.

> **Important**   The SID of a security principal identifies not only the security principal, but also the domain where its account resides. In Windows NT 4.0, a user has only one user account SID, but in Windows 2000 and later, a user might have additional SIDs located in his SID History. This means that a user's access token could possibly contain SIDs from multiple domains. This possibility is by design, and it allows the user to continue to access resources in his former domain. If SID filtering is used, it might break this process.

When an external or forest trust is created, SID filtering is turned on by default. Although it is not recommended that you do so, SID filtering can be turned off by using the netdom command.

What Is Selective Authentication?

Selective authentication is the ability to limit authentication across a trust. After a trust is complete, administrators must still grant the users in the other domain access to resources. It is not true, however, that users have no access within the trusted domain until this is done, nor is it true that there are no attacks that might be based on the new trust.

Authentication is required in two places. First, authentication is required to log on to the domain. Second, each resource the user attempts to access, checks the user's authentication credentials or requires an additional authentication. When a user attempts access across a trust, the trusting domain requires the user to authenticate, and then checks the user's credentials to determine whether the access requested is permitted. As part of the credentials check, the domain checks to see the user's group memberships on the trusting domain. In addition to belonging to any domain groups an administrator has added the trusted domain user to, this user is a member of the Everyone group and the Network group—two *implicit* groups, or groups whose membership is determined by a user's status on the network rather than by explicit placement of the user in a group. Because of the wide access that the Everyone group can potentially have within computers of the domain—especially in down-level operating systems such as Windows NT 4.0—even a user who has not been granted access to resources on a computer in the domain might be able to carry out malicious activities.

> **Exam Tip**   A user from a trusted domain can do anything that the Everyone group can do in the trusting domain. For example, the Everyone group has read access to shares by default in Windows Server 2003 and Full Control in Windows 2000 and Windows NT 4.0. Another point of access is the ability to sit down at a workstation in the trusting domain and log on to the trusted domain.

Guidelines

Follow these additional guidelines for restricting trust relationships:

Disable the Domain Info Record   The *domain info record* within the Trust properties specifies the domains that are part of the forest trust relationship. If you disable access to the domain info record, you effectively prevent any access to the domain across the trust. Figure 6-7 shows the domain info record.

Figure 6-7   The domain info record

Use a TopLevelExclusion Record To Limit Trust   A section of a domain namespace can be excluded from the trust by setting a *TopLevelExclusion record* in the Name Suffixes To Exclude From Routing tab as shown in Figure 6-8. In the example, the mo.tailspin-toys namespace is excluded from the trust.

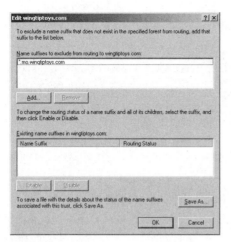

Figure 6-8   Excluding a namespace from a trust

Restrict Authentication   You can restrict authentication across a Windows Server 2003 external trust and forest trust. To restrict authentication means to require explicit permission for authentication to be granted at the server or domain level. Until this permission is granted, no user from the trusted domain will be able to access the resources on the trusting domain.

During the trust creation process, the administrator has the opportunity to select the authentication requirements. He can either select that authentication be restricted or not, and if the trust is being created as a two-way trust, each one-way trust can be independently configured for the authentication level. Figure 6-9 shows the configuration selection during the trust creation process.

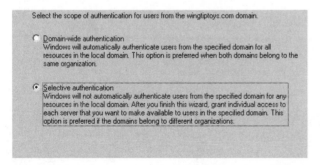

Figure 6-9   Restricting authentication during trust creation

Real-World   Fools Rush In

As a result of a recent merger, one of my clients inherited a second Windows Server 2003 forest and was tasked with providing access between domains in separate forests. A two-way trust relationship was created between two domains: one in each forest. Appropriate access was granted on servers within the trusting domains by adding user groups from the trusted domains. However, no user with membership in the trusted domain's group could access any resource on the trusting domain's member servers. A double-check of the group membership and the access rights assigned to the group on the resource showed that everything was properly set.

We found, however, that the trust had been created to require selective authentication. The administrator creating the trust was not aware of the meaning of this term but "thought" it might help protect systems exposed via the trust. He was right.

To correct the situation, we could have changed the authentication requirement for the trust. Figure 6-10 shows the trust property page on which this can be changed. Another option would have been to remove and then re-create the trust and change the authentication requirements. Or we could have added the user group to the servers where they required access and given them the permission to authenticate.

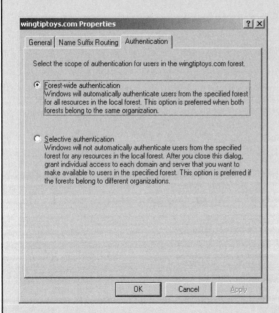

Figure 6-10   Changing the trust authentication requirements

The last option, giving the user group the permission Allowed To Authenticate was chosen. This was the right decision. Only one server was involved and only one group of users required access. By limiting the right to authenticate, we added protection for the server and for the rest of the member computers in the domain. Without permission to authenticate, access can be configured but no access will be allowed.

Grant Permission to Authenticate   After the trust is created, if selective authentication was chosen, the permission to authenticate must be granted to each group of users before they can access any resources. Two types of permission can be granted:

- To set authentication per domain in a forest trust, access the Security properties page of each domain controller in the Domain Controller organizational unit (OU) in Active Directory Users and Computers.

- To set authentication per server in a Windows Server 2003 external trust, use Active Directory Users and Computers to access the Security properties page of each server on which you want to grant access.

  On the Security properties page, you will add the Windows Groups that should be allowed to access the servers or the domain controllers and grant the Allowed To Authenticate Permission.

> **Exam Tip**   When selective authentication is in effect and a user requests access across a trust boundary, an "Other Organization" SID is added to the user's credentials. This triggers a check on the resource server or domain controller to check the user's right to authenticate. A user who is not making a request across the trust boundary has the "This Organization" SID added to her account after she authenticates. These SIDs—the "This Organization" SID and the "Other Organization" SID—are mutually exclusive. Only one of them can be within a user's credentials.

Issues that Can Prevent Networks from Supporting Trusts

For a trust relationship to be created and for access across domain and forest boundaries to occur, the network infrastructure must support trusts. Three network issues can prevent this:

- Physical infrastructure—Domain resources must be physically accessible. Routing and wiring must accommodate access.

- Name resolution—Domain Name System (DNS) must be correctly configured so that the domain name of trust peers can be resolved in both directions. If the domains are not listed in the same DNS server, you must ensure that both DNS servers can be reached by both domains.

- Firewall configuration—Access across firewalls might need to be configured. Access can be tunneled or the following ports must be opened:
  - The Local Security Authority (LSA) RPC port (also known as the NTDS fixed port, an entry made to fix the port used for RPC) is used for trust creation and to access the LSA policy database. RPC by default dynamically assigns the port for RPC replication. Setting a single, fixed value for this port will reduce the number of ports that are required open on the firewall. To set this port, add a new DWORD value called TCP/IP Port and set the value's data to the port you want to use. The new DWORD value should be added at: HKEY_LOCAL_MACHINE\SYSTEM\CurrentControlSet\Services\NTDS\Parameters.

❑   The NETLOGON RPC port is used for NTLM and for a secure channel. It can be identified at HKEY_LOCAL_MACHINE\SYSTEM\CurrentControlSet\Services\Netlogon \Parameters.

❑   Additional ports might be required, such as port 88 or Kerberos authentication and port 135 for endpoint resolution. Port 135 will be used during trust creation, and by the object picker to add groups to DACLs.

Possible Access Requirements and Recommended Trust Types

After you know the access requirements of the organization and are comfortable with the trust types, requirements, and restrictions, you are almost ready to design appropriate trust models. First, however, you must map access requirements to trust types. Table 6-3 lists possible access requirements and the recommended trust type and restriction. These best practices are, in many cases, the only way to respond to the specific needs listed.

Table 6-3   Mapping Access Requirements to Trust Types

Access Requirement	Trust Type
Reduce the trust path	Shortcut trust
Access to resources in a specific Windows NT 4.0 domain	External trust; one-way
Access to resources in a Windows Server 2003 domain from a Windows NT 4.0 domain and to the same Windows NT 4.0 domain from the same Windows Server 2003 domain	Two one-way external trusts, one in each direction
Access between every domain in a Windows Server 2003 forest and every domain in a second Windows Server 2003 forest	Two-way forest trust
Access to resources in several domains in a Windows Server 2003 forest from a single domain in another Windows Server 2003 forest	Multiple one-way trusts, one from the single domain to each of the other required domains in the other forest
Access between every domain in a Windows 2000 forest and every domain in a second Windows 2000 forest	Multiple bidirectional trusts between each domain in each forest

Guidelines for Designing Appropriate Trust Models

After you are comfortable with trust types, requirements, and restrictions, you can shorten the design process. After studying the Windows infrastructure, determining access requirements, and mapping requirements to trust types, you will still need to make design decisions. Follow these guidelines to make the best design choices:

■ **Interpret current forest and domain architecture.**   You can accomplish this by doing the following:

❑ Do not assume that this architecture will remain stable. If you know of existing Windows NT domains, or forests with Windows NT and Windows 2000 domain controllers, you should ask when these systems will be upgraded.

❑ Changes might mean you will create alternative designs depending on the expected change dates and the immediacy of the defined access requirements.

❑ Determine the reason for multiple forests. If separate forests were created to implement administrative isolation, be wary of access requests.

■ **Determine access requirements.**   You can make these determinations as follows:

❑ Do not assume requested access is legitimate or necessary.

❑ Look at all requested access before determining appropriate trust model. One situation in which to choose a forest trust over external trusts is when a large percentage of domains must be accessed.

❑ Do not choose a forest trust when the trusting domain only requires resources from one or two domains in the trusting forest.

❑ Remember that Windows 2000 forests cannot participate in forest trusts.

■ **Restrict trust access.**   You can restrict trust access in the following ways:

❑ Leave SID filtering enabled.

❑ Use selective authentication sparingly. If a small number of users require access, selective authentication is a good strategy, especially if these users are from outside the organization. Do not use selective authentication where a large number of users must access resources across multiple domains. Properly configuring selective authentication might become too cumbersome and inefficient. In situations where these users come from the same organization, there is less risk.

❑ Weigh the advantage of selective authentication—which will reduce risk by restricting access to limited domains or servers and limited users—against the increased overhead from having to restrict access in this way for multiple resources and users and the actual level of risk. Some organizations might have less risk tolerance, and for them, the extra work is not a deterrent or reason for not using selective authentication. Remember, selective authentication ensures that only those groups of users actually granted the permission to authenticate can access resources across a trust. Without selective authentication, every user in the trusted forest (or domain) has the access granted to the Everyone group in the trusting domain. The actual risk will depend on what actual access is granted the Everyone group and how much users in the trusted domain or forest are truly trusted.

❑ Use the Explicit Deny action on the Allowed To Authenticate permission instead of selective authentication when you want to prevent a small number of users access, or when you want to prevent access to a small number of domains or servers.

❑ If only a single domain must be excluded from a forest trust, disable its domain info record.

❑ If a namespace must be excluded from a forest trust, disable access to it by listing the TopLevel as Excluded.

■ **Configure the network infrastructure.**   You can accomplish this by doing the following:

❑ Tunnel access across firewalls to avoid exposing multiple ports. Ports 88, 389, 445, and 135 might be needed for inbound and outbound DACL lookups (to identify groups in an external domain) and file downloads. These ports are not, in general, good ports to leave accessible across firewalls.

❑ Test name resolution before trust configuration. This simple exercise can prevent hours of troubleshooting.

Practice: Designing Forest and Domain Trust Models

In this practice, you will practice various parts of the task of designing forest and domain trust models, including raising the forest functional level, creating a forest trust, choosing the best type of trust relationship, and choosing a technique to restrict user access to resources. Complete the following exercises. If you are unable to answer a question, review the lesson materials and try the question again. You can find answers to the questions in the "Questions and Answers" section at the end of this chapter.

Exercise 1: Raising the Forest Functional Level

Complete the following steps to practice raising the forest functional level:

> **Important**   To perform this exercise, both computers must be installed as domain controllers in their own forest.

1. Log on to the domain controller DC1 for Wingtip Toys as a member of the Domain Admins and Enterprise Admins groups.

> **Tip**   In the real world, there will be more than a single domain controller in the forest, so forest functional level must be raised by logging on to the primary domain controller emulator of the root domain in the forest as a member of Enterprise Admins.

2. Open Active Directory Domains and Trusts.

3. Right-click the Active Directory Domains And Trusts container, and select Raise Forest Functional Level.

4. In the Select An Available Forest Functional Level (shown in Figure 6-11) area, click Windows Server 2003 and then click Raise.

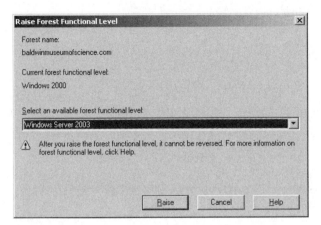

Figure 6-11   Raising the forest functional level

5. Repeat steps 1 through 4 for the Tailspin Toys domain controller.

Exercise 2: Creating a Forest Trust

Complete the following steps to practice creating a forest trust:

1. Log on as a member of the Domain Admins and Enterprise Admins groups to DC1 of Wingtip Toys. (This will be the local domain in the trust relationship wizard.)

2. Open Active Directory Domains and Trusts.

3. Right-click the domain node for the forest root domain, and select properties from the context menu.

4. Select the Trust tab, and click New Trust.

5. Enter the DNS name of the other forest. This name is taken from the root domain name of the forest—in this case, tailspintoys.com. This forest will be referred to as the specified forest in the trust wizard.

6. Select Forest Trust, and then click Next.

7. On the Direction Of Trust page, select the trust direction Two-Way Trust and click Next.

8. Select the Outgoing Trust Authentication level—in this case, Forest Wide Authentication—and click Next.

9. Select the Incoming Trust Authentication level—in this case, Forest Wide Authentication—and click Next.

10. Notice the summary information, and click Next.

11. Confirm the incoming trust, and click Next.

12. Confirm the outgoing trust, and click Next.

13. Review trust status, and click Next.

14. Review the Trust properties page, and click Finish.

    Wingtip Toys should be listed in the trusted (outgoing) and trusting (incoming) trust boxes.

Exercise 3: Choosing the Best Type of Trust Relationship

Read the following scenario and then answer the questions that follow.

Scenario   Humongous Insurance provides health insurance for employees of your company, Tailspin Toys. Humongous Insurance is working on developing new types of insurance for IT operations. To do so, they have established a Windows Server 2003 forest as the heart of an extranet and invited their customers with IT operations to participate. The forest contains three domains—two of which have resources that Humongous Insurance wants to make available to its partners.

Review Questions   Answer the following questions.

1. What is the best type of trust relationship between Tailspin Toys and Humongous Insurance to allow Tailspin Toys employees to work with Humongous Insurance resources?

   _____

2. Why is this the best type of trust relationship?

   _____

   _____

   _____

   _____

Exercise 4: Choosing a Technique to Restrict User Access to Resources

Read the following scenario and then answer the questions that follow.

Scenario   You discover that the Tailspin Toys finance department has been running its own forest. Users in the finance department have been using two accounts: one for the Tailspin Toys forest and one for the finance department forest. To remove the finance department users' need to use two accounts, you decide to create a trust between the two forests. Users in the finance department will have one account—their corporate account. Access to appropriate resources will be granted across the trust. There are only 20 Finance department employees and a single domain in the finance forest.

Review Questions   Answer the following questions.

1. What technique will you use to restrict user access to the resources in the finance department forest?

   _____

2. Why is this the best technique for this situation?

   _____

   _____

Lesson 2: Designing Authentication in a Heterogeneous Network

An authentication strategy would not be complete unless it encompassed the use of diverse systems. Today's networks are typically composed of computers running multiple operating systems. Every flavor of Windows operating system can be present, along with a mainframe computer, a midrange system such as AS-400, and one or more versions of UNIX, Linux, or both. For users to access resources on these computers, they must authenticate. Keeping in mind that most of these systems do not use the same authentication protocols, how can access be granted?

After this lesson, you will be able to

- Describe the process for designing authentication in a heterogeneous network.
- List and describe the major network authentication protocols available in Windows Server 2003.
- Identify the authentication protocols that can be used by different operating systems.
- Describe techniques for strengthening authentication processes.
- Explain the guidelines for designing authentication for a heterogeneous network.

Estimated lesson time: 60 minutes

The Process: Designing Authentication for a Heterogeneous Network

To design authentication for a heterogeneous network, follow this process:

1. Review available authentication protocols.

2. Document which systems can be configured to use which authentication protocols.

3. Review techniques for strengthening authentication processes.

4. Review best practices and guidelines for designing authentication for a heterogeneous network.

5. Design a solution.

The following sections provide the information and guidelines you need to complete this process.

Available Authentication Protocols

Windows Server 2003 does not introduce any new network authentication protocols. Instead, it maintains the ability to be backward compatible with previous versions of Windows. The following authentication protocols must be considered:

- Kerberos
- LAN Manager
- NTLM and NTLMv2
- Certificates
- Remote access protocols
- Web-based protocols

This section describes these authentication protocols in detail, except for the remote access protocols and Web-based protocols, which are examined in Chapters 7 and 13, respectively.

Kerberos

Kerberos version 5 is an Internet Engineering Task Force (IETF) RFC 1510 standard network authentication protocol that is recognized as a very secure protocol. Kerberos is the default protocol used between domain members of a Windows Server 2003 or Windows 2000 domain. The following brief steps describe the Kerberos protocol as implemented on Windows Server 2003 and some of its security benefits. The Kerberos authentication process is split into two parts: authentication and receipt of the ticket granting ticket (TGT), and using the TGT to obtain session tickets.

How Authentication and Receipt of TGT Works

This is the process:

1. The user enters her logon credentials.

2. The Local Security Authority (LSA) hashes the entered password and then uses it to encrypt the machine time. A plain-text copy of the same timestamp is packaged with the encrypted version. This package, called the authenticator, is passed by the LSA to the Kerberos package on the client.

3. The authenticator is sent to the Kerberos Distribution Center (KDC) or account database on a domain controller.

4. The KDC compares the plain-text timestamp with its own system time. If the time difference is not within the Kerberos policy "Maximum tolerance for computer clock synchronization," the request is dropped. Otherwise, the process continues.

   The Kerberos policy is part of the Account Policies of the GPO linked to the domain.

5. The KDC encrypts the plain-text timestamp using the stored password hash of the user and compares the result to the presented encrypted timestamp.

6. If the results match, the user is authenticated and sent a TGT. The TGT includes information encrypted using the password it has of the user's computer, and thus it can be used only by that computer. It also includes authorization information in the form of a list of SIDs, including the user's SID and the SIDs of the groups she is a member of.

How Obtaining Session Tickets Works

This is the process:

1. When the user requests access to a resource, a session ticket must be obtained. The TGT is returned to the KDC along with a fresh authenticator and a request for a specific resource.

2. The KDC checks the plain-text timestamp in the authenticator and rejects the request if the time difference between this stamp and its own clock is greater than the time skew. Otherwise, the inspection continues.

3. The KDC encrypts the plain-text timestamp using the user's password hash from the account database and comparing it to the encrypted timestamp in the authenticator.

4. If there is a match, a session ticket is prepared and sent to the user.

   Part of the session ticket is encrypted using the password hash of the user's machine account so that it can be read and stored by the user's computer. Part of the session ticket is encrypted using the password hash of the computer account on which the service or resource resides that the user has requested access to. This allows that computer to know that the material is provided by the KDC. (Only the KDC could know its password.)

5. The session ticket can be used to authenticate to the resource computer.

LAN Manager

The LAN Manager (LM) protocol was developed many years ago by Microsoft and was first used by the network client developed for early versions of Windows. It is a challenge/response network authentication protocol. The LAN Manager challenge/response process is as follows:

1. The user enters a password.

2. The LSA hash encrypts the password using the same algorithm used to encrypt the password for storage in the domain controller database. The plain-text password is discarded.

3. The client requests authentication from the domain controller by sending the user name.

4. The domain controller returns the challenge—a 16-bit random number called a *nonce.*

   The encrypted nonce is used to prevent replay attacks. Should the nonce be captured, an attacker can't use it to successfully authenticate without a copy of the password hash that is used to encrypt it.

5. The client uses the password hash as the key, encrypts the challenge string, and then sends it to the domain controller along with the user name. This package is called the *response.*

   If the response is captured, it might be used in a password-cracking attack if the attacker can also intercept the nonce.

6. The domain controller uses its copy of the client's password hash from its database to encrypt the challenge string. The two hashed challenge strings are compared. If they match, the client is authenticated.

The weakness of the LM authentication protocol is its use of a weak password and a weak password encryption process. The password format is weak because of the following reasons:

- All lowercase entries are converted to uppercase for storage. Thus a password composed of uppercase and lowercase letters and numbers is really only a password composed of uppercase letters and numbers. In general, creating a password composed of different types of data is more secure, and the more varied the types of data, the more secure is the password.

- The password cannot be greater than 14 characters in length. In general, the longer the password, the harder it is to crack and therefore the more secure it is.

The password encryption process is weak because the password is divided into two 7-character chunks, and each chunk is processed separately. The results are then appended together. Cracking the password is easier because two 7-character passwords can be cracked much faster than one 14-character password.

NTLM and NTLMv2

NTLM, or the Windows NT LAN Manager authentication protocol, was developed and provided by Microsoft with the first versions of Windows NT. The NTLM network authentication protocol is a challenge/response protocol. The challenge/response process is similar to that of the LM protocol with the following exceptions:

- The password itself can be much longer than 14 characters. In Windows Server 2003, it can be up to 128 characters long. Previous versions of Windows NT and Windows Server 2000 could not accept passwords of this length. However, the GUI interface provided was not designed to allow them. A custom interface could be devised. In Windows Server 2003, long passwords can be entered in the GUI.

- An MD5 hash of the full password is used. There is no division into 7-character chunks and case is preserved. NTLM also accepts all UNICODE characters, whereas LAN Manger accepted only certain ASCII characters. Cracking a 14-character NTLM password takes much longer than cracking a 14-character LM password. In fact, for good passwords and given current technology, NTLM hashes cannot be cracked within a lifetime.

- With NTLMv2, additional session security can be negotiated, including message integrity and message confidentiality including 128-bit encryption for applications that have been coded to use session security (although few have been). NTLMv2 also adds anti-reply timestamps, which require the server and client to have their clocks synchronized within 30 minutes.

Certificates

The Public Key Infrastructure (PKI) necessary to support the use of certificates in a Windows Server 2003 forest was described in Chapter 2. Certificates can also be used by other operating systems and devices on the network. You will need to check for compatibility. The other operating systems can use browser access to request and install certificates. If certificates are chosen as an authentication process for your organization, remember to require the setup of a Web-enrollment server.

Authentication Protocols That Can Be Used by Different Operating Systems

For communication between systems in a heterogeneous network to occur, a mutual authentication algorithm must exist. Many possible options exist for Windows systems. Non-Windows systems use many systems and protocols that are not compatible with Windows systems. In addition, they might be able to use compatible remote access authentication protocols such as Password Authentication Protocol (PAP) and perhaps Challenge Handshake Authentication Protocol (CHAP), and many use basic authentication to Web-based applications. Table 6-4 lists the Windows authentication protocols and indicates the operating systems for which each authentication protocol can be used.

Caution   Although the Kerberos authentication protocol is selected as being available for each operating system, this does not mean it is implemented and available on the version of the operating systems that are present in any environment.

Table 6-4   Authentication Protocols and the Operating Systems That Can Use Them

Operating System	LM	NTLM	NTLMv2	Kerberos	Certificates	Remote Access Protocols	Web-Based Protocols
Windows 95/98	Yes	No	No	No	No	Yes	Yes
Windows 95/98 with Active Directory client	Yes	Yes	Yes	No	No	Yes	Yes
Windows NT 4.0 service pack 4	Yes	Yes	Yes	No	Yes	Yes	Yes
Windows 2000	Yes	Yes	Yes	Yes	Yes	Yes	Yes
Windows Server 2003	Yes	Yes	Yes	Yes	Yes	Yes	Yes
Various mini-computers	No	No	No	Yes (some)	Yes	Yes	Yes
UNIX	No	No	No	Yes	Yes	Yes	Yes
Linux	No	No	No	Yes	Yes	Yes	Yes
UNIX or Linux Samba server	?	?	?	Yes	Yes	Yes	Yes
AS 400	No	No	No	Yes	Yes	Yes	Yes
Mainframe	No	No	No	Yes	Yes	Yes	Yes

Note   The question marks in the table are there because some Samba servers require a plain-text password to be used instead of the LM or NTLM network authentication protocol. Other Samba servers can participate and use one or more of the LM-based network authentication protocols.

Techniques for Strengthening Authentication Processes

It's not enough to simply find an authentication process that will work across disparate systems. If it were, passing passwords in clear text across the network might turn out to be the one protocol that every operating system might be configured to accept. Instead, you should seek to strengthen authentication protocols and, if this is a more secure solution, allow the use of multiple authentication protocols on the network.

Examples of choices that can be made and operations that can be implemented to strengthen authentication processes are:

- Use NTLMv2 where Kerberos cannot be used on a Windows Network
- Use Kerberos for authentication between UNIX and Windows systems
- Use certificates for authentication

The following sections describe these techniques and provide guidelines for when they are appropriate.

The NTLMv2 Technique

In a pure Windows network, or in sections of the network where communication is restricted to Windows machines, you should strengthen authentication by selecting stronger authentication protocols. Stronger authentication protocols can be selected by replacing legacy machines with Windows computers that can use the Kerberos protocol. When replacing legacy machines is not possible, and to ensure that when Kerberos is not used, the strongest authentication protocol you should specify is NTLM and possibly NTLMv2. You should also eliminate the LM hash from the account database.

Exam Tip   The security option called Network Security: Do Not Store LAN Manager Hash Value on Next Password Change can be used to prevent the storage of the LM hash. Windows 2000 service pack 2 and later and Windows XP computers can accomplish the same task via a registry edit. However, the process is not completed until the next time the user changes his password.

To select NTLM or NTLMv2:

- For Windows 2000 and Windows Server 2003 computers, use the Security Option, Network Security: LAN Manager authentication level.
- For Windows NT service pack 4 computers, a registry modification must be made.
- Windows 95/98 computers with the Active Directory client installed can also use NTLM or NTLMv2 if a registry entry is made.

Tip   Knowledge Base article 239869 (*http://support.microsoft.com/default.aspx?scid= kb;en-us;239869*) details how to make NTLM and NTLMv2 changes for improved network authentication and session security.

Kerberos Techniques

There are multiple ways in which Kerberos can be used to provide access between UNIX systems and Windows systems. Access to resources within a Kerberos realm can be provided by configuring a trust between a Kerberos realm and a Windows Server

2003 domain or by configuring Windows clients as members of a Kerberos realm. Another common scenario is providing UNIX workstations access to resources in a Windows Server 2003 domain. This also has the benefit of ensuring that the UNIX-based users are subject to the same account policy as the Windows users, and it provides a single sign-on (SSO) experience for the UNIX users. One account allows them access to both Windows and UNIX resources. The steps to produce Kerberos authentication to Active Directory for UNIX user accounts are as follows:

1. Configure accounts in Active Directory to match user accounts in the UNIX workstations. (User accounts must match exactly. The UNIX user accounts are case sensitive.)

2. Create UNIX workstation accounts in Active Directory using the host names of the UNIX workstations.

3. Create keytab files for the UNIX workstations. The keytab files include a key that is used to encrypt ticket requests. The files are created using the ktpass.exe utility provided in the Support Tools container on the Windows Server 2003 installation disk.

4. Use File Transfer Protocol (FTP) to send the keytab files from the domain controller to the respective UNIX workstation and install it.

5. Configure the appropriate files on the UNIX workstation to point to the KDC in Windows Server 2003. File names might vary. For example, on the Solaris 9 workstation, the pam.conf and krb5.conf files must be configured.

6. Synchronize clocks between the UNIX workstation and the domain controller.

See Also   Chapter 4 of the Microsoft Identity and Access Management Solution document (*http://www.microsoft.com/downloads/details.aspx?FamilyId=794571E9-0926-4C59-BFA9-B4BFE54D8DD8&displaylang=en#filelist*) presents a sample scenario and provides explicit instructions for configuring Solaris workstations to authenticate to Active Directory.

The Certificate Technique

Certificates provide a universal, strong authentication process that can be implemented across multiple operating systems. Certificates also provide authentication for IPSec policies, VPN connections, Web-based applications, and other remote access scenarios.

Guidelines for Designing Authentication for a Heterogeneous Network

A heterogeneous network does not have to use one authentication protocol. In fact, it might be impossible to do so. Instead, you might have to select the strongest protocols for use based on communication needs. Follow these guidelines to design authentication for a heterogeneous network:

- Strengthen NTLM Authentication.

  - Where possible, eliminate legacy clients and servers that require using insecure authentication protocols, such as LM, or passing clear-text passwords across the network.

  - Where it is not possible to replace Windows 98 computers, load the Active Directory client and configure the Windows 98 computers to use NTLM/NTLMv2.

  - Configure Windows NT 4.0 service pack 4 computers to use NTLM/NTLMv2.

  - Set member computer and domain controller requirements as high as possible. The exception is that NTLMv2 cannot be used by some legacy applications. If legacy applications are present on the network, some machines in some domains might require NTLM.

  - Do not weaken security to the lowest common denominator. If some Windows computers must use NTLM, you might have to reduce NTLM requirements on domain controllers, but you might be able to raise requirements to NTLMv2 in other domains or on other clients.

  - In pure Windows 2000 and later networks, do not ignore NTLM. Configure systems to require NTLMv2 wherever possible. Windows 2000 and later computers will by default use Kerberos. However, in certain circumstances, they might use LM or NTLM.

  - Where possible, remove the LM hash from the password database.

- If you must provide basic authentication for Web-based applications, use Secure Sockets Layer (SSL) to secure the process.

- Use Kerberos.

  - Use Kerberos, where possible, for authentication between Windows domains and Kerberos realms.

  - When computer-to-computer authentication is necessary within a Windows domain, use Kerberos.

  - Train administrators to map to shares using computer names instead of IP addresses where possible. In a Windows Server 2003 domain, this ensures a preference for Kerberos.

> **Exam Tip**   An example of where NTLM will be used in a pure Windows Server 2003 network is when an IP address is used with the Map Network Drive process to connect to a share. Using the IP address will mean the use of NTLM. Using the NetBIOS name of the computer will mean that Kerberos is used.

❏ Where remote access must be accomplished between Windows and other operating systems, use VPN to secure the authentication process as well as the session data.

❏ Provide Web enrollment where non-Windows and legacy Windows clients must obtain certificates.

❏ Where computer-to-computer or computer-to-device authentication is necessary outside of a Windows Server 2003 or Windows 2000 network, use certificates.

Practice: Designing Authentication in a Heterogeneous Network

In this practice, you will work with various parts of the task of designing authentication in a heterogeneous network, including hardening authentication and considering cost when designing security. Complete the exercises that follow. If you are unable to answer a question, review the lesson materials and try the question again. You can find answers to the questions in the "Questions and Answers" section at the end of this chapter.

Exercise 1: Hardening Authentication

Read the following scenario and then answer the question that follows.

Scenario   Tailspin Toys has existing Windows 98, Windows NT 4.0 Workstation, Windows 2000 Professional, and UNIX workstations. The UNIX workstations run applications critical to the research department, but there is no need for Windows users to access any UNIX applications. The UNIX workstations are not centrally managed. The users of UNIX workstations, however, do need access to resources in the Windows Server 2003 forest. Currently, they have two accounts and must use a Windows computer to access the Windows resources.

Review Question   Answer the following question.

1. How can you strengthen the authentication processes in Tailspin Toys?

_____

_____

_____

_____

_____

_____

_____

Exercise 2: Considering Cost when Designing Security

Read the following scenario and then answer the questions that follow.

Scenario   Humongous Insurance has a large number of Windows 98 client computers. When the company implemented Windows Server 2003, it discovered that the Windows 98 computers could not authenticate to Windows Server 2003 domain controllers.

Review Questions   Answer the following questions.

1. What are possible solutions to this problem?

   _____

   _____

2. What is the most cost-effective answer to this problem?

   _____

3. Why is this the most cost-effective solution?

   _____

   _____

   _____

   _____

4. What should you do to solve the problem and improve the security process? Explain your answer.

   _____

   _____

   _____

   _____

   _____

   _____

Lesson 3: Establishing Account and Password Requirements for Information Security

Just as authentication can be made more robust by selecting more secure authentication protocols, the process can also be improved by strengthening password controls. The first criteria for establishing secure account and password requirements is to not treat the development of an account policy as a trivial activity. Configuring the policy is a trivial activity; determining how to best secure an organization using these settings is not. Without implementing a proper account and password policy, your attempt to secure access to information resources will be futile.

After this lesson, you will be able to

- Describe the process for establishing account and password requirements for information security.
- Describe the qualities of strong passwords and password policies.
- Describe the password policies available for Windows Server 2003–based networks.
- Explain the technical controls for password policies and their limitations.
- Determine organizational climate and information sensitivity.
- Describe options for managing the need for multiple policies.
- Design a strong password policy.
- Explain the considerations for deciding to design an account lockout policy.
- Design an account lockout policy.
- Recommend alternatives to password-based authentication.

Estimated lesson time: 45 minutes

The Process: Establishing Account and Password Requirements for Information

Follow this process to establish account and password requirements:

1. Design a strong password policy. This includes the following steps:

   a. *Make sure you understand the qualities of a strong password policy and the password policies that you can use in Windows Server 2003–based networks.* These characteristics are implemented using technical controls, training, and enforcement.

    b. *Identify the technical controls available for password policies, and review their limitations.* To design a strong password policy, the designer must understand how to use the technical controls that are available in Windows Server 2003 and how these controls need to be supported. It is crucial that you don't just fill in the settings in the interface but that you take into account the realities of the workplace. The design should support the technical controls.

    c. *Determine the climate of the organization and the sensitivity of the information the policy will protect.* Security experts agree that a password policy must be created, but there is great disagreement about how that policy should be set. Part of your job is to determine the appropriate policy for the organization at hand. This involves more than just understanding technical issues such as how to make a complex password or that longer passwords are harder to crack. You must also examine the culture of the organization, its tolerance for risk, and the nature of the data it protects.

    d. *Identify the need, if any, for more than one password policy and how this can be managed.*

    e. *Review password policy guidelines, and design the password policy.*

2. Decide whether you want an account lockout policy, and if you do, design it. An account lockout policy is a technical control that can block account access.

3. Be aware of alternatives to password-based authentication and be ready to make recommendations. Password-based authentication will always be subject to the weaknesses of human memory and misunderstanding. Strong password policies are often obviated by human practices such as writing down passwords in obvious places, and it is difficult to convince all employees to construct strong passwords and not to share them. Therefore, it is imperative that you be aware of and ready to recommend alternatives to password authentication.

The rest of this lesson teaches the key elements of this process.

The Qualities of Strong Passwords and Password Policies

Passwords are the keys to access control. You can do much for the security of your network if you implement a strong password policy and help users to develop strong passwords.

What Makes a Strong Password?

A strong password must be defined in the context of its use. No matter the system, we know that in general long passwords are more secure than short ones. And we know that passwords that are not dictionary words or the same as account names, pet names, parents' names, and so on are harder to guess or crack. However, because password-cracking software is specific to the operating systems it is used on, and because ordinary desktop computers have the speed and memory available to crack ordinary passwords in ever reduced amounts of time, creating strong passwords requires more than following the recommendations of the assigned password policy in the domain.

Password crackers work by attempting dictionary and heuristic attacks followed by a brute-force attack. Dictionary attacks simply hash each word in the dictionary using the algorithm that is used by the authentication process, and then compare each password hash with the hashed dictionary words. Heuristic attacks make assumptions about user behavior and attempt to guess some portion of the password. They understand, for example, that users' first choice for including capital letters is at the front of a word, and their first choice for including numbers is at the end. Brute-force attacks simply try each possible permutation of the existing letters and numbers.

Modern password crackers meant for Windows systems also start with an attempt to crack the LAN Manager password. This password can be a maximum of 14 characters in length, splits the password into two seven-character words and hashes them independently, and does not distinguish between uppercase and lowercase letters. This makes it very easy to use a brute-force attack against these passwords. Users can decrease the likelihood of their password being successfully attacked by creating passwords longer than 14 characters. This means that the LM-style cracking attacks will not work, because no LM password hash will be stored. Designers can assist by designing authentication practices that limit or remove the use of LM passwords and remove the LM password hash from the account database. For more information about these methodologies, see Lesson 2 earlier in this chapter.

What Makes a Strong Password Policy?

A strong password policy has these qualities:

- Complex (consists of several types of characters), strong (follows the rules which define them) passwords must be used.

- A password history must be kept. Passwords should not be reused.

- A password change policy should require reasonable, periodic changes and not allow immediate change.

- Nothing should be done to weaken the security of password storage.

Real World   The Case of the Misdirected Corporate Password Policy

Over the last several years, it has been my privilege to teach Windows to IT auditors and to occasionally assist the auditors during an audit of their corporate Windows infrastructure. From the beginning, I found the auditors universally committed to assisting IT professionals in establishing strong security practices. In addition, I've found that IT professionals are also committed to security but are universally suspicious of auditors and the possible interference that auditors can cause in how the IT professionals administer organization's information systems.

Together, the IT auditors, IT professionals, and I quite often were able to uncover insecure practices and establish better ones. Sometimes, however, we were all hampered by previous communications failures. One such example is the case of the misdirected corporate password policy.

At the company in question, decentralization rules. Although corporate policies establish the framework for operations, local management must, in many cases, follow only general guidelines. When I visited, a new corporate information security policy had been in effect for six months. One item on its list was the requirement to have a password policy. In other words, each division did not need to follow a corporate-dictated list of password policy rules; instead, they simply had to design and use a password policy.

The division that I inspected had no password policy. Even blank passwords were allowed. When the auditor asked why, the network administrator indicated that they had established a password policy that required passwords be at least three characters and be changed every six months but that the policy had not worked.

"Not worked?!" the auditor and I cried.

"No," the network administrator said. "We got so much pushback from users and so many complaints from management that we eventually were ordered to remove the policy."

The auditor and I began questioning IT staff, management, and users. Apparently, the password policy had been implemented in the domain without any real notice and definitely without any training, counseling, or preparation. It might seem hard to believe that such a minimal policy would need any announcement. However, it was not the three-character password that was the problem, it was the abrupt change from not having to do anything to having to do something. People do not accept change well, but they can, with help. To IT staff, the change in a password policy is a few clicks. To users, it's something new and strange, something to fear. What if they can't make it work? Then they can't do their work. They will appear to be stupid. They will be looked down upon.

Instituting a password policy could have been simple: a proper announcement, staff meetings that explained the need for the policy, and even short training sessions on how to change a password, where not to write it down, reasons for not sharing passwords, and even who to go to when help was needed. If all these things had been done, even a much stronger policy could have been implemented.

Password Policies Available for Windows Server 2003–Based Networks

There are five password policies you can use in any Windows Server 2003 network:

- The password policy that is part of the Account Policy of the Security Settings portion of the Group Policy object that is linked to the domain container. This policy dictates the technical controls that will enforce a password policy for all domain accounts.

- Some security options and individual user account settings also provide technical control.

- The password policy that affects the accounts in the local database of the member or stand-alone computers.

- The written password policy. Some of this policy can be enforced with technical controls, some cannot.

- The policy that is generally practiced at the organization. Ultimately, all policies can affect the security of the information systems. Your job as a designer is to consider all these password policies—not just those that can be technically enforced—and to design an appropriate password policy and controls.

Technical Controls for Password Policies and Their Limitations

One of the first steps in designing a strong password policy is to identify the technical controls available for password policies and to review their limitations. This section describes the technical controls for password policies, the security requirements for user account configuration and security options, and the limitations of technical controls.

Technical Controls

The technical controls available for password policies have not changed in Windows Server 2003. Controls are located in the Group Policy Password Policy and are extended in the user's individual account. In addition, several security options restrict or extend the policy. The password policy is configured for the local account database in the local Group Policy, for local account databases in member computers in the Group Policy Object (GPO) linked to the container that holds the computer account, and for the entire domain user database in the GPO linked to the domain. GPO settings are located in the Windows Configuration, Security Settings, Account Policy, Password Policy container. Table 6-5 lists and defines the technical controls in the password policy.

Table 6-5   Password Policy Technical Controls

Technical Control	Default	Definition
Enforce Password History	24 passwords remembered	The number of previous passwords that are cached and cannot be reused. Multiply this number times the Minimum Password Age to determine the minimum number of days before a password can be reused. Multiply this number times the Maximum Password Age to determine the maximum number of days before a password might be reused.
Maximum Password Age	42 days	The number of days after which a password must be changed.
Minimum Password Age	1 day	The number of days before a newly changed password can be changed again. If this is not set, a user might repeatedly change her password to get around the password history restriction and reuse her original password.
Minimum Password Length	7 characters	The minimum number of characters a password must be. A password can be longer, but it cannot be shorter.
Passwords Must Meet Complexity Requirements	Enabled	Passwords must be composed of at least three of the following: uppercase letters, lowercase letters, numbers, symbols.
Store Reversible Passwords Using Encryption	Disabled	Passwords are by default hashed and then stored in the password database. Enabling this setting will prevent that from occurring and weaken password protection.

Security Requirements for User Account Configuration and Security Options

To design a strong password policy, you must also understand the security requirements for user account configuration and the security options that are available.

User Account Properties that Affect Passwords   Individual differences can be defined in the Account tab of the User's property pages. Table 6-6 lists and defines the technical controls in the individual user's account properties.

Table 6-6   User Account Properties That Affect Passwords

Property	Default	Definition
User Must Change Password At Next Logon	Enabled	Requires immediate password change regardless of maximum password period.
User Cannot Change Password	Disabled	Password must be changed by an administrator. This is a good choice for a service account. If the account becomes compromised, an attacker cannot change the password and potentially shut down the service.

Table 6-6   User Account Properties That Affect Passwords

Property	Default	Definition
Password Never Expires	Disabled	Account will never be prompted for change. This is a good setting for service accounts. Service accounts are not to be used interactively and therefore would never be able to change before they expired.
Store Password Using Reversible Encryption	Disabled	Passwords are by default hashed and then stored in the password database. Enabling this setting will prevent that from occurring and weaken password protection.

In addition to the account interface, user settings can be changed or discovered by using the net user command. This command also allows administrators to manage accounts in the local database in a way that is not exposed in the GUI, and it allows them to obtain current information about the account that is not exposed in logs or GUI. For example, the following command lists information about the Administrator account, which includes the date the password was last set and the date of the user's last logon. Partial results of the command are displayed in Figure 6-12.

Net user administrator

Figure 6-12   Displaying user properties with net user

See Also   The syntax of the net user command can be read online at: *http://support.microsoft.com/default.aspx?scid=kb;en-us;251394*.

Security Options   Security options are located in the Windows Configuration, Security Settings, Local Policy, Security Options container. Table 6-7 provides information on relevant security options.

Table 6-7   Password-Related Security Options

Option	Default	Definition
Accounts: Limit local account use of blank passwords to console logon only.	Enabled	If an account does not have a password, it cannot be used to remotely log on to the computer.
Domain Controller: Refuse machine account password change.	Disabled	If enabled, the domain controller will refuse all computer requests to change its password. Use this option to refuse all requests.
Domain Member: Disable machine account password changes.	Disabled	Prevents the computer from requesting that its account password be changed. Apply this option in an OU to prevent requests being made.
Domain Member: Maximum machine account password age.	Set for 30 days	How often a computer will attempt to change its password. Use this request to set the number of days for the request.
Interactive Logon: Prompt user to change password before expiration.	Set for 14 days	During logon, the user will be notified that she must change her password within this number of days. This number represents the number of days before the password will expire.
Microsoft Network Client: Send unencrypted password to third-party SMB servers.	Disabled	Some third-party Server Message Block (SMB) servers are not able to use the credentials, as they are normally configured when passed to a remote computer. Setting this policy means that a plain-text password will be sent to any third-party SMB server.

The Limitations of Technical Controls

Where technical controls can be used to enforce password policy, they should be used. However, the designer should understand their limitations:

■ *The password complexity requirement might not provide any additional security unless users are trained in producing strong passwords.* Using this control will force users to create passwords using characters, numbers, and symbols, and this will prevent casual password guessing. However, password-cracking products can quickly crack some these combinations, especially if they are able to use the LM password hash.

■ *Users might write down passwords in easily discovered places.* This is especially true where passwords must be complex, long, and change frequently. Research has shown that seven is the maximum number of letters or numbers that most people can easily remember.

See Also   Bell Labs did a lot of research on memory in the early days of telephones. One thing that the company learned was that the optimum number of digits people could remember was seven. This is why, at least in the United States, telephone numbers are seven digits long. You can read more at *www.hastingsresearch.com/net/05-nomenclature.shtml.*

- *Users might share passwords with co-workers.*

- *If one character in the password is changed before submitting it as a new password, the operating system sees it as a new password.* The history requirement will not prevent this type of password reuse. To an attacker who knows an old password, the obvious strategy when refused its use is to change one character and try again. Attackers know the typical user will change the last character because this change is more easily remembered.

- *Users forget their password and must have it reset.* This means somebody must have the power to do so for them. The typical resource for password changes is the Help Desk. A strong Help Desk policy, training, and enforcement practice must be used to ensure that this privilege is not abused.

- *If a password is administratively reset, the user must change his password because the person who reset it also knows it.* This can be forced by setting the account property User Must Change Password At Next Logon. However, if this is not set, the user might not remember to change her password on her own. The individual who resets the password might realize this and use the opportunity to take advantage of that knowledge.

- *There is no technical control to enforce a user-by-user change in password strength policy.* Often various areas of the organization have different needs for stronger passwords. Administrators and those with access to sensitive information should be required to use stronger passwords. However, there is no technical way to do so. The need to use one password policy per domain weakens the policy.

Planning   A domain can have only one password policy. Separate password policies can be configured in GPOs linked to OUs. However, that policy will affect only the local account database of the computers that reside in the domain.

Guidelines for Determining the Organizational Climate and Information Sensitivity

It is not enough to just understand the technical issues associated with strong password policies, you must also understand the needs of your specific organization. Military, government, and financial institutions—or areas within them—for example, might require and be able to enforce stronger policies that consist of longer passwords, longer histories, and more frequent changes. The culture of the organization, its requirements for secrecy, and the sensitivity of the data that must be protected require this. Some small businesses, manufacturers, retailers, and others not only judge themselves as less likely to be attacked but also support a culture that would not be amenable to such strict policies. Anywhere large numbers of regular people must work, it will be difficult to maintain extremely strong requirements. It might also not be necessary. Follow these guidelines to help gauge the type of policy restrictions that should be put into place:

■ Use current risk analysis reports to discover the areas within the company that might be more sensitive in nature.

■ Use current risk analysis reports to determine the organization's assumed risk.

■ Use industry knowledge to discover the sensitivity of the data that is generally part of the information systems.

■ Ask management to quantify the need to protect data and the sensitivity of the information being protected.

■ Ask the question: What would happen if the accounts were compromised?

Options for Managing the Need for Multiple Policies

You can have only one password policy per domain. Many times you need more. Within any organizations there are areas of sensitivity that require more security than others. The users who access data in these areas should use stronger passwords than most other users. There are also accounts that hold more privileged access rights: administrator accounts, privileged accounts, and accounts with delegated permissions. These privileged accounts should use stronger passwords too. Your work in discovering the organization's culture and the nature of its business might have brought these needs to your attention. Unfortunately, there is no technical control that will allow you to create separate password policies for individual accounts or groups within a domain or to vary the policy by OU. You cannot, for example, use the password policy to require administrators to use 15-character passwords without requiring everyone in the domain to do so as well. You can choose one of the following two options for managing the need for multiple password policies:

■ *Create multiple domains.* Within each domain, a separate password policy can be created. This should have been considered when the Active Directory structure was being defined. If it has been, create the appropriate policy for each domain.

■ *Extend the password policy beyond its technical controls and require users who should be using a strong password, changing it more frequently, or guarding it more strongly to do so.* This option must either be enforced by a third-party product, custom-developed code, or audit. Third-party products might include moving away from the use of passwords as authentication credentials.

Guidelines for Designing a Strong Password Policy

There are many recommendations for the settings that can be made in the physical password policy. Which one should be chosen and why? Follow these guidelines when designing password policy:

- **Consider the restrictions placed on authentication algorithms.** If LM is refused and an LM password hash is not stored in the password database, passwords are harder to crack. Where LM passwords are allowed and stored, longer passwords can be used to negate the ease of cracking LM.

- **Require the use of complex passwords.** Leave the password policy Passwords Must Meet Complexity Requirements enabled.

- **Consider the history requirement and the maximum password age requirement together.** Setting a maximum password age of 30 days and a password history of 12 might allow a user to create a favorite password for each month of the year—something like "Cococo01, Cococo02, Cococo03, and so on," where the number in the password represents the month of the year. These passwords are complex by the complexity standard and are different, but by knowing one of them just as the user does, an attacker can figure out what the policy is on almost every day of the year. (On the other days, she is only a digit away from success. Two guesses are all that's necessary.)

- **Set an account lock out policy.** But don't make your settings so restrictive that the average person can lock himself out by simply fumble-fingering his password a couple of times. More information about this subject is included in the topic that follows.

- **Consider the history requirements and the minimum password age requirement together.** Setting a history requirement does no good if the user does not have to wait before changing her password. The user can just cycle through as many passwords as necessary to return to her favorite previously used password. If a minimum password age requirement is used, the user can still cycle passwords but must do so over an extended period of time. For most users, this will not be attempted.

- **Do not enable Store Passwords Using Reversible Encryption unless you have a specific business reason to do so.** If you must provide access to users who must use systems that cannot use the Windows algorithm, provide this access by using the setting on the individual user account.

- **Do set, or leave on, the security option Prompt User To Change Password Before Expiration.** Most people find it easier to change passwords before they absolutely must do so. If this setting is not enabled, users are not warned and will suddenly have to change their password. This might result in them having to do so under stress.

Considerations for Deciding to Design an Account Lockout Policy

As mentioned earlier, an account lockout policy is a technical control that can block account access. There are benefits and drawbacks to using an account lockout policy, and you must decide what is right for your organization.

There are two schools of thought about whether using account lockout policies is a good idea. On one hand, an account lockout policy can prevent intrusion because it disables an account if multiple tries, or guesses at the password, have occurred. On the other hand, an account lockout policy can prevent legitimate but fumble-fingered or forgetful users from accessing critical data and might provide an opportunity for a successful denial of service (DoS) attack. An attacker could launch a DoS attack by rapidly attempting to crack multiple passwords. When the incorrect passwords eventually trigger account lockout, multiple users will be locked out of the domain and unable to do their work.

Self-Lockout

In spite of the real possibility that an attacker might successfully cause denial of service to an entire domain by attempting to crack the passwords of a domain with an account lockout policy in effect, I have not been seeing reports on this. However, a number of account lockout policies have caused companies harm. Several clients have told me that they abandoned account lockout policies after C-level (CEO, CIO, CTO, CSO, and so on) executives were locked out or when important sales were supposedly lost because top salesmen could not enter their password correctly and had no other way of reaching some required information.

Guidelines for Designing an Account Lockout Policy

If you decide to design an account lockout policy, you must understand the account policy lockout controls and the guidelines for designing the policy.

Account Lockout Policy Controls

When developing account controls, assume that a account lockout policy will be accepted, but keep reasons for rejection in mind. Table 6-8 lists and explains the account lockout policy.

Table 6-8   Account Lockout Policy

Control	Default	Definition
Account Lockout Duration	Not defined	Number of minutes the account should be locked out. If the setting is set to 0, an account will remain locked out until an administrator or someone given the privilege unlocks the account.
Account Lockout Threshold	0 invalid logon attempts	Number of incorrect passwords attempts that can be entered. When the setting is 0, an account is never locked out because of incorrect attempts at access.
Reset Account Lockout Count After	Not defined	Number of minutes before the number of incorrect attempts is reset to 0.

Account Lockout Policy Design Guidelines

When designing the account lockout policy, follow these guidelines:

- Set account lockout duration to a few minutes. This does prevent casual attacks, and if auditing is set and properly reviewed, it can warn that an attack is underway. It also avoids the load on administrator time and the lost user productivity if users who lock out of their accounts must wait for them to be reset by someone else.

- Consider whether you have enough staff to attend to manually resetting accounts.

- Set account lockout threshold high. If users make a few mistakes, they will not be locked. A good number is 25 because it's probably way beyond any number of attempts a valid user will make before asking for his password to be reset. However, it will stop an intruder, who will need many more attempts than that.

Alternatives to Password-Based Authentication

Because password-based authentication is subject to many human weaknesses, you must be aware of and ready to recommend alternatives to password authentication. Many alternatives exist that provide the opportunity to require two factors: something the user must possess and something the user must know. Alternatives consist of:

- Smart cards—Smart card support is built into Windows Server 2003. It replaces the use of passwords with a plastic card and a personal identification number (PIN) and requires the implementation of certificate services. Smart card usage can be configured to require logoff when removed—thus preventing it from being shared—and if users need the card elsewhere, they can ensure logoff when users leave their computers. Smart cards can be used in remote scenarios as well. Smart cards can also provide the solution for when specific groups require stronger authentication—smart cards can be used by administrators, while ordinary users continue to use passwords.

- Biometrics—Biometric authentication systems use some part of the human body to prove that the individual requesting access is who he or she claims to be. Facial or voice recognition, keyboard stroke analysis, fingerprints, retinal scans, hand geometry, and more are being successfully used.

- Tokens—RSA tokens, which provide a changing number synchronized with a server, provide a solid alternative to passwords. Other token systems, store certificates on small universal serial bus (USB) connectable devices.

Alternatives to passwords can be used to strengthen authentication practices, but their cost must be weighed against their benefits.

Practice: Designing a Strong Password and Account Policy

In this practice, you will design a strong password and account policy. Read the following scenario and then answer the question that follows. If you are unable to answer the question, review the lesson materials and try the question again. You can find the answer to the question in the "Questions and Answers" section at the end of this chapter.

Scenario

You are a security designer for Wingtip Toys. The company plans to implement a separate Windows Server 2003 domain for use by the research department. The only individuals who will have access to resources in the domain are:

- 25 toy designers
- 35 research department support staff employees
- members of the Enterprise Admins group

All computers in the research domain are either Windows Server 2003 or Windows XP Professional. It is crucial that the information in the research domain be kept confidential.

Review Question

Answer the following question.

1. Design an account policy for the research domain. Include settings for both the password and account lockout policy.

_____

_____

_____

_____

_____

_____

Design Activity: Designing a Logical Authentication Strategy

In this activity, you must use what you learned in all three lessons and apply it to a real-world situation. Read the scenario and then complete the exercises that follow. You can find answers for the exercises in the "Questions and Answers" section at the end of this chapter.

Scenario

Your consulting firm has been hired to design the authentication strategy for City Power & Light. After several meetings with key City Power & Light personnel, you have compiled the following information.

Company Background

City Power & Light got its start in the last century as the first electric power company in the Midwest. Its extraordinary growth over the years through expansion and merger have meant that little planning or direction in the way of business objectives has been applied to the IT infrastructure.

Existing Environment

A distributed management infrastructure means that each of five major locations has its own data center. Throughout the organization, Windows and UNIX client systems and servers of every type imaginable are used. The vast majority of the client and server systems are Windows. Users can have multiple accounts so that they can access the resources they need to do their job. All data centers are connected via a private, leased line. Many power plants and branch offices use the Internet for communications. At least three Windows forests exist. The Headquarters Architecture Logical diagram indicates the location of resources that all employees should be able to access. The corporate headquarters forest is the cpandl.com forest. Forests for other locations are referred to by numbers.

Interviews

Following is a list of company personnel interviewed and their statements:

- **CIO** "We have a mandate to consolidate and standardize wherever possible. The current situation will not be tolerated. There will be an umbrella security policy established in coordination with all locations and divisions, but under corporate control. Other locations can change the policy, but only where it will make their operation more secure. We are looking for specific recommendations from you on what that central, corporate security policy about authentication practices can be. We are, however, most concerned with our Windows systems and would like you to concentrate efforts first on them."

■ **Network Administrator, Western Territory**   "We are committed to improving information security. We know that practices in other locations are responsible for virus and worm infections in our environment, specifically by their executives traveling to our location. We also have difficulty accessing corporate resources. Our users have to remember too many passwords and get confused by the different requirements that different accounts have."

■ **Help Desk Employee**   "If you ask my opinion, we need a little less control, not more. I spend most of my day resetting passwords and unlocking accounts. It's just too confusing for the users and too hard for them to remember their password. Why, just last week, I had to rebuild 10 machines because their users forgot their passwords and I am not allowed to have an account on those systems or use utilities to change passwords on them."

■ **Plant Manager**   "I hope you can do something about these worm attacks. In the past, they have prevented us from getting good information on the status of operations at our plants."

■ **Finance Manager**   "You should know that there is no budget for purchasing new computer systems this quarter."

■ **Human Resources Manager**   "Our PeopleSoft systems run on UNIX, and you cannot change that."

Case Study Exhibits

Forest locations:

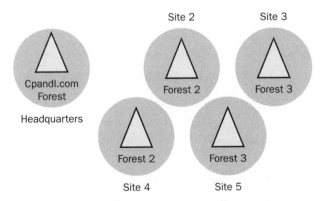

Headquarters network architecture logical diagram:

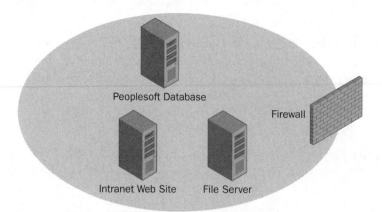

**City Power and Light Network
Shared Resources**

Business Requirements

The business requirements are:

1. Develop a password policy for the entire corporation.

2. Minimize expense of policy implementation.

3. Improve employee awareness of and compliance with the policy.

4. Provide a single sign-on experience for all users. Eliminate multiple accounts.

Technical Requirements

The technical requirements are:

1. Provide for interoperability between versions of Windows.

2. Provide for interoperability between various operating systems.

3. Have the least impact on the current level of security.

Exercise 1: Create an Account Policy

In this exercise, you will design a corporate account policy. To do this, answer the questions that follow.

> **Tip**   Remember that the account policy consists of password controls and account lockout controls.

1. What additional questions would you ask before you create the corporate account policy? Why?

_____

_____

_____

_____

_____

_____

_____

_____

_____

_____

_____

_____

_____

_____

_____

_____

_____

_____

_____

_____

_____

_____

_____

2. What are your recommendations for password length, password history, password composition, and account lockout? Explain why you made these decisions.

_____

_____

_____

_____

_____

_____

_____

_____

_____

_____

_____

_____

_____

_____

_____

_____

_____

_____

_____

_____

_____

_____

_____

Exercise 2: Provide Single Sign-On Across Windows Systems

In this exercise, you will provide a single sign-on across Windows systems. To do this, review the "Case Study Exhibits" section of the scenario and then answer the questions that follow.

Important   Although this exercise specifically requests that you pay attention only to resources in this forest, as you answer the questions, comment on how this design might be expanded to manage the other necessary parts of a total SSO experience.

1. What recommendations would you make to provide single sign-on access across Windows systems?

_____

_____

_____

_____

_____

_____

_____

_____

_____

_____

_____

_____

_____

_____

_____

2. Why did you make the recommendations that you did?

_____

_____

_____

_____

_____

_____

_____

_____

_____

_____

3. How can this design be expanded to accommodate other cross-forest access requirements?

_____

_____

_____

_____

_____

_____

_____

_____

_____

Chapter Summary

- Creating a logical authentication design does not always mean standardizing on a single authentication protocol.

- Strengthening authentication processes requires knowledge of the protocol, its weaknesses, and how its weaknesses can be mitigated.

- Forest trusts provide a way of quickly opening access between two forests without having to create multiple trust relationships.

- External trusts and forest trusts can be restricted by using:

    - Selective authentication

    - TopLevelExclusion

    - Disabling domain info records

- To design a strong password policy, you must consider the impact of each setting on the overall password policy.

- To implement a strong password policy, you must use more than technical controls.

Exam Highlights

Before taking the exam, review these key points and terms. You need to know this information.

Key Points

- You can only create a forest trust between two forests if both forests are set at the Windows Server 2003 forest functional level.

- You can obtain SSO and some interoperability between UNIX and Windows systems, and you can standardize the account policy for UNIX systems on the Windows-implemented policy by providing Active Directory accounts for UNIX workstation users, creating keys for the encryption of Kerberos messages between UNIX and the KDC, and configuring Kerberos on the UNIX workstations.

- A strong password policy takes into account the authentication protocols used in the domain. For example, if the LM password hash is both refused at the domain controller and not stored in the Active Directory password database, a password length of more than seven characters does make a stronger password. If the LM hash is stored and used, a password from eight to fourteen characters long is really no stronger than one that is seven characters.

Key Terms

Forest trust A type of trust in which every domain trusts every other domain in the other forests. Forest trusts are Kerberos style and can be one-way or two-way trusts. Forest trusts between domains in both forests are transitive, but the forest trust itself is not.

Selective authentication The ability to limit authentication across a trust.

Trust model The number and arrangement of trusts within and between forests and the way in which these trusts are restricted.

Questions and Answers

Page
6-24
Lesson 1   Exercise 3: Choosing the Best Type of Trust Relationship

1. What is the best type of trust relationship between Tailspin Toys and Humongous Insurance to allow Tailspin Toys employees to work with Humongous Insurance resources?

A one-way external trust.

2. Why is this the best type of trust relationship?

Using a one-way external trust is the best answer because it will provide the access that is required without providing access that is not required. A two-way external trust would provide Humongous Insurance potential access to the Tailspin Toys forest. A forest trust would provide too much access.

Page
6-25
Lesson 1   Exercise 4: Choosing a Technique to Restrict User Access to Resources

1. What technique will you use to restrict user access to the resources in the finance department forest?

Selective authentication.

2. Why is this the best technique for this situation?

Selective authentication is best used when access to only a few domains in the forest is required.

Page
6-35
Lesson 2   Exercise 1: Hardening Authentication

1. How can you strengthen the authentication processes in Tailspin Toys?

There are two issues to consider. First, because the UNIX workstations are not centrally managed, the accounts might have weak controls. Providing accounts to UNIX users that can access both Windows and UNIX resources will strengthen these controls. Configuring Kerberos on the UNIX workstations for use as the authentication protocol will provide secure authentication between the UNIX computers and Active Directory.

Second, while Windows 2000 and Windows XP Professional computers will use Kerberos in a Windows Server 2003 domain, Windows 98 by default will use LM. Windows NT 4.0 Workstation will use NTLM. Client computers, by default, use LM and NTLM. In addition, Windows 2000 and Windows XP Professional computers might use LM, NTLM, or both if required. Authentication processing can be made more secure if all the Windows clients are configured to use NTLMv2 when LM or NTLM is indicated.

Page
6-36

Lesson 2   Exercise 2: Considering Cost when Designing Security

1. What are possible solutions to this problem?

   Change Group Policy to allow LM, replace Windows 98 with Windows XP, or add the Active Directory Client and configure Windows 98 to use NTLM.

2. What is the most cost-effective answer to this problem?

   Reconfigure the Windows Server 2003 domain controllers to allow the use of LM.

3. Why is this the most cost-effective solution?

   It takes only a simple change to Group Policy. Another option would be to install the Active Directory client and configure workstations, but that would cost money in the form of administrator time. A third option would be to replace all the workstations, but this would also be costly.

4. What should you do to solve the problem and improve the security process? Explain your answer.

   Upgrade Windows 98 computers to Windows XP Professional. Although adding the Active Directory client to Windows 98 and configuring it to use NTLM will provide a secure authentication interface between the Windows 98 computers and the Windows Server 2003 domain, it provides no additional security benefits for the desktop computers or the overall domain. Upgrading to Windows XP Professional enables the use of Group Policy and file access security.

Page
6-50

Lesson 3   Practice: Designing a Strong Password and Account Policy

1. Design an account policy for the research domain. Include settings for both the password and account lockout policy.

   Answers may vary. The following table describes the configuration of the password and account lockout policies recommended for this research domain. Additional effort should be made to increase security with a written policy, some items of which cannot be implemented with technical controls, but must be enforced via other means. Training will help. In addition, each employee with access to the resources in the research domain should be fully aware of the policy and be convinced of the necessity of its implementation.

Table Account Policy for the Research Domain

Policy Setting	Setting	Explanation
Enforce Password History	24 passwords remembered	Requiring a password to not be reused for at least 240 days (password history multiplied by minimum password age) will most likely prevent most password reuse.
Maximum Password Age	21 days	Requiring frequent password changes reduces the opportunities for an attacker to use a password cracker on captured credentials and even on a captured password database. Note that it reduces opportunities. Weak passwords can be cracked in much less than 21 days.
Minimum Password Age	10 days	When users must wait before changing their password, they cannot easily cycle through old password choices and reuse them.

Table   Account Policy for the Research Domain

Policy Setting	Setting	Explanation
Minimum Password Length	15 characters	Requiring a minimum of 15 characters eliminates the use of password-cracking tools, which can crack only the LM hash and then use it to deduce the NTLM hash. While Kerberos will be the default authentication protocol in this domain, there are instances when NTLM can be used. In addition, unless all systems are properly configured, the LM hash is created, used (in addition to the NTLM hash) in responding to an NTLM challenge, and stored in the Active Directory database.
Passwords Must Meet Complexity Requirements	Enabled	This setting requires at least the minimum of complexity requirements.
Store Reversible Passwords Using Encryption	Disabled	This setting should not be changed from the default, as to do so would weaken security.
Account Lockout Duration	0	Administrative reset should be required to unlock locked-out accounts. This will prevent the success of an automated attack that returns to locked-out accounts after waiting for accounts to be unlocked.
Account Lockout Threshold	25	Because a locked-out account must be reset by an administrator, a large number of incorrect logon attempts can be allowed.
Reset Account Lockout Count After	15 minutes	If a research department employee incorrectly enters her credentials and knows that the count will be reset, this might prevent some lockouts that must be reset by an administrator because the employee knows she can simply wait the 15 minutes. An automated attack, however, will lock out the account unless the attacker knows the configuration of the account lockout policy and writes an attack designed to take advantage of it. (Such an attack would make 24 guesses, wait 15 minutes, and then make 24 more, and so on.)

Design Activity: Designing a Logical Authentication Strategy

Page
6-54   ## Exercise 1: Create an Account Policy

1. What additional questions would you ask before you create the corporate account policy? Why?

   Confirm that the policy should be written at two levels. First, an overall security policy that is independent of the operating system should be written. The writers should not concern themselves with whether or not the operating system can technically provide controls to enforce the policy. Second, a specific implementation recommendation for all Windows accounts should be written. Ideally, an account policy should be written without considering the available technical controls. This promotes sound and secure account policies that are not limited by an operating system with weak controls. It also forces the adoption of awareness training instead of relying on technical controls to enforce the policy. In reality, however, policies must be implemented on operating systems, and operating system knowledge might shape the direction of password controls.

Obtain information on the Active Directory infrastructure. What domains exist? What OUs have been created? What types of computer and user accounts exist in each OU? What Group Policy Objects (GPOs) have already be created and implemented? Where are Windows 98 computers located? Has the Active Directory client software been added to them? This information is important because each domain can have its own account policy. Where multiple domains and forests exist, there might be a reason for them. Stricter controls might be required. Administrators might also not understand that OU GPOs do not control account policies for Active Directory accounts. Knowing what the architecture is and what the level of administrative understanding is will influence the design of the policy implementation. Although the request does not specify the development of the training or the implementation part of the process, no designer should ignore their impact. A good design can appear to be a poor design or be unable to do its job if these details are not considered. Knowledge of Windows 98 status affects the length of the password that can be required.

2. What are your recommendations for password length, password history, password composition, and account lockout? Explain why you made these decisions.

Recommendations are as follows:

❑ **Password length**   Seven characters.

❑ **Password length rational**   Seven characters is not a difficult length for most people to remember. Longer passwords are harder and promote more frequent recording of passwords in obvious places. Also, this corporate policy is meant to be the default and other stronger account policies can require longer passwords for domains and/or computers under their management.

❑ **Password composition**   Include letters, numbers, and symbols. Ensure that symbols and numbers are within the body of the password. No names (especially obvious names such as names of the user, spouse, pet, or relatives), common dictionary terms, or specific industry or company terms should be used.

❑ **Password composition rational**   Complex passwords that place the symbols and numbers at the end or the beginning of the password are easier to crack using current cracking products. Placing these symbols in the middle makes the password more difficult to crack.

❑ **Password history**   12 passwords.

❑ **Password history rational**   Preventing password reuse is important because it reduces the likelihood that a current password will be known to more than its owner. It is difficult to know whether the user shared, wrote down, or otherwise made available a current password. It is even more difficult to know whether they ever did so. It is entirely possible that a user wrote down a password and forgot he did so. One of the advantages of frequently changing a password is that it reduces the amount of time an attacker has to crack or deduce it. If passwords are reused, the attacker has more time to discover them.

Exercise 2: Provide Single Sign-On Across Windows Systems

1. What recommendations would you make to provide single sign-on access across Windows systems?

- Create a one-way, external trust between each domain in each forest that has user accounts and the hr.cpandl.com and production.cpandl.com domains in the cpandl.com forest.

- Create access groups in the cpandl.com forest, and provide these groups the type of access required for the resources.

- Place users or groups from the other forests in these groups to provide them with the access they need.

- Remove access granted to these resources for user accounts assigned to users in other locations.

- Eliminate (disable and eventually remove) any accounts in the cpandl.com forest that were given to users from other locations to provide this access.

- Create a gateway-to-gateway VPN from location to location to tunnel trust creation and access traffic between forests.

2. Why did you make the recommendations that you did?

- Currently information indicates that at least one forest is a Windows 2000 forest and no information indicates that any of the other forests meet the requirements for a Windows Server 2003 forest functional level.

- A total of 100 percent Windows Server 2003 domain controllers in all domains in the forest is necessary to change a forest to the Windows Server 2003 forest functional level. This level, the Windows Server 2003 forest functional level, is necessary to create a forest trust.

- In addition, because only two domains at headquarters have information that must be shared with other forests, creating forest trusts might not be a good choice. Doing this might provide more access than is desired and subject the forest to attack.

- Providing access to accounts from other forests, across the forest trust, eliminates the need for users to have additional accounts just for this resource access.

- Tunneling trust creation and access requests across the firewall eliminates the need to open a multitude of ports on the firewall that might easily be exploited.

3. How can this design be expanded to accommodate other cross-forest access requirements?

Each access need requires investigation to ensure it is appropriate and to determine the best type of trust relationship. Additional one-way trusts can be created as necessary. Trusts can be made bidirectional by creating a one-way trust in the other direction. If enough trusts are needed, a forest trust can replace the current trusts.

7 Designing Secure Communications Between Networks

Exam Objectives in this Chapter:

- Design security for communication between networks.
    - Select protocols for VPN access.
    - Design VPN connectivity.
    - Design demand-dial routing between private networks.
- Design security for communication with external organizations.
    - Design an extranet infrastructure.

Why This Chapter Matters

Data traveling between trusted networks is subject to capture, diversion, and corruption. And the computers between which data travels might themselves be compromised. The people who manage the networks might be uninformed, overworked, or lack the necessary skills to protect data as it moves from place to place. For these reasons, you must understand how to secure communications between networks.

Lessons in this Chapter:

Before You Begin

This chapter presents the skills and concepts related to creating a security design framework. This training kit assumes that you have a minimum of 1 year of experience implementing and administering desktop operating systems and network operating systems in environments that have the following characteristics:

- At least 250 supported users

- Three or more physical locations

- Typical network services such as messaging, database, file and print, proxy server or firewall, Internet and intranet, remote access, and client computer management

- Three or more domain controllers

- Connectivity needs, including connecting branch offices and individual users in remote locations to the corporate network and connecting corporate networks to the Internet

In addition, you should have experience designing a network infrastructure.

Many design exercises are paper-based; however, to understand the technical capabilities that a design can incorporate, you should have some hands-on experience with products. Where specific hands-on instruction is given, you must have at least two computers configured as specified in the "Getting Started" section at the beginning of this book.

Lesson 1: Selecting Protocols for VPN Access

There are three possible protocol choices for Microsoft Windows Server 2003 virtual private networks (VPNs). Knowing which one to use where is simply a matter of understanding the characteristics and limitations of the protocols, the requirements of the planned remote access connection, and the possible types of VPNs. Thorough knowledge of the protocols and VPN types will assist you in designing secure remote access connectivity.

After this lesson, you will be able to

- Explain the purpose of a VPN.
- Describe the types of VPNs that work with Windows Server 2003.
- Describe the VPN protocol that Windows Server 2003 can use.
- Explain the uses of IPSec tunnel mode.
- Explain the considerations for comparing VPN protocols.
- Select a VPN protocol for a specific communication task.

Estimated lesson time: 30 minutes

What Is a VPN?

A *virtual private network* (VPN) is a way of connecting two networks over a third network. VPNs allow us to think of and configure the connection as if it were a connection between two computers on the same network, and they allow us to treat the data as if it were traveling on such a network. This emulation of a point-to-point connection is possible because each packet is encapsulated by adding an additional IP header. It is the information in this header that is used to route the data from one VPN endpoint to the other. Within the packet, the data can be of any type. In fact, a VPN can be used to transport NetBEUI, Internetwork Packet Exchange (IPX), or any other network protocol across a Transmission Control Protocol/Internet Protocol (TCP/IP) network. The encapsulation of the data allows us to treat the communication *as if* a physical tunnel were created between the two endpoints. Figure 7-1 shows the VPN concept. In the figure, the actual routing path of the data is shown by using solid lines. A pipe-like drawing represents the logical tunnel between the two networks.

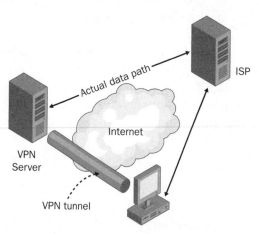

Figure 7-1   A VPN emulates a point-to-point connection.

When the client sends data to the server, the tunnel client adds the tunnel protocol header to the packet and sends the data over the network to the VPN server. The server accepts the packet, removes the header, and sends it to its destination on the internal network.

For a VPN connection to occur, both the client computer and the server computer must be using the same tunneling protocol. VPNs typically also add confidentiality (data encryption), authentication (endpoint-to-endpoint, user-to-central account database, or both), and integrity (protection from modification in transit). They can also add security features such as nonrepudiation (guaranteed to come from the identified source at a specific time) and protection from replay (packets or portions of packets cannot be reused).

Types of VPNs That Work with Windows Server 2003

Windows Server 2003 can serve as an endpoint for two types of VPNs: remote access VPNs and site-to-site VPNs. The following sections describe these VPNs.

A Remote Access VPN

A remote access VPN consists of a Windows Server 2003 server running Routing and Remote Access Services and configured as a VPN server and a compatible VPN client. The server is capable of supporting multiple VPN connections from clients. Client computers use VPN client software to connect to the VPN server. A client-to-server VPN can be created between two Windows Server 2003 computers. Most Microsoft Windows client computers can also be VPN clients. In addition, other operating system clients can have or obtain compatible client software. This type of VPN is also referred to as a client-to-server VPN.

Figure 7-2 shows a remote access VPN. In the drawing, several client computers have established connections to the VPN server. The server keeps these connections separate and routes each to its destination within the network.

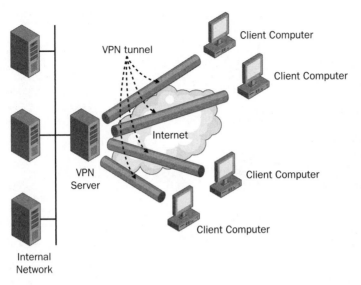

Figure 7-2   A VPN server manages multiple VPN client connections.

A Site-to-Site VPN

To create a site-to-site tunneled connection, you can install a Windows Server 2003 VPN server as a gateway on each of two networks. A demand-dial connection is then configured between the two VPN servers. A *demand-dial connection* is a connection that is completed when traffic for a specified network is received by one of the gateway servers. All traffic routed across this connection is encrypted and tunneled through the VPN, while traffic from client computers to the VPN server on one network and between the VPN server on the other network and the data's final destination is not tunneled or encrypted.

> **See Also**   For more information about site-to-site VPNs, see the "Lesson 3: Designing Demand-Dial Routing Between Private Networks" topic later in this chapter.

A site-to-site VPN can be created between two Windows Server 2003 servers, between two Windows 2000 computers, and between a combination of the two. This type of VPN is also referred to as a router-to-router VPN or gateway VPN. In this book, the term *site-to-site VPN* will be used to describe the VPN, and the term *VPN router* will be used to describe the configuration of the Windows Server 2003 computer participating in the connection.

Figure 7-3 shows a site-to-site VPN. In the drawing, the portions of the communication that are tunneled and encrypted, and those that are not, are indicated.

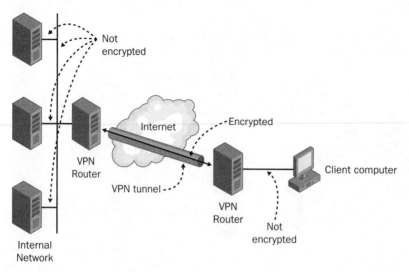

Figure 7-3   A site-to site VPN

VPN Protocols That Windows Server 2003 Can Use

Regardless of the type of VPN, three Windows Server 2003 VPN protocols can be used:

- Point-to-Point Tunneling Protocol (PPTP)
- Layer Two Tunneling Protocol over IP Security (L2TP/IPSec)
- IPSec tunnel mode

Each one will provide a secure transport for data between networks. Although they share common traits, each has its own characteristics, requirements, and limitations. You must know when each is appropriate and how they all work.

PPTP

PPTP is an Internet Engineering Task Force (IETF) standard-track protocol (RFC 2637) developed by Microsoft that is primarily used with Windows computers. The following PPTP facts should be as familiar to the security designer as a favorite T-shirt:

- Multiprotocol traffic can be encrypted (using Microsoft Point-to-Point Encryption, or MPPE), encapsulated, and tunneled across an IP network.
- The PPTP tunnel connection negotiates authentication, compression, and encryption.
- PPTP supports dynamic assignment of client addresses.
- Encryption is MPPE using the RSA/RC4 algorithm and 40-bit, 56-bit, or 128-bit encryption keys.
- To use encryption with PPTP, you must use Microsoft Challenge-Handshake Authentication Protocol (MS-CHAP), MS-CHAPv2, or Extensible Authentication Protocol-Transport Level Security (EAP-TLS) authentication.

- The initial encryption key is generated during user authentication and is periodically refreshed.

- In a PPTP packet, only the data payload is encrypted. Figure 7-4 is an example of a PPTP packet, showing the addition of headers and identifying the encrypted area.

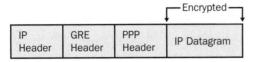

Figure 7-4 Encrypted portion of PPTP frame

L2TP/IPSec

L2TP/IPSec is a combination of Microsoft PPTP and Cisco Layer 2 Forwarding protocol (L2F). Characteristics of this protocol include:

- L2TP tunnels data across any network that can transport point-to-point traffic. IP, Frame Relay, and Asynchronous Transfer Mode (ATM) are examples of networks that L2TP can tunnel across.

- L2TP uses User Datagram Protocol (UDP) over IP messages for tunnel management.

- L2TP send encapsulated Point-to-Point Protocol (PPP) packets over UDP.

- Payloads can be encrypted and compressed.

- IPSec Encapsulating Security Payload (ESP) is used for encryption. IPSec ESP is detailed in RFC 3193.

- IPSec protection comes from an automatically generated IPSec policy that uses IPSec in transport mode.

- Although L2TP/IPSec provides user authentication, computer authentication is also required. Computer authentication is mutual—each computer must authenticate to the other.

- Computer certificates are required for computer authentication. Both client and server, or both VPN routers, must have a valid certificate.

- Each endpoint must be able to validate the certificate presented by the other. This can be an issue when the certificates used are signed by a different certification authority. Figure 7-5 shows an L2TP/IPSec packet that is showing the encrypted portion.

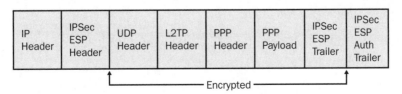

Figure 7-5 Encrypted portion of L2TP/IPSec

Uses for IPSec Tunnel Mode

IP security (IPSec) can be used without L2TP to create an encrypted tunnel. This option is usually used to create a secure connection with a non-Microsoft router or gateway that does not support L2TP/IPSec or PPTP technologies. Unlike L2TP or PPTP, IPSec tunnel mode does not require the validation of a user account. The following facts describe uses for IPSec tunnel mode:

- IP packets can be encrypted using IPSec and tunneled across an IP network.

- IPSec tunnel mode can be used for a demand-dial VPN or a client/server VPN.

- IPSec tunnel mode is not supported for client remote access VPNs.

- The use of IPSec filters to select or block communications using specific protocols or ports is not supported.

- If an IPSec tunnel mode policy is configured on a gateway, use remote access IP filters to prevent traffic outside of the tunnel from being received or forwarded. Remote access IP filters are created from the property pages of the Routing And Remote Access General Properties pages.

- IPSec tunnel mode requires both endpoints to be configured with complementary rules.

See Also For explicit instructions about how to configure an IPSec tunnel mode policy, see Microsoft Knowledge Base article 816514 "How To: Configure IPSec Tunneling in Windows Server 2003" (*http://support.microsoft.com/default.aspx?scid=kb;en-us;816514*).

Considerations for Comparing VPN Protocols

To make a decision about which VPN protocol to use, you must not only know the related characteristics and operational details of all three, you must also have a clear picture of how all three are different. Only then can you determine which of the three can be used in a specific instance, and only then can you determine which one is the best security choice for a specific VPN. As you begin to consider which VPN protocol to use, think about these things:

Encryption Considerations

Encryption considerations include:

- PPTP uses MPPE for encryption. L2TP/IPSec and IPSec tunnel mode use IPSec ESP for encryption.

- PPTP encryption begins after the PPP authentication and connection process. Therefore, the authentication process is not encrypted by MPPE. L2TP/IPSec encrypts the PPP authentication packets. This arrangement provides stronger protection because the authentication packet must first be decrypted before common password-cracking attacks can be used on the PPP packets.

Exam Tip   PPP authentication packets, if captured, are subject to password-cracking attacks that might be successful. PPTP provides no extra protection for these packets because the encryption of PPP packets begins after PPP connection and authentication. L2TP/IPSec does provide extra protection because the PPP authentication packets are also encrypted (because user authentication occurs after the formation of an IPSec security association). A successful attacker would have to intercept the packet, defeat the IPSec ESP encryption algorithm, and then apply the password-cracking software.

- PPTP uses MMPE and RC4, while L2TP/IPSec uses either Data Encryption Standard (DES) (consisting of a 56-bit key) or 3DES (consisting of three 56-bit keys) encryption.

- PPTP and L2TP/IPSec require user authentication using a PPP-based authentication protocol.

- L2TP/IPSec also requires computer authentication by using certificates. By requiring two forms of authentication, L2TP/IPSec provides a stronger authentication process. However, this requirement means that each computer must have its own computer certificate. For an implementation of client-to-server VPNs of any size, using L2TP/IPSec means you must invest in a public key infrastructure (PKI). (If the implementation is very small, you might simply purchase the computer certificates—one for each of the two site-to-site VPN computers.)

- PPTP does not require a certificate infrastructure.

- IPSec ESP requires per-packet *data origination authentication*, which provides proof that the data was sent by a specific computer. It also requires *data integrity*, which is proof that the data did not change in transit. In addition, IPSec ESP provides *replay protection*, which is protection from an attack that captures and then resends a stream of data.

- PPTP does not provide data origination authentication, data integrity, or replay protection.

- IPSec ESP and PPTP (by using MPPE) provide per-packet data confidentiality (encryption).

NAT Considerations

A PPTP VPN client can be placed behind a Network Address Translation (NAT) server if the NAT server has a PPTP NAT editor. (A NAT editor is a software addition that understands a specific protocol.) Most NAT servers have a PPTP NAT editor. L2TP/IPSec clients cannot be placed behind a NAT server unless the VPN client and VPN server understand IPSec NAT Traversal (NAT-T). NAT-T is an IETF standard-track addition that describes how the IPSec protocol can be used with a NAT server. Windows Server 2003, Microsoft L2TP/IPSec VPN client software, and the L2TP/IPSec NAT-T update for Windows XP and Windows 2000 support NAT-T.

To understand why the VPN client and server must understand NAT-T, you must examine the way that IPSec encrypts the packets and understand how NAT works. Figure 7-5 showed the portion of the IPSec-protected packet that is encrypted—which is just about everything. Not encrypted is the IP address of the source and destination computers. When a NAT server receives a packet to forward to the Internet, it replaces the source IP address. This does not cause a problem for most IP traffic because any responses will be directed to the NAT server and the NAT server can match the response with the original sending computer and forward it. However, within the encrypted IPSec-protected packet are checksums that are calculated when the packet contained the original source IP address. Because NAT cannot decrypt and then re-encrypt the packet with a new checksum, the packet is interpreted by IPSec as being corrupt or modified. This is why an unmodified Windows 2000 computer cannot support an L2TP/IPSec VPN when NAT is part of the equation. Windows Server 2003 solves that problem with NAT-T. NAT-T uses UDP encapsulates of the IPSec packet and allows it to pass through NAT. Internet Key Exchange (IKE) can detect whether NAT-T is present and uses UDP-ESP encapsulation.

Windows Server 2003 supports NAT-T. The following Windows clients, as updated or configured, also support NAT-T. You can use any of the following clients to create a VPN connection using L2TP/IPSec—even if they are behind a NAT server—as long as the VPN server is running Windows Server 2003:

> **Exam Tip** A Windows 2000 server that has been updated with the L2TP/IPSec update cannot become a Routing and Remote Access VPN server. The update is only meant for a client.

- Windows XP and the L2TP/IPSec update
- Windows 2000 and the L2TP/IPSec update
- Windows NT 4.0 and the L2TP/IPSec VPN client
- Windows 98 and the L2TP/IPSec VPN client

See Also   For more information about the L2TP/IPSec VPN client, see "Microsoft L2TP/ IPSec VPN Client" on the Windows 2000 page of the Microsoft Web site at *http: //www.microsoft.com/windows2000/server/evaluation/news/bulletins/l2tpclient.asp*.

For information about the L2TP/IPSec update for Windows XP and Windows 2000, see "Microsoft Knowledge Base Article – 818043" on the support page of the Microsoft Web site at *http://support.microsoft.com/default.aspx?scid=kb;en-us;818043*.

Guidelines for Selecting a VPN Protocol for a Specific Communication Task

Follow these guidelines for selecting a VPN protocol for a specific communication task:

- In general, if a public key infrastructure is not available, select PPTP.

- If the highest level of security is required, select L2TP/IPSec. L2TP/IPSec provides not only mutual authentication of users, but also the computer and VPN endpoint. L2TP/IPSec also provides stronger end-to-end encryption than PPTP does.

- Use IPSec tunnel mode only when interoperability issues require you to.

- If DES or 3DES is required by the organization's security policy for encryption, use L2TP/IPSec.

- Because of the CPU overhead incurred by using IPSec on VPN servers, consider either installing IPSec offload hardware or using PPTP instead.

- Use PPTP when testing VPN connectivity. It is easier to use and configure. If the VPN works with PPTP but does not work with L2TP/IPSec, the problem is related to the protocol or protocol configuration—there will be fewer things to trouble-shoot. Because PPTP does not require certificates for computer authentication and NAT is less likely to cause a problem with a PPTP VPN, using PPTP to test your VPN will allow you to verify or troubleshoot VPN network connectivity. You can then test the IPSec protocol.

Practice: Selecting VPN Protocols

In this practice, you will decide on the correct protocol for different situations. If more than one protocol is possible, list both protocols as your answer. If you are unable to answer a question, review the lesson materials and try the question again. You can find answers to the questions in the "Questions and Answers" section at the end of the chapter.

Table 7-1 lists specific scenarios and provides a blank column for entering the correct VPN protocol for each situation.

Table 7-1   Selecting VPN Protocols

Scenarios	Which VPN protocol should be used in this scenario?
The VPN server sits behind a NAT box.	
Clients must connect to a device that is not compatible with the Microsoft L2TP/IPSec VPN.	
The VPN server must operate in an environment where there is no public key infrastructure and where it serves 1000 clients.	
Users must be able to use smart cards for authentication.	
Windows 98 Seecond Edition, Windows NT 4.0, and Windows 2000 Professional clients must be able to use the VPN.	
There is concern about the use of password-cracking software on captured VPN packets.	
3DES is required for encryption.	

Lesson 2: Designing VPN Connectivity

VPNs present complicated network connectivity and security issues. In addition to selecting VPN protocols, you secure the connections between client and server by selecting and configuring client and server components and by using supporting network infrastructure.

After this lesson, you will be able to

- Explain the considerations for designing client and server VPN configurations.
- Explain the network infrastructure considerations for VPNs.
- Place VPN servers on networks.
- Provide firewall configuration information to administrators to support PPTP and L2TP/IPSec VPNs.
- Design secure VPN connectivity.

Estimated lesson time: 45 minutes

Considerations for Designing Client and Server VPN Configurations

Many VPN client and server configuration selections must match before secure communications can take place. The following components can be configured to provide security for VPN connections. You must consider all these components as you design client and server VPN configuration.

Authentication, Authorization, and Accounting Selection Considerations

Two selections are possible for controlling authentication, authorization, and accounting: Windows or RADIUS. You can select one to control all three, and you can choose one for authentication and authorization and the other for accounting. When Windows authentication is selected, the local Security Accounts Manager (SAM) database of the VPN server will be used if the VPN server is a stand-alone computer and the Active Directory directory services database will be used if the VPN server is a domain member. When RADIUS is used, the Active Directory database can also be used regardless of whether the VPN server is a domain member. When RADIUS is used, a RADIUS client (such as a Windows Server 2003 computer) passes credentials to the RADIUS server, which forwards them to Active Directory for validation. RADIUS is implemented in Windows Server 2003 as a server, the Internet Authentication Service (IAS).

Authentication Considerations

PPTP and L2TP/IPSec both require user authentication to be configured. Additionally, when using L2TP/IPSec, you must configure both computer and user authentication.

The following user authentication information should be considered in making authentication choices:

- User authentication is via PPP authentication protocols. Password authentication protocol (PAP), which sends a plain-text password across the network, is very rarely used.

- Challenge Handshake Authentication Protocol (CHAP) uses the MD5 hashing protocol to encrypt challenge strings. Only the user name crosses the network in plain text. The server must store a plain-text copy of the password, or store the password using a reversible encryption algorithm, as is the case in Windows Server 2003. CHAP is generally used only when UNIX clients are present.

- Microsoft CHAP (MS-CHAP) uses an MD4 hash, and the server can store a hashed password. The protocol provides more sophisticated error messages—including a password-expired error code, which then provides the ability to change a password during the authentication phase. The client and server independently create the encryption key MS CHAP requires for MPPE encryption based on the user's password. MS-CHAP should be used only if you have Windows 95 clients.

- MS CHAPv2 provides for mutual authentication—both client and server identify that each have knowledge of the user's password. Two encryption keys are used: one for sending text and the other for receiving text. As with MS-CHAP, the encryption keys are based on the user's password. Consequently, the strength of the encryption key is directly proportional to the strength of the user's password.

- Extensible Authentication Protocol (EAP) is an IETF (RFC 2284) extension to PPP. A choice of authentication algorithms known as *EAP – types* can be made.

- EAP is negotiated during the authentication phase of PPP.

- Because EAP allows arbitrary authentication mechanisms for PPP authentication, the dynamic addition of authentication component modules is supported. This means vendors can supply new authentication protocols at any time. (When new, stronger authentication processes are identified, the PPP protocol does not have to be rewritten—the vendor simply write an EAP type that is compatible with PPP.)

- EAP types are:
  - EAP-TLS is based on a public-key certificate and enables mutual authentication between the client and server computers that make up the VPN connection. Before data can be transmitted, a client certificate must be provided to and validated by the dial-in server and the server must provide its own, which must be validated by the client. EAP-TLS can be used with PPTP. In this case, the server must have a certificate, but the client computers do not require one. User certificates can be installed on client computers or smart cards.

❑ EAP-MD5 can be used only with L2TP/IPSec VPNs and dial-up access, not with PPTP or wireless VPNs. It is less secure than EAP-TLS because it uses passwords, not certificates. It weakens password security as well. A reversibly encrypted password must be stored in the account database, as with CHAP.

❑ EAP/MS-CHAPv2 is password based and provides mutual authentication. The client must prove its knowledge of the user password to the server, and the server must prove its knowledge of the user password to the client. Encryption keys are generated for use with MPPE based on the user's password.

Encryption Considerations

Encryption protocols are selected when the VPN is configured. L2TP/IPSec VPNs will use IPSec for encryption. PPTP uses MPPE. Encryption strength is determined by the client and server configuration. Servers must be configured to provide an encryption strength the client is capable of. Encryption strength is rated by the size of the key used. In general, the larger the encryption key, the stronger the protection. Choices include the following:

- *No encryption.* This selection provides no protection for remote access connections of any kind and is not recommended.

- *Basic.* PPTP connections will use a 40-bit key. L2TP/IPSec connections will use 56-bit DES.

- *Strong.* PPTP connections will use a 56-bit key. L2TP/IPSec connections will use 56-bit DES.

- *Strongest.* PPTP connections will use a 128-bit key. L2TP/IP Sec connections will use 128-bit Triple DES (3DES).

Remote Access Account Lockout Considerations

This feature specifies how many times a remote access authentication attempt against a valid RAS client account can fail before the account is locked out. The remote access account lockout feature can be used to protect accounts against a dictionary or brute-force password-cracking attack. In these types of attacks, hundreds of thousands of VPN connection attempts are sent across the network in an attempt to compromise a user account.

Exam Tip If smart cards are used, lockout is controlled by the design of the smart card. The manufacturer determines how many times a user can enter an incorrect PIN before lockout. Smart-card lockout recovery might require replacement of the smart card.

Setting remote access account lockout has no impact on the setting in the Group Policy Account lockout policy, nor does a setting in Group Policy affect the remote access account lockout feature. Instead, you must edit the registry to turn on the feature and edit the registry to unlock locked accounts. Before deciding to set account lockout, you should consider the following points:

- Setting lockout to apply after a specified number of attempts will foil password-cracking attacks but will also lock out legitimate users until the lockout is reset.

- A registry modification is required.

- The modification is made on the RAS server if Windows authentication is used.

- The modification is made on the IAS server if RADIUS authentication is used.

- The account lockout feature is not related to the Account Lockout Policy of Windows computers. The Account Lockout Policy works only for LAN connections, while the account lockout feature works only with remote connection attempts.

> **Note**   The *AccountLockout* subkey is added to the registry when the Routing and Remote Access or Internet Authentication Service is installed on the Windows Server 2003 computer. The subkey is located at:
>
> HKLM\SYSTEM\CurrentControlSet\Services\RemoteAccessParameter.
>
> To enable account lockout, set the *MaxDenials* value to the number of failed attempts that are allowed before lockout will occur. The number of failed attempts is reset according to the *ResetTime* value. Setting *MaxDenials* to zero disables remote account lockout.
>
> To change the time after which the number of recorded failed attempts is reset, enter the number of minutes in the *ResetTime* value.
>
> A registry subkey will be added for each user account that is locked out via remote access lockout. The subkey must be deleted to unlock the user account.

Authorization Considerations

The user's account dial-up properties specifies how authorization for remote access will be determined. The choices are displayed in Figure 7-6. Choices include the following:

- Allowed
- Denied
- Determined by remote access policies

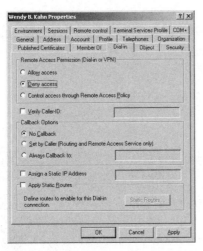

Figure 7-6   Selecting remote access authorization

Remote access policies are a set of rules that define how connections are authorized. If a client meets the specification of the remote access policies, the connection request can be accepted. If not, the connection—even one from an authenticated user—will be rejected. Remote access policies provide granular authorization. The following information should be considered when deciding whether to use remote access policies and in determining how to configure them:

■ In addition to determining whether a user is allowed to connect, remote access policies provide restrictions for accepted connections. For example, they might state the maximum connection time or an idle timeout, implement IP packet filtering, be based on required authentication and encryption protocols, or specify the hours of connection.

■ Remote access policies are configured on the remote access server if Windows authentication is chosen or on the IAS server if RADIUS authentication is selected. They are not replicated between VPN servers.

■ When IAS is used, centralized control of remote access polices is provided. Many remote access servers can use the same IAS server, and all remote access policies will reside on the IAS server.

■ Some remote access policy selections are possible only when IAS is used.

> ## Profile Packet Filtering for Remote Access Policies
>
> A remote access policy can specify IP packet filters that will restrict IP traffic on a VPN connection. This is important for two reasons:
>
> - Packet filters can be used to restrict traffic type and destination on the internal network; for example, restricting external VPN access for specific groups of clients to specific Web servers.
>
> - Packet filters can also be used to prevent other computers from using the VPN client as a router. A normal VPN connection creates a default route for the VPN client. All traffic that matches this route traverses the VPN connection. A computer might attempt to forward traffic to the remote access VPN client and thus use this connection to penetrate the network. In addition, if the client computer is configured to route traffic from other computers on a home or small office LAN, this traffic might be routed through the VPN tunnel.

Account Database Considerations

The account database for Windows network remote access connections can be the remote access server computer account database, the RADIUS server account database, or Active Directory. Consider the following things when making decisions about the account database location:

- Using Active Directory as the account database provides a single sign-on experience for the user—the same account used for LAN access to resource can be used to establish VPN remote access.

- A Windows-based user account database allows selection of authorization for remote access connections via the dial-up properties of the local or domain-based user account, remote access policies, or both.

- Accounting (audit) records can be produced that record the start and end of calls as well as predetermined intervals within a call. A RADIUS server can be configured to generate accounting requests, make these recordings separately from connection requests, and thus record information whether RADIUS is used for authentication or not.

Exam Tip   RADIUS accounting messages can provide a record of VPN connections whether or not the RADIUS server is used to provide authentication.

Network Infrastructure Considerations for VPNs

VPNs protect communications between trusted networks. To design secure VPNs, the network infrastructure must be part of the design. Network infrastructure considerations for VPNs include:

- Redundancy
- Type of VPN
- Placement of the VPN server
- Protection for VPN servers

The following sections describe the redundancy and network location considerations. VPN placement and protection are discussed in the section "Guidelines for Placing VPN Servers on Networks" later in this lesson. Types of VPNs were discussed in Lesson 1 in the "Types of VPNs That Work with Windows Server 2003" section

Redundancy Considerations

Redundancy is provided by establishing multiple VPN servers. If one VPN server fails, client sessions are disconnected. However, clients can connect again by using a different VPN server. To reduce the necessity to configure multiple connectoids (one for each VPN server), use Network Load Balancing. However, don't confuse redundancy with load balancing. Load balancing can be provided via *round-robin Domain Name System (DNS)* or clustering.

Round-robin DNS is configured by entering several weighted host records that use the same DNS name but several IP addresses. This provides load balancing because each request for name resolution will provide one of many IP addresses and thus be directed to a different computer. However, DNS has no way of knowing when a specific VPN server is not available. The IP address for a server that is not available will be provided just as often as one that is.

Network load balancing, a Microsoft clustering technology that spreads requests for a single IP address among several Microsoft Windows servers, can also provide load balancing in addition to scalability and redundancy. If a VPN server fails, client sessions will also fail and the user will be prompted to log on again. The user's new session will be managed by one of the other VPN servers in the cluster. Figure 7-7 shows Microsoft network load balancing.

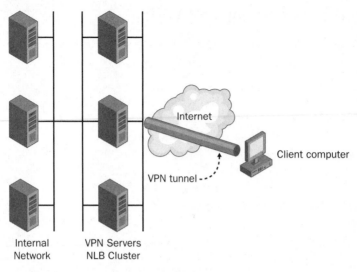

Figure 7-7   Load balancing for VPN servers

NAT Considerations

Network Address Translation (NAT) assigns an Internet-routable address to a client when the client's traffic is routed through a NAT server. By default, the NAT server will forward traffic from the external network to the internal network only if the traffic comes in response to a client request. However, most NAT servers have the capability of forwarding external requests for specific services, such as access to Web servers that are located on the internal network Two issues for VPNs are:

■ **Protocol compatibility**   PPTP VPN clients can be placed behind a NAT server and will have no difficulty. To use NAT servers and L2TP/IPSec VPNs, VPN clients and VPN servers must be configured to use NAT-T.

■ **Locating VPN and NAT services on the same server**   You can configure a Windows Server 2003 computer to be both a VPN server and a NAT server. Be careful about configuring static packet filters on the external interface of the computer. The NAT service might not be able to receive traffic from the Internet to facilitate client requests.

Guidelines for Placing VPN Servers on Networks

There are three places where you can put the VPN server on the network:

■ Place the VPN server behind the firewall.

■ Place the VPN server in front of the firewall.

■ Place the VPN server between two firewalls on a perimeter network.

Follow these guidelines for placing VPN servers on networks:

- **Placing the VPN server behind the firewall**   Guidelines include:

    ❑ Configure the firewall to allow the PPTP and/or L2TP/IPSec traffic to pass through to the VPN server.

    ❑ Use the external firewall to filter traffic and direct it to specific resources behind it. Only VPN traffic should go to the VPN server, only Web traffic should go to the Web server, and so forth.

    ❑ Use the firewall to provide intrusion detection and filter viruses, and use it to prevent denial of service attacks from reaching computers on the internal network. You must understand that VPN traffic is encrypted and cannot be inspected by the firewall. The firewall can decide only where to send the traffic.

> **Important**   The firewall can filter only on the plain-text headers of the tunneled data. All tunneled data will be passed to the firewall. However, tunneled data must be authenticated, which will prevent many possible attacks from succeeding.

    ❑ Restrict PPTP and L2TP/IPSec traffic so that it is passed only to the VPN routers. The "Firewall Configuration Information To Support PPTP and L2TP/IPSec VPNs" section provides this information.

- **Placing the VPN server in front of the firewall**   Guidelines include:

    ❑ If the VPN router is in front of the firewall, you must configure the firewall to allow any traffic that must be passed to the VPN router from the internal network. Traffic that must be passed includes management communications with a RADIUS server, with domain controllers, and with clients that need to communicate with the other site.

    ❑ Configure input and output filters on the Internet interface of the VPN router to accept VPN protocols.

    ❑ Configure the VPN router to accept only VPN protocol traffic. Routing is enabled on the external interface. If you do not block all traffic except the VPN traffic, you might forward unwanted traffic—perhaps even an attacker's traffic—through the internal interface of the VPN server and through the firewall into your network.

    ❑ Data is decrypted at the VPN router and passed to the firewall before entering the internal network. Use the firewall to filter traffic to the resources it can access, scan traffic for viruses, and perform intrusion detection.

    ❑ No filters are necessary for ESP traffic on IP protocol 50. Filters are applied after IPSec removes the ESP header.

- **Placing the VPN server between two firewalls on a perimeter network**   Use the guidelines from both of the preceding arrangements. This arrangement provides the best of both worlds because the VPN server is protected by the external firewall and the internal firewall can filter the traffic received by the VPN server.

Firewall Configuration Information to Support PPTP and L2TP/IPSec VPNs

Firewall configuration is important. Without proper configuration, one or both of two problems will exist. First, the VPN traffic, other required traffic, or both will not be able to pass through the firewall. Second, too much access will be granted to your network, thus making you more vulnerable to attack. It is not the designer's job to configure the firewall. Instead, the designer should supply the firewall administrator with the information necessary to provide secure remote access.

Tables 7-2 and 7-3 list the appropriate ports required to permit PPTP VPN traffic. Remember to consider both incoming and outgoing traffic and apply filters that meet the requirements appropriately.

See Also   Chapter 4 provides information about configuring a firewall for Active Directory authentication traffic.

Table 7-2   PPTP Input Filters: Packets That Should Not Be Dropped

Interface IP	Subnet Mask	Destination Port	Purpose
Internet interface VPN router	255.255.255.255	TCP 1723	PPTP tunnel maintenance
Internet interface of router	255.255.255.255	Protocol ID 47	PPTP tunneled data to router
VPN router Internet interface	255.255.255.255	TCP source port 1723	Only for the calling router

Table 7-3   PPTP Destination Output Filters: Packets That Should Not Be Dropped

Source Interface IP	Subnet Mask	Source Port	Purpose
Internet interface VPN router	255.255.255.255	TCP 1723	PPTP tunnel maintenance
Internet interface of router	255.255.255.255	Protocol ID 47	PPTP tunneled data to router
VPN router Internet interface	255.255.255.255	TCP source port 1723	Only for the calling router

Tables 7-4 and 7-5 provide configuration specifications for L2TP/IPSec.

Table 7-4   L2TP/IPSec Input Filters: Packets That Should Not Be Dropped

Destination Interface IP	Subnet Mask	Destination Port	Purpose
Internet interface VPN router	255.255.255.255	UDP 500	Internet Key Exchange (IKE)
Internet interface of router	255.255.255.255	UDP 4500	IPSec NAT-T (if necessary)
VPN router Internet interface	255.255.255.255	UPD 1701	L2TP traffic

Table 7-5   L2TP/IPSec Destination Output Filters: Packets That Should Not Be Dropped

Source Interface IP	Subnet Mask	Source Port	Purpose
Internet interface VPN router	255.255.255.255	UDP 500	IKE traffic
Internet interface of router	255.255.255.255	UDP 5500	IPSec NAT-T (if required)
VPN router Internet interface	255.255.255.255	UDP 1701	L2TP traffic

Guidelines for Designing Secure VPN Connectivity

Many VPN connectivity design decisions are limited by the existing network infrastructure, existing clients that must remotely access the network, and a lack of management support for sound security practices. But a secure VPN infrastructure can be developed. Use the guidelines in the following sections to do so.

Guidelines for Installation

Follow these guidelines for installation:

- Rename the external interface, naming it Internet, External, or something that will identify it as the interface configured for the Internet. Doing this will prevent you from making configuration mistakes. Configuration mistakes can weaken security on the server.

- Use the Remote Access Server Setup Wizard, and choose the Remote Access (Dial-up or VPN) selection instead of choosing Secure Connection Between Two Private Networks. The former setting prompts you to make several important security configurations; the latter does not. (With the latter setting, default settings are used.) Settings made by selecting VPN are as follows:

  - You are prompted to choose whether VPN, dial-up, or both types of access are needed. You should always select only what will be used on this computer.

  - You can choose to have packet filters for the interface allow only PPTP-related and L2TP-related traffic. If you do this, all other traffic will be dropped. This approach greatly enhances the security of the computer by ensuring only the VPN traffic can make a connection.

❑ You are prompted to decide whether to use an internal Dynamic Host Configuration Protocol (DHCP) server to assign addresses for the VPN routers that connect, or whether you want to define a range in the interface.

❑ You are prompted to decide whether to use RADIUS or Windows authentication.

Remote Access Server Configuration Guidelines

Follow these guidelines to configure the remote access server:

■ Use packet filters on the remote access server to ensure only VPN protocols are accepted on the Internet-facing connection.

■ Configure both PPTP and L2TP/IPSec VPN protocols in cases where some clients cannot use L2TP/IPSec but you want to secure communications with the highest security possible. Clients will always try to use L2TP/IPSec unless configured to use PPTP.

■ Choose most secure authentication protocols:

❑ Do not allow PAP for authentication because it requires a clear-text password.

❑ Require smart cards for authentication where possible.

❑ Where EAP is not an option, ensure MS-CHAPv2 is the only protocol selected. (By default, MS-CHAP is also selected.)

❑ Configure VPN server authentication so that MS-CHAPv2, EAP authentication types, or both are the only authentication choices. Clients that are not configured to use selected server protocols will not be able to connect.

■ Configure encryption strength to the strongest option available. This will provide 128-bit MPPE (for PPTP connections) and 3DES IPSec (for L2TP/IPSec) connections.

■ Use remote access policies:

❑ Use IAS if more than one remote access server is required. This means consistent remote access policy application and improved accounting.

❑ Use packet filters on the remote access policy profile settings for the VPN connection to ensure that only traffic originating from remote access clients is accepted. The default remote access policy Connections To Microsoft Routing And Remote Access Server has these packet filters configured.

■ If an ISP's RADIUS database is used for authentication, use IAS proxy services to direct authorization choices to internal remote access services. This provides you with control over authorization.

Guidelines for Network Deployment

Follow these guidelines:

- Place the VPN server between two firewalls on a perimeter network.

- Configure the external firewall to direct only VPN traffic to the VPN server.

- Configure the internal firewall to filter all traffic for viruses, worms, Trojans, and so on.

Practice: Designing a Remote Access Server VPN

In this practice, you will make choices for a remote access server VPN for a fictitious company. Read the scenario and then answer the questions that follow. If you are unable to answer a question, review the materials and try the question again. You can find answers to the questions in the "Questions and Answers" section at the end of the chapter.

> **Important**   Answers in this practice depend on knowledge gained in previous lessons and possibly earlier chapters.

Scenario

Humongous Insurance has decided that its dial-up remote access connections must be replaced with VPNs. More than 2000 clients use the current remote access configuration. The company has hired you to be the new tunnel administrator and has given its approval for the purchase of whatever equipment and software you recommend for the establishment of its new VPN infrastructure. The following requirements must be met:

- All VPNs must be remote access VPNs.

- The new infrastructure must be designed for the highest level of security.

- Consistency and redundancy are paramount.

- Deployment and maintenance must be automated.

Review Questions

Answer the following questions.

1. What VPN protocol will you select?

   _____

2. What authentication choices will you allow?

   _____

3. What encryption strength will you require?

   _____

4. What are the certificate requirements of this design?

   _____

5. What type of certificate infrastructure is required, and how will certificates be deployed?

   _____

   _____

Lesson 3: Designing Demand-Dial Routing Between Private Networks

After this lesson, you will be able to

■ Explain what site-to-site demand-dial routing is.

■ Design secure demand-dial routing.

Estimated lesson time: 45 minutes

What Is Demand-Dial Routing?

Demand-dial routing is the creation of an on-demand connection between two networks. When a client computer directs communications to another network, a routing device initiates a connection with the other network. Site-to-site VPNs can be created by using a demand-dial connection and a VPN tunneling protocol to create a *compulsory tunnel* (a tunnel that must be used if data travels this path) in response to a client request to route data between two networks. This can be accomplished by:

Important   Demand-dial routing is also referred to as gateway-to-gateway VPN, router-to-router VPN, or site-to-site VPN. In this book, the VPN configuration that uses demand-dial routing will be referred to as a site-to-site VPN, and the connection type will be called demand-dial routing. In this book, the term *demand-dial routing* is the same as saying *site-to-site VPN*, but you should realize that demand-dial routing can exist without the protection of a compulsory tunnel. Also, note that the VPN server used as part of a demand-dial connection is called a *VPN router*, and the VPN server to which clients connect by using VPN client software is called a *remote access VPN server*.

■ Providing two VPN servers—one on the perimeter of each network—and then configuring at least one of them to connect to the other and create the tunnel when a connection request is made.

■ Providing two VPN servers—one at each location with a dial-up connection to an ISP—and then configuring at least one of them to connect to the other and create the tunnel when a connection request is made.

A remote access VPN requires the client computer to have VPN software and a VPN tunneling protocol installed, and it requires that the client request a VPN connection. The site-to-site demand-dial VPN does not. Instead, the two VPN servers create the VPN. One of them, the *calling router*, acts as if it were the VPN client. The calling router initiates the connection with the *answering router* (the computer that plays the VPN server role) in response to a request from a client computer to connect to a computer on the other network. The client computer is unaware that anything different than normal data transfer is occurring. On the other side of the connection, the answering VPN router decrypts and routes the packet to its destination on its network. No tunnel is present—and no encryption of the data is performed—as it travels from the VPN router to the destination computer.

Although demand-dial routing was originally conceived as a link between two networks that occurs over a public telephone system (and still can be operated as one), demand-dial routing can occur over an IP internetwork by creating a connection between two VPN servers using IP addressing. In addition, although the original demand-dial connections created the tunnel in response to a client request for connection to the end network and disconnected at the end of the session, demand-dial routing with Windows Server 2003 can maintain a connection even when no client requires data transfer. Communications over the site-to-site VPN can thus be either *on-demand* or *persistent*. The following additional information about demand-dial routing provides essential data you might need to use in designing secure demand-dial routing.

Demand-Dial Routing Terminology

To understand what demand-dial routing is, you must understand the terms discussed in the following list:

- The device that provides the VPN endpoint is referred to as a *front end processor* (FEP) when used with PPTP or an L2TP Access Concentrator (LAC) when used with L2TP, but you can use either term to mean the VPN endpoint that provides the connection for the client computer, acts as a client to create a connection with another VPN endpoint, and tunnels the data between itself and the other VPN endpoint. Another name for this endpoint is *VPN router*. This is the term used in this book. When clients are required to use this tunnel for communications between two points, it is called a *compulsory tunnel*.

- When a VPN initiates or receives VPN-based demand-dial connections, it is called a *VPN router*. VPN routers used as endpoints in a demand-dial configuration can be calling routers or answering routers. Calling routers initiate the VPN connection when a packet being forwarded matches a route that uses a VPN-router interface. Connections can also be initiated by administrative request. No data packets are forwarded until authentication and authorization are completed, but once authentication and authorization is completed, the calling router forwards packets between nodes in its site and the answering router.

- An *answering router* listens for the connection request, authenticates and authorizes the VPN connection, and then acts as a router by forwarding packets between nodes in its site and the calling router.

- A site-to-site demand dial VPN can be configured to be either *one-way initiated* (which means one router is always the calling router and the other is always the answering router) or *two-way initiated* (which means either router can play either role).

- The *demand-dial interface* is both the connection point and the configuration information for the connection. It includes the type of port to use, the addressing used for the connection, the authentication methods, the encryption requirements, and authentication credentials.

Uses for Demand-Dial Routing

Uses for demand-dial routing include:

- Demand-dial routing provides a VPN tunnel between branch offices and an organization's headquarters or between any two of the organization's headquarters. Suitable connections can be arranged over the public phone system or any Internet connection.

- A demand-dial network can be created by placing Network Access Servers or NASs (which are servers placed on the perimeter of a network to serve as a gateway to some other network) configured as FEPs (or LACs) at geographic locations around the country or around the world. Client computers can make a dial-up connection to the most convenient NAS, and they can send data anywhere to any of the organization's locations that are reachable through the network. All communications will be tunneled and encrypted from endpoint to endpoint, and all communications will be tunneled to the requested location. Figure 7-8 represents such a network.

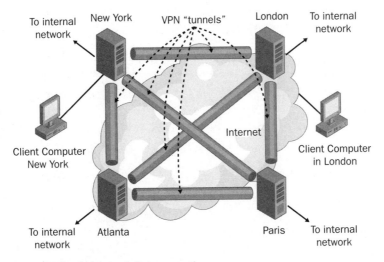

Figure 7-8   A demand-dial connection

- RADIUS provides central authentication, authorization, and accounting for a VPN.

Tunnel Facts

Multiple dial-up clients can share the compulsory tunnel. After the first client makes a connection, any subsequent requests are passed over the same tunnel. The tunnel is not disconnected until the last client has disconnected. A compulsory tunnel is created by a dial-up access server that connects to a VPN server. The user's computer is not the tunnel endpoint, the server is.

Encryption

A site-to-site VPN does not provide encryption from the client to the VPN endpoint. Instead, encryption is present only between the two VPN endpoints. This is known as *link encryption*. If you need *end-to-end encryption*, to ensure data is encrypted when it leaves the client and is encrypted across the link between the VPN endpoints, use IPSec between the client and the VPN endpoint. Figure 7-9 shows this option.

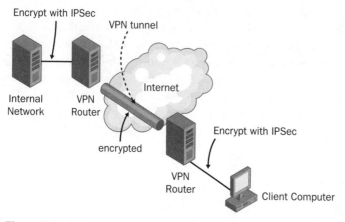

Figure 7-9   End-to-end encryption

You could also provide IPSec encryption between the destination VPN endpoint and the destination of the client's communication by configuring IPSec between the VPN endpoint and the client's destination, but this cannot be done on the fly; it must be prepared beforehand.

Features That Demand-Dial Routing and Remote VPNs Have in Common

Demand-dial routing has these features in common with remote VPNs:

- Several general commonalities, including:
  - ❑ Works the same way as dial-in properties on user accounts
  - ❑ Allows use of remote access policies
  - ❑ Has same authentication and encryption protocol choices

❑ Allows use of Windows or IAS for authentication, authorization, and accounting

❑ Allows IP address assignment

❑ Allows usage of MPPC, Multilink PPP, and Bandwidth Allocation Protocol (BAP)

❑ Allows for logging, tracing, and other troubleshooting

■ Connection endpoint configuration commonalities, including:

❑ Analog telephone connections must be configured by identifying a phone number.

❑ Internet or IP network connections must be configured using the fully qualified DNS name of the server or its IP address.

❑ A user account is used to authenticate and authorize the connection. The user account must be present and configured for remote access.

■ Common restriction options for demand-dial connections, including:

❑ Settings you can configure to specify the hours that a demand-dial connection can operate. These settings prevent the connection from being used outside of the hours specified.

❑ Settings that allow demand-dial filtering to be used to prevent IP traffic of specific types from triggering a connection, and settings that allow only specific types of traffic to make a connection.

Important   If the persistent site-to-site connection is dropped, the server will immediately attempt to re-establish the connection.

How to Address Connections

The most confusing part of demand-dial routing configuration—the part that makes configuration complex—is the configuration of connection addressing. Several factors make this so:

■ The connection uses a user account for authentication, but the user account does not belong to any user on the network.

■ The user account identified on the local VPN server must exist on the remote VPN server. This account name must match the demand-dial interface of the remote VPN server.

■ The user account must be authorized to make a remote access connection.

- The endpoint address can be either a phone number (for a connection over the public phone network) or an IP address (for a connection over an IP network such as the Internet).

- Demand-dial routing is initiated in one direction: one VPN server acts as the client and requests a connection with the second. However, both VPN servers can be configured to initiate the connection.

- Even when one end of the connection will be initiating the connection, both ends must be configured.

Although it is often difficult to immediately correctly configure the connection, using the method in the following sample scenario will help you to do so with less frustration. Refer to Figure 7-10 for the information used in the table in this sample scenario. Use a table like Table 7-6 along with the following steps to determine the correct configuration:

1. Obtain the phone numbers or IP addresses of the two computers that will participate in the demand-dial routing. Enter this information into a table, such as has been done in Table 7-6.

2. Select a name for the connection interface on the local computer. This must be the name of the user account that will be added to the remote account database.

3. Select a name for the connection interface on the remote computer. This must be the name of the user account that will be added to the local account database.

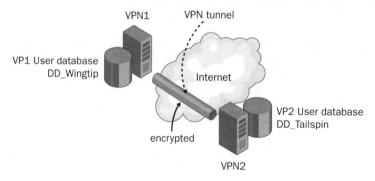

Figure 7-10   A demand-dial network

Table 7-6   **Demand-Dial Connection Interface**

Router	IP Address	Demand-Dial Interface Name	User Account Name in User Credentials
VPN1	207.209.68.50	DD_Tailspin	DD_Wingtip
VPN 2	208.147.66.50	DD_Wingtip	DD_Tailspin

4. When you set up each VPN server, use the interface name and the user account name as listed in the table. Notice that the demand-dial interface name matches the user account on the opposite VPN server. In this example, VPN1 will have a user account in its account database named DD_Wingtip. If VPN1 initiates the call, it will use this account for PPP authentication.

VPN Routers and Firewalls

VPN routers can be placed behind a firewall or outside the firewall directly on the Internet. In each case, you must consider the security of the VPN router and the configuration of the firewall. Refer to Lesson 2 in this chapter for information about VPN servers and firewalls.

Guidelines for Designing Secure Demand-Dial Routing

Demand-dial routing provides a secure method of transferring data between two networks. Authentication, authorization, accounting, and encryption choices are the same as those for remote access VPNs. There are, however, some configuration choices for the demand-dial interface. Follow these guidelines to design a secure demand-dial routing infrastructure:

- **Installation and configuration**   These guidelines include:
  - ❑ Do not make the VPN router computer a DHCP client on either the internal or external interface.
  - ❑ Where possible, dedicate the VPN router to demand dial-connections rather than allowing remote access connections. By default, both types of connections are allowed. You can prevent remote access connections by clearing the Remote Access Server check box on the General tab of the VPN Servers Properties dialog box.

- **Multiple interfaces**   These guidelines include:
  - ❑ If multiple connections with remote sites are required, use a separate remote access network interface (which can be done via a configuration choice in the remote access server console) and user account for each demand-dial connection required. This will help you monitor connections. This will result in fewer people knowing the password for an individual demand-dial user account. If you need to remove access for a specific location, you can do so by simply removing that site's interface. Because no one at that site knows the password for any other interface, nobody can reconnect without your intervention.
  - ❑ To manage multiple demand-dial interface user accounts, create a Windows group for these accounts and use remote access policies to manage the connections.

- **VPN protocols** These guidelines include:

  ❑ Use L2TP/IPSec where possible, as it provides stronger security.

  ❑ L2TP/IPSec can be used behind a NAT router in a site-to-site configuration if both VPN routers are using Windows Server 2003.

  ❑ Provide both L2TP/IPSec and PPTP if you must support VPN routers that do not support L2TP/IPSec, or for routers for which certificate services are not available.

- **Encryption** These guidelines include:

  ❑ Use the strongest encryption possible for each interface.

  ❑ Do not use operating systems as VPN routers that cannot use the highest strength encryption.

- **Authentication** These guidelines include:

  ❑ Use a local account for the user credentials (which is the default), and use a long, strong password. Schedule a periodic manual change of the password, and coordinate this with the administrator of the other VPN router.

  ❑ Where possible, use EAP for the authentication mechanism.

  ❑ EAP/MS-CHAPv2 does not require client computers to have a computer certificate. (Users use passwords as usual.) However, VPN servers still require a computer certificate. This requirement can provide a solution that is more secure and is also achievable in a network where certificate services are not available.

  ❑ EAP/TLS also requires both machine and user certificates. Although the number of certificates is small in a single demand-dial scenario, the number can get quickly out of hand if multiple sites must connect. You must weigh the increased security against the efforts required in correctly implementing, managing, and protecting a public key infrastructure.

  ❑ Do not use operating systems as VPN routers that cannot use at least MS-CHAPv2 authentication.

  ❑ Where possible, separate VPN purposes—use one computer for a demand-dial VPN router and another for remote access VPNs. This separation is especially important if you must support remote access clients that cannot use the authentication and encryption protocols that meet the security level required for VPN routers. If you must mix remote access clients with demand-dial connections, you might have to reduce the security. Because each VPN router represents a very large amount of data and numerous connections, you must ensure the highest level of protection is configured.

❑ Authentication can be configured for the VPN router as a whole (by using the VPN server properties) and for each interface (by using the interface properties). Make sure that the router as a whole includes only protocols that the interfaces need.

❑ Do not configure the user account used for authenticating the connection to require a password change at next logon. The VPN router will not be able to respond.

■ **Certificates**   These guidelines include:

❑ Ensure that certificate revocation is enabled. Set the following registry key value to 0 (zero) to ensure that CRL checking is enabled for RAS certificates. By default, it is set to 0 (zero), but it might have been set to 1 during troubleshooting. When this value—IgnoreRevocationOffline—is set to1, revocation status is ignored.

HKEY_LOCAL_MACHINE\SYSTEM\CurrentControlSet\Services \RASMan\PPP\EAP\13\IgnoreRevocationOffline

❑ These entries are available to assist in using third-party certificates that do not include CRL information or have other CRL-checking issues. When you remove the requirement to use CRL checking, you reduce the security of the connection. In a properly set up Windows Server 2003 public key infrastructure, authentication won't work unless the certificate is valid and has not been revoked. Revocation checking might fail because of the lack of a root CA certificate in the certificate store of the VPN router, an expired certificate, an invalid certificate signature, or a revoked certificate.

❑ Instead of reducing security, determine why authentication is failing. It might be supposed to fail (certificate invalid), or it might be failing because of an improper configuration.

❑ Where multiple VPN servers (remote access and demand-dial) are present, consider using RADIUS for authentication and accounting. Doing this provides a centralized service that is much more granular and robust than Windows authentication and accounting.

❑ Where RADIUS cannot be the authentication and accounting provider—or it is chosen not to be the authentication and accounting provider—you can split these roles between RADIUS and Windows. You might choose, for example, to have centralized authentication, accounting using RADIUS, or both.

❑ Use IAS for your RADIUS server, and use multiple IAS servers to provide redundancy if required.

❑ When RADIUS messages include sensitive information—such as the user password or encryption keys—the fields are encrypted using the RADIUS shared secret. The secret is configured on the RADIUS server and the VPN server. Make the RADIUS shared secret 22 characters or longer and have it be composed of a random sequence of letters, numbers, and punctuation marks. Additionally, you can use IPSec policies to protect RADIUS traffic. RADIUS, by default, uses UDP port 1812 and 1645 for authentication and ports 1813 and 1646 for accounting.

■ **Additional security settings**   These guidelines include:

❑ If necessary or preferred, limit demand-dial connection times by using the hours of operations.

❑ Set logging in the server properties (shown in Figure 7-11) so that it meets your security policy requirements. By default, only errors and warnings are recorded. This default setting will tell you only when communications are not happening. A good policy is to log all events so that you can record successful connections as well. This information will then be available for monitoring and for possible use in a forensic examination if there is an attack or your system is successfully compromised.

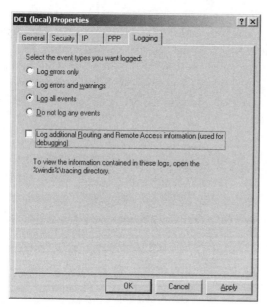

Figure 7-11   Server logging properties

❑ Use RADIUS for central authentication, authorization, and accounting for VPNs when multiple RRAS servers are required.

❑ If the system is configured for RADIUS authentication and accounting, the log files will be on the RADIUS server. You can find the log in the System-root\system32\logfiles folder. Authentication will still be recorded in the Windows event log.

❑ Use the IP packet filters interface of the VPN connection and do not, when remote access policies are used, use the settings in the profile of the policy. The profile-based settings do not apply in a site-to-site configuration.

Practice: Creating a Site-to-Site VPN

In this practice, you will design and create a site-to-site VPN. Using the brief scenario in Exercise 1, answer the questions to indicate the design choices you have made. If you are unable to answer a question, review the lesson materials and try the question again. You can find answers to the questions in the "Questions and Answers" section at the end of the chapter. Then, in Exercises 2 and 3, implement the design. You might have to make modifications to the steps in these exercises to make your site-to-site VPN match your design.

Scenario

Tailspin Toys and Wingtip Toys want to ensure that communications between the researchers in each company are secured. To accomplish this, they have decided to set up demand-dial routing between their companies. You work for Tailspin Toys and have been assigned the responsibility for providing this service. You have been provided the budget to set up the demand-dial routing, but you must have it operational by tomorrow morning at 9 a.m. You will have to configure your side of the connection, and an associate at Wingtip Toys will assist you by following your configuration instructions. The name of the Wingtip Toys computer is WT1; the name of the Tailspin Toys computer is TT1. The IP address available to you at Wingtip Toys is 207.209.68.50. At Tailspin Toys, it is 208.147.66.50. The internal network of Tailspin Toys uses 192.168.7.0/24, and Wingtip Toys uses 192.168.5.0/24.

Exercise 1: Choosing a VPN Protocol

Answer the following questions.

1. Which VPN protocol will you use?

   _____

2. Why did you choose this VPN protocol?

   _____

   _____

   _____

3. What computer or computers are required, and what services will be required on them?

   _____

   _____

4. Complete Table 7-7. Use the format DD_*site_name* for the Interface names and the format DD_*site_name* for the user name.

Table 7-7   Site-to-Site Demand-Dial Interface

Data	Wingtip Toys Computer?	Tailspin Toys Computer?
VPN router name		
IP address (external) of the other VPN router		
Interface name		
User account in the dial-out interface		
User account for dial-in		
Internal network of the other site		

Exercise 2: Implementing a Site-to-Site VPN Design

In this exercise, you will implement the design you created in Exercise 1. Complete the following steps to implement your design:

> **Important**   You will need two servers for this exercise, each of which has two network interface cards. Successful completion of the exercise involves administratively requiring the two servers to connect and demonstrating that they have connected.

1. On each server, one network interface should be configured as the external interface and one as the internal interface. Both external interfaces should be connected to a hub. This setup will simulate an internet connection. Although there is no router, both interfaces can be configured to be on the same subnet—a configuration that isn't a real-world scenario but will allow a connection to be made.

2. Log on to the Wingtip Toys computer, and select the Routing And Remote Access Service from the Administrative Tools menu.

3. When prompted, select Configure And Enable Routing And Remote Access Service and click Next.

4. Select the Remote Access (Dial-Up Or VPN) option, as in Figure 7-12, and then click Next.

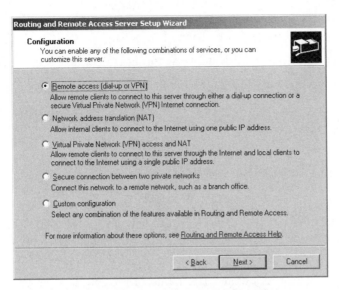

Figure 7-12   Selecting remote access configuration

Remember, this option provides significant help in setting up a secure VPN-to-VPN connection. Refer to the guidelines for more information.

5. Select VPN for the access type, and click Next.

6. Select the external interface as the interface connected to the Internet, and click Next.

    PPTP and L2TP over IPSec packet filters will be automatically configured for the interface, and all other traffic will be blocked.

7. Select a specific range of addresses, and add the range 192.168.7.100 through 192.168.7.150.

    This range of address represents addresses not assigned on the internal network. They will be available for assignment.

8. Repeat these steps on the Tailspin Toys server, but use a different IP address range: 192.168.10.100 through 192.168.10.150.

Exercise 3: Configuring Demand-Dial Routing

Complete the following steps to configure demand-dial routing:

1. In the Routing And Remote Access console of the Wingtip Toys computer, select the Network Interfaces container, and then in the details pane, select the Network Interface for the external network.

2. In the left-hand pane, right-click the Network Interfaces container and select New Demand-Dial Interface. Then click Next.

3. Enter the name for the demand-dial interface. Use the name that you entered in the table in the previous exercise. Then click Next.

4. Select Connect Using Virtual Private Networking (VPN), and then click Next.

5. Select Point-to-Point Tunneling Protocol (PPTP). Then click Next.

   PPTP is the preferred protocol when certificate services are not available.

6. Enter the IP Address for the external interface from your table. (The external interface of the Tailspin Toys computer.) Then click Next.

7. Select Add A User Account So A Remote Router Can Dial In, and click Next.

8. Add the user account information from your table.

9. Add static routes for remote networks. In this hypothetical case, the internal network of Tailspin Toys is identified as 192.168.xx and should be entered here. Click Next.

10. Complete the Dial In Credentials. The name of the interface entered in step 3 is shown as the name of the user name for the dial-in credentials (shown in Figure 7-13). Enter a password, and confirm the password.

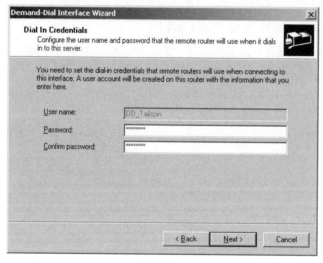

Figure 7-13 Providing dial-in credentials

This will be the user account used for PPP authentication to the Wingtip Toys site by the Tailspin Toys VPN router. The wizard will create this account on the Wingtip Toys computer. See the guidelines for the importance of setting a strong password for this account.

11. Enter the Dial Out Credentials, as shown in Figure 7-14. These are the user name and password for the Tailspin Toys VPN router. (The name is in the table from the previous exercise.) Click Next, and then click Finish.

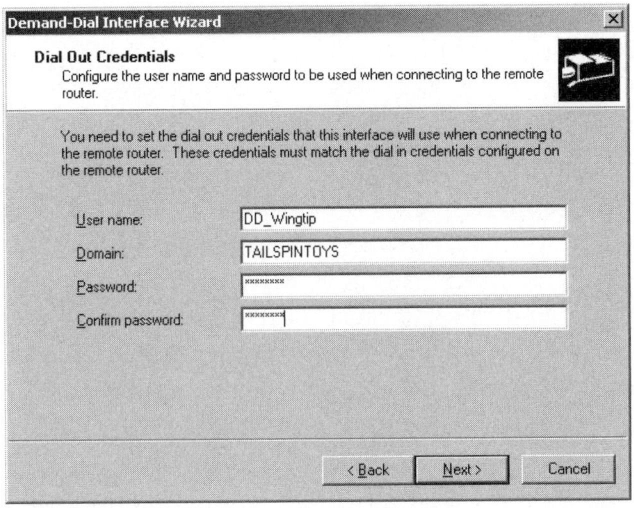

Figure 7-14   Providing dial-out credentials

The Wingtip Toys router will use this account to authenticate to the Tailspin Toys router. When you configure the demand-dial interface for the Tailspin Toys router, you must be sure to use this name to name the interface and use the password entered here for the Dial In Credentials in the wizard.

12. In the details pane of the console, right-click the demand-dial interface just created and select Properties.

13. Verify that the IP address entered is the address of the Tailspin Toys VPN router.

14. Select the Security tab, and then select the Advanced (Custom Settings) option and click the Settings button.

15. In the data encryption drop-down box, select the Maximum Strength Encryption (Disconnect if Server Declines) option, as shown in Figure 7-15.

    This will require 128-bit encryption.

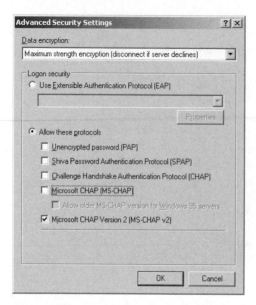

Figure 7-15 Changing security settings

16. Clear the check box for Microsoft CHAP (MS-CHAP).

17. Review your selections, and then click OK twice.

18. Right-click the interface again, and select Set_IP Demand-Dial Filters, and click the Edit button. Verify that the addresses of the Tailspin Toys internal network is listed here (see Figure 7-16). If it is not, enter it, and then click OK twice.

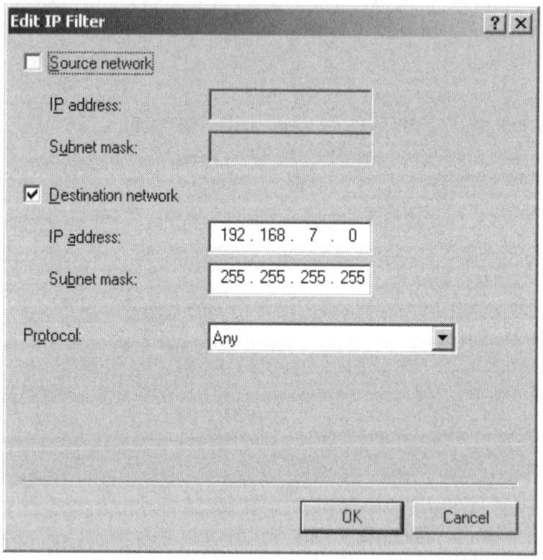

Figure 7-16 Checking network addressing

19. Check the properties of the DD_Tailspin user account. Note that the Password Never Expires check box is selected in the Account properties and that no membership in administrative groups is granted (nor is needed).

20. Repeat steps 1 through 19 with the Tailspin Toys computer, but use the information listed in the Table 7-7 for that computer.

Lesson 4: Designing Secure Communications with External Organizations

Communications with external organizations should be secured. You might decide to provide the same level of security and the same configuration arrangements that you provide for the employees of your own company. Before deciding this, you should consider the design separately to determine whether additional security is required, whether a separate network infrastructure is required, or whether additional considerations are required because of the network infrastructure of the external organization.

After this lesson, you will be able to

- Describe the methods for securing communications with external organizations.
- Determine which certificates are necessary.
- Describe ways to resolve trust issues.

Estimated lesson time: 30 minutes

Methods for Securing Communications with External Organizations

Connecting the networks of different organizations for the purpose of sharing information or doing other business activities is not an entirely new activity; however, the breadth and scope of these multiorganizational networks or extranets is new. It is also much easier these days to connect networks, and there are more ways for doing so. There are two main ways to secure communications with external organizations: using Web server applications and using VPNs. In both cases, certificates play major roles in providing secure communications. And in both cases, there are special trust relationship issues because of the need for secure communications between organizations. The following sections describe how certificates secure communications and how to resolve trust relationship issues.

How Certificates Secure Communications

Web server applications can be secured using Secure Sockets Layer (SSL). Although Web server certificates can provide server authentication to clients and securely share keys for encrypting communications between clients and a server, SSL client-side certificates provide more comprehensive security for extranets. By giving client computers certificates, you allow clients to authenticate to servers. This arrangement is even defined by some as a type of VPN connection.

See Also   The details of designing certificate-based security for client communications with a Web server can be found in Chapter 13.

VPN protocols and authentication choices for remote access services–based VPNs, as discussed in previous lessons of this chapter, also require certificates for computer and user authentication.

How to Resolve Trust Relationship Issues

When certificates are used to secure communications, the certificate must be validated before it can be used. For this to happen, the root CA certificate from the hierarchy that issued the certificates that will be presented must be available in the certificate store of the validating computer. When communications between entities in the same organization need to be secured using certificates, the availability of the root CA certificate is not usually an issue. It is likely that one CA hierarchy exists, and thus there is one root CA and one root CA certificate. Every computer that needs a copy of this certificate might already have one because it is stored in Active Directory.

However, when two or more organizations need to secure communications using certificate services, neither one has the root CA certificate of the other. To resolve this issue, you must establish a trust relationship between the organizations.

Real World   Using Security Knowledge to Resolve Connectivity Issues

I often have the pleasure of introducing consultants to the mysteries of PKI. It's a subject I like talking about, and it's also great to be able to solve a problem in five minutes that the communications consultant has been working on for hours or perhaps days. Sometimes I am contracted to solve the problem, and sometimes I answer an inquiry from a reader. The latter was the case in this example. In this example, the problem concerned VPN connections between three sites of the same company. The problem is similar to one you will have to solve when dealing with communications between multiple organizations.

I was told that all three sites used exactly the same hardware and software and were configured in exactly the same manner by local administrators using a centrally prepared instruction sheet. All three sites were part of the same company, but one site had been acquired six months previously. The purpose of the connection was to create a site-to-site demand-dial VPN between all three sites using L2TP/IPSec as the communications protocol. The reader told me that the site-to-site demand-dial VPN between Sites A and B was working just fine, but neither A nor B were able to establish demand-dial connectivity with Site C. This information, plus the requirement for L2TP/IPSec, was my first indication that the problem was trust related. I told the reader to switch to PPTP and see whether the VPN could be connected. He did, and it was. Here's how I explained why the solution worked.

When L2TP/IPSec is used to secure VPN traffic, both peers (computers on either side of a communication) must be able to present a certificate that the other peer can validate. Each computer sends to its peer a list of the root CAs that it has machine certificates from. If the peer trusts one of the CAs listed, it should be able to validate the certificate presented by its peer. If it trusts none of them, the connection cannot be negotiated. When the reader questioned the administrator at Site 3, he found that the site had its own CA hierarchy. He then examined the trusted root CA certificates in the certificate stores of Router1 and Router2 and found, not surprisingly, neither router had a copy of the Site 3 root CA. By substituting PPTP for the VPN protocol, the need for certificates was removed. A better solution would have been to develop a trust relationship based on the PKI infrastructure that was present, and that's just what we did next.

How to Determine Which Certificates Are Necessary

If you are given the task of determining where trust relationships are needed, the process is simple. To determine which certificates are necessary, complete the following steps:

Note   A fictitious scenario has been included in these steps to illustrate what should be happening.

1. Make a sketch, or examine one, of the sites and the demand-dial interfaces that will be created between the sites. Figure 7-17 shows such a sketch of three Tailspin Toys sites: New York, San Francisco, and Paris.

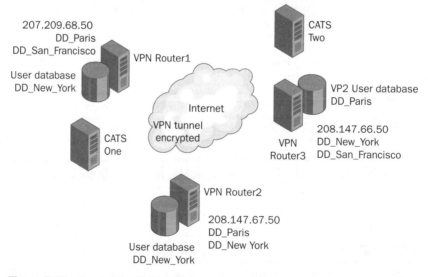

Figure 7-17   Connecting Tailspin Toys sites

2. Examine the certificate issued to the proposed VPN router for each site. You can locate this certificate by adding the Certificates snap-in for the local computer to an MMC console and looking in the Personal certificate store. If you look at the Details property page, the Issuer Information provides the name of the CA that issued the certificate, and the Certification Path property page displays the root CA in the hierarchy.

3. Make a list (List 1) of VPN routers, their site location, and the names of the root CAs you have discovered for each. Table 7-8 is a list that corresponds to the diagram in Figure 7-17.

Table 7-8   List 1

Router	Root CA
Router1	CATSOne
Router2	CATSOne
Router3	ParisOne

4. Make another list (List 2). Start by listing each VPN router, and then for each VPN router list the sites with which it must have a demand-dial interface. Table 7-9 is the list that corresponds to our example.

Table 7-9   List 2

Router	Site
Router1	San Francisco
Router1	Paris
Router2	New York
Router2	Paris
Router3	New York
Router3	San Francisco

5. Use the list created in step 3 (List 1) to determine the root CA certificate identified for each site's VPN router. Add the root CA certificate name next to the site names in List 2. Table 7-10 is List 2 with this modification.

Table 7-10   List 2 Modified

Router	Site	Trusted Root CA for Site
Router1	San Francisco	CATSOne
Router1	Paris	ParisOne
Router2	New York	CATSOne
Router2	Paris	ParisOne
Router3	New York	CATSOne
Router3	San Francisco	CATSOne

6. Examine the Root Certification Authorities store for each VPN router. Add the certificates that are present to List 2. (See Table 7-11.).

Table 7-11   List 2 Modified

Router	Site	Trusted Root CA for Site	Root Certificates Present
Router1	San Francisco	CATSOne	CATSOne
Router1	Paris	ParisOne	CATSOne
Router2	New York	CATSOne	CATSOne
Router2	Paris	ParisOne	CATSOne
Router3	New York	CATsOne	ParisOne
Router3	San Francisco	CATSOne	ParisOne

7. Examine Table 7-11. Do the routers' certificate stores include all the necessary certificates? Is a copy of the root CA certificate listed as required in List 2 present? Place a check mark beside the certificates that are missing from each router's store, as shown in Table 7-12. If a certificate that is necessary is present, the demand-dial interface, if properly configured, will be able to connect. If a certificate is missing, it will not. In this example, Router1 (in the New York site) can accept a certificate from Router2 (in the San Francisco site) because it has a match on its list of trusted CAs. Likewise, Router2 can accept a machine certificate from Router1 because there is a match on its list of trusted CAs. However, Router3 (in the Paris site) does not trust any of the CAs that Router 2 can present. A VPN site-to-site L2TP/IPSec connection cannot be made between Router2 and Router3 or between Router1 and Router3.

Table 7-12   List 2 Modified

Router	Site must connect to	Trusted Root CA for Site	Root Certificates Present on Router
Router1	San Francisco	CATSOne	CATSOne
Router1	Paris	ParisOne₂	CATSOne
Router2	New York	CATSOne	CATSOne
Router2	Paris	ParisOne₂	CATSOne
Router3	New York	CATSOne₂	ParisOne
Router3	San Francisco	CATSOne	ParisOne

To secure communications using L2TP/IPSec VPNs between Site 3 and Sites 2 and 1, both routers (Router1 and Router2) must trust the root CA of the CA hierarchy that issued at least one of the Router3 computer certificates, and Router3 must trust the root CA that issued them. The example scenario just presented identified the need for additional root CA certificate copies at all locations. To build such site-to-site connections, the next step would be to obtain and install the necessary root CA certificates for each site or use some other solution to the trust issue.

Ways to Resolve Trust Issues

For both Web server access and VPN router authentication where more than one organization is involved, trust issues can be resolved in three ways:

- A copy of the root CA certificate that is required is added to the certificate store of the Web server or of the VPN router. This might be the best solution when the number of certificates required is small. Perhaps trust of one external organization's certificate hierarchy is required on one Web server. Perhaps the number of VPN routers that require certificates is small—for example, one VPN router connection with one other company is all that is needed. However, this solution does not scale well. As the number of VPN routers that must be configured with additional certificates increases, the time needed to configure them and maintain the certificates can be unmanageable.

- All certificates used can be purchased from a common public Certification Authority. If all certificates come from the same root CA—in this case the public one—all certificates will be trusted.

- A cross-certification infrastructure can be built between the two CAs that are managed by different sites. If a cross-certification infrastructure is built, in its simplest form, all certificates issued by either hierarchy can be trusted by the other and no special configuration at the router level is required.

See Also   The technical aspects and design guidelines for cross-certification are discussed in Chapter 2.

Practice: Determining Where Trust Relationships Are Necessary

In this practice, you will examine requirements for multiple demand-dial VPNs. Your objective is to discover where it might be necessary to develop a trust relationship. Read the scenario and then answer the question that follows. If you are unable to answer the question, review the lesson materials and try the question again. You can find the answer to the questions in the "Questions and Answers" section at the end of the chapter.

Scenario

You are the security administrator for Humongous Insurance. All tunnels are remote access VPNs. The company has decided to improve security between all sites by providing site-to-site VPNs. The tunnel administrator has set up the VPN routers and configured the demand-dial interfaces, but some sites cannot connect to others. You have the following information to work with: a sketch of the necessary site-to-site VPNs (Figure 7-18) and a table that lists the trust relationships that are necessary (Table 7-13).

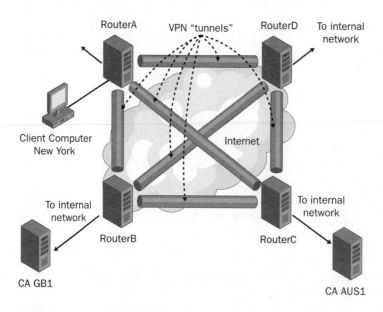

Figure 7-18   Humongous Insurance site-to-site VPNs

Table 7-13   Humongous Insurance Routers, Sites, and Certificates

Router	Root CA for this router's computer certificate	Issuer for this router's computer certificate
RouterA	KC1	GV1
RouterB	GB1	London!
RouterC	AUS1	Reef1
RouterD	KC1	NO1

Review Question

Answer the following question.

1. Using Figure 7-18 and Table 7-13, make a list of the trust relationships that are necessary. Then indicate which ones are already present and which ones need to be developed.

_____

_____

_____

_____

_____

_____

Lesson 5: Completing a Communications Design

After you have absorbed the technical components and guidelines of VPN design and used this knowledge to select VPN protocols, understand trust relationships, and design parts of a VPN infrastructure, you must learn how to put these pieces together with business drivers, interoperability concerns, and technical limitations. Only then will you be able to formulate a complete and secure communications infrastructure.

After this lesson, you will be able to

- Describe the process of designing secure communications.
- Translate business needs into technical solutions.
- Answer interoperability and technical limitations as part of the design.

Estimated lesson time: 30 minutes

The Process: Designing Secure Communications

The process of designing secure communications between networks consists of the following steps:

1. Survey remote access requirements, current network infrastructure, and the client operating system type.

2. Translate business requirements into technical solutions.

3. Answer interoperability concerns and technical limitations.

4. If communications are required with external organizations, design the trust infrastructure.

5. Select the type of VPN: either Remote Access or site-to-site.

6. Select the VPN protocol.

7. Design VPN connectivity:

   ❏ Select authentication.

   ❏ Determine certificate needs.

   ❏ Select encryption strength.

   ❏ Design authorization requirements.

   ❏ Determine whether Network Access Quarantine Control is required.

   ❏ Determine whether authentication, authorization, and accounting should be Windows or RADIUS

   ❏ Determine whether the necessary trust relationships are in place.

❏ Design the network placement of VPN servers and IAS servers.

❏ Designate a firewall configuration to support your remote access design.

These steps are not always done in exactly this order. The process is iterative. When considering business requirements, you might decide that a specific VPN protocol will be required. When considering trust relationships, you might get an idea of the certificate needs for computers but not be able to identify exactly what is needed until you have developed the design a little further.

Most of the steps just listed have been presented in the previous lessons in this chapter. However, two specific items—translating business requirements into technical solutions, and resolving interoperability concerns and technical limitations—were not. These processes were examined in Chapter 1, and you should examine that chapter again if you need to. However, a few more words are necessary to explain how you might approach these issues when designing secure communications between networks.

How to Translate Business Requirements into Technical Solutions

The business requirements for securing communications might not be directly stated. Instead, what you might see is a simple statement of requirements for communications avenues that enable employees to work while away from the office, that connect employees from different sites to headquarters, or that provide the ability to share information or sell products to business partners. In addition, you might be instructed to use the least expensive option possible. Some organizations might include statements that explicitly state the level of security wanted. For example, government connections in the United States might require compliance with the Federal Information Processing Standard (FIPS).

Your job as a security designer is twofold: first you must determine the level of security that is required, and then you must interpret this need into a technical solution. The following sections explain how to do these things.

To Determine the Level of Security Required

To determine the level of security required, you must understand the nature of the data that will be transported from site to site, understand the risks involved in transporting this information, and question management about the security posture of the organization. The security posture of an organization is both a statement of its understanding of the need for information security, its stated requirements for security, and its actual security history. You would be remiss in your obligations if you did not recommend what you consider to be appropriate security, but ultimately the decision is not yours to make. You also cannot simply always recommend only the most secure solution in total disregard of the stated requirements, technical limitations, and budgetary requirements of the project. It is OK to provide a recommendation for the most secure solution, but you should also provide an acceptable solution that takes into account the perceived risks and meets the business requirements.

To Translate Business Requirements into Technical Solutions

To translate business needs into technical solutions, you have two options: you can simply examine the possible technical solutions to the problem to see whether they meet all the stated business needs, or you can review the business needs and then come up with a specific technical solution, requirement, or limitation. Table 7-14 provides some examples of the latter approach.

Table 7-14   Translating Business Needs into Technical Solutions

Business Need	Technical Solution
The ability to securely communicate between our Paris location and our New York location must be available by tomorrow.	Use PPTP for the VPN protocol because it is less complicated to implement.
You must provide the ability for a small number of employees to use the Internet to access the corporate network.	Provide a remote access VPN infrastructure and use remote access policies. A small number of employees can be managed by using a single RRAS server.
You must provide the ability for our 5000 employees to use the Internet to access the corporate network.	Provide a remote access VPN infrastructure that includes IAS for centralized authentication, authorization (remote access policies), and accounting. To accommodate a large number of users, more than one RRAS server will be required. It will be difficult to synchronize remote access policies and manage logs on multiple servers. IAS can provide centralized management of multiple RRAS servers.
We want a solution that is so secure that it does not risk exposure of our data.	No technical solution can provide absolute security, and management should be told this. However, you can recommend smart cards as a solution that provides more protection than using passwords.

How to Answer Interoperability Concerns and Technical Limitations

To answer interoperability concerns and technical limitations:

1. Make a list of the known interoperability and technical limitations of the Windows VPN protocols and infrastructure solutions.

2. Scan the survey you made of the current environment to find items that match the list made in step 1.

3. List solutions to each issue you have identified.

4. Examine each solution against the business requirements and limitations of the project.

5. Propose a solution that will resolve the issue by meeting the business requirements and limitations.

Listing interoperability concerns and technical limitations up front allows you to avoid much redesign effort and avoid costly implementation mistakes. To make the list, you must compare your survey of existing hardware, software, and network infrastructure and your knowledge of VPN protocols and infrastructure. One way to do this is to make a list of the known interoperability and technical limitations of the current Windows VPN solutions and then scan the survey of the current environment looking for matches.

After you have practiced this technique for awhile, the obvious interoperability and technical issues might just pop out at you. After you are aware of these issues, you can then respond to them with potential solutions. You might have to modify your recommendations based on business needs, including budgetary and staffing requirements.

Example: Translating Business Requirements into Technical Solutions

Read the following description of the existing environment for Contoso, and then examine Table 7-15 for a list of the technical and interoperability issues and proposed solutions.

Contoso has only one location: Atlanta, Georgia. You must provide a VPN solution that does not require providing additional computers to employees and keeps additional expenses to the barest minimum. Two groups of employees use the Internet to communicate with Contoso:

- 2000 employees telecommute from their home to do their work. These employees:

    □ Use their own computers.

    □ Use computers that are a mix of Windows 98 second edition, Windows 2000, and Windows XP Professional.

    □ Are required to supply their own connection to the Internet.

    □ Use ISPs that block encryption. It is the policy of some ISPs to charge more for connections that can do more than simple Internet searches and downloads.

- 500 employees work at corporate headquarters. Important facts about these employees include the following:

  - 100 of them travel extensively.

  - They use company-provided laptops on which Windows XP Professional is installed.

  - Some of these employees hold executive positions within the company.

Table 7-15   Contoso Technical and Interoperability Concerns and Solutions

Problem	Proposed Solution
Employees use their own computers. This can result in a higher exposure to viruses and worms.	Require employees to use antivirus products and keep them updated. Provide this software for them (although this results in additional cost, the benefit is enormous). Require employees to keep systems patched.
Some employees are using operating systems (Windows 98) that are not natively able to use L2TP/IPSec VPNs.	Specify PPTP for telecommuters, or allow both PPTP and L2TP/IPSec. Employees might have trouble understanding how to download the L2TP/IPSec client, and providing technical support to their homes or other scripted solutions might be cost prohibitive.
Some ISPs block encryption.	The employees using these ISPs will not be able to make a VPN connection. They must be required to switch ISPs, or—if it is available—pay more for a connection using their current ISP that does allow encryption. The company might have to provide financial support for this transition.

You might have also noticed that the business requirement, although not explicitly stated, is present. This is the note that some of the traveling employees are executives. This type of statement should be followed up with questions to determine whether there is a need to provide a higher level of security for these executives or for all traveling corporate headquarter employees.

Practice: Translating Business Requirements into Technical Solutions

In this practice, you will examine business requirements and offer possible technical solutions. In Table 7-16, examine the business requirements or statements made by a member of Wingtip Toys management. For each statement, answer the question: "What technical solution will be best in this case?" Consider each statement separately, not as part of the same scenario. If there is more than one technical solution, list them. If there is no technical solution, simply enter *N/A* to indicate that there is nothing relevant to say here. If you are unable to answer the questions, review the lesson materials and try the question again. You can find the answers to the questions in the "Questions and Answers" section at the end of the chapter.

Table 7-16   Technical Solutions for Wingtip Toys Business Statements

Statements	What technical solution will be best in this case?
We require the highest level of security and will support that with any reasonable business expense.	
No additional staff will be hired for this project.	
We cannot risk the system being compromised.	
We must ensure that communications between the offices in Sydney and New York are always protected.	
Users cannot be burdened with making password changes.	

Design Activity: Designing Secure Communications

In this activity, you must use what you've learned in all five lessons and apply it to a real-world situation. Read the scenario, and then complete the exercises that follow. You can find answers for the exercises in the "Questions and Answers" section at the end of this chapter.

Scenario

You have been hired as the tunnel administrator for Humongous Insurance and have been tasked with completing the design and implementation of the Humongous Insurance extranet. You have the following information to work with.

Company Background

Humongous Insurance provides health insurance coverage for three million individuals in the United States. Health insurance sales and claims support is provided by an agency location in every state. These 50 agencies operate independently but follow guidelines created by central offices in Topeka, Kansas. Each agency manages its own staff of salespeople.

Existing Environment

Data centers for each agency are managed by the agency. Each data center includes Windows Server 2003 computers, Windows 2000 computers, and a variety of other operating systems. (Some data centers include UNIX systems, AS 4000, IBM mainframes, or all of these.) Employees at the agency headquarters are using Windows XP Professional. Salespeople and telecommuting employees have a variety of desktop and laptop systems running Windows 98 second edition, Windows 2000 Professional, and Windows XP Professional.

Interviews

Following is a list of company personnel interviewed and their statements:

- **Data Center Manager in New Orleans, LA**   "We are having trouble getting up-to-date information from headquarters. Currently, we have a dial-up connection that is often dropped without warning. It would be nice to be able to communicate also with the other state agencies."

- **Data Center Manager in Topeka, KS**   "We are looking forward to a more robust and secure communications infrastructure."

- **HIPAA Officer in Topeka, KS**   "As you know, the Health Insurance Portability and Accountability Act (HIPAA) requires that we protect the health information of our subscribers. We are under strict regulation, and any digital communication comes directly under my approval."

Business Requirements

The business requirements are as follows:

1. All communications between the sites must be kept confidential.

2. Only authorized employees are allowed to use the connection to any location using their computer.

3. Each state agency should have protected communications with headquarters and with the other sites in its region.

Technical Requirements

The technical requirements are as follows:

1. Only authorized computers can be used to connect between the sites.

2. Communications from employees not located at a site must be protected with smart cards.

3. Employees using remote access servers must use computers that meet strict configuration requirements, including the use of antivirus products and a personal firewall.

Exercise 1: Make Recommendations for Site-to-Site Configuration

Answer the following question.

1. What configuration would you recommend be used for site-to-site connections?

_____

_____

_____

_____

_____

Exercise 2: Make Recommendations for Protecting Employee Communications

Answer the following question.

1. What would you recommend to protect the communications going from remote-access employees back to the employees' offices?

_____

_____

Chapter Summary

- VPN protocol selection depends on:
    - The computer operating system and the organization's willingness to add client software.
    - The requirements for security level and speed of implementation.
    - The existing certificate infrastructure or the ability to acquire one.
- VPN network infrastructure must be considered in the development of technical solutions. Particular attention must be paid to firewall and NAT server location and configuration.
- Network Access Quarantine Control can provide additional protection for networks that are remotely accessed.
- Trust infrastructure must support proposed VPN connections when certificates are required.

Exam Highlights

Before taking the exam, review these key points and terms. You need to know this information.

Key Points

- Regardless of whether the VPN server is located behind the firewall or in front of it, you should configure the firewall to open only the required ports and configure the VPN server to protect itself by allowing only VPN traffic on its external network interface.

- Know which ports are required for VPN protocol access through the firewall.

- You configure remote access account lockout by using the registry. This has no relationship to Account Lockout in the Group Policy Account Policy settings.

- NAT-T solutions for client VPN software are available for Windows client computer software, including Windows 98 second edition, Windows 2000, Windows XP Professional, and Windows Server 2003.

Key Terms

Compulsory tunnel   A tunnel that is created to transport data between two VPN routers in a site-to-site demand-dial configuration. If no other route exists for transporting traffic from one site to another, this tunnel will be used and is therefore considered compulsory.

Remote access VPN   A type of VPN that consists of a client and server connection that is tunneled and encrypted. The client initiates the connection and must have VPN client software and VPN protocols installed.

Site-to-site VPN   A type of VPN that can be established between two VPN servers that have been configured with a demand-dial interface. A connection is made when a computer communication requires routing through the VPN server from one site to the other. The communication from the client is not encrypted, and this scenario does not require VPN client software, nor does it require that VPN protocols be installed on the client.

Split-tunnel   When a VPN tunnel is created between a client and a server, the default Microsoft VPN configuration prevents the client from accessing other networks, such as the Internet. A split-tunnel is a tunnel in which access of other networks is allowed.

Voluntary tunnel   The tunnel created when a client initiates a VPN connection with the remote access server. Because the client must initiate the connection, the tunnel is considered to be voluntary.

Questions and Answers

Pg 7-11   **Lesson 1   Practice: Selecting VPN Protocols**

The following table provides the answers:

Table   Selecting VPN Protocols—Answer Key

Scenarios	Which VPN protocol should be used in this scenario?
The VPN server sits behind a NAT box.	PPTP
Clients must connect to a device that is not compatible with the Microsoft L2TP/IPSec VPN.	IPSec tunnel mode
The VPN server must operate in an environment where there is no public key infrastructure and where it serves 1000 clients.	PPTP
Users must be able to use smart cards for authentication.	PPTP or L2TP/IPSec
Windows 98 second edition, Windows NT 4.0, and Windows 2000 Professional clients must be able to use the VPN.	PPTP or L2TP
There is concern about the use of password-cracking software on captured VPN packets.	L2TP/IPSec
3DES is required for encryption.	L2TP/IPSec

Pg 7-25   **Lesson 2   Practice: Designing a Remote Access Server VPN**

1. What VPN protocol will you select?

   L2TP/IPSec

2. What authentication choices will you allow?

   Smart cards

3. What encryption strength will you require?

   Strongest. For L2TP/IPSec, this is 3DES.

4. What are the certificate requirements of this design?

   Computer and user certificates must be used.

5. What type of certificate infrastructure is required, and how will certificates be deployed?

   A CA hierarchy configured to automatically issue and distribute computer and user certificates must be used.

Pg 7-49 **Lesson 3   Exercise 1: Choosing a VPN Protocol**

Answer the following questions.

1. Which VPN protocol will you use?

   PPTP

2. Why did you choose this VPN protocol?

   There is limited time to set up the VPN, and PPTP is less complicated. It does not require certificates. In addition, once a successful VPN is established, certificates can be obtained and the L2TP/IPSec VPN can be configured.

3. What computer or computers are required, and what services will be required on them?

   Two computers are required—one for each site. The Routing and Remote Access service must be enabled.

4. Complete Table 7-7. Use the format DD_*site_name* for the Interface names and the format DD_*site_name* for the user name.

   The following table provides the answers.

   Table   Site-to-Site Demand Dial Interface—Answer Key

Data	Wingtip Toys Computer?	Tailspin Toys Computer?
VPN router name	WT1	TT1
IP address (external) of the other VPN router	207.209.68.50	208.147.66.50
Interface name	DD_TailspinToys	DD_WingtipToys
User account in the dial-out interface	DD_WingtipToys	DD_WingtipToys
User account for dial-in	DD_WingtipToys	DD_WingtipToys

Pg 7-49   **Lesson 4   Practice: Determining Where Trust Relationships Are Necessary**

1. Using Figure 7-18 and Table 7-13, make a list of the trust relationships that are necessary. Then indicate which ones are already present and which ones need to be developed.

   Answer:

   RouterA must trust RouterB and RouterD. It trusts RouterD.

   RouterB must trust RouterA and RouterC. It trusts neither.

   RouterC must trust RouterB and RouterD. It trusts neither.

   RouterD must trust RouterA and RouterC. It trusts RouterA.

   Trust relationships must be developed between RouterA and RouterB, RouterB and RouterC, and RouterC and RouterD.

Pg 7-55   **Lesson 5   Practice: Translating Business Requirements into Technical Solutions**

The following table provides the answers.

Table   Technical Solutions for Wingtip Toys Business Statements–Answer Key

Statements	What technical solution will be best in this case?
We require the highest level of security and will support that with any reasonable business expense.	Propose smart cards, strongest encryption level, and quarantine control.
No additional staff will be hired for this project.	Automate VPN client installation using CMAK. Automate computer certificate distribution if required. Allow both PPTP and L2TP/IPSec VPN connections.
We cannot risk the system being compromised.	Propose smart cards, strongest encryption level, and quarantine control. Provide company computers, support, user training, and technical controls to prevent accidental or purposeful modification of computer software and configuration.
We must ensure that communications between the offices in Sydney and New York are always protected.	Use a site-to-site demand-dial VPN.
Users cannot be burdened with making password changes.	Require smart cards.

Design Activity: Designing Secure Communications

Pg 7-58   ## Exercise 1: Make Recommendations for Site-to-Site Configuration

1. What configuration would you recommend be used for site-to-site connections?

   Implement an L2TP/IPSec site-to-site demand-dial VPN between each site and headquarters. The state agency site should initiate all communications. Implement site-to-site demand-dial VPNs between state agency locations in each region. These VPNs connections should be initiated in either direction.

Pg 7-58   ## Exercise 2: Make Recommendations for Protecting Employee Communications

1. What would you recommend to protect the communications going from remote-access employees back to the employees' offices?

   Implement remote access VPNs at each location. Use IAS and Network Access Quarantine Control. Require smart cards.

8 Designing Security by Server Role

Exam Objectives in this Chapter:

- Design security for servers with specific roles. Roles include domain controllers, network infrastructure servers, file servers, Internet Information Services, Terminal Servers, and POP3 mail server.
  - ❑ Define a baseline security template for all systems.
  - ❑ Create a plan to modify baseline security templates according to role.

Why This Chapter Matters

We know how to design security for servers. However, configuring each server independently is not efficient or cost-effective nor does it provide a sufficiently secure process. When servers are configured one-by-one, it is difficult to provide consistency, keep up with necessary changes, and correct errors. It is too difficult to determine the status of all servers and impossible to provide accountability for changes made or not made. Therefore, the servers are more likely to be misconfigured and therefore more likely to be at risk and succumb to an attack. Furthermore, all servers are not exactly the same: they offer different services, have different levels of exposure, and do not all have the same security methods configured or implemented.

Instead of wasting time configuring each server, you can more easily secure an entire network's servers by designing security according to the role that servers must play and then automatically implementing security for all servers based on the server role.

Lessons in this Chapter:

Before You Begin

This chapter presents the skills and concepts related to creating a security design framework. This training kit assumes that you have a minimum of 1 year of experience implementing and administering desktop operating systems and network operating systems in environments that have the following characteristics:

- At least 250 supported users

- Three or more physical locations

- Typical network services such as messaging, database, file and print, proxy server or firewall, Internet and intranet, remote access, and client computer management

- Three or more domain controllers

- Connectivity needs that include connecting branch offices and individual users in remote locations to the corporate network, and connecting corporate networks to the Internet

In addition, you should have experience designing a network infrastructure.

Many design exercises are paper-based; however, to understand the technical capabilities that a design can incorporate, you should have some hands-on experience with products. Where specific hands-on instruction is given, you must have at least two computers configured as specified in the "Getting Started" section at the beginning of this book.

Lesson 1: Preparing an Infrastructure for Security by Server Role

After this lesson, you will be able to

- Describe the process of designing security by server role.
- Identify server roles.
- Explain what a security template is and why security templates are used.
- Explain how to apply security templates to servers.
- Select an implementation process for implementing security by server role.
- Design the organizational unit (OU) infrastructure for server role security.

Estimated lesson time: 30 minutes

The Process: Designing Security by Server Role

To design security by server role, you must identify the roles—or services—that servers perform on the network, establish the best security configuration for the role, and provide a means to configure and maintain the server's security. Because the process focuses on the server's role and because many servers do the same thing, a single security design can be used repeatedly. The process for designing security by server role is as follows:

1. Identify server roles.

2. Define the security for the server role.

3. Design implementation of server roles based on using security templates by:

    a. Identifying locations for server security settings, including security templates, GPOs, or any other custom settings

    b. Creating security templates and installation procedures for custom settings

    c. Deciding how to apply security templates to servers

    d. Designing an implementation strategy based on Active Directory design

    e. Using a baseline security template and incremental templates

    f. Designing an OU infrastructure to support Active Directory implementation

    g. Designing security for servers that are not members in an Active Directory domain

4. Test security templates and other security settings to ensure that the settings provide the expected protection and that the services offered by the server remain functional.

This lesson teaches what you need to know to begin this process by identifying server roles, defining security templates, deciding how to implement them, and designing the OU structure that can be used to do so. Lessons 2 and 3 continue teaching this process by showing you how to define a baseline security template and how to design an incremental security template that specifies security based on server role, respectively. Specific suggestions for server security are incorporated in the lessons and in the resources recommended by them.

How to Identify Server Roles

A server's role is the expression of the job that it performs and the services it provides. Every Microsoft Windows network includes many common roles and some roles that are unique. Common names for server roles are:

- Domain Controller
- DHCP Server
- Wins Server
- DNS Server
- File and Print Server
- FAX Server
- SQL Server
- Exchange Server
- Internet Information Server
- ISA Server
- Routing and Remote Access Server
- IAS Server
- Certification Authority

Other server roles exist. These servers might not be found on every network. They might run third-party server software, or they might simply be less common Microsoft products. But whether the computer role is common or not, it must be secured. The first step in doing so is to gather a list of the different types of server roles on your network.

Important   The process described in this chapter can be used to secure Microsoft Windows Server 2003 and Microsoft Windows 2000 servers. However, the idea of securing servers by role can be implemented for other types of servers. Although you will not be able to use the automated processes described in this chapter, you can provide more consistent security by identifying the server's role, specifying security for that role, and using the same security configuration for all like servers.

To identify server roles on your network:

1. Make a list of servers.

2. Document whether these servers are member servers in a domain or stand-alone servers.

3. Identify the services the server provides. If a server provides a service not already listed, add it to the list.

What Is a Security Template?

The basic repository for Windows Server 2003 security settings is the security template. Because the use of security templates to configure security is already built into Windows Server 2003, you should use these templates in your design. They will make the design process much easier. The security template is an .inf text file that can be

■ Edited in a text editor, such as Microsoft Notepad (shown in Figure 8-1)

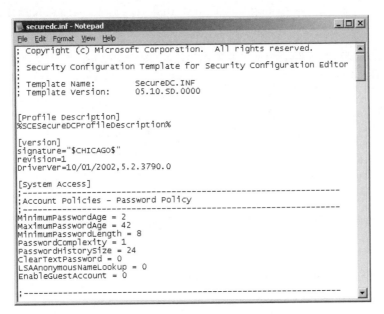

Figure 8-1   Viewing a security template in Notepad

■ Viewed and modified in the Security Templates snap-in (shown in Figure 8-2)

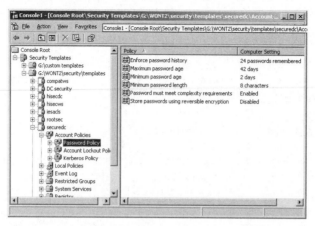

Figure 8-2 Viewing a security template in the Security Templates snap-in

■ Used by the Security Configuration and Analysis tool to help you analyze and configure security on the local server (as shown in Figure 8-3)

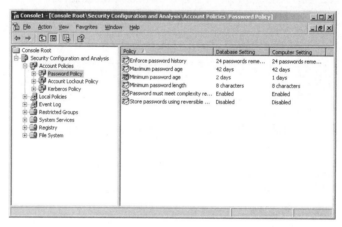

Figure 8-3 Analyzing with the Security Configuration and Analysis tool

■ Applied with a script using secedit, as in the following statement:

```
Secedit /configure /db hisecdc.sdb /cfg hisecdc.inf /log hisecdc.log
```

■ Imported into a Group Policy Object (GPO) and therefore downloaded and applied by servers that have accounts that reside within the site, domain, or OU where the GPO is applied (as shown in Figure 8-4)

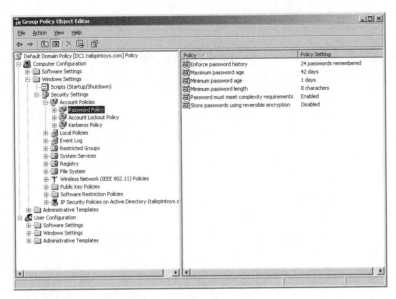

Figure 8-4   Imported into Group Policy

Sections in a Security Template

Security templates provide the ability to configure a multitude of security settings. Table 8-1 lists the sections of settings included in a security template and defines how each area is used.

Table 8-1   Security Template Sections

This Security Template Section	Can be Configured with These Security Settings
Password Policy	Password policy provides settings such as password length, renewal, history, and complexity.
Account Lockout Policy	Account lockout policy provides threshold settings.
Kerberos Policy	This policy is N/A for servers. It is applicable only when configured in a GPO linked to the domain and determines the Kerberos authentication policy for domain accounts.
Audit Policy	Audit policy settings determine which types of security events will be recorded in the computer's security event log.
User Rights	This setting determines user rights on the server. When set in GPOs linked to the domain controller OU, this setting provides rights in the domain.
Security Options	These settings provide a variety of registry entries for easier configuration in the GUI. These settings cover areas such as logon, network, communications, device driver, legal notice, and so on.
Event Log	This setting can configure event log size or overwrite policy.

Table 8-1   Security Template Sections

This Security Template Section	Can be Configured with These Security Settings
Restricted Groups	Groups added here can be used to allow policy control over their membership. Users added to the groups here are the only group members that will be allowed to remain in the local group membership. Users not present locally but added here will be added to the local group.
System Services	This setting provides the ability to set the startup mode for the service—either disabled, manual, or automatic. It also provides the ability to restrict the users and/or groups that can change this information and stop and start the service.
Registry	This setting provides the ability to set access controls and auditing controls on registry keys.
File System	This setting provides the ability to set access controls and auditing controls on files and folders.

Security Templates Necessary in the Design

Two types of templates are necessary. First, a baseline security template should be designed that, if applied, will reduce the attack surface and tightly lock down controls on Windows Server 2003 (but still allow it to run). Next, incremental templates should be developed for each server role. The incremental template will start only those services and/or loosen control for the specific server role to function. Lesson 2, "Defining a Baseline Security Template," and the topic "Guidelines for Designing Incremental Security Templates" in lesson 3 will teach you how to do so.

Methods for Applying Security Templates to Servers

After security templates are designed and tested, they must be applied to the servers before they will have any impact. There are two ways that this can be automated: using Group Policy or using secedit inside of a script. Applying security templates to the servers can also be done manually or by using the installation process.

How to Use Active Directory to Implement Security for Server Roles

Active Directory provides a very good automated solution. If security templates are imported into GPOs, the next time the GPO is downloaded by the server, the new security policy will be applied. You can use the normal hierarchical application of

GPOs to support the application of first the baseline and then the incremental templates. The normal hierarchical application of GPOs proceeds in this order:

- Local GPO
- Site GPO
- Domain GPO
- OU GPO
- Child GPO and so on, until the location of the server account is reached

If there are GPOs at each location, all GPOs are applied. If settings are not in conflict, they are merged. If a conflict exists, the last GPO applied wins. If you ensure that the baseline template is imported into a GPO that is applied before the GPO that hosts the incremental template, your security design will work. To use Group Policy to apply the templates, you must do the following:

- Build an OU hierarchy for servers. In its simplest form, a top-level OU is created and a child OU of the top-level OU is created for each server role. Figure 8-5 illustrates a simple OU hierarchy.

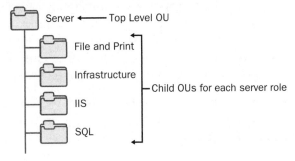

Figure 8-5   A simple server role OU hierarchy

- Add server accounts to OUs.
- Create GPOs for the top-level OU and for each server-role OU.
- Import the baseline template into the GPO of the top-level OU.
- Import the incremental templates into the appropriate server-role OU. The File and Print template, for example, will be imported into the File and Print GPO. Figure 8-6 shows the relationship between templates and GPOs.

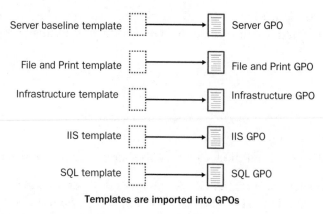

Templates are imported into GPOs

Figure 8-6 Templates are imported into GPOs

How to Use Security Configuration and Analysis or secedit to Implement Server Roles

Security Configuration and Analysis is a tool that can be used to apply a security template. When two templates are applied, the result is similar to that achieved with Group Policy. Where the settings do not conflict, they are merged. If settings conflict, the last one applied wins.

To use Security Configuration and Analysis to apply two templates, you can simply apply the baseline template and then apply the incremental template for the specific server. If you have many servers that support the same role, you can easily—after applying both templates to a server—export a new template that combines the settings of both. The new template can be used to apply security to other servers that fill the same role.

However, rather than apply templates at the console of a single server at a time, you can use secedit. You use secedit in a script that can be automatically run at logon, when booting, or as a task at some other time.

How to Use Other Methods to Apply Security Settings

There are two other methods for applying security settings: using the installation process, and manually configuring the system. To manually configure the system, you must use the Group Policy editor to edit security settings. To use the installation process:

1. Rename the baseline template **defltsv.inf**. (This template is used during installation to apply the default security settings).

2. Perform one of the following actions:

   ❑ Copy defltsv.inf to the network installation share (the place where installation files reside so that they can be used during a network install).

   -or-

   ❑ Make the new defltsv.inf file a part of a custom installation CD-ROM (that includes all other necessary installation files).

Guidelines for Selecting the Implementation Process for Security by Server Role

You might need more than one process to ensure that the correct security settings are applied to all servers. Follow these guidelines to select which implementation process to use:

- If servers are members of an Active Directory Domain, use Group Policy to apply the template security settings.

- If servers are not members of an Active Directory Domain and there are many of them, develop a script that uses secedit and use this to apply the templates.

- Apply the baseline template during installation. Apply the incremental template either later in the process or immediately after installation.

- If enough servers of a particular role type will be installed, create a combination template, rename it **defltsrv.inf**, and use it in the installation process.

- When creating default templates for installing domain controllers, make sure a domain controller template is applied before the server is promoted to a domain controller. Some services must be running that typically are not configured to be in the baseline template. If the services are not running, domain controller installation will fail.

Guidelines for Designing the OU Infrastructure for Server Role Security

To make the best use of Group Policy, design an OU infrastructure that can be used to apply the security templates. Follow these guidelines to design the OU infrastructure:

- Use a top-level OU. This is where the baseline template will be applied.

- Look for natural combinations of like server roles:
  - File Servers and Print Servers, for example, can be combined on one server or can be implemented on different computers, but a single File and Print OU might be sufficient.
  - Other combinations might be to place DNS, DHCP, and WINS servers in an Infrastructure OU.

- Look for areas where you might want to split server roles, such as:
  - When not all IIS servers should be treated the same. A natural division might be intranet servers and Internet servers.
  - When the decision to divide a server role should be based on security. Ask the question, "Would using a single incremental template for these servers weaken security?" If it would, split the server role.

- Create an OU for each server role or server role combination.

- Avoid making more OU layers than necessary. Place both Internet and intranet IIS OUs at the same level—for example, do this rather than creating an IIS OU with two child OUs named Internet and Intranet. Figure 8-7 shows an OU hierarchy that follows these guidelines.

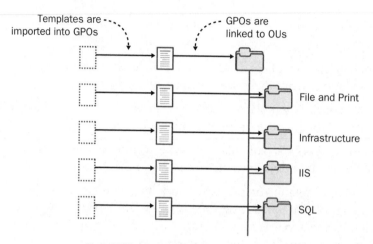

Figure 8-7   A simple server role OU hierarchy showing templates and OUs

Practice: Designing an OU Infrastructure that Can Be Used to Implement Security by Server Role

In this practice, you will design an OU infrastructure for a fictitious company. Read the scenario and then complete the exercises that follow. If you are unable to answer a question, review the lesson materials and try the question again. You can find answers to the questions in the "Questions and Answers" section at the end of the chapter.

Scenario

You are the domain administrator for Wingtip Toys and want to propose a new security plan for Wingtip Toys servers. You have decided that security by server role is the way to go. Your first step is to create the OU infrastructure. You examined how servers are used at Wingtip Toys and compiled the following information.

There are 30 servers at Wingtip Toys. Fifteen are used as file servers. There are four print servers, which are never used as file servers. The other servers include two Microsoft SQL Server servers and two servers in the Certification Authority hierarchy, including the root server, which is located in a vault. Remote access services consist of an Internet Authentication Service (IAS) server and three remote access servers. Two

IIS servers form the company intranet. An additional IIS server serves as a customer service Web site and is not a member server.

Exercise 1: Designing an OU Structure

Sketch a drawing of the OU infrastructure you will propose for Wingtip Toys. Name the OU with the type of server that it will support, and indicate how many servers will be in each OU.

Exercise 2: Justifying a Design

Answer the following questions.

1. Did you group any server roles? Why or why not?

   _____

   _____

   _____

   _____

2. How many of the OUs will require a GPO?

   _____

   _____

3. How many of the OUs need a security template designed?

   _____

Lesson 2: Defining a Baseline Security Template

Designing baselines for security is nothing new. A baseline is simply a starting point. It can represent the minimum level of security that must be applied to a server, or it can, as it is being used here, define the strongest level of security that a basic server can support, that allows the server to meet the organization's security policy, and that allows the server to still run.

After this lesson, you will be able to

- Identify which parts of a security policy can be applied to a baseline security template.
- Explain the considerations for interpreting an organization's security policy, and apply parts of it to a baseline security template.
- List sources of baseline security template samples and settings recommendations.
- Analyze baseline security template samples.
- Evaluate sample baseline security template recommendations.
- Define a baseline security template for an organization.
- Describe elements of the security configuration that cannot be completed by using security templates.

Estimated lesson time: 40 minutes

How to Identify Which Parts of a Security Policy Can Be Applied to the Security Template

You should be intimately familiar with your organization's entire security policy. However, because security templates do not offer a place to address all information security concerns, you must select items in the policy that can be expressed in the templates.

To do this, review the settings categories that are in the Security Template and identify any parts of the organization's security policy that might be fulfilled by using the template. You can use Table 8-2 as a starting point. The table lists the parts of a security template and identifies possible security policy areas and key words in an organization's security policy that might match them.

Table 8-2   Matching Security Policy to Security Templates

Security Template Section	Security Policy Sections and Key Words
Password Policy	Password policy
Account Lockout Policy	Password policy, account policy
Kerberos Policy	Authentication policy
Audit Policy	Audit policy

Table 8-2   Matching Security Policy to Security Templates

Security Template Section	Security Policy Sections and Key Words
User Rights	Authorization, user rights, access controls
Security Options	Security controls, management of information systems, access controls, legal notices
Event Log	Auditing, logging
Restricted Groups	Privilege use
System Services	Controls, proactive management, defense
Registry	Access controls, authorization
File System	Access controls, authorization

Security Policy Terminology Confusion

It is easy to get confused when talking about security policies because the term *security policy* is used to mean different things in different contexts. First, there is the organization's security policy. This is a collection of statements that identify the broad security concepts that all employees must follow. These statements are recorded in a document. Second, there is the security policy that can be designed and implemented by using technical controls in a Windows Server 2003–based computer, domain, and forest. These security policies are often implemented via the use of Group Policy policies, by applying security settings using Security Configuration and Analysis, or by directly configuring security using one of many server, domain, or server application tools. In this chapter, when the words *security policy* or *security policies* are used, they represent a reference to the written security policy document that belongs to the organization.

Considerations for Interpreting a Security Policy and Applying Parts of It to a Baseline Security Template

You might not be able to apply every security policy by using security templates, but you can apply some. Likewise, you want to be sure that nothing you implement in a security template violates security policy. For these reasons, you should examine the security policy and, where possible, map policy to templates.

Written security policies do not usually include exact parameters. They do not, for example, usually specify products or indicate exactly which user accounts can read and write files and registry keys. You will not find many references that you can directly plug into the template. Instead, your written security policy must be interpreted according to the current technology. The organization usually produces written guidelines, which suggest the current interpretation or how to interpret the guidelines, and procedures, which specify the exact steps taken to perform IT-related tasks.

For example, the security policy might state that data owners—those responsible for file content—have the right to decide who can read, write, or do both to the files. Guidelines might identify how data ownership is determined and where that information can be found. Procedures specify how to take that information and use the current technical controls to enforce the data owners' specifications. The current procedures in your organization might detail how to change the security permissions on NTFS-based files and folders. For all portions of the template, review the security policy, guidelines, and procedures so that you can use them to complete the template or at least to prevent creating a security template that violates the organization's security policy.

As you begin to interpret your security policy and apply it to the baseline security template, think about the topics in the following sections.

Important   Most written security policies are vague, but the password policy is typically an exception. Authentication is such an important facet of IT security that a written security policy might specify the exact length of the password, when it must be changed, and so on. If this information is present in your security policy, you must consider how it will affect the baseline security template. Password policy for domain accounts is configured in the default domain GPO. If a password policy is defined in a GPO linked to any other location, it will affect only the local accounts of the computers that apply the GPO. This means that only users who use local accounts to authenticate will be affected by the policy in the GPO. It does not mean, however, that you should ignore the password policy part of the baseline security template.

Consider the Use of Local Accounts

In some organizations or for some servers, local accounts are used to administer the computer or the server applications. Local accounts cannot be eliminated entirely, and therefore an attacker might attempt to compromise them. An attacker with the password for a local administrator account can do a lot of damage to the data and processes running on that computer. She might also be able to use the local administrator account to elevate her privileges in the domain. To defend against an attack on local accounts, use a GPO and establish an account policy for local accounts in addition to the account policies for domain accounts.

Exam Tip   The local Administrator account can be disabled in Windows Server 2003; however, in safe mode, the local administrator account is enabled. Although booting to safe mode requires physical access to the computer, you should still assign a strong password to the Administrator account.

Consider Current and Past Technical Limitations and Capabilities

When the written password policy was made a part of the security policy, it might not have been possible to have the additional controls that are now available in Windows Server 2003. Consider this, and attempt to interpret the nonexplicit part of the security policy. For example, keeping a password history might not have been possible and therefore might not be addressed in the security policy. However, it is now possible to use a password history to prevent users from reusing passwords.

Written password policy might specify some control that is not present by default in Windows Server 2003. Consider whether it is necessary to obtain third-party products to fulfill the policy. An example of this technical limitation might be the requirement that passwords include a punctuation mark in the middle of the password. Although Windows Server 2003 allows you to require a combination of three of four elements (uppercase and lowercase letters, symbols, and numbers), you cannot specify something as explicit as including a punctuation mark in the middle of the password. You should clarify with management whether they want to commit the resources to provide this additional control through a customer password filter DLL.

Consider the Audit Policy, User Rights, File System, Registry, and Event Logs

Consider statements in the security policy that dictate or give advice on the access that should be allowed to employees based on title, rank, security classification, or other differentiator. These statements might dictate the creation of Windows groups. Windows group creation is not done, nor is membership in groups configured, in the template. However, the use of Windows groups to define object access, object auditing, and users rights is a part of the security templates. An example of the usage of groups is to deny remote logon rights to a specific group or to audit file and folder access by Windows group.

Consider the overall tone of the security policy. The tone might indicate how strict access controls must be. For example, if the policy stresses strict security controls, you might need to apply logon rights to specific groups for specific computers by computer role. In cases where the tone is less dogmatic, this might not be necessary.

Also, consider how extensively systems will be audited. If policy demands that object access be audited, for example, you will want to make sure adequate room is available in the security event log.

Consider Security Options

The security options section provides a way to modify registry settings to improve security. The default settings in this section can be used to enforce many aspects of your organization's written security policy, including logons, passwords, network communication, object access, and user rights. The security options section can also be customized by adding entries to the security template master file using a text editor. Any security issue that can be addressed by making a registry entry can be added to the security template. Many security policy statements can be fulfilled by adding entries here.

Consider Overall Best Practices

Apply a baseline template to all servers, and use incremental templates to adjust security for specific server roles. Remember that:

■ If changes are necessary for some server role or are dictated by security policy for some server role but will weaken security, make them in the incremental templates and not in the baseline template.

■ If changes are dictated or necessary for some server role but strengthen overall security, consider making them in the baseline template. However, if they must then be relaxed for most server roles, they probably do not belong in the baseline template.

Sources of Baseline Security Template Samples and Settings Recommendations

The baseline template includes a large number of settings, and many of them cannot be simply made into yes or no decisions. You must ensure that modifications to the template follow security policy; however, you might find it difficult to make decisions about all the setting opportunities just by using your security policy. Luckily, there are other resources you can use to make these decisions.

Many organizations have documented their opinions about how security templates might be configured. They even make available copies of their recommended Windows security templates that you can download and use. Sources for security templates and security template settings recommendations include the following:

■ The "Microsoft Windows Server 2003 Security Guide" is available from Microsoft. You can download the templates and a document of almost 300 pages that specifies how they fit into the process of securing Windows servers.

■ The Microsoft guide, "Threats and Countermeasures," available at *http://www.microsoft.com/downloads/details.aspx?displaylang= en&familyid=1b6acf93-147a-4481-9346-f93a4081eea8*, provides a detailed explanation of all settings. It is designed as a companion guide to the "Microsoft Windows Server 2003 Security Guide".

- The National Security Agency offers a several-hundred-page guide and templates that address security in Windows 2000.

- The "Microsoft Windows 2000 Security Operations Guide" provides documentation, recommendations, and templates for Windows 2000.

- *Microsoft Certified Professional Magazine*, which you can view at *www.mcpmag.com*, provides a conference CD-ROM and attack analysis, as well as a discussion on how the Windows Security Conference held in July 2002 built a secure network using Microsoft Windows 2000 templates provided in the Windows Security Operations Guide. The network was presented on the Internet, attacks were invited, and none were successful.

On the CD   The "Microsoft Windows Server 2003 Security Guide," "Threats and Countermeasures," and "Microsoft Windows 2000 Security Operations Guide" are included in the Supplemental Information section on the CD.

Guidelines for Analyzing Baseline Security Template Samples

The best and most comprehensive templates and explanations for the use of security templates are in the "Microsoft Windows Server 2003 Security Guide" (identified in the rest of this section as "the guide"). In addition to providing and explaining a member server baseline template, the guide also provides templates and recommendations for domainwide security and infrastructure and for many common server roles. This is an impressive piece of work and should be a part of your security toolkit. However, you should not blindly implement the provided templates (nor should you do so for any other preconfigured security template offering). The following guidelines specifically address the Microsoft guide and its templates, but they can be used in a similar fashion to review other guides and templates.

- **Examine the guide and all templates.**   The guide provides a solution that identifies three levels of security. Select the level—Legacy client (servers must be accessible to clients other than Windows 2000 and XP Professional), Enterprise Client, or High Security—that matches your needs. The level names allude to the operating systems that can be present if this template is used for the servers. Table 8-3 defines the operating systems that are allowed in each level. You might also find that all three templates are applicable.

Table 8-3   Operating Systems Allowed at Security-Guide Levels

Operating System	Legacy Client	Enterprise Client	High Security
Windows 98	Yes	No	No
Windows NT 4.0 Workstation	Yes	No	No
Windows NT 4.0 member servers	Yes	No	No

Table 8-3   Operating Systems Allowed at Security-Guide Levels

Operating System	Legacy Client	Enterprise Client	High Security
Windows NT 4.0 domain controllers	No	No	No
Windows 2000 Professional	Yes	Yes	Yes
Windows 2000 member servers	Yes	Yes	Yes
Windows 2000 domain controllers	Yes	Yes	Yes
Windows XP professional	Yes	Yes	Yes
Windows Server 2003 member servers	Yes	Yes	Yes
Windows Server 2003 domain controllers	Yes	Yes	Yes

■ **Do not use one source exclusively.**   You might find that information from other template recommendations is useful. You should also use product documentation, TechNet resources, books, and whitepapers to supplement the guide.

■ **Examine the recommendations in light of your security policy.**   For example:

❑ Examine each section of the template recommendations, but don't disregard how sections or parts of sections work together. See the topic "Considerations for Interpreting a Security Policy and Applying Parts of It to a Baseline Security Template" earlier in this lesson.

❑ Each part of the Account Lockout Policy is dependent on the other parts. You cannot simply make a choice on one without considering the others.

■ **Ensure that design recommendations are tested.**   The specific recommendations might have been tested but cannot possibly be judged safe for your organization. You might have legacy clients or applications that will be broken by settings that might not affect others. You might have requirements beyond those which can be reproduced in someone else's test.

■ **Consider the template designer and its intended audience.**   This can have an affect on the security settings in the template and whether or not they are applicable in your organization or correct for using in the model defined in this chapter. For example:

❑ The Microsoft templates were developed to meet this book's definition of *baseline*—that is, a rigorous security standard that is then adjusted to allow specific server roles to be implemented on the network.

❑ Other templates might define *baseline* as a common security standard that most can live with. The gold standard templates from the Center of Internet Security (CIS), for example, represent the agreement of many organizations and might or might not provide the level of security your organization requires in a baseline template.

How to Evaluate Sample Baseline Security Template Recommendations

There are many design decisions to be made when using security templates to define security for servers. It is easy to give guidelines and provide thoughts for your consideration. It is more difficult to tell you exactly what to do.

Information security consultants are famous for responding to requests for specific settings with the words "it depends." To help you learn how to evaluate template recommendations, Table 8-4 provides explanations for some recommendations in the guide's templates—both as described in the document and also as explained elsewhere. Sections that are explained in other chapters—such as Password Policy, Account Lockout Policy, and Auditing—are not commented on here. Table 8-4 also provides commentary on the settings. For a comprehensive explanation, read the guide and refer to other resources, some of which are provided in the "Sources of Baseline Security Template Samples and Settings Recommendations" topic earlier in this lesson. To evaluate baseline security template recommendations, perform the following tasks:

- Read the security template setting and the choices presented. Choices might be to simply enable or disable, or they might be more explicit.

- Use resources to determine what the setting will do. Sometimes it will be self evident, such as the setting that states the minimum length for a password. Other settings might seem vague or might just need to be researched.

- Use your own knowledge and other resources to determine the impact a specific setting might have when combined with other settings.

- Determine whether the setting can restrict, lock down, or eliminate something and therefore make a server more secure.

- Determine whether the setting restricts, locks down, or eliminates something that might cause the server to not run.

- Determine whether the setting adheres to or violates your organization's security policy.

- Consider each setting in the template, and make a decision about whether changes are needed to make servers more secure or whether secure baseline settings should be reinforced by including them in the template.

Table 8-4   Evaluating Template Settings

Setting	Purpose	Comments
Access this computer from the network	A user right that determines the users that can connect to a computer over the network. Used by SMB, HTTP, NetBIOS, CIFS, and COM+. The guide recommends removing the Everyone group in the High Security template and just allowing Administrators and Authenticated Users. Although anonymous is not in this group in Windows Server 2003, Guest account and groups are.	This is a good place to restrict access to only those who need it, depending on computer role. Use the High Security recommendation, and make other decisions in the incremental templates. Restricting access further here might cause problems, especially if few server roles really need restrictions.
Adjust memory quotas for a process	A user right to adjust memory available to a process. In the wrong hands, it can cause a denial of service attack, as too much memory is used by a single process and none or little is available for others. The guide recommends High Security restrict this right to Administrators, NETWORK SERVICE, LOCAL SERVICE.	By default, this setting is not defined in other templates and the member server default is Administrators, NETWORK SERVICE, LOCAL SERVICE. The reason for repeating this information in the template is to be able to reapply the defaults. If an administrator granted this right to other users, thus making an attack or misuse more likely to succeed, a GPO that uses this template will maintain the defaults. This is a good use of templates, and you might consider using this strategy to protect other critical security settings.
Debug programs	A user can attach a debugger to a process or to the kernel, providing access to sensitive operating system components. Debugging shouldn't be occurring on a production computer. Revoke for all security groups and accounts. No one should have this privilege.	There have been cases where a user with this right was able to elevate his privileges to administrator and thus take over a computer. Note how the template removes a right that could prove dangerous in the wrong hands—a right that is not necessary anyway in a production environment.

Table 8-4   Evaluating Template Settings

Setting	Purpose	Comments
Deny access to this computer from the network	Can be used to explicitly deny remote access. As you know, no access is given without specific permission. However, judicious use of this right will prevent many "accidents"—situations where some action provides unintended access. Note that the templates explicitly deny access to the ANNONYMOUS LOGON, Built-in Administrator, Guests, Support_388945a0, Guest, and all non-operating systems service accounts.	Restricting the accounts entered here should not cause a problem, and the same accounts are recommended for each level. You might, however, review your applications and other requirements. For example, if anonymous access is required for some legacy application, then denying the anonymous logon the right to log on will break that application.
Shut down the system	The member server default gives backup operators, power users, and Administrators this right. The guide recommends that it should be given only to Administrators in the High Security level template.	If a server can be shut down, any number of attacks can be carried out that will provide the attacker with complete control of the server. Reducing the number of people who can shut down the server reduces this threat. Remember, though, that someone with physical access to the computer could use the power switch to shut the server off without shutting it down. You should also consider ways to protect against this possibility—or at least make it harder to access the power switch and perhaps more noticeable when someone does.

Guidelines for Defining a Baseline Security Template for an Organization

After you have reviewed specific recommendations for settings in security templates, understand what each setting can be used for, and have identified where the baseline security template can be used to enforce the organization's security policy, you are ready to define the baseline security template you will use. Follow these guidelines to define a baseline security template:

■ **General guidelines.**   Apply security policy to the security settings by using the following:

❑ Where there is a question as to whether to lock a setting down, disable a service, or otherwise choose between a restrictive setting or a less restrictive setting, choose the more restrictive setting unless you know that it will prevent the server from running.

❑ Do not make settings in the baseline policy that affect only one server role. You will make those settings in the incremental policies.

■ **Password policy guidelines.** Follow specifics, guidelines, or both from the security policy, and establish a policy. Having no password policy, or a weak one, on a server can empower an attacker.

■ **Account lockout policy guideline.** Set the number of lockout attempts high enough so that a small number of mistakes will not lock out an account.

■ **Kerberos Policy guideline.** Do not apply the Kerberos Policy, which is only valid when configured in the default domain GPO.

■ **Audit policy guidelines.** Turn on auditing for logon events, privilege use, and object access. Settings in the template will determine auditing events recorded on servers. Without these security events, an attack could go unnoticed or information that would identify attackers would be missing. Configure object-level access auditing in incremental templates or at the server. Objects might vary by server, and placing a large number of items in the template might cause performance issues.

■ **User rights guidelines.** Carefully restrict user rights to those needed. Remember that most rights should be assigned only to administrators on sensitive servers to reduce the attack surface.

■ **Security options guidelines.** Because some settings affect communications between servers and other computers on the network, remember to review settings on domain controllers and clients before making changes from the defaults.

■ **Event log guidelines.** Event-log size defaults for Windows Server 2003 might be adequate for many servers. If extensive auditing is configured, event log sizes might need to be larger. Review needs for server roles when compiling incremental templates, and monitor servers. You might need to adjust log sizes later.

■ **Restricted groups guidelines.** Use restricted groups to control the local Administrator group membership. Membership in this group is overlooked. Non-IT employees can be assigned administrator privileges to provide them the ability to administer a server application. By default, they can add others to the Administrators group. Limit the local Administrators group to membership approved by IT.

■ **System services guideline.** Ensure permissions for setting system services start-up mode and for stopping and starting services is restricted to the Administrators group.

■ **Registry and file system guidelines.** Do not set registry or file systems permissions in the baseline security template. The baseline template will be reapplied periodically even if changes are not made. Having a lot of permission settings can increase network activity and Active Directory replication without providing enough additional benefit.

Elements of the Security Configuration that Cannot Be Completed Using Security Templates

The process of developing a single baseline security template and incremental templates and designing an OU hierarchy is not the end of the security configuration story. There are several other elements of the security configuration:

- Domain controller security
- Stand-alone computer security
- Security for computers on perimeter networks
- Server application security

Domain Controller Security

Domain controllers are automatically placed in their own OU and should not be moved. A default domain controller GPO exists. The domain controller plays such a specialized role that security for the domain controller should be designed independently of the other servers. You might, however, use knowledge gained in developing baseline and incremental templates to develop a template that can be used to secure domain controllers. Several basic differences should be explored, and these differences will result in modifications to the baseline template before it is used with domain controllers:

- The password policy, account lockout policy, and Kerberos policy must be configured in the default domain GPO, not in the default domain controller GPO. No settings should be configured for these areas of the domain controller template.

- The audit policy configured represents the audit information that will be collected on the domain controller. The Audit Account Logon Events and Audit Logon Event settings are critical. The former setting records events relative to Kerberos activity and logon activity at the domain controller (relative to domain-level accounts), and the latter refers to network logon activity.

- Many more events will be collected at the domain controller, so the security event log should be larger.

- Additional services are required beyond those of an ordinary server. Services include the File Replication Service service and Distributed File System service.

- Domain controllers must have the File And Printer Sharing For Microsoft Networks setting enabled in the network configuration settings.

- Domain controllers can also be Domain Name System (DNS) servers. This additional role requires additional security configuration.

Stand-Alone Computer Security

Stand-alone computers cannot be configured using an OU infrastructure and GPOs linked to the OUs. However, baseline and incremental templates can still be developed to provide consistent security for these servers. The delivery mechanism can be script and task-scheduled based.

Security for Computers on Perimeter Networks

Computers on perimeter networks offer special security challenges. They can be stand-alone computers or domain members. The way that security is applied will depend on their status. They will require additional security configuration and protection beyond what security templates can apply.

Server Application Security

Although this chapter develops the concept of using security templates and Group Policy to apply security via server role, do not lose sight of the security configuration that must be done outside of security templates. Security templates are operating system tools for security. Server applications all have unique requirements and tools for configuring security. A complete plan for applying security by security role should include these requirements, dictate baseline security for each role, and provide information about how security is applied.

> **See Also**   Many other chapters in this book supply more information about securing common Microsoft server applications such as Routing and Remote Access server (Chapter 7), Certification Authority (Chapter 2), and Internet Information Server (Chapter 13).

Practice: Using a Security Policy to Define the Baseline Template

In this practice, you will examine parts of a fictitious company's security policy and identify whether or not these parts can be implemented in the baseline template. You will also identify whether these parts of the security policy should be implemented and, if they should, where in the template you can do so. Read the scenario and then complete the exercises that follow. If you are unable to answer a question, review the lesson materials and try the question again. You can find answers to the questions in the "Questions and Answers" section at the end of the chapter.

> **Important**   This is a continuation of the practice at the end of Lesson 1.

Scenario

You finish designing the Wingtip Toys OU infrastructure and now need to create a baseline security template. You decide to review relevant parts of the security policy:

- Password policy—Passwords must be used to manage access to all computers. Passwords must be at least 7 characters long. No controls will lock users accounts unless a large number of false tries have been entered.

- Certificate services policy—The root CA server will be protected by keeping it offline and keeping it in a locked and protected area or room. Access to the room will be limited. All Certification Authority servers will be managed by assigning management roles and enforcing role separation.

Exercise 1: Deciding Whether a Password Policy Should Be Implemented in a Baseline Security Template

Based on the password policy, answer the following questions.

1. Could this password policy be implemented in the baseline template? If so, where?

_____

_____

2. Should this password policy be entered in the baseline template? Why or why not?

_____

_____

Exercise 2: Deciding Whether a Certificate Services Policy Should Be Implemented in a Baseline Security Template

Based on the certificate services policy, answer the following questions.

1. Could this certificate services policy be implemented in the baseline template? If so, where?

_____

_____

_____

2. Should this certificate services policy be entered in the baseline template? Why or why not?

_____

_____

_____

Lesson 3: Designing Incremental Security Templates Based on Server Role

The incremental security template is primarily used to relax the security settings imposed by the baseline security template to allow additional services on the servers to run. An incremental template is developed for each server role so that only the necessary services and settings are applied to each server.

After this lesson, you will be able to

- Decide when to group server roles.
- Design incremental security templates.

Estimated lesson time: 20 minutes

Guidelines for Deciding When to Group Server Roles

After you have identified server roles on your network, you might find that several of them can be placed into a similar category—for example, file servers and print servers. Follow these guidelines to decide when to group server roles:

- **Group server roles when doing so will not compromise the security of either computer.**   Because grouping server roles might enable more services on some computers than is necessary for their function, this weakens the security on these servers. However, the risk might be acceptable depending on the environment in which the server runs.

- **In highly sensitive environments, do not group server roles.**   For example, do not group server roles when implementing DNS services to the Internet on a file server for internal documents.

- **Do not group server roles unless there is some common ground.**   For example, do not group database servers with network infrastructure servers. The administrators of the database server will likely require a greater amount of trust from the organization than those of the network infrastructure server because of the value of the information in the databases. Often, you can group the following server roles:

  - ❑ WINS, DHCP, and DNS servers can be grouped as Infrastructure Servers.

  - ❑ File servers and print servers can be grouped as File and Print Servers.

Guidelines for Designing Incremental Security Templates

Designing incremental security templates for server roles consists of determining where security settings in the template need to be changed from those set in the baseline template. In general, this is not an onerous task because few settings need to be changed. However, security for server roles generally involves much more than modifications made to the security templates. Settings specific to the role usually must be made to server applications running on the server. Application-specific settings are not part of the security templates. Follow these guidelines when designing incremental security templates:

- General guidelines:
    - Rename the Guest and Administrator accounts and their descriptions. Do not give them the same name for every server. By varying the name in this way, an attacker who discovers the name will not have the names for all servers.
    - Disable the Guest account, and disable the Administrators account if it will not be used.
    - Configure recommended services in the templates even if you configure them on the servers before templates are applied. Configuring them in the templates ensures they are not disabled on the local server. Configuring them in the templates makes the Administrators group the only group that can change the startup mode of the service.
- File server guidelines:
    - Set the DFS service to Automatic only if you are using file servers to provide DFS services.
    - Set the File Replication Service (NTFRS) to Automatic only if you are using file servers to provide this service.
- Print server guidelines:
    - Set the Print Spooler service to Automatic.
- Infrastructure server guidelines:
    - Set the DHCP Server service to Automatic if DHCP servers are used on the network.
    - Set the WINS service to Automatic if WINS servers are used on the network.
    - Set the DNS service to Automatic if DNS is used on the network.
- IIS server guidelines:
    - Grant the user right "Deny access to this computer from the network" to the ANONYMOUS LOGON, Built-in Administrator, Support_388945a0, Guest, and all non-operating system service accounts.
    - The baseline policy included the Guests group in the user right "Deny access to this computer from the network". However, IIS uses the ISUR_servername account as a member of the Guests group for anonymous access by Internet users.

- ❑ Set the HTTP SSL service (HTTPFilter) start up mode to Automatic.

- ❑ Set the World Wide Web Publishing service to Automatic.

- ❑ Do not enable (or install) other Web server services unless required by the Web server and approved by management. Recommendations about when to use which components are available online as well as in the "Microsoft Windows Server 2000 Security Guide".

- ■ IAS server guidelines:

  - ❑ Set the IAS service to Automatic.

- ■ Certificate Authority (CA) server guidelines:

  - **a.** Set the security option "Restrict CD-ROM access to locally logged-on user only."

  - **b.** Set the security option "Restrict floppy access to locally logged-on user only."

> **Note** Restricting access to floppy drives and CD-ROM drives prevents anyone from using the device (floppy or CD-ROM) when someone is logged on locally to the Certification Authority. Because key information can be copied to or from a CD-ROM or floppy, it is a good idea to block access.

  - **c.** Remember that the restrictions apply only when someone is logged on locally.

  - **d.** Set the security option "System Cryptography: Use FIPS compliant algorithms for encryption, hashing and signing" if your organization is required to meet US government standards for digital encryption, hashing, and signing.

  - **e.** Set the Certificate servers (certsvc) to Automatic.

  - **f.** Disable the Computer browser service. CA servers do not require this service.

  - **g.** Add audit SACLs (records to gather success or failure of access) to registry keys as listed below to audit for changes to certificate services role configuration. Role configuration for certificate services is explained in Chapter 2. For HKLM\SYSTEM\CurrentControlSet\Services\Certsrv\Configuration and its subkey, set auditing to Failed for Everyone Full Control.

  - **h.** For KLM\SYSTEM\CurrentCOntrolSet\Services\Certvc\Configuration and all subkeys, set auditing to Successful for Everyone for all Special permissions. Set the audit type to Failed for Everyone Full Control on the path %SystemRoot%\system32\CertLog.

  - **i.** Add the audit SACLs for the CA logs and database. Set the audit type to Successful for Everyone Modify on the path %SystemRoot%\system32\CertSrv. If these paths have been moved, set the SACLs at the correct location.

Practice: Designing an Incremental Template for a Perimeter Network Server

In this practice, you will develop a list of items to consider when developing an incremental template for a perimeter server and sketch an OU infrastructure that can provide security in the perimeter network. Read the scenario and then complete the exercises that follow. If you are unable to answer a question, review the lesson materials and try the question again. You can find answers to the questions in the "Questions and Answers" section at the end of the chapter.

> **Important**   This is a continuation of the practice at the end of Lesson 2.

Scenario

While developing your baseline and incremental templates, you've had to struggle with what to do with the servers on the perimeter. You have identified two file servers that sit on the perimeter partner network. There is a partner network that is a segmented network area that provides access to researchers from a partner toy company, Tailspin Toys. The network is segmented from the internal Wingtip Toys network by a firewall that restricts traffic between the internal network and the partner network. Researchers from Wingtip Toys can access the partner network across the boundary between internal and partner networks, and researchers from Tailspin Toys can access the partner network via a special Web site and via a special VPN. The file servers contain research documents. A separate forest has been established, and the file servers are member servers in a domain in this forest.

Exercise 1: Planning Security for File Servers

Answer the following question.

1. How will you provide security for these file servers?

   _____

   _____

   _____

   _____

   _____

   _____

   _____

   _____

   _____

Exercise 2: Designing an OU Structure to Include a Perimeter Network

Sketch a drawing of an OU infrastructure that can provide security in the perimeter network.

Design Activity: Completing the Design—Domain Control Templates

In this activity, you must use what you learned in all three lessons and apply it to a real-world situation. Read the scenario and then complete the exercises that follow. You can find answers for the exercises in the "Questions and Answers" section at the end of this chapter.

> **Important**   This is a continuation of the practice at the end of Lesson 3.

Scenario

Your design is almost complete. You are now ready to design security templates for the domain. As you begin the process, your boss returns the initial part of your proposal. He is not pleased. He believes that you have not created a plan that will provide adequate security for the servers at Wingtip Toys. He wants to see your plan for domain controller security and additional notes on security by server role. You have the following information to work with.

Company Background

Wingtip Toys is a distributor for toys of all kinds. It designs 80 percent of the toys it sells but has them manufactured by another company. Competition is stiff and there is concern that competitors might be engaging in corporate espionage.

Existing Environment

Thirty servers and four domain controllers are all located at corporate headquarters. Recently, a CA hierarchy was added to the network and the use of certificates for EFS was implemented.

Interviews

Following is a list of company personnel interviewed and their statements:

- **C.I.O.**   "What kind of cockamamie idea is this? You have defined pretty stringent security of these servers. Aren't you going to break something? Where is the security for the domain controllers? These "incremental" templates don't seem to do much except start some services. Where is the rest of your security plan?"

- **Security Manager**   "Where are you getting your security ideas? Does this plan follow the security policy? This is a very interesting idea. Can you tell me how this will work? Now, as I understand it, the servers that are domain members will all get this policy. What about those that are not? What about servers in the DMZ?"

- **Help Desk**   "Oh, can we do the same thing for the desktop computers? Isn't a desktop computer a computer role?"

Case Study Exhibits

The following network logical diagram shows domain member relationships, indicates stand-alone servers, and shows a DMZ:

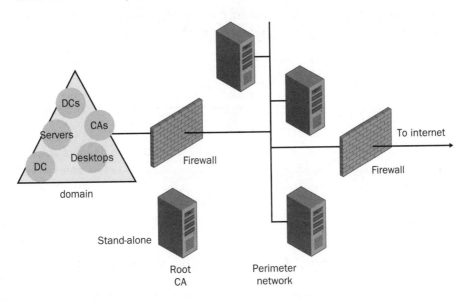

Business Requirements

The business requirements are:

1. Changes in computer security must not interfere with performance.

2. Changes in computer security must not interfere with the ability of employees to get their jobs done.

Technical Requirements

The technical requirements are:

1. Servers must not be able to perform any service they do not absolutely need to do.

2. Servers must be able to do the job they are required to do.

3. No user should be able to log on interactively to the servers unless the user is an administrator.

4. User network access to servers should be restricted. Only users who must have access to a server should be able to access it over the network.

Exercise 1: Revise a Security Plan to Add Security for Domain Controllers

In this exercise, you will outline the configuration of a security template for domain controllers. You do not have to specify every security setting, but you should address broad categories that are different from the server security templates. Answer the following question.

1. What areas must be addressed to adapt the baseline server template so that domain controllers will be able to function?

_____

_____

_____

_____

_____

_____

_____

_____

Exercise 2: Design Additional Server Security Based on Role

In this exercise, you will provide your plan for providing additional server security based on role. To do so, answer the following question.

1. What additional security elements should be addressed for server roles?

_____

_____

_____

_____

_____

_____

_____

_____

_____

_____

_____

_____

Chapter Summary

- Security templates should be designed to apply security based on the role that a server will perform on the network.

- Use the "allow the absolute minimum of function, maximum of security" dictum to design security templates.

- If a service is not used, disable it.

- If a setting can be locked down, lock it down.

- Use incremental templates to provide a server with the ability to perform its function.

Exam Highlights

Before taking the exam, review these key points and terms. You need to know this information.

Key Points

- Server roles are the categories that indicate the specific function that a server plays on the network.

- Baseline and incremental templates are combined with an OU infrastructure to deliver the maximum security configuration to servers on a network while still allowing them to perform their function.

- Baseline templates should be configured to the maximum security settings that will allow a server to still run, and incremental templates relax this security so that a server can play a specific role.

- Security templates should be configured with the organization's security policy in mind.

Key Terms

Baseline template   A security template that is configured to lock down a Windows computer to the maximum amount for a specific network.

Incremental template   A security template that, when used to configure security settings on a computer, relaxes security so that a specific server role can be implemented.

Security template   A list of security configurations in a file. The file can be used to configure security on a computer or analyze security on a computer, or it can be imported into a Group Policy object and used to configure security on multiple computers.

Server role   The job that a server plays on the network, such as file server or print server.

Questions and Answers

Page
8-13

Lesson 1 Exercise 1: Designing an OU Structure

Sketch a drawing of the OU infrastructure you will propose for Wingtip Toys. Name the OU with the type of server that it will support, and indicate how many servers will be in each OU.

OU structure might vary; however, the number of servers should work out the same. In other words, there should be only one CA in the CA OU because the other CA is offline. There are only two IIS servers in the IIS OU because the other IIS server is identified as not belonging to the domain. This figure shows a recommended design:

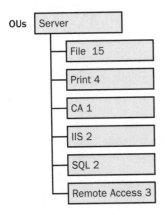

Page
8-13

Lesson 1 Exercise 2: Justifying a Design

1. Did you group any server roles? Why or why not?

   File and Print servers might seem to be a group that could be made, but the information indicates that print servers are never file servers. RRAS and IAS servers are grouped because they are used for remote access and because the security configuration that can be done in the security template is similar.

2. How many of the OUs will require a GPO?

   Answers may vary. The recommended design needs seven. You should have one baseline GPO and one incremental template for each server OU.

3. How many of the OUs need a security template designed?

   Each OU needs a security template designed.

Page
8-27
Lesson 2   Exercise 1: Deciding Whether a Password Policy Should Be Implemented in a Baseline Security Template

1. Could this password policy be implemented in the baseline template? If so, where?

   Yes. This could be placed in the baseline template in the password policy and account lockout policy sections.

2. Should this password policy be entered in the baseline template? Why or why not?

   Yes. Although this does not represent the domain password policy, servers should have a password policy.

Page
8-27
Lesson 2   Exercise 2: Deciding Whether a Certificate Services Policy Should Be Implemented in a Baseline Security Template

1. Could this certificate services policy be implemented in the baseline template? If so, where?

   No. The protection instructions cannot be entered. The management role assignment cannot be entered. However, protection for this role assignment can be a part of a template.

2. Should this certificate services policy be entered in the baseline template? Why or why not?

   No. Although a part of the policy can become a part of a template, it should not be part of the baseline template. Instead, it should be part of the incremental template designed for the OU that will include the CA servers.

Page
8-31
Lesson 3   Exercise 1: Planning Security for File Servers

1. How will you provide security for these file servers?

   A baseline template for the partner domain should be developed. It should be a high-security template, enforcing the most restrictive level of security. An OU infrastructure can provide OUs that map to server roles, such as the file servers. An incremental template should be developed for the file servers that will allow them to function as file servers while protecting them. In addition to allowing them to share files, you should include file and registry ACLs in the templates to ensure consistency and recurring application of the security settings. If common files are stored on both servers, security settings for these files should also be provided in the templates.

Lesson 3   Exercise 2: Designing an OU Structure to Include a Perimeter Network

Page
8-32 Sketch a drawing of an OU infrastructure that can provide security in the perimeter network.

Answers may vary. This picture provides an answer:

Perimeter Network Domain

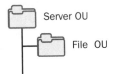

Server OU

File OU

Design Activity   Completing the Design—Domain Control Templates

Exercise 1: Revise a Security Plan to Add Security for Domain Controllers

Page
8-34

1. What areas must be addressed to adapt the baseline server template so that domain controllers will be able to function?

   Services, password policy, Kerberos policy, audit policy, event logs, security options, and user rights. Additional services will need to be set to Automatic. Because the password policy for the domain is controlled by the default domain policy, the domain controller policy should not have a password policy. The audit policy of the domain controller needs both account logon events and logon events set for success and failure. The event logs need to be set to a larger size. Security options for domain controllers need to be configured. User rights should not restrict domain user network access.

Exercise 2: Design Additional Server Security Based on Role

Page
8-34

1. What additional security elements should be addressed for server roles?

   Each server role has specific security issues, many of which cannot be addressed within the security templates. To provide better security plans that address server roles, additional research must be completed. Items to consider include server administration specific to the server roles, security based on the primary application the server is running. For example, Certification Authority administration and user roles can be further configured to provide separation of duties. Routing and Remote Access servers might need packet filters configured to prevent harmful traffic from entering the network. Microsoft SQL Server databases can be secured based on the database purpose. Microsoft Exchange Server, SQL Server, IIS, and all other server roles have security configurations and best practices that are specific to the server role and cannot be configured using security templates. Communications between each server might require special treatment, and IPSec in transport mode might be used to do so.

9 Designing Access Control for Enterprise Data

Exam Objectives in this Chapter:

- Design an access control strategy for data.
- Design an access control strategy for directory services.
- Analyze auditing requirements.
- Create a delegation strategy.
- Design the appropriate group strategy for accessing resources.
- Design a permission structure for directory service objects.
- Design an access control strategy for files and folders.
    - Design a strategy for the encryption and decryption of files and folders.
    - Design a permission structure for files and folders.
    - Design security for a backup and recovery strategy.
    - Analyze auditing requirements.
- Design an access control strategy for the registry.
    - Design a permission structure for registry objects.
    - Analyze auditing requirements.

Why This Chapter Matters

If an attacker is able to gain access to the network, you must have additional defenses in place. Two of those defenses are the object permissions that you set on files, folders, and registry keys and appropriate use of the Encrypting File System. Used properly, these defenses can limit the damage an attacker can do. Object-level permissions also allow you to protect objects from unauthorized use by employees and others you authorize to access the network. Permissions set on objects in Active Directory directory services, however, provide additional benefits. By setting permissions on objects in the Active Directory, you can lessen the administrative burden, provide autonomy for divisions and departments within your organization, or both.

Lessons in this Chapter:

Before You Begin

This chapter presents the skills and concepts related to creating a security design framework. This training kit assumes you have a minimum of 1 year of experience implementing and administering desktop operating systems and network operating system in environments that have the following characteristics:

- At least 250 supported users

- Three or more physical locations

- Typical network services such as messaging, database, file and print, proxy server or firewall, Internet and intranet, remote access, and client computer management

- Three or more domain controllers

- Connectivity needs, including connecting branch offices and individual users in remote locations to the corporate network and connecting corporate networks to the Internet

In addition, you should have experience designing a network infrastructure.

Many design exercises are paper-based; however, to understand the technical capabilities that a design can incorporate, you should have some hands-on experience with products. Where specific hands-on instruction is given, you must have at least two computers configured as specified in the "Getting Started" section at the beginning of this book.

Lesson 1: Designing the Access Control Infrastructure

The first step in designing access control for enterprise data is to understand the basic principles of access control in Microsoft Windows Server 2003 and how to use that structure to secure objects such as files, folders, and registry keys.

After this lesson, you will be able to

- Control access to data in Windows Server 2003.
- Describe how the access control process works.
- Explain how permission inheritance affects access.
- Describe where permissions are stored.
- Explain how inheritance affects the use of deny permissions.
- Design an appropriate group strategy for accessing resources.
- Design a permission structure for files and folders.
- Design a permission structure for registry keys.

Estimated lesson time: 60 minutes

How to Control Access to Data in Windows Server 2003

Access to data in Windows Server 2003 is controlled by having a robust authentication mechanism, setting permissions on data objects, encrypting files, and protecting data during transport. Previous chapters—Chapter 2, Chapter 3, and Chapter 7—detailed authentication, IPSec Policies, and VPNs, respectively. This chapter will explain permissions and the Encrypting File System.

Several basic principles and best practices provide the backdrop for a security designer's work:

- While permissions vary depending on the type of data, the way access is granted does not. Once a security designer has a firm understanding of the access control process, she can couple that knowledge with the permission structure for each Windows Server 2003 object and design access control for them.

- Permissions should never be granted to user accounts; instead, Windows groups should be used. If permissions are granted to user accounts, it becomes difficult to manage them. Determining what access the user has will be difficult, as will removing that access when an employee leaves the company.

- File encryption is an additional protection, but it must be carefully managed. If users do not understand how to use the encrypting file system, they will possibly either have a false sense of security (and might, for example, leave unencrypted copies of their sensitive files around) or find themselves unable to access files that they have encrypted.

- To design access control for data in Windows Server 2003, apply these steps:

    a. Identify the access control process.

    b. Explain Permission Inheritance.

    c. Design a group strategy for access control.

    d. Design a permission structure for files and folders.

    e. Design strategy for encryption and decryption of files and folders.

    f. Design a permission structure for registry keys.

    g. Design access control for directory services, which includes creating a delegation strategy and designing a permission structure for directory service objects.

    h. Design security for backup and recovery.

    i. Analyze auditing requirements.

How the Access Control Process Works

The access control process in Windows Server 2000 relies on the evaluation of the permissions set on an object and the security identifiers (SIDs) that are assigned to the security principal. Two separate data structures or collections of data are used in the evaluation process.

The data object is assigned a *security descriptor*, a construct that includes a Systems Access Control List (SACL) and a discretionary access control list (DACL). SACLs are used in auditing and will be discussed further in Lesson 3, "Analyzing Auditing Requirements." DACLS contain a number of Access Control Entries (ACEs). ACEs identify a permission and indicate to whom it is assigned. ACEs are assigned to objects at object creation and can be modified by a security principal with the change permissions permission. Each ACE contains a SID, a permission, and an action (either Allow or Deny).

> **See Also**   Permissions are uniquely defined according to the type of object. For example, you can "read" a file, but you "query value" for a registry key. Although permissions for files, folders, and registry keys can be listed and defined in short tables, there are so many objects in the Active Directory—and each one might have unique permissions—that it is impossible to provide a comprehensive list of Active Directory object permissions within a document of any normal size. For explicit information on object permissions, see the "How to Design a Permission Structure for Files and Folders" and "How to Design a Permission Structure for Registry Keys" sections in this lesson and the "Guidelines for Designing the Delegation and Permission Structure for Active Directory Objects" section in Lesson 2.

An access token is created for the user or computer at logon. The access token is assigned to any process the security principal runs. Hence, when a user starts Microsoft Word, his access token is assigned to the running winword.exe process. You can see this by opening the Task Manager and adding the User Name column to the Processes tab. The access the user has to documents will depend on the permissions set on the documents and the contents of the access token. The access token contains a list of SIDs, including the SID of the security principal and the SIDs of the groups of which the user account is a member.

What Is the Security Reference Monitor?

The *Security Reference Monitor* is a kernel-level component that runs in the %systemroot%\System32\Ntoskrnl.exe process. The Security Reference Monitor resolves requests for object access, builds a security descriptor for a new object, and validates a given security descriptor. The concept of a security reference monitor is a standard security model in operating systems that is used to evaluate all access to objects.

The basic access control process works like this:

1. The user or a process acting on behalf of the user attempts to access an object. Access attempts can be things like "Open a file for reading and writing," "Query a registry key," or even "Reset a password."

2. The security reference monitor compares the SIDs contained in the access token to the SIDs in each ACE for the ACL.

3. If no matching SIDs are found, access is denied implicitly.

4. If a matching SID is found, the request is evaluated based on the contents of the ACE according to the following rules:

   ❑ If the permission in the ACE matches some part of the request, the action of the ACE is evaluated. Otherwise, access will be denied.

   ❑ If the action is Deny, access is denied.

   ❑ If the action is Allow, any other requested permissions must be processed.

5. Each ACE is evaluated until either access is denied or an Allow ACE is found for every requested permission—in which case, access is granted.

The Airport Access Control Concept

In its simplest form, access control in Windows Server 2003 acts like a security guard and the physical controls at the airport. For each request or attempted action, the security guard or the physical control evaluates the request or action against a list of permissions that are associated with credentials. If a person wants to move to the gate area, she must have a picture ID and a boarding pass for a flight leaving that day. A guard inspects these credentials before providing access. If a person attempts to enter a secured area, he must know the door code or have the correct badge. As long as the guards are properly trained and the controls are properly implemented, security at the airport can control access—every person must have the proper credentials before they can do what they want to do. If something is not properly managed, if credentials can be falsely obtained, if controls are weak, or if security is ill-designed, then security will not work.

In Windows Server 2003, the same truths hold true. Credentials must be restricted to those who need access and access controls need to be well designed. For Windows Server 2003, the credentials are the SIDs, the controls are permissions, and the security guard is the Security Reference Monitor process.

How Permission Inheritance Affects Access

Permissions can be configured on each object independently; however, many Windows objects are part of hierarchical structures and might inherit the permissions applied to all parent objects. Permission inheritance makes it easy to configure like permission settings on many items at the same time. For example, if the same permission sets will apply to a large number of files and folders that are underneath a top-level folder in the file system, an administrator can configure the permission settings once, on the top-level folder, and the permissions will be inherited by every file and folder that falls beneath the top-level folder. Figure 9-1 displays the Advanced Security Settings for the Administrators group on the chngmgmt\servers\fileservers\ folder. For each permission type, the Inherited From column displays the location from which permissions are inherited.

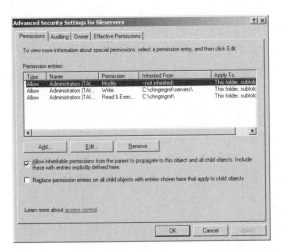

Figure 9-1   Permission inheritance information is located on the Permissions tab of the Advanced Security Settings dialog box

Permission inheritance can also be configured to apply only to some objects in the path underneath a top-level folder or to none of them at all. In addition to the permissions that are inherited by the object, permissions can be configured directly on the object. The following examples illustrate possible inheritance scenarios.

Scenario 1: Full Inheritance

Figure 9-2 shows full inheritance. All permissions boxes are grayed to indicate this. All permissions from the parent folder chngmgmt are inherited by the child. Figure 9-3 shows the the result of this on the Permissions tab in the Advanced Security Settings dialog box for this folder. Notice that the Allow Inheritable Permissions From Parent to Propagate to This Object and All Child Objects. Include These With Entries Explicitly Defined Here check box is selected.

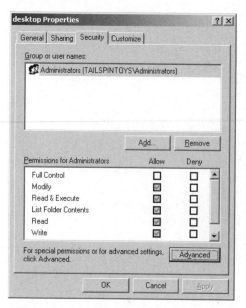

Figure 9-2   Full inheritance is indicated by grayed permissions boxes

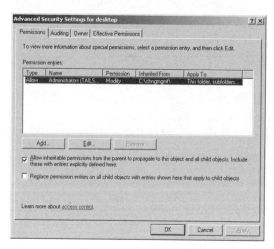

Figure 9-3   Viewing the Permissions tab on the Advanced Security Settings dialog box confirms that all permissions are inherited

Scenario 2: Inherited and Applied Directly to the File

Figure 9-4 shows a file that both inherits permissions from its parent and has permissions applied locally. The Full Control permission box is not grayed to indicate that it is applied to the local folder and not inherited. Figure 9-5 shows the Permissions tab on the Advanced Security Settings dialog box, which confirms this. It shows that the Full Control permission is not inherited. The Allow Inheritable Permissions From Parent to

Propagate to This Object and All Child Objects. Include These With Entries Explicitly Defined Here check box is selected. Permissions that are inherited are grayed-out. (They cannot be changed or removed except by removing inheritance or changing them on the parent folder.) Permissions that are assigned directly on the file are not grayed-out.

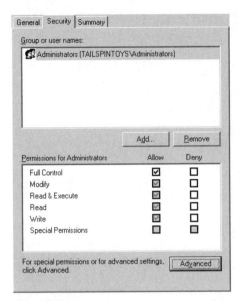

Figure 9-4   A file with both inherited and locally assigned permissions

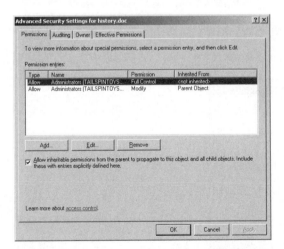

Figure 9-5   Inherited permissions and locally applied permissions

Scenario 3: Blocked Inheritance

Figure 9-6 shows a file that does not inherit permissions from its parent folder. The permissions are directly set on the file. The permission boxes are not grayed out. Figure 9-7 shows the the result of this on the Permissions tab in the Advanced Security Settings dialog box. You should note that the Allow Inheritable Permissions From Parent to Propagate to This Object and All Child Objects. Include These With Entries Explicitly Defined Here check box is not selected.

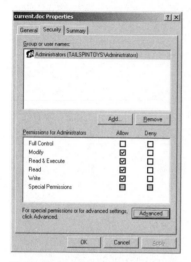

Figure 9-6   Locally set permissions are not grayed out

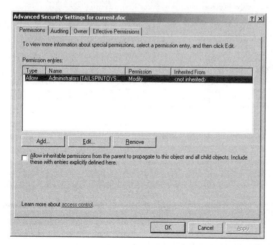

Figure 9-7   Inheritance is blocked

Scenario 4: Inheritance with Multiple Tiers

Permissions can be inherited from multiple tiers. If many levels of the hierarchy have permissions and inheritance is not blocked, all permissions will apply successive layers. Figure 9-8 shows this scenario.

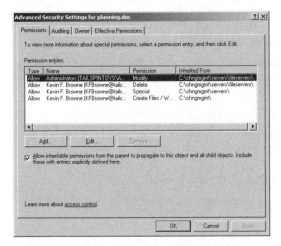

Figure 9-8   Inheritance from multiple parents

Where Permissions Are Stored

The first version of the NTFS file system stored security descriptors with each file and folder, and with each registry key. If a permission was changed on a folder, all files and folders below that folder inherited the permission change and each file and folder security descriptor was modified accordingly. Registry key security descriptors were managed the same way. The registry key contained its own security descriptor and if permissions changed on a parent key, the security descriptor of every child key also changed.

Windows 2000 NTFS changed that. In the Windows 2000 version of NTFS—and in Windows Server 2003 and Windows XP—security descriptors are stored in a special hidden object in the file system. Each file and folder, instead of including a security descriptor, contains only a pointer to the security descriptor. In addition, the file system now stores only unique security descriptors. That is, if a file has only the Allow Accountants Read permissions, a security descriptor is stored. If 10 files or 100 files have this same descriptor, still only one copy is stored. When a permission set is changed, the change is made only to the one security descriptor. Files and folders that inherit this change in setting do not receive the information that permissions have changed. However, when a user next attempts to access the file, the new security descriptor will be evaluated, and thus the new permissions will be applied. This new way of storing and managing permissions makes permission evaluation much more efficient.

> **Note**   Registry permissions, however, are stored as they were in Windows NT; security descriptors are stored with the registry key.

How Inheritance Affects the Use of Deny Permissions

A common mantra used to explain Windows NTFS permissions is "If access is denied, it doesn't matter whether another permission allows access because the user will be denied access." This mantra is wrong. Instead, the rule that applies is that after a Deny permission is encountered, it does not matter whether an Allow permission exists because the access will be denied. This is not the same thing. The following cases provide two examples in which both Deny and Allow permissions for the same access permission exist but a different answer results. A third case extends the problem to permissions inheritance from multiple folders.

Case A: Permissions on the File Only, No Inheritance

In this case, no permissions are inherited. Permissions are assigned explicitly on the file. The Allow Read permission is assigned to the Accountants group, and the Deny Read permission is assigned to John Smith. When John, a member of the Accountants group, attempts to read the file, will he be able to? John will be denied permission because permissions are first sorted and then evaluated in the following order:

1. Directly applied Deny permissions

2. Directly applied Allow permissions

3. Inherited Deny permissions

4. Inherited Allow permissions

For Case A, because there are no inherited permissions, the permissions are sorted and evaluated in this order:

1. Directly applied permission: Deny John Smith Read

2. Directly applied permission: Allow Accountants Read

Because the rule says that once a Deny is found the Allow doesn't matter, John will be denied access.

Case B: Permissions Inherited and Directly Applied on the File

1. Directly applied permissions: Allow Accountants Read. In this case, the file account_numbers.txt, which is in a folder called Important, has both inherited and directly applied permissions. The permissions Allow Accountants Read and Deny John Smith Read are assigned to the Important folder. These permissions are inherited by the accont_numbers.txt file. The account_numbers.txt file also has the

directly assigned permission Allow Accountants Read. The permissions are sorted in the following order:

2. Inherited Deny permissions: Deny John Smith Read

3. Inherited Allow permissions: Allow Accountants Read

Because the Accounts group Allow Read permission is the first permission in the list, John will be given permission to read the file. If we return to the mantra, "If access is denied, it doesn't matter whether another permission allows access because the user will be denied access." You can see that it is wrong. The directly applied Allow permission takes precedence over the inherited Deny permission.

Case C: Inheritance from Multiple Folders

One question remains. What will be the effect if multiple objects exist in the inheritance path and each object provides permissions that are inherited? Figure 9-9 shows a multiobject inheritance path. It also indicates two permissions set at each level. For purposes of simplification, assume that inheritance is not blocked at any level and that all permissions applied at each level are inherited by the file quarterlyreport.doc. Will John be able to read the file or not?

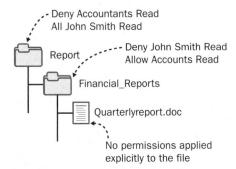

Figure 9-9   What are the effective permissions?

The rule you must follow here is that the closer the parent object is to the child, the higher on the evaluation list order it will be. That is, permissions on parent objects close to the child object are given more weight than those set further away. For Case C, the permissions are sorted in the following order:

1. Directly applied Deny permissions: N/A

2. Directly applied Allow permissions: N/A

3. Inherited Deny permissions (inherited from the Financial_Reports folder): Deny John Smith Read

4. Inherited Allow permissions (inherited from the Financial_Reports folder): Allow Accounts Read

5. Inherited Deny permission (inherited from the Reports folder): Deny Accountants Read

6. Inherited Allow Permissions (inherited from the Reports folder): Allow John Smith Read

John will not be able to read the folder.

The permissions that are applied when John attempts to access the file are called the *effective permissions.* You can calculate the effective permissions by using the Inheritance sort order, or you can access the Effective Permissions tab. This tab can be accessed from the Security tab of the object, by clicking the Advanced button, and then selecting the Effective Permissions tab. Figure 9-10 displays the tab for the history.doc file for Kevin Browne.

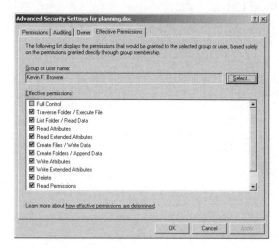

Figure 9-10   Effective permissions are displayed on the Effective Permissions tab

How to Design an Appropriate Group Strategy for Accessing Resources

To design a group strategy for accessing resources, you perform the following steps:

1. Define the roles that users hold. User roles include administrative roles—such as Administrator and Backup Operator—that are defined as default groups and other roles—such as Accounting Manager or Payroll Clerk. For every job function in which a user must access computer resources, a role should be defined.

2. Define the resources that must be accessed by each role. Resources include files and folders, registry keys, and Active Directory resources.

3. If a default group meets the needs of this role, use the default group; otherwise, create groups for each role. The rights of default groups are defined in the User Rights portion of the Local Policy for servers and the User Rights portion of the Default Domain Controller GPO for domains.

> **Important**   Additional rights can be assigned to groups but not listed in the User Rights container. For example, the Administrators group will always be able to take Ownership of objects, even if they are not listed as having the Take Ownership right in the User Rights container.

4. Create and/or use Universal, Global, Domain Local, and Machine Local Groups as necessary to facilitate group management. Information on these groups is included in the "What Are the Windows Group Types and Scopes?" section.

5. Apply permissions on the container for each role (group) that must have access.

The following sections provide additional information you must have to complete these steps and present guidelines for designing an appropriate group strategy for accessing resources.

What Are the Default Groups?

Windows groups are created to assist in the definition of user roles in Windows Server 2003. Groups can be default or custom. Many default groups exist that define an administrative role. Default groups are listed in Table 9-1. The table also indicates where the group exists. Some groups exist in the local Security Accounts Manager (SAM) of a single server. Others reside on domain controllers. Groups that reside on domain controllers can be located in the Built-in container or the Users container. The Built-in container contains groups that were present on the stand-alone server before it was promoted to be a domain controller. Figure 9-11 displays the contents of the domain controller Built-in group and the location of the Users group. In Table 9-1, a *Y* indicates the group is present and an *N* means it is not.

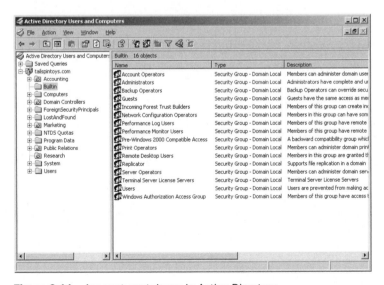

Figure 9-11   Account containers in Active Directory

Table 9-1   Default Windows Server 2003 Groups

Group	Local SAM Stand-Alone Server	Active Directory Built-In Container	Active Directory Users Container
Administrators	Y	Y	N
Account Operators	Y	Y	N
Backup Operators	Y	Y	N
Guests	Y	Y	N
Incoming Forest Trust Builders	N	Y	N
Network Configuration Operators	Y	Y	N
Performance Log Users	Y	Y	N
Performance Monitor Users	Y	Y	N
Pre–Windows 2000 Compatible Access	Y	Y	N
Print Operators	Y	Y	N
Remote Desktop Users	Y	Y	N
Replicator	Y	Y	N
Server Operators	Y	Y	N
Terminal Server License Servers	Y	Y	N
Users	Y	Y	N
Windows Authorization Access	Y	Y	N
Cert Publishers	N	N	Y
Dns Admins	N	N	Y
DnsUpdateProxy	N	N	Y
Domain Admins	N	N	Y
Domain Computers	N	N	Y
Domain Controllers	N	N	Y
Domain Guests	N	N	Y
Domain Users	N	N	Y
Enterprise Admins	N	N	Y
Group Policy Creator Owners	N	N	Y
RAS and IAS Servers	N	N	Y
Schema Admins	N	N	Y

The Windows Authorization Access group is new in Windows Server 2003. This group is not used for user administrative roles. Instead, it is used to provide service accounts permission to read user access token data. It is often used in role-based access control application designs You can read more about how this group is used in the article, "Role-Based Access Control for Multi-tier Applications Using Authorization Manager," at *http://www.microsoft.com/technet/treeview/default.asp?url=/technet/prodtechnol /windowsserver2003/maintain/security/athmanwp.asp.*

What Are the Windows Group Types and Scopes?

Each group that is created must be a specific group type, and each group type has a scope. Group scope defines where a group can be used and what types of users and groups can be members. Group types and their scope are as follows:

- Universal groups—These groups can be used only in forests that are in Windows 2000 or Windows Server 2003 functional mode. Universal groups can contain members from any group in the forest and can be given access permissions to any object in the forest.

- Global groups—These groups can contain only members from their own local domain. They can be given access permissions to any object in the forest.

- Domain local groups—These groups can contain members from any domain in the forest but can be granted access only to objects within their own domain. An advantage of domain local groups over machine local groups is that domain local groups are created in Active Directory and can be granted access to objects within their own domain.

- Machine local groups—These groups can contain members from any domain in the forest but can only be granted access to objects within their own computer. A machine local group is created in the local SAM of the server.

What Is Group Nesting?

Groups can be nested within other groups. The advantage of group nesting is that it requires less work when assigning privileges and permissions. For example, if a local machine group is created and used to grant Read permission to a set of documents that all employees should have access to, membership in this group will provide any employee the ability to read the documents. However, in a large forest of many domains, adding each user account to the group would be inefficient and unmanageable for many reasons, including the following:

- The increased time it would take to add each employee's account as a member in the group.

- The time and difficulty involved in determining when a user left the company, and therefore, in determining when the user should be removed from the group.

- The difficulty involved in knowing when new employees are added.

- The limited knowledge of a particular group's administrator. The administrator in charge of managing the group will be part of the administrative structure of the domain that the computer belongs to. She will not have knowledge of users in the other domains.

To more easily manage the problem of working with many members in a group, you can adhere to the following best practices regarding group strategy. The strategy uses the employee example, but it can be modified for many circumstances.

- Create a global group in each domain for employees.

- Place all domain accounts that belong to employees in the global group in their respective domains.

- Nest the global groups, one for each domain, in the local group. In this example, nesting means to make the global group a member of the local group.

- Grant the local group access to all resources that all employees can access.

- If access to resources on other servers is required, use a domain local group or create a machine local group where the need is.

- Manage the membership of the global groups at the domain level. Instead of placing user accounts directly in the machine local group account, you can create global groups at each domain and each employee's account will be placed in the global group created in his or her domain.

What Are the Nesting Rules?

The previous example shows the nesting rules that are followed in a Windows 2000 mixed functional level domain: global groups can be nested in local groups. In a Windows 2000 native functional level domain or Windows Server 2003 functional level domain, additional nesting rules apply:

- Domain local groups can nest in domain local groups from their own domain.

- Global groups can nest in other global groups and in universal groups.

- Universal groups can nest in local groups, global groups, and other universal groups.

Improve Security by Using Group Nesting

We know that unused accounts should be disabled and removed as soon as possible. We know that it is important to remove and re-assign privileges and permissions when an employee changes a job. However, IT might be the last to know when employees leave the company or are transferred to another job. When IT does receive notice, if permissions have been assigned to these user accounts, locating and removing the employees' access across the enterprise is a difficult and time-consuming process.

On the other hand, if privileges and permissions are assigned to groups, we only need to remove the user accounts from the groups they are a member of to remove their privileges. There are far fewer groups in the user's domain than there are resources in the enterprise. Even a manual search, group by group, is far less trouble than attempting to find every place that a user account might be assigned access. When best practices are followed, removing a user's access to resources is greatly simplified. When best practices are followed, the possibility that some unknown access permission will provide inappropriate access is reduced.

Guidelines for Designing an Appropriate Group Strategy for Accessing Resources

Follow these guidelines when designing group strategy for accessing resources:

- Create groups that represent user roles. Doing this will make it easy to determine which resources they should have access to.

- Give these groups the privileges and access that is required.

- Never assign privileges and permissions to individual user accounts.

- Use group nesting to ease the security burden. Nest multiple groups that contain users into a single local group. Give this group access. Not only is it easier to manage group memberships but resource access can be easily removed. Removing access to a resource is a quick way of preventing or limiting intrusion if you know or suspect that your system has been compromised.

- Use built-in operating system groups where the permissions and privileges given the operating system groups exactly meet the needs of the user role.

- Protect administrative groups. Do not allow a user with less privilege to manage groups that have more privileges.

- Create group accounts and user accounts in organizational units (OUs), and then assign management privileges over these groups by delegating control of the OU.

- Limit the administrative authority of these managers. Do not provide users who manage groups with rights outside the OU.

- Use a naming structure that clearly indicates the group scope. For example, preface domain local groups with DLG_ and global groups with GG_.

How to Design a Permission Structure for Files and Folders

To design a permission structure for files and folders, you must be able to explain the design considerations, understand how share permissions and file system permissions interact, and apply the guidelines for designing access control for files and folders.

Considerations for Designing a Permissions Structure for Files and Folders

When designing a permission structure for files and folders, consider two main issues. First, you can influence the inheritance of permissions by selecting from the following options:

- The check box: Allow Inheritable Permissions From Parent to Propagate to This Object and All Child Objects. Include These With Entries Explicitly Defined Here. This option allows permissions to be inherited from folders at a higher level in the file hierarchy.

- The check box: Replace Permission Entries On All Child Objects With Entries Shown Here That Apply To Child Objects. Selecting this option will force the propagation of permission settings to child objects. (Permissions are applied automatically when a new object is created.) If permissions require updating, you must select this box.

- The Apply Onto box can be set when a new permission is assigned. The depth in the hierarchy to which the permission is extended depends on this setting. The options within the list include the following:

    - This Folder, Subfolders And Files—Any files or folders created beneath this folder will inherit the permissions set.

    - This Folder Only—Only files and folders added to this folder will inherit the permissions set. (Subfolders of folders added to this folder and any files in them will not inherit these permissions.)

    - This Folder And Subfolders—Only subfolders added will inherit the permissions; files will not.

    - This Folder And Files—Only the folder and its files will receive permission.

    - Subfolders And Files Only—Only subfolders and their files will inherit permissions. Files in this folder will not.

    - Subfolders Only—Only subfolders will inherit permissions. Files in this folder will not.

    - Files Only—Only files in this folder will inherit permissions.

- An additional check box on the Object page: Apply These Permissions To Objects And/Or Containers Within This Container Only.

You can also prevent a specific folder hierarchy or a single file from inheriting any permissions at all even if the parent folder is set to push permissions down to the subfolder or file, by deselecting the check box Inherit From Parent The Permission Entries That Apply To Child Objects. Include These With Entries Explicitly Defined Here.

How Share Permissions and File System Permissions Interact

Security descriptors are also attached to shared folders. The DACLs assigned to shares are processed only when a remote user attempts to connect to a share through the network redirector. The effective permissions that must be evaluated to determine whether the user can connect and which permissions they will be able to use once connected are the result of combining the permissions from both the share and the underlying folder.

> **Exam Tip**   Share permission for Windows Server 2003 is set to Everyone Read by default. This is a departure from previous Windows operating systems, which assigned the Everyone Full Control access permission by default.

To evaluate the effect of combining share and folder permissions remember this single rule: The most restrictive setting wins. However, do not get caught in the trap of simply looking at all permissions—you must evaluate each access attempt both at the share and at the folder, and then choose the most restrictive. When you evaluate the access permissions on each object, use normal rules. Remember that permissions are cumulative. You will then have two results and can select the most restrictive conclusion.

For example, in Figure 9-12, the Accountants group has Read and Write permissions on the Vendors share and Read permission on the Vendor folder. The Managers group has Modify permission on the Vendors share and Read and Write permissions on the Vendor folder. John is a member of both the Accountants group and the Managers group. He attempts to remotely modify a file in the folder. If you simply look for the most restrictive permission, you will draw the conclusion that John cannot modify the file because he has only Read permission. However, if you evaluate the permissions on the share, you will see he has Modify permission on the share and Read and Write permissions on the folder. Clearly, the most restrictive of these two is Read and Write. John can modify the file.

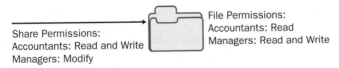

Figure 9-12   Determining permissions

Guidelines for Designing Access Control for Files and Folders

Follow these guidelines when designing access control for files and folders.

Do these things:

- Keep your permission structure simple. Where permissions change and where it is possible, provide a separate top-level folder for these files and subfolders.

- Protect sensitive subfolders by removing their ability to inherit permissions from parent folders. You can see an example of this by looking at the system folder. A change to the root of the volume will not, by default, propagate to the system folder.

- Set explicit permissions on shares that will give approved groups the access they are authorized to have.

- Set folder permissions on folders that are shared. Folder permissions control access by any user logged on at the console. Not only do you want to ensure that access is controlled for both remote and local access, but you might want these permission sets to be different. When the permissions sets are different, it might be harder to determine exactly what access remote users will have, but you will have the control necessary no matter how the data is accessed.

- If many folders and files require the same permissions, place them in a hierarchy, apply the permissions at the top of the hierarchy, and propagate them throughout the hierarchy.

Don't do these things:

- Do not share folders that provide sweeping access to top-level folders. Apply access only for areas of the file system that need it. Do not provide looser access at the parent folder and stronger access controls at one of its subfolders. An attacker can take advantage of weak access controls at the parent folder and traverse the file structure to attack files and folders deep within it. If these folders and files need stronger protection, make the share at their level the only way to remotely access them, or make the share at a parent level require stronger protection.

- Do not use the FAT or FAT32 file system.

- If you use an alternative method to remotely access data on the disk (for example, terminal services, remote assistance, or webDAV—a component that allows users to manage content on a Web server), make sure it is also secured. Don't let these alternatives subvert file system security.

- Do not change default permissions on system files and folders without extensive research and testing. Weakened permissions put your computer at risk, and stronger protection might prevent the operating system from running.

- Do not relax the default permission on shares by changing it to Everyone Full Control.

How to Design a Permission Structure for Registry Keys

To design a permission structure for registry keys, you must first understand the registry key permission structure and then follow the guidelines for designing one.

The Registry Key Permission Structure

The registry key permission structure is similar to the file system permission structure:

- Registry keys inherit permissions from parent registry keys.

- The inheritance model is similar—substitute the words "registry key" and "subkey" for "folder" and "file", respectively, in the inheritance model described for files and folders. You can select different structures, either restricting the inheritance and how far it goes or preventing inheritance.

- Effective permissions are a result of combining inherited and explicitly assigned permissions.

- Explicitly defined permissions take precedence over inherited permissions.

There are also differences between the registry key permission structure and the file system permission structure:

- Permission names are different, and there is a smaller range of permissions.

- Security descriptors are stored with the registry key, not in a separate structure.

- File permissions on registry files control access to the file, but it is not necessary to modify data in registry keys. Registry key permissions control access to registry key data.

Guidelines for Designing a Permission Structure for Registry Keys

Follow these guidelines for designing a permission structure for registry keys.

- Do not change system registry keys without extensive research and testing.

- Do not change registry file permission keys. Providing file permissions to the registry files is not necessary to provide access to registry keys.

- Do not provide users with the ability to modify registry key values where this is not necessary. To understand where it is and is not necessary requires research.

- Use test systems to validate permission settings, and then apply new settings to production systems via a tested script, program, security templates, or Group Policy. Once tested, these systems provide a way to ensure that modifications will be consistent across multiple computers and that accidental applications of the wrong changes won't crash systems or weaken security. Modify registry permissions and data programmatically where possible. It is easy to damage the ability of the operating system to function by wanton exercise of direct permission and data entry.

- Use application products that follow Windows guidelines for software development. In most cases, changes to registry key permissions will not be through extensive design. The reasons for changing permissions are in large part because of the addition of new software. The installation package should set the required permissions for application-related registry keys.

- If applications require elevated privileges (the user must be an administrator, for example), do not provide access by adding users to the Administrators group. Instead, evaluate the need for changing permissions to registry keys to allow users the access required without providing them elevated privileges on the computer. Often, as is the case with many older applications, applications are said to require administrator rights, but they really only need permission to write information to the HKEY_Local_Machine registry hive.

Practice: Evaluating Permission Inheritance

In this practice, you will test your knowledge of permission inheritance by evaluating the effective permissions on files, folders, and registry keys. If you are unable to answer a question, review the lesson materials and try the question again. You can find answers to the questions in the "Questions and Answers" section at the end of the chapter.

In each of the following examples, examine the list of groups that are assigned access to the secret.txt file. There are two lists: a list of ACLs that applies to folders or files, and a list of groups that user Christie Moon is a member of. The location in the file hierarchy where ACLs are assigned access is also shown in a figure for each example. The ACLs and group memberships do not change, but the location of the folders do. Examine the list of groups that Christie Moon belongs to. If Christie attempts to modify the file, will she be successful or will she receive an access denied message?

The following ACLs are applied:

- Marketing Folder:
    - ❏ Marketing – Allow Read
    - ❏ Managers – Allow Modify
- Plan Folder
    - ❏ Maintenance – Deny Full Control
    - ❏ Marketing – Allow Modify

- Plan.doc file

    - Marketing – Allow Read

    - Managers – Allow Modify

- Plan share

    - Marketing – Deny Full Control

    - Managers – Allow Read

In addition, Christie is a member of the Managers group and the Supervisors group.

Review Questions

Answer the following questions.

1. Given the file structure in the following picture and assuming remote access, what type of access does Christie have?

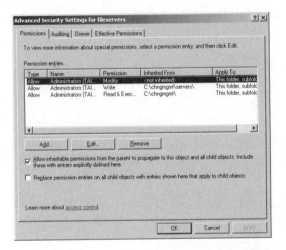

_____

_____

2. Given the following file structure and assuming local access, what type of access does Christie have?

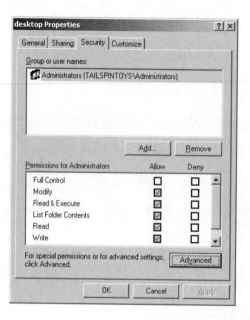

3. Given the following file structure and assuming remote access, what type of access does Christie have?

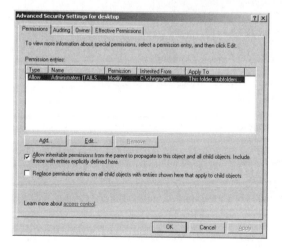

Lesson 2: Designing the Delegation and Permission Structure for Active Directory Objects

Permission setting and access control analysis on Active Directory objects is similar to the analysis you perform for files and folders. The differences are that Active Directory objects have many, many more permission types. These permission types can grow if Active Directory–enabled applications such as Microsoft Exchange Server are added to the domain; and the range of access that these permissions can supply is much more varied.

After this lesson, you will be able to

- Describe the object permission structure for Active Directory.
- Use delegation to distribute administration duties.
- Design the delegation structure for Active Directory.
- Design the object permission structure for Active Directory.

Estimated lesson time: 25 minutes

The Object Permission Structure in Active Directory

The object permission structure for Active Directory has many similarities with that of the file system. Objects are arranged in a hierarchical structure, and permission inheritance can be managed to ensure the propagation of permissions throughout a section of the structure or to prevent inheritance by sensitive objects. Like files, folders, and registry keys, Active Directory objects have their own unique permission sets. There are two differences between Active Directory objects and the other objects that can be protected by permissions:

- There are many Active Directory object types, and each type has some permissions common with all other object types and its own set of unique permissions.

- To the Active Directory, all activity is seen as a matter of access, and all management over this activity is seen as access control. It's as if rights have become permissions. Some permissions available for Active Directory objects can be leveraged to provide granular control over whole categories or divisions of the Active Directory infrastructure.

Important   The blurring of the distinction between rights and permissions is also present in one particular file system permission. There is a file permission named WRITE_OWNER, which provides the account with this permission the ability to change ownership on the file. The Change Ownership right is a user right that is assigned using the User Rights portion of a Group Policy Object (GPO). An example of an Active Directory permission that sounds like a right is the Reset Password permission. Users have the right to change their passwords. You can give one user the ability to change another user's password by setting the Reset Password permission on the account object in the Active Directory.

The permissions that are available for each object in Active Directory and their default settings are defined in the objects schema in the Active Directory Schema. It would be impossible to list all of them in this book; indeed, there does not seem to be a publicly available comprehensive list of all possible permissions. Nor is there any guide that might help you determine the exact impact of every possible set of permissions. And there might never be. However, you can investigate and learn about the major permission sets and then use them to gain a security advantage.

You can also plan and undertake management of Active Directory objects by using the permissions that you do understand. You can delegate administration of Active Directory objects by assigning permissions at the container or object level. However, best practices dictate that you should do so at the container level in most cases. For example, for delegation of authority at the object level look at the discussion on securing a Certification Authority in Chapter 2. In that case, you assign administration of a single CA by assigning permissions on that CA object. For an example of delegating authority at the container level, see the following discussion of managing OUs.

See Also   An excellent reference on Active Directory object permissions in Windows 2000 is the five-volume set, "Active Directory Developer's Reference Library," published by Microsoft Press. You will not find a comprehensive list of object permissions; however, you will find much information explaining how Active Directory object permissions work. Much of this information remains true for Windows Server 2003. Updated documentation is located on the Microsoft Developers Network Web site at *http://msdn.microsoft.com*.

How Active Directory Object Permissions Can Aid Security

To understand how Active Directory object permissions can aide security, you can study the effect of object permission changes on an OU object. OUs contain user and computer accounts, among other objects, and any permissions set on OUs can affect the management and security of the computer accounts and user accounts that reside in the OU. Examining the available permissions can help you determine how to design a permission infrastructure that will do the best job at increasing security. Open the Security Property page (shown in Figure 9-13) of any OU object in Active Directory Users and Computers. As it does for files and folders, this page presents a broad list of permissions. These permissions, like similar ones for files and folders, are actually composite permissions.

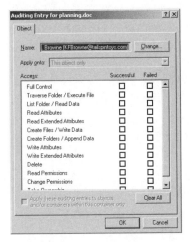

Figure 9-13   Security properties for an OU

> **Tip**   In addition to using the object editor to change Active Directory permissions or using the Delegation Of Authority Wizard, you have three additional ways that these permissions can be modified. You can use the dsacls command. For example, the dsacls `"ou=market-ing,dc=tailspintoys,dc=com"` `/I:s` `/g` `"tailspintoys.com\Help_Desk":rpwp;` `lockouttime;user` command will give the Help_Desk group permission to unlock locked user accounts in the Marketing OU of the Tailspintoys.com domain. You can also use the ADS-IEdit tool (Adsiedit.msc) or programmatic methods to edit Modify permissions on Active Directory objects.

To explore the permissions behind Full Control, for example, click the Advanced button, and then click the Edit button. Two additional pages of permissions are displayed, one labeled Object and the other labeled Properties. The object page (shown in Figure 9-14) is a list of over 70 permissions that define access to these types of objects if they are present within the OU. The Property page displays a list of more than 70 permissions and defines access to the properties of objects within the OU container. Table 9-2 lists some permissions of each type and provides information about how they might be used. The first seven permissions represent the comprehensive permissions on the first security page. (Six are visible in the figure.)

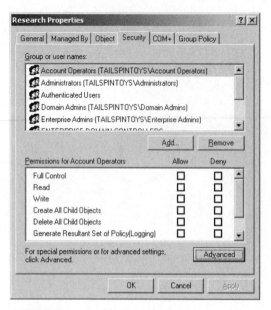

Figure 9-14   OU object permissions

Table 9-2   OU Object Permissions

Permission	Suggested Use
Full Control	Granting full control provides complete authority over all objects present and future in the OU, including creation and deletion of objects not currently defined.
Read	Examine the properties of all objects in the OU.
Write	Modify the properties of all objects in the OU.
Create All Child Objects	Create any OU valid object in the OU, including a sub OU.
Delete All Child Objects	Delete any object in the OU, including a sub OU.
Generate Resultant Set of Policy (Logging)	Create a report that details the result of Group Policy application for any computer or user object in the OU. (To execute this permission, the user will need permission to access the remote computer and access to the remote computer cannot be blocked.)
Generate Resultant Set of Policy (Planning)	Create a report that details the possible result of Group Policy application for any computer or user object in the OU.
Create Account Objects	Create user and computer objects.
Create Computer Objects	Create computer objects.
Create User Objects	Create user objects.
Create Group Objects	Create groups.
Create Organizational Unit Objects	Create OUs.

Table 9-2   OU Object Permissions

Permission	Suggested Use
Create Shared Folder Objects	Create a shared folder object in the OU. The shared folder must already exist.
Write All Properties	Modify any object's properties.
Write adminDescription	Write the description of the Administrator account.
Write Name	Write the name of the object—for example, the name of the user or the name of the computer.
Write Street	Write the street name of the user account.
Modify Owner	Modify the owner of the object.

If you open these pages for yourself and examine the complete lists presented there, you will discover that these pages do not present all the permissions associated with all objects in the OU. The Reset Password permission is missing, as are many permissions that provide control over user accounts. To change many of the permissions on Active Directory objects, you must use the Delegation of Authority wizard.

How to Use Delegation to Distribute Administration Duties

You can use the Delegation of Control Wizard to give designated groups of users access to and control over objects in Active Directory. To do so:

1. Determine which group of users should have the authority that you will delegate.

2. If no Windows group that contains these users exists, create one and give these users membership in it.

3. Use the Delegation of Control Wizard to assign the permissions to the group.

4. Review the permissions granted, and test the operation of this privilege.

> **Tip**   The Reset Password permission is the most commonly requested delegation task. Another task is the right to unlock locked user accounts. This task can be delegated by defining a custom task, selecting user objects, selecting the specific property, and then selecting the Read LockoutTime and Write LockoutTime permissions.

The best way to learn what each permission can be used for or what combination of permissions will result in the action you want is to research the issue in product documentation and on the Microsoft Windows TechNet and MSDN Web sites.

The best way to learn how to use the wizard is just to use it. A brief explanation of the steps—with accompanying figures showing the delegation of the Reset Password permission for users in the Marketing OU to a custom group called Help Desk—follows:

1. Open Active Directory Users and Computers.

2. Right-click the Marketing OU, and select Delegate Control.

3. Use the Add button to select the Help Desk group, and click Next.

4. Explore the capabilities of the wizard by selecting the Create A Custom Task To Delegate option button, and then click Next.

5. Select the Only The Following Objects check box, select an object, and then click Next.

6. Examine the permissions (see Figure 9-15).

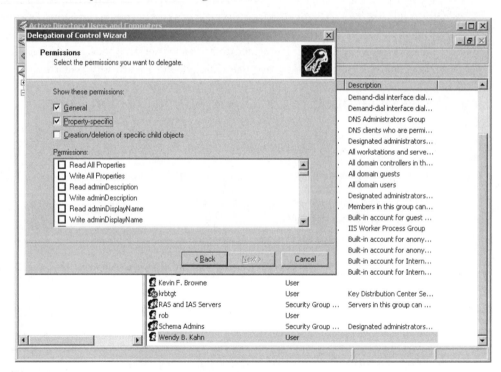

Figure 9-15   Examining the permissions

7. Return to the Tasks To Delegate page by clicking Back twice.

8. Select Reset User Passwords And Force Password Change At Next Logon (shown in Figure 9-16), and then click Next.

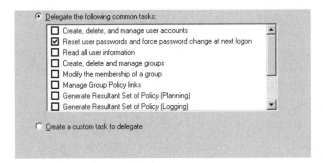

Figure 9-16   Verifying that the reset permission is set

9. Click Finish.

To inspect the changes to the OU permissions:

1. Right-click the Marketing OU, and select Properties.

2. Select the Security tab.

3. Click the Advanced button.

4. Select the Help Desk group, and click the Edit button.

5. Examine the list of permissions (shown in Figure 9-17).

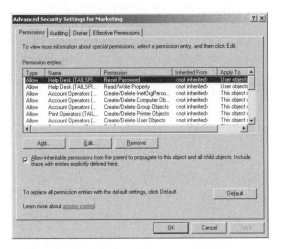

Figure 9-17   Examining the list of permissions

There is no "un" delegate authority wizard. The only way to remove delegation is to visit the properties page of the object in Active Directory and remove the permission; consequently, you should document changes you are making.

Guidelines for Designing the Delegation and Permission Structure for Active Directory Objects

Delegation of authority is accomplished by changing permissions on objects in the Active Directory. Whether the Delegation of Authority Wizard is used, the permissions are directly modified, or their changes are scripted or hanged in some other fashion, the end result is the same. Neither delegation nor permission structure for Active Directory can be discussed without talking about the other. Therefore use the following guidelines when designing the permission structure and delegation structure for Active Directory objects:

- Design the Active Directory OU infrastructure to support delegation of administration of users, computers, and groups.

- Delegate authority at the object container level rather than assigning Full Control over the container. Full Control provides too much authority over the container, its current objects, and objects and object types that might be added.

- Delegate authority over large object containers such as users, computers, and groups at the object container level rather than doing so at the object container. For example, delegate the authority for the Reset Password permission to all users in the Marketing OU rather than delegating authority over resetting the password to Jeff Smith, a user in the Marketing OU.

- Delegate authority to Windows groups, not to individual users.

- Delegate authority over logical groups of permissions. For example, delegate authority over the Reset Password and Change Password At Next Logon permissions or over address-related properties of user accounts rather than over address-related and account-related properties. (For example, Human Resources might need the ability to change a user's address and phone number but not to change whether the password should be kept in the account database in reversibly unencrypted form.)

- Train users who will be given elevated privileges because of changes in Active Directory Permissions.

- Create custom Microsoft Management Console (MMC) consoles for use by groups that will manage some aspects of Active Directory. Restrict their use of MMC consoles to these consoles.

- Assign responsibility for areas of the Active Directory schema, and ensure that all changes to Active Directory object permissions are reviewed.

- Document changes that will be made, and keep documentation up to date.

- Test any proposed changes in a test network, not in production.

Practice: Reviewing a Permission Structure Design

In this practice, you will review the design of a permission structure for the Finance OU of Tailspin Toys. Read the scenario and then answer the question that follows. If you are unable to answer the question, review the lesson materials and try the question again. You can find the answer to the question in the "Questions and Answers" section at the end of the chapter.

Scenario

You are the senior security designer for a security firm named Contoso, Ltd. Your company has been contracted to examine the design for the Active Directory permission structure for Tailspin Toys. You have been asked to provide your analysis of the structure of the Finance OU in an initial meeting with Tailspin Toys in a few days. You have been given the following design for the Finance OU:

Finance OU: Groups in the Finance OU and Their Active Directory Permissions   The design includes three Windows groups: Finance, Managers, and Clerical. The delegated permissions for each group are as follows:

- The Finance group has no delegated permissions.
- The Managers group is delegated Full Control of all objects in the OU.
- The Clerical group is designated Help-desk-type access, such as resetting passwords, unlocking accounts, adding new user accounts, and so on.

Review Question

Answer the following question.

1. What are your suggestions, criticisms, and additions to this design? Explain the reasons behind your suggestions.

   _____

   _____

   _____

   _____

   _____

   _____

   _____

   _____

   _____

Lesson 3: Analyzing Auditing Requirements

Access controls are established to keep people out. Auditing is used to document when they get in. If attackers penetrate your defense (and they will), if employees attempt access beyond their assigned privileges (and they will), and if systems are not correctly configured and therefore allow improper use of resources (and they will), then audit records of operations provide an accurate account of what happened and can alert you to an attack in progress.

After this lesson, you will be able to

- Analyze auditing requirements.
- Use Windows Server 2003 audit polices and SACLs.
- Explain auditing considerations.

Estimated lesson time: 30 minutes

How to Analyze Auditing Requirements

To analyze auditing requirements, you must:

- **Review legal requirements for maintaining documentation on data access.**   This includes legislation such as the Heath Insurance Portability and Accountability Act (HIPAA), which specifies provisions for access to private patient, customer, or employee data. If there are legal requirements that specify access control, auditing that access might also be required.

- **Review legal requirements for attack documentation that will facilitate prosecution.**   The time to specify the collection of access information and privilege-use information is before an attack.

- **Review each computer role for specific auditing requirements.**   The role a computer plays in the network might greatly influence the need for auditing, and it might introduce special auditing requirements because of server applications installed on the server, the nature of the data stored there, the location of the computer, and who has access to it.

- **Determine what parts of the GPO Audit Policy is required for each computer role.**   It is not a particularly good idea to enable every audit policy for success and failure.

- **Determine what object auditing is required.**   Object auditing requires the configuring of SACLs directly in the security descriptor of the object. It is not necessary nor practical to audit access to every object. Instead, determine which objects might require auditing.

- **Determine the ability to produce activity and security logs for specific products.** Many products and services create their own logs, and these logs can also provide valuable security information. Many services and server applications automatically log operation and security information to special logs. Some of these products and services can be configured to collect more or less information. Examples of these logs are shown in Table 9-3.

Table 9-3 Examples of Logs That Might Hold Security Information

Log Name	Contents of Log
DCPromoUI.log	Report of the Active Directory service installation and removal process. It includes the name of the source domain controller used for replication. This information is a useful record that shows when promotion or demotion occurred on a specific server.
DCPromo.log	Report of security settings used during promotion or demotion.
Netsetup.log	Log of the events that occur when joining a computer to a domain.
Ntfrs.log	Log of events that occur each time file replication runs.
Netlogon.log	Log of errors that occur when the Net Logon service attempts to dynamically create a DNS record.
Userenv.log	Log of events during the computer processing of Group Policy and user profiles.
DHCPSrvLog	Log of DHCP server events.

- **Determine how audit logs should be managed, including controlling the size, location, and retention functions.** The security event log can be configured to modify its size and record-retention function. Security Event logs are located on each Windows Server 2003 computer, and there are no built-in capabilities for centralizing the collection of these audit records.

- **Determine your analysis requirements of audit logs.** Auditing includes more than the collection of audit records. Logs must be analyzed, as they can provide information that might indicate an attempted or successful attack, document appropriate usage of sensitive records, provide information that can empower the creation of secure solutions to access needs, and document security incidents.

What Is an Audit?

Before you can analyze auditing requirements, you must understand several auditing terms. The following terms are defined according to their use in this book:

- An *audit policy* is a written document that specifies the organization's IT audit policy. The document can specify what will be audited, when it will be audited, and who will do the auditing. It can include items that are not auditable via technical means. An audit policy can also be the audit policy section of a Group Policy Object (GPO). An audit policy can include instructions on what objects will be audited if object auditing is enabled in the GPO audit policy. Access to objects such as files, folders, registry keys, printers, and Active Directory objects can be audited.

- The term *auditor* has a legal meaning, as does the term *audit*. For example, officially, an audit can be performed only by an auditor (someone who is certified as an auditor). Care should be taken to identify exactly what is meant when either the term *auditor* or *audit* is used. In this book, all reference to *audit*, *auditor*, and *auditing* refer to the collection of data from the logs and its analysis. We are not using the term in the legal sense. If your organization's policy is that a formal IT audit be completed, it will usually specify the use of its own internal auditors or an outside firm and will not allow this requirement to be replaced by any self-auditing that IT might do by reviewing logs.

- The term *audit* can also have another meaning. Some individuals and organizations use the term to mean an evaluation, especially a security vulnerability evaluation or even a penetration test. This is not the meaning used in this chapter.

How to Use Windows Server 2003 Audit Policies and SACLs

The following sections describe what the Windows Server 2003 audit policies and SACLs can be used for, describe how object access can be audited, and then explains how to analyze events.

What the Windows Server 2003 Audit Policies and SACLs Can Be Used For

The audit policy is a component of the Local Security Policy container in a GPO. The configured audit policy will determine the types of events recorded in the security log of the computers whose accounts are in the container to which the GPO is linked. The default domain controller policy specifies the audit events recorded on domain controllers, while GPOs linked to the domain and to OUs will determine the events logged to the security logs on servers and desktop computers. Table 9-4 lists the audit policies and how the records that they will collect can be used. You can configure all polices in this table for success, failure, or both, or you can choose not to configure them at all. You cannot restrict their collection of events except for the Object Access category.

This category, when enabled, allows object access events to be recorded if auditing is also configured on the objects.

Table 9-4   Audit Policies

Policy	Description
Audit Account Logon Events	Provides information on events that occur where the account used to log on resides. Use this event in an Active Directory domain to examine the domain logons, including ticket information. These records will be in the security event log of the domain controller where logon occurred. Logon failures might indicate an attack or might simply indicate time-synchronization problems between a client and the domain controller. These events are also recorded on workstations and servers when local accounts are used. Log for failure to detect attacks. Log for success to determine whether an attack was successful.
Audit Account Management	Account management includes creating, deleting, and modifying accounts. Events are recorded where the account is located. Audit for success to track management. Compare to authorized account creation, deletion, and changes (a manual effort) to discover creation of unauthorized additions and deletions. Audit for failure to catch attempts at creation and deletion by unauthorized individuals.
Audit Directory Service Access	Audit records regarding access to Active Directory objects will be collected only if SACLs are set on Active Directory objects. Because of the large number of Active Directory objects, it would be futile, impractical, and unnecessary to audit access to every object. Instead, analyze objects for sensitivity and set auditing on these objects. Audit for success and failure here, and set requirements for success, failure, or both at each object audited.
Audit Logon Events	Events are recorded on the computer where the access token is created. If a domain account is used, events are recorded both on the workstation and on the domain controller—one for the account logon event on the domain controller, and one for the logon event on the workstation. Events on the domain controller are recorded when Group Policy is read. Use these events to help determine where an attack might have originated, or to determine why a GPO was not applied. Audit for failure to uncover attacks; audit for success to discover whether attacks were successful.
Audit Object Access	This policy is similar to the one that determines whether Active Directory objects can be audited, albeit specific to file, printer, and registry permissions. Set it for success and failure in the GPO, and then set SACLs on objects as required.
Audit Policy Change	If the security policy is changed, it is recorded. If GPOs are used to configure all audit policies for member servers and workstations, any record of policy changes will take place on the domain controller and it is not necessary to audit for policy changes on workstations and servers. A success event is also logged when a policy is refreshed. This does not indicate a policy change, just a policy refresh. You can determine whether a policy was changed by comparing the policy recorded in the event with the approved security policy.

Table 9-4   Audit Policies

Policy	Description
Audit Privilege Use	If this event is enabled for success, each time a user successfully uses a privilege an event will be recorded. This means a lot of events will be recorded. If audited for failure, only failed attempts at privilege uses will be recorded.
Audit Process Tracking	If set for success, each action of any running process is recorded. This can mean enormous logs and is not necessary. The time to audit a process is during development, before the approval of a purchase or implementation (to determine whether the application is doing only what it is supposed to do), and when it is necessary to troubleshoot permission issues. None of these things should be done on production computers.
Audit System Events	Records events such as shut down and start up. These events are useful because many attacks require system shut down, reboot, or both to succeed.

How Can Object Access Be Audited

Object access auditing must be enabled in the audit policy to succeed; however, for security events to be recorded, you must configure the SACLs on an object. The choices for file object auditing are shown in Figure 9-18, and the choices for directory object auditing are shown in Figure 9-19.

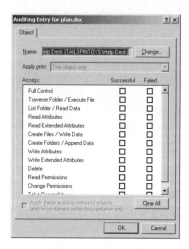

Figure 9-18   File object access auditing configuration

Figure 9-19   Directory object access auditing configuration

How to Analyze Events

After auditing requirements are analyzed and audit policies are configured, the security event logs will begin to collect security events. What then? Logs are of no use unless they are collected, analyzed, and archived. You must determine the purpose of security event collection before establishing an audit policy. You must establish policies and procedures for reviewing the logs and analyzing the events. Analyzing event logs is not simply a process of reviewing events one by one in the logs. This is too time-consuming and might not reveal much useful information unless the reviewer is intimately familiar with each of the large number of events that can be issued and what combinations of events might mean. Instead of approaching security event logs as a large number of records to review, follow this process to analyze events:

1. Determine events or event combinations that will alert you to specific attacks.

2. Ensure that you are auditing for these events.

3. Log and archive security event logs in a central location.

4. Filter logs for these events on a periodic basis, and set alerts. The time frame for analysis will depend on the sensitive nature of the events, the risk tolerance of the organization, and the current analysis of the likelihood of attack.

5. Map event alerts to specific incident-response procedures.

Examples of events and event combinations follow.

Example of Authentication   A large number of authentication failures can mean an attack has occurred or is occurring. The threshold for recorded failure events will vary according to the number of user accounts and what is normal for your organization. The number of failed logon events that is normal for your organization depends on the sophistication of your users, the severity of your password policy, and the number of accounts users have. Other circumstances can also affect this number. You will have to audit failed logons for a while to determine what is normal. This number can change over time. The events that indicate failed logon are listed in Table 9-5. You should filter security logs for these events.

Table 9-5   Failed Logon Events

Event ID	Description
675	Preauthentication failed. Logged at the domain controller when a user enters an incorrect password.
529	Logon failure. Logged when an invalid user account is used or a valid user account was used with an invalid password.
530	Logon attempt occurred outside of the allowed time.
531	Logon attempt was made using a disabled account.
533	Logon attempt was made using an expired account.
534	Logon attempt was made using a type that is not valid on this computer by this account. Logon types are network, interactive, batch, service, unlock, Network-Cleartext, NewCredentials, Remote Interactive, and CachedInteractive. Allow and Deny of logon type is set in the User Rights portion of Group Policy. If, for example, a group that a user is a member of is assigned the Deny Network Logon right at a file server and the user attempts to access a share on that server, the event 534 will be recorded.
535	Logon attempt was made after the password had expired.
536	Logon attempt was made when the Net Logon service was not running.
537	Logon failure occurred for a reason that was undetermined or was not one of the reasons listed.
539	Logon failure. An account was locked out.

An example of a failed logon event is shown in Figure 9-20. Notice the logon type, user name, and server name.

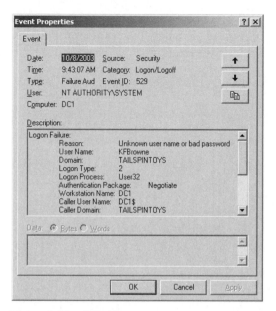

Figure 9-20   Failed logon

If a number of failed logon events for a specific account have occurred, look for a successful logon event. Successful logon events might also indicate a successful Kerberos ticket issuance. Successful logon events are listed in Table 9-6.

Table 9-6   Successful Logon Events

Event ID	Description
528	Successful logon.
540	Successful network logon.
672	An authentication service (AS) ticket was issued. An AS ticket is issued when a request for access to a service is requested.
673	A ticket granting service (TGS) ticket was issued. A TGS ticket is issued when authentication is successful.
674	An AS or TGS ticket was successfully renewed.
538	Successful logoff.
551	Successful user-initiated logoff.

A successful logon event is shown in Figure 9-21. Notice that the User name is indicated in the User field. This is the field that can be filtered on in the Event log. Shown in Figure 9-22 is a successful logoff event. It might be important to track and match logon with logoff and then, from the time stamps on the records, determine that a user was logged on when a security event occurred. User logoff and logon events can be matched by logon ID. The examples given, Figure 9-21 and Figure 9-22, are the logon and logoff events for Kevin F. Browne. You can verify this by comparing the logon ID and verifying that they are the same. By the time stamps, you can tell that Kevin was logged on for approximately four and a half minutes.

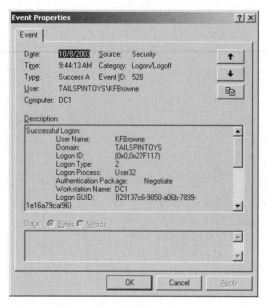

Figure 9-21   Successful logon

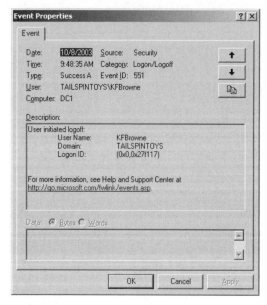

Figure 9-22   Successful logoff

Example of Taking Ownership   By default, administrators have the user right to take ownership. To protect confidential information, data owners might request that the IT administrator not have access privileges on sensitive files. This can easily be done by removing the administrator's group access permissions on the files. However, the administrator can take ownership of the file and give herself any access she wants. Nothing can prevent her from doing so. However, you can audit files that are configured to block administrator access by auditing for this event and tracking object access events.

Figure 9-23 shows the configuration for auditing for use of the Take Ownership permission. To ensure that the administrator is caught, you should also audit for privilege use. Two possible events can be recorded. If the administrator attempts access while logged on interactively to the server on which the file resides, the Se_TakeownershipPrivilege, event 578, is recorded. This is a privilege usage event. However, if she takes ownership remotely, the file Take Ownership permission (WRITE_OWNER) is used. This is object access event 560. With all this noted, remember that administrators can also delete audit logs, either in their entirety or by individual events. If you have untrustworthy administrators, the only solution is to not allow them to be administrators.

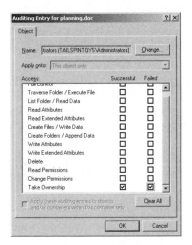

Figure 9-23   Auditing for Take Ownership

See Also   To prevent an administrator from reading a file, you can encrypt the file. However, if you do so, make sure the administrator is not the file recovery agent. To learn why and what you can do to prevent administrators from reading sensitive files, see Lesson 5, "Designing a File Encryption and Decryption Strategy" later in the chapter.

Auditing Considerations

When analyzing auditing requirements, consider the following:

- Auditing requirements are different based on computer role. Choose an auditing policy that provides the information necessary for each computer role.

- Auditing provides little value unless events are reviewed. A policy should be established to review security logs.

- Auditing requirements can change over time. One example would be when specific users are suspected of unauthorized file access, tampering, or improper access. In this situation, you could set up auditing on sensitive files for these users or the groups that they are in, record security events, and then analyze the information. When the information needed is accumulated, you would remove the auditing requirements.

- Centralizing the collection of auditing events is essential to sound security event record management and might be required by regulations or industry rules.

- Auditing process activity is not a good idea, in general, for production servers. It is a sound strategy for periodic use on test systems.

- Recording privilege access events will also generate a large number of events. Weigh the need to manage logs that this will create, and determine whether this is a worthwhile event.

- Setting object access auditing on files, folders, registry keys, and Active Directory objects can be affected by inheritance rules. When setting object auditing, you can set the requirements on a parent object and require that audit settings are pushed to subobjects by inheritance. You can also prevent the inheritance of SACLs by clearing the Allow Inheritable Auditing Entries from the Parent to Propagate to This Object and All Child Objects. Include These With Entries Explicitly Defined Here check box. Figure 9-24 illustrates this concept. The Marketing folder has inheritance blocked. Setting auditing for parent folders will have no affect on the Marketing folders.

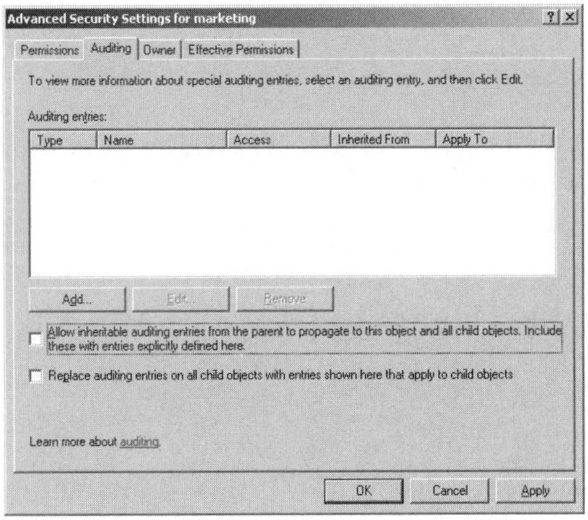

Figure 9-24   Blocking inheritance

Practice: Determining What to Audit and Analyzing Audit Records

In this practice, you will create a list of audit requirements for a fictitious company, and then analyze common records found in the security log. Complete the exercises that follow. If you are unable to answer a question, review the lesson materials and try the question again. You can find answers to the questions in the "Questions and Answers" section at the end of the chapter.

Exercise 1: Determining What to Audit

Read the following scenario and then answer the question that follows.

Scenario   You are an IT auditor at Wingtip Toys. You are asked to specify the audit requirements for a file server in the research department. The file server will store confidential research information. Files are protected by EFS encryption. Communications between researchers' workstations and the file server are protected by IPSec. Only the researchers and their workstations are allowed to access the file server.

Review Question   Answer the following question.

1. What should be audited? Explain why you made each recommendation.

_____

_____

_____

_____

_____

_____

Exercise 2: Analyzing Audit Records

Read the scenario and then answer the questions that follow.

Scenario   You are an IT Security officer. Your job is to review audit records. On Monday morning, you find these audit records.

Audit records:

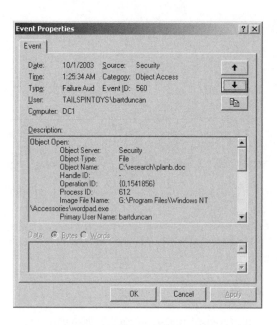

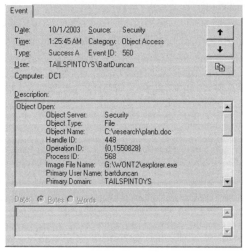

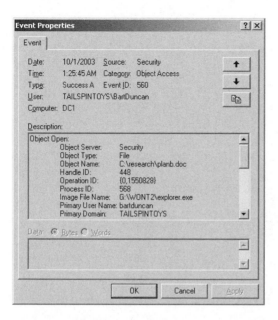

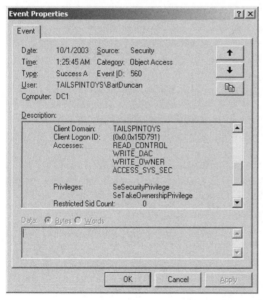

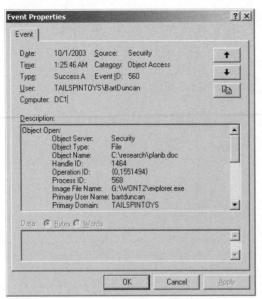

Domain controller audit records:

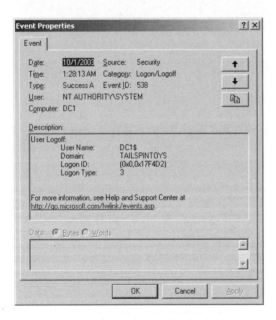

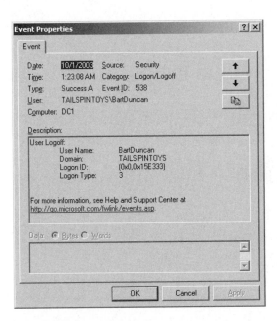

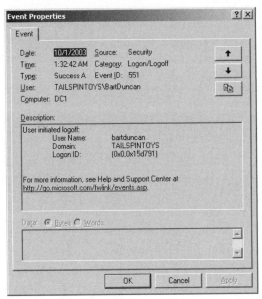

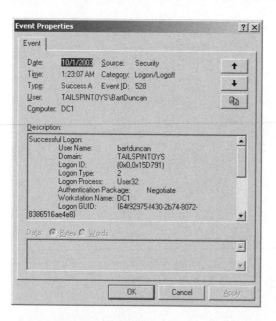

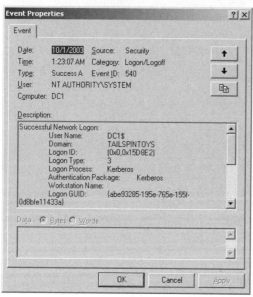

Review Questions   Answer the following questions.

1. What do the first five audit records tell you?

   _____

   _____

   _____

   _____

   _____

   _____

   _____

   _____

   _____

   _____

2. You wonder why a researcher was looking at files in the middle of the night. This is abnormal activity for Tailspin Toys. You want to trace any other activity by this user during the night. You must first find out the time at which this researcher, Bart Duncan, was logged on. Examine the domain controller audit records. What time was Bart logged on?

   _____

   _____

Lesson 4: Designing Security for Backup and Recovery Operations

When disaster strikes, you must be able to recover IT operations and data. This is accomplished by using backup procedures, recovery procedures, backup media, and backup personnel. If the backup operations and recovery procedures are not designed with security in mind, the recovery operations might fail as well. If security is not provided for the media, the media might be stolen and its data recovered by unauthorized people, or it might be used to destroy current data by overwriting it with new data. If personnel are not trained in the secure handling of backup media and in the processes necessary for recovery, the outcome of recovery operations is put at risk.

After this lesson, you will be able to

- Ensure that necessary cluster backup information and data are available.
- Explain the purpose of shadow copy.
- Explain the considerations for designing secure backup operations.
- Design security for backup and recovery operations.

Estimated lesson time: 30 minutes

How to Ensure That Necessary Cluster Backup Information and Data Are Available

A *server cluster* is a group of computer systems that are configured to work together to ensure the continuous availability of critical applications and to increase the computing power available to the application. Common uses for server clusters are to run mission-critical Microsoft SQL Server applications and messaging systems such as Microsoft Exchange Server.

Cluster backup is the process of making a backup copy of both the cluster data and configuration information, such as cluster disk signatures and partitions. When both data and configuration are properly backed up, the cluster can be restored if complete failure occurs. To ensure that the information and data necessary are available for restoration:

1. Perform an Automated System Recovery (ASR) backup on each node in the cluster. An ASR backup backs up the local system state data, system services, and any disks that are part of the operating system. An ASR backup of a cluster node will back up the cluster disk signatures and partitions.

2. Back up the cluster disk from each node. You should also back up the cluster quorum. The quorum should be backed up because it is the source of information on the current cluster configuration, application registry checkpoints, and cluster

recovery log. If the cluster service is running on a node and you perform a system state backup, you will automatically back up the quorum data.

3. Back up each application running on the nodes.

Tip   Backup operators do not have the default permissions to back up clusters. You can give them this privilege by adding them to the security descriptor for the cluster service. Should you? That will depend on the sensitivity of the cluster data. In very secure environments, backup of secure systems is reserved for the administrators only.

See Also   For more information on backing up clusters, see the article "Backing Up and Restoring Server Clusters" at *http://www.microsoft.com/technet/treeview/default.asp?url= /technet/prodtechnol/windowsserver2003/proddocs/entserver/SAG_MSCSusing_9.asp.*

What Is Shadow Copy?

Shadow copy backup provides a way for users to recover deleted files and for administrators to recover servers. The default process allows the ordinary backup process to back up open files You can configure the file system to automatically back up portions or the entire disk to another volume or to a storage area network (SAN), a subnetwork of shared computers that contains only disks for data storage. If shadow copy is used to back up volumes to a SAN, the copy can be transported to a backup server, backed up to tape, and sent to offsite storage. The backup to tape occurs offline—that is, it is being made from a backup server, not the production server. When shadow copies are available, recovery can be much quicker.

See Also   A whitepaper about fast recovery is available on the Windows page of the Microsoft Web site at *http://www.microsoft.com/windows/storage/productinformation/white-papers/W2K3ActDirFastRecov.doc.*

A user with normal user privileges can restore a file that belongs to her by using Windows Server 2003 or by using the shadow copy client. The shadow copy client is available for Windows XP and Windows 2000 service pack 3 and later. Two services are used:

- The Volume Shadow Copy Service, which supports the creation of single point-in-time shadow copies or snapshots of volumes. Data can be stored on Direct Attached Storage (DAS) or storage area networks.

- The Virtual Disk Service provides the interface and support for the volume management and provides programming interfaces.

Considerations for Designing Secure Backup Operations

Data can be lost for many reasons, including hardware failure, software failure, malicious code (viruses, worms, and Trojans), natural disasters—such as tornadoes and floods—and theft. To prevent the total loss of data if any of these events occur, all data—from files and folders and registry keys to the Active Directory database—should be backed up. Backup operations, however, include more than inserting a tape in a drive and forgetting about it. You must ensure that the backup that is made is verified, and you must protect the backup. When preparing a design for backup operations, consider the following security issues:

- **Data transport**   Creating a good backup and transporting backup media to and from the site need to be considered. A procedure that outlines how backups are verified, where they are stored while on site, and how they are transported should be prepared and followed. The process of returning backups to the site must also be considered. For example, many organizations specify that backups can be returned only by authorized personnel. This requirement is designed to prevent accidental or malicious restoration of old data over valid current data.

- **Data media**   Will tapes, disks, CD-ROMs, or storage area networks be used? You will need to plan security differently for some types of storage. SANs are subnetworks of disks, and security must be planned for the network, disks, and the secure transport of data to the SAN across the production network or via an alternative network connection. Tapes and CD-ROMs can be secured by providing temperature-controlled, clean, and lockable areas. Media must also be rotated and retired. Media does wear out and should be replaced as necessary to ensure good backups will be available should they be needed. Tape backup wears out quickly and is more susceptible to errors than disks. Storage, both on site and off, should be appropriate for the type of media used.

- **On-site storage location**   Is an on-site fireproof location available? The availability of such a location supports sound management practice and secures backups against damage that might be caused by fire. It does not obviate the need for off-site storage. There also need to be procedures in place that dictate the proper use of storage. A fireproof vault cannot protect its contents if it is open. It is common practice in many data centers to leave the door of the vault open, and this is a bad practice.

- **Off-site storage location**   Best practices indicate that off-site storage should also be provided, and backup media should be taken off-site on a daily basis. The location should be far enough away that the same incident, such as flooding, a chemical spill, or weather does not take out both the site of operations and the backup site. The off-site storage location can also be the location where operations can be moved if a disaster prevents the immediate resumption of activity in the data center. If the recovery site and the storage location are different, make sure there is a way to move backup media to the recovery site.

- **The backup process**   If backups are not started automatically, you must plan a foolproof method of starting them manually. If backups are started automatically, you must have a way of validating that backups are made.

- **Auditing and verifying**   You must audit whether backup was done according to schedule, and you must verify that a valid backup was taken.

- **Storage area networks**   Transfer of data across the network to storage area networks for backup is a legitimate practice. You must secure the data transfer, and you must secure the data location.

- **Disaster avoidance planning**   The best backup plan includes disaster avoidance, which includes ensuring the physical safety of servers and backup media—not just in the data center, but at remote sites as well. Storing a server in a locked cabinet under the sink is not a valid or secure plan. Leaving backup media out, transporting it in the trunk of a car on a hot day, and so on are not sound plans. Providing process redundancy and possibly redundancy by supporting a remote data center for use during a disaster might be the difference between a business failure and a recovery.

- **Disaster recovery**   A disaster recovery plan is an essential part of a business continuity plan. A business continuity plan attempts to ensure the survival of the business after a disaster. The goal of a business continuity plan is to ensure the business's survival. The goal of a disaster recovery plan is only one step in that process. Its goal is to ensure that business operations continue during an outage or a disaster. Disaster recovery plans can include moving data center operations to remote locations, using manual procedures while data center operations are in recovery, or both. Business continuity includes the rebuilding of the data center and the rest of the business—putting the business back into full and normal operations.

- **Backup and recovery procedures**   A plan must be practiced. Written procedures should be validated by testing. Can you restore Active Directory if all domain controllers fail? Can you rebuild the root CA? Security for backup is validated when this type of recovery is successful. Practicing recovery is an essential part of backup security. It will help you discover security holes in your backup procedures, which are good things to discover before you really need to recover critical systems.

- **Security for media**   Media, whether it is blank or contains backups, should be secured. If a backup can be stolen, an attacker can restore critical or sensitive files on his own computer and gain access. If an attacker can obtain backup media and make it unusable or inaccessible, any event failure will be a total disaster.

- **Backup data selection**   The following types of data need backup and protection: system state for every server and Active Directory service.

- **Backup storage identification** Ensure that a record of backup, which includes identification of media or backup location, is made and is available to the recovery team.

- **Backup type selection** Backup types are normal, incremental, and differential. A backup type is usually selected to improve performance or to minimize the number of tapes that are required. Backup tapes can cause security problems if they are not properly labeled or if tapes necessary for recovery are overwritten. For example, if incremental backup is used, every tape between the last full backup and the most current backup must be available for recovery. If differential backup is used, only the most recent incremental backup and the last full backup are required.

Guidelines for Designing Security for Backup and Recovery Operations

The elements of good backup operations are easy: back up the data to sound media, store it in a safe place, do these two things frequently, and audit the practice. But the elements of securing the backup process are much broader, and more choices must be made. Follow these guidelines when designing security for backup and recovery operations:

- Ensure that personnel who perform backup are trained and understand their job. Audit their activity to ensure the job is being done correctly and securely.

- Ensure secure storage, both off-site and on-site, for storage media.

- Ensure that only authorized individuals can bring backup media on-site. This prevents a malicious or unqualified individual from using the media to restore old data over new, or from using backups to build new servers and then provide themselves access to sensitive data.

- Ensure that media is transported in a secure fashion. Media should be permanently labeled. Media should be transported in locked containers.

- Develop backup and restore strategies and test them.

- Separate the user rights of backup and restore. By default, the Backup Operators group has both privileges. By separating these rights, you make sure that the person who backs up the data does not have privileges to restore the data. In this manner, you prevent a disgruntled employee from restoring old data over new.

- Back up data on system and boot volumes and system state.

- Create an Automated System Recovery (ASR) data set backup when the operating system changes. Operating system changes include the addition of hardware and drivers and the installation of a service pack. If you have an ASR backup set, recovery will be easier. ASR protects only the system—a backup of data at the same time is required.

- Create and use a backup log. Keep information on the date, media, any errors encountered, the results, and so forth.

- Test backup processes by doing a trial restore. Restore to test machines in case recovery fails.

- Do not disable the default volume shadow copy backup method. If you do, open files will not be backed up.

Practice: Reviewing a Backup Plan

In this practice, you will review a plan for backup and answer questions about the plan. Read the scenario and then answer the question that follows. If you are unable to answer the question, review the lesson materials and try the question again. You can find the answer to the question in the "Questions and Answers" section at the end of the chapter.

Scenario

Wingtip Toys contracted with Contoso, Ltd. to design a disaster recovery plan. The Chief Technical Officer (CTO) must review the disaster recovery plan and approve or disapprove payment for the job. You are a new employee and a new member of the IT security team. The CTO asks you to examine the plan and give him your opinion about how good the plan is. He wants to know if you think anything else can be done to ensure that the plan promotes secure operations and is a sound disaster recovery plan. He provides you with the following summary of the plan.

Disaster and Recovery Plan for Wingtip Toys: Executive Summary   Disaster   and recovery planning is a critical support operation for Wingtip Toys and will consist of the following elements:

- All server data will be automatically backed up daily to a special storage area network. The SAN will be separate from the SAN used for production data.

- Data in the SAN will also be placed on tape and shipped to off-site storage on a daily basis.

- Weekly recovery tests will be conducted. Each test will be over some functional area—for example, one week's test might be recovery for file server data in the research department, while the next week's test might be recovery of the public Web site.

- An annual disaster recovery drill will test the company's ability to move to an alternative location and bring up IT operations from a complete disaster to full recovery.

Review Question

Answer the following question.

1. What do you tell the CTO?

_____

_____

_____

_____

_____

_____

_____

_____

_____

_____

_____

_____

_____

_____

Lesson 5: Designing a File Encryption and Decryption Strategy

File ACLs can manage access to files, but sometimes an additional layer of protection is necessary. If an attacker can gain access to your network, she might be able to compromise an administrator account and thus access sensitive files. If a laptop contains sensitive files and is lost, the added protection of encryption, if properly managed, can prevent unauthorized individuals from reading the files. In these cases and in others, the Encrypting File System (EFS) can be used to add a layer of protection. If, however, its use is not properly managed and users aren't trained in using it, EFS offers little protection and can even block legitimate access to encrypted data.

After this lesson, you will be able to

- Ensure recovery of EFS encrypted files.
- Disable EFS.
- Describe the platform differences that affect the use of EFS.
- Explain the considerations for designing server-side storage for EFS.
- Design secure encryption and decryption of files.

Estimated lesson time: 30 minutes

How to Ensure Recovery of EFS Encrypted Files

If the key necessary to decrypt an encrypted file is damaged or lost, how can you ensure that the encrypted file can be decrypted? EFS is a straightforward system for personal file encryption and decryption that requires minimal configuration before use. Its operation is transparent to the user.

The most important part of your EFS strategy must be to ensure recovery. If EFS recovery is ignored, data can be lost. When files are encrypted using EFS, there are two ways in which the file can be decrypted:

- The private key that is associated with the public key used in the encryption process can be used in the decryption process.
- If a file recovery agent is designated before the file is encrypted, the private key that is associated with the public key of the file recovery agent can be used in the decryption process.

Warning There are many ways in which EFS keys can become unavailable. The keys are stored in the user's profile so that if the profile is deleted or becomes corrupted the EFS keys are lost. Access to the private EFS key is removed when the user password is reset in Windows XP and Windows Server 2003. The rationale for this is to prevent an administrator or other user with the Reset Password permission from resetting the user's password, logging on as the user, and decrypting the EFS encrypted files. If the user changes her password by using the change password function, access to EFS encrypted files will not be lost. Finally, keys are just data blobs—any data stored on the computer can become corrupted.

If neither of these keys is available or if the keys are corrupted, the file cannot be decrypted. To ensure that the data in encrypted files will not be lost, an organization must either disable EFS or design an EFS recovery process. Several options can be used to design EFS recovery:

- Train users how to back up and safely store EFS keys. If a backup of a key is available, it can be imported into the profile of a user account and used to decrypt the file.

- Ensure the existence of a file recovery agent or agents.

  ❑ By default, the first administrator account to log on in the domain is the recovery agent.

  ❑ By default, on a Windows Server 2003 stand-alone server, there is no default recovery agent. This is also true of Windows XP. If either Windows Server 2003 or Windows XP is joined in a domain, the domain recovery agent will be used.

  ❑ Recovery agent keys must be backed up.

- Design a file recovery process. Self-signed recovery agent certificates can be used, or a PKI/CA solution can be deployed.

- Deploy key recovery solutions using a public key infrastructure (PKI).

  ❑ A Windows Server 2003 Enterprise Server must be used to establish a certificate authority (CA).

  ❑ A custom template for EFS must be created and deployed.

  ❑ Key recovery agents must be created.

See Also Chapter 2 explores the design of certificate services.

Considerations for Using a File Recovery Strategy That Uses Self-Signed Certificates

File recovery is the process of either restoring a backup of the original keys and then continuing to use the files, or using a file recovery agent to decrypt a file and then returning the file to the owner for encryption. Relying on self-signed certificates makes it difficult to ensure EFS file recovery for more than a few users. Consider the following when designing a file recovery strategy that uses self-signed certificates:

- **Consider users and EFS key backup.**   Users do not understand the need to back up encryption keys, or they might back up keys and not store them safely. If a backup key is available to an attacker, it can be used to obtain access to the data in encrypted files. There is no centralized way of organizing and storing backup keys. An administrator would have to collect backup files from all users (or make them himself) and provide a secure storage area. It is impractical to manage the storage of thousands of backed-up keys.

- **Consider the file recovery agent keys.**   The recovery agent keys can also be damaged or lost. File recovery keys also need to be backed up. They also need to be available before files are encrypted. Creating or making available the recovery agent certificate (and thus the public key) after a file is encrypted does not provide a way to recover the file if the user's keys are damaged or lost.

- **Consider the file recovery agent.**   The default file recovery agent is an administrator. Determine whether the administrator is the right person for this responsibility. In many organizations, sensitive files are encrypted to prevent unauthorized individuals within the organization from reading them. If the administrator is the recovery agent, you must ensure that she is authorized to read the encrypted files, because she will be able to.

- **Consider the storage of backed-up keys.**   EFS keys are backed up by exporting them to a file. The file should be password-protected and stored safely. What is a safe place? Is it safe to allow users to store this data in a place of their choosing? Should a central place be designated? How practical is the storage and maintenance of backup keys?

- **Consider the password protection of EFS keys.**   The password is chosen by the user and might be weak. It must be remembered in order to recover the keys. Users might back up the keys and never need them, or not need them until a lot of time has passed. They might not remember the password and thus be unable to install the backed-up keys. They might not trust their memory and therefore write down the password and keep it with the backup keys, thus making the keys available to anyone who can access the disk.

- **Consider the protection offered by the password for backed-up keys.**   The keys do not have to be imported back to the original account for which they are issued. They can be imported into any account if the password used to export the keys is known. If the password is weak or stored with the backed-up keys, the keys might easily be used in a successful attack on EFS.

- **Consider the safety of keys that have been backed up.**   Backed-up keys can also be damaged or lost. Just as you should verify data backups, you should also verify backed-up encryption keys by importing them into an account. However, providing all users with an additional account to do so is impractical and might prove to be a security liability, as users might forget to delete the account profile or otherwise remove the encryption keys and thus provide another account that can access their files.

- **Consider removing file recovery agent keys from the network.**   If file recovery agent keys are stored in the owner's profile, the owner can read files that were encrypted when the keys were available. This access is transparent. Although access can be audited, the recovery agent has already read the file. If the recovery agent private key is backed up and removed from the network, the file recovery agent cannot transparently read the file. She must import the key and then read the file.

Considerations for Designing File Recovery Using a Certification Authority

File recovery can be a management nightmare and an iffy situation when self-signed certificates are used. One solution is the development of a PKI to manage EFS. Before doing so, consider the following:

- **Consider the PKI design.**   If no PKI exists, a considerable investment in time must be spent planning the PKI and the use of the PKI to deploy EFS certificates.

- **Consider CA security.**   The security of the EFS encrypted files is dependent on the security of the CA that issues the EFS certificates and EFS recovery agent certificates. This server should be secured.

- **Consider EFS key backup.**   Establishing a PKI for the management of EFS certificates does not automatically provide EFS key backup. You still should back up critical EFS keys such as those issued to file recovery agents.

- **Consider file recovery agents.**   You can create as many file recovery agents as you want. It might be appropriate to create file recovery agent accounts for specific OUs. This can split the responsibility and provide tighter control over EFS encrypted files.

■ **Consider the file recovery process.**   The process of file recovery must be designed, including designating file recovery agents and outlining the process for file recovery. Best practices include:

❑ Keeping the file recovery agent private keys off-line. The public keys are needed in the encryption process. The private key is needed only for recovery.

❑ Providing off-line recovery stations. Encrypted files are moved to these stations for recovery.

❑ The file recovery agent keys are imported into an account on the workstation and used to decrypt the files.

❑ Decrypted files are then safely moved to the owner's computer.

❑ The file recovery agent keys are then exported and removed from the file recovery station.

Considerations for Designing Key Recovery for EFS

A Windows Server 2003 Enterprise Edition computer with the certificate services can be configured to issue EFS certificates with a file archival property. When properly implemented, the EFS keys are archived at the CA and can be recovered as necessary. This implementation was described in Chapter 2.

How to Disable EFS

If your EFS policy is not to use it, or if you want to ensure recovery of EFS files and need time to design and deploy a solution, you should disable EFS. There is a risk with any technology. By default, EFS is available to anyone with a user account. Without proper training and a file recovery process in place, the information in EFS files can be lost. This is because the EFS keys required to decrypt the file can be lost or damaged. If the EFS keys are not present and undamaged, EFS encrypted files cannot be read.

EFS is disabled by clearing the Allow Users To Encrypt Files Using Encrypting File System (EFS) check box. Figure 9-25 shows the check box. This check box is located on the Properties page for the Encrypting File System policy in the GPO. The local Security Policy can be used to disable EFS on a single system, while the domain GPO can be used to disable EFS for the domain. This option is available by opening the GPO and navigating to the Security Settings area of the GPO. Right-click the Encrypting File System policy, and select properties to locate this option. In Windows 2000, EFS could be disabled simply by deleting all recovery agents. This method will not work in Windows XP or Windows Server 2003, as both allow EFS to not have a recovery agent.

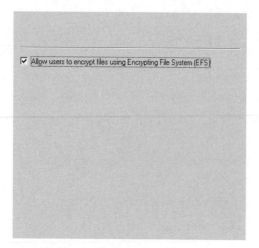

☑ Allow users to encrypt files using Encrypting File System (EFS)

Figure 9-25   Disabling EFS

Platform Differences That Affect the Use of EFS

EFS has been available since the introduction of Windows 2000. In addition to improved file and key recovery options, two major differences in EFS between Windows 2000, Windows XP after service pack 1, and Windows Server 2003 are the default designation of encryption protocols and the ability to share an EFS file.

Table 9-7 displays the encryption protocols and strengths available for EFS by platform.

> **Exam Tip**   The default encryption protocol used in Windows XP post–service pack (SP) 1 and Windows Server 2003 is 256-bit Advanced Encryption Standard (AES). This encryption protocol is very strong, but the encryption protocol used by default in Windows 2000 is 56-bit DES-X. You must not attempt to open Windows XP or Windows Server 2003 EFS encrypted files on a Windows 2000 computer. Because the files encrypted on the Windows XP post–SP 1 computer have been encrypted with a different encryption algorithm, you will not be able to read them using Windows 2000. You might also corrupt the encrypted file by trying to do so.

Table 9-7   Encryption Protocols

Operating System	DES-X	3DES	AES	Default
Windows 2000	Yes	Yes	No	DES-X
Windows XP Professional	Yes	Yes	Yes	DES-X
Windows XP Professional post–SP 1	Yes	Yes	Yes	AES
Windows Server 2003	Yes	Yes	Yes	AES

The encryption protocol is changed by either editing the registry or using the Group Policy Security Option: System Cryptography. Use FIPS Compliant Algorithms For Encryption. If this security option is enabled, 3DES will be used for encrypting files. The registry can be edited to select the default EFS encryption algorithm. The key, AlgorithmID (a REG_WORD value), is changed by using one of the values listed in Table 9-8.

Table 9-8   EFS Encryption Algorithm Choices

Value	Encryption Algorithm
0x6604	DESX
0x6603	3DES
0x6610	AES

The value is located at:

HKEY_LOCAL_MACHINE\SOFTWARE\Microsoft\Windows NT\CurrentVersion\EFS

How EFS Files Are Shared

By default, EFS in Windows 2000 was a personal file encryption product. The account used to encrypt the file and the file recovery agent can encrypt and decrypt the file. It was possible to programmatically provide file-sharing of EFS encrypted files.

Windows XP Professional introduced the ability to share encrypted files using the GUI. The person who encrypts a file can determine who can decrypt the file by importing the EFS certificate of the person he wants to allow to encrypt the file and making it available in his certificate store. This process can be done while setting up sharing on the file. Sharing is configured from the Advanced property pages of the file. In Figure 9-26, Kevin Browne is providing Bart Duncan the ability to work with the encrypted file secret4.txt. The main problem with sharing EFS files is twofold: there is no way to document which files are so shared, and each person who is given access can also provide access for others.

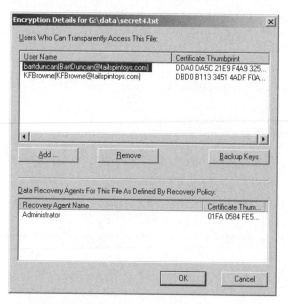

Figure 9-26   Sharing an encrypted file

How Offline File Storage Encryption Works

Windows Server 2003 enabled the encryption of offline storage. Offline file storage is a process that provides online storage of files on a file server and on the desktop. When a user is online, she works with files stored on the server. Files can be periodically or manually synched with the desktop. When the desktop system is not connected to the network, the user can still work with the files because she is working with a locally stored copy of the file.

Windows 2000 introduced the offline file storage system, but you could not encrypt the offline file storage. This meant that sensitive files could be exposed if the computer was stolen. Users who traveled with company-issued laptops had the convenience of bringing files along with them, but they could not protect the files with encryption.

Windows Server 2003 and Windows XP Professional provide the solution to that problem. The offline file storage area can now be encrypted. However, the entire storage area must be encrypted—you cannot choose to encrypt file by file or just for the user. Offline files are encrypted with the SYSTEM account's private key. Consequently, EFS offers little protection against a skilled attacker who has taken physical possession of the computer.

Considerations for Designing Server-Side Storage for EFS

EFS encrypted files can be stored on file servers or on Web servers by using WebDAV. Consider the following when designing server-side storage for EFS:

- **Consider file server preparation for EFS file storage.**   The file server must be configured for delegation. Doing this creates some element of risk. When a server is configured for delegation, the user account can be used by the server to request a service ticket from the Kerberos Distribution Center (KDC). There is no restriction on what type of service ticket can be requested, received, or used.

- **Consider the need for EFS key storage on the file server.**   To store EFS files on the server, the server must be able to encrypt and decrypt the files. The user's EFS keys must be available on the server. If roaming profiles are used, this is not a problem because the user's profile can be downloaded to the file server. If roaming profiles are not used, the user must log on interactively to the server and either import a copy of his EFS keys or allow a new certificate to be created and stored on the file server.

- **Consider the use of a local profile on the server.**   When a local profile is created and EFS keys are generated, they are not the same key as that used in the local file system. This means that an EFS encrypted file from the file server cannot be decrypted using the user's local computer EFS keys.

- **Consider file transport between servers.**   When a file server is used to store the EFS files, EFS files are not encrypted while they traverse the network. Instead, they are decrypted on the workstation, traverse the network in plain text, and are encrypted on the file server. To protect files in transport, consider the use of IPSec to encrypt the files.

- **Consider using WebDAV.**   WebDAV is implemented in Internet Information Services (IIS) and allows users to store files on the Web server. If an IIS server is configured to do so, users can store EFS encrypted files on the Web server by using WebDAV.

- **Consider WebDAV communications.**   Unlike simple file storage, WebDAV does not require that the EFS encrypted file be decrypted before transport. EFS encrypted files can be transported across the network and remain encrypted.

Guidelines for Designing Secure Encryption and Decryption of Files

Follow these guidelines when designing secure encryption and decryption of files:

- Disable EFS until you can develop an EFS policy.

- Determine who should be allowed to use EFS, and train these users.

- Partition the use of EFS. It is not necessary to allow all users to encrypt files. You can enable and disable EFS in a GPO and link the GPO to any container where you need to either enable or disable the use of EFS.

- If EFS will be used, harden it. This can be done by:

  ❑ Ensuring the encryption of temporary folders. Applications can write files to temporary folders. If these folders are not marked by encryption, clear-text copies of your sensitive data might reside in them.

  ❑ Setting the page file to delete at shut down. The page file can also contain clear-text copies of encrypted documents. Should an attacker be able to obtain physical access to the computer, the page file is protected while the system is running, but when the system is shut down, the attacker might be able to gain access.

- Use file recovery or key recovery where large numbers of users must be allowed to encrypt files.

- Use key recovery in high-security situations.

- If file recovery is used, design a process for file recovery. Require backup of file encryption keys, and train users how to do it.

- If file recovery using a PKI will be used:

  ❑ Design a process for file recovery.

  ❑ Create file recovery agents for special accounts. These accounts should not be accounts that are used for user or administrator chores. They can be assigned to and used by authorized file recovery personnel when the need arises.

  ❑ Disable and protect file recovery agent accounts until they are needed.

  ❑ Export file recovery keys, and consider removing the file recovery private key from the network.

  ❑ Provide a separate file recovery station, and import file recovery keys only when necessary to recover files.

  ❑ Back up all file recovery agent keys, and store them in a safe place.

- If key recovery using a PKI will be used:

  ❑ Enforce role separation.

  ❑ Design the key archival and key recovery process. (See Chapter 2 for additional information on key archival.)

  ❑ Use unique accounts for key recovery agents. Key recovery agents should not be CA administrators or Certificate Managers.

  ❑ Use special accounts for key recovery agents.

Practice: Designing a Secure Encryption and Decryption Strategy

In this practice, you will design a secure encryption and decryption strategy for a fictitious company. Read the scenario and then answer the questions that follow. If you are unable to answer a question, review the lesson materials and try the question again. You can find answers to the questions in the "Questions and Answers" section at the end of the chapter.

> **Important**   You will need to use your PKI knowledge from your study of Chapter 2 and the material you learned earlier in this chapter to complete this practice.

Scenario

You are the CA Administrator for Tailspin Toys. You have been asked to participate in the design of a secure encryption and decryption plan for Tailspin Toys. Tailspin Toys would like its research department employees to encrypt research documents. It is critical that documents be protected at all times. Documents will be stored on a central file server in the research department area.

Review Questions

Answer the following questions.

1. What are your recommendations for this design?

   _____

   _____

   _____

   _____

   _____

   _____

2. What training will you recommend for the researchers?

   _____

   _____

   _____

   _____

   _____

Design Activity: Designing Data Access Security

In this activity, you must use what you learned in all five lessons and apply it to a real-world situation. Read the scenario and then complete the exercises that follow. You can find answers for the exercise in the "Questions and Answers" section at the end of this chapter.

Scenario

You are the Security Administrator for Tailspin Toys. Tailspin Toys just purchased Coho Winery. Your job is to visit Coho Winery to review its data-protection processes. When you begin the process of interviewing Coho Winery employees, you find they have no data-protection strategy in place. You must immediately design a plan for data access security. Review the following information, and answer the questions provided.

Company Background

Coho Winery was a family-owned business for 100 years. It was established by Nicole Holliday and her good friend Brian Hodges. When Brian Hodges' son died last year, he left no family to inherit the winery, and it was sold to pay back taxes. The new owners know a lot about producing good wine but little about business management. Tailspin Toys was able to purchase the winery very cheaply.

Existing Environment

IT operations at the winery were established 20 years ago, as it was felt that the business side of the winery was being swallowed up in paperwork. Brian Hodges, Jr., then in his 60s, hired his neighbor's son, Andrew Hill, to manage the business side and gave him the responsibility of implementing and managing IT operations.

Interviews

Following is a list of company personnel interviewed and their statements:

- **Andrew Hill**   "We got a good operation here. We have 100 servers. Forty of those servers are in a Web farm. We sell lots of wine over the Internet. Most of it is not produced here. We just bottle and label, bottle and label. We got a lot of wine-related gift items, gift baskets, stemware, kitchen stuff, and the like. If you can slap a grape or a bottle of wine on it, we sell it. We're doing so well I don't know what we are doin'. Hah!"

- **Network administrator**   "When I started two years ago half the data was inaccessible because someone had set up NTFS and screwed things up. We had hundreds of groups. We had more groups than users. We had user accounts that had never been used. Groups too. Users were assigned direct access to files. What a mess. I had to literally remove all access to data files except for administrators and wait to see who screamed. Trouble was, a lot of people were administrators, so there wasn't much screaming. I'm trying to clean up things a little as I go on, but it's hard to remove administrative privileges that people have had for a long time. We also have a lot of legacy applications, so users often need to be administrators anyways."

- **IT auditor from the auditing firm Fabrikam**   "Thank you for hiring my company to do this review. Coho Winery has no IT auditing in place. None. We would be happy to design an auditing policy for Coho Winery. Here are the results of my audit."

- **Backup operator**   "Yes. I make all the data backups every night. Then I put the tapes in the trunk of my car. At the end of the week, I take them to my house. I got a spare room. Where do I live? Oh, just down the road. I could get those tapes in a minute if we need them."

- **Help desk**   "What problems? I can solve all the problems. People call me with their problems. I solve them. Excuse me, my phone is ringing. I don't get paid to talk. Probably Sally can't get to another file she needs. She is always deleting things then wanting them back, or can't get to something because she doesn't have access."

Business Requirements

The business requirements are:

1. There is little to no budget for additional equipment.

2. Operations cannot be interrupted.

Technical Requirements

The technical requirements are:

1. Technical access controls need to be strengthened.

2. IT auditing needs to be designed and implemented.

Exercise 1: Analyze Hot Spots

You know that a lot of work has to be done to bring IT operations up to Tailspin Toys standards. But you must make an immediate report to your boss on the situation to detail the critical nature of the problem and areas that must be changed immediately. Answer the following question.

1. What are five immediate areas of concern? Explain why these are concerns.

   _____

   _____

   _____

_____

_____

_____

_____

_____

_____

_____

_____

Exercise 2: Make Changes to Backup

Your boss has read your report and asked you to return to Coho Winery and begin implementing sound access controls for IT. He will be sending help and giving you the authority to make changes. He asks you to decide what will provide the most security and to implement that first. Answer the following questions.

1. What change do you want to implement first? Why?

_____

_____

_____

_____

_____

_____

2. Employees are used to having their own way. The backup operator and network administrator might be resistant to change. What can you do to help them see why these changes must be made?

_____

_____

_____

_____

_____

Chapter Summary

- Access control provides additional layers of defense. Permissions, audit, backup, and EFS can all work together to manage access to resources.

- Delegation of authority is used to reduce administrative workload and to provide separation of duties and autonomy for divisions and departments within the company.

- Backup plans for data are essential. They should include provisions for protecting the backup data, media, and operations.

- Encryption and decryption of files should be managed carefully. Encryption has little effect if it is easy to discover the user's password or to become the file recovery agent. When a sound protection and recovery mechanism is provided, EFS can provide exquisite control over access to sensitive information.

Exam Highlights

Before taking the exam, review these key points and terms. You need to know this information.

Key Points

- Being able to analyze audit records is almost as important as analyzing auditing requirements.

- PKI provides a sound way of implementing both EFS file recovery and EFS key archival.

- The Delegation of Authority Wizard provides administrative control by assigning permissions to objects in Active Directory. To remove this authority, you must edit the permissions assigned to the objects.

- Explicit permissions, even explicit Allow permissions, have precedence over inherited permissions.

- If permissions are inherited from many parents, the permissions inherited from the parent closest to the object are evaluated before those from objects that are further away.

- SACLs also follow inheritance rules.

Key Terms

Access Control Entry (ACE)   A piece of metadata that identifies a permission and indicates to whom it is assigned. ACEs include a SID, a permission, and the Allow or Deny action. Discretionary Access Control Lists (DACLs) are composed of ACEs.

Security descriptor   A construct that includes a Systems Access Control List (SACL) and a Discretionary Access Control List (DACL).

Security Reference Monitor   A kernel-level component that runs in the *%system-root%*\System32\Ntoskrnl.exe process. Security Reference Monitor resolves requests for object access, builds a security descriptor for a new object, and validates a given security descriptor.

Questions and Answers

Page
9-24

Lesson 1   Practice: Evaluating Permission Inheritance

Answer the following questions.

1. Given the file structure in the following picture and assuming remote access, what type of access does Christie have?

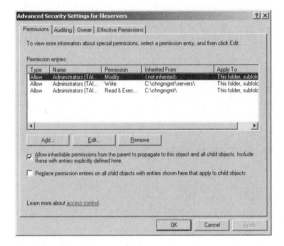

Christie has Read access.

2. Given the following file structure and assuming local access, what type of access does Christie have?

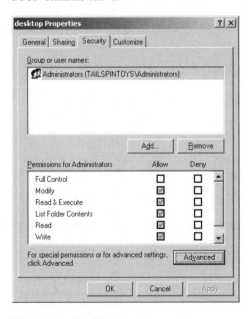

Christie has Modify access.

3. Given the following file structure and assuming remote access, what type of access does Christie have?

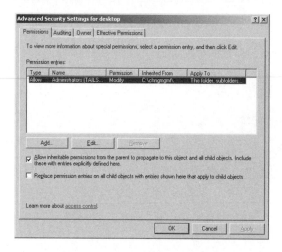

Christie has No Access access.

Lesson 2   Practice: Reviewing a Permission Structure Design

Answer the following question.

1. What are your suggestions, criticisms, and additions to this design? Explain the reasons behind your suggestions.

Answers may vary. Managers should not be given Full Control over objects in the OU. This gives too much power and is not necessary to manage the OU. Managers also typically do not understand nor really care about administering IT functions. This appears to be more of a power issue. Likewise, clerical employees might not be the best group to give Reset Password permissions and other IT functions to. Allowing all clerical workers this level of control is not a good idea. The newest clerical worker in the finance department could reset passwords on manager accounts and perhaps gain access to sensitive documents. Instead, I recommend creating a special Help Desk group and delegating to this group the authority to create and manage accounts. You can put trusted clerical personnel into the Help Desk group, add executive assistants, or do both. Membership in the group, however, should not be automatic.

Page
9-47

Lesson 3   Exercise 1: Determining What to Audit

1. What should be audited? Explain why you made each recommendation.

Audit for success and failure for logon and account logon, privilege use, policy change, and object access. Set SACLs on folders that will contain sensitive research documents. As files are added to the folders, they will inherit the audit settings. Establishing this level of audit will provide an audit trail of researchers' activity on the file server. It will also provide information on potential attempts by unauthorized individuals to access files and servers.

Page
9-48

Lesson 3   Exercise 2: Analyzing Audit Records

Answer the following questions.

1. What do the first five audit records tell you?

These audit records tell you that an attempt was made to access the research server in the middle of the night by someone who was unauthorized. And that later an authorized access attempt was successful. The file planb.doc was accessed.

2. You wonder why a researcher was looking at files in the middle of the night. This is abnormal activity for Tailspin Toys. You want to trace any other activity by this user during the night. You must first find out the time at which this researcher, Bart Duncan, was logged on. Examine the domain controller audit records. What time was Bart logged on?

Bart was logged on from 12:14 a.m. until 3:15 p.m.

Page
9-59

Lesson 4   Practice: Reviewing a Backup Plan

Answer the following question.

1. What do you tell the CTO?

Answers may vary. First, ask for the entire plan. If the CTO really expects a good review, he will provide it. Executive summaries are just that—notes to give the big picture. This summary does not tell you everything you need to know. It leaves out answers to the following questions, which are necessary to judge the plan:

- ❑ How will the SAN be secured? Firewalls should be used to allow only backup traffic in and nothing out. If data needs to be recovered, you can easily change the configuration so that data can flow back where it is needed, or a server can be restored in the SAN network area and then moved to its normal location.

- ❑ How will the backup media that is moved off site be handled? Its handling needs to be secured.

- ❑ How are staff members trained? Where are the written procedures for the processes and identification of duties?

- ❑ Where is the off-site location for data storage and for resuming operations if this should be necessary? Both are mentioned in the plan, but no details are given. This place should be far enough away so that it wouldn't also be affected by a natural disaster or other conditions that cause the problems at the normal site.

Page
9-71

Lesson 5   Practice: Designing a Secure Encryption and Decryption Strategy

Answer the following questions.

1. What are your recommendations for this design?

Disable EFS on the researchers' computers until the solution can be implemented. Design file archival for EFS. Add extra protection for the server to be used. Use IPSec to encrypt communications between the file server and the researchers' computers. Use ACLs on the file server to control access to files. Researchers can use and share EFS files at will, but ACLs can prevent access to files by unauthorized personnel. Do not give researchers Ownership or Change permission because these permissions would allow them to change the ACLs. Create a custom Windows group and include all the researchers who can share the encrypted file or files. By creating such a group, you will make it easier to identify which researchers should be sharing with each other. Creating such a group will also make it easier for the administrators to manage ACLs because the Windows group can be given NTFS permissions to access the files. (However, EFS encrypted files must be shared with individual accounts, not with groups.)

Lock down EFS on the desktop. Encrypt temp folders. Although the policy will be to store EFS encrypted files on the file server while the researchers are working on the files, the files can be written temporarily to disk. Configure the research workstations and the file server to erase the contents of the page file on shutdown. Creating a policy for the use of EFS by the researchers and the storage of files on the server is a must. Designate a key recovery agent, but do not provide this individual with key recovery agent keys until it is necessary to recover keys.

2. What training will you recommend for the researchers?

Answers may vary. All researchers should be trained in the use of EFS. They should be instructed on the policy. Instruct researchers on how to share EFS files. Train someone in the research department as a key recovery agent.

Design Activity: Designing Data Access Security

Page
9-73

Exercise 1: Analyze Hot Spots

You know that a lot of work has to be done to bring IT operations up to Tailspin Toys standards. But you must make an immediate report to your boss on the situation to detail the critical nature of the problem and areas that must be changed immediately. Answer the following question.

1. What are five immediate areas of concern? Explain why these are concerns.

Answers may vary. Here are some hot spots:

❑ Recovery might not be possible if a disaster were to occur. The tapes are often stored in a car trunk, and the permanent off-site storage location is an employee's house nearby. This raises questions about the security of the tapes. What if the employee were fired? What if a disaster—for example, a tornado—wiped out the data center and the employee's house?

❑ The help desk appears to have too much power. The employee spoke of giving Sally access where she doesn't have permission.

❑ There are too many administrators. The network administrator said so. Also, this was indicated by the help desk employee's interview and by the network administrator's statement that there were few complaints when he removed most access except administrators.

❑ There is no IT audit. There appears to be none at all, according to the auditor.

❑ Apparently free-flowing operations are still like those by a tiny mom-and-pop shop. There might be many more deficiencies in operations. There is a need to do an overall assessment of IT technical controls and probably of other operations.

Page
9-74

Exercise 2: Make Changes to Backup

Your boss has read your report and asked you to return to Coho Winery and begin implementing sound access controls for IT. He will be sending help and giving you the authority to make changes. He asks you to decide what will provide the most security and to implement that first. Answer the following questions.

1. What change do you want to implement first? Why?

   A backup plan. If a sound backup and recovery plan is not in place, there could be no business to manage.

2. Employees are used to having their own way. The backup operator and network administrator might be resistant to change. What can you do to help them see why these changes must be made?

   Show them why the current plan might not be the best. To both people, bring up the problem of a hot trunk and backup tapes. To both, bring up the wild chance of a tornado taking out both the business and the employees' homes. To the network administrator, explain the issue of how the employee might respond if he were fired. For both, set up a recovery drill. Provide a test network and computers. Let them know it's a drill, but ask them to restore a critical database, file server, or domain controller.

10 Designing a Secure Client Infrastructure

Exam Objectives in this Chapter:

- Design a client authentication strategy.
    - Analyze authentication requirements.
    - Establish account and password security requirements.
- Design a security strategy for client remote access.
    - Design remote access policies.
    - Design access to internal resources.
    - Design an authentication provider and accounting strategy for remote network access using Internet Authentication Services (IAS).

Why This Chapter Matters

Without careful planning and analysis, tomorrow's business and technical requirements can easily reduce security and leave networks vulnerable to attacks. Access via mobile devices such as telephones and Personal Digital Assistants (PDAs) demand new approaches to authentication and access control. New requirements for access to an organization's data as a result of merger, acquisition, or access to new markets might require a relaxation in technical controls. Carefully designed and implemented security barriers become worthless in the face of new technologies.

Many of these demands are the result of the need to connect client computers to networks at any time, from any device, and from anywhere.

Lessons in this Chapter:

Before You Begin

This chapter presents the skills and concepts related to creating a security design framework. This training kit assumes you have a minimum of 1 year of experience implementing and administering desktop operating systems and network operating system in environments that have the following characteristics:

- At least 250 supported users

- Three or more physical locations

- Typical network services such as messaging, database, file and print, proxy server or firewall, Internet and intranet, remote access, and client computer management

- Three or more domain controllers

- Connectivity needs that include connecting branch offices and individual users in remote locations to the corporate network, and connecting corporate networks to the Internet

In addition, you should have experience designing a network infrastructure.

Many design exercises are paper-based; however, to understand the technical capabilities that a design can incorporate, you should have some hands-on experience with products. Where specific hands-on instruction is given, you must have at least two computers configured as specified in the "Getting Started" section at the beginning of this book.

Lesson 1: Designing the Client Authentication Infrastructure

The design of an authentication infrastructure prepares the organization's network for its current needs to secure access to resources and provides the groundwork for future authentication needs. In many cases, the authentication requirements and the password policy's established requirements can be met by ordinary client computers. Today's networks, however, must be accessible to many different computing devices.

After this lesson, you will be able to

- Explain the process of designing a client authentication infrastructure.
- Analyze authentication requirements.
- Analyze authentication requirements for Windows clients.
- Analyze authentication requirements for non-Windows clients.
- Analyze authentication requirements for communications with ISPs and mobile carriers.
- Explain the considerations for establishing account and password security requirements.
- Design a client authentication infrastructure.

Estimated lesson time: 30 minutes

The Process: Designing a Client Authentication Infrastructure

To design a client authentication infrastructure, security designers follow this process:

1. *Analyze network and resource access needs.* This includes the needs of employees, customers, and partners.

2. *Determine network and resource connection points.* Connection points can be remote access servers, RADIUS servers, Web sites, Internet connections, ISPs, telephony carriers, and so on.

3. *Determine whether additional connection points are required.* Analyze, for example, the need for mobile devices to connect to the network. If there is a need, but no access point, determine the best possible way to provide access without compromising security.

4. *Identify clients.* Clients include:

   ❑ Wired clients, such as Microsoft Windows–based computers and non-Windows clients

   ❑ Wireless clients, such as computers with wireless access cards and mobile devices such as telephones and PDAs

   ❑ Special clients, such as RADIUS clients used to connect to RADIUS servers such as Microsoft Internet Authentication Service

5. *Identify the authentication protocols and requirements of clients and servers.* Requirements include authentication to servers and local authentication—for example, authentication to a mobile device such as a smart phone or PDA.

6. *Analyze computer and user authentication requirements.*

   ❑ Computer authentication requirements can include IPSec policy authentication requirements, authenticating switch requirements, RADIUS client to RADIUS server requirements, and so on.

   ❑ User authentication requirements include LAN requirements (such as NTLM and Kerberos), remote access authentication requirements (such as MS-CHAP and EAP authentication requirements), and Web authentication requirements (such as anonymous and SSL).

7. *Examine the organization's security policy.* Do this to determine the account and password security requirements.

8. *Determine whether authentication protocols and specifications available on clients meet authentication requirements set by the security policy.* If authentication requirements set by the security policy cannot be met by clients, determine whether additional software or devices can provide the authentication specified by policy.

Which clients will be used depends on the architecture of the organization. However, you should plan for the integration of all types of clients, even if they are not used at the current time. This chapter provides assistance on analyzing client authentication requirements and how they relate to the security policy.

How to Analyze Authentication Requirements

The main task of analyzing authentication requirements is to understand what each client offers and how that might fit in the organization's security policy. The first step is to identify clients.

Guidelines for Identifying Clients

Identification of clients is an important first step and will point to areas within and outside of the organization that must be considered when gathering authentication requirements.

Don't make the mistake of considering only current clients as identified by IT. If, for example, no managed mobile devices are connecting to the network, it's almost a given that some employees are using devices such as PDAs to store organization-related data and synching with direct cables or through wireless means with the organization's desktops, their own computers, or both. Other areas of the organization might also be researching, planning, or starting to provide access for phones that can store and synchronize data.

Telephony clients can access the organization's network through carriers. Devices on the carrier's network can be the first access point that the organization's mobile devices authenticate to. Devices on the carrier's network will also need to communicate with devices on the organization's network, and authentication between carrier and organization devices will also need to be considered. Weak security at the carrier's network could weaken security for your network. An attacker might be able to compromise the carrier's network and then attack yours. Weak authentication between devices on the carrier's network and yours can also endanger your network. Spend time understanding the security policy and preparations of the carrier and assuring the security of the connection between the two networks.

Consider as well RADIUS clients and RADIUS proxies. Consider whether they are located on the organization's network or that of a service provider such as an Internet service provider (ISP). In this case, your users also authenticate to a network that is not under your control. Weak security on the part of the ISP can put your network at risk. Weak security on the connection between your two networks can also provide attackers an entry point.

How to Collect Authentication Requirements

When collecting and analyzing authentication requirements, remember this question: Can a user using a specific device securely authenticate to the device and/or securely authenticate to the organization's network? The designer cannot stop with the "can" part of the equation but must keep the "securely" part in mind. The definition of a secure connection will depend on the organization's specification in its security policy, the designer's knowledge of best practices, and an analysis that might be device specific. (Some devices might not meet requirements even if their specifications appear to say they will. For example, device specifications might state a capability, such as using a virtual private network [VPN], that will meet the security policy requirement, but in practice the device might not manage more than a few connections.) To analyze authentication requirements for clients, follow these steps:

1. Collect information on each of the technologies and authentication processes that might be used to connect to the organization's resources:

   ❑ Technologies for computer (or computing device) authentication

   ❑ Technologies for user authentication

   ❑ Network authentication, including LAN and remote access authentication

   ❑ Device-specific authentication

   ❑ Modification of authentication credentials capabilities

2. Determine where authentication processes might be weakened because of the need to use less secure technologies or weaker password processes.

3. Determine where a technology can use a stronger authentication process or stay the same.

4. Determine where a technology cannot meet the organization's security policy.

5. Determine where integration with existing directories will mean a separate directory.

6. Determine where single sign-on cannot be achieved.

7. Determine whether alternative authentication technologies, such as biometrics or smart cards, can be used to strengthen the authentication process.

The following sections apply the preceding steps to current technologies.

Guidelines for Analyzing Authentication Requirements for Windows Clients

Authentication by Windows computers (computer authentication) and by users using Windows computers (user authentication) is discussed in Chapter 3 (IPSec), Chapter 6 (authentication infrastructure), Chapter 7 (remote access and VPNs), and Chapter 12 (wireless networks). These chapters define Windows authentication protocols, remote access authentication protocols, and 802.1x wireless authentication. Analyze the following Windows clients authentication needs:

■ Analyze wired clients located on the LAN. Consider authentication requirements and capabilities.

❑ Determine whether wired clients can use Kerberos and NTLMv2.

❑ If clients cannot, can they be configured to do so?

❑ Analyze secure client and server authentication processes as much as possible, considering security policy, client capabilities, and administrative ability to harden clients.

❑ Analyze the availability and need for going beyond passwords to using smart cards, biometrics, or token-type devices for a higher level of security.

❑ Analyze whether cached credentials will be allowed when there are problems with network access to domain controllers. Unless restricted, Windows clients cache successful authentication credentials that can be used to log on should a domain controller not be available.

■ Analyze wireless windows clients. Wireless clients often require a relaxation in authentication requirements for computing devices and computers. Some wireless clients, for example, use a four-digit PIN number as authentication. Your password policy might require a longer length. Other wireless networks do not require authentication at all. Consider upgrading or adding updates that provide 802.1x wireless authentication. Consider products that improve the authentication capabilities of wireless devices.

- Analyze windows clients that will be used to remotely access the network. Windows clients can be configured to use Point-to-Point Protocol (PPP) authentication, but consider which ones can connect using smart cards or other more secure forms of authentication.

- Analyze clients that will be used both on the LAN and remotely. These clients will need to be evaluated for both LAN and remote authentication needs.

- Analyze computer authentication using certificates. Can all clients use certificates for LAN-based secure connections using IPSec? Can all remote clients use certificates across a dial-up connection, VPN, or both?

- Analyze client-to-Web server authentication. Can clients participate in a Secure Sockets Layer (SSL) or Transport Layer Security (TLS) connection?

- Analyze client application authentication requirements. What type of authentication is required by applications? If the authentication requirements of an application do not meet security policy, can anything be done to correct this? For example, if a clear-text authentication is required by an application, a solution using SSL might be the answer.

- Analyze Windows client authentication to non-Windows hosts such as UNIX and Mainframe computers. These authentication processes require special configuration, the use of additional Windows services, (Services for UNIX), Windows servers (Host Integration Server), or third-party products.

- Analyze Windows client authentication synchronization requirements. It might be necessary to synchronize user data and passwords among multiple directories. Microsoft Identity Integration Server 2003 Enterprise Edition is a possible solution for providing single sign-on across multiple directories.

> **Note**   When you look, it's interesting what you find. For example, 802.1x authentication capabilities are part of Windows XP Professional and Windows Server 2003, and they can be added to Windows 2000 (via the 802.1x Authentication Client). These capabilities are also available for Windows 98, Windows Millennium Edition, and Windows NT 4.0 Workstation for customers with Premier and Alliance support contracts.

Guidelines for Analyzing Authentication Requirements for Non-Windows Computer Clients

Non-Windows computers must also be considered. Non-Windows authentication issues arise when you have any of the following situations:

- Non-Windows clients on the LAN

- Non-Windows clients used by customers and partners to remotely access your organization's information

- Non-Windows servers that Windows clients must authenticate to

- Non-Windows servers that different clients must authenticate to

Use the following processes and considerations to analyze non-Windows clients and servers:

- Determine the authentication protocols that are native to each operating system.

- Are any of the choices also available to Windows clients and servers? UNIX computers and many others can use Kerberos to communicate with Windows computers. What would be required to do so?

- Do services exist that resolve authentication issues—for example, Client Services for Netware, Services for UNIX?

- Do products exist that resolve authentication issues—for example, Host Integration Server?

- Do these services and products synchronize passwords between the operating systems if different directories must be used?

- What changes if the non-Windows computer will be used to access Windows computers remotely?

- What are the weaknesses or strengths that might be introduced? One example of a weakness that could be introduced is the need to use Password Authentication Protocol (PAP) for remote access. (PAP uses a password in the clear).

- Are there mitigations for weaknesses? What are the processes that are in place to avoid the issues mentioned here? Are there other things that can be done?

Guidelines for Analyzing the Authentication Requirements for Communications with ISPs and Mobile Carriers

To provide access using mobile devices such as telephones and PDAs, you might need to use special Microsoft servers such as Microsoft Mobile Information Server and Microsoft Internet Authentication Server. These computers might need to authenticate with an ISP or with a carrier server or device (and you will want the carrier's device to authenticate with your server). Authentication is between computers or between computing devices, and this is different than analyzing authentication requirements between users and computers. You will need to work with the ISP to find the most secure authentication solution. Possibilities include:

- IPSec

- SSL

- VPN

> **Tip**   All these choices also include the ability to encrypt all the data between the two computers. Make sure that you explore the compatibility and performance issues that this might introduce.

Guidelines for Analyzing the Authentication Requirements for Mobile and Other Nontraditional Computing Devices

Facilitating mobile communications is the stated business objective of many projects that provide employee and partner access to the organization's data. Your goal should be to ensure that these projects do not provide avenues that can be exploited by those unauthorized to do so. Requiring strong authentication is the first line of defense. To design authentication processes that will protect both the data on these devices as well as the use of these devices to access the organization's data, you must consider the following items:

- Authentication to the device. Many devices do not require authentication. They might offer simple PIN number or password choices. Third-party options might provide stronger authentication.

- Data synchronization. Devices might provide the ability to synchronize directly to a local PC. Synchronization over a LAN or remote connection is possible.

- Authentication to networks via the device. Many devices include built-in processes for creating a wireless or wired network connection.

You must also investigate each device to determine its capabilities and needs. For example, most cellular voice-only phones do not provide device authentication. If you have physical possession of the phone, you can use it to make a call. Other cellular phones, many with limited data capabilities, do provide simple authentication schemes such as the need to enter PIN numbers before they can be activated. Still other phones, smart phones (phones that can become clients in remote applications or provide capabilities similar to PDAs), and PDA/phone combinations might provide more sophisticated authentication schemes. You can no longer assume that a device holds no data storage, synchronization, or direct-connection capabilities.

Guidelines for Analyzing Authentication to the Device

Even if telephones or PDAs are not used in remote applications, nor approved for use in remote connections to data systems, sensitive data might be stored on them. If the device is lost or stolen, this data might be recovered by someone who would use it for malicious purposes. By default, many of these devices do not require authentication, you simply turn them on. If the device contains a mechanism for authentication, it might be a simple PIN or password system that can be easily broken or circumvented by putting the device into maintenance mode. Collect the following information, and analyze the results when considering authentication to computing devices:

- Does the device offer onboard authentication?

- Is it turned on by default?

- What is the strength of the authentication?

- Is there a way around it?

- Can devices be configured to require authentication?

- Can someone who has physical possession of the device go around the authentication process? Maintenance back doors might allow access to data. Auxiliary memory, such as compact flash cards, might be removed and used in another, unprotected device.

- Are authentication applications available for use with the device?

- What identification and authentication process is in place when synching data between the device and a PC?

If your analysis determines that the authentication techniques provided by the device are not adequate to protect the data that might be stored on it, select a product that can strengthen authentication. You should also propose this product as a requirement that must be used with the device.

Auxiliary Authentication for PDAs

Several software and hardware products are available to strengthen computing devices. Product types include hand signature, picture-based passwords, biometrics, smart cards, tokens, and application software that enables programmers to develop custom solutions. The following types of authentication products might provide a solution for your organization:

- Certicom   Security   Builder   (*http://www.certicom.com/products/security-builder/securitybuilder_feat.html*) provides developers the opportunity to build encryption, digital signature, and key exchange into applications.

- Communication Intelligence Corporation (CIC) makes products such as Pen OP and Sign-On for Pocket PC, which are handwritten signature analysis authentication products, and InkTools, a software developer kit that can be used in developing custom applications. (*http://www.penop.com/products/inktools/*).

- Vasco   (*http://www.vasco.com/documents/literature/pdf/DP_pocketPC.pdf*) makes Digipass, which is a token device that uses one-time passwords. (One-time passwords are passwords that are not reused. They are often implemented by performing some type of calculation based on information only known to the device and a server.)

- Pointsec makes a picture-based authentication system, Pointsec for Pocket PC (*http://www.pointsec.com/solutions/solutions_pocketpc.asp*). To use this product, you create a password by selecting, in a specific order, four pictures from nine displayed on the screen. To log on, you must select each of the four pictures in the correct order. To remember your password, you can make up a story that goes with the pictures—for example, "Girl loves man and dog."

- BioHub is a fingerprint authentication device that fits into a CompactFlash (CF) card slot in a Pocket PC. It compares a live fingerprint with a fingerprint template stored in the Pocket PC.

- HP makes a Pocket PC with a built-in fingerprint reader (*http://h10010.www1.hp.com/wwpc/us/en/sm/WF05a/215348-64929-215381-314903-f44-322916.html*).

Other sources of authentication products for Pocket PC can be found on the Windows Mobile page of the Microsoft Web site at *http://www.microsoft.com/windowsmobile/resources/whitepapers/security.mspx#authentication*.

Guidelines for Analyzing the Network and Remote Authentication Requirement for Mobile Devices

Additional authentication requirements are necessary when mobile devices connect to networks. The way in which they authenticate might depend on the type of connection and communication protocols used. Many devices can connect in a number of ways. For example, wired network interface cards and wireless cards can be used to connect PDAs to LANs. PDAs might have built-in wireless connectivity. Phones, Pocket PC phones, and smart phones use various traditional and modern telephony communication protocols. In addition to authenticating the initial access, these protocols might also be able provide data synchronization and they might require additional authentication for connections to internal applications.

Products You Might Need to Provide Secure Client Access

The authentication protocols available for use by these devices might depend on the communication protocol, the data source that must be accessed, and the devices that must be used for connectivity. Thus, a Pocket PC might use Microsoft SQL Server Remote Data Access (RDA) to access data in a SQL Server database. RDA uses authentication and encryption via Microsoft Internet Information Services (IIS), including anonymous, basic, and SSL. Thus, a third-party application—such as ScoutIT from Aether—might be used as an intermediary between devices and Microsoft Active Directory. These products enforce the desired authentication and security levels for each user by storing information in a management database. Other similar products are available from Computer Associates and XcelleNet.

Access over the Internet might use built-in capabilities. Pocket Internet Explorer, for example, supports NTLM and SSL. Remote access can also be provided by the VPN client. Synchronization over the Internet can be provided via Microsoft Server Active Synch and uses enterprise authentication credentials.

Mobile phones and pagers might use Wireless Authentication Protocol (WAP) and the Wireless Transport Layer Security (WTLS) protocol, which provides encryption of all data, including authentication data.

An introduction into the security and management requirements of mobile devices is available in the article, "Managing Mobile Devices in the Enterprise," on the TechNet page of the Microsoft Web site at (*http://www.microsoft.com/technet /treeview/default.asp?url=/technet/itsolutions/mobile/evaluate/mblmange.asp*).

Analyze the following information with regard to authentication and mobile devices:

- **Analyze the communication protocols used by the devices.**   Determine what authentication protocols can be supported by these protocols.

- **Analyze device authentication options.**   Determine whether the device can use authentication protocols or services already in use in your organization, such NTLM, SSL, or MS-CHAP.

- **Analyze password options.**   Devices might be restricted to 4-digit or 7-digit options. Determine whether this meets current password policy requirements. Determine whether this will require a change in the domain password policy. Determine whether there is a way to accommodate reduced password length without weakening the password policy.

- **Analyze products that improve authentication to devices themselves.**   These products can strengthen network authentication by preventing access to the device that uses a different authentication scheme to access the network. Some of these authentication products, if tampered with, destroy data that is resident on the mobile device. Determine what problems this might cause and whether this is an acceptable or preferred security solution for the organization.

■ **Analyze intermediary needs for authentication.** Intermediary needs are the requirements related to the equipment of ISPs and mobile communication carriers. The mobile device might be required to authenticate to the ISP or carrier's device, and the carrier's device might need to authenticate to computers on the organization's network. Figure 10-1 shows an example of this. In the figure, mobile devices connect to the carrier's network. A Microsoft Mobile Information Server Carrier Edition computer on the carrier's network connects to a Microsoft Mobile Information Server (MMIS) on the organization's network.

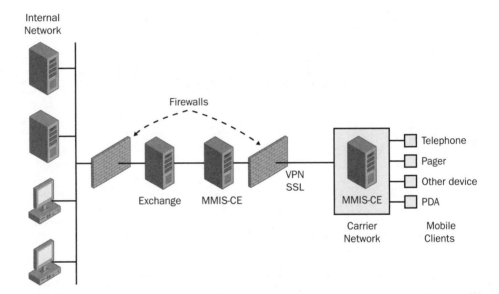

Figure 10-1 An MMIS and MMIS Carrier Edition connection

■ **Analyze the requirements of intermediary systems.** Determine how the requirements of intermediary systems will affect authentication between intermediary systems, between devices and intermediary systems, and between intermediary systems and systems on the organizations network. Figure 10-1 shows the path between the mobile device and the points along which there might be or should be authentication.

■ **Analyze the weaknesses inherent in permitting communications across public networks or networks not under the direct control of the organization.** Determine where authentication can strengthen the security posture of these communications and mitigate the effect of potential weaknesses.

■ **Analyze products that might be used to resolve communication issues with diverse carriers.**   For example, you could analyze MobileSys Globility Access (*www.mobilesys.com/products/globility/index.html*), which is a private global wireless data network that provides access to Short Message System (SMS) and wireless carriers around the world. Figure 10-2 shows where this product would fit in the communications schema. Determine the authentication issues and whether using such a product will strengthen or weaken authentication.

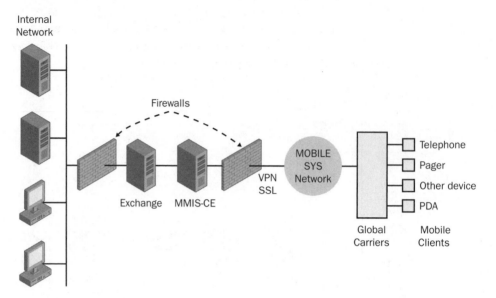

Figure 10-2   An example of a third-party connection configuration

Note   Microsoft Mobile Information Server is a mobile application server. It can be used to provide mobile employees, customers, and partners with access to data from a range of wireless devices. MMIS provides secure authenticated access to the Windows network. MMIS works with the WAP gateway at the wireless carrier. There is a Mobile Information Server Carrier Edition, but MMIS works with other carrier-side gateways. MMIS adds a new tab, Wireless Mobility, to the Active Directory Users and Computers user Account properties. On this tab, you can authorize wireless connectivity and synchronization.

Guidelines for Analyzing Authentication Required for Mobile Employees

Mobile employees must also have access to authentication technologies that will prove their identity and employment status to multiple organization locations. Many employees are required to travel from location to location and require access to network resources and location facilities. Organizations cannot rely on simple recognition of employees by receptionists and guards; they must require stronger methods of authentication.

Traditional employee badges, even picture-ID badges, are not sufficient, as they can be easily counterfeited. The use of traditional employee badges cannot be relied on, as they do not have technical enforcement options. It is often quite easy to use social engineering techniques to escape the badge requirement. In addition, it is difficult to communicate information such as employment status and authorization using traditional badges.

One possible solution is the use of smart badges. Smart badges are devices that include a picture ID, employment numbers, physical device access codes, and other digital mechanisms on a smart card. Smart badges provide traditional recognition and documentation, but they also incorporate data that can solve the problems inherent in traditional badges. Used as a smart card, they can provide network authentication; used a physical access device, they can be swiped to automatically open doors, lockers, and other areas. In addition, when smart cards are used to provide digital authentication, they can provide tracking information on employee activity. A record of locations and secured areas visited, as well as network activity, can be tracked. When issued to contractors, similar access and tracking can be provided.

You will need to analyze the needs of your organization for such devices and for the systems that produce and read them.

Considerations for Establishing Account and Password Security Requirements

You must thoroughly document account and password options on other directories and management devices that might be required to provide mobile device access. There are two aspects that need to be analyzed:

- Consider what account and password characteristics are available when any client device of any user connects from anywhere.

- Consider the account and password policy requirements dictated by the organization's security policy. These make it more difficult for an account to be compromised. Keep in mind that it's sometimes difficult to provide access and maintain a strong security posture.

 See Also   User account and password options are presented in Chapter 6.

Only by doing this analysis—by analyzing all clients, including mobile device technical requirements and security policy—can you develop a sound, secure client authentication infrastructure. Where technical capabilities inherent in mobile devices or in their connectivity requirements are lacking, you might determine that third-party products or custom development is required to secure access.

Guidelines for Designing a Client Authentication Infrastructure

Designing a client authentication infrastructure requires knowledge of diverse products, communications protocols, and security policy. It also requires strong analytical ability. It might also require the ability to stand firm on security policy and seek alternative solutions to the technical and business constraints inherent in client connectivity.

Follow these guidelines when designing a client authentication infrastructure:

■ **Do not put access above the need to provide secure access.**   Every opening you provide for your users can become a point of attack and result in damage to your network or data theft.

■ **Select products that provide a range of authentication options, including third-party options where appropriate.**   In a heterogeneous network, you might need to provide options beyond the primary authentication protocol used in your network. For example, you might be using MS-CHAPv2 as your remote access standard, but discover that a particular ISP users must use at some location does not provide that option. If the products you have standardized on are not flexible, you might need to authorize the purchase of additional devices.

■ **Seek to improve authentication security with existing devices.**   You should not assume that products are installed with only the most secure authentication choices. The default implementations of authentication, especially for remote access, might allow the use of weak protocols. In addition, previous products used on the network, or used to connect remotely to the network, might have required the use of less secure authentication protocols. Reviewing current authentication and comparing it against the needs of clients on the network can result in an improvement simply by eliminating the need to use older, less secure authentication protocols. It is also true that new authentication protocols and processes, such as the use of EAP and smart cards, can strengthen authentication.

■ **Look for solutions that maintain or provide single sign-on opportunities.**   When single sign-on is available, users have only one account and password to remember and maintain. When users have many passwords to remember and maintain, there is a larger chance that passwords will be written down where they can be stolen.

■ **Design an overall infrastructure, but divide it into areas of design that specify client types.**   For example, divide it into areas such as mobile devices, remote access Windows clients, and so on. Each type of device and each specific client has unique qualities that must be addressed. Rarely will one solution fit all.

■ **When a product must be used, and using it might weaken authentication throughout the network, seek a solution that can overcome this problem. Do not weaken all security when new products are introduced.**   Instead, determine whether authentication can be managed by intermediary devices or applications so that other authentication processes can remain at their level. For example, if PDA users are restricted to a four-digit password, or mobile phone users can use only a four-digit PIN number as authentication, do not reduce the security policy in the domain to a minimum password length of four digits. Instead, you can require PDA users to use a VPN client that does support stronger password requirements or secure tokens, and use the capabilities of Microsoft Mobile Information Server to manage authentication for mobile phone users.

Practice: Designing a Client Authentication Infrastructure

In this practice, you will design a client authentication infrastructure for a fictitious company. Read the scenario and then answer the questions that follow. If you are unable to answer a question, review the lesson materials and try the question again. You can find answers to the questions in the "Questions and Answers" section at the end of the chapter.

Scenario

You are the security designer for Wingtip Toys. You have just joined the company and have been asked to participate in the review committee for the purchase of mobile access services and devices. Wingtip Toys realizes that some employees' only remote access needs are to send and receive e-mail. The sales department is developing a custom application for sales order entry and catalog information retrieval. Your goal is to consider the security implications of possible purchases. Your first goal is to consider authentication.

Review Questions

Answer the following questions.

1. What are the types of clients that might be used in this scenario? Why do you consider these clients?

   _____

   _____

   _____

   _____

2. What information will you need to consider to analyze the authentication requirements of these devices?

   _____

   _____

   _____

   _____

Lesson 2: Designing a Secure Remote Access Strategy for Client Computers

Each remote access attempt can be a desired connection or an attack. Each remote access can expose sensitive data. Each remote access can be crucial to the survival of the organization. You must design a secure remote access strategy that allows and protects authorized connections and blocks attacks. To do so requires more than just meeting the authentication requirements of clients and of the organization's security policy. A secure remote access strategy also includes a wide range of constraints and data-protection specifications. This lesson describes how to design secure access to internal resources by using Microsoft remote access products.

***

After this lesson, you will be able to

- Describe the process for designing a secure remote access strategy for client computers.
- Design remote access policies.
- Design access to internal resources.
- Explain the considerations for designing authentication and accounting for remote network access by using IAS.
- Design an authentication and authorization strategy by using IAS.

Estimated lesson time: 40 minutes

***

The Process: Designing a Secure Remote Access Strategy for Client Computers

To design a comprehensive secure remote access strategy for clients, security designers follow a process that looks like this:

1. *Analyze the authentication requirements of the clients and security policy.* Lesson 1 explained how to do this task.

2. *Design client access to internal resources.* This process includes remote access via dial-up and VPNs across the Internet. Web-based access through an Internet application should be considered and is discussed in Chapter 13.

3. *Design remote access policies.* Remote access policies include the written security policies of the organization and the remote access policies that can be established using Microsoft Remote Access Services and Internet Authentication Service. The design of an organization's security policies is beyond the scope of this book.

4. *Design an authentication and accounting strategy by using Internet Authentication Services (IAS).*

The rest of this lesson teaches what you need to know to complete steps 2, 3, and 4 in this process.

Guidelines for Designing Client Access to Internal Resources

Designing client access to internal resources is only one part of designing access to internal resources. The later part of the process consists of many activities. An appropriate design might not include all the following processes, but all these actions should be considered:

- Determine the types of access that will be allowed, and design access specific to the users and remote access clients.

- Design infrastructure to support secure remote access.

- Design the use of managed VPN Client Connections.

- Analyze the client authentication infrastructure.

- Develop guidelines for client security, and train users.

- Analyze remote access servers such as RRAS and IAS.

- Analyze the need for Network Access Quarantine Control.

- Design remote access policies to provide secure access and reject unauthorized access.

Many of these processes have been discussed in previous chapters and earlier in this chapter. The client authentication infrastructure is discussed in Lesson 1. Remote access policies are analyzed in the "How to Design Remote Access Policies" section. The use of VPNs, remote access servers, and Network Access Quarantine Control are discussed in Chapter 7 and in the "Considerations for Designing Authentication and Accounting for Remote Network Access Using IAS" section later in this chapter. Chapters 2 and 3 present information about network infrastructure design. This section will discuss the use of managed client connections and securing client connections.

Considerations for Designing Managed Client Configuration

Remote access client connections do not have to be managed. A single compatible client can be manually configured to access a network using a dial-up connection, a VPN server, or both. However, this process is tedious and difficult to maintain. It is also difficult to provide a consistent configuration. If you must manually configure a client, almost all the design decisions remain the same. The difference between manual configuration and using managed client configuration is that with the former you do not have to consider the creation of Connection Manager (CM) profiles, nor do you have to consider securing them or their deployment. However, Connection Manager profiles ensure a consistent user experience and make it easier to configure clients. Use the following information in designing client configuration:

- **Considerations for Connection Manager profiles**   A large number of remote access clients can be deployed by creating Connection Manager (CM) profiles. CM includes:

  - ❑ A client dialer, which resides on the client and ensures approved use of the client-side connection capability while also ensuring a successful connection. The user, for example, can select a phone number and use help. The dialer automatically can create the dial-up connection if a user selects a VPN connection, and it can run custom actions during the different phases of the connection process. A custom dialer (the profile) can be created by the network administrator to meet the organization's specifications for dial-up and VPN connections.

  - ❑ The Connection Manager Administration Kit (CMAK), which is used by an administrator to create the profile. The profile is a self-extracting executable that can be provided to a user via a Web site, e-mail, CD-ROM, or other distribution mechanism. When run by the user, the profile creates the preprogrammed connections. A profile can be created for most versions of Windows.

  - ❑ Connection Point Services (CPS), which provides the ability to create, distribute, and update custom phone books. Phone books provide the Point of Presence (POP) entries, telephone numbers, or VPN addresses used to access a dial-up network, the Internet, or a VPN server. When users travel, they have all the required phone numbers needed to access approved connection points or proxies to them. A Phone Book Server, a Windows Server 2003 computer running IIS (including the FTP Publishing service), and an Internet Server Application Programming Interface (ISAPI) extension are used to update clients. Figure 10-3 shows the use of these components. In the figure, a client uses the client dialer to reach a RADIUS proxy and, through it, a RADIUS server on the corporate network. The client also queries the Phone Book Server for an updated list of numbers.

- **Client configuration**   Considerations include:

  - ❑ Authentication selection for the client must match at least one of the approved authentication configurations on the server.

  - ❑ Encryption strength selection on the client must match at least one of the approved encryption strength settings on the server.

  - ❑ VPN protocol selection on the client must match at least one VPN protocol selected on the server.

  - ❑ If certificates are required, a valid certificate of the right type must be installed on the client computer or smart card.

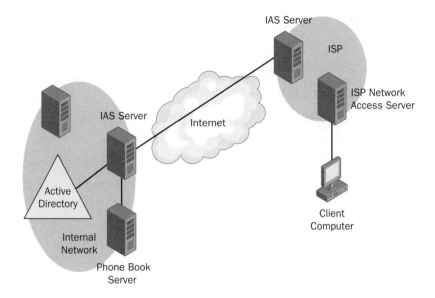

Figure 10-3   Managed connections

- **Client routing**   Considerations include:

  ❑ At VPN connection time, a Windows-based VPN client creates a new default route for the connection.

  ❑ Because the VPN route is the default route, the IP address of the tunnel server can still be reached, other routes configured on the client can still be used, and all other Internet locations are not reachable as long as the client is connected to the VPN server.

  ❑ If the client needs simultaneous access directly to the Internet (not through your intranet) and to your VPN-accessible intranet (which is not a particularly good security arrangement), you might need to configure split-tunneling. Split-tunneling is a technique used to provide client access to more than one network even when a VPN connection is present.

  ❑ A VPN client can be prevented from creating a new default route (one in which the client will be able to directly access the Internet and your intranet) in the Advanced TCP/IP Properties dialog box for the VPN connection. Figure 10-4 is a screen shot of this page with the Determining Routing For VPN Remote Access Clients check box deselected. If this setting is disabled, a route is created—it just does not become the default route. User selection of this element can be prevented by configuring Group Policy.

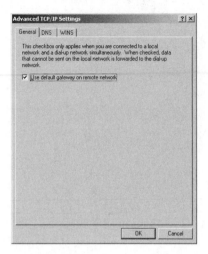

Figure 10-4   Allowing Internet access

Guidelines for Client Security

Follow these guidelines for client security:

- Educate users on remote access security and the necessity of using antivirus products, keeping antivirus products up to date, using a personal firewall, not attempting to change security configuration, not sharing company-provided computers, and establishing password-controlled access to their home computers.

- Use Network Access Quarantine Control to enforce as many of these restrictions as possible.

- Deploy smart cards for authentication wherever possible.

- Configure or upgrade Windows clients to use only MS-CHAPv2 or EAP authentication types.

Guidelines for Using Connection Manager Profiles and Phone Books

Follow these guidelines:

- If Connection Manager phone books are used and File Transfer Protocol (FTP) is used to update the phone book files on the phone book server, be sure that the FTP services are stopped or disabled after the phone book is transferred and that they are started only when new changes must be transferred.

- Do not allow anonymous FTP access to the Phone Book Server (PBS).

- Protect administrative connections to the PBS server using IPSec.

- Protect Connection Manager profiles and the distribution process. This is important because:

  ❑ Profiles contain scripts and access data that might provide an attacker with valuable information. Although connections are password protected, providing an attacker with all the server configuration information and access numbers reduces the amount of work the attacker has to do to successfully attack your network.

  ❑ If an unauthorized individual is allowed to access and modify profiles, that person can mount a denial of service attack (by providing incorrect information in profiles that later get distributed to users and that don't work), weaken VPN communications (by configuring less secure options, such as weaker encryption strength), and access a lot of information that might provide ideas and data for other types of attacks.

How to Design Remote Access Policies

In the organization's security policy, remote access policies determine the who, what, when, and where of remote access. When remote access connections use Microsoft Routing and Remote Access Services (RRAS) and IAS, your job as a security designer is to translate these policies into remote access policies—ordered sets of rules that determine whether a connection can proceed (is authorized) or whether it is rejected. Remote access policies specify the when and how of remote access connections to these services.

Remote access policies are composed of the following:

- One or more conditions, such as time of day, day of week, connection type, or Windows group membership.

- Remote access permissions, either Deny or Allow.

- A profile that specifies constraints that apply to an authorized connection.

To design remote access policies, you must first understand how they work, the constraints of the dial-in properties page, how to use remote access policies to control remote access, the conditions used by RRAS and IAS, and profile properties.

How Remote Access Policies Work

To design remote access policies, you must understand how they work. Connection attempts can be made via wired or wireless connections. They can arrive via the Internet, the WAN, a dial-up connection, and a direct connection to a carrier or ISP. When the connection reaches the remote access server, remote access policies are processed to determine whether the connection should be accepted or rejected. The decision is based on a combination of remote access policy conditions, permission, and profile constraints as well as the settings on the user account dial-in property page. An exception to this process is new in Windows Server 2003 when IAS is used as the authentication provider. The exception hinges on the value of the remote access policy profile. The advanced page attribute Ignore-User-Dialin-Properties is set to false (the default) or true, as indicated in Figure 10-5. This attribute is not evaluated until the connection attempt has met the remote access policy conditions; however, it can make a significant difference in policy processing. Ignoring user account settings is important if a setting there might interfere with the connection (for example, if a wireless access point cannot be dialed like a phone line, yet a user's account setting can specify that call-back should be used). This attribute can also be used to configure remote access policies for authentication switches, another component that cannot be "dialed." Two procedures that explain remote access policy evaluation follow.

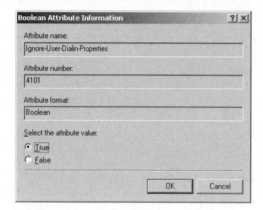

Figure 10-5   Ignore-User-Dialin-Properties

User Account Dial-in and Remote Access Policies Are Evaluated   When Windows authentication is selected (that is, when no IAS server is used) or if the IAS Ignore-User-Dialin-Properties attribute is set to false, the following process is used to evaluate a connection attempt.

The dial-in property page allows specification by the user (the page is set to Allow or Deny) or by Remote Access Policy. If the dial-in property page specifies access by user (as shown in Figure 10-6), the following events occur:

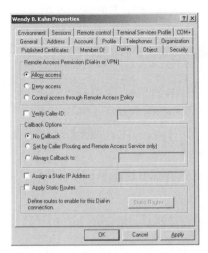

Figure 10-6   Specifying user account access

Exam Tip   If all remote access policy conditions are not met by the connection attempt, the next remote access policy is evaluated. Remote access policy profile constraints and user account dial-in properties are evaluated only if remote access policy conditions are met.

1. The connection attempt is compared to the first remote access policy conditions. By default, a remote access policy permits connection at any time of day or on any day of the week. (If no remote access policies exist, the connection is rejected.)

2. If the connection attempt meets the remote access policy conditions, the value of the Ignore-User-Dialin-Properties attribute (which is set in the profile of the policy) is checked. For this procedure, it is set to false.

   a. The remote access setting of the user account is checked.

   b. If the user account setting is Grant, then continue. The remote access policy profile connection settings and the user account settings are applied. If the connection settings do not match, the connection is rejected; if they match, the connection is accepted.

   c. If the user account setting is Deny, the connection attempt is rejected.

   d. If the user account setting is neither Allow nor Deny, it is set to Control Access Through Remote Access Policy. The remote access permission setting of the policy is checked. If it is Deny, the connection is rejected. If it is allow, then continue.

    e. If the connection settings in the user account and the policy profile all match, the connection is allowed. The user account dial-in property page and the remote access policy profile constraints are evaluated.

    f. If the connection settings in the user account and the policy profile do not all match, the connection is rejected.

3. If the connection attempt does not match all of a remote access policy's conditions, the next remote access policy is evaluated.

4. If no remote access policy matches the connection attempt, the connection attempt is rejected.

5. If the connection is allowed, it is constrained by the profile setting in the remote access policy.

User Account Dial-in Is Not Evaluated   When RADIUS authentication is selected (an IAS server will be used) and the IAS Ignore-User-Dialin-Properties attribute is set to true, the following process is used to evaluate a connection attempt.

1. The connection attempt is compared to the first remote access policy's conditions. By default, a remote access policy permits connection at any time of day or on any day of the week. (If no remote access policies exist, the connection is rejected.)

2. If the connection attempt meets the remote access policy conditions, the value of the Ignore-User-Dialin-Properties attribute (which is set in the profile of the policy) is checked. For this procedure, it is set to true.

    a. The remote access policy permission is checked. If it is Allow, then continue. If it is Deny, the connection is rejected.

    b. The remote access policy profile constraints are evaluated. If the connection settings in the policy profile all match, the connection is allowed. If the connection settings in the policy profile do not all match, the connection is rejected.

3. If the connection attempt does not match all of a remote access policy's conditions, the next remote access policy is evaluated.

4. If no remote access policy matches the connection attempt, then the connection attempt is rejected.

5. If the connection is allowed, then it is constrained by the profile setting in the remote access policy.

Constraints of the Dial-in Properties Page

After you understand how remote access policies work, you need to gain knowledge of the constraints that they can place on remote access connections in order to design remote access policies that meet your security policy. With the exception noted earlier, each remote access connection is subject to two sets of constraints: those on the user account dial-in property page, and those in the remote access policy. You will use your knowledge of both to design remote access policies.

Dial-in account properties are the first barrier to remote access. By default, user accounts are denied access, as shown in Figure 10-6. The dial-in properties page offers the following constraints:

- *Allow*. The connection is permitted. (Remote access policy conditions and restrictions can still terminate the connection.)

- *Deny*. Unless user dial-in properties are ignored, the connection attempt will always be refused.

- *Control Access Through Remote Access Policy*. This choice is available only for stand-alone Windows 2000 and Windows Server 2003 remote access servers and Windows 2000 and later native and functional mode domains. (The Administrator and Guess accounts on stand-alone servers and on Windows 2000 and later native and functional mode domains are set to Control Access Through Remote Access Policy by default. New accounts will also be set this way. In Windows 2000 Mixed functional mode domains, the default is Deny access.

- *Verify Caller ID*. If used, this constraint checks to see that caller is calling from a phone number entered in this location. If some number that is not on the list is used, the connection is terminated. Caller ID must be supported by the caller, the phone system between the caller and the remote access server, and between the remote access server and the call answering equipment. The call answering equipment must be able to provide the remote access server with the number, and the remote access server must also have the correct driver to pass the information to the Routing and Remote Access Service. If this setting is configured but these specifications are not met, the connection is denied.

- *Allow Callback*. The server will disconnect and dial the number entered in the property pages or the number indicated by the client if the property pages are configured to allow this. The length of the number allowed is longer in Windows Server 2003—up to 128 characters, as opposed to 48 in Windows 2000.

- *Assign a Static IP*. A static IP address can be entered in the property pages and used by the client when accessing resources on the network.

- *Apply Static Routes*. The static routes defined in the property pages are added to the routing table of the RRAS server when the connection is made by this user.

Note   Windows Server 2003 computers also have dial-in property pages in their computer accounts. Computers can be authorized to remotely connect and be authenticated as if they were users. For example, an 802.1x Ethernet client uses EAP-TLS and an installed computer certificate to authenticate to an authenticating Ethernet switch. For more information about 802.1x and wireless connections to Windows Server 2003 networks, see Chapter 13.

Exam Tip   User accounts in a Windows NT 4.0 domain or a Windows Mixed domain functional mode domain can be configured only for the Allow, Deny, and Allow Callback options.

When to Ignore Dial-In Properties

Sometimes you'll have a need to ignore dial-in properties. You might need to do this because clients—such as those using an authenticating switch or wireless connection—might not understand some parts of the dial-in user account properties and therefore would disconnect a legitimate session. You can configure a remote access policy to ignore the dial-in properties by configuring the Ignore-User-Dialin-Properties attribute of the Advanced tab of the profile settings of the remote access policy. You can even choose to apply this condition for some types of connections and not for others. By setting the attribute to false, you allow dial-in to be used; by setting the attribute to true, you prevent dial-in from being used. A good example of such a use is to create two remote access policies—one for wired connections, and one for wireless. If authorized remote access user Kevin F. Browne uses a wired connection, the properties of his user account dial-in page are considered. When he uses a wireless connection, they are not.

How to Use Remote Access Policies to Control Remote Access

To examine the remote access policies, open the Routing and Remote Access console and expand the RRAS server container. Select the Remote Access Policy to view in the detail pane the policies that have been configured. Figure 10-7 shows the two default policies: one specifies Microsoft-specific access, and the other covers all attempts by defining a schedule of 7 days a week/24 hours a day. To review any remote access policy, double-click the policy in the details pane. Figure 10-8 shows the property pages of the default policy. To configure access, you create new remote access policies. When a connection is attempted, remote access policy conditions, remote access profiles, and user account dial-in properties are evaluated. Many remote access policies are used only by IAS.

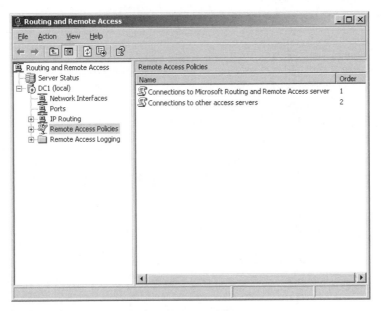

Figure 10-7   Viewing remote access policies

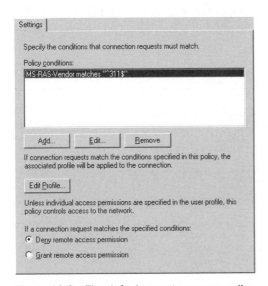

Figure 10-8   The default remote access policy

Conditions Used by RRAS and IAS

Table 10-1 lists and describes the conditions that can be set in a remote access policy used when Windows authentication is selected and therefore the remote access policies are evaluated by the RRAS server.

Table 10-1   Conditions Used by RRAS

Attribute	Description
Authentication Type	The authentication type being used—for example: CHAP, EAP, MS-CHAP, or MS_CHAPv2.
Called Station ID	The phone number of the network access server (NAS) or Routing and Remote Access server (must support passing the called ID).
Calling Station ID	The phone number from which the call was placed.
Day and Time Restrictions	The day of the week and the time of day of the connection attempt. The day and time used are those of the authorizing server (the RRAS server).
Tunnel Type	The tunnel type created by the requesting client. Possible tunnel types include: Point-to-Point Tunneling Protocol (PPTP) and Layer Two Tunneling Protocol (L2TP). This attribute can be used to specify profile settings, such as authentication method or encryption strength.
Windows Groups	The name of the group to which the user or computer account is attempting to connect.

Table 10-2 lists and describes the remote access policy conditions that can be configured in a remote access policy that is evaluated when RADIUS is chosen as the authentication provider (by IAS).

Table 10-2   Conditions Used by IAS

Attribute	Description
Authentication Type	The authentication type being used—for example: CHAP, EAP, MS-CHAP, or MS_CHAPv2.
Called Station ID	The phone number of the network access server (NAS) or Routing and Remote Access serer (must support passing the called ID).
Calling Station ID	The phone number from which the call was placed.
Client Friendly Name	The name of the RADIUS client requesting authentication. This is configured in the Friendly Name on the Setting tab in properties of the RADIUS client in IAS. It is a character string (used by IAS).
Client IP Address	The IP address of the RADIUS client or the RADIUS proxy.
Client Vendor	The vendor of the NAS requesting authentication.
Day and Time Restrictions	The day of the week and the time of day of the connection attempt. The day and time used are those of the authorizing server (the RRAS or IAS server).
Framed Protocol	The type of framing of the incoming packets—for example: PPP, SLIP, Frame Relay, and x.25 (used by IAS server).
NAS Identifier	The name of the NAS. It is a character string (used by IAS).

Table 10-2   Conditions Used by IAS

Attribute	Description
NAS IP Address	The IP address of the NAS (the RADIUS client) that sent the message.
NAS Port Type	The type of media used by the access client; for example, you might choose aysnch (for analog phone lines), ISDN, tunnels, virtual (for VPNs), or IEEE 802.11 wireless or Ethernet (for Ethernet connections such as Ethernet switches).
Service Type	The type of service that is requested—for example: framed (such as a PPP connection) or login (such as a Telnet connection).
Tunnel Type	The tunnel type created by the requesting client—for example, PPTP or L2TP. It can be used to specify profile settings, such as authentication method or encryption strengths.
Windows Groups	The name of the group to which the user or computer account is attempting to connect.

Profile Properties

If all conditions of a remote access policy are met, an Allow or Deny permission is processed, either by using the user account property or the remote access policy. If the permission is Allow, the profile of the remote access policy is evaluated. The profile can further restrict the connection. Its characteristics can also restrict an authorized connection. Profiles parameters are listed in Table 10-3.

Table 10-3   Profile Properties

Property	Description
Dial-in constraints	This page is where dial-in constraints are set. The constraints included are: idle time, connection limit, days and times, specified number, and specific media (async, ISDN, virtual, or 802.11).
IP	This page specifies choices for client IP address assignment and is where IP packet filters can be defined if desired. There are four possibilities for IP address assignment. The choices are: the access server must supply the address; the client can request an IP address; address assignment is specified by the access server; or a static IP address is listed in the profile. If there is an IP address in the user account, it overrides the profile setting. IP packet filters are defined on this page and apply to remote connection traffic. Both output, which is the traffic to the client, and input, which is the traffic from client packet filters can be written. IP packet filters are not applied to dial-on-demand connections.
Multilink	This page is used to set the number of ports a multilink connection can use and specifies Bandwidth Allocation Protocol (BAP) policies. (The RRAS server must have multilink and BAP enabled for these to work.)

Table 10-3   Profile Properties

Property	Description
Authentication	This page enables authentication types that can be used. It also enables or denies whether users are allowed to change their passwords by using MS-CHAP. (This setting must match the settings for RRAS.)
Encryption	This page defines the encryption choices that can be negotiated between the client and the server. Choices are: No Encryption, Basic (dial-up and PPTP connections will use 40-bit key MPPE; L2TP/IPSec connections will use 56-bit DES), Strong (PPTP connections will use56-bit MPPE; L2TP/IPSec connections will use 56-DES), and Strongest (PPTP connections will use 128-bit MPPE; L2TP/IPSec connections will use 3DES).
Advanced	This page provides the ability to define RADIUS attributes that will be used in the remote access policy profile. Attributes can be used to constrain an authorized connection between the RADIUS server and the RADIUS client.

To Design Remote Access Policies

Design remote access policies based on user needs and on the organization's remote access policy. Follow these steps to design remote access policies:

1. Divide remote access policy needs into three groups: users, computers that will authenticate to switches or use wireless connections, and RADIUS clients. RADIUS clients can be RRAS servers or other Network Access Servers (NAS).

2. Follow these steps for users:

   a. Determine whether access should be allowed or denied based on user Dial-in properties or based on routing and remote access policies.

   b. Design a remote access policy that sets conditions that meet security policy. If the authorization decision will be based on user Dial-in properties, configure the user account dial-in property page to either Allow or Deny connections. If the authorization decision is based on the remote access policy, configure user accounts to Control Access Through Remote Access Policy. Use the Windows group membership of the user and the remote access policy group membership condition to control Deny and Allow access settings.

   c. Create a profile for each remote access policy to meet policy constraints or set constraints on an authorized connection.

3. Follow these steps for computers:

   a. Configure computer accounts by placing them in groups and setting each computer's account dial-in property to grant access based on the remote access policy. Ensure that switches are configured to use EAP and IAS as the RADIUS server.

    b. Use the computer group as a condition in the policy.

    c. Set the access method to Ethernet or wireless.

    d. Configure authentication—for example, provide computers with certificates if EAP-TLS is the preferred authentication choice.

    e. Delete the default policies on the RRAS or IAS server.

4. Follow these steps for RADIUS clients:

    a. Preconditions: Ensure that RRAS or NAS is added as a RADIUS client and that RRAS or NAS is configured.

    b. Set conditions. Ensure that client-vendor matches the client configured and that the NAS port defined is the one used by the vendor. (For example, choose asynchronous if a modem is used.)

    c. Set profile settings. These might be vendor specific and are set on the Advanced page of the profile.

    d. Delete default policies.

Example: Creating a Remote Access Policy

This example provides a fictitious scenario and an example solution.

Scenario

You are a new security designer. Your boss asks you to provide access to the sales and marketing department employees from anywhere during normal business hours plus or minus two hours, but only from their homes at other times. The employees must use a VPN to connect, and they must use the strongest encryption setting. Normal business hours are 9 a.m. to 5 p.m. Monday through Friday. All sales and marketing employees are members of the SAandMA Windows group.

Solution

Create two remote access policies: one based on normal business hours, and the other based on the other hours of the week. The user dial-in properties are set to provide access based on remote access policies, and a home phone number is entered in the Verify text box. An example user dial-in property page from a remote access policy is displayed in Figure 10-9. The policy specifications are listed in Table 10-4.

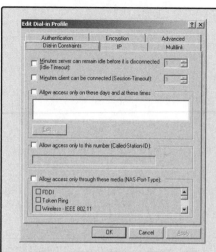

Figure 10-9   User dial-in properties

Table 10-4   Remote Access Policy 1

Policy Part	Configuration
Remote Access Policy 1 Name	SAandMA Daytime
Conditions	Time-of-day constraints: 7 a.m. to 7 p.m., Monday through Friday.
Windows Groups	SAandMA
Permissions	Grant remote access permission.
Profile	Dial-in Constraints: Select the Allow Access Only Through These Media (NAS-Port-Types) check box. Then, check the Virtual (VPN) check box. (See Figure 10-10.)
	Encryption: Deselect all boxes except Strongest Encryption (MPPE 128 bit). (See Figure 10-11.)
	Advanced page: Add the Ignore-User-Dialin-Properties attribute (shown in Figure 10-12), and set it to true (which will ignore the requirement to verify the user's phone number).
	User account Dial-in Properties: Select the option button Control Access Through Remote Access Policy.

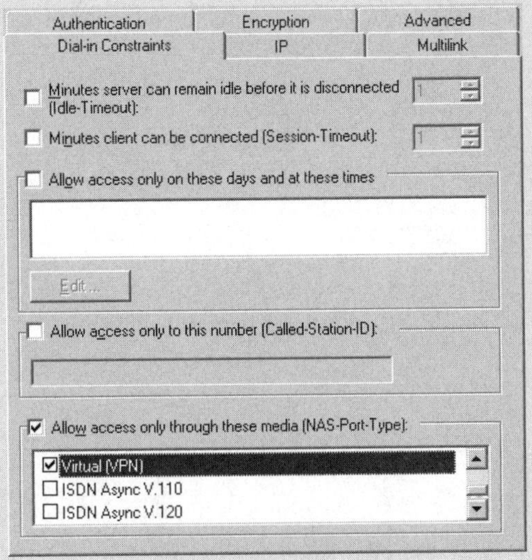

Figure 10-10   Restricting connections to VPN

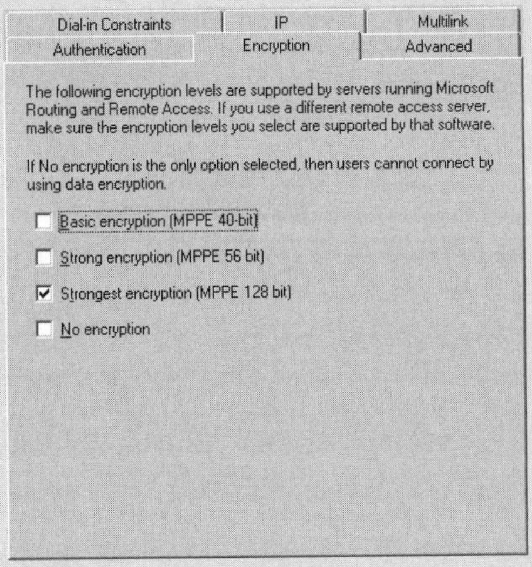

Figure 10-11   Requiring strongest encryption

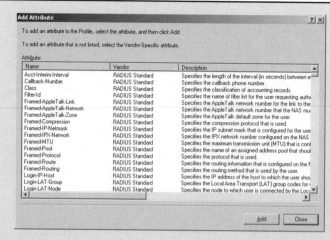

Figure 10-12   Selecting an attribute (The property page for this attribute is displayed in Figure 10-5.)

Policy specifications for policy 2 are listed in Table 10-5.

Table 10-5   Remote Access Policy 2

Policy Part	Configuration
Remote Access Policy 2 Name	SAandMA Anytime
Conditions	Time-of-day constraints: 7 days a week/24 hours a day is OK.
Windows Groups	SAandMA
Permissions	Grant remote access permission.
Profile	Dial-in Constraints: Select the Allow Access Only Through These Media (NAS-Port-Types) check box, and then select the Virtual (VPN) check box.
	Encryption: Deselect all check boxes except Strongest Encryption (MPPE 128 bit).
	Advanced page: The Ignore-User-Dialin-Properties attribute is set to False or not configured. (The requirement to verify the user's phone number will be evaluated.)
	User account Dial-in Properties: Set these properties to Control Access Through Remote Access Policy.

Considerations for Designing Authentication and Accounting for Remote Network Access Using IAS

This section explains what the Internet Authentication Service (IAS) is, describes how to design remote network access by using IAS, and then provides considerations for RADIUS configuration, network locations, and Network Access Quarantine Control.

What Is IAS?

IAS is a Microsoft implementation of RADIUS. RADIUS is an IETF standard for managing remote access to networks. IAS can be used for many purposes, including:

- Providing centralized authentication, authorization, and accounting for remote access connections.

- Allowing one remote access server or RADIUS server to provide centralized authentication or accounting for remote access connections, while allowing another remote access computer or RADIUS server to provide the service not provided by the first. (For example, a RADIUS server at an ISP can provide authentication, while a RADIUS server on the organization's network can provide accounting.)

- Supporting 802.1x authentication for wireless connections and authenticating switches.

- Serving as a RADIUS proxy and directing connection requests to RADIUS servers.

- Providing Network Access Quarantine Control.

How to Design Remote Network Access Using IAS

To design remote network access using IAS:

1. Determine whether IAS is really necessary. If simple remote access connections are all that is required and a single RRAS server is all that is necessary, IAS should not be configured.

2. Determine whether IAS is needed as a RADIUS server or as a RADIUS proxy.

3. Determine whether IAS will be the authentication, authorization, and accounting provider or whether it will provide only some of these functions.

4. Consider IAS configuration and network location.

5. Consider Network Access Quarantine Control.

6. Design remote access policies.

Considerations for RADIUS Configuration and Network Locations

When RADIUS is used, the VPN client establishes a connection to the VPN server, but the VPN server acts as a RADIUS client and uses the RADIUS server to authenticate and authorize the client. Figure 10-13 shows this process.

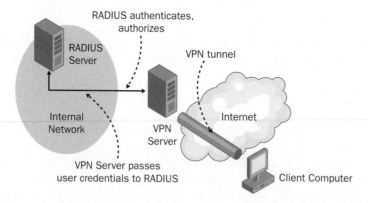

Figure 10-13   RADIUS provides central authentication, authorization, and accounting for VPN connections

Consider the following points when designing RADIUS authentication:

- When RADIUS is used, remote access policies on the RADIUS server dictate authorization policy.

- Active Directory can be used by the RADIUS server as its account database. The RADIUS server must be able to communicate with Active Directory.

- The VPN server must be able to communicate with the RADIUS server.

- The VPN server passes user credentials to the RADIUS server. This data is encrypted using the RADIUS shared secret. This shared secret must be configured on both the VPN server and the RADIUS server.

- RADIUS can also provide proxy services to other RADIUS servers. Many organizations use ISP-based RADIUS servers to forward authentication requests from an organization's mobile users to the organization's RADIUS servers.

In addition, consider the following new Windows Server 2003 IAS options:

- Supports a RADIUS proxy. A RADIUS proxy forwards or routes messages between access servers and other IAS servers.

- Allows network authentication and authorization to be mapped by the IAS proxy to different computers. Authentication can be directed to an external RADIUS server (a non-Windows account database can be used), and authorization can be directed by remote access policies.

- Supports 802.1x wired and wireless connections and authenticating switches.

- Supports Protected Extensible Authentication Protocol (PEAP) for 802.11 wired and wireless clients. PEAP uses Transport Layer Security (TLS) for end-to-end communication.

- Provides for enhanced EAP configuration using remote access policies. Windows 2000 allowed only a single EAP type. Windows Server 2003 remote access policies support several.

- Supports ignoring user dial-in properties. (User dial-in properties might modify some setting that is contrary to policy. To ensure full control of settings resides with Remote Access policy, use this setting.)

- Supports configuring RADIUS clients by IP address range.

- Supports computer authentication, and therefore supports wireless or authentication-switch access clients.

- Supports user certificate purpose-checking. Certificate types are determined by the certificate Enhanced Key Usage (EKU) extension.

- Supports user authentication–based remote access policies.

The RADIUS server can be a third-party RADIUS server, or it can be implemented using Windows Server 2003 IAS. Several options are available for the use of the RADIUS server. Figures 10-14, 10-15, and 10-16 show these options.

Figure 10-14 shows a simple IAS/RRAS design.

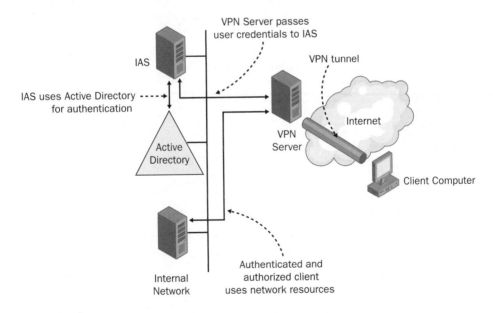

Figure 10-14   A simple IAS design

Figure 10-15 shows the integration of an ISP's remote access infrastructure. The ISP's access server sends connection requests to an IAS proxy, which forwards the connection to an IAS server on the Wingtip Toys network.

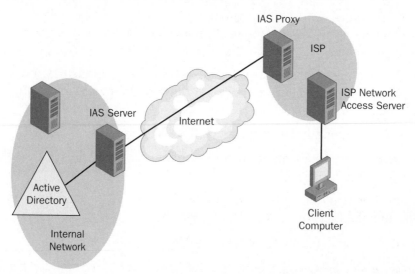

Figure 10-15 IAS and ISPs

Figure 10-16 shows how IAS can be used as a RADIUS proxy with multiple forests. Remote access requests are received by an IAS proxy. The domain name portion of the user name is used to determine which IAS server to send the request to. The figure represents the configuration for Humongous Insurance, which has a second forest for its Contoso Research division. The IAS proxy is configured to send requests from employees of Humongous Insurance to an IAS server in the Humongous Insurance forest and from employees of Contoso Research to an IAS server in the Contoso forest.

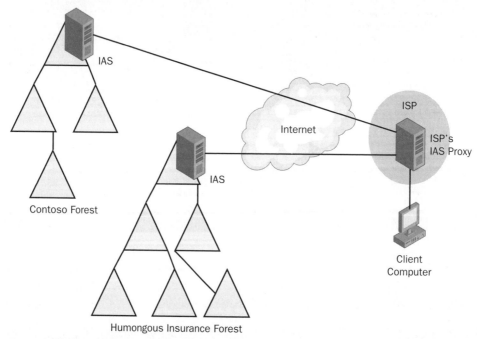

Figure 10-16 IAS and multiple forests

> **See Also**   Some IAS options are used to secure and support wireless connectivity. These options are discussed in Chapter 12.

Network Access Quarantine Control Considerations

Network Access Quarantine Control is a new feature of Windows Server 2003 that can prevent access to a private network until the configuration of a remote computer has been validated. Validation is performed by comparing the remote computer against a list of required attributes provided in a script. The script is created by network administrators in compliance with a security policy. For example, administrators might want to ensure that clients have the latest service packs and hotfixes or up-to-date antivirus software before they connect to the corporate network. The process works like this:

1. A remote access computer requests a connection.

2. The user is authenticated.

3. The remote computer is assigned an IP address.

4. The connection is placed in quarantine mode, which limits network access by using IP filters.

5. The provided script is run on the RAS client computer.

6. After the script completes the *notifier* component on the RAS client, it notifies the *listener* component on the remote access server that the RAS client either met the quarantine policy or failed to meet it. If the client fails the policy check or the notifier does not respond within a predetermined period of time, the client will be disconnected. If the client passes the check, the quarantine IP filter will be removed.

Figure 10-17 shows the network components. The client in the figure can be Windows XP, Windows Server 2003, Windows 2000, Windows Millennium Edition, or Windows 98 Second Edition.

RADIUS provides central authentication, authorization, and accounting for the VPN. In Figure 10-17, note the following required components:

- A remote client that has been provided with a Connection Manager profile created with the Windows Server 2003 Connection Manager Administration Kit. The profile contains a network policy compliance script and a notifier component.

- A remote access server running Windows Server 2003 and the quarantine notification listener service.

- A RADIUS server running Windows Server 2003 and Internet Authentication Service (IAS) configured with a quarantine remote access policy. The policy specifies two quarantine settings: the IP filter and the quarantine timeout setting.

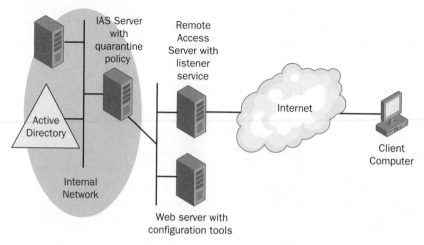

Figure 10-17   Network components for quarantine control

Note   The network access quarantine notifier and listener components (rqc.exe and rqs.exe) as well as a sample quarantine script are provided in the Windows Server 2003 Resource Kit Tools and are downloadable from the Downloads page of the Microsoft Web site at *http://www.microsoft.com/downloads/details.aspx?familyid=9d467a69-57ff-4ae7-96ee-b18c4790cffd&displaylang=en*. Additionally, you can use the Windows Server 2003 SDK to write your own custom components.

Guidelines for Designing an Authentication and Authorization Strategy Using IAS

Follow these guidelines to design authentication and authorization strategies when using IAS:

- When the user account dial-in permission is set to Control Access Through Remote Access Policy, specify connection access as dependent on Windows Groups. Otherwise, all user accounts will be allowed access if they meet the conditions and profile constraints of a remote access policy.

- Always set the user account dial-in permission to Control Access Through Remote Access Policy where possible. This eases the management burden because access can be managed by Windows groups instead of the administrator having to visit each user account page.

- Configure shared password settings:

  - Select the Message Authenticator attribute with the shared secret when PAP, MS-CHAP, and MS-CHAPv2 authentication protocols are allowed. This parameter ensures the entire RADIUS message is encrypted. (When EAP authentication types are used, the Message Authenticator attribute is used by default.)

❑ Create 22-character or longer shared secrets composed of a random sequence of letters, numbers, and punctuation. Change this password often. This will help protect the IAS server and the RADIUS clients from password-cracking attacks.

❑ Configure each RADIUS client, RADIUS server, and RADIUS Proxy pair (each connection path) with a different shared secret.

❑ Do not specify RADIUS clients by address range. If you specify RADIUS clients by address range, you must use the same shared password for all RADIUS clients—and this is not a good security practice.

■ Do not allow PAP authentication. PAP passwords are passed in the clear.

■ Where possible, specify EAP for authentication and use EAP types that require certificates.

■ Configure Network Access Quarantine Control.

■ Specify the use of Terminal Services for remote administration, or specify the use of IPSec between the administrative workstation and the IAS computer.

■ Configure IPSec policies to encrypt RADIUS traffic between RADIUS clients and IAS.

Practice: Designing a Remote Access Policy

In this practice, you will design remote access policies to the specific conditions given to you. Read the scenario and then answer the question that follows. If you are unable to answer the question, review the lesson materials and try the question again. You can find the answer to the question in the "Questions and Answers" section at the end of the chapter.

Important   It is not necessary to configure the policy on an RRAS or IAS server.

Scenario

You must refuse connections if MS-CHAP or PAP is used for authentication. You must grant access if other authentication protocols are used, if the connection is requested during the normal business hours of 9 a.m. to 5 p.m., or if the user is a member of the Dial-Up Windows group and encryption is used. You can assume all user accounts have been configured to Control Access Through Remote Access Policy.

Review Question

Answer the following question.

- What should the remote access policies be? Use Tables 10-6 and 10-7 to indicate your design for remote access policy 1 and 2. If you believe that more than two policies are necessary to meet this scenario's specifications, copy the table to the extra space below or use scratch paper to design the additional policies.

Table 10-6   Remote Access Policy 1

Policy Part	Configuration
Remote Access Policy Name	
Conditions	
Windows Groups	
Permissions	
Profile	

Table 10-7   Remote Access Policy 2

Policy Part	Configuration
Remote Access Policy Name	
Conditions	
Windows Groups	
Permissions	
Profile	

Design Activity: Designing a Secure Client Infrastructure

In this activity, you must use what you learned in both lessons and apply it to a real-world situation. Read the scenario and then complete the exercises that follow. You can find answers for the exercises in the "Questions and Answers" section at the end of this chapter.

Scenario

Wide World Importers is going to provide sales personnel with mobile devices instead of laptops for remote communication with sales offices. Sales personnel will be able to send and receive e-mail and use a custom application to access sales catalogs, review customer information, discover order status, and place new orders. The application has not been developed yet. As the security administrator, you must begin the process of designing a secure client infrastructure for this project. While beginning your preliminary research, you also find areas where remote access security can be improved. You have the following information to work with.

Company Background

Wide World Importers is a wholesale provider of toys and gifts, with offices in Tokyo, New York, San Francisco, Zurich, and Hamburg. Sales continue to grow, and Wide World Importers believes this is because of its personal approach. Although customers have full access to on-line ordering and order tracking, most sales are entered by sales personnel, who visit major customers on a regular basis.

Existing Environment

Data centers in each location store product information. Customer data is regionalized, but catalog contents are replicated worldwide. Current remote access connections are provided for dial-up and Internet access via Microsoft Routing and Remote Access Services and Internet Authentication Services. Sales, marketing, and management personnel use Windows 2000 and Windows XP Professional laptop computers to access the data center.

Interviews

Following is a list of company personnel interviewed and their statements:

- **Sales VP** "I have mixed feelings about this. On the one hand, it will be great for the many sales people who do not use their laptops until they get back to their hotels. They say the clunky computers get in the way between them and their customers. It's been an uphill battle to get sales people to use computers. Those that do, however, benefit by being able to check inventory and orders while at the customer site and also by being able to show customers pictures in the on-line catalog. We'll be able to do most of this with the new equipment, but I wonder about the size of the picture on the mobile devices."

- **Salesperson** "This is great! It's so little. I can really travel light now."

- **General Business Manager, New York** "Aren't we going to have some problems here? These devices are so little. Won't they get lost?"

- **Marketing VP** "We need to be sure that competitive data is not lost if the device is lost or stolen. We especially need to be sure that someone couldn't use the device to place orders or cancel them or re-route them. I read this article today about how corporate espionage is being carried out by stealing PDAs at the airport and then using the data on the PDAs to construct customer lists and socially engineer the company's employees to give out sensitive information. We've got to watch out for that."

- **CTO** "Can't we do something about the people who connect with computers that are not kept up to date with patches? I've some proposals here by some companies who say they can provide a filter to keep those connections out."

- **IT Administrator** "I want to ensure that any carrier equipment authenticates to our network."

- **Auditor** "We just got a solid password policy implemented. I understand some mobile devices can't meet our policy. I would not advise weakening our policy."

Business Requirements

These are the business requirements:

1. Sales personnel must not have to become computer geeks to use these devices. Security should not lock authorized users out.

2. Data on mobile devices must not be available if the device is lost or stolen.

3. The password policy must remain strong.

Technical Requirements

These are the technical requirements:

1. Any third-party equipment in between the client's and the organization's servers must protect the connection and data transferred.

2. Only authorized connections should be made.

3. Wherever possible, remote access users must not be able to connect if their systems are not up to date.

Exercise 1: Create a Top-Level Design

Answer the following question.

1. Provide a top-level design that details the possible equipment, software, and network configuration that can provide a security infrastructure for these new remote access requirements. Generalizations are necessary at this stage in the design, but what would you look for?

_____

_____

_____

_____

Exercise 2: Analyze Authentication Requirements

Answer the following question.

1. What are the authentication requirements of the clients in this new design?

_____

_____

_____

_____

_____

Exercise 3: Design Remote Access Policies

Answer the following question.

1. What remote access policy or policies will be necessary for these new remote access requirements?

> **Important** It is not necessary to configure these remote access policies, nor to specify in detail the conditions and profile constraints because the specific mobile devices are unknown. Simply indicate what policies should seek to do.

_____

_____

_____

_____

Chapter Summary

- A client authentication strategy must be developed that considers LAN-based and WAN-based clients, wireless clients, and remote access clients.

- Account and password security policy should be interpreted in client access plans and not weakened because of the restrictions of modern devices.

- Third-party authentication products can assist in securing authentication and protecting data on mobile devices.

- RRAS and IAS remote access policies should reflect the remote access security policy of the organization.

- The authentication, authorization, and accounting capabilities of IAS should be used.

Exam Highlights

Before taking the exam, review these key points and terms. You need to know this information.

Key Points

- Remote access policies can secure remote access through the application of remote access conditions, profile constraints, and user account dial-in properties.

- Network Access Quarantine Control can be used to ensure the status of remote access clients meets an organization's security policy with respect to updates, virus protection, and security configuration.

- Securing connections between RADIUS servers, RADIUS proxies, RADIUS clients, and other remote access devices is as important as securing connections between users' devices and user accounts and servers on the network.

Key Terms

Authentication provider   A computer or computing device that accepts authentication credentials from a client and uses a directory to authenticate or reject a connection attempt. IAS is an example of an authentication provider.

Authentication switches   Switches that can authenticate a connection from a client. IAS can be used by the switch as the authentication provider.

Network Access Quarantine Control   A process that inspects a device that has requested connection against a list of specifications—such as service pack and patch status. If the client does not meet the listed specifications, Network Access Quarantine Control quarantines it to some area of the network where it can download updates to bring it up to specification, or it rejects the connection attempt. If the client meets all requirements, the normal network connection is provided.

Questions and Answers

Page
10-17

Lesson 1 Practice: Designing a Client Authentication Infrastructure

1. What are the types of clients that might be used in this scenario? Why do you consider these clients?

Answers may vary. Laptop computers might be used, but mobile devices such as PDAs and smart phones or PDA/phone combinations might also be used. The company has indicated that some employees only need to use e-mail and that others might be using a custom application. Both of these requirements can be met by mobile devices.

2. What information will you need to consider to analyze the authentication requirements of these devices?

You must consider whether RRAS, IAS, or both will be used. If only laptops are used, will only Windows laptops be used? Should VPNs be specified? What does the security policy say about passwords and accounts? Are any of the clients incapable of meeting the security policy? If mobile devices are used, what are the carriers' requirements? How will the carriers' and the organization's equipment authenticate? How will mobile devices authenticate to the carrier? How will users authenticate to mobile devices?

Page
10-43

Lesson 2 Practice: Designing a Remote Access Policy

The following tables provide the answers.

Table Remote Access Policy 1—Answer Key

Policy Part	Configuration
Remote Access Policy Name	Must Not PAP or CHAP. (The name might vary.)
Conditions	Include all versions of CHAP except MS-CHAPv2; include PAP; and include the allow unauthenticated choice.
Windows Groups	Not Applicable
Permissions	Deny remote access permissions.
Profile	Not Applicable

Table Remote Access Policy 2—Answer Key

Policy Part	Configuration
Remote Access Policy Name	Allow Dial-Up Group
Conditions	Windows Groups: Dial-Up Day and Time Restrictions: 9 a.m. to 5 p.m., Monday through Friday allowed
Windows Groups	Not Applicable
Permissions	Grant remote access permissions.
Profile	Encryption: Deselect the No Encryption check box.

Design Activity: Designing a Secure Client Infrastructure

Page
10-47

Exercise 1: Create a Top-Level Design

1. Provide a top-level design that details the possible equipment, software, and network configuration that can provide a security infrastructure for these new remote access requirements. Generalizations are necessary at this stage in the design, but what would you look for?

Answers may vary. There are two specific areas where the current design will change. First, Network Access Quarantine Control should be added to prevent current remote access clients from connecting with potentially dangerously configured systems. This can be done with current equipment, but the actual process must be designed to meet an agreed-upon policy and then new client access profiles must be developed. Second, providing remote access for mobile devices will depend on the type of device that is used and the type of communications protocols that they use. However, the use of a carrier will most likely be necessary, and connection specifications should not be left entirely to the carrier after the carrier is selected. The security of the connection between clients and the carrier and the carrier and Wide World Importers is critical. Also important is the design of authentication requirements.

Page
10-47

Exercise 2: Analyze Authentication Requirements

1. What are the authentication requirements of the clients in this new design?

Answers may vary. Three areas need to be considered:

Salespeople must be able to authenticate in a sure fashion to the devices. Because of concerns about sensitive data, a third-party authentication application should be selected that offers secure authentication other than a password, and which destroys all data on the system after some limited number of false attempts. Sales people will need training in synchronizing data over the network or to their own computer so as not to lose data.

Authentication before accessing e-mail and the custom application should be separate from authentication to the device. This adds another layer of security. Should an unauthorized user be able to get around device authentication, she will have another hurdle before she can access or modify data over the network.

Authentication between carrier equipment and the Wide World Importers network should also be strong.

Page
10-47

Exercise 3: Design Remote Access Policies

1. What remote access policy or policies will be necessary for these new remote access requirements?

Answers may vary. A remote access policy should be configured that will allow authorized user (by Windows group) access that is based also on the requirements of the equipment that becomes part of the design. Restrictions based on time and so on should be considered in the overall security policy for the new applications, and they should be added to the remote access policy profile.

11 Designing a Secure Client System

Exam Objectives in this Chapter:

- Design a strategy for securing clients. Considerations include desktop and portable computers.
    - ❏ Design a strategy for hardening client operating systems.
    - ❏ Design a strategy for restricting user access to operating system features.

Why This Chapter Matters

A network is only as secure as its weakest point. Client computer systems are often that weakest point. If client systems are compromised, an attacker might be able to elevate his privileges on the client system to attack other computers in the network. If client controls are weak, intruders and authorized computer and network users might obtain access to resources that they should not have access to. When client computer system security is not a part of security, there is no security.

Lessons in this Chapter:

Before You Begin

This chapter presents the skills and concepts related to creating a security design framework. This training kit presumes that you have a minimum of 1 year of experience implementing and administering desktop operating systems and network operating system in environments that have the following characteristics:

- At least 250 supported users
- Three or more physical locations
- Typical network services such as messaging, database, file and print, proxy server or firewall, Internet and intranet, remote access, and client computer management
- Three or more domain controllers

- Connectivity needs that include connecting branch offices and individual users in remote locations to the corporate network, and connecting corporate networks to the Internet

In addition, you should have experience designing a network infrastructure.

Many design exercises are paper-based; however, to understand the technical capabilities that a design can incorporate, you should have some hands-on experience with products. Where specific hands-on instruction is given, you must have at least two computers configured as specified in the "Getting Started" section at the beginning of this book.

Lesson 1: Designing a Strategy for Securing Client Computers

To design a secure client system, you must know how networks and client systems work, but you must also have an overall understanding of what needs to be done to secure clients. This foundation knowledge will help you better organize activities, prioritize efforts, and prevent conflicts. This lesson provides that foundation knowledge.

After this lesson, you will be able to

- Describe the techniques for designing a security strategy for client computers.
- Explain the process for designing an organizational unit (OU) infrastructure for client computers.
- Explain the considerations and guidelines for designing an OU infrastructure for users.

Estimated lesson time: 30 minutes

Techniques for Designing Security for Client Computers

Securing client computers involves both securing the client computing device (computer, PDA, smart phone, and so on) and locking down what users of the device can do to it and with it. This chapter will concentrate on designing a strategy to secure client computers running Microsoft Windows by using Windows tools. The following sections describe the components of the security strategy that you must think about and the techniques that you must use.

Components of a Security Strategy for Client Computers

The components of a security strategy for client computers include:

- Designing an OU infrastructure for computers
- Designing an OU infrastructure for users
- Designing the GPO infrastructure for user and computer OUs
- Designing a strategy for hardening client operating systems
- Designing a strategy for restricting users

Techniques

In Chapter 8, you learned how to design server security by server role. The techniques learned there can be applied to designing security for client devices and users. Ultimately, the design of secure clients must be based on a security policy but interpreted in a manner necessary for each type of client. To proceed, use the following techniques:

■ Separate client computers by operating system roles such as desktop or remote computers (laptops and desktops).

■ Group user accounts by the job that they do. Dividing client computer and user accounts in this manner allows the design to address specific types of users and computers.

■ Develop Group Policy Objects (GPOs) that address the management and security concerns of each computer and user role.

■ Secure computer and user accounts that are not part of an Active Directory directory service infrastructure. Security templates, systems policies and scripts, as well as third-party products can be used to manage and secure these computers and the users who work with them.

Tip This lesson will not directly address client computers other than those with accounts in Active Directory; however, many of the techniques discussed can be used on stand-alone client computers.

The next sections in this lesson will address designing an OU infrastructure to support this type of design. Using OUs and GPOs is the way to secure Windows clients that are members of a Windows Server 2003 or Windows 2000 domain. However, some workstations might not be joined in a Windows domain. Securing these clients will require other techniques. Techniques for securing stand-alone Windows clients are addressed in Lessons 2 and 3, which present the design details for securing computers and clients, respectively.

The Process: Designing an OU Infrastructure for Client Computers

Like servers, client computers play various roles. Client computers are tools that users use to do their work, but computer roles do not always parallel user roles and different operating systems provide somewhat different controls. To design an OU infrastructure, consider that the reason for doing so is to be able to implement Group Policy policies that secure the computers placed in each OU. To design an OU infrastructure:

1. Decide whether GPOs will be applied to all computer accounts in the OU or whether filtering by computer group will be used.

2. If GPOs will be applied to all computer accounts in the OU, consider the following:

    a. If computer management requires the use of top-level client computer OUs that represent geographical, departmental, or functional parts of the organization, use child OUs for each operating system and for different computer roles as shown in Figure 11-1.

   b. If no special management directives require computer management by geographical, departmental, or functional part of the organization, create OUs for
   each operating system and create child OUs to represent client computer
   roles—such as laptop, desktop, and administrator workstation—as illustrated
   in Figure 11-2.

3. If GPOs will be filtered by computer group, determine how you will group computers and design an OU hierarchy that does not cover these groups. Examples of
   such an OU hierarchy are:

   ❑ If groups will represent a computer operating system, create an OU infrastruc-
      ture that does not include OUs based on a computer operating system.
      Instead, add computer accounts to computer groups based on operating sys-
      tem, and filter GPOs by these groups. Figure 11-3 shows this type of hierarchy.

   ❑ If groups will represent a computer role, create an OU infrastructure that does
      not include OUs based on computer role. Instead, add computer accounts to
      computer groups based on a computer role, and filter GPOs and the OU level
      by these groups.

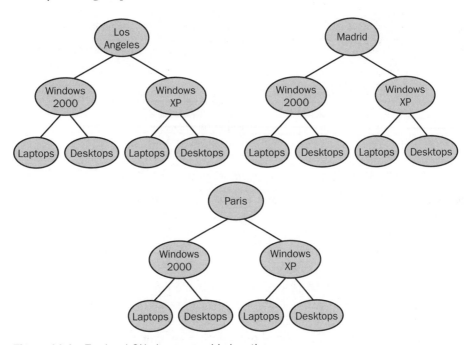

Figure 11-1   Top-level OUs by geographic location

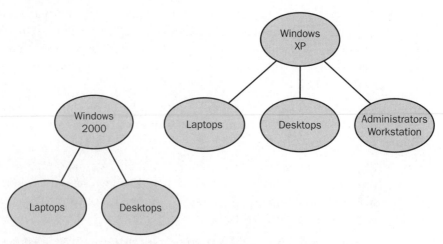

Figure 11-2   Top-level OUs by operating system

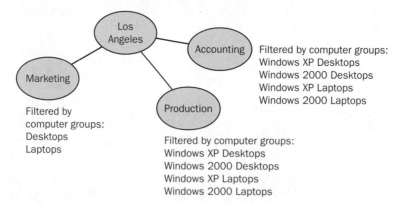

Figure 11-3   OUs filtered by computer groups

Figures 11-1 and 11-2 represent options that both require OUs based on operating system and computer role. This is because both the operating system and computer role might require different GPOs. Management of computer configuration by operating system requires a different Group Policy, and one of the easiest ways to introduce this is by linking a Group Policy policy to an OU. Different versions of Windows require a different Group Policy policy because the range of configuration options varies and because it is possible that a change implemented for one operating system might cause a problem for the other. Computer roles—such as desktop, laptop, kiosk, administrator workstation, and high-security workstation—might also require a different GPO.

Warning   Although Group Policy works in a similar manner for Windows 2000, Windows XP Professional, and Windows Server 2003, there are many differences in the options that can be set. Applying a Group Policy policy to computers that cannot use settings in the policy is counterproductive and might be harmful. It can also cause much confusion, because a review of the Group Policy settings can lead an individual to believe that security configurations or other solutions are in place when actually they are not (because they cannot be implemented on the different version of the operating system). For these reasons, you must design an OU infrastructure that allows you to apply Group Policy policies on an operating-system basis.

The exact infrastructure design might vary because of the types of clients and the roles that they play. Computer accounts might reside in OUs created to serve geographical, departmental, or functional needs. The management of these computers might be delegated to users within these areas of the organization, and they might control or have input into the client computer security policy for their area. Where client computer security policy is based on the security policy of the organization, control over Group Policy should not be delegated at the OU level. By not delegating control over Group Policy at the OU level, you can prevent OU administrators from lowering the security of computers whose accounts are in OUs.

After the OU design is completed, GPOs are designed and can be linked to each OU. Figure 11-4 shows an OU hierarchy for client computers based on geographical top-level OUs with its respective GPOs, and Figure 11-5 shows a hierarchy created strictly by computer role.

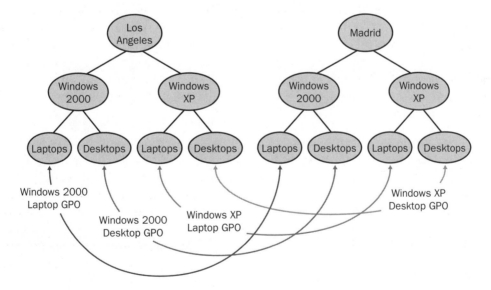

Figure 11-4   Geographical top-level OUs are often used to support local administration at distant locations.

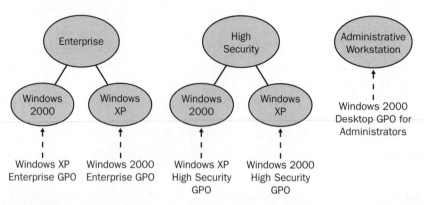

Figure 11-5   Top-level OUs designated by computer and user roles allow management of homogenous groups

Considerations and Guidelines for Designing an OU Infrastructure for Users

Like computers, users also play roles on the network. If you have followed convention, the roles of your users are represented in Windows groups. Group Policy policies, however, do not apply to Windows groups but to OUs, and therefore to the user and computer accounts within the OUs.

When designing an OU infrastructure for users, the primary consideration is management of the accounts. To some, *management of accounts* simply means creation, deletion, user properties management, and group membership management. To others, management of accounts means these things as well as complete control over the user's ability to use the computer. Unlike server role management, management of user accounts can be a political issue as well as an ease-of-management issue. The design of OUs might be up to IT administration, but the authority for controlling what users do on the desktop might not be. Your OU design must accommodate the dual needs of delegating control over user accounts and locking down the desktop according to user role.

These two management issues can result in an OU structure in which OUs represent each user role; that are designed around geographic location, department, or functional area; or that simply collect user accounts into a few OUs for management purposes. Some OU infrastructures might be a combination of these designs. Figures 11-6 through 11-9 provide examples of such OU infrastructures. In any of these cases, all user accounts within the OU might need to have the same settings applied. It might also be that this is not so. If possible, you should place user accounts that play the same role in the same OU. However, if it is not possible to use OUs as user role containers—if, for example, users are placed in OUs by department—you can filter the Group Policy policy by Windows group.

How to Use OUs as User Role Containers

To use OUs as user role containers, determine user roles and create an OU for each role. For example, use an OU for administrators, one for users, one for managers, and one for the help desk. The deciding factor in whether or not to create another OU is whether the users need to be treated differently. Users who work the help desk, for example, might require more access to their computers than most other users. Administrators require the most control; clerical workers require the least control. Figure 11-6 shows an example of such an OU infrastructure.

Figure 11-6   Top-level user OUs might collect user accounts by role

How to Use OUs as Management Containers

When the OU infrastructure must accommodate simple user management and is designed by geographic location (shown in Figure 11-7), department (shown in Figure 11-8), and so forth, you might find that you have little to no ability to produce top-level OUs that represent user roles. However, in many cases, you will be able to create child OUs to accommodate user roles or you might need to create multiple GPOs for a single OU and filter their application by user group. Figure 11-9 shows an OU infrastructure that uses child OUs to accommodate user roles. The user accounts will be in the child OUs. If user roles are universal—that is, a specific role requires the same desktop configuration—you can create a single GPO and either link it to each user role OU in the domain that includes users that fill that role or copy it to another domain and link it to the appropriate OUs.

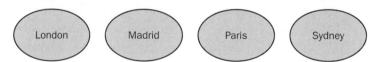

Figure 11-7   Top-level OUs for users might be by geographic location

Figure 11-8   Top-level OUs for users might be by department

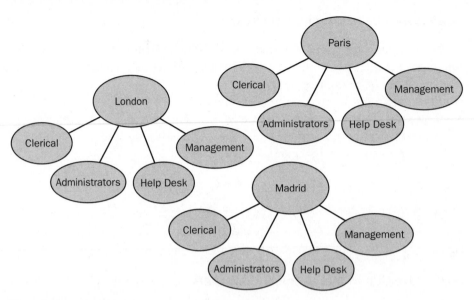

Figure 11-9   Using child OUs for user roles

Practice: Designing an OU Infrastructure for Client Computers

In this practice, you will design an OU infrastructure for client computers at a fictitious organization. Read the scenario and then answer the questions that follow to create your design. If you are unable to answer a question, review the lesson materials and try the question again. You can find answers to the questions in the "Questions and Answers" section at the end of the chapter.

Scenario

You are a security designer for Humongous Insurance. Your boss has asked you to adjust the current OU infrastructure to improve security for client computers. Top-level OUs already exist for each geographic area that Humongous Insurance serves. Client computer accounts are assigned to OUs based on their geographic location. OUs are New York, Paris, Sydney, San Diego, and Johannesburg. Each location has a data center and manages its own computers and users. Your boss wants to improve client computer security by applying security by computer role. The New York and Paris locations have 100 percent of their computers running Windows XP Professional. Sydney and San Diego have 100 percent of their computers running Windows 2000 Professional. Johannesburg has a mixture of Windows 2000– and Windows XP Professional–based computers. At each data center, administrative computers are on a separate subnet and are accessible only to administrators.

Review Questions

Answer the following questions.

1. What should the OU infrastructure look like? Design the OU infrastructure by sketching it below.

2. Why did you create the OUs that you did?

   _____

   _____

   _____

   _____

   _____

   _____

   _____

   _____

   _____

   _____

   _____

Lesson 2: Designing a Strategy for Hardening Client Operating Systems

An OU infrastructure alone won't provide security for client systems. The Group Policy policies that will link to the OU must be designed, and a strategy must be developed to harden client operating systems that are not member servers or to address security settings that cannot be maintained via Group Policy. To complete the design, you must use security templates, administrative templates, software restriction policies, and local computer tools. This lesson teaches you how.

After this lesson, you will be able to

- Explain the process for designing a strategy for hardening client operating systems.
- Design security templates for basic operating system hardening.
- Design administrative templates to manage application features.
- Explain what the IEAK can be used for.
- Design software restriction policies to manage application use.
- Design the implementation of security structures.

Estimated lesson time: 50 minutes

The Process: Designing a Strategy for Hardening Clients

Client computers are hardened by configuring security settings and securing applications. To design a strategy for Windows 2000 and Windows XP Professional client computers, security designers follow a process like this one:

1. Design baseline and incremental security templates for each OU.

2. Design administrative templates for each OU.

3. Design software restriction policies for each OU.

4. Design an implementation strategy for security templates, administrative templates, and software restriction policies.

The following topics teach what you need to know to complete these steps.

Guidelines for Designing Security Templates for Basic Operating System Hardening

In Chapter 8, you used security templates to design security for server roles. You created a very restrictive baseline template and an incremental template that added the necessary functions for specific roles. You can do the same for client computers.

> **Tip**   Remember that the baseline template is used to present the maximum security policy with the minimum amount of services.

The security template available for use with client computers is the same as that available for servers. The exact settings you should make in the baseline template will depend in part on the settings made for servers, your organization's security policy, and your ability to determine just how little you can enable in the base template and still have a computer that works. Fortunately, you can find recommendations for the baseline template settings in the document "Windows XP Security Guide," located at *http://www.microsoft.com/downloads/details.aspx?displaylang=en&familyid= 2d3e25bc-f434-4cc6-a5a7-09a8a229f118*. In addition to including a printed document, the guide includes security templates you can adjust for the specific requirements of your design and use in security implementation. Two baseline templates are included: one for Enterprise clients and one for High Security clients.

> **On the CD**   The "Windows XP Security Guide" is included in the Supplemental Information section on the CD.

In addition, incremental templates are included in the guide. Two computer roles are defined—laptop and desktop—and therefore, four incremental templates are defined—two for each of the two computer roles. If you choose to use these templates to complete your security template design, you need to adjust the baseline and incremental templates to match your organization's requirements and develop any additional computer role incremental templates. The provided incremental templates are:

- Enterprise Client Desktop
- Enterprise Client Laptop
- High Security Desktop
- High Security Laptop

Regardless of whether or not you decide to use the provided Microsoft Windows XP templates, use this technique: develop a baseline template for importing into a GPO on top-level OUs, and develop incremental security templates for importing into GPOs linked to computer role OUs.

Considerations for Security Template Contents

You can find recommendations for security settings from many sources, including the Windows XP Security Guide and other documentation on the Microsoft Web site. Many of these recommendations can be implemented in Group Policy by creating a security template and then importing it into a GPO. Consider the following audit policies and user rights in your plans to secure client computers:

- **Terminal Services and Remote Assistance**   Consider granting the Deny Log On Through Terminal Services right to the Everyone group. Doing so will prevent any use of terminal services to manage the client computer. This right is also necessary for the use of Remote Assistance. If your organization's policy is to have help desk employees who use Remote Assistance to manage client systems, create a Windows group and grant that group the Allow Log On Through Terminal Services right. (Do not, in this case, grant the Deny Log On Through Terminal Services right to the Everyone group, as that will also deny access to the Help Desk group.) You might also choose to grant the Allow Log On Through Terminal Services right to Administrators. You might want to have one policy for sensitive systems in which you deny the right to the Everyone group, and another one for less sensitive systems in which the help desk operators are given access. An example of a sensitive group in regard to this setting is laptops. Securing them from remote assistance access can help prevent them from becoming victims to remote attacks while being used outside the organization.

- **System Time**   Consider restricting the ability to make changes to system time to Administrators. Windows XP, for example, grants this right only to Administrators and Power Users. Because users sometimes must be made Power Users to run legacy applications, many users are likely to have this right. Changing the system time can have an adverse effect on domain logons and other network operations, as the time difference between the client and server must be small for Kerberos to validate access requests. An incorrect time on a client computer will also skew audit records, which results in the audit record having little value. You might also need to consider, however, that granting this right where necessary is far preferable to granting full administrator privileges.

- **Restrict the Log On Locally right**   Consider restricting this right. Users need this right to log on at the console of the client computer. They also need this right to use Terminal Services or access Internet Information Services (IIS) remotely. By restricting this right to Administrators and Users, you prevent Guest logon. By further restricting this right on sensitive systems to custom Windows groups, you prevent access by domain users who are not authorized to use the system.

- **System monitoring**   Consider allowing only Administrators to have the Profile Single Process right. This right allows users to use monitoring tools for system performance. It is not necessary in order to use the System Monitor. However, if the System Monitor is used to collect data using Windows Management Instrumentation (WMI), sensitive information might be available that would assist an attacker. Restricting this right to Administrators prevents all others from obtaining that data.

- **Backup and restore**   Consider splitting these rights by giving the right to back up files and directories only to Backup Operators and reserving for Administrators the right to Restore Files And Directories. A user who has the Restore Files And Directories right can restore an old backup over current information and thus destroy the current data. Backup Operators have access to backup tapes and disks. By restricting the Restore right to Administrators, you prevent rogue backup operators from accidentally or maliciously damaging systems.

■ **Audit policies**   Consider the need for audit records on the client system. Audit records on client systems might be perceived to be of less importance than those on server systems. However, the value of audit records is twofold. One value is their ability to assist in intrusion detection. The other is to determine what happened, who did what, and when something happened. Therefore, you should consider enabling auditing. Table 11-1 lists recommendations for auditing for Windows clients.

Table 11-1   Auditing Considerations for Windows Client Computers

Audit Policy	Client Systems	High Security Client Systems	Rationale
Audit account logon events	Success/Failure	Success/Failure	Tracks use of domain account logon records. Also, records remote connections to the client. If file and print sharing is enabled to provide access for remote administration, records of administrators' connections will be recorded here, as will attempts at connection by others.
Audit account management	Success/Failure	Success/Failure	Records changes to accounts and group memberships. These changes can be checked against authorized changes. A change here in an environment where local accounts are not used might indicate a successful attack.
Audit logon events	Success/Failure	Success/Failure	Logs domain account usage. Tracks local logon and use of local accounts.
Audit object access	Success/Failure	Success/Failure	Provides the opportunity to track usage or attempted usage of local files systems and registry objects. Audit settings must be made to the objects. However, if audit of object access is not configured in the audit policy, object access auditing will not be done.
Audit policy change	Success	Success	Records changes to user rights, audit policy, and trust policy.

Table 11-1 Auditing Considerations for Windows Client Computers

Audit Policy	Client Systems	High Security Client Systems	Rationale
Audit privilege use	None	Failure	Records failed attempts at use of privileges that are not assigned. This can produce many records that might not be of value on ordinary client systems, but records of failed attempts at privilege use on sensitive systems are of value.
Audit systems events	Success	Success/Failure	Tracks systems events, which are things such as shutdown and restart. These events can be the results of attempted or actual attacks, but this policy more likely will just be recording normal usage. Client systems are often shut down at the end of the day, and monitoring system events might result in many hours of effort to produce insignificant results.

Consider the following security options, event log settings, restricted groups, services settings, and object permission settings in your security template design:

- **Cached logon credentials** Consider limiting the number of logon credentials that are cached locally. These credentials are used when a domain controller is not available. Setting cached logon credentials to 0 prevents logon if no domain controller is available. This setting might be appropriate for highly sensitive client computers, but it is not acceptable for laptop computers, as they will frequently be used where domain controllers are not available for logon. Consider setting sensitive laptops to 1. However, remember that the last logon is the one that will be cached. If an administrator or technician logs on to the laptop for any reason, her or his credentials will be cached. Unless the authorized user of the laptop logs on and off before disconnecting from the network, the authorized user will not be able to log on to the laptop until it is connected to the network.

- **Credential storage** Consider enabling the security option Do Not Allow Storage Of Credentials Or .NET Passports For Network Authentication. If you enable this option, users will not be able to store Passport credentials and credentials used to log on to remote servers and workstations on their client computers, and therefore they will have to type them in each time they want to use them. Not storing credentials makes the access to applications, Web sites, databases, and so on safer. However, when users have multiple passwords to remember, they are more likely to write them down, use a weak password, or both. You will have to evaluate which approach poses the most risk for your organization.

- **Allow Floppy Copy And Access To All Drives And Folders When Using Recovery Console**   Consider disabling this setting for all client computers. If an attacker can use the recovery console, he can copy the local Security Accounts Manager (SAM) and attack it on a computer where he is administrator. He can also copy sensitive files that might be protected otherwise, or access and delete sensitive files. This setting is sometimes enabled to allow technicians an easier way to repair a computer. This might be acceptable for some client systems, especially those that do not store sensitive information, but it is not acceptable for systems that require a high security level.

- **Certificate Rules and Software Restriction Policies**   Consider enabling the security option System Settings: Use Certificate Rules On Windows Executables For Software Restriction Policies when certificate software restriction policies will be used. Disabling this setting will result in certificates not being checked to see whether they are invalid because of revocation. Disabling this setting might improve performance. See the "Guidelines for Designing Software Restriction Policies to Manage Application Usage" section for more information.

- **Security Event Log Settings**   Consider estimating what the proper size of the Security event log should be and monitoring log growth. If you find that a larger log is needed to accommodate the number of records, you can make it larger. Your objective should be to capture all records. To do this, schedule archiving of the log on a periodic basis and create a large enough file size to accommodate all records created between archives. If the log is filling faster than you anticipated, either archive logs more frequently or enlarge the log size.

- **Restricted Groups**   Consider using restricted groups to control management of local group management. Adding a group here allows you to maintain membership of a local group by policy. A user with local administrative privileges might be able to add members to a local group, but then, at the next policy refresh, membership will revert to the membership identified here.

- **File System and Registry Key Permissions**   Consider recommendations in the Windows XP Security Guide for Secure Clients. Settings are adequate for most clients; additional hardening might be necessary on sensitive client computers. Any changes, however, should be thoroughly tested before being made in a production environment.

- **System Services**   Control startup values for services by making changes in this area of Group Policy. Consider disabling, at a minimum, the services listed in Table 11-2. Evaluate the need for other services on a case-by-case basis. Set permissions on all services to ensure, except in unique circumstances, only administrators can stop and start services and change the startup value. If there is a valid need for an ordinary user to start a service—for example, when he needs to execute a program that runs as a service—grant him the right to start the service but not to change its startup mode. In the table, two choices are given. One, labeled

Client, is for ordinary clients computers; the other, Secure Client, represents the preferred service status for computers that require a higher degree of security.

Table 11-2   System Services to Consider Disabling

Service User Interface Name	Service Name	Client	Secure Client
Alerter	Alerter	Disabled	Disabled
Background Intelligent Transfer Service	BITS	Manual	Disabled
ClipBook	BlipSrv	Disabled	Disabled
Fax Service	Fax	Manual	Disabled
FTP Publishing Service	MSFtpsvr	Disabled	Disabled
IIS Admin Service	IISADMIN	Disabled	Disabled
Messenger	Messenger	Disabled	Disabled
Net Meeting Remote Desktop Sharing	Mnmsrvc	Manual	Disabled
Network DDE	NetDDE	Manual	Disabled
Network DDE DSDM	NetDDEdsdm	Manual	Disabled
Remote Registry Service	Remote Registry	Automatic	Disabled
Telnet	TlntSvr	Disabled	Disabled
World Wide Web Publishing Service	W3SVC	Disabled	Disabled

Guidelines for Designing Security Templates

In addition to making a decision about certain security template items, follow these guidelines when designing security templates:

- **Set strong password policies**   Set a strong password policy for local account databases. Domain password policies are set in the default GPO linked to the domain. However, local accounts on clients use the password policy in the GPO linked to the OU in which the computer account resides. Even if local accounts are not used, they exist. A password policy should be assigned to the baseline security template that provides a strong password policy for local accounts.

- **Restrict remote access to the client computer**   Restrict remote access by granting the Access This Computer From The Network right to Administrators and Users. Doing this will prevent anonymous access and also override attempts by applications that grant this right to the Everyone group or other groups.

- **Debug programs**   Do not grant this right to any users of production systems. This powerful right can be abused to gain access to sensitive system information and components. Attacks exist that can exploit this right to grab hashed passwords and other security information. Enabling this setting will not inhibit developers from using application debugging utilities such as those included with Microsoft Visual Studio .NET.

- **Restrict remote shutdown rights**   Grant this right only to Administrators or those authorized to repair and maintain systems. Anyone who can shut the system down remotely can cause a denial of service (DoS) attack and might be able to cause data loss or complete other attacks that require a reboot.

- **Ensure the security of the Security Event log**   Enable the Event Log setting Prevent Local Guests Group From Accessing Security Log in Group Policy. By default, the Guests group does not have access to the Security Event log. However, including this setting in policy ensures that it will remain that way. Set the security log retention method to As Needed, and monitor the log to ensure that it is archived, it is cleared periodically, and no events are lost.

- **Follow recommendations for using security options**   Security options provide the ability to easily enable and disable security functions on client computers. Several of the security options are long-standing security guidelines for Windows systems, and others are newer and might not be present in all versions of Windows. These guidelines are detailed in Table 11-3.

Table 11-3   Security Option Recommendations to Follow When Creating Security Templates

Option	Recommendation
Limit Local Account Use Of Blank Passwords To Console Logon Only	Set to Enabled to prevent access using accounts with no passwords over the network. Of course, on all client computers no account should have blank passwords, and this can be controlled by local security policy. However, if users have local Administrator rights, they can change the local password policy. They can change this security option as well, but they might not see a need to because they are only wanting easier local access.
Rename Administrator Account	Reduce the attack surface by obscuring the name of this powerful account. Enabling this setting does not change the description of the Administrator account.
Do Not Display Last User Name	Enable this setting to ensure an attacker is not given account names. The last logon name is normally displayed when a user attempts to log on at the console. This scenario provides an attacker with a valid account name; the attacker then only has to guess the password. If no account name is provided, an attacker must guess both the account name and password.
Message Text For Users Attempting To Log On	Provide a logon warning prepared by your legal department that identifies the restrictions on logon on this computer. Doing this will not prevent an attacker from logging on if the attacker knows or can deduce an authorized account and password, but it will prove that she was not "invited" in.

Table 11-3   Security Option Recommendations to Follow When Creating Security Templates

Option	Recommendation
Allow Anonymous SID/Name Translation	Disable this setting to prevent an anonymous user from requesting security IDs (SIDs) of other users or using a SID to gain a user name. If this setting is enabled, for example, an anonymous user can use the well-known local administrator SID to determine its account name. You should change the name of the administrator account to make it more difficult for password-cracking attacks to occur.
Do Not Allow Anonymous Enumeration Of SAM Accounts, and Do Not Allow Anonymous Enumeration Of SAM Accounts And Shares	Enable both of these settings to prevent enumeration of local client computer accounts and client computer shares. If an attacker can enumerate accounts, he has the information he needs to mount a password-cracking attack. If an attacker can enumerate share names, he can begin an attack on the shares. Many vulnerability scanning and auditing security programs require that File And Printer Sharing be enabled on the client computer. By obscuring the shares, you at least make it more difficult for any attacks to occur.
Restrict Anonymous Access To Named Pipes And Shares	Enable this setting to block anonymous user access to named pipes and shares. Named Pipes are communication connection points that are used by programs such as Microsoft SQL Server and others. Authenticated connections will still be allowed.
Do Not Store LAN Manager Value On Next Password Change	The LAN manager password hash is easily attacked. By removing any storage of this credential, you reduce the ability of an attacker to compromise an account.
LAN Manager Authentication Level	Use this setting to determine how LM, NTLM, and NTLMv2 are used for network authentication. Settings on the client must be synchronized with the settings made at the domain and server level. If they are not, domain authentication to the domain or to local server accounts might not work.
Minimum Session Security For NTLM SSP Based (Including Secure (RPC) Clients)	Use this setting to determine a session's security level for compatible applications. Settings on the client must be synchronized with the settings made at the domain and server level.
Allow Automatic Administrative Logon	Disable this option, which would allow anyone to log on as Administrator simply by using the Recovery Console.
Clear Virtual Memory Pagefile	Enable this setting to clear the page file at shutdown and thus remove any sensitive information that might have been placed there. The information in the page file might include things such as passwords and plaintext (not encrypted) versions of EFS encrypted files.

How to Design Administrative Templates to Manage Application Features

This section first describes what administrative templates are and then explains how to configure and use administrative templates and how to analyze administrative template settings to control application features.

What Are Administrative Templates?

Administrative templates are files that can be loaded into a GPO and provide a way for an administrator to specify operating system utility and application settings. When a GPO is applied to a computer, the registry changes are made. Administrative templates provide a vast range of controls, some of which apply security for applications and many of which are not directly security related, but are instead simple application configuration related. Many of the application features can become security issues if users are allowed to configure them. The reasons for this are not always obvious, but best practices tell us that the following application features should be managed:

- Version control should be managed so that you'll know what you have to patch and how to fix it.

- The number of user settable options should be reduced to as close to zero as possible.

- Security items such as encryption and authentication should be configured to the securest setting the clients and servers can both use.

 Tip Unlike security templates, administrative templates cannot be configured and then linked to GPOs. Administrative templates are, however, distinct files and can be created, loaded, or unloaded from a GPO and then used to establish security settings.

Operating system administrative templates are part of the operating system product and are installed by default. They are either computer-based or user-based and are used to modify values in the user or computer hives of the registry. In addition to operating system administrative templates, application-specific templates are available.

 See Also Templates for Microsoft Office, for example, are provided with the Microsoft Office Resource Kit and can be downloaded from *http://www.microsoft.com/office/ork/2000 /appndx/toolbox.htm#word2kmsu*.

Office templates can also be used in the Systems Policy Editor, a tool provided for Windows 98 and Windows NT 4.0 that can be used to apply Systems Policy. Systems Policy is a way to provide a logon download of registry settings that are applied to a client at logon.

How to Configure and Use Administrative Templates

To configure and use administrative templates, open a GPO and navigate to the Administrative Templates section of the computer or user node of the GPO. The location is shown in Figure 11-10. Double-click a specific container in the template to change its settings. An open template container property page is shown in Figure 11-11. When the GPO is downloaded by the client, the settings will be applied. Administrative template settings will be displayed in the Group Policy Management Console.

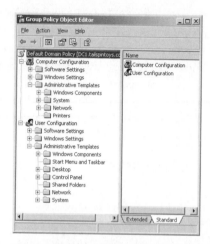

Figure 11-10 Administrative templates have their own node in Group Policy

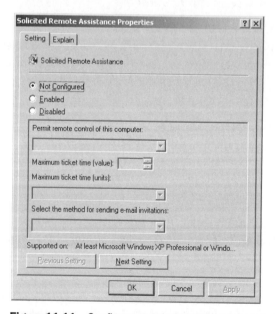

Figure 11-11 Configure an administrative template setting by making changes in its property pages

How to Analyze Administrative Template Settings for Control of Application Features

Administrative templates allow the administrator to establish configuration settings for windows components, the system, the network, printers, the desktop control panel, and shared folders. Each of these sections has subsections on specific areas such as NetMeeting, Internet Explorer, Logon, Group Policy, DNS Client, Active Desktop, and so on. You should analyze the need to use settings, and how to set them, for each section and subsection. This means you must literally inspect hundreds of settings. The best way to do this is follow this simple approach.

1. Pick a subsection that is important to your operations.

2. Read the Explain text (shown in Figure 11-12) of each item in the subsection.

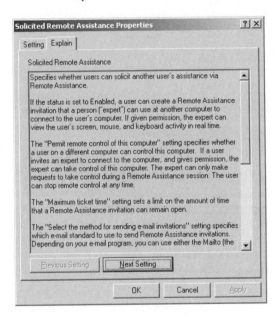

Figure 11-12   The Explain tab text of an administrative template documents the meaning of the setting

3. If you have questions about the item and the effect it will have, use additional resources such as the Windows XP Security Guide and online documentation.

4. Decide which settings must be configured to comply with security policy.

5. Decide which settings must be configured to comply with company policies.

6. Test the settings in a test network

7. Implement the settings in local or domain Group Policy.

Example: Analyzing the Administrative Template Settings for Terminal Services

This example uses the technique (described in the lesson) on the Terminal Services subsection of the Computer Configuration, Administrative Templates, Windows Components section. This section is shown in Figure 11-13.

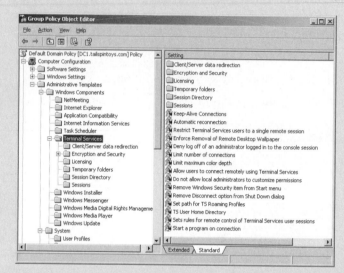

Figure 11-13   The Terminal Services section of administrative templates provides a way to control terminal services.

Scenario

Tailspin Toys will be implementing terminal services to manage desktop applications for the employees in the research area. It is imperative that security be strong. You, as the security designer, have been asked to prepare a list of key terminal services–specific settings that will make management of terminal services easier and more secure. Included with the request is a pointer to security policy, which states that any communications that researchers do across the network must be encrypted and that researchers are not allowed to store data on their desktops. Your company's long-standing operations policy recommends that strong controls be implemented for the research department and that few application configuration options be available to users.

Determining Available Options

The first part of your plan is to determine what options are available in administrative templates and how you should recommend they be set.

1. *Pick a section.* The section is the Terminal Services Section, and there are six subsections.

2. *Read the Explain text.* Open each item, and select the Explain tab.

3. *Use additional resources.* Some settings, such as Do Not Allow Drive Redirection, are explained well, but it's difficult to really see any security choice that needs to be made. And many of the settings use double negatives, as this one does. If you enable a "Do Not," that means it does, right? The Explain tab for this setting indicates that drives are mapped, and you know that to be true from experience. When using a terminal services session, the user has access to his own drives. So what? You reference a copy of the Windows XP Security Guide and find the issue. To make client drives available to the client when the user is in a terminal services session, the terminal services server maps the client drives to itself. This means a possible attack vector is added. If someone should be able to access the terminal services server and client drives were mapped, the attacker might be able to obtain data from the client. You know that research team members sometimes store the results of their work on the local computer. You decide that this setting should be enabled; researchers should not be allowed to access their local drives when using a terminal services session.

4. *Decide which settings must be configured to comply with security policy.* Security policy requirements include the encryption of communications. You note that the Set Client Connection Encryption Level setting allows you to require 128-bit encryption.

5. *Decide which settings must be configured to comply with company policies.* Company policy says to restrict certain activities of the researchers. Table 11-4 provides guidelines for terminal services application features. Five recommendations that meet Tailspin Toys requirements are included in the table. For a full review of terminal services settings, see the administrative template for any GPO.

6. *Test settings in a test network.* There are other parts of terminal services that must be tested. You provide the testers with a copy of a table similar to 11-4 to use in their tests. Create a GPO that includes settings for terminal services and test it as well.

7. *Implement your design in a local or domain group policy.* When the design is approved and tested, administrators will implement it in the domain.

Devising Recommendations

Table 11-4   Recommendations for Tailspin Toys Terminal Services Settings

Setting	Discussion
Allow Time Zone Redirection	Disable this setting to prevent client systems from changing the zone related to their session. By default, Time Zone Redirection is not allowed, and the time for the session is the server time. Not all clients can do time zone redirection, and it is wise to keep times correct on the server. Otherwise, you might not be able to figure out the real time that files on the server were accessed.
Do Not Allow Clipboard Redirection	Enable this setting to prevent researchers from sharing data between the client and the terminal services server. If this setting were enabled, researchers could take server-side data and use the clipboard to capture and move data from the server to the client computer.
Always Prompt Client For Password Upon Connection	Enable this setting to make researchers log on before they can start a terminal server services session. If this setting were to be disabled and a researcher were to leave her desk while still logged on but not in a terminal services session, an intruder or fellow worker would be able to open a terminal services session and access the researcher's data.
Set Client Connection Encryption Level	By default, the data sent between client and server is encrypted at the highest level that the client supports. Setting encryption to the High Level ensures 128-bit encryption. If the client cannot use 128-bit encryption, the session is terminated.
Do Not Allow Drive Redirection	Enable this setting to prevent researchers from accessing their local drives when using a terminal services session. This will also prevent an intruder from gaining access to the researchers' computers.

What Is the IEAK?

The Internet Explorer Administration Kit (IEAK) provides a way to develop, deploy, and maintain a customized browser. It is another automated way to manage security settings. Like knowledge of security templates and administrative templates, knowledge of IEAK is a necessary part of the security designer's toolbox. IEAK tools include the Internet Explorer Customization Wizard and the IEAK Profile Manager. The following items can be customized:

- Privacy Settings. Match browser privacy settings with Web site privacy policy. Prevent cookies from sites that do not match the privacy settings from downloading.

- Security Zones. Establish settings for each security zone.

- Designate approved software publishers.

- View and Manage certification authority settings.

- Quick Launch Bar. Remove links to channels or the Internet Connection Wizard from the bar.

- Hide other configuration parts such as the Security tab.

- Use standard Windows administrative template files to select configuration settings.

- Use custom administrative templates .

See Also   The latest version of the IEAK can be downloaded from the Internet Explorer Administration Kit page of the Microsoft Web site at *http://www.microsoft.com/windows /ieak/default.asp*.

Guidelines for Designing Software Restriction Policies to Manage Application Usage

This topic explains what software restriction policies are, provides the questions you must answer during the design process, describes the types of software restriction policies there are, and then provides guidelines for designing these policies.

What Are Software Restriction Policies?

Software restriction policies are tools in Group Policy that can be used to restrict or allow software to run on Windows XP Professional computers, Windows Server 2003 computers, or both. These policies do not have anything to do with software configuration; they simply determine whether or not the software will run. A single software restriction policy can be created in a GPO, but each policy can have multiple rules. Designing software restriction polices is a two-part process. First, the general properties of the policy must be designed, and then the policies themselves must be designed.

Considerations

There are five major questions to answer in the design process for the software restriction properties.

1. Should the Security Level be unrestricted or disallowed? Software restriction policies, by default, allow all software to run, as shown in Figure 11-14. You must configure a policy to prevent software from running. But is this the way it should be? Should you allow all applications to run (the Unrestricted Security level) and then deny through a policy the few that should be allowed to run? Or should you allow no applications to run (the Disallowed Security Level) and allow applications to run in a policy?

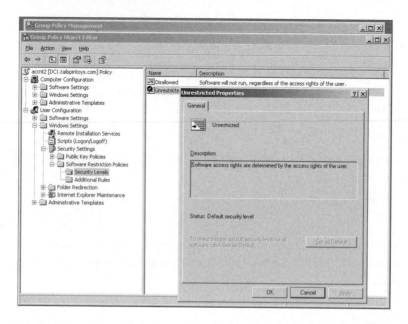

Figure 11-14   Security levels determine whether all software can run or whether no software can run

2. Should software restriction policies apply to all users or to all users except administrators? Determine whether it will be harder for administrators to do their job without the ability to run the software that will be disallowed. The option is configured as shown in Figure 11-15.

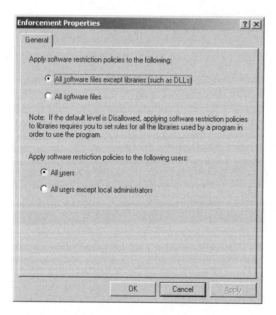

Figure 11-15   You must determine whether administrators are exempt from software restriction policies

3. Should dynamic-link libraries (DLLs) be exempt? For example, if an executable is allowed to run, will you need to also write an allow policy for all of its DLLs?

4. What file types are considered to be executable? You can add and remove file types, as shown in Figure 11-16, that should be checked and for which you can write software restriction policies.

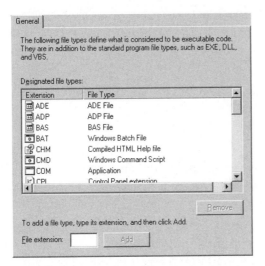

Figure 11-16   If new file types become available, you can add them to the File Type property and write software restriction policies.

5. Should users, local administrators, or enterprise administrators select trusted publishers? See Figure 11-17.

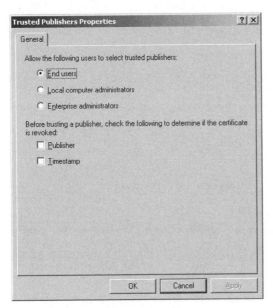

Figure 11-17   Restrict administration of trusted publishers by adding only the necessary administrative group.

After policy is designed, the rules themselves are designed. If the security level will be unrestricted (the default), then you write policies that will prevent software from running. If the security level will be disallowed, you must write policies that will allow software to run.

 Important   To include certificate software restriction rules, you must configure the Security Option, System Settings: Use Certificate Rules on Windows executables for software restriction policies.

Types of Software Restriction Policies

There are four types of software restriction policies:

- *Certificate*. Certificate rules allow or restrict software by checking for a signature by a trusted publisher. If the signature is valid and the publisher is approved, the software will be either allowed to run or is not allowed to run, depending on the security level set in the rule.

- *Hash*. Hash rules create a hash of a selected executable. When an attempt is made to run an executable, it is hashed and the hash is checked against existing, restricted hashes. If a match is found, the software is allowed to run or is prevented from running, depending on the security level set in the rule. The hash of an executable will never change, so regardless of where the software is located the policy can still take effect. If a new version of the software is released, the hash will not match and the software is not restricted by the policy.

- *Internet Zone*. Windows installer package software is allowed or restricted based on the Internet Zone it is downloaded from. Other types of software are not restricted by these rules.

- *Path*. A path rule designates a Windows file or registry path in which software will be either allowed or denied. If the software is copied to another path, the policy will not apply. Four default registry paths are set. The default paths allow system software to run even if the security level is set to Disallowed.

Guidelines for Designing Software Restriction Policies

Follow these guidelines when designing software restriction policies:

- Use path rules with caution. If the security level is set to Unrestricted and your path rule security level is set to Disallowed, users will not be able to run the executables in the path. However, if they can copy the executables to another location, the path rule will not be in effect and they will be able to run the executables.

- If you need to absolutely prevent unauthorized software from running on the computer, set the software restriction policy security level to Disallowed. A security level of Disallowed will prevent all software from running. Rules can then be written for software that you want to run using any of the rules.

- Do not remove the four Additional Rules that are set by default. These rules will allow system software to run if you set the security level to Disallowed.

- If the security level will be set to Disallowed, you must apply rules to allow anything that you want to run, including startup programs, logon scripts, and so on.

- For every rule that allows or restricts software, design rules that enable or restrict associated software. Associated software is software that might be started by the other software.

- Design software restriction policies for computers in the computer configuration portion of the GPO, and design them for users in the user configuration section of a GPO.

How to Design the Implementation of Security Structures

During the design process, you will examine and design security templates, administrative templates, and possibly software restriction policies and IEAK profiles. Before any of these elements can be implemented, you must design the process that will be needed to do so. To design the implementation for these security structures:

1. Determine whether computers are domain members or stand-alone computers.

2. For domain member computers, combine security templates, administrative templates, and software restriction policies into GPOs and link them to appropriate OUs.

3. For stand-alone computers, add a security template, an administrative template, and software restriction policies to the local GPO, or use a custom script to implement the equivalent registry changes.

4. For all computers, design IEAK profiles to manage security settings in Internet Explorer.

Practice: Analyzing Administrative Template Settings to Control Application Features

In this practice, you will analyze the administrative template settings for terminal services and provide recommendations for hardening terminal services. Read and follow the instructions, and then complete the table that follows. If you are unable to complete the table, review the lesson materials and try again. You can find answers to this practice in the "Questions and Answers" section at the end of the chapter.

> **Important**   This is a continuation of the practice at the end of Lesson 1. Complete this practice as if you are still a security designer for Humongous Insurance.

Spend time learning about each selection in the Terminal Services section of the administrative templates in Group Policy. Use the Explain tabs and any additional resources that you need, such as the results from searching the Technet Web site or the Windows XP Security Guide. Then use Table 11-5 to record at least five recommendations for hardening terminal services (making sure they are things that can be done with Group Policy), and provide your reasons for making these recommendations. You cannot use any recommendations that were already used in this lesson.

Table 11-5   Recommendations for Hardening Terminal Services

Setting	Recommendation and Reasons

Lesson 3: Designing a Strategy for Restricting User Access to Operating System Features

If users can access and modify operating system features, they can destroy the computer they are working with, obtain information that might be used to attack other computers on the network, and elevate their privileges on the computer and possibly on the network. An attacker, after she gains any access to the computer, might be able to do the same. Even if these disrupting and business-crippling events do not occur, there is the potential for lost productivity and increased network maintenance costs as a result of the misconfiguration of operating system features, the presence of unapproved third-party software, and the lack of consistency.

After this lesson, you will be able to

- Explain the process for designing a strategy for restricting user access to operating system features.
- List Windows Groups that you can use to restrict user access to operating system features.
- Design the use of administrative templates to restrict user access to operating system features.

Estimated lesson time: 30 minutes

The Process: Designing a Strategy for Restricting User Access to Operating System Features

Users access operating system features to perform common administrative tasks. These tasks include operations such as adding and removing applications and printers, changing the configuration of an operating system feature such as networking or display, and scheduling an application or task to run at a specific time. These tasks can also include simple things such as selecting a desktop background or screen saver.

It would be easy to insist that no user should have any access to operating system features. However, implementation of such a design would soon fail. For example, administrators and users who use laptops and are often far away from the organization's help desk maintenance technicians need the ability to do some things for themselves. Other users might work at remote sites where no administrative assistance is available. In some organizations, it is also traditional to give users choices in configuration operations in the area of desktop appearance. It might be preferable in many instances to provide users the ability to perform some functions, rather than prevent them from working, or give them full administrative privileges.

A more workable strategy for restricting user access to operating system features is:

1. Place users in groups that provide limited access to operating system features.

2. Identify administrative template settings that restrict user access to operating system features.

3. Design GPOs that restrict user access to operating system features based on client computer role and user needs.

4. Link GPOs to OUs that contain computer and user accounts that should be restricted.

5. Filter GPOs by user group as necessary.

The following sections provide the information you need to complete steps 1 through 3. Steps 4 and 5 are operational steps that you should already know.

Windows Groups You Can Use to Restrict User Access to Operating System Features

This topic describes the benefits of using Windows Groups and provides examples of the groups you can use to provide limited operating system privileges.

The Benefits of Using Windows Groups

Placing users in Windows Groups that provide some administrative privileges has two benefits. First, giving users who need *some* administrative privileges only the administrative privileges they need is a good security practice. A user cannot abuse a privilege that he does not have. Second, if you use GPOs to restrict user access to operating system features, you can filter a GPO by these groups if the user account is in an OU that would remove access to the operating system features these groups need to use.

Example Groups

Example groups that can be used to provide limited operating system privileges are:

■ *Network Configuration Operators.* Network Configuration Operators can make changes to Transmission Control Protocol/Internet Protocol (TCP/IP) settings and renew and release TCP/IP addresses on domain controllers in the domain.

■ *Print Operators.* This group can manage, create, share, and delete printers.

■ *Remote Desktop Users.* This group can remotely log on to the desktop.

■ *Power Users.* This group can create user accounts; modify and delete the account they have created; create local groups; add and remove users from the groups they have created; and add or remove users from Power Users, Guests, and User groups. They can also create shared resources.

Guidelines for Designing the Use of Administrative Templates to Restrict User Access to Operating System Features

Before you can design the use of administrative templates to restrict user access to operating system features, you should understand a few important concepts. This topic describes how administrative templates are used, provides guidelines for deciding which administrative template to use, shows how to translate a security policy into technical controls, and lists the administrative template settings that manage remote access. Then, guidelines are provided for designing the use of administrative templates to manage user access to the operating system.

How Administrative Templates Restrict User Access

Administrative templates can be used to restrict user access in the following two ways:

- Administrative templates in the Computer Configuration area of a GPO can be used to restrict all users of the computer to which the GPO is applied.

- Administrative templates in the User Configuration area of a GPO can be used to restrict access by users to which the GPO is applied.

Guidelines for Deciding Which Administrative Template to Use

There are hundreds of administrative templates. How do you decide which ones to use and how to set them? You must use your knowledge of your organization's security policy and your knowledge of the impact that the ability to use the operating system feature has. You can gain much information from reading the Explain tabs of the administrative template settings, but you must also use your ability to analyze the threat that might come from using the feature. To do the latter, you must use your knowledge of what the operating system feature or utility does. The rest of this lesson provides a sample analysis of how to translate a security policy into the technical controls and guidelines for restricting user access to operating system features.

How to Translate Security Policy into Technical Controls

In this scenario, a security policy will be translated into the use of administrative templates and membership in Windows Groups.

Scenario   Humongous Insurance has added a security policy that states:

"No user shall use remote administration applications or operating system features to remotely access or manage a client computer."

To apply technical controls that will assist the fulfillment of this policy, the following steps are taken:

- The user right Access This Computer From The Network is assigned only to administrators and domain controller computers.

- The following services are disabled in the GPOs designed for restricting user access to operating systems features:

  ❑ Terminal services

  ❑ Remote Desktop Assistance

  ❑ Telnet

  ❑ World Wide Web Publishing

- The Remote Desktop Users group is added to the Restricted Groups section of GPOs designed for OUs. No members are added to the group. When Group Policy is refreshed, any members who have been added to the group will be removed.

- Settings in administrative templates that might provide users with remote access to client computers are modified in GPOs designed for user OUs. A listing of these settings is provided in the "Administrative Template Settings that Manage Remote Access" section.

- If a user OU does not already have a GPO used for the purpose of managing user access to operating system features, a new GPO is created and linked to the OU.

Administrative Template Settings that Manage Remote Access

Two sets of Administrative Templates exist: those for computers and those for users. Often, there are similar settings in both templates. Computer settings control the activity of every user that logs on to a computer. User settings control only users whose accounts are in the OU where the settings are applied. Each user logging on to the same computer can have a different experience when user settings are used. The following lists show an example of settings that follow this rule. Both have similar-sounding settings.

The following Computer Configuration administrative template settings can be used to manage remote access:

- **NetMeeting** Configure the Computer Configuration, Administrative Templates, Windows Components, NetMeeting setting to enable the Disable Remote Desktop Sharing setting for sensitive computer clients. This setting will prevent the use of this tool by users to share items on the desktop with other users. Providing remote users access to resources on a client system in any manner is a security risk. Allowing NetMeeting desktop sharing is like giving users the right to create shares and provide unrestricted access into the data files of their computer.

- **Windows Messenger** Set Do Not Allow Windows Messenger To Be Run to Enabled. This prevents the use of Windows Messenger and MSN Messenger. Instant messaging applications provide access to files on the users' desktops and can serve as vectors for viruses, worms, and Trojan horses.

- **Terminal Services**   Disable the setting Allow Users To Connect Remotely Using Terminal Services to prevent terminal services connections.

- **Remote Assistance**   If you disable the Solicited Remote Assistance setting, users will not be able to solicit remote assistance. If you disable the Offer Remote Assistance setting, no one will be able to offer remote assistance.

The following User Configuration administrative templates can be used to prevent remote access and administration of client computers.

- **NetMeeting**   In the Application Sharing folder, enable the following settings to prevent the use of any application-sharing feature. Alternatively, restrict remote access to shared application information by enabling the Prevent Control setting but allowing some sharing through the following options:

  ❑ Enable Disable Application Sharing

  ❑ Enable Prevent Sharing

  ❑ Enable Prevent Desktop Sharing

  ❑ Enable Prevent Sharing Command Prompts

  ❑ Enable Prevent Sharing Explorer Windows

  ❑ Enable Prevent Control

- **Windows Messenger**   Enable the Do Not Allow Windows Messenger To Be Run setting to prevent Windows Messenger from being used. Instant messaging applications can be used to copy files to a remote desktop. These files might contain code that could allow an attacker to gain control of the desktop.

Guidelines

Follow these guidelines when designing the use of administrative templates to manage user access to operating system features:

- Use other operating system features to control user access. Administrative templates are a powerful feature that can be used to manage users. However, they are not the only feature. If, for example, you want to prevent users from using terminal services, there are settings in administrative templates that can assist you. However, if no one should use terminal services to connect to specific computers, you should also take the direct step of disabling terminal services, and possibly providing an IPSec policy to block any attempts at using terminal services.

- Use combinations of operating systems features to gain the maximum control over user access. An example of doing so would be applying the controls described in the previous bullet point.

- Use administrative templates to apply restrictions selectively to users. A different policy can be designed for an OU or even, using filtering by groups, for members of specific Windows Groups whose accounts are in the OU.

- Use both computer configuration and user configuration administrative templates when features are present in both.

Practice: Translating a Security Policy that Controls User Access to Operating System Features

In this practice, you will make a list of technical controls that can be used to fulfill a security policy and then expand one control by providing details. Review the security policy and then answer the questions that follow. If you are unable to answer a question, review the lesson materials and try the question again. You can find answers to the questions in the "Questions and Answers" section at the end of the chapter.

Security Policy

The security policy states, "Users shall not be able to configure their computers."

Review Questions

Answer the following questions.

1. What technical controls can be used to prevent users from configuring their computers?

_____

_____

_____

_____

_____

_____

_____

_____

_____

_____

_____

_____

_____

2. Select one aspect—such as Internet Explorer, Control Panel, or the Desktop—and describe at least five administrative template settings that will fulfill this part of the security policy. Use the Explain tabs and the Windows XP Security Guide to help you find the answers.

_____

_____

_____

_____

_____

_____

_____

_____

_____

_____

_____

_____

_____

_____

_____

_____

_____

_____

_____

_____

_____

_____

_____

_____

_____

Design Activity: Designing Technical Controls to Manage the Use of Laptop Computers

In this activity, you must use what you learned in all three lessons and apply it to a real-world situation. Read the scenario and then complete the exercise that follows. You can find answers for the exercise in the "Questions and Answers" section at the end of this chapter.

Scenario

Your company, Contoso, Ltd., has been contacted to present a proposal for assisting Humongous Insurance in designing controls for employees who use laptop computers. As the technical assistant for the sales team, you are asked to provide a top-level design of the technical controls to manage laptop users and a list of specific controls and recommended settings that can be added to the proposal. Your job is to provide the sales team with solid information and recommendations for the things to tell Humongous Insurance in the proposal, but the sales team will decide what and how much to include in the proposal. Your preliminary design—a list of steps to take—must be ready for the team meeting tomorrow. You and the sales team have been allowed to conduct preliminary interviews and have gathered the following information.

Company Background

Humongous Insurance is a large national insurance company with multiple locations.

Existing Environment

Many employees spend part of their time at the office and part of their time traveling. Some employees work almost entirely from their homes or from various locations while they are traveling. All employees that must travel are issued company laptops with all the software necessary to do their jobs. Laptops are running either Windows 2000 or Windows XP Professional. Microsoft Office is installed on all laptops, as are personal firewalls and antivirus software. GPOs that contain restrictive administrative template settings are linked to OUs that contain user and computer accounts. There are some OUs that contain computer accounts for both laptops and desktops. All laptop computers are members of a Windows Server 2003 domain.

Interviews

Following is a list of company personnel interviewed and their statements:

- **Chief Security Officer**   "We have a very restrictive desktop lockdown program. If there is a way to configure an application so that you must be an administrator to configure it, we do it. If there is a control that can be locked down and/or removed from the user interface, we do so. We have developed a large number of custom-written profiles that describe the tasks a user must do and how much his computer can be locked down and still allow him to do it. These have been translated into GPOs and are applied to all desktop computers used at company offices. However, we cannot link these GPOs to OUs that contain laptop computers because this prevents the laptop users from being able to do their job."

■ **Network administrator** "The laptop users have too much access to their computers' utilities and configuration. We are constantly seeing problems caused by the changes that they make. They delete software, reconfigure network settings, add software that causes problems, change settings in Control Panel, and generally are like young puppies to whom everything is a chew bone. If a setting can be changed, I can guarantee you that some laptop user has changed it."

Business Requirements

The business requirements are:

1. Computer problems must not interfere with the user's productivity.

2. Help desk costs must be reduced.

Technical Requirements

The technical requirements are:

1. Laptop users must have limited access to operating system and application features. Specifically, they might need to be able to modify network configuration, add a printer, and do some other limited configurations, but they must not be able to control everything.

2. A way to update and maintain any configuration settings must be available without returning the laptop to the help desk for maintenance.

Exercise 1: Create a Preliminary List of Technical Controls to Manage the Use of Laptop Computers

In this exercise, you will prepare a list of recommendations to provide a solution for Humongous Insurance. Answer the following question.

1. What should Humongous Insurance do to control the use of laptop computers? Prepare a list of recommendations and provide supporting evidence or reasons why you have included each item.

_____

_____

_____

_____

Chapter Summary

- Designing a secure client system means considering all aspects of computer and network security as it affects client computers.

- Key areas of concern are hardening the client computer operating system and restricting user access to operating system features.

- Administrative templates are extremely useful tools for securing both key areas. However, they are not the only solution and should be combined with controls that secure computers—controls such as security templates and software restriction policies, group membership, communication protection, and local computer access controls.

Exam Highlights

Before taking the exam, review these key points and terms. You need to know this information.

Key Points

- Watch double negatives in administrative templates. Enabling a setting that begins with the word "Disable" disables the feature. Disabling the same feature actually enables it. Enabling a setting that begins with the words "Do not allow" disables a feature. Disabling the same setting actually enables it.

- If you set the software restriction policy security level to Disallowed, no software other than crucial operating system features can run unless you create a software restriction rule that allows the software to run.

- If you set the software restriction policy security level to Unrestricted, all software can run unless a rule is developed to prevent specific software from running. However, some rules—such as path rules—can be circumvented, so using an unrestricted security level and rules is not a sure solution to preventing unauthorized software from running.

- Use administrative templates—both computer and user configuration settings—to manage access to application features and to prevent user access to operating system features. If there is a conflict, computer settings usually win.

- Design an OU infrastructure to support the application of administrative templates in unique GPOs. Administrative templates cannot be imported into GPOs; instead, the settings must be configured directly in the GPO.

Key Terms

Security levels   A setting in a software restriction policy that determines whether all software is allowed to run (Unrestricted) or no software is allowed to run (Disallowed). It is also a setting in a software restriction policy rule that determines whether the rule means that the software is permitted to run (Unrestricted) or prevented from running (Disallowed).

Software restriction policies   Tools in Group Policy that can be used to restrict or allow software to run on computers running Windows XP Professional and Windows Server 2003.

Software restriction rule   A specific declaration within a software restriction policy that allows a specific software program to run or prevents it from running.

Questions and Answers

Page
11-10

Lesson 1 Practice: Designing an OU Infrastructure for Client Computers

1. What should the OU infrastructure look like? Design the OU infrastructure by sketching it below.

Answers may vary. The following graphic shows a recommended design.

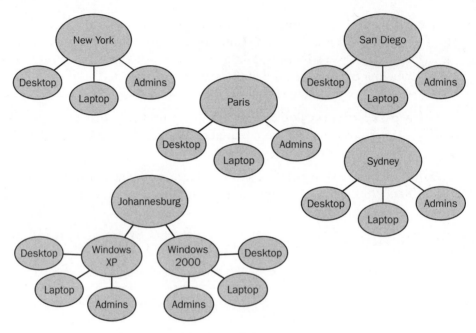

2. Why did you create the OUs that you did?

Answers may vary. The geographical OUs are already in place with computer accounts. This structure is left as is because each geographic area manages its own computers. Leaving this structure in place will also leave delegated management tasks in place. Within each OU, child OUs are created for each role and computer accounts are moved there as appropriate.

All locations except Johannesburg are limited to one client operating system. However, in Johannesburg, both Windows XP and Windows 2000 Professional clients exist. At this location, two child OUs are created—one for each operating system—and then child OUs for each computer role are created within them. This arrangement allows for the development of a baseline GPO for the operating system OU, which supports the organization's security policy, and it allows for the development of incremental GPOs for each computer role that might adjust that policy to meet the needs of the computer role.

Lesson 2   Practice: Analyzing Administrative Template Settings to Control Application Features

1. Spend time learning about each selection in the Terminal Services section of the administrative templates in Group Policy. Use the Explain tabs and any additional resources that you need, such as the results from searching the Technet Web site or the Windows XP Security Guide. Then use Table 11-5 to record at least five recommendations for hardening terminal services (making sure they are things that can be done with Group Policy), and provide your reasons for making these recommendations. You cannot use any recommendations that were already used in this lesson.

The following table provides one answer. Answers may vary.

Table   Recommendations for Hardening Terminal Services—Answer Key

Setting	Recommendation and Reasons
Allow Reconnection From Original Client Only	Enable this setting to prevent users with Citrix ICA clients from reconnecting to a session from a computer other than the computer that they started the session with. This might prevent a hijacked session, one where the original user does not end a session before logging off, and another user, who has obtained the original user's credentials, reconnects to the session. Unfortunately, this setting works only when Citrix clients are used.
Set A Time Limit For Active But Idle Terminal Services Sessions	Enable and set a time limit. If a user leaves her desktop unattended after starting a session, this timeout will disconnect the session after the specified time. This can prevent someone from simply using the session at the user's desktop while the user is away. The interloper would have access to anything that the original user would because the interloper is using her credentials.
Start A Program On Connection	Enable this setting to restrict a user's activity on the terminal server. The Start button is not displayed, and when the user ends the designated program, the session is automatically terminated.
Set Rules For Remote Control Of Terminal Services Sessions	Enable this setting to prevent any viewing or remote control of a session. If an administrator can view a session, he can view sensitive information. If he can remotely control it, he can act as the user. Neither of these capabilities is desirable where users do confidential or sensitive work.
Deny Log Off Of An Administrator Logged In To The Console Session	Enable this setting to prevent an administrator from forcing the logoff of another administrator when the first administrator is connected to the console. If the first administrator is forced off the session, all data not saved is lost. This might not be a good idea.

Page
11-38

Lesson 3 Practice: Translating a Security Policy that Controls User Access to Operating System Features

Review Questions

1. What technical controls can be used to prevent users from configuring their computers?

   Answers may vary. Recommended answer:

   ❑ Administrative Template settings in a GPO

   ❑ An IEAK profile

   ❑ Direct application of registry settings

   ❑ Custom scripts

   ❑ Third-party applications

   ❑ Not making users administrators or power users on their computer

2. Select one aspect—such as Internet Explorer, Control Panel, or the Desktop—and describe at least five administrative template settings that will fulfill this part of the security policy. Use the Explain tabs and the Windows XP Security Guide to help you find the answers.

   Answers may vary. Answer for Internet Explorer:

   ❑ Enable the Disable Automatic Install Of Internet Explorer Components setting. This setting prevents the automatic installation of components when a Web site is visited that needs them. The user will be prompted and allowed to install or not install the component. Many Web sites offer Internet Explorer components for download. There is no way to determine whether the Internet Explorer component is good, has an inherent flaw, or harbors malicious code. You should provide an alternative way for updating Internet Explorer. However, letting users simply respond to a request that lets any Web site download code to the browser is a potential problem.

   ❑ Enable the Disable Periodic Check For Internet Explorer Software Updates setting. By default, Internet Explorer will check for new updates every 30 days and notify users if one is available. By enabling this setting, users won't know of and download updates. Enabling this setting assists in maintaining version control. An alternative way of updating Internet Explorer—such as using Software Update Services—should be put into place so that client computers can be updated with security patches.

   ❑ Enable the Disable Software Update Shell Notifications On Program Launch setting. By default, the user is notified if channels, a technology for updating software, are used to install new components. When this is enabled, channels aren't used. Enabling this setting also prevents users from interfering with shell updates.

❑ Enable the Security Zones: Do Not Allow Users To Add/Delete Sites setting. When a site is added to a security zone, the settings assigned to that zone affect how the site can be accessed. Because some zones might be set to more restrictive settings, you should not allow users to change which zone a site can be set to or to add an unknown site explicitly.

❑ Enable the Security Zones: Do Not Allow Users To Change Policies setting. Security settings for each security zone make up a policy by which user activity and Internet Explorer response is controlled. If users were able to change this policy, they might do so in a manner that would put the company at risk.

❑ Enable the Security Zones: Use Only Machine Settings setting. This setting ensures a uniform application of security zone settings. When this setting is disabled, users can choose their own settings. If this is enabled, no user can change the settings, and this is what you want.

Design Activity: Designing Technical Controls to Manage the Use of Laptop Computers

Page
11-41

Exercise 1: Create a Preliminary List of Technical Controls to Manage the Use of Laptop Computers

1. What should Humongous Insurance do to control the use of laptop computers? Prepare a list of recommendations and provide supporting evidence or reasons why you have included each item.

Answers may vary. Recommendations:

❑ Make laptop users members of the Network Configuration Operators group so that they can make changes as necessary to their network configuration.

❑ Make laptop users members of the Print Operators group so that they can manage a printer connected to their laptop.

❑ Remove laptop user accounts, both user and computer, from general OUs. The goal is to be able to manage them differently. Create a new OU, and place laptop accounts in it.

❑ Design software restriction policies that allow only approved software on the laptop computers. This will keep users from installing or running unauthorized software.

❑ Create IEAK profiles to manage Security Zones and other aspects of Internet Explorer configuration and block user access to these configurations. Controlling Security Zone configuration is a good way to protect systems. Tight controls for Internet sites and relaxed controls for intranet sites can be established.

❑ Review the current administrative template settings for computers and users that do not travel. Determine changes that will be needed to relax control so that users can do their job while away from the office.

Section V
Creating a Security Design for Wireless Networks and Web Servers

Designing security for networks is a large task, and no one element should be ignored. However, two areas where security is paramount, where security is often weak, and where attackers delight in testing their acuity are wireless networks and Internet Information Services (IIS).

Never has it been so easy for anyone to access data from any device at any time. Mobile devices now come with default wireless access, and wireless access points (APs) are very inexpensive and make computing more convenient. However, mobile devices are so difficult to secure that wireless seek-out-and-remove exercises are rapidly becoming a major security initiative within many organizations. Many organizations are finding that employees are using their own money to purchase wireless APs. They are finding that even departmental and approved wireless APs are not secured. Yet it is not difficult to design secured wireless access. Chapter 12 will tell you how.

Web servers represent one of the few instances where outsiders are invited into your information systems.

Your job as a designer is to make sure that that invitation is not abused. Chapter 13 will help you do that. The chapter will help you create IIS security designs that accomplish the following:

- Ensure that invited guests cannot stray outside of areas approved for them.
- Provide every protection possible for Web site content and Web server operations.
- Ensure that default and planned security is not removed without cause.

12 Designing Security for Wireless Networks

Exam Objectives in this Chapter:

- Design public and private wireless LAN with security.
- Design 802.1x authentication for wireless networks.

Why This Chapter Matters

If you don't design and implement secure wireless networks, unsecured wireless networks will appear across the enterprise. Unsecured wireless networks allow unauthorized and unauthenticated access to your corporate network from both harmless guests who wish to piggyback on your connection to the Internet and from attackers.

Lessons in this Chapter:

Before You Begin

This chapter presents the skills and concepts related to creating a security design framework. This training kit presumes that you have a minimum of 1 year experience implementing and administering desktop operating systems and network operating systems in environments that have:

- At least 250 supported users
- Three or more physical locations
- Typical network services such as messaging, database, file and print, proxy server or firewall, Internet and intranet, remote access, and client computer management
- Three or more domain controllers
- Connectivity needs that include connecting branch offices and individual users in remote locations to the corporate network, and connecting corporate networks to the Internet

In addition, you should have experience designing a network infrastructure.

Many design exercises are paper-based; however, to understand the technical capabilities that a design can incorporate, you should have some hands-on experience with products. Where specific hands-on instruction is given, you will need at least two computers configured as specified in the "Getting Started" section at the beginning of this book.

Lesson 1: Designing Security for Wireless Networks

It is imperative that you develop and use a secure design for wireless networks. Doing this is difficult because the wireless standards themselves, and therefore the equipment built to meet the standards, have many security failings. To counter these limitations, you must know what they are.

After this lesson, you will be able to

- Explain the purpose of an 802.11 wireless network.
- Describe secure and insecure wireless network topology options.
- Describe wireless network security features.
- Explain the process for designing security for wireless networks.
- Describe the threats introduced by wireless networks.
- Design security for 802.11b wireless networks.
- Design security for 802.11i (WPA) networks.

Estimated lesson time: 40 minutes

What Is an 802.11 Wireless Network?

In this chapter, a *wireless network* is a network that consists of two or more connected 802.11 wireless computing devices in either:

- **Infrastructure mode**   Wireless clients connect to a wireless access point (AP) that might or might not be connected to a wired network.

   -or-

- **Ad hoc mode**   Wireless clients connect directly to each other without using an AP.

Other types of wireless networks, such as the cellular phone network or other wireless communications networks, are not covered in this chapter.

Several versions of the 802.11 wireless standard—including 802.11b, 802.11a, 802.11i, and 802.11g—have been or are being implemented in commercially available devices. However, the most prevalent systems are 802.11b. Another standard, 802.1x, is not a standard that defines a wireless network; instead, it defines a security protocol (encryption and authentication) for 802.11 wireless networks that also can be used for wired networks. Table 12-1 lists and defines the current 802.11 wireless standards. In the table, the acronyms WEP and WPA are used. These terms indicate encryption processing, which is fully defined in the section "Wireless Network Security Features" later in this lesson. For more information about the standards, see the Institute of Electrical and Electronics Engineers (IEEE) wireless Web site at *http://standards.ieee.org/wireless.*

> **Note**   The 802.11 standard is also referred to as *Wireless Fidelity* or *WiFi*.

Table 12-1   Current 802.11 Wireless Standards

Standard	Wired Equivalent Privacy (WEP) or WiFi Protected Access (WPA)?	Information
802.11b	Both	The most common wireless network with a speed of 11 megabits per second (Mbps) and a frequency of 2.4 gigahertz (GHz).
802.11a	Both	A newer standard that is not compatible with 802.11b. It has a speed of 54 Mbps and a frequency of 5 GHz.
802.11g	Both	Gigabit wireless. A newly completed standard said to be 100 % backward-compatible with 802.11b. It has a speed of 54 Mbps and a frequency of 2.4 GHz.
802.11i	Not applicable	A draft standard expected to be ratified in late 2003 to improve security.
WPA	Not applicable	An interim standard similar to 802.11i.
802.1x	Both	A security standard for 802.11 networks that provides authentication and encryption. 802.1x requires the use of a RADIUS server.

Secure and Insecure Wireless Network Topology Options

The typical wireless network configuration consists of an access point—a server that connects clients to an internal network—and client computers. Figure 12-1 shows this arrangement, which is known as a Basic Service Set (BSS). The wireless access point serves as a bridge between the wireless and wired network.

When a wireless network is configured in this manner, any wireless client that can successfully connect to the wireless AP is connected to the internal network. When several APs are used but are connected to the same wireless network, the arrangement is known as an Extended Services Set (ESS). The ESS creates a single logical network segment and is identified by a single Service Set Identifier (SSID). An example ESS is shown in Figure 12-2. Security consists of wireless AP controls, as discussed later in the section titled "The Process: Designing Security for Wireless Networks."

A more secure approach requires the wireless client to use a virtual private network (VPN) to access the internal network. Figure 12-3 shows this arrangement. In the figure, note the use of a firewall to protect the internal network from potential attacks from unauthorized wireless clients.

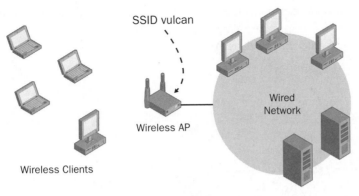

Figure 12-1   A simple wireless network uses a wireless access point as a bridge to a wired network.

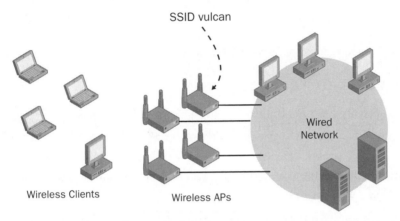

Figure 12-2   Several wireless APs can be combined to create a single logical subnet.

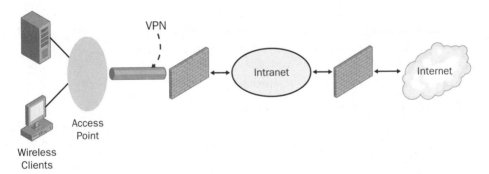

Figure 12-3   When a VPN is required in order to access the internal network, client-to-server communications can be secured, as can the wired network.

Another approach uses a RADIUS server and the 802.1x authentication protocol to provide additional security both at the AP and at the juncture of wireless and wired networks. As shown in Figure 12-4, Microsoft Internet Authentication Server (IAS) can be used as the authentication server in this arrangement. In the figure, the dotted lines represent the request for connection from the wireless client to the AP, which then must go to IAS and be authenticated by Active Directory.

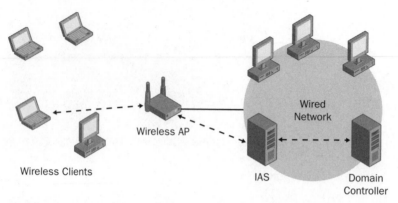

Figure 12-4   IAS provides a secure border control for wired/wireless network connections.

Wireless Network Security Features

Although the security features built in to 802.11 networks are few, there are options. The following authentication and encryption choices must be made as part of the design process.

- **Authentication options for 802.11**   The 802.11 standard defines the following two types of authentication:
    - ❏ Open System Authentication—No authentication is done unless it is combined with Media Access Control (MAC) address restriction on the AP.
    - ❏ Shared Key Authentication—A shared secret is used. There is no method defined for key distribution. The key configured on the AP must be known to the person manually configuring the client. The process is difficult to maintain especially in a large environment or when shared keys are frequently changed to increase security.

- **Encryption for 802.11**   Wired Equivalent Privacy (WEP) encrypts the data sent between wireless nodes using RC4. No key management protocol is defined. Keys must be manually distributed and added to wireless clients. Manual changes are required. The following two keys are defined:
    - ❏ A global key that protects multicast and broadcast traffic from a wireless AP to its clients.
    - ❏ A session key that protects unicast traffic between the AP and its clients and that protects multicast and broadcast traffic sent from clients to the AP.

- **WiFi Protected Access (WPA)**   This is an interim standard that follows the proposed 802.11i wireless standard. This standard provides improved encryption by using the Temporal Key Integrity Protocol (TKIP). TKIP provides integrity. Authentication is provided by the use of the Extensible Authentication Protocol (EAP).

- **802.1x**   This is a new security standard for 802.11 networks that uses RADIUS for authentication and provides key management.

The Process: Designing Security for Wireless Networks

In spite of the options listed in the previous section, the typical 802.11 wireless access point offers little in the way of security. In many cases, it is deployed using the system defaults and does not support the relatively new WPA or 802.1x standards. The access point is connected to the wired network and then turned on. Computer systems with wireless cards can easily connect to the network.

To design security for an 802.11 network, follow this process:

1. Be aware of the threats that wireless networks introduce.

2. Advise management of the threats, propose a wireless security policy that outlaws unapproved wireless networks and specifies the wireless security standards for your organization, or if appropriate, do both.

3. Design wireless security for 802.11b networks:

    ❑ Design security for wireless clients.

    ❑ Design secure configuration of wireless networks.

    ❑ Provide a more secure network topology.

4. Design security for 802.11i (WPA) networks.

5. Design wireless security using 802.1x authentication.

Guidelines for these design steps are provided below, with the exception of number 5. The subject of designing wireless security using 802.1x authentication is discussed in Lesson 2.

Threats Introduced by Wireless Networks

The following threats are present wherever wireless networks exist:

- **Attacks by an intruder with a wireless connection to your network**   Attacks can be of any type that could be launched from a wired connection, including password-cracking attacks, attempts to find weak controls, broadcast monitoring (whereby an attacker sniffs data as it traverses your network), or even the launching of a worm, virus, or Trojan horse attack. While use of a switch instead of a hub as a connection point for the wireless AP might prevent casual listening to all traffic on the network, Address Resolution Protocol (ARP) spoofing can be used to trick the switch into routing data through the intruder's client.

■ **Worm and virus attacks by a passive intruder**   Even if the intruder means no harm and is just seeking free access to the Internet, if his computer is infected with a worm or virus, he might spread it to your network.

■ **Secure Sockets Layer (SSL) and Secure Shell (SSH) hijacking**   This type of attack might be accomplished by an attacker against wireless networks that rely on SSL VPNs for access security. In this attack, the intruder uses an ARP spoofing technique and attempts to substitute his server credentials. The client gets a warning that the credentials have changed and is asked to accept them. If a user accepts the credentials, the communications destined for the client's internal network are now redirected to the attacker's rogue server.

■ **Unauthorized connections by anyone with a computing device and a wireless network card to an unsecured wireless access point**   Access to the wireless network does not require a wired connection. A connection to your wireless network might be made just as easily from the parking lot of your building, the sidewalk outside its front door, or the offices on the floor above as it is from your business offices. While a wireless connection does not remove the protections you have in place using authentication, access controls, and encryption, a wireless connection does allow unauthorized individuals access to your network, inside your firewall. Any connection to your inside network is a potential threat.

■ **Attacks on your wireless clients from other wireless clients**   Joining your wireless client to an unsecured wired network places you on a network with unknown participants. This is like being connected to the Internet without a firewall. Any attack that might be mounted over the Internet can also be used against clients on a wireless network.

■ **Attacks from rogue access points that have created unauthorized access points to the network**   Employees might connect a wireless access point to their authorized network connection. They do this to make it easier to move around the general area of their office without a wire or to allow visitors to their area to connect to the network. An intruder might seek to connect a rogue wireless access point to an unattended network jack. If the intruder is successful, he now has a connection to your network from outside your facilities.

■ **Logon credentials capturing (also known as the Evil Twin attack)**   An attacker might attempt to capture logon credentials by placing a fake access point near the legitimate one. If her access point has a stronger signal, she can entice clients to attempt to log on to her wireless network instead of the real one. When clients attempt to log on, she might be able to capture logon credentials that can be used in an attack on the client's real networks.

■ **Attacks against WEP**   Such an attack might be mounted and be successful at obtaining the WEP encryption keys. If the keys are obtained, an attacker can decrypt wireless data. In addition to gaining sensitive information, the attacker might also obtain information necessary to join the wireless network protected by WEP.

■ **Jamming or Denial of Service (DoS) attacks**   Just as a DoS attack against a wired network can work by overloading the network with too much activity, similar attacks can make a wireless network unavailable.

■ **Disruption**   Other devices—such as baby monitors, cordless phones, and Bluetooth devices—work at the same 2.4 GHz frequency and can disrupt the wireless network.

Wireless Attack Resources

Many of the threats listed in the "Threats Introduced by Wireless Networks" section are widely known, but many network administrators are not aware of them. You can locate more information at the following locations. If you find links for attack tools and want to download them to learn how to defend your network, consider the source and protect your network and client.

■ A Dsniff FAQ explaining SSH and HTTPS hijacking can be found at *www.monkey.org/~dugsong/dsniff/faq.html*.

■ Airsnort is a program that can be used to attack WEP-encrypted data. If enough data can be captured, encryption keys can be recovered. Information about Airsnort can be found at *http://airsnort.shmoo.com/* and *http://sourceforge.net/projects/airsnort*.

■ Netstumbler scans for wireless networks and logs SSIDs and the access point's MAC address. If you add a GPS receiver, it logs the latitude and longitude of the AP. You can turn off the broadcast of SSIDs by the AP to hide the access point from Netstumbler (*www.netstumbler.com*).

■ Information on the Pocket PC MiniStumbler can be found at *www.netstumbler .com*.

Guidelines for Designing Security for 802.11b Wireless Networks

To design wireless security for 802.11b networks, you must design security for wireless clients and provide a more secure network topology and proper wireless access point configuration to secure the wireless network from wireless attacks. The following sections provide the guidelines that you need to do these things.

Guidelines for Designing Security for 802.11b Wireless Clients

Wireless clients also need defenses against attacks that might be directed towards them. Remember, enabling a wireless client is similar to plugging it into an untrusted wired network. You do not know who might be near enough to attack the wireless client, either through a connection to the wireless AP or by making a direct connection to the client. Use the following guidelines to design security for clients:

■ Use personal firewalls on wireless clients.

■ Use a VPN client to connect to the network using a wireless client. Doing this adds another layer of encryption and authentication.

■ Secure the client. Ensure file and print services are turned off.

■ Use hardening techniques to secure the client operating system.

Guidelines for Providing Proper Wireless Access Point Configuration and a More Secure Network Topology

In addition to designing proper security for wireless clients, designing security for 802.11b networks consists of providing proper configuration of the wireless access point and providing a more secure network topology configuration.

Design Considerations for Securely Configuring Wireless Access Points   By default, many wireless access points are configured in the least secure mode and many wireless access points remain highly insecure. Wireless networks are subject to different attacks than wired networks, and they introduce new threats to the wired network. The following security configuration can be implemented to protect the wireless access point and the wired network that it is connected to.

■ Secure the network name.

    ❑ Change the default Server Set ID (SSID). The SSID identifies the wireless access point and thus its wireless network. If the wireless access point is correctly configured, only clients that are configured with the same SSID can communicate with it. Think of the SSID as a simple shared password. As with a shared password, eventually everyone knows it and its use provides no security at all. All wireless access points come configured with a default SSID. (Some default passwords are *tsunami, 101, Default SSID, WLAN, intel, linksys,* and *wireless.*) Because default SSIDs are widely known, using the default SSID provides no security. Changing the SSID might provide little protection, however, because many wireless access points broadcast their SSID and many wireless clients listen and identify the network to the user, or they might even automatically attempt to connect to it. Even if WEP is configured, the SSID is not encrypted. The 802.11 standard does not call for encryption of the wireless management packets. Still, having a unique SSID is a start.

❑ Turn off the SSID broadcast. Some wireless access points can be configured not to broadcast the SSID. This will prevent an attacker from obtaining the SSID by sniffing for the broadcast. However, the SSID will be transmitted in the clear when a legitimate client connects to the access point. An intruder needs only to sniff and wait for a legitimate client to connect and capture the SSID. Turning off the broadcast is not a significant security step, but it does keep the casual interloper off the network.

■ Secure WEP.

❑ Configure WEP. WEP can be configured to use 40-bit or 12-bit encryption. Turning on WEP provides encryption of the data packets between the wireless client and the access point. However, known flaws in WEP allow an attacker to discover the WEP encryption keys. Still, an attacker is not lurking around every corner armed with an attack tool and interested in listening in to your network. Using WEP will prevent the mildly curious from sniffing your wireless communications and prevent the interloper who claims to only desire free Internet access from connecting to your network. Newer APs can be programmed to overcome some of the weaknesses of WEP and yet remain compatible with existing wireless network cards. If these APs are in use, many of the less sophisticated attacks against WEP can be repulsed. Use of WEP might just provide a sound legal advantage because an attacker armed with tools to break your encryption can hardly claim that she was merely seeking free Internet access.

❑ Change the default WEP keys. Access points might come configured with default WEP keys. Change these keys. These keys are well known and will certainly be used to test any wireless network that is using WEP.

■ Secure the Simple Network Management Protocol (SNMP).

❑ Change the SNMP community word. Some access points run an SNMP agent. This provides a network management tool for network administrators, and if the community word is left at the default, it is a tool that can be used by attackers to configure the access point. If the attacker can do so, he can nullify any security you might have put into place. Common default SNMP community words are *public* and *comcomcom*.

❑ Ensure the SNMP agent is not vulnerable to the SNMP vulnerability exploited by the PROTOS tool developed by the University of Oulu. Newer SNMP implementations are not subject to this attack, and patches are available to protect older implementations.

■ Use Open System Authentication. In many wireless implementations, including Windows XP, the wireless authentication shared key is the same as the wireless encryption key. Shared key authentication uses a challenge and response mechanism, which is subject to attack. If an intruder can capture the challenge and response, he might be able to deduce the shared key and therefore have both the authentication key and the encryption key for your wireless network.

- Protect access to base-station administration tools. Many access points have Web-based administration tools that are available across a wireless connection. These administration tools might be unprotected by default or protected by a default password. The password should be changed before the access point is connected to the wired network.

- Ensure secure clients. Authorized wireless clients can pose a risk to the entire network if they store sensitive information for authentication and communication with the access point. If the client is not secure, this information can be easily obtainable by an attacker. Some wireless networks are accessible via custom clients. The clients might store the SSID in the registry. Encryption keys might be stored in the registry—unencrypted. This is not an issue with Windows XP because any SSIDs are stored in the interface and clearly visible.

- Specify a wireless access point configuration standard in the wireless security policy. A standard configuration for all access points will ensure that the security you specify is applied uniformly to all base stations.

- Filter MAC addresses. 802.11b wireless networks can provide some security if you specify the MAC addresses of authorized clients. This might not be practical on a large or dynamic network because the access points must be manually configured. It also is not foolproof security. The MAC address is transmitted in the clear and therefore can be sniffed. With proper tools, an intruder can configure her wireless computer to spoof an approved MAC address.

- Search for rogue wireless access points and remove them. Access points can be searched for by searching for SNMP agents. Web and telnet interfaces also might have banner strings that can identify an access point. Matching this information to authorized access point information helps to identify rogue APs. APs might also have a unique TCP/IP fingerprint that can be used to identify them. A wireless sniffer can also identify the presence of an AP by sniffing for 802.11 packets in the air. Checking the IP address of the packets can help you determine what networks they are on.

See Also   A large number of packets must be captured to break WEP. This might take longer than the intruder wants to wait. However, successful attacks on a busy network have taken as little as 15 minutes. To read more about the WEP issue, you can find documentation on WEP insecurities by researchers at Berkeley at *www.isaac.cs.Berkeley.edu/isaac/wep-faq.html*. An attack using this knowledge can be read about at *www.cs.rice.edu/~astubble/wep /wep_attack.html*. Note that the problem is not with the specific encryption algorithms (RC4) used by WEP but with their implementation.

Guidelines for Increasing Wireless Security through Network Topology Where wireless access points are placed on the LAN is important. You do have choices. Should you firewall the AP? Follow these guidelines to increase wireless security:

- **Carefully select and correctly position the antenna to limit the exposure of wireless networks.** When you do this, better coverage and access is provided for authorized users, and intruders have less chance of obtaining access to the network. Directional antennas and low transmitter power can eliminate some of the wireless leakage (wireless access from outside your facility). Connect the wireless access point to a switch instead of a hub.

  A switch does not broadcast all data to all its nodes, thus a wireless client can not easily sniff wired network traffic on the network connected to a switch.

- **Use a wireless DMZ.** Think of wireless access points as untrusted networks. They are. Use firewalls and VPNs to protect access to your networks from the access point.

- **Use 802.1x security.** This standard uses a key management protocol that provides keys automatically and can change them rapidly at set intervals.

> **Tip** Use a wireless honeypot. A wireless honeypot generates thousands of counterfeit 802.11b access points. You can hide the real wireless network among this plethora of beacon frames. This will confuse attackers. While it might only be a temporary setback to a determined attacker, it can cause a large number of less sophisticated or less determined attackers to look elsewhere to indulge their curiosity or to obtain free Internet access. You might also be able to monitor connection attempts and know when you are under sustained attack. You can find information about a commercial wireless honeypot at *www.blackalchemy.to/project/fakeap*.

Guidelines for Designing Security for 802.11i (WPA) Networks

The IEEE 802.11i proposed standard (ratification due at the end of 2003) includes security improvements to the 802.11 standard. An interim standard, WiFi Protected Access (WPA), has been implemented in some wireless devices. This standard improves security by using several techniques and the capabilities of existing wireless devices. An upgrade that provides Windows XP Professional WPA capabilities can be downloaded from the Microsoft Web site.

WPA security includes WPA authentication. If a RADIUS server is available, WPA supports EAP. If a RADIUS server is not available, a preshared key can be used. Encryption is required. Rekeying of unicast and global encryption keys is required by the standard. The Temporal Key Integrity Protocol (TKIP) changes the key for every frame. Key changes are synchronized between the client and the AP. The global encryption key is advertised to connected wireless clients by the AP. A technique called Michael provides integrity. Its 8-byte *message integrity code* (MIC) is encrypted with the data and the integrity check value of 802.11. The use of the Advanced Encryption Standard (AES) is optional, as some existing equipment might not be able to support the addition of the AES protocol.

To support WPA, changes must be made to the following items:

- **Wireless access points** You need to create a different beacon frame with new 802.11 WPA information containing the SP security configuration, a specification of encryption algorithm, and wireless security configuration. A firmware update might be available for existing wireless APs.

- **Wireless network adapters** The firmware must be updated to support the WPA information element, WPA two-phase authentication, TKIP, and optionally Michael. A firmware update might be available from the wireless card manufacturer. To be compatible with Windows XP (service pack 1) and Windows Server 2003, the network adapter must pass the adapter WPA capabilities and security configuration on the *Wireless Zero Configuration Service*.

- **Wireless client programs** Wireless client programs must be updated so that they can configure WPA authentication and WPA encryption algorithms. Windows XP Home and Professional (service pack 1 and later) or Windows Server 2003 will need the Windows WPA update client. The client will also modify the wireless configuration GUI to support new WPA options.

Guidelines for Securing Wireless 802.11 Networks

Follow these guidelines to secure wireless 802.11 networks:

- Use WPA if it is supported by your wireless hardware.

- Use 802.1x if it is supported by your wireless hardware.

- If neither WPA or 802.1x is available, use open system authentication and configure WEP.

- If 802.1x, WPA, or both are not an option, use a VPN.

- Design the location of APs to eliminate or at least reduce the amount of wireless access to your networks that can be found from outside your network.

Practice: Securing a Rogue Access Point

In this practice, you will design security for an access point that has just been discovered on a fictitious company's network. Read the scenario and answer the question that follows. If you are unable to answer the question, review the lesson materials and try the question again. You can find the answer to the question in the "Questions and Answers" section at the end of the chapter.

Scenario

You attend a meeting in the executive suite of Tailspin Toys. You find that a wireless access point provides network access for the executive suite. By asking a few questions, you determine that the access point was given to the president of the company by his wife. You find that the AP was simply plugged into the network. As the security officer for Tailspin Toys, you must do something. You decide that the best course of action is not to attempt to get the AP removed but to provide a security design. Your boss likes the idea, and asks you to list the five most important things that can be done to secure the rogue access point.

Review Question

Answer the following question:

1. What five ideas for securing the rogue access point would you give to your boss? Be sure to justify your ideas.

_____

_____

_____

_____

_____

_____

_____

_____

_____

_____

_____

_____

_____

_____

Lesson 2: Designing Security Using 802.1x for Wireless Networks

Even if you have taken every security precaution in configuring your 802.11 wireless network, it is difficult to prevent unauthorized connections. Anyone who can connect can detect and receive all data on that network and potentially on your wired network. Even WEP-encrypted data might be successfully attacked. An attacker can connect from outside your facilities, disrupt your network, infect it, steal data, and then be gone without a trace. 802.1x can provide a solution to such problems if properly implemented and managed. This lesson will show you how to design a solution like this.

After this lesson, you will be able to

■ Explain how 802.1x improves wireless security.

■ Describe the infrastructure requirements of 802.1x.

■ Explain how 802.1x authentication works.

■ Design security using 802.1x.

■ Design authentication using 802.1x.

Estimated lesson time: 40 minutes

How 802.1x Improves Wireless Security

802.1x is an Internet Engineering Task Force (IETF) standard that was created to address the security issues of 802.11. 802.1x is not a replacement for 802.11; instead, think of 802.1x as the security addendum for 802.11. 802.1x does add considerable security support to 802.11 wireless networks; however, hardware and software upgrades are necessary, as are changes to the wireless support infrastructures.

Security changes come with the addition of authentication improvements, validation and revocation checking procedural changes, and key management. A RADIUS server is required to perform authentication and can provide authorization and auditing improvements. The following sections describe these changes.

Authentication Improvements

Microsoft Internet Authentication Services (IAS) can be used as the RADIUS server. Both computer and user authentication flexibility is added by the ability to use Extensible Authentication Protocol (EAP) types, including the following:

■ **PEAP-EAP-MSCHAPv2**   Protected Extensible Authentication Protocol (PEAP) EAP-MSCHAPv2 passwords are protected by Transport Layer Security (TLS). Mutual authentication is provided because the server also is authenticated by the client. The RADIUS server is used for authentication and must have a certificate, but client computers do not need them. Instead, the user provides a user ID and password.

- **EAP-TLS**   This type provides certificate-based, mutual authentication. Both the RADIUS authentication server and wireless clients must have certificates.

- **EAP-MD5**   No certificates are required, and authentication is not mutual. The user provides a user ID and password for authentication. This option is not considered secure because there is no protection for the user credentials, and the credentials are subject to dictionary attacks as with Challenge Handshake Protocol (CHAP) protocol, which EAP-MD5 is based on.

Certification Validation and Checking Procedures

When certificates are used for authentication, it is important that validation and revocation checking is enabled. When IAS is the RADIUS server, Windows XP is the client, and certificates are used, the following certificate validation and checking procedures are followed:

1. IAS checks client certificates

    - for valid dates.

    - to see whether it is possible to construct a certificate chain.

    - if configured, for required key usages and application policies present in the certificate.

    - to ensure they have been signed with the client's private key.

    - to check for revocation.

2. Windows XP checks the server certificate

    - for valid dates.

    - to see whether it is possible to construct a certificate chain.

    - for required key usages in the certificate.

    - to ensure the certificate has been signed with the server's private key.

> **Tip**   During authentication, Windows XP cannot check the revocation status of the IAS server certificate because network access is not available during EAP-TLS authentication. You can, however, enable an extra certificate check. You can explicitly select the trusted root CAs to which the server certificate can chain. This process will produce a trust decision prompt to users. While properly making a trust decision might seem inconsequential, it is sometimes a difficult issue for end users. Management of the list can be provided by using update string values on WLAN clients through Active Directory directory services wireless network policies. This solution might not be warranted except in high security situations because of the need for user training and the potential management details involved in constantly updating the list.

Key Management

Key management is the process of key change and distribution. One of the failings of 802.11 wireless networks is that there is no key management. By default in 802.11 wireless networks, encryption keys are manually recorded in access points and clients. To change the keys, a new key must be entered both at the access point and on every client—an operation that is merely tedious when there are a few clients but near impossible with any frequency when there are many clients. The lack of key management is answered in 802.1x by dynamic key assignment. *Dynamic key assignment* means that encryption keys are distributed to the clients automatically; it is not necessary to manually enter keys. Keys can also be frequently changed without manual intervention.

Frequent key changes improves security because it makes it more difficult to crack the key and limits the harm done if an attacker deduces a key. Ideally, keys should be changed before any cracking tool can deduce them. Simply put, if the keys are changed often enough, an attacker will not be able to capture enough information in time to crack the encryption keys. Before he can do so, they will be changed.

> **Note**   802.1x can be implemented with both WPA and WEP 128-bit encryption.

Windows XP and IAS will perform dynamic key assignment during certificate authentication. Therefore, key exchange—the process of ensuring that client and server both have the same session keys—is protected. Keys are refreshed periodically by forcing the Windows XP client to reauthenticate to the server every 10 minutes. Dynamic key exchange and refresh, also known as *rekeying*, is possible only when certificates are used for authentication.

> **Exam Tip**   Rekeying is not possible if EAP-MD5 is used as the authentication choice because passwords, not certificates, are used.

Infrastructure Requirements of 802.1x

Using 802.1x to improve the security of an 802.11 network is not a trivial task. Extensive infrastructure changes for the wired and wireless network might be necessary. Some of these changes are upgrades or replacements of wireless hardware and software. In addition, if they are not already part of the network infrastructure, RADIUS and possibly public key infrastructure (PKI) will need to be added to the wired network. The following sections describe the infrastructure requirements of 802.1x in detail.

IAS Requirements

IAS on Windows Server 2003 and Windows 2000 Server can be configured to be used as the RADIUS server in the wireless network. The wireless access point becomes the RADIUS client. Wireless clients connect to the AP, but authentication and authorization is performed by IAS via Active Directory. IAS blocks or accepts connections from the AP based on two types of IAS policies: remote access policies and connection request policies. These policies are described below:

- IAS remote access policies are used to constrain client access and manage connections. The NAS-Port-Type Matches "Wireless – Other Or Wireless-IEEE 802.11" policy (as shown in Figure 12-5) can be used to identify incoming requests from wireless clients. Additional remote access policies (for example, Windows groups, authentication EAP method, and so forth) can also be used, as described in Chapter 11.

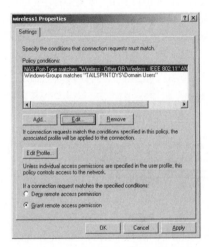

Figure 12-5   Using the NAS-Port-Type wireless remote access policy to identify wireless clients

Two profile attributes must be set on the NAS-Port-Type wireless remote access policy to ensure smooth functioning:

- ❏ Ignore-Users-Dial-in should be set to True to ensure settings such as Call Back are not sent to wireless APs.

- ❏ Termination-Action should be set to RADIUS Request, as shown in Figure 12-6, to ensure that when XP clients re-authenticate, wireless APs don't disconnect them.

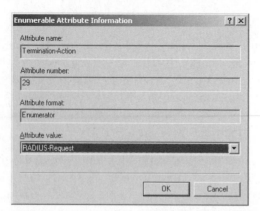

Figure 12-6   Setting the Termination-Action attribute to prevent the AP from disconnecting Windows XP clients during re-authentication

■ Connection request policies are used to manage RADIUS requests from wireless APs. Wireless APs must be identified on the IAS server to prevent rogue access points from participating in your wireless and wired networks. Connection request policies can set date and time restrictions and ensure that authentication is made against Active Directory.

PKI Requirements

If a public key infrastructure (PKI) is not established in the network, you must make a decision about how to manage the certificate requirements of 802.1x. If PEAP-EAP-MSCHAPv2 is the authentication protocol of choice, only a server certificate is necessary, and it is not necessary to implement a full-fledged PKI. However, if EAP-TLS is chosen, implementation of a Microsoft certificate services–based PKI can provide the necessary certificate infrastructure. Automatic computer certificate distribution makes the process easier. If an Enterprise CA is installed on a Windows Server 2003 Enterprise server, custom templates—which add the ability to customize key use and application requirements information on the certificate for use with wireless networks—can be designed. This can assist in constraining client connections because certificate validity checks can be based on this information.

Wireless Hardware and Software Requirements

New or upgraded APs, wireless network cards, and client software are necessary. Windows XP service pack 1 and Windows Server 2003 have the necessary client software. An 802.1x upgrade for Windows 2000 Server is available for download.

Tip   Free 802.1x clients for Windows 98, Windows Millennium Edition, and Windows NT 4.0 are available to Microsoft customers who have a support agreement.

Active Directory Requirements

Group Policy settings can be used to manage client configuration. A wireless policy is located in Group Policy (shown in Figure 12-7) at Computer Configuration/Windows Settings/Security Settings/Wireless Network (IEEE 802.11) Policies/.

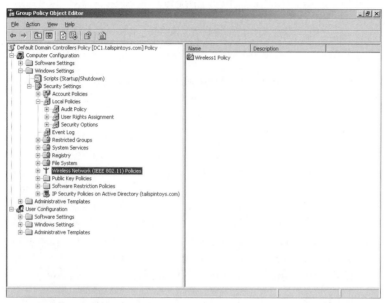

Figure 12-7   Using the Group Policy wireless policy to manage client configuration

Settings on the General Tab   The General tab of the policy (shown in Figure 12-8) includes the following settings:

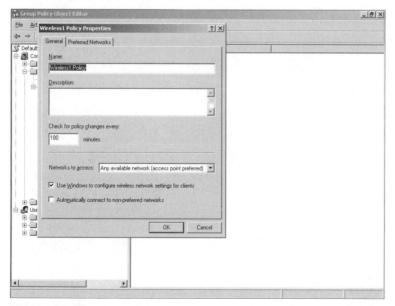

Figure 12-8   The General tab controls the type of wireless network that clients can connect to.

- A Networks To Access box that provides three choices:

  ❏ Any Available Network (Access Point Preferred)—This policy will select an access point over an AD Hoc network; however, connection to an AD Hoc network is not prevented.

  ❏ Access Point (Infrastructure) Networks Only—Set this policy to prevent connections to AD Hoc networks.

  ❏ Computer-To-Computer (AD Hoc) Network Only—Set this policy to prevent connection to an AP.

- A Use Windows To Configure Wireless Network Settings For Clients check box. This box is selected by default. This setting sets the preference for Windows configuration over any third-party wireless client software.

- An Automatically Connect To Non-Preferred Networks check box. This box is cleared by default. If selected, it allows automatic connection to any available wireless network—not a particularly good idea if you are attempting to design a secure wireless infrastructure. Allowing a client to connect to just any wireless network might expose the client to wireless attacks from other participants. Allowing automatic connection might mean that the client connects to a network without the user's knowledge. The user might think her network is not accessible by attackers when the network cable is unplugged, but because of this feature, the user might actually be connected and under attack without knowing it.

Adding Preferred Networks   Adding preferred networks to the policy provides clients with preconfigured settings that will enable them to automatically connect to approved APs. Client configurations for approved networks are configured by using the Add button on the Preferred Networks tab, as shown in Figure 12-9.

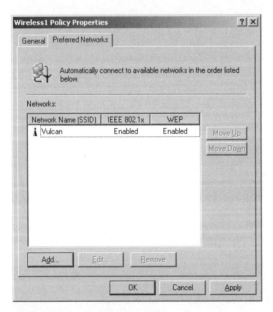

Figure 12-9   Adding preferred networks on the Preferred Networks tab

AP settings for 802.1x wireless network connections are configured on the Network Properties and IEEE 802.1x tabs. The Network Properties tab (shown in Figure 12-10) should include the SSID. Follow these guidelines regarding the checkboxes:

■ Select the Data Encryption (WEP Enabled) check box to provide encryption of data.

■ Do not select the Network Authentication (Shared Mode) check box. Open mode is required to allow authentication via IAS.

■ Select the The Key Is Provided Automatically check box to allow dynamic key exchange.

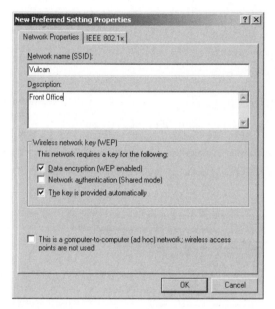

Figure 12-10   Configuring wireless network properties for all APs on the Network Properties tab

The IEEE 802.1x tab (shown in Figure 12-11) provides a place to configure 802.1x-specific properties:

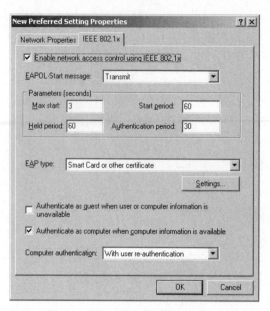

Figure 12-11 Configuring 802.1x properties on the IEEE 802.1x tab

■ Select the Enable Network Access Control Using IEEE 802.1x check box.

■ Configure the EAPOL-Start Message box and parameters to match the requirements of the AP:

❑ Transmit

❑ Do Not Transmit

❑ Transmit Per IEEE 802.1x

■ Set the EAP Type box according to the type selected on the AP: either Smart Card or Protected EAP (PEAP).

■ In either case, use the Settings button to further configure EAP settings. A new properties page (shown in Figure 12-12), identified as the properties page of the EAP Type chosen, can then be completed:

Figure 12-12   Specifying smart card or other certificate properties to ensure connectivity and to designate the trusted root certificate servers whose certificates can be used

❑   If Use My Smart Card or Use A Certificate On This Computer is chosen, the dialog box allows you to determine which will be used. When a certificate on the computer choice is made, the additional Use Simple Certificate Selection (Recommended) check box is provided. Choosing the simple certificate selection allows Windows XP to determine the correct computer certificate to use by the certificate properties.

❑   If PEAP is chosen, a further authentication method is chosen in the Select Authentication Method box (shown in Figure 12-13), either Secure Password (EAP-MSCHAPv2) or Smart Card Or Other Certificate. If EAP-MSCHAPv2 is selected, clicking the Configure button presents the opportunity to select Automatically Use My Windows Logon Name And Password (And Domain Name If Any). (See Figure 12-14.) Be sure to click OK to verify, and be sure to return to the dialog box shown in Figure 12-12 to continue exploring the other selections described below.

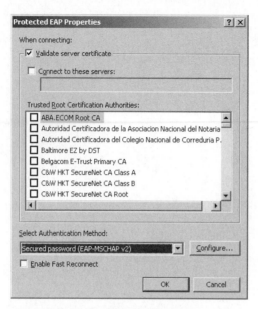

Figure 12-13 Selecting PEAP authentication: either MSCHAPv2 or certificates

Figure 12-14 If password authentication is chosen, the user's logon credentials can be automatically used if so desired.

❑ Select the Validate Server Certificate check box to require validity checks. (See Figure 12-12.)

❑ If desired, enter the fully qualified domain name suffix of the acceptable CA in the Validate Server Certificate, Connect To These Servers box. This will mean that users will be presented with a trust validation box.

❑ In the Trusted Root Certification Authorities area, select a check box next to the trusted root CA used to validate certificates. If you have implemented a PKI, your server's name should be available. If you have purchased a server certificate, select the check box for the trusted root CA of the issuing company.

❑ Select the Use A Different User Name For The Connection check box if the user requires wireless connection using a different account than he or she has logged on with.

You can also configure computer authentication behavior on the IEEE 802.1x tab (shown in Figure 12-11). Choices are:

- Authenticate As Guest When User Or Computer Information Is Unavailable. This choice is useful if guests will be allowed to access the wireless network.

- Authentication As Computer When Computer Information Is Available. This allows the computer to authenticate even if no one is logged on. This is a good thing if the computer must maintain a connection to the network.

- Computer Authentication. Within this drop-down list, three choices are possible:

  - User Re-Authentication. The computer will authenticate every time the user does.

  - User Authentication. The computer will authenticate when the user logs on.

  - Computer Only. The computer will authenticate only when the computer is started.

How 802.1x Authentication Works

This section describes the physical infrastructure components of the 802.1x authentication process and then explains how the process works.

Physical Infrastructure Components of the 802.1x Authentication Process

The 802.1x authentication process is combined with the authorization process and includes these components:

- A wireless client or supplicant
- A wireless AP with two ports:
  - An uncontrolled port to which any client can request and through which a client can negotiate a connection with the controlled port
  - A controlled port that grants access to authenticated and authorized clients
- A RADIUS server (in this example, IAS) or authenticator that serves as the control agent
- An authenticating server (the Windows Server 2003 domain controller) that can validate the presented client credentials

These components are shown in Figure 12-15. In the figure, the client has requested access but has not been authenticated; therefore, the second, controlled port is not available to it.

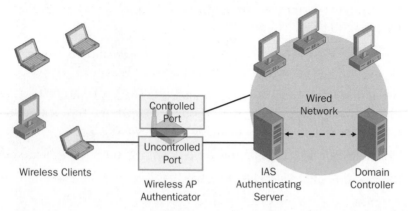

Figure 12-15   The physical infrastructure components for 802.1x authentication

The 802.1x Authentication Process

The physical infrastructure components are used in the process shown in Figure 12-16. The process is similar to that described in Chapter 7 when IAS was used as the RADIUS server for a remote access solution. One of the differences between that process and this process is that the wireless AP, as the RADIUS client, uses two ports: an uncontrolled port at which any client can request network access, and a controlled port through which only authenticated and authorized clients can access LAN resources. The numbers in the figure correspond to the steps in the process as listed below.

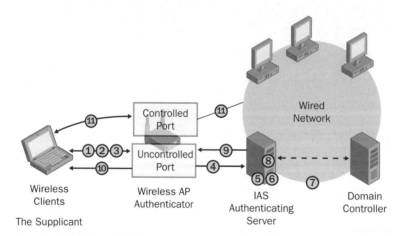

Figure 12-16   The 802.1x authentication process

1. A wireless client, the supplicant, requests a connection to the AP. The client cannot connect directly to the controlled port but must negotiate a connection using the uncontrolled port.

2. The AP requests identity information.

3. The supplicant returns this information.

4. The AP creates a RADIUS Access Request message that includes the supplicant's credentials and sends it to IAS (the authenticator).

5. IAS checks its Connection Request Policies to see whether the AP is approved and meets any constraints.

6. If the AP is authorized to submit a request and meets any constraints, IAS checks its Remote Access Policies to see whether the client is authorized.

7. If the client is authorized, the credentials from the Access Request message are forwarded to the domain controller (the authenticating server) for authentication.

8. If the client is authenticated (confirmation is returned to IAS from the domain controller), IAS checks its Remote Access Policy policies for any constraints that must be applied to the connection.

9. IAS returns notice of accepted authentication and authorization to the AP in a RADIUS Accept message.

10. The AP generates the WEP keys and passes them to the client.

11. The client is allowed access to the network through the controlled port.

Guidelines for Designing Security Using 802.1x

802.1x provides many security advantages over 802.11 used alone. Follow these guidelines when designing security for 802.1x:

- Use Group Policy to set client settings. Using Group Policy will provide uniformity and ensure the wireless access policy is being followed.
  - ❑ Set network to Access Point (Infrastructure) Networks Only.
  - ❑ Do not select the Automatically Connect To Non-Preferred Networks check box.
- Use SSL or SSH when remotely managing wireless access points. This will prevent capture of configuration data.
- Use IAS remote access policies to control connection authorization. Provide full-time staff with authenticated unrestricted access; provide contractors and business partners with authenticated, restricted access to specific networks and applications; and provide visiting guests access to the Internet, VPN access back to their own organizations, or both.
- Use IAS remote access policies to control session specifications, encryption strength, IP packet filters, and static routes.
- Use IAS connection policies to validate APs and restrict their access.

- Use Active Directory and a wireless network policy to leverage automatic configuration of networking clients. (A different policy can be configured for each GPO.)

- Mitigate the threat of WEP attacks by increasing the frequency of session key change. A lot of data must be captured by the attacker before he can deduce the keys. If the keys are changed before he obtains enough information, he will have to start all over again.

- Use the "Guidelines for Designing Authentication Using 802.1x" section that follows.

Guidelines for Designing Authentication Using 802.1x

Authentication is a critical part of the security design process for 802.1x. Follow these guidelines when designing authentication for wireless networks that will use 802.1x:

- Consider PEAP-EAP-MSCHAPv2 when user computers are not members of a domain. EAP-MSCHAPv2 requires little infrastructure change, does not require PKI, and is supported by Windows XP, Windows 2000, and Pocket PC 2002.

- Use PEAP-EAP in small organizations where a certificate infrastructure is not needed for other purposes.

- Use PEAP-EAP as a transition authentication choice where PKI implementation is in process.

- Do not use PEAP-MD5. The password used is not protected and is subject to dictionary attacks.

- Use certificate revocation. Checking for revoked certificates can prevent the use of stolen laptops and the credentials on them in attacking your network.

- Check for valid server certificates to prevent a man-in-the-middle attack.

- Use Group Policy policies to manage client authentication.

Practice: Selecting Authentication Protocols

In this practice, you will test your understanding of authentication protocol choices for 802.1x. Review the situations in Table 12-2, and evaluate each situation on its own merits (that is, each row in the table represents a different wireless design). In the second column of the table, record your choice of authentication protocol. In the third column, present your reasons for making this choice. If you are unable to answer a question, review the lesson materials and try the question again. You can find answers to the questions in the "Questions and Answers" section at the end of the chapter.

Table 12-2   Selecting Authentication Protocols

Situation	Use This Authentication Protocol	Why?
PKI is already deployed, and IAS is used for remote access.		
PKI is not deployed. Budget funds are small, and IT personnel are scarce.		
PKI is not deployed. Information is extremely sensitive, and the highest degree of security is required.		
Security policy states that rekeying must occur.		

Design Activity: Securing a Network from a Free Wireless Access Site

In this activity, you must use what you learned in both lessons and apply it to a real-world situation. Read the scenario and then complete the exercise that follows. You can find answers for the exercise in the "Questions and Answers" section at the end of this chapter.

Scenario

The Baldwin Museum of Science has a community center and promotes the use of the center for public activities. It also organizes public events such as music concerts, poetry readings, and art displays. The museum's delicatessen is open 12 hours a day and provides special coffee drinks, and in the evening it transforms itself into a wine bar. Many people use the museum as a place for relaxation and as an alternative work space. The museum would like to provide a free wireless access point so that visitors can connect to the museum Web site and access the Internet while visiting the museum.

As network administrator for the Baldwin Museum of Science, you do not want a wireless AP in the museum because you fear the security implications. Your boss tells you that you must implement wireless APs in the delicatessen and that you have 24 hours to come up with a secure Internet access plan.

Company Background

The Baldwin Museum of Science was established in 2002 to honor the technical genius of people using technology to better the world. The museum hosts a permanent collection of artifacts from the early computing era as well as a historical exhibit that covers the development of technology since early times. In addition, the museum holds educational workshops on technology concepts and provides scholarships. The response from the IT community has been phenomenal, and the museum is now looking for more space and will soon double its workforce.

Existing Environment

A small network consisting of 10 servers and 200 Windows XP Professional desktop computers supports the museum staff. The museum Web site is hosted offsite but is designed and updated from the museum.

Future Plans

The museum would like to host traveling shows from museums around the world. Next year, in particular, they would like to host a show that includes World War II cryptographic artifacts, including the only known existing example of the Japanese purple machine, an infamous German enigma machine, and many examples of code books and resources used during that era.

When museum officials inquired about hosting the show, they found that the museum did not meet the security requirements of the show promoters. Specifically, the museum uses ordinary locks on its doors, and while employees have ID badges, the badges could be easily counterfeited. Changes in IT infrastructure as well as the way the museum manages its day-to-day activities will need to be made.

Interviews

Following is a list of museum personnel interviewed and their statements:

- **Museum curator** "We really believe that giving our visitors wireless access to our Web site and the Internet will foster a sense of community as well as allow scholars to do research while examining the exhibits. We can even provide more interesting and educational tours. A proposal is sitting on my desk that would rent Pocket PCs to guests. The Pocket PCs would provide pictures and audio lectures for guests as they tour the museum. They can also look up more information, view pictures of exhibits in other museums and private collections, and ask questions directly of museum staff, all through the Pocket PC. Frankly, I don't understand what the problem is with putting in this access. I did so at my home for under $200.00."

■ **Security Chief** "My job is to protect the museum exhibits. We have good physical security, but it could be better. I have proposed smart badges. These badges will provide our staff with entrance into the building and into the private areas of the museum. I can even locate staff members by these badges if need be. More importantly, we can then implement tighter physical security at all museum entrances, back rooms, storage areas, and offices. Secondly, I want to tag every exhibit item and know if any are moved from where they are supposed to be."

Case Study Exhibits

The current network includes a single Windows Server 2003 domain with a single firewall. All desktop computers and servers are on the same physical subnet.

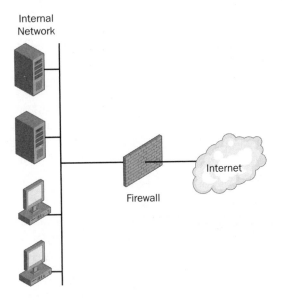

Business Requirements

These are the business requirements:

1. Guests must be able to access the Internet using their own PCs from the delicatessen area.

2. No special configuration other than entering an SSID (if visitors are not using a wireless device that can identify the wireless network, or if it is decided not to broadcast the SSID) should be necessary.

3. Future needs for wireless access must be considered.

Technical Requirements

These are the technical requirements:

1. Guests must not be able to access the museum network but must be able to access the museum Web site.

2. The infrastructure must be extensible to support future needs.

Exercise 1: Design a Secure Wireless Network

Answer the following questions.

1. How will you design the wireless network? Sketch a design, and describe the elements that you will put into place.

_____

_____

_____

_____

_____

_____

_____

_____

_____

_____

_____

_____

_____

_____

_____

_____

_____

_____

_____

_____

_____

_____

_____

_____

2. How will this design support the future wireless access needs of the museum?

_____

_____

_____

_____

_____

_____

_____

_____

_____

Chapter Summary

- Wireless networks that rely on an 802.11 infrastructure alone are difficult to secure at all.

- Adding 802.1x improves the authentication and encryption processes and makes the wireless network securable.

- Rogue wireless APs present a strong challenge to the security of the network. Efforts both in policy awareness and rigorous detection and elimination of rogue APs must be undertaken.

Exam Highlights

Before taking the exam, review these key points and terms. You need to know this information.

Key Points

- PEAP-EAP-MSCHAPv2 authentication is a good choice for small networks and for networks in which a PKI is not in place because only a server certificate is required. Authentication on the client side will require only user passwords. In addition, secure key exchange and rekeying is possible.

- EAP-TLS is the authentication method of choice where high security is required. It will, however, require PKI because both server and client certificates are necessary. Client authentication is accomplished with the use of computer certificates.

- EAP-MD5 is not considered a good authentication choice. Mutual authentication and rekeying is not possible. While authentication does follow a secure challenge and response protocol, the password material is subject to capture and dictionary attacks.

- 802.11 wireless networks that do not support 802.1x are subject to attacks on the WEP encryption. If enough data can be captured, the keys can be deduced.

Key Terms

Open System Authentication   An 802.11 wireless network identification scheme. This is not authentication at all, but merely identification.

Rekeying   The process of periodic changing of encryption keys during an encrypted session.

Service Set Identifier (SSID)   The name used to identify the wireless network.

Shared Key Authentication   An 802.11 wireless network authentication scheme. A shared secret is used.

Questions and Answers

Page
12-16
Lesson 1 Practice: Securing a Rogue Access Point

1. What five ideas for securing the rogue access point would you give to your boss? Be sure to justify your ideas.

Answers may vary. Here are five recommended ideas:

❑ Set up a VPN, and configure executive computers to use the VPN to access the wireless network. This will ensure that only authorized users can access the network through the wireless AP and provide encryption for the data they send.

❑ Use WEP. Encrypting message content will make it much more difficult for intruders to determine the information within the messages. If a VPN is implemented, this might not be necessary.

❑ Change the placement of the AP itself to minimize any signal leakage. If the signal can be located only from within the executive suite, the opportunity for access from intruders is lessened.

❑ Enter the MAC addresses of the executive computers, and allow only these computers to connect. This limits connection unless someone is able to determine and then spoof the MAC address of an executive computer. Although this type of spoofing is possible, taking these measures does provide some protection.

❑ Block administrative access via the AP's Web interface. Require access via a serial port. This will prevent a wireless connection from being able to change the AP configuration to favor the attackers.

Page
12-32
Lesson 2 Practice: Selecting Authentication Protocols

The following table provides the answers to this practice.

Table Selecting Authentication Protocols—Answer Key

Situation	Use This Authentication Protocol	Why?
PKI is already deployed, and IAS is used for remote access.	EAP-TLS	Certificate issuance is not a problem. Mutual authentication will occur.
PKI is not deployed. Budget funds are small, and IT personnel are scarce.	PEAP-EAP-MSCHAPv2	Passwords can be used. A large investment in PKI infrastructure is not needed.

Table   **Selecting Authentication Protocols—Answer Key**

Situation	Use This Authentication Protocol	Why?
PKI is not deployed. Information is extremely sensitive, and the highest degree of security is required.	EAP-TLS	A higher level of security can be obtained. No passwords are used.
Security policy states that rekeying must occur.	EAP-TLS	Certificates are required to support rekeying.

Design Activity: Securing a Network from a Free Wireless Access Site

Page
12-36
Exercise 1: Design a Secure Wireless Network

1. How will you design the wireless network? Sketch a design, and describe the elements that you will put into place.

Answer:

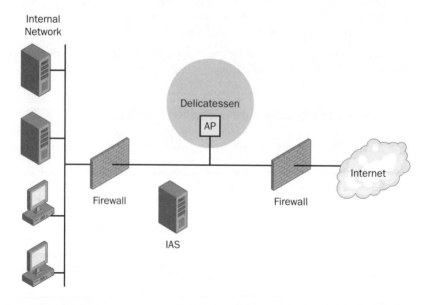

An 802.1x wireless AP will be placed in the delicatessen area and physically secured. This AP will be one that can support both 802.11b and 802.11g wireless access cards and those cards that do not have 802.1x capabilities as well as those that can. The AP will be separated from the museum network by a firewall but allowed access to the Internet. A Microsoft IAS server will be deployed, and the wireless AP will be configured as a RADIUS client of the IAS server. The IAS server will be configured to allow guest access but will limit the hours of that access to public museum hours. A connection policy will be implemented on the IAS server to

prevent connections by rogue APs. Maximum logging will be configured both on the IAS server and inside the museum network. The logs will be filtered and reviewed to detect intrusion attempts and any possible successes.

Although no museum computers currently have wireless network cards, a wireless policy will be developed and implemented in Group Policy at the domain level that restricts museum computers to authenticated, encrypted 802.1x access. If wireless cards are added to employee computers, Group Policy will prevent them from using the wireless network unless the connection is authenticated and encrypted. PEAP-EAP-MSCHAPv2 will be implemented as the authentication choice because this will not require the implementation of PKI. A server certificate will be obtained to support protected employee use of the wireless network. A remote access policy will be implemented on the IAS server to enforce these constraints. The initial implementation will allow only wireless access to the Internet. Employee access via museum computers will require authentication and encryption between the client and IAS server to protect the client computer.

A security policy will be written that bans any APs that are not authorized by IT and provides authority to scan, search for, and remove such APs.

2. How will this design support the future wireless access needs of the museum?

Because the infrastructure includes 802.1x-capable infrastructure, sound and secure support for authenticated and encrypted access to the museum network will be available. Although there is no deployment of PKI, this could be added to support future museum security improvements such as smart badges and more secure locks and exhibit tags. The use of client certificates is also supported by the wireless infrastructure and could easily be added. As new plans for the use of wireless access by both employees and guests are developed, the infrastructure can easily be expanded to meet these plans.

13 Designing Security for IIS

Exam Objectives in this Chapter:

- Design security for Microsoft Internet Information Services (IIS).

  - Design security for Web sites with different technical requirements through enabling the minimum required services.

  - Design a monitoring strategy for Internet Information Services.

  - Design an IIS baseline based upon business requirements.

  - Design a content management strategy for updating an IIS server.

- Design user authentication for Internet Information Services.

  - Design user authentication for the Web site using certificates.

  - Design user authentication for the Web site using authentication from IIS.

  - Design user authentication for the Web site using RADIUS for IIS authentication.

Why This Chapter Matters

Web sites serve as easily identifiable targets for targeted and nontargeted attacks. Public Web servers, by their very definition, must be accessible to everyone, and thus attacks can easily be directed to them. Web servers also run standardized applications and must be able to respond to standard protocols. Because these applications are well-known and understood by many, it is easy for attackers to create or adapt readily available attacks at them. Also, because Web servers are both accessible by the public and often provide access to resources on the public network, they can provide unintended portals for attacks on the private network of your organization.

IIS is also a high-profile attack target simply because it is the most identifiable and accessible Microsoft product. You must provide superior hardening and protection for IIS and your Web-based applications. If you don't, you are hanging up a welcome sign—inviting every malicious hacker and disgruntled former and present employee in and providing them the opportunity to destroy your network.

Lessons in this Chapter:

Before You Begin

This chapter presents the skills and concepts related to creating a security design framework. This training kit presumes that you have a minimum of 1 year of experience implementing and administering desktop operating systems and network operating systems in environments that have the following characteristics:

■ At least 250 supported users

■ Three or more physical locations

■ Typical network services such as messaging, database, file and print, proxy server or firewall, Internet and intranet, remote access, and client computer management

■ Three or more domain controllers

■ Connectivity needs that include connecting branch offices and individual users in remote locations to the corporate network, and connecting corporate networks to the Internet

In addition, you should have experience designing a network infrastructure.

Many design exercises are paper-based; however, to understand the technical capabilities that a design can incorporate, you should have some hands-on experience with products. Where specific hands-on instruction is given or desired, you will need at least two computers configured as specified in the "Getting Started" section at the beginning of this book.

Lesson 1: Designing IIS Security Baselines

Securing IIS involves a combination of developing security for Microsoft Windows Server 2003 and using IIS-specific knowledge and controls. Windows Server 2003 hardening baselines were introduced in Chapter 8. This lesson focuses on designing security for IIS. This lesson goes beyond the simple IIS incremental template mentioned previously and provides specific baselines for IIS services.

After this lesson, you will be able to

- Explain the process of designing security for IIS.
- Reduce the Web server attack surface.
- Control access to Web servers, Web sites, applications, and server resources.
- Explain how data in transit can be protected.
- Explain the considerations for designing a secure content management strategy.
- Design monitoring and maintenance strategies for IIS.
- Design access control for databases on the Web server.
- Configure Web servers to isolate Web sites and applications.

Estimated lesson time: 90 minutes

The Process: Designing Security for IIS

IIS 6.0 is installed in a locked-down fashion. With this version of IIS, many security issues will be based around deciding what services, components, and configuration need to be done to enable an application to run or to create a useful Web site that fits a business need. In the rush to "just get it to work," services might be started and components might be added that are not needed.

Your job as a designer is not only to design security controls that need to be put into place but to ensure that the security that is already established is not modified without reason. One way to enforce this process is to design a security baseline for IIS that meets business needs and then require that any change to that baseline meet stringent requirements for security and business needs. To design security for IIS that meets business needs, follow these steps:

1. *Understand the business needs.* Do not design security in a vacuum. The first step is to understand the business needs. Remember that one of these needs, however, is to provide a Web server that has security that cannot be breached. Each section of this lesson and Lesson 2 provides explicit suggestions for how the dual requirements of meeting business needs and providing a secure Web server and sites can be met.

2. *Design a reduced attack surface for the Web server.* Harden the server running Windows Server 2003. Examine the default security of IIS, and select services and components that need to be enabled or implemented. Know what exists by default for both the Web server and for Windows Server 2003.

3. *Design isolation and control for access to Web servers, Web sites, applications, and server resources.* Use ACLs and identities to isolate Web sites and protect server resources. Isolate applications in application pools. *Application pools* are a group of Web sites and applications that can use the same worker process. Each application pool serves as an isolation boundary—an application running outside of the application pool has no access to the processes or Web site running inside the application pool.

4. *Design authentication for the needs of the Web site.* Enable only the authentication types necessary. The design of authentication for IIS is taught in Lesson 2 of this chapter.

5. *Design how data will be protected in transit.* Protect sensitive data—such as logon credentials, user identities, and credit card numbers—while it is in transit. Protect data transported between IIS and database servers.

6. *Design a secure content management strategy.* Provide a secure process for managing Web site content. Only authorized people should be able to add, change, or remove content.

7. *Design monitoring and maintenance strategies for IIS. Design monitoring for security issues, performance issues, and reliability issues.* Design a patching and updating process. Design remote administration.

8. *Design security for databases used by Web sites and applications.* Databases provide storage for and process data used in Web applications. Securing this data is often an exercise in securing the database.

9. *Configure Web servers to isolate Web site and applications.* Many Web Servers host more than one Web site, and many sites host many applications. Keeping sites and applications isolated from one another is an essential security technique.

These design steps are interdependent, and the elements that are used in a specific design will depend on the business needs of a Web site, as well as the requirements of the Web server. A Web server is often used to host multiple Web sites; therefore, designing security for the Web server will also include designing security for each Web site hosted. The security needs of each site might be similar (for example, when an organization wants to host multiple departmental Web sites on a single Web server), or the security needs might be diverse (if, for example, an ISP needs to host thousands of Web sites, each from a different customer, on a single server).

Therefore, the first step in designing security for IIS is to understand the choices that can be made and then apply them to the specific needs of a Web server/Web site combination. This lesson follows that approach, as does the list of steps just shown. The first five steps, which can be approached in any order from a design standpoint, should be followed in order during implementation. They discuss the options that are available and provide some suggestions as to when they should be used. Additional security is also necessary for the Web site/Web server combination, the design of content management, and the monitoring and maintenance parts of the design.

Guidelines for Reducing the Web Server Attack Surface

To reduce the Web server attack surface, you must secure Windows Server 2003 and then enable only needed IIS components and services. The following sections provide guidelines for how to do these things.

Guidelines for Securing Windows Server 2003

The first step in reducing the attack surface for the Web server is to reduce the attack surface of the Windows Server 2003 server on which the Web server runs. Many chapters in this book detail strategies that can help you do so. This section outlines a few Web server–specific details.

Disable or Restrict Use of Unnecessary Services and Components   One of the first areas of concern should be the services running on the Web server. The design should include recommendations that specify possible services that can be disabled. Two purposes can be served here. First, in most cases, simply disabling a service ensures that any vulnerabilities discovered in its code cannot be exploited before the patch is released. Second, removing the capability that the service provides can prevent inadvertent or intentional damage to the Web server. Services are, after all, designed to be used to do something. Each "something" adds risk. For example, the remote registry service is designed to allow administrators to remotely modify the registry. If this service is enabled on the Web server, this ability could be used by an attacker to damage the Web server. However, if the service is disabled and administration is carried out either locally or through terminal services, the remote registry services should be disabled to prevent an attack using the service.

Chapter 8 provides recommendations for services that should be disabled in a locked-down environment. If you use the baseline templates described there to apply security for the server, you will use an incremental template as the IIS baseline. In that template, you will enable services that are required for the IIS server to run.

One additional thought to remember: not every Web server is only a Web server. While dedicating the server to just be a Web server is preferred, this might not always be possible. Remember to define clearly any additional roles the Web server computer will have to perform, as you might need to enable services and other settings for it to do so. The following sections provide Web server–specific information about Windows that might be different from or required in addition to the generic recommendations provided in Chapter 8.

Do not enable services that were disabled to conform to the recommendations evaluated in Chapter 8 or because of other considerations. Evaluate additional enabled services to see whether they can be disabled as well. Some services that should be evaluated include the following:

- **Automatic updates** The server update process should be reviewed for Web servers. You can choose a different path for Internet servers than for intranet servers. All Web servers should be updated; however, you might want to develop an update process that is specific to Web servers. Critical Web servers might be running specialized software and hardware, which can result in issues with updates. A higher degree of testing might be necessary. In addition, unexpected downtime because of some problem with an update might have a higher cost than if the same specialized software or hardware were located on a less critical server. For these reasons, consider disabling the automatic update services, but do design an update process.

- **BITS** The Background Intelligent Transfer Service (BITS) is used to provide background file transfers. It is used when automatic updates are enabled. If automatic updating is disabled, this service should be disabled as well.

- **Remote Registry Service** This service is used to allow Administrators and Backup Operators remote access to the registry. In a high-security server, such as an Internet server, disable this service and provide alternative remote management methods, or require administration from the console.

- **Terminal Services** Do not install terminal services in application mode. If terminal services is required for administration, it is available in administrative mode. You do not want ordinary users to be able to obtain terminal services access to the Web server.

- **SMTP Service** Simple Mail Transfer Protocol (SMTP) services can be installed on the Web server to provide e-mail services for Web applications. If it will not be used, it should not be installed. If it is used, it should be secured. Security configuration includes:

  - Assigning SMTP operators. SMTP operators are users who can configure and manage SMTP.

  - Preventing relay. Allowing uncontrolled relay can result in someone using this server to send unsolicited e-mail (spam) and in a reduction in performance.

See Also   Knowledge Base article 324281 provides instructions on how to prevent relay by requiring authentication and then setting Relay Restrictions. Relay restrictions can be used to prevent relay from any computer or restrict relay to specific groups of computers. Knowledge Base article 324285 provides further information on security options for SMTP.

- ❑ Authenticating use of SMTP services. More information can be found in Lesson 2.

- ❑ Configuring Transport Layer Security (TLS) encryption. Users can be required to use TLS, which is similar to Secure Sockets Layer (SSL), to connect to and communicate with the SMTP server. This requirement will secure data using encryption, but it does not implement user authentication.

- **Additional IIS services and components**   Do not install additional Web server components, such as the Network News Transfer Protocol (NNTP) service, unless there is a clear business need for the service and a security design has been prepared.

Manage Access to Files and Folders   In addition to managing services, you must address these areas of Windows Server 2003: the file system location and the use of access control lists (ACLs) on files, folders, and registry keys. The following list summarizes several Web-specific issues:

- Locating the Web server content on a dedicated disk separate from the operating system. Doing so can prevent *directory traversal attacks*. Directory traversal attacks are attacks where an individual obtains access to a subdirectory and attempts to traverse the directory to gain access elsewhere. Thus, an attacker might have access to a content folder and seek to gain access to a sensitive folder, such as an operating system folder that contains the Security Accounts Manager (SAM) database. It is much more difficult to move from one disk to another than it is to simply traverse the directory.

- Removing permissions. Except for Administrators and SYSTEM Full Control, permissions on the root of the disk volume can be removed. (Removing SYSTEM Full Control can cause problems with backup and defrag software.)

- Using a top-level folder to contain all the subfolders that will contain Web sites and applications.

- Providing a subfolder for each Web site and Web application.

- Ensuring that anonymous accounts used for access to the Web sites do not have access elsewhere on the server.

- Ensuring that Windows groups and accounts given permissions on Web pages do not have access elsewhere on the server.

- If you have multiple Web sites on the server, ensuring that users accessing one site cannot access another site.

- Ensuring proper file and folder permissions are set that support permissions set on Web accessible folders. More information on this topic can be found in the "Guidelines for Controlling Access to Web Servers, Web Sites, Applications, and Server Resources" section.

Guidelines for Enabling Only Needed IIS Components and Services

IIS is not installed by default on Windows Server 2003. When it is installed, the bare minimum Web server components and services are installed, unless the person installing it or the scripted installation process selects additional services and components. After installation, additional services and components can be installed.

Insist on Minimum Requirements Lists for Web-Based Application Requirements
Essential to the design of a Web server is determining which services and components are needed for the applications that will be running on the Web server and where these services or components can themselves be restricted. The application developers, or the company that produced the commercial Web-based applications, should indicate which services are needed. As part of your security design for a specific site, you should request this information and insist that only the specific services and components that are needed be installed.

Lock Down the Default Installation   A default installation of IIS provides only a few services and components. However, if the Web server will be a dedicated Web server, you can also disable a few of those. The following list provides information on the default services and components installed by IIS and notes where these elements might not be required and thus can be disabled:

- **Application Server Console**   An MMC snap-in that provides administration for all Web Application Server components. On a dedicated Web server, this snap-in is not necessary. IIS Manager can be used.

- **Enable Network COM+ Access**   Provides services for COM+ components in distributed applications. Disable this feature unless it is required by applications running on the Web server.

- **Internet Information Services**   Can provide basic Web and FTP services and is a required service. However, not every subcomponent needs to be enabled. The following subcomponents must be enabled:

  - Common Files—Files that must be present for the Web server to run.

  - Internet Information Services Manager—The administrative interface for IIS. Disable it if the Web server will not be managed locally.

  - SMTP—Used to provide support for the transfer of mail and not necessary for the Web server function. Unless this service will be used, disable it.

❑ World Wide Web Service—Provides basic Web services, such as static and dynamic Web pages. This feature must be enabled or all components will be disabled.

After installation, you might need to perform additional configuration that can further restrict the use or functioning of the services.

Enable Only Necessary Components   The business needs of the organization will dictate the Web applications that will run on the server. In an ideal world, the security designer will be called upon to assist in the application design to ensure that the best choices are made at that time to support security. If this is not the case, the designer's job is to minimize exposure while supporting the applications.

Enable Essential Web Service Extensions   By default, only static Web pages can be used. To provide support for dynamic Web pages and other Web services, additional services and extensions must be added, such as Active Server Pages, ASP.NET, FrontPage Server Extension, WebDAV, Internet Server API (ISAPI) Extensions, and so forth.

Do not change the status of All Unknown ISAPI Extensions to Allowed. (See Figure 13-1.) This creates a security risk because many ISAPI extensions are created to extend Web services and are not reviewed for security vulnerabilities. Requiring review and approval for the use of an ISAPI extension is a sound security practice and assists in the effort to reduce the attack surface. This is an issue over which people primarily concerned with business needs can butt heads with those primarily concerned with security. It is relatively easy to write or locate an ISAPI extension that provides some extra service or function. It is a lot harder to write or review for security the ISAPI extension. Providing a review process can help ensure that the business needs and the security requirements are both considered.

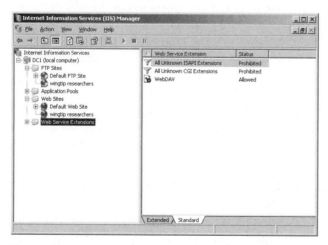

Figure 13-1   Keeping the All Unknown ISAPI Extensions as Prohibited

Enable Only Essential MIME Types   A number of MIME types commonly in use on Web servers are approved for use by default. Approval of these MIME types simply allows well-known data formats to be used in Web page and application development. Should additional MIME types be necessary, you can add them. But do not add types that are unnecessary. Removal of MIME types to restrict usage to those approved on the Web site is also easy to do using the interface (as shown in Figure 13-2).

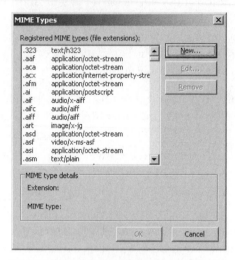

Figure 13-2   Adding and removing MIME types as required

Use Web-Specific User Roles Appropriately   Web sites and applications support special user roles. Understanding these roles and limiting them to only the access and permissions that they require is important to the security of the Web server, Web sites, and applications. These roles include the following:

- **Anonymous access account**   In a default installation, the IUSR_*computername* account (where *computername* is the name of the server on which the Web server is installed) is created. Its purpose is to provide and control anonymous access to the Web site. When a visitor accesses a Web page, the anonymous account is used and the visitor does not have to log in. You can control the visitor's access to the Web server, site, and application by setting NTFS permissions. If an organization provides a public Web site, anonymous access is usually required. However, that does not mean sensitive folders and files on the Web server must be available to anonymous access. Protect files via Web permissions and NTFS permissions, and require authentication to access them.

- **IWAM_*computername***   This is an account provided for compatibility with IIS 5.0. It is possible to run the Web server in IIS isolation mode instead of the worker process isolation mode provided in IIS 6.0. When applications are run in IIS isolation mode, they are run in the context of the highly privileged local system account. Applications can also be run out-of-process, and then the IWAM_*computername* is used. This account has fewer privileges on the server.

- **Process identity**   A *process identity* is the Windows account that a process runs under. When anonymous access is allowed, the IUSR_*computername* is the process identity.

- **Application pool identities**   An *application pool identity* is a user account that is the process identity for the worker processes that service an application pool. Each application pool can and should have a separate application pool identity. Assign permissions to the application pool identity to restrict and grant the access to resources, such as files on an NTFS partition or data in a Microsoft SQL Server database. Web sites and applications running in the application pool have the same rights and permissions granted to the application pool identity. For more information on application pools and application pool identities, see the "How to Isolate Web Sites and Applications" section.

- **IIS_WPG group**   This is a default group that is added when IIS is installed. This group has default access to write to log files, access to the metabase, and other access required for most IIS applications to run. This group provides an easy way to provide the application pool identities with the access required. Instead of applying the proper access permissions directly to each new user account created as an application pool identity, the new account can be added to the IIS_WPG group.

For any specific Web site or Web application, running processes require access to Web pages, scripts, and other resources on the Web server and on other servers, such as databases and file servers. If you know the process identity of the application, you can control it via NTFS permissions. If you can participate in the design of the Web application and Web site, you can give administrators the ability to appropriately control and monitor Web site usage. For example, you can do the following:

- Restrict access to specific Web pages or database content stored in SQL Server by requiring the process to run in the identity of the user

- Isolate applications from one another by running them under the identity of the application pool

- Restrict anonymous access to the Web server by allowing the application to run under the IUSR_*computername* account

> **Tip**   The default application pool identity is the NetworkService account. This is a low privileged account. A unique account should be specified and needs to be added to the IIS_WPG group in order to have access to the IIS metabase and content. The IIS_WPG group has, by default, permissions that will allow most Web sites and applications to run.

Guidelines for Controlling Access to Web Servers, Web Sites, Applications, and Server Resources

Many IIS-specific features can be used by themselves, and many interoperate with operating system permissions to provide additional security for Web sites. Follow the guidelines in the following sections to control access to Web servers, Web sites, applications, and server resources.

Restrict Access from Specific IP Addresses or Domain Names

You can restrict access to the Web site or application by blocking specific domain names and IP addresses, or by allowing only specific domains and IP addresses. You can, for example, restrict access to intranet sites to computers on your internal network or some portion of your internal network. You can block specific IP addresses from which attacks are occurring. Access cannot be blocked by a portion of a Web site or an application.

Tip   Use address ranges instead of domain names where possible. If domain names are used, a reverse lookup must be done each time a request for access is received, and this will reduce performance.

To block access, leave the default setting (in which all users are allowed to access the site) and then specify the domain or IP address range to be blocked. To restrict access to specific domains or address ranges, disable default access (in which no users are allowed to access the site) and then add the domain names and IP address ranges of the exceptions that you want to make (as shown in Figure 13-3). Restricting access to intranet Web sites to specific internal subnets not only makes good security sense, but it meets the business needs of restricting certain types of data to specific employees and preventing access by outsiders who penetrate the internal network. Wireless users, for example, can be given IP addresses from a range that is blocked from accessing certain internal Web sites. Visitors and intruders might gain access to the network, but access to the internal Web site is prevented.

Warning   You should note that IP addresses can be easily spoofed. If this is done, these controls will not prevent unauthorized use. These controls should still be used, however, because they will prevent much abuse.

Figure 13-3   Allowing access by disabling the default access and then adding the specific IP addresses or domains that can access the site

Use Web Site Permissions

Web site permissions are used by IIS to determine what type of action can occur within a Web site or virtual directory. Web site permissions are not used in place of NTFS permissions but work with them. Web site permission only affects those who visit the Web site. NTFS permissions affect both Web site visitors and those who access the file system through some other means. If the NTFS settings and the Web site permissions conflict, the most restrictive permission will be the one that determines the action that can take place.

Web site permissions include the following:

- **Read**   Read is the default permission and is required to view the content and properties of directories and files. If all pages on the Web site are scripted content, such as Active Server Pages (ASP), the read permission is not required and can be removed.

- **Write**   Write allows the Web site visitor to change the content and properties of directories and files.

- **Script Source Access**   Script Source Access permits access to source files. If Script Source Access and Read are set, visitors to the Web site can read scripts; if Write is set, they can modify the source files. This permission is necessary when using WebDAV.

- **Directory Browsing**   Directory Browsing allows users to view file lists.

- **Log Visits**   Log Visits places a log entry for each visit to the Web site.

- **Index This Resource**   Index This Resource permits the indexing service to index the resources and therefore allows searches to be made.

- **Execute**   Execute is divided into the following three levels of access:

    ❑ None—No scripts or executables can run on the server.

    ❑ Scripts Only—Only scripts can run on the server.

    ❑ Scripts And Executables—Both scripts and executables can run on the server.

> **Caution**   When WebDAV is enabled, you should require authentication for the site and set appropriate file permissions. WebDAV provides an opportunity to change data on the Web site, and access to these sites should be carefully controlled.

Use NTFS Permissions

NTFS permissions must be set to allow the type of access required, and they should be set to explicitly deny access to sensitive files. The following access is required for the Web site to be functional:

- Administrators can manage content of Web sites and applications.

- Users can read content of Web sites and applications.

- Users can perform other functions as required and allowed by the Web site application.

- Application pool identities can read the content of the Web sites and applications.

- Application pool identities can perform other functions as required and allowed by the Web site.

Set Permissions on Web Sites and Virtual Directories

Follow these guidelines when determining permissions to set for Web sites and virtual directories:

- **Remove the Read permissions if the entire site uses scripted content.**   Removing excess permissions is always a good idea.

- **Do not set Write and Scripts Only permissions or Write and Scripts And Executables permissions on the same directory.**   Doing so will allow visitors to add scripts or modify scripts and execute them.

- **Do not set Write and Script Source Access permissions or Read and Script Source Access permissions on the same directory.**   Allowing visitors to read scripts might allow them to read sensitive data such as passwords. Allowing visitors to write scripts might allow them to do harm to the data or Web server.

- **Enable logging.**   Recording who is accessing the Web server and what is happening on the Web server can help you detect possible attacks and understand how an attack occurred, as well as gather evidence that might assist in locating and prosecuting the person who attacked the site.

- **Keep different file types in separate directories, and set appropriate NTFS permissions.**   Recommendations on the best way to do this are outlined in Table 13-1.

Table 13-1   Recommended File Permissions

File Type	Extensions	Administrators	System	Everyone
CGI	.exe, .dll, .cmd, .pl	Full control	Full control	Execute
Script files	.asp	Full control	Full control	Execute
Include files	.inc, .shtm, .shtml	Full control	Full control	Execute
Static content	.txt, .gif, .jpg	Full control	Full control	Read-only

How Data in Transit Can Be Protected

This section explains what data must be protected in transit. It then describes how SSL is used to protect data, how IPSec is used to protect data, how a VPN is used to protect Web server data, and how a remote server is used to protect data.

What Data Needs to Be Protected in Transit?

Data on the Web server must be protected from unauthorized access and modification. Data exchanged between the Web server and its clients and between the Web server and any other servers that it interfaces with should also be protected. Examples of these needs include the following:

- A client enters confidential information such as a Social Security number or credit card number into a form on a Web site.

- Data is added to or retrieved from a SQL Server database by an application on the Web server.

- Administration of Web servers is done remotely.

- Content is added, replaced, or otherwise managed remotely.

Three technologies used to protect data in transit are SSL (or TLS), IPSec, and virtual private networks (VPNs). All three may be used to protect data accessed by Web applications on remote servers.

How SSL/TLS Is Used to Protect Data

SSL is commonly used to support client/Web server applications such as e-commerce and remote e-mail access. SSL can also be used to support communications between SQL Server and IIS and between IIS and ISA Server. SSL support between client and server and between IIS and SQL Server consists of server authentication and the encryption of data between the two computers. If ISA Server is the firewall in front of the IIS Web site, SSL can be configured to tunnel from the client directly to the IIS server or to be received by the ISA server and then passed to the IIS server. TLS is an IETF standard version of SSL and may be used in the same way.

How SSL Processing Works

SSL provides authenticated access and encryption of data traveling between a client and a server. A server certificate is required, but SSL can also be configured to use or require the use of client certificates. Where only a server certificate is used, the Web server can be authenticated because its server certificate is signed by a trusted Certification Authority (CA). During the authentication process, a session key is calculated by the server and securely passed to the client. Client and server can then encrypt and decrypt all data that is passed between them.

On the Internet, server certificates from public CAs can be validated by the client because a copy of the root server certificate of the public CAs is stored on the client computer. Private CAs belonging to organizations (for example, Windows Server 2003 CAs installed by the organization) can also be used to issue SSL server certificates. However, because a copy of the root server certificate is not present by default in a client certificate store, a warning will be given to users of such sites. Users can accept the server certificate as trusted, but they should not.

On the intranet, an organization might choose to use its own internal, private CA to issue SSL server certificates. This approach has the advantage of reduced cost, and it limits exposure because no outside organization is responsible for the security of the organization's SSL certificates and thus site communications. However, if the PKI that produces the server certificate is not securely managed, the security of the Web site communications can be more easily compromised.

In addition to producing SSL server certificates for Web sites, an organization's CA can be used to produce client certificates and, where highly sensitive information must be accessed or must traverse the network, client certificates can be required by the SSL-protected Web site. For more information about the use of client certificates for Web site authentication, see Lesson 2 of this chapter.

How IPSec Is Used to Protect Data

IPSec can be used to protect communications between IIS and other servers that IIS must communicate with and between the administrative workstation and the IIS server. IPSec can also block communications that are not authorized. By requiring an IPSec-negotiated transport for data passed between computers, the confidentiality of the data is protected and the computers with which the IIS server will communicate are restricted. Blocking communications that are not authorized is important because doing so can eliminate attacks based on other protocols. IPSec blocking policy could be set, for example, to block all access except through port 80 (HTTP), port 443 (HTTPS) and, if required, 3389 terminal services. Access can also be controlled by blocking some types of access by specific server.

Two examples of using IPSec are shown in Figures 13-4 and 13-5. In the first figure, an administrative workstation on the internal network is used to administer an IIS server in the perimeter network. If the administrator workstation attempts a connection to the IIS server, an IPSec session is negotiated. IPSec policies on the IIS server and on the administrative workstation identify the IP addresses of each other and require certificates for authentication. In the second figure, data requested from the SQL server is returned. Both the request and response are encrypted. In the remote administration example, the data passes through the firewall because appropriate ports are configured.

Administrative
Workstation

IIS

Figure 13-4 IPSec can be used to protect remote administration sessions.

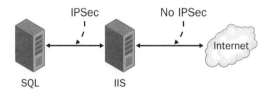

SQL

IIS

Figure 13-5 IPSec can be used to protect data traveling between the Web server and a database.

How a VPN Is Used to Protect Web Server Data

Remote administrative sessions, content management sessions, and client access to highly sensitive Web servers can be protected by using a VPN. As shown in Figure 13-6, VPNs can be established from the internal network as well as from the external network.

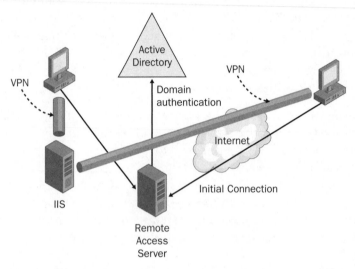

Figure 13-6   VPNs can be used to protect communications from both internal and external networks.

How a Remote Server Is Used to Protect Data

It is possible to store Web site content on remote servers and increase reliability, performance, and security. It is also possible to reduce security. In addition to placing data in a SQL Server database on a separate server, data can be stored on file servers and Network-Attached Storage (NAS) devices. Data on remote SQL Server databases and Windows file servers can be secured using SQL Server permissions, file system permissions, or both. Data on NAS devices will have to be secured using any methods provided by the device manufacturer.

An example of this type of storage is provided in Figures 13-7 and 13-8. In Figure 13-7, clients access IIS and all data is stored on remote databases. Although IIS is located on the perimeter network, the file servers are located on the internal network behind the interior firewall. If the IIS server is compromised, an attacker will have to penetrate a second firewall to access the data. In Figure 13-8, data from several IIS servers at an ISP is stored on a high-end server with high-speed RAID. A similar configuration might store data on a file server cluster.

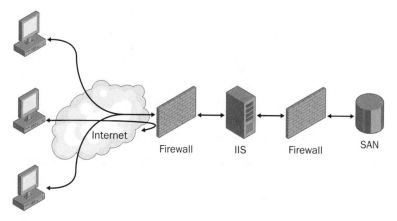

Figure 13-7   Distributed information is collected at IIS and stored remotely on the private network.

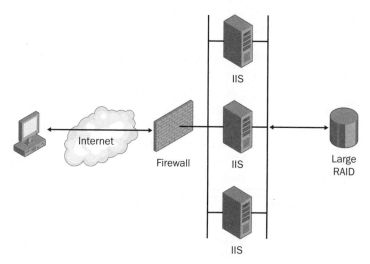

Figure 13-8   Distributed information is collected at IIS and stored on a high-end RAID server.

If data on remote servers should log access, or if it requires authenticated user access, user credentials can be forwarded by IIS to the remote servers. Use constrained delegation to limit the risk that code running on the remote servers might use the delegated user credentials for unintended or malicious activity.

Considerations for Designing a Secure Content Management Strategy

When a Web site is first deployed, all content can be added to the site when the site is not accessible externally. However, after a site is deployed, it must be updated.

The methods for content management must be securable and secured, and the ability to change and update content must be granted only to authorized users. You can move content to the Web server by using FTP, Microsoft FrontPage publishing, WebDAV, copy and paste, or third-party Web publishing products. There are two security issues with all of these methods: managing authentication and authorization for the file movement, and securing the data. Content can also be modified directly on the server, although this is not recommended. Regardless of the method you choose, unauthorized users or guests should not be able to make content changes on the Web site. The entire process of content management must be secured—from ensuring that proposed changes are approved to securely moving the content from test servers to the Web site. To design secure content management, consider the following items:

- **The content management approval process**   New content for Web sites must be approved. A process should be developed and enforced that identifies who can approve changes to site content.

- **Content update production**   New content should be developed and tested on a test server. Developers should not have the ability to write to the production server, and all changes should be made on the test server first, and then content can be moved to the Web server.

- **Automatic updates of content**   Content should be moved to the Web server in a secure manner. Automatic updates from test servers is not a secure method unless the test server is as secure as the production server. It makes no sense to allow changes made to an insecure server to automatically propagate to the production server. If the test server is compromised, any content the attacker designs will be automatically posed to the production Web server. Instead, consider transfer of content changes to a secondary server and then, after inspection, movement to the production site.

- **Updating content using FTP**   An FTP site or sites for updating content should be created on a separate server from the production Web server. Access to FTP sites can be authenticated, but authentication credentials will traverse the network using clear text. Consider the following options:

  ❑ Using a VPN to access the FTP server

  ❑ Limiting access to the FTP site to specific servers

- **Updating content using FTP user isolation**   When designing a content refresh strategy using FTP, consider using FTP user isolation. The user with credentials for this site cannot traverse the directory structure to access other sites.

> **See Also**   For more information about FTP user isolation, see the "Guidelines for Designing Authentication Using RADIUS" section in Lesson 2 of this chapter.

- **Securing data transfer**   Consider using IPSec policies to authenticate both the client and server computer, protect user credentials, and protect the content while it crosses the network.

Guidelines for Designing Monitoring and Maintenance Strategies for IIS

Designing monitoring and maintenance strategies for IIS combines the monitoring and maintenance strategies described for all networked systems—such as firewalls and intrusion detection—and adds Windows-specific operating system security and IIS-specific strategies such as backing up the metabase and managing IIS-specific logs. It is also necessary to include a design for secure administrative practices.

The following sections explain the components of a backup strategy for IIS, describe IIS log file formats, and then provide guidelines for designing monitoring and responding to alerts; reviewing security policies, processes, and procedures; encrypting communications; and designing secure remote administration. This topic addresses only IIS-specific issues.

How the Entire Process of Designing Monitoring and Maintenance Strategies Works

This lesson teaches how to design monitoring and maintenance strategies for IIS. However, it's important to know that the entire design should include the following tasks:

1. Design a backup strategy for IIS.

2. Design a strategy for applying service packs and security patches.

3. Ensure the Windows Server 2003 auditing design includes object auditing for the Web server.

4. Design the use of file and folder access Systems Access Control Lists (SACLs) for Web site content. Include at least monitoring of modification and deletion of content.

5. Review the security policy, process, and practices to ensure security policy compliance, and recommend changes to security policy as necessary.

6. Use intrusion detection systems to monitor network activity. A correctly configured and monitored intrusion detection system can alert on suspicious events. A trained individual or team can use this information to prevent intrusions or reduce their impact.

7. Specify the configuration of Windows Server 2003 logs on the IIS server.

8. Specify logging of Web site access. Design with log type, specifications in conjunction with security, performance, and log size in mind.

9. Design strategies for monitoring log content and responding to alerts.

10. Design secure remote administrative practices.

Components of a Backup Strategy for IIS

In addition to Windows Server 2003 system backup, a backup strategy for IIS should include the following items:

- **Backup of Web pages**   Web pages should be designed and modified on test servers. If a well-designed update process is followed, a test server is a complete backup of the current Web site. However, a normal backup should be made to ensure recovery because test servers are often reconfigured to "test" the next new pages or changes and might not, in reality, be a complete backup at any one specific point in time.

- **Backup of database data**   Many Web sites store data on an external SQL Server database. The database will also require backup.

- **Backup of the metabase**   The IIS metabase is the structure that stores IIS configuration settings. The metabase in IIS 6.0 consists of two plain-text XML-formatted files—MetaBase.xml and MSSchema.xml—in the %*SystemRoot*%\System32\Inetsrv folder. Backup is via the IIS Backup/Restore Configuration task in the IIS administration interface and can also be scripted. The backup can be encrypted by entering a password. This will prevent the restore of an old metabase over the current one. Instructions for creating a script and for using the built-in administration tool are documented in Knowledge Base article 324277. An additional security feature makes a backup history file when changes are made to the metabase and saved to disk, and the history can be rolled back if necessary.

IIS Log File Formats

To design appropriate logging of IIS data, you must understand the capabilities and specifications for logging that can be set. IIS logging should be established to log Web site access. This data serves as a record of Web site access and can be reviewed to determine the nature of attempted attacks, trace a user's activity on the site, and provide forensic evidence that might be used to locate the source of an attack or in legal prosecution. Daily, weekly, or monthly log files can be specified. A separate log can be recorded for each application and Web site on the server, unless the central binary log file format is used. In addition to five log file formats, custom log file modules can be created. Table 13-2 summarizes the properties of the different log file formats.

See Also   To learn more about how to create custom IIS log file formats, see the article, "Custom Logging Modules," on the TechNet page of the Microsoft Web site at *http://www.microsoft.com/technet/treeview/default.asp?url=/technet/prodtechnol/windowsserver2003/proddocs/standard/log_custommodules.asp*.

Table 13-2   Properties of Different IIS Log File Formats

File Format	W3C	IIS	NCSA	ODBC	Binary
Customizable?	Yes	No	No	No	N/A
Data separated by	Spaces	Commas	Spaces	N/A	Unformatted
Time zone	Greenwich Mean Time	Local Time	Local Time	Local Time	Local Time
Can be separate for each site and application?	Yes	Yes	Yes	Yes	No
Available for FTP sites as well as Web sites?	Yes	Yes	No	Yes	Yes
Comments	Awkward at first to consider time, but very useful when many sites are involved.	Records more information than other fixed formats.	Available for Web sites only, not FTP.	Kernel mode caching is disabled, and performance might suffer.	Preserves memory resources.

Tip   If the SMTP service is installed and started on Web servers, access can be logged. To do so, you must enable protocol logging for SMTP. This is done in the property pages for the SMTP virtual server.

Guidelines for Designing Monitoring and Responding to Alerts

Follow these guidelines for designing monitoring and responding to alerts:

- Choose a log file format based on the properties that will be the most useful. For example:

  ❑ The IIS log file format will record the target file accessed, but the NCSA log file format will not.

  ❑ The central binary log file format can be the most efficient and can conserve memory, CPU, and disk space. However, because all data from all sites is logged to one log and because the format is binary, the log file might be more difficult to assess.

- Set or maintain log folder permissions. Because the log file location can be moved, be sure to set proper permissions at the custom location. When central binary log files are used, set the folder permissions to:

  ❑ SYSTEM and Administrators Full Control

  ❑ Everyone Read

- Set or maintain log file permissions. When central binary log files are used, set file permissions to:

  ❑ SYSTEM Full Access

  ❑ Administrators Read And Delete

  ❑ No Access Is Approved For The Group Everyone

- On a stand-alone Web server, audit the Local GPO for compliance with baseline security policy.

- On domain member Web servers, audit the domain GPO and GPOs that are applied to Web servers.

- When auditing GPOs ensure

  ❑ User rights provide only those necessary.

  ❑ Only administrators can log on locally, and only administrators have the ability to log on to Web servers using terminal services.

  ❑ Only necessary services are enabled.

- Create custom log file formats where it is necessary to log data that cannot be specified in the available log file formats.

- Audit firewall configuration. Specifically, ensure that ports are closed that are known attack vectors and that are not necessary for Web server functions, such as TCP and UDP ports 135, 137–139, and 445.

- Audit the use of periodic virus scanning both on the Web server and on network gateways.

> **Tip** Network segmentation and firewall configuration are also important parts of Web server security. Review network segmentation and Web server location information in Chapter 4. Any Web site design should include reference to Web server location and firewall configuration, either to indicate the proposed server placement and necessary firewall controls or to indicate how the new application or Web site will need to work with the current environment.

Guidelines for Reviewing Security Policies, Processes, and Procedures

Security policies, processes, and procedures should be periodically reviewed. Follow these guidelines for doing so:

■ When new security risks are identified, ensure that current security practices, Web site configuration, and server configuration adequately deal with the risk. For example, if a new worm is discovered, will the server be vulnerable?

■ If new processes or procedures for securing Web servers and Web sites are developed, review the applicability for your Web servers and sites.

■ If new application development processes or new application security review capabilities become available, review their appropriateness for your application's development and review processes. For example, will redesigning a Web application as a .NET framework application improve your ability to secure it? Will designing Web applications as Web services increase or reduce the security risk to the application data? Can new development tools that check for buffer overflows in applications be used in Web development?

■ If new tools for vulnerability analysis are available, determine whether they will be of value in discovering and correcting vulnerabilities in Web servers, Web sites, and applications.

■ Conduct periodic Web application, Web site, and Web server threat analysis reviews. Threat analysis reviews allow administrators, developers, management, security personnel, users, and others to use their knowledge of the Web server and how it is used to speculate on potential risks to that environment. The discovery of unknown security risks should result in a security review to determine whether any new action is required to reduce or eliminate the risk.

■ When Web server changes are made, evaluate changes to determine whether security has been reduced. A change management process should be in place that approves and monitors changes to Web server and Web site configuration as well as application changes. Part of this process should ensure a security review of the changes proposed. In addition to Web site access logging, changes should be logged. Monitoring changes to ensure only authorized changes have been made and to determine whether the security analysis was correct will help discover potential problems before they become problems and discover potential attacks.

■ Review the use of intrusion detection systems (IDSs) and vulnerability analysis systems that are in place to determine whether they are doing the necessary job and whether the information they produce is being used.

Guidelines for Encrypting Communications

Follow these guidelines for encrypting communications:

- Use SSL to encrypt application data and authentication credentials for connections between clients and IIS.

- Use SSL or IPSec to secure data connections between IIS and databases or other server resources and IIS.

- Use IPSec or a VPN to secure authentication credentials and encrypt data connections between administrative workstations and IIS and between clients used for content management and IIS.

Guidelines for Designing Secure Remote Administration

There are those who say that all Web servers should be administered only from the console to avoid possible compromise via remote administration methodologies. However, for large Web sites and organizations with multiple Web servers, administration via the console is impractical (although such organizations might consider it for specific sensitive IIS servers). Instead, remote administration is done via the Internet Information Services Manger or terminal services. A third option, using the Remote Administration (HTML) tool, is generally avoided because it offers too many possibilities for remote compromise. The rationale is that HTML access to the server from the Internet must be possible (unless, of course, it is an intranet-only Web server); therefore, the administration tool might be used in an attack. On the other hand, access via other administrative tools—such as terminal services or the Internet Information Services Manager—can be blocked at the firewall.

Follow these guidelines when designing secure remote administration:

- Do not install the Remote Administration (HTML) tool.

- Use the Internet Information Services Manager for both console and remote administration. (This tool is now available for Windows XP.)

- Consider using terminal services. You can use the Internet Information Services Manager tool on the remote IIS server over terminal services, and you do not need to add administration tools to Windows XP. You can use terminal services from Windows 2000 Professional and other Windows operating systems as well. Terminal services sessions are encrypted, and the user using them is authenticated. In addition, unless the IIS computer has the terminal service installed and is configured to allow other users and groups, only Administrators can connect and use the service.

- Consider the use of IPSec to secure administrative traffic from the administrative workstation and the IIS server.

- Require VPN access to the network in order to administer IIS across the WAN if such administration is authorized.

Guidelines for Designing Access Control for Databases on the Web Server

Backend databases, databases installed on a server other than the Web server, are often a part of an IIS application. However, databases can also be installed directly on the Web server. To secure databases use the following guidelines:

- **Use the security features of the database.**   Many databases have built-in controls that specify user accounts and provide granular access controls for administration, applications, and data tables.

- **Control Web-based access to the database.**   Some database access controls, such as those produced by the Microsoft FrontPage 2000 to provide access to a database, include provisions for authentication before the database can be accessed. If the application is developed in-house, provide controls over access via Web pages.

- **Control Web-based access to databases that use ODBC.**   Set password settings for the Data Source Name (DSN). The DSN is used by an active server page or other application to refer to the database.

- **Use NTFS as appropriate to restrict access.**   Databases can restrict access via database resident controls. The NTFS permissions set on the database file itself might not be relevant except to provide system and administrative access for file management.

- **Use Web authentication methods to control access to the Web server.**   The use of user credentials for database access can be configured. Consider whether this is the appropriate solution for the type of database access required.

Guidelines for Configuring Web Servers to Isolate Web Sites and Applications

This section provides reasons for isolating Web sites, explains how to isolate Web sites and applications, and then teaches how to configure Web servers to isolate Web sites and applications.

Reasons for Isolating Web Sites

In some situations, a single Web site will be hosted on a Web server. However, there are many instances where multiple Web sites run on a single server. Two examples are:

- An organization runs multiple departmental Web sites on a single server for convenience, ease of management, and cost reduction.

- An ISP provides hosting services for many organizations and places multiple Web sites on each Web server that it uses.

In both cases, there are good reasons for isolating Web sites from one another including:

- **Performance and reliability**   If a specific Web site crashes or performs poorly, this action will not affect other sites.

- **Protection**   If a Web site is compromised, the attacker will be prevented from accessing other Web sites.

- **Maintenance**   If a Web site needs to be taken offline for maintenance or restarted, this will not affect other Web sites.

- **Meeting business consolidation needs**   Many departments within an organization might have departmental Web sites. It is cost prohibitive to establish and maintain a server for each department. A Web server with multiple Web sites, however, can meet this need and provide a better opportunity to secure and maintain security for all Web sites.

- **Meeting ISP shared-hosting needs**   An ISP might host thousands of Web sites. Using isolation, the ISP can do so on a few servers.

> **Off the Record**   An alternative to isolation is the use of virtual machines. In this scenario, a server runs each Web site in its own virtual machine, literally using a sandbox technique. Because each site runs in its own machine, none has access to the other. However, in this case, multiple operating system licenses are required, as are operating system security configuration and maintenance. You should also be aware that not all virtual machines create such a sandbox. There are mainframe virtual machine technologies that do so, but many PC-type virtual machines do not do exactly the same thing.

How to Isolate Web Sites and Applications

To isolate Web sites and applications, run IIS 6.0 in worker process isolation mode and specify that applications and Web sites hosted on the same server belong to separate application pools. Each application pool uses virtually mapped memory that is not available to other processes. Use file system ACLs to support isolation. You can also tighten security by providing isolation within the metabase. Administration of specific application pools can be restricted to the Web site author and administrator.

Why It Is Important to Understand Impersonation

Impersonation, a concept that indicates a process can run under different security credentials, is basic to all Windows operating systems. Impersonation becomes especially interesting when applied to application pools. Although a worker process runs in its application pool under the application pool identity, it also is allowed to impersonate its own—or run under security credentials different from its own—base identity. When a worker process is created, it is given a process token associated with the application pool identity, and by default, everything the worker process does is done using this context. It can do only what it has been given the rights and permissions to do. However, if a user request is processed (that is, if a user accesses the Web site in the application pool), the thread (which can be one of many a process utilizes) that services the request is given a token associated with the user: the authenticated user's token. For each action (such as reading a Web page or executing a script) that the user attempts, her token is validated against the ACL of the resource. This concept is extended as well if the request involves the use of an ISAPI extension. Hence, NTFS permissions must be set to allow or restrict users and the application pool identity.

If this concept is misunderstood, it can result in a compatibility problem. For example, it can result in Web applications that will not run, except for running anonymously or when using the administrator account. Unfortunately, this could result in an unsophisticated IT administrator, in an attempt to solve the compatibility problem, giving users who must run the application membership in the local administrators group on the Web server. To prevent this situation, application designers, Web site administrators, as well as domain administrators should be educated on the application identity concept and the correct configuration for any Web applications should be well documented. In addition, applications should be tested using accounts other than that of an administrator to ensure that once deployed, they will work correctly for all authorized users.

How to Configure Web Servers to Isolate Web Sites and Applications

To configure Web servers to isolate Web sites and applications:

1. List the Web sites and applications hosted on the server.

2. Group Web sites by organization or business unit within the organization.

3. Divide groups from step 2 into subgroups that require similar rights and permissions.

4. Remove from subgroups any sensitive applications that must be isolated from all other applications.

5. For each of these applications and for the remaining groups specify that a unique application pool be created.

6. Designate a unique service account, the application pool identity, for each application pool, and specify the rights this identity needs within the Web sites.

7. Specify user rights and permissions required by the application pool identity for each application pool. Include both ordinary rights and additional user rights that might be necessary for a specific application or Web site. Do not grant rights and permissions that are not necessary.

Examples: Designing IIS Security Baselines Based on Business Needs

The best way to learn how to design IIS security baselines based on business needs is to examine possible business needs, answer those needs with a description of IIS features that the business needs appear to suggest are required, and then identify how security can be established that will allow the business needs to be met but will add minimal risk to the IIS environment. The following examples are provided as potential solutions to such a project. In Table 13-3, business needs are identified in the first column, IIS features that might be required to support those needs are provided in the second column, and suggestions for security to accommodate the business needs are shown in the third column.

Table 13-3   Designing IIS Security Baselines—A Business and Security Needs Matrix

Business Need	IIS Feature	Security
Multiple departmental Web sites.	Virtual Web sites	Use worker process isolation mode and separate application pools for each department.
Content management for departmental sites must be under the control of the department.	FTP site for content upload	Protect data and FTP basic authentication using IPSec.
E-mail access from the Internet.	Microsoft Outlook Web Access	Secure with SSL. Require client certificates.
Remote administration of Web sites at branch locations.	HTML-based administration tool	Do not use an HTML-based tool. Instead, provide VPN access to the Web server.

Practice: Designing IIS Security to Meet Business Needs

In this practice, you will provide security for proposed business requirements related to IIS. In Table 13-4, review the business need in the first column and the proposed IIS feature in the second column. Then, propose a proper security solution for each business need. If you are unable to answer a question, review the lesson materials and try the question again. You can find answers to the questions in the "Questions and Answers" section at the end of the chapter.

Table 13-4   Designing IIS Security for Business Needs

Business Need	Proposed IIS Feature	What is your proposed security solution?
An ISP must host 2000 Web sites.	Virtual Web sites.	
Content management for the sites hosted for the ISP must be provided for each Web site. Each Web site owner must not be able to change content on other sites.	FTP site for content upload.	
E-mail access from the Internet. There is no budget for implementing PKI.	Outlook Web Access, Windows authentication.	
Large amounts of data storage are needed.	Store data on a storage area network (SAN).	
Mail relay from internal mail servers to ISP mail server.	Provide SMTP service on the Web server.	

Lesson 2: Designing User Authentication for IIS

Your design must always specify the types of access to Web site content that should be made available. Start by designing authentication because it is the first place where you can block access or provide secure access. The design should specify the type of authentication that is allowed. Anonymous access might be required for access to public Web sites but does not have to be provided. Basic authentication and Windows integrated authentication both require accounts and passwords, but neither is the proper solution in all cases. Authentication choices provide secure access to Web information and applications. Support for improved authentication security and support for authorization controls via ACLs based on the authenticated user's identity are also benefits of well-designed user authentication.

After this lesson, you will be able to

- Explain the process for designing user authentication for IIS.
- Design authentication for Web sites and servers.
- Describe IIS authentication methods.
- Design IIS user authentication using certificates.
- Design authentication using RADIUS.
- Describe the options that are available when designing authentication for FTP.
- Explain the considerations for designing authentication for SMTP.

Estimated lesson time: 40 minutes

The Process: Designing Authentication for IIS

Designing authentication for Web site access does not just involve providing access by the public to static Web pages. To select the proper authentication methods, you must evaluate access requirements for data access, e-commerce, B2B e-commerce and other partner access, administration, and content management. Authentication design also involves designing authentication for other IIS servers, such as FTP sites and Web sites.

To design authentication for IIS, security designers follow a process like this:

1. *Review or learn the authentication methods that are available.* As IIS evolves, authentication methods do as well. The security designer must know what the use of each method requires, as well as any caveats in its use.

2. *Use best practices and guidelines regarding the use of IIS authentication to accomplish the following tasks:*

   a. *Select authentication methods based on access requirements.* Public access to public Web sites usually requires only anonymous authentication. Where Web site access includes access to or communication of sensitive information, you should use stronger authentication requirements.

b. *Select authentication methods based on data to be accessed.* The sensitivity of the data that will be accessed and communicated will dictate the methods of authentication that can be used.

c. *Select authentication based on network location of clients and Web servers.* Access by clients on the intranet might require and allow different authentication methods than access by clients from the Internet or partner sites.

d. *Select authentication methods based on client and server characteristics.* Some authentication methods require specific clients; others, such as certificate authentication, require client certificates.

e. *Select authentication methods based on your ability to change client, server, and network characteristics.* To implement secure access to intranet sites from the Internet, certificates might be required for clients. This can necessitate changes to client operating systems, browsers, server configuration, and network infrastructure.

3. *After selecting authentication methods, create a secure design for their implementation.* Many forms of IIS authentication, such as anonymous or Windows integrated, require little additional design. However, some forms of authentication—such as certificate authentication, authentication used when using RADIUS, or authentication used when FTP and/or SMTP are part of IIS—have their own design issues.

Steps 1 and 2 can be done in any order.

Guidelines for Designing Authentication for Web Sites and Servers

Follow these guidelines when designing authentication for Web sites and servers:

- Use Windows integrated authentication on the local intranet where there is less risk of credentials being captured and cracked.

- Use digest authentication only if all clients are members of the same domain or trusted domain as the IIS server and only if other authentication techniques are not preferred.

- Use anonymous authentication when public access is required. No user will need to provide credentials.

- Use certificate authentication when highly secure access is required and a mechanism for secure certificate distribution is available. Certificate authentication, when properly designed and managed, has been shown to be less vulnerable to attack than password authentication.

- Use SSL to secure basic authentication where basic authentication must be used. Examples of this are the use of Outlook Web Access for remote mailbox access. Basic authentication passes credentials in clear text. When SSL is used, the credentials and other communications are encrypted.

- Use VPNs to protect administrative access and content management access. Using a VPN ensures that the communication is protected and can, if IPSec is used, ensure that the connection is from an authorized administrative console.

- Use RADIUS for authentication, authorization, and audit of Web site access via VPNs to Web sites. RADIUS can provide centralization of remote access policies when multiple remote access devices are used. It also provides the ability to protect wireless access, and it provides additional services such as quarantine control.

- Restrict access to SMTP virtual servers by requiring authentication for relaying and providing authentication for use of SMTP services. This will prevent the use of SMTP in sending spam. It also ensures that access is limited to authorized connections.

- Protect remote basic authentication to FTP sites by using VPNs and LAN basic authentication FTP access using IPSec. Basic authentication passes credentials in the clear. Using VPNs and IPSec will encrypt these credentials.

IIS Authentication Methods

IIS provides a range of authentication methods that allows the design of anonymous access or authenticated access by Windows account or .NET passport account. Each method is desirable for certain uses. The typical IIS installation will provide several IIS authentication methods depending on the data that site users will be accessing. IIS authentication methods are defined in Table 13-5.

Table 13-5 Authentication Methods

Authentication Method	Description
Anonymous	The user does not have to enter credentials to access Web pages to which the anonymous user account has been granted access. This allows public access to a public Web site. You constrain this access by setting NTFS permissions on files and folders on the Web site and server. If a user attempts access on a file or folder for which the anonymous user account does not have access, an attempt to authenticate the user will be made. Anonymous use will always be checked first, even if other settings are also made. This means a log of user access will indicate usage by the anonymous account.
Integrated Windows	NTLM or Kerberos authentication will be used. It is not supported over a proxy connection. Internet Explorer 4.0 or later must be used.
Digest authentication for Windows domain controllers	This authentication type requires a user ID and password. Credentials are passed over the network as an MD5 hash. This authentication type also requires Internet Explorer 5.0 or later. Clients and servers must be members of or trusted by the same domain, and passwords must be stored by using reversible encryption.

Table 13-5   Authentication Methods

Authentication Method	Description
Basic	With this authentication type, credentials are passed over the network in clear text. Basic authentication requires a user account and password. This authentication type can be used by all Web clients.
.NET passport	With this authentication type, requests must include valid Microsoft .NET passport credentials. If no credentials are detected in the request, the request is redirected to the .NET passport logon page on the Internet. If selected, all other authentication types are unavailable.

Exam Tip   In general, if multiple authentication types are available, IIS will select the most secure type first and then attempt the other less secure types. However, there are two exceptions. If IIS anonymous authentication is available, that will be used first; if .NET passport authentication is chosen, no other authentication type is available.

Guidelines for Designing IIS User Authentication Using Certificates

When applications require strong authentication, user certificates can be used. In the IIS interface and documentation, these certificates are referred to as client certificates. Certificate authentication is configured in a two-step process: certificates must be mapped to Windows user accounts, and the use of client certificates must be configured on the IIS Web site. Certificates can be issued by a Windows Certification Authority managed by the organization or a third-party public CA.

Important   In this book, and in documentation of wireless clients and remote access, the term *client* is used to represent the computer used to access the server or access point. The term *client certificate* is often used to represent a certificate or the certificate issued to a computer or device. However, in the IIS interface and documentation, the term *client certificate* refers to the use of a certificate issued to a user. Be careful when reading any discussion of client certificates because the meaning can be different depending on the topic discussed. In this chapter, to discuss the use of certificates for user authentication in IIS, the term *client certificate* will mean the same thing as *user certificate*.

Two types of certificate mapping and certificate trust lists (CTLs) can be used. Directory Services (DS) mapping or IIS mapping types can be selected, or a list of trusted Certification Authorities can be identified by creating a CTL. Certificate revocation lists (CRLs) are checked by default, and the process can be configured for better control over CRL refresh.

How to Use Certificate Mapping

Directory Services mapping can be enabled from the Directory Security tab of the Web Sites Properties dialog box, as shown in Figure 13-9. If users have been issued certificates by a Windows Enterprise Certification Authority, the certificate will already be mapped to their user account in Active Directory.

Figure 13-9   Enable the use of certificates already mapped to accounts in Active Directory.

Alternatively, IIS mapping—either one-to-one or many-to-one—can be used. With IIS mapping, certificates must be mapped to a Windows account from within the IIS Web site property pages. Requirements for certificate mapping are configured by clicking on the Secure Communications box from the Directory Security page of the Web site properties. As shown in Figure 13-10, there are two choices for certificate mapping: one-to-one and many-to-one.

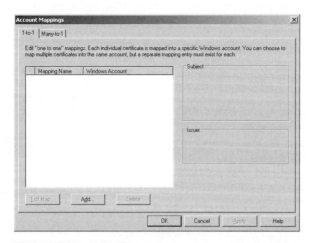

Figure 13-10   Use IIS mapping to map certificates for use on a specific IIS server.

One-to-one mapping requires a certificate to be explicitly mapped to a user account. To do this, you will need to export user certificates to a certificate file, and then add the certificate and specify a Windows account using the one-to-one property page Add button. The certificate is mapped for use on a specific IIS server. When a client presents a certificate for authentication, it is checked against the copy of the certificate stored by the server. The map must be exact. If anything is different, authentication is denied.

Many-to-one mapping allows you to write wildcard rules that will then accept any certificate that meets the rules. In Figure 13-11, a rule to allow any certificate issued by the root1 CA is being written. Figure 13-12 shows the Many-To-1 tab after successful completion of the mapping. The Web server will accept any client certificates issued by the CA. If users are issued new certificates from the CA, the certificates will be accepted. Notice that a single Windows account is chosen for the mapping.

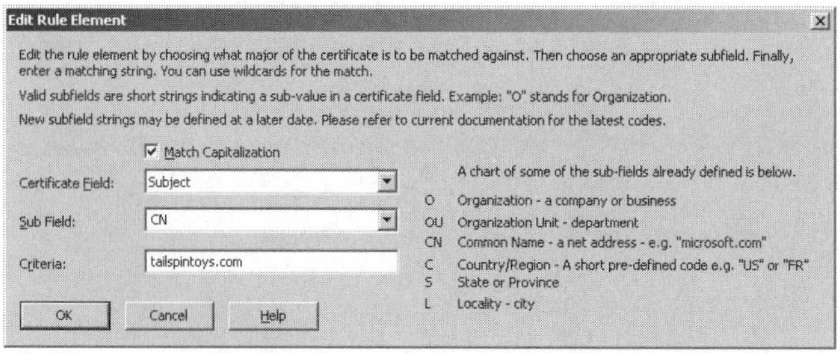

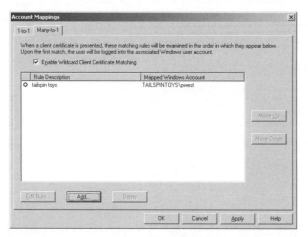

Figure 13-11   Designate the CA from which certificates will be accepted.

Figure 13-12   Using many-to-one mapping, all access authorized by the rules is mapped to a single Windows account.

How to Use Certificate Trust Lists

A *certificate trust list* (CTL) is a list of certificate characteristics that will allow a certificate to be accepted for authentication. A CTL is created only at the Web site level and thus is a good choice for use by departments or groups within an organization. For example, the research group at Wingtip Toys might specify that at the research Web site on an IIS server in the partner perimeter network, all certificates from the tailspin-toys.com domain be accepted. CTLs are not mapped to Windows user accounts. A CTL is created by using the New button on the Secure Communications dialog box to add certificates to the list. If this is the first CTL, you must select the Enable Certificate Trust List check box as well, as shown in Figure 13-13. Figure 13-14 shows the contents of the trust list—in this case, a single certificate.

Figure 13-13   A CTL is based on information provided in the subject or issuer field of the presented certificate.

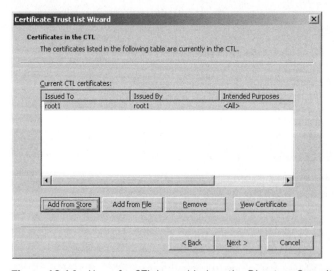

Figure 13-14   Use of a CTL is enabled on the Directory Security, Secure Communications page.

How to Manage CRLs for IIS

A certificate revocation list must be checked to ensure that a certificate presented for authentication has not been revoked. CRLs are cached and used until the next CRL publication. IIS, however, should be configured to allow CRLs to be downloaded more often. If, for example, certificates have been revoked and the CA administrator manually publishes a CRL, IIS can download the new CRL without waiting for the current, cached CRL to expire. If IIS is not configured to download CRLs more frequently, information on certificates that are revoked might not be available as quickly as necessary. A user certificate that has been compromised might have been revoked, yet it could be used to access data on the server because the CRL was not updated. To manage CRLs, configure the following metabase properties:

- CertCheckMode can be used to enable and disable CRL checking. (CRL checking is enabled by default.)
- RevocationFreshnessTime can be used to refresh the CRL even if the cached CRL is still valid.
- RevocationURLRetrievalTimeout is used to set the default interval.

Guidelines for Designing Client Authentication Using Certificates

Follow these guidelines for designing client authentication using certificates:

- **Use IIS mapping if there is a need for advanced wildcard mapping.** Wildcard mapping is easier and more flexible using IIS mapping.
- **Use DS mapping when all users already have Active Directory accounts.** Doing this will save time and allow access to multiple servers.
- **Use DS mapping when authentication at many servers is necessary.** Otherwise, IIS mapping would have to be repeated at each server. DS mapping is not entered at the server.
- **Use IIS mapping in a small network or where greater control over issuance and revocation is required.** In a small network, a PKI might not be established, as it would be cost prohibitive to provide certificates for all users. A single Web server might be all there is to manage. When DS mapping is used, all users with certificates have access. When IIS mapping is used, the user certificate must be explicitly mapped—just having a certificate will not gain the user access.
- **Use one-to-one mapping for greater security.** One-to-one mapping provides accountability. You can audit and prove who accesses the server. In many-to-one mapping, all user access will be recorded as coming from a single account.
- **Use many-to-one mapping where similar access by a large number of users is required and where there is no requirement for accountability.** Access by every user will be recorded as access by the common account. Many-to-one mapping can be quickly set up, but it does not provide accountability.

Guidelines for Designing Authentication Using RADIUS

RADIUS authentication can be used wherever remote access—either dial-up or VPN access to Web sites—is required. Dial-up and VPN access might be required for administration and content management. It might be provided for users seeking access to mailboxes on a Microsoft Exchange server or other secured intranet sites. It might already be in place to secure wireless access to intranet Web sites.

> **See Also**   For more information about the design of RADIUS authentication for VPNs, see Lesson 2, "Designing VPN Connectivity," in Chapter 7. For more information about wireless access using RADIUS, see the topics *Secure and Insecure Wireless Network Topology Options* and *Guidelines for Designing Security for 802.11i (WPA) Networks* in Chapter 12.

> **Note**   While there is no direct configuration option for IIS users to be authenticated using RADIUS, you could write an ISAPI filter that redirected access requests to the Web server to a RADIUS server. In this model, all access—even anonymous access—is redirected to the RADIUS server. If Microsoft Internet Authentication Server is used, remote access policies can also be used to constrain user access. A third-party ISAPI filter–based product (RadIIS) is available from TCP DATA at *http://www.tcpdata.com/radiis_overview.htm*.

Follow these guidelines when designing authentication to Web sites using RADIUS:

- Select RADIUS authentication when designing VPNs to be used for access to Web sites.

- Require the dial-up property of user accounts that will access Web sites using RADIUS to be via remote access policies.

- Configure remote access policies that are based on Windows groups. Use groups that are designed to manage and control access to Web sites. For example, a group created for Web site administrators should be used to authenticate remote access for Web site administration.

- Add RADIUS logs to the list of logs that must be reviewed.

- Encrypt communication between the RADIUS client and RADIUS server.

Options Available When Designing Authentication for FTP

FTP site authentication is restricted to anonymous and/or basic authentication or FTP user isolation. Anonymous access uses the IUSR_*computername* account by default but can be configured to use any Windows account. Anonymous access is similar to anonymous access for IIS. Users don't need to know the account and password. When basic authentication is used, user credentials are passed across the network in the clear, so it might be beneficial to use IPSec policies to protect these credentials or require VPN access.

A new authentication possibility in IIS 6.0 is the ability to use *FTP user isolation*. FTP user isolation is a methodology where a specific folder is assigned as the FTP site location and is accessible only by using a specific user account and password. In this scenario, the FTP user isolation mode—either Isolate Users or Isolate Users Using Active Directory—is chosen when the site is created. Figure 13-15 shows the FTP User Isolation page of the FTP Site Creation Wizard.

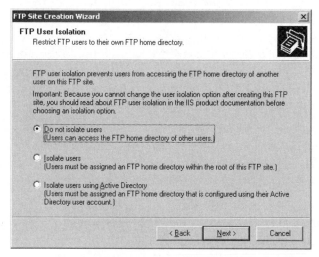

Figure 13-15   Selecting the user isolation mode during FTP site setup

Isolate Users is configured after the site is created by using the Directory Security page to delete the anonymous account and entering a specific domain or local users account. The account name must match the name of the directory on the file server used to store FTP site data.

> **Tip**   Using user isolation has the additional security benefit that a user can see only his FTP directory. To the user, it looks like his FTP folder is the root of FTP.

Isolate User Using Active Directory authenticates users against a specific container in the Active Directory. This reduces the amount of searching that might be done in the Isolate Users mode. Configuration consists of adding the user account to the Directory Security pages of the FTP site and then modifying the FTPRoot (the file server share) and FTPDir (the home directory FTP site location for the user account) properties of the user object in Active Directory.

> **Note** To read or set the FTPDir and FTPRoot properties of a user account, use the script, issftp.vbs, located in the system32 folder.

Considerations for Designing Authentication for SMTP

Consider the following items when designing authentication for SMTP:

- **Restrict relay to prevent spam.** Authentication for relaying, sending, and receiving e-mail can be configured. You configure authentication using the SMTP Access properties page. Configure authentication for mail relay by configuring authentication and then using the relay restrictions configuration. You can either prevent all relay, identify approved computers that can relay, or set the Allow All Computers Which Successfully Authenticate To Relay setting. In the third case, all computers are blocked unless they can meet authentication requirements. You can also configure SMTP to provide the authentication credentials it requires to forward messages to another server that requires authentication.

- **Disable anonymous authentication.** You can configure authentication requirements for incoming messages by requiring anonymous, basic (clear text), or Windows integrated authentication. Allowing anonymous authentication will encourage spam.

- **Provide authentication for the outbound message.** Do this if the SMTP virtual server is used to relay e-mail from your domain to servers under your management, to those at ISPs, and to other servers with which you have relaying arrangements.

- **Use TLS.** Consider securing client basic authentication connections to the SMTP server by requiring TLS. Consider securing relays between authorized servers by requiring TLS.

Practice: Selecting Authentication Methods for IIS

In this practice, you will select authentication methods for IIS based on business needs. Much of the design work for authentication for IIS consists of analyzing the business needs and selecting the most secure authentication choice or choices that will fulfill these needs. In Table 13-6, review the scenarios and then indicate the authentication method or methods that you would choose for each scenario. In the third column, briefly explain why you chose the method or methods that you did. If you are unable to answer a question, review the lesson materials and try the question again. You can find answers to the questions in the "Questions and Answers" section at the end of the chapter.

> **Tip** Assume that the proper Web and NTFS permissions have been set on the site.

Table 13-6   Selecting Authentication Methods

Scenario	Authentication Method	Rationale
Public Web site		
Public Web site with some files that restrict access by Windows groups.		
Intranet site, some of which should be accessible to all users and some of which is restricted by Windows groups.		
An e-commerce site. SSL is configured.		
Outlook Web Access Server. No PKI is in place in the enterprise.		
Partner site. You must be able to hold individual users at the partner company accountable. That is, you must be able to tell, based on the Windows account, that a specific partner employee accessed the site.		

Table 13-6 **Selecting Authentication Methods**

Scenario	Authentication Method	Rationale
A specific company-operated CA is configured to issue certificates only to employees in the research department. A research department Web site needs to be restricted so that only employees of the research department can access it.		
Outlook Web Access and a PKI are already established. You want the highest level of security.		

Design Activity: Designing Security for IIS

In this activity, you must use what you learned in both lessons and apply it to a real-world situation. Read the scenario and then complete the exercise that follows. You can find answers for the exercise in the "Questions and Answers" section at the end of this chapter.

Scenario

As the Web site administrator for Tailspin Toys, your job has been to design and maintain the Web site look and feel. Web hosting is outsourced. When you were hired, the Web site was a collection of product pages, marketing hype, and a disorganized customer information database. You've built a world-class Web site that attracts a large audience because of the child safety pages, interactive toy demonstrations, virtual toy factory, and all-occasion gift selection workshop. The workshop is personalized by the use of the image of a friendly grandmotherly type woman, Mrs. Claus. Your "Letters to Mrs. Claus" newsletter boasts 150,000 subscribers.

Recently, your boss informed you that the Web site is going to be moved in-house. You might remain the Web site administrator if you can prove that you can handle the Web server administration duties as well. To prove your ability to handle the extra responsibilities, she asks you to provide a server administration plan. You have some training and background in server administration because that is what you did while job hunting for a Web site administration position. You do not want to lose your job and feel that a key part of the administration plan should be IIS security. You start your administration plan by designing security for IIS. You have the following information to work with.

Company Background

Tailspin Toys is an international wholesaler and retailer of toys. The company originally specialized in flying toys such as kites and toy airplanes, but it now sells many different types of toys. In addition to children's toys, the company markets many products to adults—from expensive, remote-controlled model airplanes to marble chess sets. If kids of any age will play with it, Tailspin Toys will sell it.

Existing Environment

No public Web servers are hosted by the organization. There is a perimeter network that provides a location for the Exchange front-end server. Windows Server 2003 is specified as the server platform of choice for new servers. All client computers run Windows XP Professional or will by the year's end. All laptop computers run Windows XP Professional. PKI has been implemented.

The current Web site does not provide any e-mail services. Customer comment forms are filled out from a Web page and posted to the Web site. Contact e-mail addresses are provided, but the Web server is located on the current Tailspin Toys network.

Interviews

Following is a list of company personnel interviewed and their statements:

- **Marketing representative** "Oh, good. I wanted to talk to you. Now that the Web site will be hosted here, I want to be able to make changes on my own."

- **Human Resources employee** "We'd like to be able to advertise jobs on the site and collect resumes."

- **Salesperson** "That server can't have any downtime."

- **ISP manager** "Oh, you don't want to move your Web site. We can't guarantee security if you do so. Data storage? We can provide you unlimited use of our Microsoft SQL Server. We provide bandwidth on demand. Applications? Yes, all your applications use ASP. We just began discussions with you—all about moving to .NET."

Business Requirements

These are the business requirements:

1. Uptime must be 24 hours a day, every day.

2. Consumers must not notice a difference in their Web site experience.

3. Additional services must be added. If something will increase revenue or improve customer relations, it should be done.

Technical Requirements

These are the technical requirements:

1. All services provided by the current hosted site must be provided.

2. Security must protect the Web site and data from attack.

Exercise 1: Choose Security to Meet Business and Technical Needs

Answer the following question.

1. As you start to do your security design, you realize that security issues you need to resolve fall into multiple categories. You make the following list of categories. Review the categories in Table 13-7, and then indicate the type of security that will meet the business and technical needs of the Web site for each category.

Table 13-7 Choosing Security to Meet Business and Technical Needs

Category	What type of security will meet the business and technical needs of the Web site?
Authentication	
Content management	
Web permissions	
NTFS permissions	

Table 13-7   Choosing Security to Meet Business and Technical Needs

Category	What type of security will meet the business and technical needs of the Web site?
Remote storage of data	
Remote administration	
Web site services and extensions	

Chapter Summary

- Securing IIS is a task composed of securing the server running Windows Server 2003 and applying IIS-specific security.

- Key factors to consider when designing IIS security baselines are IIS-related services and extensions, process isolation, Web and NTFS permissions, and authentication.

- Authentication via certificate mapping can provide secure access to internal resources such as e-mail and intranet sites. Partner access using certificates provided by partners can also be provided via certificate mapping.

Exam Highlights

Before taking the exam, review these key points and terms. You need to know this information.

Key Points

- Application pools can be used to set up process isolation and to provide security for multiple Web sites installed on the same server.

- FTP user isolation mode provides the ability to create multiple virtual FTP roots. Authorized users of FTP sites cannot use directory traversal to access other FTP sites on the same server.

- Using RADIUS for authenticated access to Web sites can provide a way to securely manage authentication in situations in which many authorized users must securely access a public Web site.

- Always protect basic authentication by encrypting communications between client computers and the Web server. SSL can be used with or without client certificates to protect access from the Internet. IPSec can be used to protect communications from the internal network to the IIS server.

Key Terms

Application pool identity   A user account that is the process identity for the worker processes that service an application pool.

Application pools   A group of Web sites and applications that can use the same worker process. Application pools are isolated from interactivity.

FTP user isolation   A method in which a specific folder is assigned as the FTP site location and is accessible only by using a specific user account and password. Each FTP site appears to the user as if it is the FTP root.

Page
13-31

Lesson 1   Practice: Designing IIS Security to Meet Business Needs

The following table provides the answers.

Table   Designing IIS Security for Business Needs—Answer Key

Business Need	Proposed IIS Feature	What is your proposed security solution?
An ISP must host 2000 Web sites.	Virtual Web sites.	Use worker process isolation mode and separate application pools for each department.
Content management for the sites hosted for the ISP must be provided for each Web site. Each Web site owner must not be able to change content on other sites.	FTP site for content upload.	Protect data and FTP basic authentication using VPNs. Provide authentication via RADIUS.
E-mail access from the Internet. There is no budget for implementing PKI.	Outlook Web Access, Windows authentication.	Use basic authentication and secure with SSL. A server certificate will be required. Alternatively, require VPN access to the network to access e-mail.
Large amounts of data storage are needed.	Store data on a storage area network (SAN).	Provide a firewall to secure access to the SAN from the Web site. Allow traffic from the Web server only.
Mail relay from internal mail servers to ISP mail server.	Provide SMTP service on the Web server.	Restrict mail relay to that from specific mail servers on the internal network. Require TLS for mail transfer. Insist on authenticated and secure traffic between the ISP and your Web server SMTP services.

Lesson 2 Practice: Selecting Authentication Methods for IIS

The following table provides the answers.

Table Selecting Authentication Methods—Answer Key

Scenario	Authentication Method	Rationale
Public Web site	Anonymous.	There is no need to restrict read access.
Public Web site with some files that restrict access by Windows groups.	Anonymous and basic. However, you should consider providing additional protection—such as SSL or a VPN—for user credentials.	The public should be restricted, but access to private information should be allowed. Basic authentication allows authorization security. SSL or a VPN protects user credentials.
Intranet site, some of which should be accessible to all users and some of which is restricted by Windows groups.	Windows integrated.	A Web site that allows access to internal users is at less risk. Capture of Windows credentials used on the internal network is still possible, but it is less likely to happen than when this type of authentication is used on a Web server accessible from the Internet. SSL can be implemented if the nature of the data requires a higher degree of security.
An e-commerce site. SSL is configured.	Anonymous.	The user's private information (such as credit card number) is secured via encryption provided by SSL. Anyone who can provide valid credit card information can make a purchase on the site. Anyone should be able to access the site.
Outlook Web Access Server. No PKI is in place in the enterprise.	SSL. Basic authentication.	This configuration will protect Windows credentials as they cross the Internet. Any browser can be used with basic authentication.
Partner site. You must be able to hold individual users at the partner company accountable. That is, you must be able to tell, based on the Windows account, that a specific partner employee accessed the site.	SSL. Client authentication is required. One-to-one certificate mapping is used.	Each user must provide a copy of his or her certificate and use the certificate for authentication. Because the certificate is mapped to an account, use of the Web site can be monitored.

Table   Selecting Authentication Methods—Answer Key

Scenario	Authentication Method	Rationale
A specific company-operated CA is configured to issue certificates only to employees in the research department. A research department Web site needs to be restricted so that only employees of the research department can access it.	Certificate mapping. Many-to-one.	This configuration allows access to be restricted to a specific CA.
Outlook Web Access and a PKI are already established. You want the highest level of security.	SSL. Require client certificates.	This approach requires the server and users to authenticate.

Design Activity: Designing Security for IIS

Page 13-46

Exercise 1: Choosing Security to Meet Business and Technical Needs

Answer the following question.

1. As you start to do your security design, you realize that security issues you need to resolve fall into multiple categories. You make the following list of categories. Review the categories in Table 13-7, and then indicate the type of security that will meet the business and technical needs of the Web site for each category.

   The following table provides the answers.

   Table   Choosing Security to Meet Business and Technical Needs—Answer Key

Category	What type of security will meet the business and technical needs of the Web site?
Authentication	Anonymous access should be available. No other IIS authentication choice should be enabled. Certificate mapping should be enabled. This will allow employees who need access to special areas on the Web site to have it.
Content management	A separate server will be provided to allow FTP site creation. FTP user isolation will be used to allow authorized users for different parts of the Web site to upload content to unique locations. You will review content changes, make sure proper approval is obtained, and move the content to the production server.

Table Choosing Security to Meet Business and Technical Needs—Answer Key

Category	What type of security will meet the business and technical needs of the Web site?
Web permissions	Separate folders for static content and for executables will be maintained. Permissions will be set on the static content as Read. Permissions on executables will allow execution, but they won't allow Write permissions. Any data that users must enter into forms will be written to databases on a SQL Server server, not to local Web pages. Some content is accessible only to certain users. These folders will be given Read permission but will be controlled through the use of NTFS.
NTFS permissions	NTFS permissions will parallel Web permissions when anonymous access is allowed. NTFS permissions will control Web access to restricted areas of the Web site and will deny access to the anonymous account. Other NTFS permissions will be set on folders and files that should not be Web accessible.
Remote storage of data	A SQL Server database will have to be installed and secured. IPSec policies will be written to secure data written to the database.
Remote administration	Remote administration will be allowed only via terminal services. An IPSec policy will be used to protect data and for computer authentication.
Web site services and extensions	ASP will need to be enabled, but no other extensions will be enabled unless it is determined that some application requires them. The FTP service will not run on the Web server.

Glossary

!Special Administration Console (!SAC)   A Windows Server 2003 recovery console that provides command-line support and can be accessed through an out-of-band remote management port using terminal software that supports VT-UTF8, VT100+, or VT100. SAC and !SAC are command-line consoles that are different than the Windows Server 2003 command-line environment.

802.11   A standard for wireless networks.

802.1x   A new security standard for 802.11 networks that uses RADIUS for authentication and provides key management. 802.1x is an IETF standard created to address the security issues of 802.11. The 802.1x standard is not a replacement for 802.11. Instead, 802.1x should be thought of as the security addendum for 802.11. The 802.1x standard does add considerable security support to 802.11 wireless networks; however, hardware and software upgrades are necessary, as well as changes to the wireless supporting infrastructures.

Access Control Entries (ACEs)   Data structures that identify permissions and indicate to whom they are assigned. ACEs are assigned to objects at object creation and can be modified by a security principal with the Change Permissions permission. Each ACE contains a security identifier, a permission, and an action (either Allow or Deny).

ad hoc mode   A type of wireless network where wireless clients are connected directly to each other without using an access point.

answering router   In a site-to-site (router-to-router) virtual private network (VPN), the router that listens for the connection request, authenticates and authorizes the VPN connection, and then acts as a router by forwarding packets between nodes in its site and the calling router.

anti-replay protection   A process or configuration that ensures that authentication and other successful negotiation packets cannot be re-used by another computer to form a successful connection.

application pool identity   A user account that is the process identity for the worker processes that service an application pool. Each application pool can and should have a separate application pool identity. Web sites and applications running in the application pool have the same rights and permissions granted to the application pool identity.

application pools   An IIS group of Web sites and applications that can use the same worker process. Each application pool serves as an isolation boundary—that is, an application running outside of the application pool has no access to the processes or Web site running inside the application pool.

authentication   A process through which security principals (users, computers, and processes) can prove their identity before connecting to the network or to some resource contained by the network. In a traditional network, authentication is supported by technologies that rely on passwords. Today, additional authentication tools—such as certificates, smart cards, biometrics, tokens, and even unique devices—are supported.

Authentication Header (AH)   One of two subprotocols of IPSec. AH provides superior packet authentication. This is because AH provides protection for the data packet and the IP header. The AH header contains a field, named Authentication Data, that includes an integrity check value (ICV) or authentication code. This value is checked to validate message authentication and integrity. The ICV is calculated over the Internet Protocol header, the AH header, and the data payload. Encapsulating Security Payload (ESP), in contrast, does not sign the whole packet.

Authority Information Access (AIA)   A location—such as a URL, a file system path, or an LDAP—where a copy of the certificate authority certificate can be obtained.

authorization   The process that dictates what a security principal can do after it is authenticated. System privileges and object-based access control lists (ACLs) are the primary methods of authorization used in the Microsoft Windows family of operating systems.

Automated System Recovery (ASR)   An ASR backup backs up the local system state data, system services, and any disks that are part of the operating system. An ASR backup of a cluster node will back up the cluster disk signatures and partitions.

autonomy   A state or condition in which external control is possible even while local control is the way things are done.

Basic Service Set (BSS)   A single-access-point wireless-network configuration consisting of an access point or server that connects clients to an internal network and clients. The wireless access point serves as a bridge between the wireless and wired networks.

bidirectional trust   A trust relationship that extends in both directions.

border controls   Controls that sit at the junction between trusted and less trusted segments of a network. They can be firewalls, remote access servers, intrusion detection systems, packet filtering routers, virtual private network servers, or a combination of these things that are located on a border between the internal private network and an external network such as the Internet.

border gateway   A hardware or software device that separates an organization's internal, private network from a network that does not belong to it, such as the Internet.

bridge CA   A Certificate Authority (CA) that becomes the link between multiple hierarchies. If the bridge CA is part of the certificate chain, the certificate will be validated.

Business Drivers   The objectives that propel a business forward and continue to make it profitable.

business continuity plan   A plan that consists of an analysis of the major risks to an organization's survival and of a plan for the mitigation of, or other response to, the risks.

business impact analysis (BIA)   A type of risk analysis, usually undertaken as part of the business continuity plan process. For each risk, it is determined what will happen if risk becomes reality. For each risk, it is determined exactly how much time in days or hours can pass before the business goes out of business. Each risk is then ranked according to this time factor. This ordered list helps management assign resources to mitigate the risk or to respond to the results if the risk becomes a reality.

CA Administrator   A Windows Server 2003 CA role. The CA Administrator configures and maintains the certificate authority (CA).

California law SB 1836   An amendment to the California Information Practices Act that says if you do business with residents of California, have their unencrypted information in your databases, and are then hacked, you must notify each of those California residents that his or her personal information might have been compromised. This law is a California law that affects every state in the United States.

calling routers   In a site-to-site virtual private network (VPN), the routers that initiate the VPN connection when a packet being forwarded matches a route that uses a VPN-router interface.

certificate authority (CA)   An entity or an organization that manages and controls the production of public or private certificates. *CA* is also the name used to describe the computer device and the software that produces or controls the issuance or revocation of certificates and the infrastructure for certificate use in the network.

certificate authority (CA) hierarchy   An organized collection of CAs. The first CA in a CA hierarchy is the root, and there can be only one root. All other CAs joined in the hierarchy are subordinate to the root and must receive a CA certificate from another CA. A CA hierarchy can contain both stand-alone and enterprise CAs.

certificate chain   Defines the path from the root certificate authority (CA) through the layers of the intermediary and issuing CAs to the specific certificate being validated.

certificate distribution   The process of getting the certificate to the device from which it will be used.

certificate enrollment   The process used by user and computer accounts to obtain a certificate.

certificate manager   A Windows Server 2003 CA role. The certificate manager manages certificates, approves and denies certificate enrollment and revocation requests, reactivates certificates placed on hold, and recovers archived keys. This role uses the Issue And Manage Certificates permission.

certificate practice statement (CPS)   A formal document that specifies how the public key infrastructure (PKI) will be operated and managed. It is, as the American Bar Association states, "A statement of the practices which a certification authority employs in issuing certificates."

certificate policy statement   A statement of the practices that indicates how a certificate is used, how keys are managed, requirements for enrollment, requirements for revocations, and so on.

certificate revocation   The process of revoking a digital certificate or withdrawing approval for a digital certificate.

certificate revocation list (CRL)   A list of certificates that have been revoked along with the reason they were revoked.

certificate services   Services through which public key and private key algorithms are implemented. Certificate services include the issuing, use, and maintenance of certificates.

certificate trust list (CTL)   A list of certificate characteristics that will allow a certificate to be accepted for authentication. A CTL is created only at the Web-site level and thus is a good choice for use by departments or groups within an organization.

cluster backup   The process of making a backup copy of both the cluster data and configuration information, such as cluster disk signatures and partitions. When both data and configuration are properly backed up, the cluster can be restored if complete failure occurs.

complete mediation   The security principle that states all access avenues should be checked. Examples are that program input should be checked by the program; administrators should protect shares with proper permissions; users should not be allowed to install unapproved software; auditors should be reviewing whether all of these things, and any other access controls, are being implemented properly.

compulsory tunnel   A virtual private network (VPN) tunnel that must be used if data travels the path two networks created by a site-to-site VPN.

confidentiality   The process that keeps private information private. Data, communications, and even code can have requirements for protection. While authorization can protect digital information, there are many ways to subvert authorization, including taking ownership of an object, placing a copy of the data on another computer, capturing information as it flows across a network, and so forth. Providing layers of security is a maxim of good security. Confidentiality allows you to do this. Confidentiality is most often obtained on a network by using encryption.

Connection Manager (CM)   A program that includes a client dialer, the Connection Manager Administration Kit (CMAK) (used to create the profile), and Connection Point Services (CPS) (used to create and distribute custom phone books).

Connection Manager Administration Kit (CMAK)   A tool used by an administrator to create the profile. The profile is a self-extracting executable that can be provided to a user via a Web site, e-mail, CD-ROM, or other distribution mechanism. When run by the user, the profile creates the preprogrammed connections. A profile can be created for most versions of Windows.

Connection Point Services (CPS)   Services that provide the ability to create, distribute, and update custom phone books. Phone books provide the Point of Presence (POP) entries, telephone numbers, or virtual private network (VPN) addresses used to access a dial-up network, the Internet, or a VPN server. When users travel, they have all the required phone numbers needed to access approved connection points or proxies to them. A Phone Book Server, a Windows Server 2003 computer running IIS (including the FTP Publishing service), and an Internet Server Application Programming Interface (ISAPI) extension are used to update clients. The client also queries the Phone Book Server for an updated list of numbers.

critical update   A released fix that addresses a critical non-security-related update.

CRL Distribution Point (CDP)   A location—such as a URL, a file system path, or an LDAP—where the certificate revocation list (CRL) can be found.

cross-certification   The process whereby two CA hierarchies can form a trust relationship so that certificates on each CA hierarchy will be trusted by the other.

data integrity   A quality that means the data of a system is not changed without authorization.

data origin authentication   A type of authentication that verifies whether each packet received came from the server that negotiated the connection.

defense in depth   A security principle that says you should not rely on one defensive technique but use many. If one defensive technique fails, the other might prevent the intrusion or at least give you time to deal with it.

delta CRL   A certificate revocation list (CRL) that is published between the normal publication periods of the CRL. Delta CRLs contain only newly revoked certificates.

demand-dial connection   A connection that is completed when traffic for a specified network is received by one of the gateway servers. All traffic routed across this connection is encrypted and tunneled through the virtual private network (VPN), while traffic from client computers to the VPN server on one network and between the VPN server on the other network and the data's final destination is not tunneled or encrypted.

demand-dial interface   In a virtual private network, the interface that is both the connection point and the configuration information for the connection. It includes the type of port to use, the addressing used for the connection, the authentication methods, the encryption requirements, and authentication credentials.

demand-dial routing   The creation of an on-demand connection between two networks.

dependent administrative functions   Functions of administration that can be split into two parts. For the job to be completed, both operations are necessary.

Diffie-Hellman group   A parameter that indicates the strength of the key used to secure the Quick Mode negotiation in IPSec when the master key is being calculated. The larger the group number, the larger the key.

digital certificate   A collection of related data that binds an identity to a cryptographic key pair. Certificates can be used for authentication, authorization, non-repudiation, and other security controls.

Directory Service mapping   A type of certificate mapping for Internet Information Services (IIS). If it is enabled, the certificates bound to the Active Directory account of a user can be used for authentication to IIS.

directory traversal attacks   Attacks where an individual obtains access to a subdirectory and attempts to traverse the directory to gain access elsewhere. Thus, an attacker might have access to a content folder and seek to gain access to a sensitive folder such as an operating system folder that contains the Security Accounts Manager database.

discretionary access control lists (DACLs)   A list of Access Control Entries (ACEs) used to control access to objects in Windows NT and later Windows operating systems.

diversity of mechanism   A security principle that states if every computer is the same and if every defense mechanism is the same, then they will fail the same way; therefore, use a variety of mechanisms. This principle is also addressed by providing redundancy and multiple paths. For example, you can design a classic perimeter network (also known as a DMZ, or demilitarized zone, and a screened subnet) or border network with two firewalls. One firewall should be between the Internet and the border network, and the other should be between the border network and the internal network. Do not use the same firewall at each border. If an intruder successfully penetrates the external firewall, you do not want her to be able to use the same attack on the internal firewall.

DNS cache poisoning An attack on the Domain Name System (DNS) that gives false information in response to a DNS server. If no protection against this attack exists, the false information might be placed in the DNS server cache and given out in response to a request. Clients are then redirected either to a computer under the control of the attacker, or they are simply sent to an incorrect address.

DNS footprinting An attack in which an attacker obtains Domain Name System (DNS) zone data and thus has domain names, computer names, and IP addresses. This information can be used to further compromise systems.

DNS IP spoofing An attack in which an attacker might attempt to use valid IP address obtained from Domain Name System (DNS) zone information in IP packets created by the attacker. Because these packets now appear to come from a legitimate source on the network, the attacker might be able to use them to gain information or compromise other resources.

EAP-MD5 An Extensible Authentication Protocol (EAP) type that can be used only with Layer Two Tunneling Protocol/Internet Protocol security (L2TP/IPSec) VPNs and dial-up access, not with Point-to-Point Tunneling Protocol (PPTP) or wireless VPNs. It is less secure than EAP-TLS because it uses passwords not certificates. It weakens password security as well. A reversibly encrypted password must be stored in the account database, as with the Challenge-Handshake Authentication Protocol (CHAP).

EAP/MS-CHAPv2 An Extensible Authentication Protocol (EAP) type that is password based and provides mutual authentication. The client must prove its knowledge of the user password to the server, and the server must prove its knowledge of the user password to the client. Encryption keys are generated for use with Microsoft Point-to-Point Encryption based on the user's password.

EAP-TLS (Extensible Authentication Protocol/Transport Layer Security) An EAP type that is based on a public key certificate and enables mutual authentication between the client and server computers that make up the virtual private network (VPN) connection. Before data can be transmitted, a client certificate must be provided to and validated by the dial-in server and the server must provide its own, which must be validated by the client. EAP-TLS can be used with Point-to-Point Tunneling Protocol (PPTP). In this case, the server must have a certificate, but the client computers do not require one. User certificates can be installed on client computers or smart cards.

economy of mechanism   A security principle that states that complexity is the enemy of security. The more complex security is, the more likely it is to fail. When a security strategy is hard to understand, people don't use it or configure it incorrectly. For example, if a smart card must be in the smart card reader to keep a session going, make the smart card the employee ID badge. Because an ID badge must be worn at all times, the user's smart card will always be available to the user. Only one card is therefore necessary for both approved functions.

effective permissions   Permissions that are applied to an object. Effective permissions may be a combination of permissions assigned on the object and inherited permissions.

Emergency Management Services (EMS)   A new feature in Windows Server 2003 that provides assistance in remote administration. Windows Server 2003 can start and operate without most video card support and, depending on the hardware, without legacy keyboard controllers. If properly equipped, the out-of-band management port (typically the serial port) can support Remote Installation Services (RIS).

Encapsulating Security Payload (ESP)   One of two IPSec subprotocols that provides an end-to-end encryption enrollment agent.

Extended Services Set (ESS)   A wireless network in which several access points are used but are connected to the same wireless network. The ESS creates a single logical network segment and is identified by a single Service Set Identifier (SSID).

Extensible Authentication Protocol (EAP)   An Internet Engineering Task Force (IETF) (RFC 2284) extension to Point-to-Point Protocol (PPP). A choice of authentication algorithms known as *EAP – types* can be made.

external trust   A trust that is created between a domain in a forest and either a Windows NT 4.0 domain or a domain in another forest.

feature pack   A new feature or features released for a current product. The feature pack only adds functionality and is usually part of the next release of the product.

Federal Information Processing Standard (FIPS)   A standard for data processing mandated for some United States government operations. This standard specifies cryptographic algorithms and other security-related processing functions. Meeting these standards might require special software, certain cryptographic algorithms, and security devices such as Fortezza cards.

file recovery   The process of either restoring a backup of the original keys and then continuing to use the files, or using a file recovery agent to decrypt a file and then returning the file to the owner for encryption.

filter action   The action taken if an IPSec policy is triggered. Each rule must have one and only one filter action. The filter action is taken if the policy is triggered because of something in the filter list. If a filter list contains filters that include the destination port on the local computer for telnet ftp and nntp and a filter action of block, any traffic received that is destined for these ports is dropped.

filter list   A list of the filters that makes up an IPSec rule. Each rule can have multiple filters. Filters specify information about the source and destination computers. Filters also provide information about the protocol, including source and destination ports, source and destination IP addresses, and source and destination mask.

forest trust   A forest trust can be created between two Windows Server 2003 forests.

FTP user isolation   A method in which a specific folder is assigned as the File Transfer Protocol (FTP) site location and is accessible only by using a specific user account and password.

functional levels   Windows server 2003 domain and forest designations that cannot be set if their restrictions on domain controller operating system are not met. Both domain and forest functional levels are available. In each case, a functional level can be configured when domain controller requirements are met.

Graham Leach Bliley   A United States law that financial institutions (that is, any company that provides financial products or services) must obey. The law controls how they must manage the privacy of customer financial information. It restricts use and disclosure of nonpublic personal information.

Health Insurance Portability and Accountability Act (HIPAA) of 1996   A United States national standard for the protection of health information. The act describes privacy and security standards for electronic exchange of patient health information. This applies to the IT department at doctors' offices, hospitals, and insurance carriers, and it might apply to other businesses as well (for example, to businesses that have benefit plans, because their healthcare plans might come under the restrictions of the law).

Homeland Security Act of 2002   A United States federal act that provides increased surveillance powers for law enforcement agencies, including surveillance conducted on the Internet. The act includes provisions to make it easier for federal agencies to obtain customer information from Internet service providers (ISPs).

hotfix   A package consisting of one or many files that provides a fix for a product problem. A hotfix addresses a specific customer problem and is available only through a support relationship with Microsoft. Other terms that have been used in the past are *quick fix engineering (QFE) update*, *patch*, and *update*.

IIS certificate mapping A process that maps a Windows account to a certificate by using a feature of IIS. After the certificate is mapped to an account, the certificate can be used to authenticate to IIS.

impersonation A concept basic to all Windows operating systems, which becomes especially interesting when applied to application pools. Although a worker process runs in its application pool under the application pool identity, it also is allowed to impersonate, or run under security credentials different from its own, base identity.

in-band management The administration, either directly via the console or remotely via the network, of a server that is running normally.

incident response The process that defines what happens when an attack or suspected attack occurs.

incoming forest trust builders A default user group in Windows Server 2003 whose members can create incoming trusts. Incoming trusts are those in which users in the external forest can be granted access and privileges in the internal or local forest.

incoming trust A type of Windows Server 2003 trust in which the accounts in the local domain can be given access to resources in the specified domain.

infrastructure mode A type of wireless network in which wireless clients connect to a wireless access point (AP) that might or might not be connected to a wired network.

integrated service pack A release or product with the service pack already applied.

integrity The ability to guarantee that information is not arbitrarily changed. Changes can be made to data, but only when authorized. Many networks and systems maintain integrity by providing authentication and authorization controls. When data is sent over a network, additional controls are needed. Network communications has long supported the use of algorithms that check integrity by comparing the result of a calculation that includes the data sent with the result of that same calculation that includes the data received. If there is a difference in results of the two calculations, then the data has changed. These calculations detect accidental changes made because of poor communications and trigger a repeated transmission. These calculations cannot protect the integrity of data from malicious interference. Modern communication protocols such as IPSec use encryption to protect the data that is sent from being tampered with.

intermediate CAs Certificate authorities (CAs) that do not issue end-use certificates and that obtain their CA certificate from another CA. The intermediate CA is only used to issue CA certificates for other CAs.

intrusion protection system (IPS)   A system built to react to and stop an attack without administrative intervention that has recently emerged on the market. IPS products detect attacks and can be programmed to respond to them. For example, the device might immediately block all traffic from the identified interloper.

IPSec driver startup modes   A configuration that specifies which, if any, IPSec will be in place during startup. Modes are: Permit, which permits all inbound and outbound traffic; Block, which blocks all inbound and all outbound traffic until a persistent policy is applied; and Stateful, which allows Dynamic Host Configuration Protocol (DHCP) and all outbound traffic initiated by the computer during startup, as well as inbound traffic that is sent in response to outbound traffic.

isolation   A state or condition that indicates a clear, precise boundary. It is used to describe an administrative condition in which there is no way for administrators from one network to administer another network.

issuing CA   The certificate authority (CA) that issues end-use certificates.

keep up to date   A security principle that states that system patches should be installed when they are released and new security configuration information should be used to update systems.

key archival   The process in the Windows Server 2003, Enterprise Edition certificate authority (CA) that stores the private keys of certificates if configured to do so.

key management   The process of key change and distribution and possible archival.

least privilege   A security principle that states that people should be given only the privileges and access to data that they absolutely need. For example, users shouldn't be administrators on their desktops, and you should delegate administrative authority at the organizational unit (OU) level where possible, not domain-wide.

legacy system   Any infrastructure component—such as hardware, operating system software, network devices, or applications—that is technically out of date. For example, Windows 2000–based computers might be defined as legacy systems in a predominately Windows XP Professional and Windows Server 2003 network, and recently produced IBM-style mainframes that host hundreds of Linux servers running Apache Web sites would not be defined as legacy systems (at least not until the next version is placed on the market).

link encryption   The type of encryption in a site-to-site virtual private network (VPN). It does not provide encryption from the client to the VPN endpoint. Instead, encryption is present only between the two VPN endpoints.

local domain   In a Windows Server 2003 trust, the local domain is the domain from which the trust wizard is being run.

many-to-one mapping   A type of Internet Information Services (IIS) certificate mapping in which many certificates are mapped to one user account.

metabase   The Internet Information Services (IIS) structure that stores IIS configuration settings. The metabase in IIS 6.0 consists of two plain-text xml-formatted files— MetaBase.xml and MSSchema.xml—in the *%SystemRoot%*\System32\Inetsrv folder.

Microsoft Security Response Center (MSRC) severity rating   A system that applies a rating to an announced vulnerability.

***Name* constraint**   Designates namespaces that are permitted in the certificates presented. The certificate authority (CA) enforces all constraints defined in its certificate. This allows specification of which namespaces from the other hierarchy will be trusted. Specific namespaces can also be excluded. For example, a common best practice would be to prevent the partner hierarchy from issuing certificates that use your namespace.

NAT-T   A process that uses User Datagram Protocol (UDP) to encapsulate the IPSec packet and allows it to pass through Network Address Translation (NAT). Internet Key Exchange (IKE) can detect whether NAT-T is present and, if it is detected, use UDP-ESP encapsulation.

Network Access Quarantine Control   A new feature of Windows Server 2003 that can prevent access to a private network until the configuration of a remote computer has been validated. Validation is performed by comparing the remote computer against a list of required attributes provided in a script. The script is created by network administrators in compliance with a security policy. For example, administrators might want to ensure that clients have the latest service packs and hotfixes or up-to-date antivirus software before they are connected to the corporate network.

Network Address Translation (NAT)   A process that assigns an Internet-routable address to a client when the client's traffic is routed through a NAT server. By default, the NAT server will forward traffic from the external network to the internal network only if the traffic comes in response to a client request. However, most NAT servers have the capability of forwarding external requests for specific services, such as access to Web servers that are located on the internal network.

network load balancing   A Microsoft clustering technology that spreads requests for a single IP address among several Microsoft Windows servers. It can also provide load balancing in addition to scalability and redundancy. If a VPN server that is using network load balancing fails, client sessions will also fail and the user will be prompted to log on again. The user's new session will be managed by one of the other VPN servers in the cluster.

nonrepudiation   A method of providing undeniable proof that a security principal is the source of some data, action, or communication. Nonrepudiation can, for example, verify the assertion that the user did use her credit card to make an online purchase or that the boss did send the e-mail giving me the day off. In both cases and in many other digital situations, the use of public key/private key technologies can be used to implement nonrepudiation.

nontransitive trust relationship   An attribute of trusts. When multiple trust relationships exist, trust does not extend from trust to trust. That is, if domains A and B trust each other and domains B and C trust each other, domains A and C do not trust each other. Windows NT 4.0–style trusts are nontransitive.

one-to-one mapping   A type of Internet Information Services (IIS) certificate mapping in which each certificate is mapped to only one user account.

one-way trust   A trust relationship that extends in one direction. All Windows trusts can be created in a single direction. However, a bidirectional trust can be created by creating two trust relationships, one in each direction.

Open System Authentication   A wireless access point (AP) authentication mechanism in which no authentication is done unless combined with Media Access Control address restrictions on the AP.

outgoing trust   In Windows Server 2003, a trust in which the accounts in the specified domain can be given access to resources in the local domain.

out-of-band management   Management of a server by using a serial port or special device.

perimeter network   An area that defines a network that is neither part of an organization's internal network nor part of the external network but is under the control of the organization. Also known as a DMZ, because of its resemblance to a demilitarized zone agreed upon between hostile nations.

process identity   The Windows account that a process runs under. When anonymous access is allowed in Internet Information Services (IIS), the IUSR_*computername* is the process identity. When process isolation is used, the default process identity is the network service.

Protected Extensible Authentication Protocol (PEAP)   An authentication protocol used for 802.11 wired and wireless clients. PEAP uses Transport Layer Security (TLS) for end-to-end communication.

Protected Extensible Authentication Protocol (PEAP) EAP-MSCHAPv2   An authentication protocol in which passwords are protected by Transport Layer Security (TLS). Mutual authentication is provided because the server also is authenticated by the client. The RADIUS server is used for authentication and must have a certificate, but client computers do not need them. Instead, the user provides a user ID and password.

psychological acceptability   A security principle that recognizes that the human element is the most important security asset. This principle dictates that you make security unobtrusive, hide its complexity, use acceptable processes, and obtain user buy-in. For example, if you choose to use biometrics, which might include fingerprinting and retinal scans, consider user acceptance. Your users might find the processes to be an invasion of personal privacy. Voice recognition and hand geometry might be more readily accepted by users.

public key infrastructure   The sum of the components implemented to provide certificate services on a network.

qualified subordination   The process of setting constraints on a trust relationship between certificate authority (CA) hierarchies. A qualified subordination can use multiple constraints and even limit which types of certificates from a partner will be trusted.

quorum disk   The cluster quorum disk, often just referred to as the quorum disk, is the source of information on the current cluster configuration, application registry checkpoints, and cluster recovery log.

reduce the attack surface   A security principle that says the fewer avenues of attack that are available, the less there is to protect and the less chance there is of the network being compromised. For example, to decrease the number of avenues of attack you should disable unneeded services, not install unnecessary services or applications, and protect sensitive data with encryption.

remote access policies   Ordered sets of rules that determine whether a connection can proceed (is authorized) or whether it is rejected. Remote access policies specify the when and how of remote access connections to these services and are part of Routing and Remote Access Services (RRAS) and Internet Authentication Service (IAS).

remote access VPN   A virtual private network (VPN) that consists of a Windows Server 2003 server running Routing and Remote Access Services and that is configured as a VPN server with a compatible VPN client.

remote administrative practices   Any administration practices that do not take place at the console. However, some security practices change when the remote administration takes place over the WAN or Internet as opposed to over a local LAN. The risk of interception is higher during these more remote activities, and additional security is required.

Remote Assistance   A Windows Server 2003 and Windows XP utility that allows users to send an invitation or request help with the system they are logged on to. The invitation, if accepted by the recipient, allows access to the system that sent the invitation. Although this might seem similar to Remote Desktop for Administration, Remote Assistance differs in several respects. Remote Assistance requires an invitation. Remote Desktop for Administration can be controlled, but it does not require a local user to send an invitation. With Remote Assistance, both the person sending the invitation and the invitee can see what is being controlled on the local machine. It can be used as a teaching mechanism. Remote Desktop for Administration does not do this. The user has a say in decisions made and is prompted to approve the takeover of her systems. A password is required to use the invitation. Remote Desktop for Administration requires that the user be an Administrator. Further, Remote Desktop for Administration requires the knowledge of a distinct password, which should be passed to the administrator through an alternative medium (for example, over the telephone).

Remote Data Access (RDA)   A process used to access data in a SQL Server database. RDA uses authentication and encryption via Microsoft Internet Information Services (IIS), including anonymous, basic, and Secure Sockets Layer (SSL).

Remote Desktop Connection (RDC)   A process that can be used to connect to a Windows XP Professional computer running the Remote Desktop. The connection provides full access to the file system, ports, printers, and audio, and it provides smart card sign-on to Windows Server 2003 from Windows Server 2003, XP Professional, and Windows CE .NET.

Remote Desktop for Administration   A tool, also known as the remote desktop tool, that can be used to administer Windows Server 2003. The tool is provided in Windows XP and for Windows Server 2003 can be used to access a Windows Server 2003 computer and administer it. Terminal services on Windows Server 2003 does not have to be installed to use Remote Desktop for Administration. It is built on the Windows 2000 model of terminal services for administration.

Remote Desktop Protocol (RDP)   A protocol used by terminal services. This protocol does not have a mechanism for authenticating the server that the client is connecting to. Consequently, an attacker could spoof the Terminal Server to intercept logon credentials.

Remote Desktop Web Connection   An Active X control/com object that can be used to connect remotely to Windows XP and Windows Server 2003.

replay protection   Protection from an attack that captures and then resends a stream of data.

risk   The probability of suffering a loss.

risk management   The process of identifying risk and deciding what to do about it.

role separation   A technical control in a Windows Server 2003 certificate authority (CA) that divides CA administration duties into roles. The roles can also be enforced.

root enterprise CA   A certificate authority (CA) that is integrated with Active Directory and can be installed only on a Windows Server 2003 or Windows 2000 server that is a member server in an Active Directory domain.

root stand-alone CA   A certificate authority (CA) that is not integrated with Active Directory.

round-robin DNS   A load-balancing solution that is configured by entering several weighted host records that use the same Domain Name System (DNS) name but several IP addresses. This provides load balancing because each request for name resolution will provide one of many IP addresses and thus be directed to a different computer. However, DNS has no way of knowing when a specific VPN server is not available. The IP address for a server that is not available will be provided just as often as one that is.

Sarbanes-Oxley Act of 2002 (Public Company Accounting Reform and Investor Protection Act)   A United States federal act that targets publicly traded or registered companies by placing many restrictions on the operation of public accounting firms and including strict requirements for records retention to prevent document destruction. Many private firms are also complying with the act.

Secure Sockets Layer (SSL)   A protocol that provides certificate-based server authentication and encryption between a client and a server. Client authentication to the server is optional.

security boundaries   Borders beyond which security authority does not extend. Strictly speaking, no security principal, right, or privilege that is valid on one side of the border is valid on the other. Security boundaries provide isolation of administrative authority.

security descriptor   A construct that includes a Systems Access Control List (SACL) and a discretionary access control list (DACL) and can be assigned to a Windows object.

security design framework   A collection of items or components that should be considered when creating any information security design.

security patch   A released fix that addresses a vulnerability in a specific product.

security policies   Concise statements of required behavior. Security policies do not dictate the implementation of security procedures.

security procedures   Detail how the security policies are carried out.

Security Reference Monitor   A kernel-level component that runs in the %system-root%\System32\Ntoskrnl.exe process. The Security Reference Monitor resolves requests for object access, builds a security descriptor for a new object, and validates a given security descriptor. The concept of a security reference monitor is a standard security model in operating systems that is used to evaluate all access to objects.

security update processes   The ways in which security changes can be made.

security updates   Any updates that must occur in direct response to either new knowledge of a practice that will improve security or a security patch released in response to a newly discovered vulnerability.

segmented networks   Networks separated by devices that might obstruct the free flow of communications between computers on opposite sides. Devices such as routers, switches, firewalls, Network Address Translation (NAT) servers, virtual private network (VPN) servers, and proxy servers are often used to segment networks. Networks are often segmented to obscure the existence and composition of the network, to protect elements of one network from another, or for both reasons. In other words, segments are created to define areas of trust.

selective authentication   The ability to limit authentication across a trust.

separation of duties   A security principle that states that whenever possible you should separate the functions of critical operations and assign different parts of the operation to different roles within the organization. For example, programmers should not have network administration privileges; those with backup rights shouldn't have restore rights; and auditors shouldn't be able to modify systems.

server cluster   A group of computer systems that are configured to work together to ensure the continuous availability of critical applications and to increase the computing power available to the application. Common uses for server clusters are to run mission-critical Microsoft SQL Server applications and messaging systems such as Microsoft Exchange Server.

service pack   A cumulative set of hotfixes, security patches, critical updates, and updates to the release of a product. It might include resolved problems not made available elsewhere, and it might include customer-requested design changes and features.

service processors   Devices that can be used to provide out-of-band administration for both normal administration and administration that requires Emergency Management Services (EMS). Another name for a service processor is application-specific integrated circuits (ASICs). They provide connections via out-of-band ports, which can be serial ports, USB ports, Ethernet ports, or modem connections.

Service Set Identifier (SSID)   The wireless network name.

SHA1   An integrity algorithm, it is required for organizations subject to Federal Information Processing Standards (FIPS) regulations.

shadow copy backup   A type of backup that provides a way for users to recover deleted files and for administrators to recover servers. The default process allows the ordinary backup process to back up open files.

Shared Key Authentication   A wireless network authentication type in which a shared secret is used. There is no method defined for key distribution. The key configured on the access point must be known to the person manually configuring the client.

shortcut trust   A trust created between two domains within the same forest. This trust does not provide any new access benefits. It does, however, reduce the trust path length and make operations more efficient. Shortcut trusts are useful to optimize performance if a large number of domain trusts must be crossed for resource authentication or if a parent domain in the trust patch exists in a remote location over a slow WAN link.

SID filtering   A process that does not allow the use of security identifiers (SIDs) from outside the forest to be used to access resources within the forest. When a user attempts to access resources across forest boundaries, SIDs are dropped from the user's access credentials if they do not come from the forest in which the user's account resides.

site-to-site VPN   A virtual private network (VPN) in which a VPN server serves as a gateway on each of two networks. It is not necessary to use a VPN client.

Special Administration Console (SAC)   Provides command-line support, and can be accessed through an out-of-band remote management port using terminal software that supports VT-UTF8, VT100+, or VT100. SAC and !SAC are command-line consoles that are different from the Windows Server 2003 command-line environment.

special cryptographic service providers (CSPs)   Code provided by vendors so that their devices will work with certificate services. By default, three third-party CSPs (Schlumberger cryptographic service provider, Infinean SICRYPT Base Smart Card CSP, and Gemplus GemSAFE card CSP v1.0) are available, but vendor CSPs can be added as needed.

specified domain   A domain in a Windows Server 2003 trust that is not the local domain. A trust is created between the local domain, the domain within which the trust configuration is begun, and a specified domain.

split DNS   A DNS configuration method in which the namespace is divided and a subdomain is used for internal addressing. The internal Domain Name System (DNS) namespace is a subdomain of the external DNS namespace. For example, if the fictitious company Humongous Insurance uses this structure, humongousinsurance.com is the external domain and local.humongousinsurance.com is used as the internal DNS subdomain.

SSL and Secure Shell (SSH) hijacking   An attack that might occur against wireless networks that rely on Secure Sockets Layer (SSL) virtual private networks (VPNs) for access security. In this attack, the attacker uses an Address Resolution Protocol (ARP) spoofing technique and attempts to substitute his server credentials. The client gets a warning that the credentials have changed and is asked to accept them. If a user accepts the credentials, the communications destined for the client's internal network are redirected to the attacker's rogue server.

storage area network (SAN)   A subnetwork of shared computers that contains only disks for data storage.

subordinate CA   A certificate authority (CA) that is a child CA of a root CA in a hierarchy and receives its CA certificate from a root CA.

subordinate enterprise CA   A subordinate certificate authority (CA) that is integrated with Active Directory.

subordinate stand-alone CA   A subordinate certificate authority (CA) that is not integrated with Active Directory. The subordinate stand-alone CA can be installed on a Windows Server 2003 or Windows 2000 server that is or is not an Active Directory domain member server.

symmetric key encryption   A type of encryption that uses a single key and an algorithm to convert plain text, which is easily understood, into cipher text, which is not. One of encryption's weaknesses is the problem of keeping the encryption key safe.

technical constraint   Any reason why a security design cannot be implemented as designed due to limitations of technology. The reason for the technical constraint can be insufficient interoperability between disparate systems, legacy system issues, or simply the existence of applications and hardware components that pose conflicts or that cannot support the proposed design.

terminal concentrators   Hardware devices that are used to provide serial access to several servers from a single networked device. This device can then be used to monitor a large number of servers from one location.

threat modeling   The act of brainstorming about new threat conditions by using known lists of possible attacks. Defenses for the possible threats can then be created.

transitive trust relationship   A type of domain relationship in which multiple trust relationships exist and trust extends between all trusted and trusting domains. Windows 2000 and Windows Server 2003 domains within a forest are in a transitive trust relationship: all domains trust all other domains.

trust, but audit   A security principle that states that users and administrators must have the privileges they need to do their job, but no one is completely and permanently above suspicion. The principle is based on the reality that people change, temptation can be great, and anger can make some people overstep their usual reluctance to break the rules. It also emphasizes that provisions for auditing should be part of any security design and that reviewing audit logs can provide valuable information.

trust model   The number and arrangement of trusts within and between forests, as well as the way in which these trusts are restricted.

trust relationship   A conjoining of domains that allows authentication and access across domain boundaries, forest boundaries, or both.

trusted domain   In a one-way trust, the *trusted* domain is the domain whose accounts can be given access to resources in the trusting domain.

trusting domain   In a one-way trust, the *trusting* domain is the domain whose resources can be accessed by accounts in the trusted domain.

trusts   Relationships between domains that provide the ability to share resources across security boundaries.

update rollup   A collection of security patches, critical updates, updates, and hotfixes released together. They might be concerned with only one product component, such as Microsoft Internet Explorer.

update   A released fix that addresses a noncritical, nonsecurity-related bug.

USA Patriot Act   A United States federal law established to deter and punish acts of terrorism. The act includes a directive for the U.S. Secret Service to develop a national network or electronic crime task force, and it amends the federal criminal code to allow wire, oral, and electronic communications surveillance for terrorism offenses, chemical weapons–related crimes, and computer fraud and abuse. Allowable surveillance now includes interception of computer trespassers and wiretaps to monitor teleconferences.

use of fail-safe defaults   A security principle that states that systems should always be configured to choose the most secure default action. For example, ports on firewalls should always be closed by default. You must open those for which you want to provide access. No access, such as access to a file, should be possible unless it is explicitly given.

volume shadow copy   A service that empowers the end user to recover previous editions of files or to restore files that have been accidentally deleted.

VPN router   A virtual private network (VPN) that initiates or receives VPN-based demand-dial connections. VPN routers used as endpoints in a demand-dial configuration can be calling routers or answering routers.

WiFi Protected Access (WPA)   An interim standard that follows the proposed 802.11i wireless standard. This standard provides improved encryption by using the Temporal Key Integrity Protocol (TKIP). TKIP provides integrity. Authentication is provided by the use of the Extensible Authentication Protocol (EAP).

Wired Equivalent Privacy (WEP)   An encryption algorithm used to encrypt the data sent between wireless nodes using RC4. No key management protocol is defined. Keys must be manually distributed and added to wireless clients. Manual changes are required. Two keys are defined. A global key protects multicast and broadcast traffic from a wireless access point (AP) to its clients. A session key protects unicast traffic between an AP an its clients, and it also protects multicast and broadcast traffic sent from clients to an AP.

zone replication   The process of transferring zone records between primary and secondary Domain Name System (DNS) servers. That is, all changes to zone data are made on the primary DNS server and replicated to one or more secondary servers.

Index

H

In-depth, daily administration guides
for Microsoft Windows Server 2003

Microsoft® Windows® Server 2003 Administrator's Companion
ISBN 0-7356-1367-2

The in-depth, daily operations guide to planning, deployment, and maintenance. Here's the ideal one-volume guide for the IT professional who administers Windows Server 2003. This ADMINISTRATOR'S COMPANION offers up-to-date information on core system-administration topics for Windows, including Active Directory® services, security, disaster planning and recovery, interoperability with NetWare and UNIX, plus all-new sections about Microsoft Internet Security and Acceleration (ISA) Server and scripting. Featuring easy-to-use procedures and handy workarounds, this book provides ready answers for on-the-job results.

Microsoft Windows Server 2003 Security Administrator's Companion
ISBN 0-7356-1574-8

The in-depth, daily operations guide to enhancing security with the network operating system. With this authoritative ADMINISTRATOR'S COMPANION—written by an expert on the Windows Server 2003 security team—you'll learn how to use the powerful security features in the latest network server operating system. The guide describes best practices and technical details for enhancing security with Windows Server 2003, using the holistic approach that IT professionals need to grasp to help secure their systems. The authors cover concepts such as physical security issues, internal security policies, and public and shared key cryptography, and then drill down into the specifics of key security features of Windows Server 2003.

To learn more about the full line of Microsoft Press® products for IT professionals, please visit:

microsoft.com/mspress/IT

In-depth technical information and tools for
Microsoft Windows Server 2003

Microsoft® Windows Server™ 2003 Deployment Kit: A Microsoft Resource Kit
ISBN 0-7356-1486-5

Plan and deploy a Windows Server 2003 operating system environment with expertise from the team that develops and supports the technology—the Microsoft Windows® team. This multivolume kit delivers in-depth technical information and best practices to automate and customize your installation, configure servers and desktops, design and deploy network services, design and deploy directory and security services, implement Group Policy, create pilot and test plans, and more. You also get more than 125 timesaving tools, deployment job aids, Windows Server 2003 evaluation software, and the entire Windows Server 2003 Help on the CD-ROMs. It's everything you need to help ensure a smooth deployment—while minimizing maintenance and support costs.

Internet Information Services (IIS) 6.0 Resource Kit
ISBN 0-7356-1420-2

Deploy and support IIS 6.0, which is included with Windows Server 2003, with expertise direct from the Microsoft IIS product team. This official RESOURCE KIT packs 1200+ pages of in-depth deployment, operations, and technical information, including step-by-step instructions for common administrative tasks. Get critical details and guidance on security enhancements, the new IIS 6.0 architecture, migration strategies, performance tuning, logging, and troubleshooting—along with timesaving tools, IIS 6.0 product documentation, and a searchable eBook on CD. You get all the resources you need to help maximize the security, reliability, manageability, and performance of your Web server—while reducing system administration costs.

To learn more about the full line of Microsoft Press® products for IT professionals, please visit:

microsoft.com/mspress/IT

Get a **Free**
*e-mail newsletter, updates,
special offers, links to related books,
and more when you*

register online!

Register your Microsoft Press® title on our Web site and you'll get a FREE subscription to our e-mail newsletter, *Microsoft Press Book Connections.* You'll find out about newly released and upcoming books and learning tools, online events, software downloads, special offers and coupons for Microsoft Press customers, and information about major Microsoft® product releases. You can also read useful additional information about all the titles we publish, such as detailed book descriptions, tables of contents and indexes, sample chapters, links to related books and book series, author biographies, and reviews by other customers.

Registration is easy. Just visit this Web page and fill in your information:

http://www.microsoft.com/mspress/register

Microsoft®

System Requirements

The exercises for this training kit emphasize security design and not implementation; however, the book does contain a few hands-on exercises to help you learn about designing security for a Windows-based network. To complete the hands-on exercises, you must meet the following minimum system requirements:

- **Microsoft Windows Server 2003, Enterprise Edition** A 180-day evaluation edition of Windows Server 2003, Enterprise Edition, is included on the CD-ROM.
- **Computer and processor** 133 megahertz (MHz) minimum is required. Use the Intel Pentium/Celeron family, the AMD K6/Athlon/Duron family, or a compatible processor. (Windows Server 2003, Enterprise Edition supports up to eight CPUs on one server.) 733 MHz is recommended.
- **Memory** 128 megabytes (MB) of memory is the minimum required (maximum 32 gigabytes [GB] of RAM). 256 MB or more is recommended.
- **Hard disk** 1.55 to 2 GB of available hard-disk space is required. (More room will be required to install additional operating system features and to practice some of the techniques described.)
- **Drive** A CD-ROM or DVD-ROM drive is required.
- **Display** VGA or hardware that supports console redirection is required.
- **Peripherals** A keyboard and Microsoft Mouse, or a compatible pointing device, or hardware that supports console redirection is required.
- **Miscellaneous** Internet access and networking requirements:
  - ❑ Some Internet functionality might require Internet access, a Microsoft Passport account, and payment of a separate fee to a service provider. Local and/or long-distance telephone toll charges might apply. A high-speed modem or broadband Internet connection is recommended.
  - ❑ For networking, you must have a network adapter appropriate for the type of local-area, wide-area, wireless, or home network to which you want to connect and access to an appropriate network infrastructure. Access to third-party networks might require additional charges.

Uninstall Instructions

The time-limited release of Microsoft Windows Server 2003, Enterprise Edition, will expire 180 days after installation. If you decide to discontinue the use of this software, you may need to reinstall your original operating system, depending on which partition you have the operating system installed. You may also need to reformat the partition on which the operating system was installed to remove conflicting configurations that may interfere with another installation.